KNOWLEDGE ECONOMY, INFORMATION TECHNOLOGIES AND GROWTH

Knowledge Economy, Information Technologies and Growth

Edited by
LUIGI PAGANETTO
University of Rome Tor Vergata, Italy

Routledge
Taylor & Francis Group

LONDON AND NEW YORK

First published 2004 by Ashgate Publishing

Reissued 2018 by Routledge
2 Park Square, Milton Park, Abingdon, Oxon OX14 4RN
605 Third Avenue, New York, NY 10017

First issued in paperback 2021

Routledge is an imprint of the Taylor & Francis Group, an informa business

A Library of Congress record exists under LC control number: 2002190861

Notice:
Product or corporate names may be trademarks or registered trademarks, and are used only for identification and explanation without intent to infringe.

Publisher's Note
The publisher has gone to great lengths to ensure the quality of this reprint but points out that some imperfections in the original copies may be apparent.

Disclaimer
The publisher has made every effort to trace copyright holders and welcomes correspondence from those they have been unable to contact.

ISBN 13: 978-0-815-39007-7 (hbk)
ISBN 13: 978-1-351-15456-7 (ebk)
ISBN 13: 978-1-138-35630-6 (pbk)

DOI: 10.4324/9781351154567

Contents

List of Figures

List of Tables

List of Contributors

Leonardo Becchetti. Year of birth: 1965. Place of birth: Rome.

2000 Associate Professor Faculty of Economics University of Rome 'Tor Vergata'.

1996 PhD Economics, University of Oxford (technological innovation and finance) Supervisor Philip Aghion.

1993 MSc Economics, London School of Economics.

Some publications:

– Becchetti, L., 'The Effect of Bond plus Equity Warrant Issues on Stock Volatility: An Empirical Analysis with Conditional and Unconditional Volatility Measures', *Applied Financial Economics*, 6, 1996, pp. 327–35;

– (with Bagella, M.), 'The Optimal Financing Strategy of high-tech Firms: The Role of Warrants', *Journal of Economic Behaviour and Organisation*, 35, 1998, pp. 1–23;

– with Becchetti, C.), 'A Chartist Approach to Stock Exchange Series (CASES) Decomposition: Theoretical Justifications and Empirical Analysis', *Advances in Investment Analysis and Portfolio Management*, 5, 1998, pp. 31–69;

– (with Rossi, S.), 'The Positive Effect of Industrial District on Export Performance of Italian Firms', *The Review of Industrial Organisation*, 16/1, 2000, pp. 53–68;

– (with Bagella, M. and Carpentieri, A.), '"The First Shall Be Last'. Size and Value Strategy Premia at the London Stock Exchange', *Journal of Banking and Finance*, 2000, pp. 893–920;

– (with Paganetto, L.), 'The Determinants of Suboptimal Technological Development in the System Company-Component Producers Relationship', *International Journal of Industrial Organisation*, forth. (and *CEIS Working Paper No. 102)*, 2001;

– (with Bagella, M. and Caggese, C.), 'Finance, Investment and Innovation: A Three Pillars Approach based on A Priori Identification, Direct Revelation an Econometric Estimation', *Research in Economics (Ricerche Economiche)*, forthcoming 2000.

Massimo G. Colombo. Year of birth: 1958. Place of birth: Milan, Italy. Professor of Engineering Economics, University of Pavia and Politecnico di Milano.

Some publications:

–   (with Delmastro, M.), 'Some Stylized Facts about Organization and its Evolution', *Journal of Economic Behavior and Organization*, 40, 1999;

–   (with Delmastro, M.), 'A Note on the Relation between Size, Ownership Status and Plant's Closure: Sunk Costs vs. Strategic Size Liability', *Economic Letters*, 69, 2000, pp. 421–2;

–   (with Cantwell, J.), 'Technological and Output Complementarities, and Inter-firm Cooperation in Information Technology Ventures', *Journal of Management and Governance*, 4, 2000, pp. 117–47;

–   (with Delmastro, M.), 'Technology Use and Plant Closure', *Research Policy*, 30, 2001, pp. 21–34;

–   (ed.), *The Changing Boundaries of the Firm*, Routledge, London, 1998.

Francesco Daveri. Year of birth: 1961. Place of birth: Piacenza, Italy. Professor of Political Economics, Faculty of Law, University of Parma.

Some publications:

–   (with Tabellini, G.), 'Unemployment, Growth and Taxation in Industrial Countries', *Economic Policy*, April, 2000;

–   (with Faini, R.) 'Where do Migrants Go?', *Oxford Economic Papers*, October, 1999;

–   *Economia dei Paesi in via di sviluppo*, il Mulino, Bologna, 1996.

Marco Delmastro. Year of birth: 1969. Place of birth: Rome. PhD in Economics, University of Warwick, 2000. Officer of the Authority Garante della Concorrenza e del Mercato.

Some publications:

–   'The Determinants of the Management Hierarchy: Evidence from Italian Plants', *International Journal of Industrial Organization*, 2001;

–   (with Colombo, M.G.), 'A Note on the Relation between Size, Ownership Status and Plant's Closure: Sunk Costs vs. Strategic Size Liability', *Economic Letters*, 69, 2000, pp. 421–27;

–   (with Colombo M.G), 'Some Stylized Facts about Organization and its Evolution', *Journal of Economic Behavior and Organization*, 40, 1999;

- (with Colombo, M.G.), 'Technology Use and Plant Closure', *Research Policy*, 30, 2001, pp. 21–34.

Adriaan Dierx. Year of birth: 1957. Place of birth: Venlo, Netherlands. PhD in economics at the University of Pittsburgh. Responsible for analysing structural reforms in EU product markets. He has published a number of papers as well as chapters in books on the sectoral impact of the euro, European market integration and competitiveness, metropolitan growth and migration.

Alberto Heimler. Director of Study, Authority Garante della Concorrenza e del Mercato. President, 'Competition and Regulation', Work Group OCSE. He is author of numerous articles in the international economic literature.

Fabienne Ilzkovitz. Head of the unit 'Internal Market and national markets of goods and services; competition policy; competitiveness analysis' in the Directorate General for Economic and Financial Affairs of the European Commission. Professor of European Economic Policy and European Integration at the Université Libre de Bruxelles and of International Economics in a Brussels Business School (ICHEC). She has published several papers and contributed to several books dealing with European integration, international aspects of EMU, competition policy and industrial economics.
Some publications:
- (with Dierx, A. and Schmidt, J.H.), 'Economic and Monetary Union', in M. Darmer and L. Kuyper (eds), *Industry and the European Union: Analysing Policies for Business*, Edward Elgar, Aldershot, 2000;
- (with Dierx, A., Schmidt, J.H. and Meiklejohn, R.), *The Control of State Aids : A Proposal for a Co-ordinated Approach*, ed. C.D. Elhermann, '1999 Competition Workshop' organized by the European Institute of Florence;
- (with Dierx, A., Meiklejohn, R. and Mogensen, U.), 'Liberalisation of Network Industries: Economic Implications and Main Policy Issues', *European Economy*, No. 4, 1999;
- (with Dierx, A.), 'From the Single Market to the Single Currency: New challenges for European companies', in A. Dierx (ed.), 'L'euro et l'intégration européenne', published by the Euro Institute under the direction of J.V. Louis and H. Bronkhorst, P.I.E., Peter Lang, 1999;
- (with Dierx, A. and Mogensen, U.), 'ICT in Europe. Issues and challenges', *Papeles de economia espanola*, No. 81, 1999;

–   (with Dierx, A. and Nicodème, G.), 'Des nouveaux défis pour l'Union Européenne', *Les Cahiers économiques de Bruxelles*, 2001;
–   (with Dierx, A.), 'Du marché unique à la monnaie uniqu: l'impact sectoriel de l'euro', *Revue du CEPII*, 4th quarter 1999.

Dale W. Jorgenson. Year of birth: 1933, Place of birth: Bazeman, Montana. Professor of Economics at Harvard University. He was elected to membership in the American Philosophical Society in 1998, the Royal Swedish Academy of Sciences in 1989, the US National Academy of Sciences in 1978 and the American Academy of Arts and Sciences in 1969. He was elected to Fellowship in the American Association for the Advancement of Science in 1982, the American Statistical Association in 1965, and the Econometric Society in 1964. He was awarded honorary doctorates by Uppsala University and the University of Oslo in 1991. Jorgenson is President of the American Economic Association. He has been a member of the Board on Science, Technology, and Economic Policy of the National Research Council since 1991 and was appointed to be Chairman of the Board in 1998. He is also Chairman of Section 54, Economic Sciences, of the National Academy of Sciences. He served as President of the Econometric Society in 1987. Jorgenson received the prestigious John Bates Clark Medal of the American Economic Association in 1971. This Medal is awarded every two years to an economist under 40 for excellence in economic research. The citation for this award reads in part: Jorgenson is the author of more than 200 articles and the author and editor of 20 books in economics. His collected papers have been published in nine volumes by The MIT Press, beginning in 1995. The most recent volume, *Econometric Modeling of Producer Behavior*, was published in 2000.
Some publications:
–   (with Stiroh, K.J.), 'Information Technology and Economic Growth', *American Economic Review*, May, 1999;
–   (with Stiroh, K.J.), 'US Economic Growth and the Industry Level', *American Economic Review*, May, 2000;
–   *Postwars US Economic Growth and International Comparison of Economic Growth*, The MIT Press, 1995;
–   *Economic General Equilibrium Modeling and Energy, The Environment and Economic Growth*, The MIT Press, 1998.

Michael T. Kiley. Year of birth: 1970, Place of birth: Bridgeport, Connecticut. Profession: economist. Professional affiliation: Division of Research and Statistics, Board of Governors of the Federal Reserve System, USA

Some publications:

–   'Partial Adjustment and Staggered Price Setting', *Journal of Money, Credit, and Banking*, 2001;
–   'Price Stickiness and Business Cycle Persistence', *Journal of Money, Credit, and Banking*, February, 2000;
–   'The Supply of Skilled Labour and Skill-biased Technological Progress', *Economic Journal*, October, 1999;
–   Predicting Tax Rate Changes: Insights from the Permanent Income Hypothesis', *Journal of Macroeconomics*, Winter, 1998.

Andreas Kopp. Education: University of Göttingen (MA in economics), European University Institute and University of Giessen (PhD). Previous affiliations: research officer at the University of Giessen, Kiel Institute of World Economics, visiting researcher at the University of California, Berkeley, Hamburg Institute of International Economics, currently visiting professor at the Technical University of Dresden

Some publications:

–   *Institutional Economics of Backward Agriculture*, Tübingen. 1992;
–   'Population Growth: Cause or Effect of Inequality in Developing Countries?', *Acta Demographica*, 1995–96, pp. 15–27;
–   (co-author), 'Social Policies in the Transition Economies of Middle and Eastern Europe', *Kieler Studien*, No. 273, Tübingen, 1996;
–   (with Carillo, M.), 'La escuela alemana de ciencia económica regional', *Regiones y Desarrollo*, Vol. III, No. 5, 1999), pp. 1–29;
–   *Uncertainty and the Theory of Agglomeration*, Berlin (forthcoming).

Gilles Le Blanc. Year of birth: 1969. Place of birth: Rome. Lecturer in Economics, Paris School of Mines and Visiting Researcher, London School of Economics.

Some publications:

–   'Les nouveaux districts des technologies de l'information : l'exemple de Denver aux Etats-Unis', in DATAR (ed.), *Réseaux d'entreprises et territoires – Regards sur les systèmes productifs locaux*, La Documentation Française, Paris, 2001, pp. 97–116;
–   'Télécommunications', in *Dictionnaire du Web*, Dalloz, Paris, 2000;
–   (with Bomsel, O.), 'Dépenses militaires, restructuration de l'industrie d'armement et privatisation de la défense 1994–1999', *Arès*, Vol. XVIII, No. 46, 2000, pp. 41–54;

–   'Dynamiques industrielles et réglementaires des télécoms: une comparaison Etats-Unis/France', in IFRI, *La Documentation Française*, 1999, Paris.

David Andrés Londoño Bedoya. Year of birth: 1970. Place of birth: Santafé, Colombia. Current Assistant of Political Economics at the Faculty of Economics of University of Rome 'Tor Vergata' and Researcher at the Department of Economics and Institutions.
Some publications:
–   (co-authored with Becchetti, L.), 'Political Business Cycle, Liberalisation and Privatisation of an Electrical Utility: The Impact on Shareholder Value', presented at the 27th EARIEConference, Université de Lausanne, 2000;
–   (co-authored with Becchetti, L.), *Investment Subsidies: Which Firms Get Them and What is Their Impact on Investment and Efficiency*, 2000;
–   *Effetti della Liberalizzazione e della Privatizzazione del Settore Elettrico in Italia. Il Ruolo della Governance*, under commission of the Centre for International Studies on Economic Growth CEIS, University of Rome 'Tor Vergata', 1999.

Lisa M. Lynch. Year of birth: 1956. Place of birth: Waterbury, Connecticut. She is the William L. Clayton Professor of International Economic Affairs at the Fletcher School of Law and Diplomacy at Tufts University. She is co-editor of the Journal of Labor Economics and a Research Associate at the National Bureau of Economic Research and the Economic Policy Institute. A former Chief Economist at the US Department of Labor, Professor Lynch has published more than 50 papers and books on issues such as the impact of technological change and workplace practices (especially training) on productivity and wages, determinants of youth unemployment, and the school-to-work transition. Her work has appeared in professional journals such as *The American Economic Review*, *The Review of Economics and Statistics*, *Industrial and Labor Relations Review* and *The Journal of Econometrics*.
Some publications:
–   (co-author), *Opportunity Knocks: Training the Commonwealth's Workers for the New Economy*, 2000;
–   *Training and the Private Sector: International Comparisons*, 1994;
–   *Strategies for Workplace Training*, 1993;

- 'How to Compete: The Impact of Workplace Practices and Information Technology on Productivity', *Review of Economics and Statistics*, August, 2001.
- (profiled in the August 1998 issue of *Scientific American*), 'Beyond the Incidence of Training', *Industrial and Labor Relations Review*, 1998;
- 'Wage Inequality and Long Term Unemployment: Is Human Capital the Answer?', *Swedish Economic Policy Review*, 1998;
- 'Human Capital Investment and Productivity', *American Economic Review*, 1996;
- 'The Economics of Youth Training in the US', *Economic Journal*, 1993;
- 'Private Sector Training and the Earnings of Young Workers', *American Economic Review*, 1992.

Donato Masciandaro. Year of birth: 1961. Place of birth: Matera, Italy. Professor in Monetary Economics, University 'Bocconi' of Milano and Professor of Economics, Faculty of Economics, University of Lecce. Previously Consultant to United Nations.
Some publications:
- 'Introducing E banking in Italy: Trends and Perspectives', *Journal of International Banking Regulation*, 2001;
- (ed., with Riolo, F.), *Internet banking. Tecnologia, Economia e Diritto*, V Rapporto sul Sistema Finanziario, Fondazione Rosselli, Edibank, Milano, 2000.
- (with Di Torrepadula, I.), 'E-Commerce e ruolo delle banche: prime riflessioni', in D. Masciandaro and F. Riolo (eds), *Internet banking. Tecnologia, Economia e Diritto*, V Rapporto sul Sistema Finanziario, Fondazione Rosselli, Edibank, Milano, 2000, pp. 137–48;
- (with Bagella, M.), 'Le banche ed Internet tra efficienza ed integrità', in D. Masciandaro and F. Riolo (eds), *Internet banking. Tecnologia, Economia e Diritto*, V Rapporto sul Sistema Finanziario, Fondazione Rosselli, Edibank, Milano, 2000, pp. 137–48.

Antonio Nicita. Year of birth: 1968. Place of birth: Siracusa, Italy. Research of Political Economics, University of Siena.
Some publications:
- (ed., with Pagano, U.), *The Evolution of Economic Diversity*, Routledge, London, 2001.

- (ed., with Franzini, M.), *Economic Institutions and Environmental Policy*, Ashgate, Aldershot, 2001.

Luigi Paganetto. Year of birth: 1940. Place of birth: Genova, Italy. Dean of the Faculty of Economics and Business Administration, Full Professor of International Economics and President of the Center for International Studies on Economic Growth at the 'Tor Vergata' University of Rome. Editor 'CEIS-Il Mulino' series and member of the editorial boards of *Sviluppo economico*. Member of: ENEA technical scientific committee, Council of the Ministry for Foreign Affairs Institute, Council of Ente Cassa di Risparmio of Rome, Board of Directors of Poligrafico dello Stato, member of the Italian private employers' association Confindustria's Technical-Scientific Committee, adviser to the Italian Prime Minister's Office, Information Society – Chairman of the Committee, Member of the Italian export credit agency SACE's board of experts. Author of several articles and books in Macroeconomic Theory, International Economics and Italian and European Industrial Economics.

Some pubblications:
- (ed., with Phelps, E.S.), *Finance, Research, Education and Growth*, Macmillan, London, forthcoming;
- (ed., with G. Tria), *Istituzioni e governo dell'economia*, Il Mulino Bologna, 1999;
  Borsa, investimenti e crescita, Bologna, 2000;
- (with Scandizzo, L.P.), *La Banca Mondiale e l'Italia: dalla ricostruzione allo sviluppo*, Il Mulino Bologna, 2000;
- (with Scandizzo, L.P.), *Crescita endogena ed economia aperta*, Il Mulino, Bologna, 2001;
- (ed., with Pietrobelli, C.), *Scienza, tecnologia e innovazione: quali politiche?*, Il Mulino, Bologna, 2001.

Patrick Rey. Year of birth: 1957. Professor of Economics, University of Toulouse. Research Director, Institut d'Economie Industrielle (IDEI). Consultant for OECD, World Bank, European Commission, Ministère de l'Economie and Commissatiat Général au Plan (France); also consultant in US and EU competition cases.

Some publications:
- 'Competition Policy and Economic Development', *Development Themes of the 21st Century*, Villa Borsig Workshop Series, 1998, pp. 92–103;

- (with Aghion, P. and Dewatripont, M.), 'Competition, Financial Discipline and Growth', *Review of Economic Studies*, Vol. 66, No. 4, 1999, pp. 825–52;
- 'On the Form of State Aid', *European Law Journal*, 1999;
- (with Comanor, W.S.), Vertical Restraints and the Market Power of Large Distributors, *Review of Industrial Organization*, Vol. 17, No. 2, 2000, pp. 135–53;
- (with Crémer, J. and Tirole, J.), 'Connectivity in the Commercial Internet', *Journal of Industrial Economics*, 2000.

Pasquale L. Scandizzo. Year of birth: 1942. Place of birth: Salerno, Italy. MSc, PhD in Economics, University of California, Berkeley. Full Professor Professor of Political Economy, the 'Tor Vergata' University of Rome. President of the Institute of Studies on Economic Planning (ISPE) from 1990 to 1993. Senior Consultant with The World Bank, FAO, The Interamerican Development Bank. Since 1994, President, Fondazione Cassa di Risparmio di Salerno. Chairman, Sichelgaita Research Institute on Economics and Social Development, Salerno. Scientific director of *Sviluppo Economico* and co-editor of the labour economics journal *Labour* and *Open Economies Review*. Author of 20 books and monographs and more than 100 articles in academic journals.

Kevin J. Stiroh. Year of birth: 1967. Place of birth: New Jersey, USA. Harvard Univerity MA, PhD Economics, 1955. Senior Economist A, Federal Research Bank of New York. Professional memberships: American Economic Association, National Association of Business Economists.
Some publications:
- 'ICT Drives the US Productivity Revival', *Economic Trends*, 2001;
- 'Is IT Driving the US Productivity Revival?', *International Productivity Monitor*, 2001;
- 'The Economic Impact of Information Technology', *Encyclopedia of Information Systems*, Academic Press, San Diego, CA, 2001;
- (with Morgan, D.P.), 'Bond Market Discipline of Banks: The Aset Test', *Journal of Financial Services Research*, 2001;
- (with McGuckin, R.H.), 'Computer and Produsctivity: Are Aggregation Effects Important?', *Economic Inquiring*, 2001;
- (with Morgan, D.P.), *Bond Market Discipline of Banks*, in *The Changing Financial Industry Structure and Regulation: Bridging States, Countries and Industries: Proceedingss of the 30th Annual Conference on Bank*

Structure and Competition, Federal Reserve Bank of Chicago, May, 2000, pp. 496–526.

Marc van Wegberg. Year of birth: 1957. Place of birth: Hunsel, The Netherlands. Professor, University of Maastricht, Faculty of Economics and Business Administration, Department of Management Science, Section Organization Studies.
Some publications:
–   (with Vercoulen, F.), *Standard Selection Modes in Dynamic, Complex Industries: Creating Hybrids between Market Selection and Negotiated Selection of Standards*, Maastricht: NIBOR Working Paper, nib98006, 1998;
–   'Architectural Battles in the Multimedia Market', in Nicholas W. Jankowski and Lucien Hanssen (eds), *The Contours of Multimedia: Recent Technological, Theoretical and Empirical Developments*, John Libbey Media, Luton, 1996, pp. 32–46;
–   (with van Witteloostuijn, A.), 'Strategic Management in the New Economy: Modern information technologies and multichannel contact Strategies', in Joel A.C. Baum and Henrich R. Greve (eds), *Advances is Strategic Management: Multi-Unit Organization and Multimarket Strategy*, vol, 18, JAI Press, Greenwich, CT, 2001, pp. 265–306.

Robert D. Willig. Professor of Economics and Public Affairs at Princeton University. Consultant and advisor for the Federal Trade Commission and the Department of Justice on antitrust policy, for OECD, the Inter-American Development Bank, and the World Bank on global trade, competition, regulatory and privatization policy, and for governments of diverse nations on microeconomic reforms. Member of the editorial boards of the *American Economic Review*, the *Journal of Industrial Economics*, *Utility Policy*, the MIT Press Series on Regulation, and the *Electronic Journal of Industrial Organization and Regulation Abstracts*. He is the author of *Welfare Analysis of Policies Affecting Prices and Products, Contestable Markets and the Theory of Industry Structure*, and numerous articles in the professional economics and legal literature. He is the co-editor of the *Handbook of Industrial Organization*, and an editor of *Can Privatization Deliver? Infrastructure for Latin America*.

Martin Zagler. Year of birth: 1968. Place of birth: Linz, Austria. Visiting Researcher, British Library for Political and Social Sciences, London School of Economics, London. Program Coordinator, Ludwig-Boltzmann-Institute for Growth Research, Vienna.

Some publications:

– *Economic Growth and Unemployment in Europe*, Palgrave Macmillan, Basingstoke, forthcoming 2002;

– *Endogenous Growth, Market Failures, and Economic Policy*, Macmillan, Basingstoke and St Martin's Press, New York, 1999;

– (with Helmenstein, C.), 'Economic Performance: Between a New Economy Boom and Bust', *Wirtschaftspolitische Blätter*, 2001;

– 'Budgetpolitik und Budgetkonsolidierung', in E. Theurl, R. Sausgruber and H. Winner (eds), *Kompendium der österreichischen Finanzpolitik*, Springer, Heidelberg, 2001;

– 'Efficiency, Innovation and Productivity: On the Impact of Unemployment on Endogenous Growth', in H. Hagemann and Seiter (eds), *Growth Theory and Growth Policy*, Routledge, London, 2001.

Foreword

This volume focuses on the information and communication technology (ICT) revolution and its impact on economic growth.

Even though the emergence of the knowledge economy is at the centre of attention by media and is often a subject of the economic policy debate, economic research on the issue is still relatively underdeveloped and many aspects of it are still awaitig deep theoretical and empirical scrutiny.

One important question is whether, as many economists and opinion leaders maintain, the knowledge economy and the information technologies have fostered the birth of a 'new economy' which, by inducing a strong productivity growth in most sectors, is behind the impressive growth of GDP experienced by the American economy. Empirical research has in fact been unable to provide a conclusive answer to such question.

The book debates this issue and provides the opportunity to discuss the economic and social effects of the ICT revolution. It also focuses on the functioning and the micro-economic structure of the ICT sector, as well as on its impact on various industries, on the financial system and on the labour market. It analyses the role of the ICT revolution on regional development and it addresses important policy issues such as its consequences for antitrust legislation and government regulation.

Introduction

The technological revolution originated by the progressive convergence of software and telecommunications and fostered by the advancements in the digital technology is significantly changing the microeconomic and macroeconomic scenario in the industrialized countries.

This revolution is a challenge for economic paradigms as it urges to change the ways in which knowledge and technology are usually conceptualized. Its first consequence is in the important distinction between *knowledge products* and *access to knowledge*.

Knowledge products (software, databases) are weightless, expandable and infinitely reproducible. They are generated in a process in which the same consumer is usually involved and create value, by increasing productivity of labour or by adding value to traditional physical products or traditional services. Knowledge products are nearly public goods. Expandibility and infinite reproducibility make them non-rivalrous, and copyright protection makes them much less excludable than other type of innovation (Quah, 1999). As a consequence, they are not the ultimate reasons either for the deep differences in productivity and growth between the US and Europe in the recent years, or for the divide between industrialized and developing countries.

The crucial non-public factor which is responsible for the observed international dispersion in productivity and growth is information and communications technology (ICT) bottlenecks: i) the diffusion and capillarity of the network and therefore its ability to carry the largest amount of knowledge products in the shortest time; ii) the access of individuals to the network in which knowledge products are immaterially transported; and iii) the power and availability of terminals (PCs, second generation mobile phones) which process, implement and exchange knowledge products which flow through the network.

In this framework, it is immediately clear that the development of financial markets and regulation in the telecommunication sector play a crucial role and may affect both ICT diffusion and its impact on growth. Insufficient access provision and excess taxation may crucially limit the diffusion of personal computers and internet accesses (Quah, 1999). Liberalization in the telecommunication sector may reduce the costs of accessing the network and well developed financial markets make it easier to finance projects which aim to implement the capacity of the network and the quality of 'terminals'.

It is therefore essential to concentrate on the role that political, cultural, economic and social infrastructures have in determining the ability of each country to benefit from knowledge good spillovers, including its capacity of increasing the availability of skilled human capital and information infrastructures and promoting a drastic adjustment in education and training.

This is the framework in which contributions collected in this book are placed. These contributions aim to answer three crucial issues: i) is the ICT-productivity nexus robust; ii) which are the crucial issues in the microeconomics of telecommunication which need to be tackled in order to improve our regulatory stance and to foster diffusion of innovation in the economic system; and iii) does a closer inspection at these issues contribute to explain the observed productivity and growth dispersion and, in particular, the different performance between Europe and the US?

On the first issue the book presents new macro and micro evidence which confutes, at least for the period under observation, the famous Solow saying 'we find computers everywhere, except in the productivity statistics'. The methodological approach followed by some contributions in this book overcomes the first vintage empirical research which generally did not find relevant productivity improvements associated with ICT investments (Bender, 1986; Lovemann, 1988; Roach, 1989; Strassmann, 1990). This research has several limits: i) the adoption of simple bivariate correlations between aggregate productivity and aggregate ICT capital stock does not take into account the impact of all controls which also affect aggregate productivity (Lehr-Licthenberg, 1999); ii) the incapacity of investigating into the ICT-productivity nexus to find that the link between the two variables occurs through a positive effect on productive variety (Milgrom-Roberts, 1988). Contributions collected in this book therefore show that, going beyond an aerial view, we discover several intermediate effects of ICT which may help to explain the paradox. More specifically, by deconstructing ICT into its software, hardware and telecommunication components, it is possible to find that ICT modifies the trade-off between scale and scope economies. If software investment increases the scale of firm operations, telecommunications investment creates a 'flexibility option' easing the switch from a Fordist to a flexible network productive model in which products and processes are more frequently adapted to satisfy consumers' taste for variety.

A second crucial focus of this book is regulation. Once we recognize that limits in the diffusion and access to the network reduce local appropriability of quasi-public knowledge products, we easily understand that the microeconomics and governance of the telecommunication sector may make the difference.

With this respect the traditional dilemma of the optimal patent length translates into the trade-off between the incentive to innovate for telecommunication firms and an ex-post monopolistic power which may significantly reduce access to other competitors at a certain node of the service chain, limiting de facto a cheap access to knowledge products on the net. In this respect the book discusses the concept of essential facility which may ease the trade-off by imposing an access obligation to owners and try to identify the optimal pricing of access which may reconcile the above mentioned conflicting goals.

Another typical feature of ICT product and services is its systemic nature, namely its complex architecture which must ensure full compatibility of several component products (Becchetti-Paganetto, 2000). The issue of product standards becomes therefore crucial both for individual producers and the regulator which must guarantee a certain degree of flexibility to avoid the creation of new monopolistic positions. Finally, our analysis of microeconomics and regulation of ICT presents also an investigation of the effects of the technological revolution on localization highlighting causes and consequences of new clustering patterns in high-tech sectors on industrial activity and on employment growth. This poses new challenges but also opportunities for underdeveloped areas such as the south of Italy. Catching up is somewhat easier as it depends on the access to the internet, the quality of human capital and the physical infrastructure but is not heavily conditioned as in previous industrialization phases, by large sunk investment in physical capital which were an unsurmountable barrier and made impossible to bridge the gap in more mature sectors.

A third crucial issue which in some way must incorporate the previous two (ICT-productivity nexus and the microeconomics and regulation of new technology) is how different patterns in the diffusion of ICT have affected the recent US–Europe divide in productivity and growth.

Why, as it is clearly shown by aggregate evidence presented in this volume, do European countries invest and accumulate fewer resources in new technology than the US?

Some interesting clues to answer this question are scattered throughout the book. Empirical analysis on micro data show that the adoption of ICT technologies crucially depends on managers' education and propensity to risk and also on corporate governance structures. A more dispersed shareholdership without interlocked directories and opaque cross-participation among different companies generates a more transparent governance with a clearer focus on shareholder value. The example of the Italian banking sector shows that the larger Italian banks with complex shareholding patterns in which foundations and the government still play a relevant role adopt new technologies at a far slower pace. On the same time, in the labour market, more educated and more flexible workers are more prepared to gain from innovation in terms of higher productivity.

The conclusion of the book is therefore that the ICT revolution needs several complementary factors to fully operate its beneficial impact on productivity and growth. Among them a highly educated human capital which is capable to earn the higher returns to talents generated by the ICT revolution, an evolved corporate governance structure which, driven by the goal of increasing shareholders' value, accelerates the adoption of innovation, a well developed financial system which supports entrepreneurial risk with the availability of equity finance, a more evolved regulatory framework capable to ease the typical dilemmas of the telecommunication sector on product standards and optimal pricing access to essential facilities.

Crucial differences on the above mentioned complementary factors provide a comprehensive picture of the determinants of the US–Europe productivity gap in the last years and lay down the path we need to follow in the following years if we really want to benefit from the last technological revolution.

PART I

Chapter 1

Technology-based Entrepreneurs: Does the Internet Make a Difference?

Massimo G. Colombo and Marco Delmastro

1   Introduction

In the 1990s, growing attention has been devoted by economists and policy makers to entrepreneurship and new technology-based firms (NTBFs). The reason may be traced to the evidence that small and new firms account for a substantial share of the new jobs created in those countries such as the US that have displayed a strong employment record.[1] In addition, the view has been rapidly gaining ground that high-growth start-ups, especially those operating in high-tech industries play a crucial role for the renewal of the economic system. In particular, they are believed to provide the US with an innovation-based competitive advantage in key sectors of the so-called 'new economy' such as software, e-commerce and communication equipment. Such view is corroborated by the success stories of Microsoft, Oracle, Cisco, America-on-line, Yahoo!, and other Internet outfits.

The concern that Europe is a laggard in the NTBF sector triggered a policy-oriented research effort aimed at analysing factors that favour or inhibit the birth of NTBFs and influence their post-entry performances (see EC, 1996a and 1996b). In particular, a conspicuous body of new evidence was developed on the characteristics of high-tech entrepreneurs in numerous European countries (for a survey see Storey and Tether, 1998a).

One of the objectives of the present chapter is to supplement the evidence provided by such studies with comparable data relating to Italian founders of NTBFs. Note that Italy is a very interesting case. On the one hand, propensity towards entrepreneurship is especially high in Italy (see, for instance, Blanchflower and Oswald, 1999) and small firms account for a disproportionately high share of total employment.[2] On the other, Italy exhibits a poor performance in high-tech industries, with the ratio of research expenditures to GNP being close to 1 per cent, that is less than half the value of France or the UK.

Moreover, it is important to emphasize that the evidence provided by previous studies on the characteristics of high-tech entrepreneurs mainly concern manufacturing industries. This work aims to extend such evidence to service industries which are related to or have been rejuvenated by the development of Internet. For one thing, as was said earlier, sectors such as e-commerce, other Internet services, software and multimedia content are at the core of the 'new economy' and are presently dominated by young, highly successful US firms, even though there is evidence that Europe is catching up.[3] What is even more interesting, Internet involves a technological revolution which is likely to have quite disruptive consequences on established technical knowledge and consolidated business models. In addition, markets for Internet services still are in the very early stage of the life cycle, especially in Italy which so far has been a latecomer in the diffusion of the new technology. So arguments inspired by evolutionary theories of technical change suggest that the characteristics of Internet entrepreneurs may differ from those of founders of NTBFs in other industries. In this paper, we intend to address empirically such research question. This would provide some initial insights into whether policy measures that are traditionally considered as suitable to support NTBFs also apply to Internet start-ups.

For this purpose, we consider a sample composed of 241 entrepreneurs which between 1984 and 1999 established 116 new firms that operate in ICT manufacturing and service industries and are located in Northern Italy. We analyse entrepreneurs' age at foundation of the start-up, educational qualifications, prior working experience, and motivations of the self-employment choice. We devote particular attention to differences in the personal characteristics of founders according to the sector of operation of the start-up. In particular, we investigate whether entrepreneurs in Internet related activities are different from those operating in other ICT industries (especially in manufacturing).

The findings of the study highlight a country-specific effects which may be traced to the characteristics of the Italian institutional setting, with Italian high-tech entrepreneurs being less educated and having less specific working experience than their counterparts in other European countries. We also show that Internet entrepreneurs generally are younger and even less educated (especially in technical fields) than the other sample founders. They quite often are at their first professional experience; if they have prior working experience, it generally is in unrelated industries.

The remaining of the chapter is organized as follows. In the next section we present the data set. In Section 3 we analyse the aforementioned personal characteristics of founders of Italian NTBFs. In Section 4 we turn attention to motivations of the self-employment choice. Some summarizing remarks which also highlight the policy implications of the findings of this work, in Section 5 concludes the chapter.

2 The Data Set

The data set used in this paper has been developed at Politecnico di Milano in 1999. The sample is composed of 241 founders of 116 Italian NTBFs that operate in one of the following information and communications technology (ICT) sectors: Internet (namely Internet service and access provision and e-commerce), software, multimedia content, and manufacturing industries of ICT (i.e., communication equipment, computers and electronics).[4] Such sectors can be regarded as representative of the universe of NTBFs, at least in Italy.[5] In this chapter, a NTBF has been defined as a young firm founded after 1984, which at the date of foundation was independent (i.e. not controlled by another firm).

Table 1.1 presents the composition of sample founders by sector of operation. Only 10 per cent of entrepreneurs operates in manufacturing, while the remaining 90 per cent is distributed among Internet (25 per cent), multimedia content (8 per cent) and, above all, software (56 per cent). So, most founders operate in services; these sectors either belong to the new paradigm of Internet or have been recently rejuvenated by it (as in the case of both software and multimedia content).

Table 1.1 Industry composition of founders of NTBFs

Sector	Number of founders	%
Internet (ISP, e-commerce)	60	24.9
Software	136	56.4
Multimedia content	20	8.3
ICT manufacturing	25	10.4
Total sample	241	100.0

Data collection was carried out in 1999 by the following process. The first step consisted in identifying target firms that complied with the above mentioned criteria relating to age and sector of operations and were located in Northern Italy.[6] Unfortunately, data provided by official national statistics did not allow to obtain a reliable description of the universe of firms from which a representative sample could be extracted. Therefore, we had to resort to a number of other sources. These include lists of newly established firms provided by the Milan Chamber of Commerce and national industrial associations (AIIP, ANIE, ANEE), on-line and off-line firm directories (such as Kompass), and lists of participants in industry expositions. Information provided by the national financial press, specialized magazines and other sectoral studies was also considered. Altogether, 343 firms were selected for potential inclusion in the sample.

Second, the selected firms were contacted by phone by educated interviewers who explained to the entrepreneurs the purpose and other details of the survey, and checked for compliance with the requirements for consideration in the survey. This reduced the size of the 'universe' to 260 firms. Then a questionnaire was sent to such firms either by fax or by e-mail. The questionnaire has a quantitative/qualitative nature. The first section contains information on characteristics of the entrepreneurs such as age, education, prior working experience, and motivations of the self-employment decision. The second section comprises further questions concerning the characteristics of the start-up firms and their post-entry performances in terms of growth and innovative activities. The final (qualitative) section is devoted to factors that promote or inhibit growth and innovation. In this chapter, we will focus on the first section of the questionnaire; results relating to the other sections will also be mentioned when they are pertinent to the objective of the study.

Lastly, the data set was completed by telephone and through some direct interviews with the selected entrepreneurs; this final step was crucial in order to obtain missing data and to check the accurateness of answers.

3   The Characteristics of Founders of Italian NTBFs

Age

The age at which an agent takes the self-employment decision clearly depends on aspects such as his risk aversion, financial constraints and the need for technological and market competencies which may have been acquired through both education and prior working experience (Roberts, 1991). Empirical studies show that this choice usually occurs when an individual is between 30 and 40.[7] On the one hand, both risk aversion and the cost of leaving an employment position are positively correlated with age, due to family concerns and career patterns (see, for instance, the job shopping models of Johnson (1978) and Miller (1984)). This effect would decrease the age of the self-employment choice, with other things being equal. On the other hand, entrepreneurship may not be an option for younger workers due to lack of professional and relational skills and liquidity constraints. As to this latter aspect, the older an individual the larger the amount of capital he can build up to start a new business (Evans and Jovanovic, 1989).

In high-tech environments, raising capital may be even more difficult because information asymmetries are more severe. So, technology-based starters are generally found to be older than other starters (see, for instance, Donckels, 1989). In particular, this effect is likely to depend on the specific nature of the sector in which new firms operate: financial (and knowledge) barriers to entry are influenced by industry characteristics.

Table 1.2 sheds some light on the age profile of NTBF founders depending on the industry. First, at the date of firm's foundation, the average age of Italian high-tech entrepreneurs is 33, which is in line with the international evidence (see footnote 7). Second, and more interesting, there are sizable differences in the age of entrepreneurs across sectors of operations of the start-ups. In particular, Internet-based founders represent the youngest category (average age equal to 28), whilst entrepreneurs of ICT manufacturing firms are the eldest (40). In order to gain further insights we have proceeded to compute t-tests between the average age of entrepreneurs of different sectors. These tests confirm that the above mentioned differences are statistically significant at conventional levels.

Table 1.2   Age of founders of Italian NTBFs

Sector	Minimum	Average[a]	Maximum
Internet (ISP, e-commerce)	19	28.5 **	46
Software	18	33.3	53
Multimedia content	21	36.4 *	63
ICT manufacturing	23	39.9 **	67
Total sample	18	33.0	67

Notes

a   T-test of the difference between the average age of founders belonging to a given sector and that of the rest of the sample.
*   Significance level greater than 10%.
**   Significance level greater than 1%.

A thorough analysis of the determinants of such phenomena lies beyond the scope of the chapter. Nonetheless, some preliminary remarks are in order. First, it is worth emphasizing that in manufacturing the minimum optimal scale is substantially higher than in services, especially those linked to Internet. Accordingly, the start-up size of sample firms is equal to 18 employees in ICT manufacturing industries and to four in the other sectors (in particular, three employees for Internet, four for software and five for multimedia content). Thus, an individual needs a larger amount of financial resources to set up a new firm in manufacturing. Given that entrepreneurs of Italian NTBFs usually use their personal savings to finance their activities (Giudici and Paleari, 2000),[8] it follows that those that operate in manufacturing industries need to wait longer before being able to leave their previous job, having accumulated sufficient financial resources to found a start-up. This argument helps explain why entrepreneurs in ICT manufacturing industries are significantly older than those that operate in services.

However, we think that there is more than that as to cross-sectoral differences in the age of sample entrepreneurs. An additional reason fur such differences, which explains in particular the younger age of Internet entrepreneurs, resides in the industry life cycle and the nature of technological changes associated with Internet. While the manufacturing sectors of ICT are based on consolidated technological trajectories which originated in the 1970s and early 1980s, Internet is a new competence destroying technological paradigm;[9] markets for new services arising from it are still in their infancy, especially in Italy. It follows that in ICT manufacturing sectors, market and technological competencies accumulated by founders of NTBFs through education and prior working experiences (in particular, in incumbent firms operating in the same industry of the start-up) play a key role in determining post-entry performances. Conversely, the new paradigm of Internet makes prior knowledge largely obsolete. In order to be successful, new innovative ideas radically departing from consolidated technological patterns and new business models based upon untried capabilities and skills must be developed. Under such conditions, barriers to entry are lower, as newcomers enjoy a knowledge advantage with respect to incumbent firms (see Gort and Klepper, 1982; Agarwal and Gort, 1996)[10] and, what is more important for the purpose of the present chapter, their extent is only loosely related to entrepreneurs' education and previous working experience. The remainder of the chapter is dedicated to analyse these issues in greater detail.

Education

The education of NTBF founders is generally recognized as a key element to understand the post-entry performance of high-tech start-ups (Jo and Lee, 1996). Empirical evidence show that entrepreneurs working in high-tech environments have an excellent education career. For instance, Autio et al. (1989) find that 90 per cent of Finnish founders of NTBFs have followed higher education. A similar result has been found for UK (85 per cent with graduate degree and 48 per cent with doctorate; see Westhead and Storey, 1994), Belgium (80 per cent have followed higher education; see Donckels, 1989) and Germany (more than 50 per cent with an engineering degree; see Licht et al., 1995).

Before proceeding with the evidence of educational attainments of founders of Italian NTBFs, a preliminary remark is in order. Italian graduate degrees can be hardly compared to most European degrees. Indeed university education programs generally are longer: they last for no less than four or five years, depending on the specific topics (four years for social sciences and most scientific degrees, five years for engineering), and the average time needed for graduation is longer than six years (again, it depends on the specific field).

Table 1.3 presents evidence on the level of educational attainment of Italian technology-based entrepreneurs. The low percentage of graduate entrepreneurs (38 per cent) may thus be partially due to the Italian institutional context.[11] In addition, only 20 per cent of founders has a graduate degree in sciences directly linked to the ICT sectors such as electronic and telecommunication engineering and computer sciences; 5 per cent has a degree in other technical branches (i.e. other fields of engineering, mathematics, physics and chemistry), 10 per cent in social sciences and 3 per cent in humanities or medicine.

Besides institutional factors, the low level of educational attainment of sample founders may also be due to industry-specific effects. Indeed, while prior evidence relating to other countries is based on samples of entrepreneurs working in high-tech manufacturing, in this study the overwhelming majority of start-ups is in industries directly (ISP, e-commerce) or indirectly (software, multimedia content) connected with Internet. Table 1.4 distinguishes findings on education attainments depending on the sector in which NTBF founders actually operate. Chi-squared tests for multinomial distributions have also been performed in order to detect the existence of significant differences across sectors. The tests, which for sake of synthesis are illustrated in the Appendix (see Table 1.A1), show that the null hypothesis that such differences are statistically insignificant can be rejected at conventional levels, with the only

Table 1.3   **Education of founders of Italian NTBFs**

Education	Number of observations	%
ICT graduate degree[1]	48	19.9
Other technical graduate degree[2]	12	5.0
Economic graduate degree[3]	23	9.6
Other graduate degree[4]	8	3.3
ICT high school[5]	28	11.6
Other high school[6]	122	50.6
Total sample	241	100.0

Notes

1   Graduate degree in: electronic and telecommunications engineering, computer science.
2   Graduate degree in: other engineering, mathematics, physics, chemistry.
3   Graduate degree in: economics, law and political sciences.
4   Graduate degree in: humanities, medicine, architecture.
5   High school leaving certificate in: electronics, computer sciences and telecommunications.
6   Other high school leaving certificate.

Table 1.4   **Education of founders according to the sector of operation of the start-ups**

Education[1]	Internet		Software		Multimedia content		ICT manufacturing	
	Obs.	*%*	*Obs.*	*%*	*Obs.*	*%*	*Obs.*	*%*
ICT graduate degree	7	11.7	29	21.3	3	15.0	9	36.0
Other technical graduate degree	3	5.0	9	6.6	0	0.0	0	0.0
Economic graduate degree	6	10.0	13	9.6	4	20.0	0	0.0
Other graduate degree	1	1.7	3	2.2	3	15.0	1	4.0
ICT high school	6	10.0	13	9.6	0	0.0	9	36.0
Other high school	37	61.6	69	50.7	10	50.0	6	24.0
Total sample	60	100.0	136	100.0	20	100.0	25	100.0

Note

1   See Table 1.3

exception of the software industry. Again results show two opposite patterns depending on the stage in the life cycle of ICT sectors. In ICT manufacturing, the level of educational attainment of founders of NTBFs is significantly higher than that of Internet entrepreneurs, even though it still is lower than in other European countries. 40 per cent of founders is graduated and 72 per cent has followed an ICT education (either through a higher education degree, 36 per cent, or by means of an ICT high school, 36 per cent). Conversely, Internet entrepreneurship is composed of young businessmen with a rather poor education background: of them only 28 per cent has a graduate degree and 22 per cent has followed an ICT education. Founders of NTBFs in the software and multimedia content industries have an intermediate profile. On the one hand, as concerns higher education, they are similar to those of ICT manufacturing industries: 40 per cent and 50 per cent of founders of firms operating in software and multimedia content provision has a graduate degree, respectively. On the other hand, as to technical competencies, they look very similar to Internet businessmen: only 31 per cent and 15 per cent of them have followed an ICT education, respectively.

To sum up, we have found that the evidence on educational attainments of founders of Italian NTBFs in ICT industries significantly differs from that of prior studies relating to other countries. This may be due to institutional factors (i.e. a country-specific effect) that in Italy lower the percentage of the self-employment population with higher education degrees. However, the findings also show that there are considerable differences depending on the sector in which businessmen operate. In ICT manufacturing industries the share of entrepreneurs with a technical educational background is considerably higher than in other sectors, in accordance with the view that technical competencies acquired through education are key for the post-entry performance of new firms. At the other end of the spectrum there are Internet-based activities. Founders of ISP and E-business firms are found to have a significantly poorer technical education background: 73 per cent of them has not followed any technical education versus only 28 per cent of founders of ICT manufacturing firms.

Prior Working Experience

In order to complete the picture of the characteristics of high-tech entrepreneurs, we present evidence on the prior working experience of founders of NTBFs. Because high-tech start-ups depend heavily on founders' knowledge and skills, we expect these latter to have developed considerable experience in related technological and market activities. In order to gain insights into the working background of Italian technology-based founders, we have divided prior employment status; a) depending on whether the sample entrepreneurs already had working experience or not; and b) as far as the former group of founders is concerned, according to the sector of operation of the firm in which founders were previously employed. Within ICTs we have distinguished between four industries: 1) electronics; 2) computer industry; 3) telecommunications (both the production of communications equipment and the provision of telecommunication services); and 4) software and E-business. Moreover, competencies deriving from a working experience in traditional and multimedia publishing may be important, at least for entrepreneurs working in the provision of multimedia content. Thus, we have defined a 'spin-off' as a founder who was previously employed in anyone of the aforementioned industries (that is, ICT industries and publishing).

Table 1.5 shows findings on working background. 42.4 per cent of sample founders can be defined as spin-offs, given that before founding the firm they were working within ICT industries or in publishing. Of these, only 13.7 per cent were previously employed in the electronic, computer or telecommunication industry, that is in sectors dominated by large firms and research organizations which are recognized by previous studies as the main incubators (together with public research organizations) of successful high-tech start-ups (see Carayannis et al., 1998). Some 25.7 per cent were previously employed in software houses and Internet companies; these usually are, at least in Italy, very small firms.[12] More than 37 per cent of sample founders had prior working experience in sectors outside ICTs and publishing, and 20.3 per cent had no working experience.

Table 1.5   Prior working experience of founders of Italian NTBFs

	Observations	%
Electronics	10	4.1
Computer industry	11	4.6
Telecommunications (equipment and services)	12	5.0
Software, Internet	62	25.7
Publishing (traditional and multimedia)	7	3.0
Working experience in other industries	90	37.3
First working experience	49	20.3
Total sample	241	100.0

Again we observe sizable differences in the entrepreneurs' working profile depending on the sector in which they decide to entry (see Table 1.6). Founders of Internet companies are mainly at their first working experience (40 per cent); if they have a working background this derives either from software (21.7 per cent) or from a sector other than ICTs and publishing (31.7 per cent). Similarly, founders of multimedia content companies and software houses were previously employed in firms operating in the software industry or outside ICT. However, in this case the percentage of founders at the first working experience is significantly lower than that of Internet businessmen (16.2 per cent and 10 per cent for software and multimedia content, respectively). Finally, founders of ICT manufacturing firms have a very different working profile: most (68 per cent) are spin-offs having a prior working experience in a ICT sector, and only 4 per cent of them is at the first working experience. Again, we run chi-squared tests for multinomial distributions to asses the robustness of the empirical findings. The results are reported in the Appendix (see Table 1.A2). For each sector in which the sampled entrepreneurs operate out of the four considered, the distribution of founders across the various categories of working background turned out to be significantly different, at conventional levels, from the one of the remaining entrepreneurs.

Table 1.6   Previous working background according to the sector of operations of the start-ups

	Internet		Software		Multimedia content		ICT manufacturing	
	Obs.	*%*	*Obs.*	*%*	*Obs.*	*%*	*Obs.*	*%*
Electronics	0	0.0	4	2.9	3	15.0	3	12.0
Computer industry	2	3.3	9	6.6	0	0.0	0	0.0
Telecommunications	0	0.0	0	0.0	0	0.0	12	48.0
Software, Internet	13	21.7	42	30.9	5	25.0	2	8.0
Publishing	2	3.3	4	2.9	1	5.0	0	0.0
Working experience in other industries	19	31.7	55	40.5	9	45.0	7	28.0
First working experience	24	40.0	22	16.2	2	10.0	1	4.0
Total sample	60	100.0	136	100.0	20	100.0	25	100.0

It is quite interesting to combine the results on founders' age at the time the start-up was established and education so as to sketch out the average duration of their working experience before becoming self-employed. We concentrate attention on the findings concerning Internet companies and ICT manufacturing firms. As to founders of these latter firms, the average age, at the date of firm's foundation, is 37 for those with a high school leaving certificate and 44 for those with a higher education degree. Considering that in Italy students leave on average the high school at 19 and the university at 27, this implies 18 (for founders with high school) and 17 years (for those with higher education) of professional experience before the foundation of a NTBF. This period proves to be much shorter for Internet entrepreneurs. Indeed, by doing the same calculation one derives that prior professional experience lasts for only 9 and 4 years for founders of Internet companies with high school leaving certificate and higher education degree, respectively.

Summing Up: The Characteristics of Italian NTBF Founders

In order to gain further insights into the relation between the characteristics of founders of NTBFs and the sector of the start-up, we have computed bivariate correlations. Table 1.7 illustrates variables that capture founder's characteristics. *Age* is the standardized value of founder's age at the date of start-up. *Education* and *ICT degree* are two measures of the level of education attainment of NTBF founders. In particular, *Education* is a categorical ordered variable which is 2 when the founder has a technical higher education degree, 1 if he has another graduate degree, and 0 otherwise (i.e. high school). *ICT degree* is a dummy variable that captures technical skill acquired through education: it is one for founders with ICT education (either high school leaving certificate or graduate degree). Prior working experience is evaluated through the variables *spin-off* and *first job*. The former is a dummy variable that equal one for founders with prior working experience in ICT and related sectors: electronics, computer industry, telecommunications, software, e-business, and publishing. The latter is a dummy variable which is one for founders with no working background.

Table 1.8 presents bivariate correlations between measures of characteristics of NTBF founders and industry dummies. As stressed before, it emerges a scenario with two opposite types of high-tech entrepreneur. On the one hand, individuals that decide to start an Internet activity are significantly younger, less educated and with few (if any) prior working experience. This may be the outcome of two complementary explanations. First, the advent of the new Internet paradigm and the associated birth of new markets have created new business opportunities which encourage entry of a large number of new entrepreneurial firms. So, lower entry barriers and business expectations of an

Table 1.7   Definition of variables describing the characteristics of founders of Italian NTBFs

Variable	Description
ICT manufacturing, software, Internet, multimedia content	Dummy variables, equal to 1 when the NTBF Founder operates in ICT manufacturing, software, Internet, and multimedia content provision respectively; 0 otherwise
Age[a]	Founder's age at the date of firm's foundation.
Education[b]	Categorical variable, which is 2 for founders with ICT or other technical graduate degree, 1 for founders with other graduate degree (e.g. social sciences, humanities), 0 for founders with high school leaving certificate
ICT degree[b]	Dummy variable, equal to 1 for founders with ICT education (either with graduate degree or with high school); 0 otherwise
Spin-off	Dummy variable, equal to 1 for founders with prior working experience in ICT sectors
First job	Dummy variable, equal to 1 for founders at first job; 0 for founders with some prior working experience (inside or outside ICT sectors)

Notes

a   Standardised value, null mean and unity variance.
b   For a definition see Table 1.3.

expanding market have caused an excess of entry of newly established firms (Camerer and Lovallo, 1999), the majority of which is run by entrepreneurs who lack both managerial and technical competencies. In the long run, competition will lead to a shake out, selecting efficient firms and forcing less efficient ones to exit. Second, as was said earlier, Internet is a competence destroying paradigm. Therefore, technological and managerial knowledge related to previous experience becomes very fast obsolete, and reproducing consolidated patterns of behaviour may be detrimental to business success. E-founders are thus more likely to be both less educated than other ICT entrepreneurs and at their first working experience. If one focuses attention on e-founders that do have prior working experience, they are less likely to be spin-offs.

On the other hand, founders of ICT manufacturing firms are older, more educated (at least as regards technical education) and with more professional experience in ICT sectors. Indeed, ICT manufacturing industries are in a more mature stage of the life cycle and enjoy lower industrial turbulence. Moreover, they are based on rather consolidated technological knowledge. In this case, competencies acquired through both education and professional experience are crucial.

In an intermediate position, software and multimedia content are industries which have been partially revitalized by the advent of Internet. Within these sectors, the markets is populated by entrepreneurs in their mid-to-late 30s with good educational attainments (but not specifically technical) and some working experience inside and outside ICTs.

4   Motivations of the Self-employment Decision

The interviewed entrepreneurs were asked to choose one or more (out of six) motivations and factors which have been the most important ones to shape the start-up decision.[13] Selected motivations are of four types. First, entrepreneurs may be induced to start a new business because of negative future prospects of the mother firm.[14] Of these defensive motivations, concern about future career developments within the mother firm and scepticism about prospects of the mother firm seemed to us as the most relevant ones. Turning attention to psychological factors, we concentrate on entrepreneurs' willingness to manage autonomously their working time and aversion to a hierarchical corporate culture. By following the income choice approach (see Blanchflower and Oswald, 1998), we include motivations regarding an expected increase in the entrepreneur's income by becoming self-employed. Within this approach, the self-employment decision of a potential founder working for a firm occurs when the discounted utility from present and prospect income flows within the company (or with other possible employment relations) is lower than the discounted expected utility of the income flow from the independent activity. A similar framework applies to the case of an individual at his first job experience. In this case he compares the discounted expected utility of the income flow from the independent activity with an outside market option (i.e. the income potentially assured by an employment relation). Of course, the choice depends highly on an individual's risk aversion and degree of myopia, capital constraints and environmental uncertainty. Finally, entrepreneurs may be of a Schumpeterian type, being mainly motivated by the willingness of introducing a product or process innovation.

Table 1.8 Bivariate correlations

Sector	Age	Education	ICT	Spin-off education	First job
Internet	-0.2904 ***	-0.1257 **	-0.1223 **	-0.1630 **	0.2814 ***
Software	0.0308	0.0683	-0.0160	0.0244	-0.1175 *
Multimedia content	0.1115 *	0.0113	-0.1071 *	0.0163	-0.0772
ICT manufacturing	0.2608 ***	0.0569	0.2963 ***	0.1768 ***	-0.1381 **

Notes

*** Significance level greater than 1%.
** Significance level greater than 5%.
* Significance level greater than 10%.

Table 1.9 Ranking of motivations influencing the self-employment choice (per cent)[a]

Motivation	Total sample	Internet	Software	Multimedia content	ICT manufacturing
Desire to manage working time	47.8	52.6	47.2	40.0	50.0
Belief in introducing an innovation	46.7	52.6	49.1	40.0	30.0
Perceive potential for higher income	40.2	63.2	39.6	10.0	30.0
Aversion to hierarchical corporate culture	32.6	36.8	34.0	20.0	30.0
Concern about future career developments	17.4	26.3	17.0	0.0	20.0
Scepticism about prospects of the mother firm	13.0	10.5	11.3	10.0	10.0

Note

a   Percentage of founders quoting a motivation; multiple choices are allowed.

Table 1.9 shows findings on motivations of the self-employment choice of founders of Italian NTBFs. In particular, column 2 reports the ranking of motivations for the entire sample of founders, and columns 3 to 6 present rankings once we distinguish the four industry categories of high-tech entrepreneurs. As prior empirical evidence has found (see Storey, 1982; Vivarelli, 1991), the desire to manage working time turns out to be most important factor underlying the self-employment choice: 48 per cent of sample founders indicate this factor as a major determinant of the start-up choice. Given the high-tech nature of start-ups, innovation related motivations have a similar importance, with the percentage of NTBF founders indicating this factor being as high as 47 per cent. Also, the prospect of earning a higher income in the new venture scores a high value (40 per cent), though lower than the one of the previous two factors. Instead, defensive motivations (i.e. concern about future career developments within the prior company and scepticism about prospects of the mother firm) do not seem to be very common causes of a corporate spin-off (17 per cent and 13 per cent, respectively). Finally, aversion to hierarchical corporate culture is in the middle of the list (fourth motivation with a percentage equal to 32.6 per cent), pointing again to the non-marginal role played by psychological motivations of entrepreneurs. In other words, besides economic rational calculations the self-employment choice heavily depends on the particular structure of entrepreneurs' preferences.

As for all other characteristics of high-tech founders, also motivations are significantly related to industry factors. Within E-founders, start-up motivations are linked to high profit expectations associated with the take-off of the market for Internet-based services. Indeed, within this category of founders the perceived potential for income increase scores a percentage as high as 63.2 per cent (the highest value in our sample). This confirms, at least partially, that in the infancy of a new industry overconfidence and excess of entry characterize entrepreneurs' behaviour (Camerer and Lovallo, 1999).[15] After an industry shakeout when industrial turbulence decreases and competitive selection forces are at work, profit expectations are less positive. Indeed, within the manufacturing sectors of ICT entrepreneurs' motivations to establish a new firm are relatively more defensive (30 per cent of them quote the bad prospects of the mother firm versus 13 per cent of the total sample and 10.5 per cent of Internet founders).

5 Conclusions

In this chapter we have analysed the personal characteristics of 241 founders of NTBFs that operate in ICT sectors and are located in Northern Italy. We have considered both manufacturing (i.e. electronics, communication equipment, computers) and service (software, multimedia content, ISP and e-commerce) sectors. Due to the prominent position of ICTs within Italian high-tech industries and, within ICTs, the predominance of northern regions, the sample can be regarded as representative of Italian high-tech entrepreneurs.

In this perspective, the first contribution of this work to the literature is that it allows to compare the evidence on such characteristics of Italian entrepreneurs as their age at foundation's time, educational background, prior working experience, and motivations of the self-employment choice with that provided by previous studies relating to other European countries. Such comparison highlights the existence of a country-specific effect. Even though Italian entrepreneurs are on average in their mid-30s like their European counterparts, they have lower educational qualifications, especially in technical fields. In addition, among sample entrepreneurs the percentage of spin-offs, that is of entrepreneurs having prior working experience in sectors related to the activity of the new firm, is considerably lower than in other countries. These findings suggest that the institutional setting may deeply influence the self-employment decision. For instance, the long duration of high education programs in Italy is likely to negatively affect the propensity of graduated individuals to setting up a new firm: as risk aversion rapidly increases with age, the later an individual graduates, the less likely that he will take the self-employment choice. Beyond the characteristics of the education system, there may be other institutional factors, related for instance to the organization of the labour and financial markets in Italy and to national corporate law, that may influence risk aversion of highly educated individuals, and consequently the birth rate of NTBFs and the personal characteristics of high-tech entrepreneurs. We think that a thorough analysis of the impact of the institutional context based on international comparisons, would considerably extend our understanding of the phenomenon of NTBFs.

Nonetheless, institutional differences with respect to other countries only offer a partial explanations of the data presented in this work. It has been shown in the previous sections that there are sizable cross-sectoral differences as to the characteristics of Italian high-tech entrepreneurs, with founders of ICT manufacturing and Internet firms being at opposite extremes. The former are on average in the early 1940s at the date of establishment of the start-up;

they are more educated, at least as regards technical education, and generally have developed professional experience in ICT industries before becoming self-employed. The latter are younger and less educated; quite often, they are at the first working experience. If they do have prior working experience, it usually is in sectors unrelated to the activity of the new firm. In addition, as to the motivations of the self-employment choice, among e-founders expectations of a substantial income increase play a key role. On the contrary, in the ICT manufacturing category defensive motivations are relatively more important. Software and multimedia content industries, which have been rejuvenated by the commercial success of Internet, turned out to be in an intermediate position.

Such evidence allows some intertwined and complementary explanations relating to the industry life cycle and the nature of the technological changes connected with the development of Internet. Internet has been described by previous studies as a new technological paradigm. Due to its competence destroying nature, prior knowledge and skills, pertaining to both the technological and managerial spheres, rapidly become obsolete. Innovative technical ideas and new business models, which depart from consolidated ways of thinking, are required for business success in Internet activities. In addition, markets for Internet services still are in their very infancy, especially in Italy. This has a series of implications. On the one hand, barriers to entry are lower in Internet-based industries due to the knowledge advantage enjoyed by newcomers with respect to incumbent firms. In addition, there may be overconfidence on the part of Internet entrepreneurs as to the profit potential associated with the new technology. Excess entry of unfitted individuals may well result. On the other hand, distinctive capabilities in Internet activities are likely to be only loosely related to those developed by an e-founder through education or in previous professional occupations. Therefore the fact that e-founders exhibit lower educational qualification and less (and more unrelated) working experience than other ICT entrepreneurs comes as no surprise.

In order to be able to discriminate between the above arguments, further empirical evidence is needed. In particular, one should try to relate the post-entry growth and innovative performances of NTBFs that operate in different sectors to the personal characteristics of entrepreneurs. This study is high in the authors' research agenda.

Nonetheless, it is important to emphasize that the results so far obtained clearly show that Internet does make a difference, even though we are only able to presume why. Such evidence has important policy implications.

As a result of the considerable attention which in the 1990s has been devoted by the economic literature to NTBFs as a key driver of economic renewal, wide consensus has developed as to the main obstacles that inhibit growth of such firms and the policy measures that are most suitable to remove them. In this context special emphasis has been placed on such factors as the inadequacy of the banking system, the need for specialized financial institutions such as venture capital firms which are better suited to deal with problems arising from information asymmetries, the lack of marketing and managerial skills on the part of high-tech entrepreneurs, and the difficulty experienced by NTBFs in hiring skilled personnel. The idea that NTBFs are 'special' and thus require ad hoc policy measures has gained ground among economists and then also among policy makers (see for instance Storey and Tether, 1998b). We agree with such argument. Nonetheless, we also claim that there is a case for paying more attention to cross-sectoral differences than it has been done so far. In other words, it is important to adjust policy measures according to the idiosyncratic characteristics of different industrial settings. Such reasoning especially applies to Internet-based activities. Building a coherent policy framework to effectively support Internet start-ups, a move which in our view will play a key role for the competitiveness of Europe, goes far beyond the objectives of the present work. Suffice here to mention that recognizing that activities related to Internet have special requirements is a necessary premise to this end. For instance, indirect demand-side support policies aimed at favouring the self-sustained take-off of a European mass market for Internet services[16] might turn out to be as effective as highly popular supply-side policy measures such as those aimed at increasing the supply of PhDs in science and technology fields or those targeting failures of financial markets.

Notes

1   According to data from the US Small Business Administration, between 1992 and 1996 small and medium firms (i.e. number of employees lower than 500) created 11.8 million of new jobs, while larger firms lost almost 650.000 jobs. In addition, Acs et al. (1999) show that for the five years period from 1990 to 1995 births of new establishments (which actually also include new branches of existing firms) contributed 25.9 per cent to the net job creation rate of 7.1 per cent. Gross job creation was found to be heavily concentrated among high growth new firms, especially those that are in innovative industries (see Birch and Medoff, 1994; Kirchhoff, 1994; Reynolds and White, 1997). See also OECD (1996).

2   In 1992, Italian firms with fewer than 20 employees accounted for 38.7 per cent of total employment, a value that is five times as large as that of the US and three times as large as that of the UK (see OECD 1998).

3   This is indirectly witnessed by the growing attention that the international economic and financial press is devoting to European e-firms (see for instance the cover stories of *Business Week*, 31 January, 7 February and 6 March 2000).

4   These sectors correspond to the following four-digit industries (NACE-CLIO classification): communication equipment 31.30, computers 30.02, electronics 32.20.

5   The two most important high-tech sectors that were not considered are pharmaceuticals (inclusive of biotechnology) and aerospace. According to 1996 Italian census data (ISTAT 1999), the number of small and medium size firms (i.e. number of employees lower than 500) in such industries is only 1.4 per cent of the number of firms that operate in the ICT industries taken here into consideration. Absent more precise data on the age distribution of firms, there is no reason to believe that such proportion is substantially altered when one focuses attention on NTBFs.

6   The decision to confine the analysis to Northern Italy was due to practical reasons; as the identification of target firms was a very time consuming process, we were forced to concentrate efforts in geographical areas where the likelihood of finding ICT-based NTBFs was sufficiently high. In this respect, note that Northern Italy accounts for over 50 per cent of Information Technology expenses of Italian firms and over 65 per cent of total employment in the industries considered in the present work (see again ISTAT 1999).

7   Autio et al. (1989) studying a sample of Finnish founders of NTBFs find an average age equal to 34. In the French case NTBFs' founders are on average 37 years old at the date of foundation (GMV Conseil, 1989). They are between 30 and 50 in the UK (Westhead and Storey, 1994).

8   Indeed 95 per cent of sample founders have financed their start-up using their personal income.

9   For a definition of technological paradigm and technological trajectories see Dosi (1982). On the difference between *competence destroying* and *competence enhancing* technological change see Tushman and Anderson (1986). Finally, for a thorough analysis of the characteristics of the Internet paradigm see Colombo and Garrone (1997).

10   Note that the large number of new entrants may also be the result of overconfidence on the part of e-founders as to the profit opportunities of start-ups. This issue will be addressed in greater detail in Section 4.

11   Note also that since risk aversion is positively related to age, the later an individual graduates, the less likely he takes the self-employment choice. Thus, an institutional system in which individuals graduate very late will have a disproportionate number of entrepreneurs with a very low level of educational attainment. Indeed, individuals with higher degrees, being older will generally take the employment choice.

12   In 1996, 87 per cent of software houses had five or fewer employees, versus 41 per cent of firms in the communications equipment sector and only 1 per cent in the computer and other office equipment industry.

13   For evidence on the role of entrepreneur's personal motivations on firm's post-entry performance see Arrighetti and Vivarelli (1999).

14   Note that these factors apply only to entrepreneurs with previous job experience.

15   The concepts of overconfidence and excess of entry are nicely summarized by the following words of Joe Roth, chairman of Walt Disney Studios: 'If you only think about your own business, you think, "I've got a good story department we're going to go out and do this". And you don't think that everybody else is thinking the same way. In a given weekend in a year you'll have five movies open, and there's certainly not enough people to go around' (*Los Angeles Times*, 1996, quoted in Camerer and Lovallo, 1999).

16 Examples of such measures include subsidization of Internet wide-band access, introduction of PCs in schools, and the development of Internet-based public services so as to capture indirect network externalities. For more details see Colombo and Delmastro (2000).

References

Acs, Z.J., Armington, C. and Robb, A. (1999), 'Measures of Job Flow Dynamics in the US', CES research paper 99–1.

Agarwal, R. and Gort, M. (1996), 'The Evolution of Markets and Entry, Exit, and Survival of Firms', *The Review of Economics and Statistics*, 78, pp. 489–98.

Arrighetti, A., Vivarelli, M. (1999), 'The Role of Innovation in the Post-entry Performance of New Small Firms: Evidence from Italy', *Southern Economic Journal*, 65, pp. 927–39.

Autio, E., Kanerva, R., Kaila, M. and Kauranen, I. (1989), *New, Technology-based Firms in Finland*, Helsinki: Sitra Publication Series.

Birch, D. and Medoff, J. (1994), 'Gazelles', in Solmon, L.C. and Levenson, A.R. (eds), *Labor Markets, Employment Policy, and Job Creation*, Boulder, CO and London: Westview Press.

Blanchflower, D. and Oswald, A. (1998), 'What Makes an Entrepreneur?', *Journal of Labor Economics*, 16, pp. 26–60.

Blanchflower, D. and Oswald, A. (1999), 'Measuring Latent Entrepreneurship across Nations', mimeo, University of Warwick.

Camerer, C. and Lovallo, D. (1999), 'Overconfidence and Excess of Entry', *American Economic Review*, 89, pp. 306–18.

Carayannis, E., Rogers, E., Kurihara, K. and Allbritton, M. (1998), 'High-technology Spin-offs from Government R&D Laboratories and Research Universities', *Technovation*, 18, pp. 1–11.

Colombo, M.G. and Delmastro M. (2000), 'New Technology-based Firms in ICT Industries: A Policy Perspective', paper prepared for 'Compostela 2000. Programa Europa Mundi: The Construction of Europe, Democracy, and Globalisation', Santiago de Compostela, April 2000.

Colombo, M.G. and Garrone, P. (1997), 'The Multimedia Paradigm: An Evolutionary Approach', *Communications and Strategy*, 28, pp. 215–43.

Delapierre, M. (1998), 'NTBFs: The French Case', *Research Policy*, 26, pp. 989–1003.

Donckels, R. (1989), 'Tech versus Common Starters: Comparison by Means of 32 Case Studies', Brussels: Small Business Research Institute.

Dosi, G. (1982), 'Technological Paradigms and Technological Trajectories', *Research Policy*, 11, pp. 147–62.

EC (1996a), 'New Technology-based Firms (NTBFs) in Europe', EIMS Publication No. 31.

EC (1996b), 'Review of Studies on Innovative Fast Growing SMEs', EIMS Publication No. 42.

Evans, D. and Jovanovic, B. (1989), 'An Estimated Model of Entrepreneurial Choice under Liquidity Constraints', *Journal of Political Economy*, 97, pp. 596–615.

Giudici, G. and Paleari, S. (2000), 'The Provision of Finance To Innovation: A Survey Conducted among Technology Based Small Firms', *Small Business Economics*, pp. 37–53.

GMV Conseil (1989), 'La creation d'enterprises innovantes', Rapport pour la Ministere de l'Industrie, Paris.

Gort, M. and Klepper, S. (1982), 'Time Paths in the Diffusion of Product Innovations', *Economic Journal*, 92, pp. 630–53.

ISTAT (1999), *Censimento Intermedio dell'Industria e dei Servizi*.

Jo, H. and Lee, J. (1996), 'The Relationship between an Entrepreneur's Background and Performance in a New Venture', *Technovation*, 16, pp. 161–71.

Johnson, W. (1978), 'A Theory of Job Shopping', *Quarterly Journal of Economics*, 92, pp. 261–78.

Kirchhof, B.A. (1994), *Entrepreneurship and Dynamic Capitalism: The Economics of Business Formation and Growth*, Wesport, CN and London: Greenwood, Praeger.

Licht, G., Nerlinger, E. and Berger, G. (1995), *Germany: NTBF Literature Review*, Mannheim: ZEW.

Miller, R. (1984), 'Job Matching and Occupational Choice', *Journal of Political Economy*, 92, pp. 1086–120.

OECD (1996), *SMEs: Employment, Innovation and Growth. The Washington Workshop*.

OECD (1998), 'Small Businesses, Job Creation and Growth: Facts, Obstacles and Best Practices', http://www.oecd.org/dsti/sti/industry/smes/prod/smes.pdf.

Reynolds, P.D. and White, S.B. (1997), *The Entrepreneurial Process: Economic Growth, Men, Women, and Minorities*, Wesport, CN and London: Greenwood, Quorum Books.

Roberts, E.B. (1991), 'The Technological Base of the New Enterprise', *Research Policy*, 20, pp. 283–98.

Storey, D.J (1982), *Entrepreneurship of the New Firm*, London: Croom Helm.

Storey, D.J. and Tether, B.S. (1998a), 'New Technology-based Firms in the European Union: An Introduction', *Research Policy*, 26, pp. 933–46.

Storey, D.J. and Tether, B.S. (1998b), 'Public Policy Measures to Support New Technology-based Firms in the European Union', *Research Policy*, 26, pp. 1037–57.

Tushman, M.L. and Anderson, P. (1986), 'Technological Discontinuities and Organizational Environments', *Administrative Science Quarterly*, 31, pp. 439–65.

Vivarelli, M. (1991), 'The Birth of New Enterprises', *Small Business Economics*, 3, pp. 215–23.

Westhead, P. and Storey, D.J. (1994), *An Assessment of Firms Located on and off Science Parks in the UK*, London: HMSO.

Appendix

Multinomial chi-squared tests on the distributions of NTBF founders by educational qualification are based on a smaller number of categories than those considered in Table 1.4 due to small number problems (i.e. we want to avoid situations in which a category has a null value for some sectors). Thus, we have proceeded to aggregate the six categories into three: 1) technical graduate degree (i.e. ICT and other technical graduate degrees); 2) other graduate degree (i.e. economic and other graduate degrees); and 3) high school living certificate (i.e. ICT and other high school). The null hypothesis is that the distribution does not depend on the specific sector of operation of the start-up. Results of multinomial tests are presented in Table 1.A1.

Table 1.A1   Education of NTBF founders according to the sector of operation: multinomial tests

Sector	Test (2)
Internet	17.251 ***
Software	2.713
Multimedia content	61.831 ***
ICT manufacturing	62.241 ***

Notes

*** Significance level greater than 1%.
Degrees of freedom in parenthesis.

As for education, the number of categories of founders' working background has been reduced with respect to those of Table 1.6. in this case we have run multinomial chi-squared tests on the distributions of founders by working experience after reducing the number of classes from seven to four: 1) working experience in ICT manufacturing (i.e. electronics, computer industry and telecommunications); 2) software and Internet background; 3) other working experience (i.e. publishing and working experience outside ICT); and 4) first working experience. Again the null hypothesis is that there are no sectoral biases.

Table 1.A2 Working experience of NTBF founders according to the sector of operation: multinomial tests

Sector	Test (3)
Internet	140.829 ***
Software	21.973 ***
Multimedia content	33.407 ***
ICT manufacturing	395.429 ***

Notes

*** Significance level greater than 1%.
Degrees of freedom in parenthesis.

Chapter 2

The Effect of Multimarket Scope on Firms' Compatibility Choice

Marc van Wegberg

1   Introduction

The knowledge economy exists in vertical value chains that tend to run in three levels of activity:

technology suppliers → network operators → content, service providers.

The technology providers supply information and communications technology (ICT) products such as computer hardware, connection equipment, and software. Network operators acquire these ICT products to create physical data and voice communication networks. On these networks, service providers run services (applications) to distribute information goods (content) or to enable communication between people. Products from different companies need to connect together to make these services work. Pieces of hardware and software need to interoperate. Compatibility is the condition that describes the connectivity and interoperability of these technologies, components, and products. Compatibility is an important condition for a flourishing knowledge economy.

There is much debate about what causes firms to prefer their technologies to be compatible (see Shapiro and Varian, 1999, for a topical textbook, and Katz and Shapiro, 1994, and Matutes and Regibeau, 1996, for surveys). Public sympathy tends to be with those who support compatibility and standards. There is rightly much support for the Internet custodians in the IETF (Internet Engineering Task Force) and the World Wide Web Consortium. But private companies have more to think about than public sympathy. They may come out in favour of incompatible technologies. For example, videogame consoles by Sega and Nintendo are incompatible with each other (Van Wegberg, 1996).

In the literature about compatibility choice, an important insight is that a firm's choice of (in)compatibility depends both on the absolute size of the market demand created by a new technology and the firm's share of the associated revenues (Shapiro and Varian, 1999, p. 198). An incompatible technology, based on a proprietary standard, may increase or safeguard the firm's appropriation of revenues. Incompatibility may be the price to pay if suppliers want to appropriate revenues from their technology development efforts. Compatible technologies, on the other hand, protect users' investments in these technologies. They may increase the absolute size of market demand. An innovator may decide to give up control over its technology in order to trade-off its share of total revenues for the total size of revenues.

The basic argument in this chapter is that we need to understand a firm's compatibility choice in the broad context in which it operates. That is, we need to look beyond the direct effects of compatibility choice for the market place. Firms tend to be active in multiple markets. Their compatibility choice for a technology may have direct effects in one market, that have indirect consequences in its other markets. As a result, the choice of compatibility may work out differently for a pure player, a firm that is active only in the one product market that is directly concerned, than for multimarket firms with interests in related markets. A pure player needs to recoup its technology efforts in the market directly affected, so it tends to focus on the appropriability of its investments (the appropriability motive). A multimarket firm can afford to focus on growing the market, knowing that it can recoup its investments in other markets that are positively affected by the growing market (the market demand size motive). When the market directly affected by a standard has spillovers on other markets, the market demand size motive when choosing a standards' regime may be more important than the appropriation motive.

We first discuss the problem at hand. Then we discuss a simple model that highlights the compatibility choice in a context with multiple markets, multimarket firms, and cooperation. A brief example of mobile Internet economics illustrates the issues in a real world context. The appraisal points to future research issues that our model opens up.

2   Product Portfolio, Compatibility Choice, and Standardization

Compatibility is a technical feature of the relationship between two or more components in a system. There are various forms of compatibility (Farrell and Saloner, 1986; Katz and Shapiro, 1986; Matutes and Regibeau, 1996). The common feature of compatible products is that they enable their users to share resources. Efficiency tends to be the underlying motive for developing compatible technologies and products. If a product enables communication, such as a telephone, different products are called compatible if their users can communicate with each other. All users who use different, but compatible, products together form a network. This is a direct network externality (Katz and Shapiro, 1985 and 1986).

Another form of compatibility occurs when individual products are components that need to be combined to be of use to the user. Potentially complementary components need to be compatible for the user to be able to actually combine them in a system (Matutes and Regibeau, 1988). Complementary systems can also lead to an indirect network externality, that is, sales of either compatible product benefit users of the other compatible product indirectly, by stimulating sales, investments, and improvements of the complementary product. Another indirect externality occurs if interchangeability of parts facilitates mass production when that leads to economies of scale. In short, if products are compatible, they enable a positive network externality to their users.

The choice to make products (in)compatible has important effects on the demand side of the market. Suppliers may agree with each other up-front to make their products compatible. Compatibility is likely to benefit the users (all else remaining equal) by enabling positive network externalities. It increases the network users can communicate with (the direct network externality), it increases the scale at which components are built, or it enables the provision of more, better or cheaper complementary products, like hardware and software (indirect network externalities).

A firm may also, however, prefer that its product is incompatible with those of a rival. It may be costly to achieve compatibility, as this may require R&D investments, or building an adapter (Katz and Shapiro, 1985). If their products are incompatible, each firm will try to generate the network externalities mentioned above (such as economies of scale) by fierce competition. Firms are more willing to compete for customers today, if they believe that these customers form a network (an installed base) that increases the utility of their product for future customers. The associated price cutting may make this scenario more attractive to users than the case when firms agree *ex ante* on compatible products (Katz and Shapiro, 1986). Incompatibility may also stimulate firms to do R&D, when each needs to build up an installed base of users. Their greater incentive to do R&D may be socially beneficial (Farrell and Katz, 1998), except when the firms overinvest in R&D (Kristiansen, 1998). Once the products are introduced in the market, their compatibility may facilitate customer switching between their product and their rivals' products, thus increasing competition *ex post*.

Suppliers may prefer their products to be compatible, in order to slow down an R&D race, and to avoid wasteful duplication of R&D effort. Compatibility may also prevent a crippling price war *ex ante* (before a standard is established) to built up market share.

In an evolutionary context, Metcalfe and Miles (1994) distinguish between short term and long term effects of compatibility. The short-term effect of standardization is to create order and reduce variety. It reduces variety for producers (fewer technologies to choose from) or consumers (by eliminating products that do not use the technology that got standardized). Standardization also, however, expands the market, which itself tends to arouse creativity and variation. Demand growth and large market size stimulate the development of compatible and complementary products.

There are various ways to achieve compatibility. One way is to formulate a standard, a set of specifications, such that products that satisfy these specifications, are compatible. Another is to build an adapter (an interface, converter or a gateway) that couples different products to integrate their networks (e.g., Choi, 1996a). Creating an adapter makes two products partially compatible, which shows that the compatibility choice does not have to be an all or nothing affair (De Palma, Leruth and Regibeau, 1999). The choice of compatibility can be unilateral, if one firm decides to build an adapter, or bilateral, if all suppliers have to agree on a standard (Matutes and Regibeau, 1988). In this chapter we focus on the latter route, the definition of a standard.

Firms can follow several paths in establishing a standard. Each contender may develop the technology, and then introduce a product in the market. Competition in the market for customers may settle the standard. The technology developers may license their technology to rival producers, in order to increase the bandwagon behind their technology. In this case, competition for rival suppliers' adoption decisions may settle the standard. Firms may cooperate to develop a technology together. Competition then takes the form of a battle between alliances. Finally, all relevant firms may cooperate up-front to develop and adopt a technology. If there is a standard setting organization, firms may develop a technology and submit it to the organization. The latter will take charge for a certification, adoption, diffusion, and user feedback process

In these scenarios, cooperation increases from the licensing strategy up to the institutionalized standard setting process. Firms face a trade-off between a larger chance of adoption (by cooperation) and a loss of control and appropriation (if cooperation implies a loss of revenue or control to the partners). Technology developers can choose which mode of standardization to adopt. They will try to anticipate which mode best serves their interests. In this chapter we focus on the first and third standardization mode in Table 2.1: go it alone or cooperate to develop the industry-wide technology standard.

Table 2.1   Modes of standardization

	Cooperation	Appropriation	Control	Who chooses standard?
Develop technology and launch product	None	Via market sales	Total	Users
Develop and license technology	Individual development Joint adoption	Via market sales and licensing revenues	Via licensing contracts	Users and suppliers
Alliance to develop and adopt technology	Joint development and adoption	Share licensing revenues, and product sales	Negotiation	Suppliers (and users if rival alliances exist)
Submit technology to standardization institute	Joint development; adoption stimulated by institute	Share in licensing revenues (if collected), and market sales	Participation in process	Standardization institute, its members (users, if members, or if rival technologies hit the market)

A proprietary standard offers control and revenues to the firm. This offers incentives for the firm to invest in its technology. If firms develop competing technologies, they may experiment and choose different avenues of technological development (Choi, 1996b). A cooperative standardization process reduces the scope of this experimentation, and may thus lead to a loss of revenue.

A collective process may slow down innovation, relative to independent actions by the competing firms. Farrel and Saloner (1988) show that bargaining in a collective process delays adoption of a standard, compared with the case of uncoordinated choice of technology. However, having one agreed upon standard can also speed up diffusion and adoption by users, as these need not fear that they buy the wrong standard. Users may postpone or avoid adoption, if they anticipate that they may end up with the standard that loses out later, thus forcing upon them the costly switch to the standard.

Cooperation may take the form of an industry-wide alliance or of competing alliances. In the latter case, the product market (both suppliers and buyers) still face a choice between competing (incompatible) technologies. Axelrod, Mitchell, Thomas, Bennett and Bruderer (1995) explore competing alliances, when firms can choose between two competing standard setting alliances. Firms face a quandary: they will tend to avoid an alliance that contains close rivals, but they will also prefer the largest alliance (in terms of the combined market share of its members). In the real world case of competing Unix versions, they succeed largely in predicting which firms will join a particular Unix alliance.

Table 2.2 summarizes the factors that affect the choice of compatibility. New inputs in this debate may come from looking at the wider context in which firms choose compatibility of their products.

The standardization strategy and compatibility choice tend to be part of a larger environment. Firstly, an individual standard is often part of an architecture of complementary standards that together define a system, a family of products and technologies that provide services to users (Henderson and Clark, 1990). This systemic approach connects standardization policy to the overall architectures and the associated competitive environments. Secondly, the product market concerned interacts with each firm's overall portfolio of activities. A firm may be active in markets indirectly affected by the standard. The markets can be linked on the demand side or on the supply side. Thirdly, firms increasingly form clusters or networks. An individual standard can form a small part of the activities that go on in the network. The network context may well determine the choices individual firms make concerning a compatibility choice. We believe that much future research on standardization will focus on this wider, systemic/multimarket/cluster environment.

A firm's multimarket scope may reflect linkages among its product markets. A demand side link exists when, for example, the products are complementary (see Matutes and Regibeau, 1989; and Church and Gandal, 1996). A supply side link exists when, for example, there is an economy of scale or learning by doing effect in an input that the production processes for both markets share. This will lead to an economy of scope (Teece, 1980; Baumol, Panzar and Willig, 1982; Van Witteloostuijn and Van Wegberg, 1992). A shared brand name or reputation can lead to an (informational) economy of scope. It is also possible that one market's product is an input in either the production process or consumption process in the other market. The positions of these products

Table 2.2   Factors that have an effect pro or contra (+ or −) compatibility choice

Factor	Effect on compatibility choice	Literature
Resource sharing (direct or indirect network externality; complementarity)	+	Fundamental argument for standardization Katz and Shapiro (1985)
R&D costs of compatibility	−	Farrell and Katz (1998); Kristiansen (1998)
R&D competition if products are incompatible	− (suppliers)/ + (customers)	Katz and Shapiro (1986)
Price cutting to sell incompatible products	+	Choi (1996a)
An adapter can create costly, partial compatibility	+	Choi (1996b)
Competition between incompatible technologies supports experimentation	−	
Time consuming negotiations may be needed to develop a standard	−	Farrell and Saloner (1988)
To avoid direct rivals, firms may create competing alliances	−	Axelrod et al. (1995)
A high customer preference for product variety benefits from standardization of technology and components	+	Metcalfe and Miles (1994)

in the value chains of suppliers and customers will determine the potential for synergies among the markets.

This chapter explores the effect of the firm's multimarket scope on the compatibility choice. If at least one firm prefers incompatibility, competition in the market place will decide about the market shares of these technologies. We will focus on the long-term effects, rather than on the diffusion process. The outcome of this game depends on many factors, including the following:

- which competitive position and market share do the two firms have in the market concerned?
- which outside interests do the two technology developing firms have?

We will call an outside interest *weakly synergetic*, if the firm's other interests benefit from or correlate with market demand size in the focus market. The link is weak, in that we do not assume tight links between those markets, such as shared technology, compatibility, etc. If a multimarket firm is active in weakly synergetic markets, its overall performance tends to correlate with the demand size of the focus market, rather than its share in that market. We suggest the following propositions:

- *proposition (1a)*: a multimarket firm active in weakly synergetic markets tends to prefer a collectively agreed standard (the market size motive);
- *proposition (1b)*: if the firm is active only in the focus market, it will choose the standardization strategy that maximizes its value within that market (the appropriation motive). It will tend to prefer incompatible technologies.

A Model

Two firms seek their preferences for the compatibility of their products. The question is: does a firm for whom the product is part of a wider product line address the standardization issue differently than a pure player?

Say, two firms develop a new product technology. The new product (product A) has a positive network externality on the demand side. The utility of the product A to each user increases in the number of users of compatible technologies. Users may prefer a single compatible technology. The suppliers may not be so sure. They may cooperate to develop a single technology. If they do not cooperate, each develops its own technology. Either way, they subsequently compete in the product market. Depending on the anticipated technology development costs, competition, and product demand, firms will prefer cooperation or going it alone.

The outcome may change if one firm is a multimarket firm that also supplies a weakly synergetic market B. This supplier may be more interested in the total number of users of product A than in its own market share. This may change his preferences for compatibility.

Assumptions There are two markets, market A and market B. In market A, there are two suppliers, firms 1 and 2, with their product A_1 and A_2. A buyer (j) derives a net utility from product A_i of

$$U_j = \alpha_j v_i + \beta N_i - p_i, \tag{1}$$

where v_i indicates the quality of the product and N_i the size of the network (i.e., the demand). If the products are compatible, both products have the same network (called N_A), otherwise each product has its own network (N_i). The consumer chooses the product that gives the largest net consumer surplus. If the net consumer surplus is negative, she does not buy at all. The α_j are uniformly distributed over an interval $[\alpha^{min}, \alpha^{max}]$ with a density of γ, which implies that there are $N = \gamma (\alpha^{min} - \alpha^{max})$ potential buyers.

We assume that firms compete in prices p_i (Bertrand competition). Each maximizes gross profits, given the investments made to develop the technology. Marginal costs are given and identical for both firms at c. The quality levels are given, and different. We assume that firm 1 has the high quality product: $v_1 > v_2$. We assume, therefore, that quality differences are unrelated to marginal costs. An example where this tends to hold are information goods.

Market B is of a complementary good to market A. Product B, that is, has a higher utility to customers who also use product A than for those who did not buy A. It does not matter here whether a customer bought A_1 or A_2, nor does it matter whether A_1 and A_2 are compatible. We should not think of A and B as compatible products, therefore, like computer hardware and software. See Church and Gandal (1996) for that. Instead, think of market A as computers and market B as for media with information about computers. People who have a computer probably derive more utility from reading about this market.

Only buyers in market A are willing to buy product B. For convenience, we assume market B is a monopoly, and the inverse market demand function is: $p_B = \alpha - \frac{b}{N_A} q_B$ where N_A is the number of buyers of product A. In market B, these buyers are homogeneous (that is, each has his own demand curve for product B: $p_B = a - b q_B$). The monopolist's marginal production costs are zero, for convenience. Product B will always be supplied, therefore, and the market outcomes are: $q_B = \frac{a}{2b} N_A$; $p_B = a/2$; $\pi_B = \frac{a^2}{4b} N_A$; $CS_B = \frac{a^2}{8b} N_A$, where CS is the total consumer surplus. The consumer surplus per individual buyer, CS_j, is $\frac{a^2}{8b}$. If we define $d = \frac{a^2}{8b}$, we can restate that

$$\pi_B = 2dN_A, \quad CS_j = d, \text{ and } CS = dN_A. \tag{2}$$

For convenience, we assume that consumers are myopic, that is, if they decide about buying product A they do not anticipate on the consumer surplus they realize later if they buy product B. This helps to focus on how expectations by suppliers in market A of sales in market B affect their decision making in market A.

Before firms 1 and 2 can supply a product in market A, they need to develop one first. We will assume that there are given fixed costs for developing a new product technology: F for firms 1 and 2, if their products are incompatible, and G if the two cooperate for compatible products (with $F <= G <= 2F$). If compatibility is an afterthought, the fixed costs G will equal 2F, as each firm develops its own technology. If compatibility has to be designed into the products from the ground up, compatible products demand joint development, and G will realize some economy of scale: $G < 2F$. For convenience, we abstract from characteristics of research and development such as being endogenous, uncertain, and subject to spillovers (imitation).

With these basic assumptions we have the simplest possible model that can explore mechanisms discussed in this chapter. More complex models might attempt to be more descriptively realistic.

Case 1: cooperate or not in developing a network product In this case, the suppliers in market A (firms 1 and 2) are independent from the supplier (firm 3) in market B. Market A opens up before market B, which means that both suppliers and customers first decide about buying and selling in market A, before they decide about market B.

Case 1A: compatible products If the firms in market A cooperate to develop compatible goods, they develop a single network, which means that consumer surplus is $U_j = \alpha_j v_i + \beta N_A - p_i$ where N_A is the total number of buyers. Among the consumers with increasing α's from α^{min} to α^{max}, there are two critical consumers: the consumer with the quality preference α'' who is indifferent between buying product 2 (the low quality product) and not buying, and the consumer with α' who is indifferent between products 1 and 2. The sales and network levels of products 1 and 2, and total demand, are:

$$N_1 = \gamma \, [\alpha^{max} - \alpha'], \; N_2 = \gamma \, [\alpha' - \alpha' \, '], \text{ and } N_A = \gamma \, [\alpha^{max} - \alpha' \, '] \tag{3}$$

The consumer who is indifferent between product 2 and not buying has a consumer surplus of zero:

$$\alpha' \, ' v_2 + \beta N_A - p_2 = 0, \text{ with } N_A = \gamma \, [\alpha^{max} - \alpha' \, ']. \tag{4}$$

We assume that this marginal consumer exists, at least for a price p_2 equal to the marginal cost c:

Assumption: $\alpha^{min} < \dfrac{c - \beta \gamma \alpha^{max}}{v_2 - \beta \gamma} < \alpha^{max}, \; 0 < v_2 - \beta \gamma \text{ and } 0 < \beta \gamma \alpha^{max}.$

Remember that consumers do not anticipate on their consumer surplus in market B. The consumer who is indifferent between products 1 and 2 faces the following equality:

$$\alpha' v_1 + \beta N_A - p_1 = \alpha' v_2 + \beta N_A - p_2. \tag{5}$$

Solve these three equations in α', $\alpha' \, '$, and N_A, to get:

$$\alpha' \, ' = \frac{p_2 - \beta \gamma \alpha^{max}}{v_2 - \beta \gamma}$$

$$\alpha' = \frac{p_1 - p_2}{v_1 - v_2} \tag{6}$$

$$N_A(p_1, p_2) = \gamma \, \frac{\alpha^{max} v_2 - p_2}{v_2 - \beta \gamma}$$

This gives the following demand levels, which we express as functions of the prices:

$$N_1(p_1, p_2) = \gamma \, [\alpha^{max} - \frac{p_1 - p_2}{v_1 - v_2}], \text{ and}$$

$$N_2(p_1, p_2) = \gamma \, [\frac{p_1 - p_2}{v_1 - v_2} - \frac{p_2 - \beta \gamma \alpha^{max}}{v_2 - \beta \gamma}]. \tag{7}$$

The firms have gross profits $\pi_i(p_1, p_2) = (p_i - c)N_i$:

$$\pi_1(p_1, p_2) = (p_1 - c)\,\gamma\,[\alpha^{\max} - \frac{p_1 - p_2}{v_1 - v_2}],$$

$$\pi_2(p_1, p_2) = (p_2 - c)\,\gamma\,[\frac{p_1 - p_2}{v_1 - v_2} - \frac{p_2 - \beta\gamma\alpha^{\max}}{v_2 - \beta\gamma}]. \tag{8}$$

This is gross of the development costs of the new product (G). Each firm chooses its price to optimize its profits, given the price of its rival. The first order conditions for optimality of profits then define the reaction curves:

$$p_1(p_2) = \frac{1}{2}\,(p_2 + c + \alpha^{\max}(v_1 - v_2))$$

$$p_1(p_2) = \frac{1}{2}\,\frac{cv_1 + p_1 v_2 - c\beta\gamma - p_1\beta\gamma + (v_1 - v_2)\alpha^{\max}\beta\gamma}{v_1 - \beta\gamma} \tag{9}$$

The second order conditions for optimality hold if $\beta\gamma < v_2 < v_1$. Equations (9) determine the equilibrium prices as:

$$p_1 = \frac{-(3cv_1 - 2v_1^2\alpha^{\max} + 3c\beta\gamma + \alpha^{\max}\beta\gamma(v_1 - v_2))}{4v_1 - v_2 - 3\beta\gamma}$$

$$p_2 = \frac{-(2cv_1 - cv_2 - v_1 v_2^2\alpha^{\max} + 3c\beta\gamma - \alpha^{\max}\beta\gamma(v_1 - v_2))}{4v_1 - v_2 - 3\beta\gamma} \tag{10}$$

Substitute these to get sales:

$$N_1(p_1, p_2) = \gamma\,\frac{2v_1\alpha^{\max} - c - \alpha^{\max}\beta\gamma}{4v_1 - v_2 - 3\beta\gamma}$$

$$N_1(p_1, p_2) = \gamma\,\frac{(v_1 - \beta\gamma)(\alpha^{\max}(v_2 + \beta\gamma) - 2c)}{(v_2 - \beta\gamma)(4v_1 - v_2 - 3\beta\gamma)} \tag{11}$$

$$N_A(p_1, p_2) = \gamma\,\frac{c(3\beta\gamma - 2v_1 - v_2) + \alpha^{\max}(3v_1 v_2 - v_1\beta\gamma - 2v_2\beta\gamma)}{(v_2 - \beta\gamma)(4v_1 - v_2 - 3\beta\gamma)}$$

The equilibrium prices also define profits:

$$\pi_1(p_1, p_2) = (v_1 - v_2) \frac{(2v_1 \alpha^{max} - c - \alpha^{max} \beta \gamma)^2}{(4v_1 - v_2 - 3\beta\gamma)^2}$$

$$\pi_2(p_1, p_2) = (v_1 - v_2)\gamma \frac{(v_1 - \beta\gamma)(\alpha^{max}(v_2 + \beta\gamma) - 2c)^2}{(v_2 - \beta\gamma)(4v_1 - v_2 - 3\beta\gamma)^2} \qquad (12)$$

Case 1B: incompatible products Each firm now has its own network, which means that consumer utility of product i for consumer j is $U_j = \alpha_j v_i + \beta N_i - p_i$. This modifies the characteristics of the indifferent consumers. The consumer who is indifferent between product 2 and not buying has a net consumer surplus of zero:

$$\alpha''v_2 + \beta N_2 - p_2 = 0, \text{ where } N_2 = \gamma[\alpha' - \alpha''] \text{ (from equation 3).} \qquad (13)$$

The consumer who is indifferent between products 1 and 2 has identical net consumer surplus from both goods:

$$\alpha'v_1 + \beta N_1 - p_1 = \alpha'v_2 + \beta N_2 - p_2, \text{ where } N_1 = \gamma[\alpha^{max} - \alpha'] \qquad (14)$$
(from equation 3).

These four expressions in four variables (α', α'', N_1, N_2) give solutions:

$$\alpha' = \frac{-p_1 v_2 + p_2 v_2 + p_1 \beta\gamma + v_2 \alpha^{max} \beta\gamma - \alpha^{max} \beta^2 \gamma^2}{Numa}$$

$$\alpha'' = \frac{p_2 v_1 - p_2 v_2 - p_1 \beta\gamma - p_2 \beta\gamma + \alpha^{max} \beta^2 \gamma^2}{Numa}$$

$$N_1 = -\frac{p_1 v_2 \gamma - p_2 v_2 \gamma - v_1 v_2 \alpha^{max} \gamma + v_2^2 \alpha^{max} \gamma - p_1 \beta\gamma^2 + v_1 \alpha^{max} \beta\gamma^2}{Numa} \quad (15)$$

$$N_2 = -\frac{p_2 v_1 \gamma - p_1 v_2 \gamma - p_2 \beta\gamma^2 + v_2 \alpha^{max} \beta\gamma^2}{Numa}$$

where $Numa = v_1 v_2 - v_2^2 - v_1 \beta\gamma - v_2 \beta\gamma + \beta^2 \gamma^2$.

As a result, we now have the demand levels written as functions of the prices. Anticipating consumers' demand levels, the firms choose their price levels to maximize their gross profits. Given the profit functions, which as before are $\pi_i(p_1,p_2) = (p_i - c)N_i$, for $i = 1$ and 2, we can derive the first order conditions of optimality. Reformulated, these conditions are the reaction curves of the prices. Together, they determine the prices that will prevail:

$$p_1 = \frac{c(3v_2 - 2\beta\gamma)(v_1 - \beta\gamma) + \alpha^{max}(v_2^2\beta\gamma + 2v_1^2(v_2 - \beta\gamma) - 2v_1(v_2^2 + v_2\beta\gamma - \beta^2\gamma^2)),}{Nump}$$

(16)

$$p_1 = \frac{c(2v_1 + v_2 - 2\beta\gamma)(v_2 - \beta\gamma) + v_2\alpha^{max}(v_1 v_2 - v_2^2 v_1\beta\gamma) - 2v_2\beta\gamma + 2\beta^2\gamma^2),}{Nump}$$

where $Nump = 4v_1 v_2 - v_2^2 - 4v_1\beta\gamma - 4v_2\beta\gamma + 4\beta^2\gamma^2$.

The second order conditions for optimality imply that $\beta\gamma < v_2 < v_1$ (as in the previous case 1A) and that $0 < Numa$. It will not come as a surprise that these prices lead to tedious expressions for the profit levels:

$$\pi_1(p_1,p_2) = \frac{(\gamma(v_2 - \beta\gamma)(c(-v_1 v_2 + v_2^2 + 2v_1\beta\gamma + v_2\beta\gamma - 2\beta^2\gamma^2) + \alpha^{max}(v_2^2\beta\gamma + 2v_1^2(v_2 - \beta\gamma) - 2v_1(v_2^2 + v_2\beta\gamma - \beta^2\gamma^2)))}{-Nump*Numa}$$

(17)

$$\pi_2(p_1,p_2) = \frac{(\gamma(v_1 - \beta\gamma)(v_2\alpha^{max}(-v_1 v_2 + v_2^2 + v_1\beta\gamma + 2v_2\beta\gamma - 2\beta^2\gamma^2) + c(-2v_2^2 - v_2\beta\gamma + 2\beta^2\gamma^2 + 2v_1(v_2 - \beta^2\gamma^2))))^2}{-Nump*Numa}$$

Comparing the outcomes of case 1 Firms compare their profits in case 1A, where products are compatible, to case 1B, where they are not. In order to be able to focus on the interaction with the other market B, we want to avoid complicated bargaining procedures. We will simply state that firms prefer the outcome that offers the largest total profits. This assumption implies that firms are able to exchange side payments, that is, when going from compatible to incompatible products, if one firm would gain and the other lose, the one that gains compensates the one that loses. How will they pay the side payment? Well, in the case that their products are compatible, they form an alliance to develop their technology in the first place. They may not share the development costs on a 50-50 basis. Instead, they may share costs such that if they achieve compatibility, the one that gains will compensate the loser.

In view of this discussion, we will call the difference between total profits when products are compatible and when they are not, the *compatibility bonus* to the firms:

$$Bonus_{case1} = [\pi_1(p_1, p_2) + \pi_2(p_1, p_2)_{case1A} - [\pi_1(p_1, p_2) + \pi_2(p_1, p_2)_{case1B}. \quad (18)$$

A similar expression holds for total sales. An analytical solution from comparing the total profit levels in these two cases would be hard to interpret. A solid, and obvious, analytical result is when $\beta = 0$ when there is no network effect (see the utility function (1)): the profits and sales when products are compatible equal those when they are not; the compatibility bonus is zero.

We therefore turn to a numerical solution. We assume that $\alpha^{min} = 0$, $\alpha^{max} = 1.5$, $c = 0.3$, and $v_2 = 0.5$. For values of β in the interval $[0.01, 0.05]$ and v_1 in the interval $[1.3, 2]$, the second order conditions for optimality and the other assumptions hold. The compatibility bonus is negative, so for these parameter values, the firms will prefer products to be incompatible. The sales bonus is positive: compatibility increases sales but reduces profits. Compatibility enhances the quality of products with the same network benefit. This makes the products better substitutes for each other. The result is more competition, lower prices, and higher sales as well as lower profits. Compatibility also has a direct effect on sales: by increasing the relevant network of each product (from its own sales to total industry sales), it increases the utility of the products, and thus increases sales.

Case 2: standardization when one supplier sells a complementary product
We now consider the case where the low-quality firm in market A, firm 2, has merged or acquired firm 3 in market B. This may change the preferences for compatibility of their products in market A.

Case 2A: compatible products The situation is similar to the case 1A up to the profit functions in equations (8). Firm 2 includes in its overall profits its profits in market B ($2N_A d$):

$$\pi_2(p_1, p_2) = (p_2 - c)\gamma[\frac{p_1 - p_2}{v_1 - v_2} - \frac{p_2 - \beta\gamma\alpha^{max}}{v_2 - \beta\gamma}] + 2d\gamma\frac{\alpha^{max}v_2 - p_2}{v_2 - \beta\gamma}. \quad (19)$$

This reflects the fact that for each customer in market A, firm 2 earns an additional profit of $2d$ in market B. There are N_A customers in market B, where

N_A is as in equation (6). Computations are similar to case 1A. For incompatible products, case 2B, results are derived similarly to case 1B.

We simulate numerically, to get some grip on these cumbersome formulae. We take a value of d = 0.2. We again see that sales in case A exceed those in case B: compatibility increases sales. This time, in contrast with the previous case, the profit compatibility bonus is positive: compatibility increases profits. The reason is, of course, that compatibility, as it increases sales, increases the profits made in market B, which the firms now factor into the compatibility decision of firms 1 and 2.

Results of looking at markets A and B together We are interested in the effect of market B on the relative profitability of compatible products. That is, do activities in weakly synergetic markets tend to increase the compatibility bonus?

For the parameter values simulated, the two firms will prefer incompatibility in case 1 and compatibility in case 2. That is, if they include in their considerations the feedback effect of sales in market A on sales in market B, then they will switch from preferring incompatibility to compatibility. This confirms propositions 1a and 1b: the presence of a multimarket firm tips the market from preferring incompatibility to compatibility.

Secondly, consider the compatibility bonus in case 1, where markets A and B are separately supplied, and the compatibility bonus in case 2, where A and B are jointly supplied. Figure 2.1 looks at the difference between the latter and the former: the gain in compatibility bonus due to market B. Figure 2.1 tells us that market B increases the compatibility bonus, at least for all parameter values considered. Both the parameter β and v_1 tend to increase this profitability bonus.

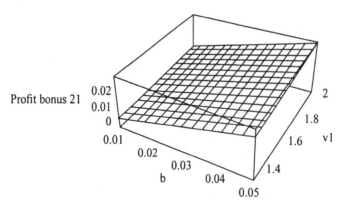

Figure 2.1   Gain in compatibilità bonus

How does the size of profitability in market B, the parameter d, influence the profitability bonus? If we define the difference between the compatibility bonus in case 2 and the one in case 1 as a function, we can compute the first derivative of this function to d. If we simulate the size of the first derivative, evaluated at the same parameters as before, including that d = 0.2, then the next figure shows the result. Figure 2 shows that the derivative of the differential compatibility bonus to d is positive for the parameter values simulated. A higher parameter β and v_1 tend to increase this effect of d on the profitability bonus.

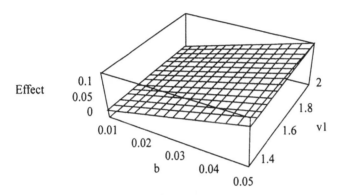

Figure 2.2   Effect of market B profitability on the profitability bonus

Figure 2.3 offers a different view on the compatibility bonus. It reports the profits of firm 2 only. The upper curve is firm 2's profit compatibility bonus from case 2, where it is a multimarket firm, active in both markets A and B. The lower curve is firm 2's compatibility bonus in case 1 where it only serves market A. In both cases its compatibility bonus is positive. Since firm 2 is the low-quality firm, it always benefits from compatibility (at least for the simulated parameter values). The higher v_1 is (on the x-axis), the smaller the market share of firm 2 in market A, all else remaining equal. It benefits more from compatibility when it is a multimarket firm than when it is single-market supplier. The difference of these compatibility bonuses increases when v_1 increases, that is, when its market share in market A decreases. The multimarket firm gains from an increasing v_1, as a higher v_1 increases total demand in A and thus in market B, while the single-market firm is hurt by an increase of v_1, which decreases its market share in market A.

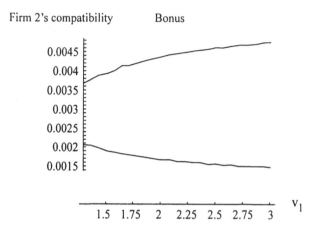

Figure 2.3   Profit compatibility bonus of a multimarket firm

A Case in Point

An Internet technology may illustrate our model. Our main sources is the web journal *C:Net*. The Wireless Application Protocol, or WAP, will enable digital mobile telephones to download and display websites, provided that the telephone has a WAP-enabled browser, and a server has a WAP enabled website. WAP technology fits in the three tier approach:

technology providers → network providers → service providers
(handsets and servers)   (GSM operators)   (WAP sites)

The WAP forum maintains and supports the standard. Its pioneering members include Ericsson, Nokia and Intel. 3Com, makers of the popular PalmPilot handheld computer, developed an alternative technology for mobile Internet access, WebClipping. The WebClipping approach uses a mobile telephone as modem and a Palm handheld to display the on-line information. In August 1999, 3Com adopted the WAP for its Palm handheld. Nokia and Ericsson sell handsets and mobile telephone equipment. These markets are expected to benefit hugely from WAP technology, as it will bring e-commerce to mobile telephones, thus increasing the utility of mobile telephony to users. To support their equipment markets, they can give away WAP technology for free. 3Com, instead, makes money from selling handheld computers and, increasingly, licensing its software to competing sellers of handheld computers (such as Acer, Handspring, IBM and Sony). It tried to keep its WebClipping technology proprietary in order to be able to license it and optimize the usefulness of its Palm technology. This may explain its reluctance to participate in the WAP forum. The growing support for the WAP forced it, however, to adopt this technology.

3 Appraisal

This chapter has shown that if firms expand their product scope to become multimarket firms, this changes their preferences for (in)compatibility of products in any particular product market. In the specific case explored here, the multimarket firm has a greater preference for compatibility. The scope enhancing mergers that we observe in Information and Communication Technologies and e-commerce may thus increase the firms' willingness to participate in industry-wide standard setting processes. This indicates a willing view on these mergers. Since multimarket firms have different preferences with regard to standards than do single-market firms, firms may merge in our model, in order to change their preferences. Once mergers give rise to multimarket firms, these may form alliances with the remaining pure players to establish compatible technologies. In our model, at least, mergers and alliances can be complementary rather than substitutes.

To arrive at this result we made some simplifying assumptions that later work may relax. We did away with bargaining processes by invoking the Coase theorem (Milgrom and Roberts, 1992) that firms bargain to an efficient (for them) outcome. We also focused on the product market effects of compatibility choices, while ignoring the effects on technology development processes. More elaborate multimarket spillovers may also be a meaningful area for further research.

References

Axelrod, R., Mitchell, W., Thomas, R.E., Bennett, D.S. and Bruderer, E. (1995), 'Coalition Formation in Standard-setting Alliances', *Management Science*, 41(9), September, pp. 1493–508.

Baumol, W.J., Panzar, J.C. and Willig, R.D. (1982), *Contestable Markets and The Theory of Industry Structure*, New York: Harcourt Brace Jovanovich.

Choi, J.P. (1996a), 'Do Converters Facilitate The Transition to a New Incompatible Technology? A Dynamic Analysis of Converters', *International Journal of Industrial Organization*, 14, pp. 825–35.

Choi, J.P. (1996b), 'Standardization and Experimentation: Ex Ante vs. Ex Post Standardization', *European Journal of Political Economy*, 12, pp. 273–90.

Church, J. and Gandal, N. (1996), 'Strategic Entry Deterrence: Complementary Products as Installed Base', *European Journal of Political Economy*, 12, pp. 331–54.

De Palma, A., Leruth, L. and Regibeau, P. (1999), 'Partial Compatibility with Network Externalities and Double Purchases', *Information Economics and Policy*, 11(2), July, pp. 209–27.

Farrell, J. and Katz, M.L. (1998), 'The Effects of Antitrust and Intellectual Property Law on Compatibility and Innovation', *The Antitrust Bulletin*, Fall–Winter, pp. 609–50.

Farrell, J., Monroe, H.K. and Saloner, G. (1998), 'The Vertical Organization of Industry: Systems Competition versus Component Competition', *Journal of Economics and Management Strategy*, 7(2), Summer, pp. 143–82.

Farrell, J. and Saloner, G. (1986), 'Installed Base and Compatibility: Innovation, Product Preannouncements, and Predation', *American Economic Review*, 76(5), December, pp. 940–55.

Farrell, J. and Saloner, G. (1988), 'Coordination through Committees and Markets', *RAND Journal of Economics*, 19(2), Summer, pp. 235–52.

Henderson, R.M. and Clark, K.B. (1990), 'Architectural Innovation: The Reconfiguration of Existing Product Technologies and the Failure of Established Firms', *Administrative Science Quarterly*, 35, pp. 9–30.

Katz, M. and Shapiro, C. (1985), 'Network Externalities, Competition, and Compatibility', *American Economic Review*, 75(3), June, pp. 424–40.

Katz, M. and Shapiro, C. (1986), 'Product Compatibility Choice in a Market with Technological Progress', in D. Morris et al., (eds) (1986), *Strategic Behaviour and Industrial Competition*, Oxford: Clarendon Press, pp. 146–65.

Katz, M. and Shapiro, C. (1994), 'Systems Competition and Network Effects', *Journal of Economic Perspectives*, Spring, 8(2), pp. 93–115.

Kristiansen, E.G. (1998), 'R&D in the Presence of Network Externalities: Timing and Compatibility', *Rand Journal of Economics*, Autumn, 29(3), pp. 531–47.

Matutes, C. and Regibeau, P. (1988), '"Mix and Match": Product Compatibility without Network Externalities', *RAND Journal of Economics*, 19(2), Summer, pp. 221–34.

Matutes, C. and Regibeau, P. (1989), 'Standardization across Markets and Entry', *Journal of Industrial Economics*, 37(4), June, pp. 359–71.

Matutes, C. and Regibeau, P. (1996), 'A Selective Review of the Economics of Standardization: Entry Deterrence, Technological Progress and International Competition', *European Journal of Political Economy*, 12, pp. 183–209.

Metcalfe, J.S. and Miles, I. (1994), 'Standards, Selection and Variety: An Evolutionary Approach', *Information Economics and Policy*, 6, pp. 243–68.

Milgrom, P. and Roberts, J. (1992), *Economics, Organization and Management*, Englewood Cliffs: Prentice-Hall.

Shapiro, C. and Varian, H.R. (1999), *Information Rules: A Strategic Guide to the Network Economy*, Boston, MA: Harvard Business School Press.

Teece, D.J. (1980), 'Economies of Scope and the Scope of the Enterprise', *Journal of Economic Behavior and Organization*, 1, pp. 223–47.

Van Wegberg, M. (1996), 'Architectural Battles in the Multimedia Market', in N. Jankowski et al. (eds), *The Contours of Multimedia: Recent Technological, Theoretical and Empirical Developments*, John Libbey Media, Ch. 3, pp. 32–46.

Van Witteloostuijn, A., and van Wegberg. M. (1992), 'Multimarket Competition: Theory and Evidence', *Journal of Economic Behavior and Organization*, July, 18(2), pp. 273–82.

Internet Sources

C:Net (http://www.news.com/?cnet.tkr).
WAP forum (http://www.wapforum.org/).

Chapter 3

Information Technology Revolution and Italian Banks: A New Schumpeterian View?

Donato Masciandaro

1   Introduction

The aim of the chapter is to analyse effects and causes accompanying the introduction of new information technologies in the Italian banking systems. The chapter's outline is as follows. Using as database the news in the years 1997–2000, Section 2 illustrates in a comparative perspective the recent applications of Internet technologies to the classic banking activities in the Italian context, using the following categories: payment services, trading, asset management, lending and origination. Section 3 goes in depth, providing an empirical study on the introduction of e-banking in the first 110 individual Italian banks up to May 2000: the result is that the move to e-banking seems to have been easier for banks that were already innovative, large, private and particular mutual loan banks – 'Popolari' – and located primarily in the north. Section 4 discusses in a short run perspective a possible model to analyse the introduction of e-banking in Italy, using a simple theoretical model consistent with the more recent theories of bank behaviour, based on the role of managerial incentives. If the Internet revolution is interpreted as a structural and idiosyncratic shock, the model shows the level of e-banking investment is inversely related to the banker's conservatism. Introducing an 'e-banking condition', its likelihood, the banker's propensity to risk being equal, is: a) directly proportional to the probability of success of the e-banking investment; b) inversely proportional to the unrecoverable expected costs of the investment; c) directly proportional to the relative expected profitability; d) indirectly proportional to the reputation costs for the manager (more precisely, the initial progressiveness of said costs);

In a long-run perspective Section 5 concludes and offers recommendations, advancing a 'new Schumpeterian' view which states that at least some individual banks could become active protagonists in the changes that the way of producing, distributing and purchasing may register in the coming times.

2   Internet Banking Abroad and in Italy: Macrotrends

The development of new technologies, especially the Internet, with their possible applications to traditional economic activities, has also had considerable impact on banking and financial activities. There have been many profound changes in just the past few years, and some them have so deeply affected the structural characteristics of the financial industry as to alter the very nature of the intermediaries who operate there.

To conduct this type of analysis, we shall start from the following reference scheme and classification proposed and proceed to examine the impact these new technologies and the advent of the Internet have had on the individual categories of activity conducted thus far by traditional banks.

Banking activities can be divided into the following categories:

- payment services (ranging from the use of current accounts, credit/debit cards, services related to electronic commerce and new products of the 'electronic money' type);
- trading (the service of buying and selling securities on behalf of clients);
- asset management (managing customer assets, especially the sale of mutual funds shares and related advisory services);
- lending (granting loans to private individuals, particularly consumer credit and mortgage loans);
- origination (the issue of equities, otherwise known as IPOs, or bonds).

The Internet revolution is day-by-day impacting all the sector of the banking system. We shall then define what we mean by the Internet, that is, the medium on which most, if not all, banking and financial services are now carried, and will increasingly be carried out in the future. We use the term 'Internet' to include a wide variety of methods that can be used to disseminate information electronically. The term generally refers to an informal network of computers (the so-called World Wide Web) which connects millions of users throughout the world. The Internet not only provides new methods of communication but also helps disseminate information in an easier, more immediate, ubiquitous, flexible and economical way. The Internet is accessible to anyone with a PC, a modem for connecting and a contract with a service provider.

Use of the Internet in banking and financial intermediation is growing, of course, in direct proportion to the use and capillary spread of the Internet in the population. According to the latest estimates, the number of users is between 80 and 100 million in the USA and 40 and 50 million in Europe alone. According to projections, this figure is destined to exceed 80 million (30 per cent of Europe's adult population) by the end of 2002. Regarding Italy, the data processed by the SDA Bocconi Internet Observatory and Eurisko indicate the number of Web users at 5 million (including occasional and office users).

Payment Services

Money has undergone several revolutions throughout history: from the day when goods were used for bartering, to metallic currency and then to paper, finally arriving, after many years, to electronic transfers of money, which initially concerned only the wholesale sector and later also retail, with the spread of 'plastic' money (credit and debit cards).

However innovative they may be, the new forms of currency, such as EFT, e-checks, EBPP (see below) and credit/debit cards, still use traditional money, such as bank deposits, as their underlying base. What has changed, sometimes considerably, is the ways these new forms are accessed and transferred. The latest revolution is the birth of true electronic money, detached from traditional currency, which may assume various configurations (from 'smart cards' to cybermoney). The future could bring the closing of the circle in currency evolution, with a possible return to bartering, this time in electronic form, however.

In this section we shall analyse the various forms of currency, starting with the electronic transfer of traditional money, particularly via the Internet, and ending with electronic currency (e-money or e-cash).

As we said, the first systems for the electronic transfer of funds concerned the wholesale sector. In the USA the Fed, right from its inception, began to develop such systems, to permit the transfer of deposits held by banks at the central bank. More generally, 'wire transfers' permit banks, large companies and governments to effect transactions of large unit amounts (the average value is around US$4 million). One of the larger systems, supported by private banks, is called CHIPS (Clearing House Interbank Payments System), characterized by the international nature of its participants and the transactions. The total transfers effected on CHIPS has mushroomed in the past 20 years from US$16 trillion in 1977 to US$310 trillion in 1999.

These payment systems are in most cases supported by networks operated by major telecommunications companies, which ensure universal access to their services. There are a few private networks, however, developed by major financial institutions (e.g. Chase or Citibank) and, lastly, the VANs (value-added networks) that transform the data received (e.g. by authorizing a credit or validating the use of a credit card). One of the better examples of a VAN is SWIFT, which provides banks with instructions for effecting payments (formally, this network would be termed a message transfer system and not an EFT, but it is treated like an EFT, considering that the messages it transfers are considered sufficient to authorize payment and given the high level of security provided).

Shifting our attention from the wholesale sector of electronic payments, ACH is an automated payment mechanism, without the use of paper documents, designed for small unit value payments, originally developed by the Federal Reserve and now offered by private players, such as VISA and Chase. The level of security provided is not comparable to that of Fedwire or CHIPS, but the cost level is quite low and its use by both consumers and companies is growing rapidly. The payments made most frequently are those related to pension schemes, utility services and loans.

While the large transfers of money through the electronic networks described above were developing, retail flows had not yet taken electronic form. Not until the 1960s, in the USA, did alternative electronic payment systems for consumers begin to develop, based on credit, such as credit and debit cards. After surpassing initial diffidence and an inevitable learning curve, these cards have become an authentic new form of money used and honoured worldwide.

The functioning of the credit card system has remained basically unchanged over the years: the cards furnished by issuers, or by banks belonging to a network, are offered to depositors and other creditworthy customers, to whom the banks of the system grant a line of credit (in the event the amount of purchases in a given period exceeds a predetermined limit). Participating merchants are credited the amounts deriving from the transactions with cardholders net of a commission (a percentage on the amount of the purchase charged with the card) by their banks. These banks then apply to the banks of the cardholders (and collect an 'interchange fee' on the transaction), which in turn debit the amount to their customers, plus interest if they pay beyond a certain period of time when the credit is basically granted without interest. The network uses its own clearing system, with no intervention by the central bank.

The advantages for merchants are, basically, the high degree of security associated with the transactions, the reduced use of checks (whose payment is not assured, is slower and associated with a greater probability of losses), the handling of less cash and probably a greater propensity to spend on the part of credit cardholders. Cardholders can drastically reduce their need for cash, enjoy interest-free credit for a certain number of days, keep better records of their transactions, benefit from 'rewards programmes' and enjoy favourable predetermined conditions if they exceed their spending limits.

With the increasing competitive pressure in this sector, and particularly with the entry of commercial banks to rival the initial card issuers (especially American Express and Diners Club), the commissions paid by merchants, as well as the commissions paid by cardholders, have sharply declined. Cardholders have also been offered increasingly attractive rewards programmes.

The 1980s brought further competitive pressure to this sector. On the one hand, there was the issue of credit cards by new institutions (financial and not, particularly mass retailers and telecommunications companies); on the other, the introduction of technological innovations such as debit cards and ATMs, which enable holders to obtain cash easily, thus reducing credit card use. The effect has been to further reduce margins, with lower commissions and interest rates.

In the 1990s it was possible to pay at most retail outlets either by credit card or by debit card (in which case the amount is instantly debited to the holder's deposit balance). The phenomenon has also become global, no longer regarding just the USA whence it started, which means greater risks for the system (particularly credit risks) that must now adapt to much different economic, cultural and regulatory conditions.

Regarding development prospects in the credit card sector, companies may choose from three different models: specialization in loans to cardholders (unsecured loans), creation of a vertical portal that offers a vast range of financial services and a focus on e-commerce.

This last model, in particular, has the issuers of credit cards concentrating on stimulating the use of their cards as the payment medium for online purchases. They must therefore be capable, first of all, of attracting to their credit card network customers with a high propensity for purchasing on the Internet and, secondly, of exploiting the data on consumer purchases and preferences to further stimulate online commerce.

The issuers most likely to succeed in the implementation of this strategy must have an international presence, a significant presence in the business cards segment (American Express, for example, is extremely well positioned in both areas and can also exploit the advantage of directly controlling its own payments system, without the presence of the banks, thus gleaning better information on the transactions of its customers) and strong relationships with companies that could be main e-commerce players (in the USA, for example, the best positioned in this sense are some commercial banks that issue credit cards, such as Citigroup, Bank One, Bank of America and Chase).

The growth of payment by credit card in e-commerce, however, must not make us forget the dangers implicit in the nature of the Web. Electronic payments, once made only on private and secure networks, now find their best prospects for growth in the use of an insecure private network like the Internet. Data protection and encryption techniques must therefore become increasingly sophisticated and secure to preserve the integrity of the transactions. Thus far the most common means of payment have employed an encryption system known as SSL (secure sockets layer), while a new, more complex standard, such as SET (secure electronic transactions), could emerge as the winning new standard, by remedying the defects of the former.

The Internet will be a crucial factor for the credit card sector not only through the growth of online commerce, and the consequent increase in the number of transactions, but also as a distribution channel:

- thanks to the Internet, which offers the possibility of online application and customization, the costs of acquiring new cardholders may be drastically reduced, with a significant impact on issuers' profitability;
- The Internet favours the birth of 'affinity groups', to which issuers offer to create a highly characterized card that gives holders a sense of belonging that normal, undifferentiated cards cannot furnish;
- cardholders will increasingly visit the issuers' sites to monitor their credit situations, thereby creating increased 'traffic' and a new source of revenues from advertizing;
- the cards may be supplemented with electronic purses (see below) and capture a large share of the online purchases, if these new instruments obtain wide distribution.

With the development of the Internet, competition to leading incumbents in the credit card sector could come from alternative products, such as e-cash and e-checks (see below), and from possible new issuers. Regarding the first problem, even after probable acceptance by consumers within a reasonable period of time, the new instrument will be favoured only for small transactions, while credit cards will continue to maintain the competitive advantage given by rewards programmes. Regarding new entrants, the risk that a few leaders in e-commerce may decide to issue cards of their own, without the collaboration of the current players, seems rather unlikely.

Before examining the concept of e-money, there are three more instruments that simply permit faster access to deposits of traditional money in banks, therefore lacking the characteristics of true electronic money (see below). The first of these is the e-check, whereby we can order our bank to pay a certain amount to a third party indicated by us, who sends the digital check to his own bank, which then credits the funds to him after receiving them from our bank, through a clearing house operation.

Then there are EBPPs (electronic bills presentment and payment), which let us make recurrent payments online, such as those associated with utility services. The sending and payment of utility bills online could prove to be a formidable opportunity per credit card issuers but particularly for banks: both consumers and the companies would prefer to handle their accounts electronically, without the mailing of envelopes and without 'paper' payments, by sending e-mail or by visiting a website.

The site could be that of the utility company or, which would be more convenient for consumers, a single site associated with numerous companies requiring this type of service. In the latter case, consumers could learn the details of their bills and pay them with just a few mouse clicks.

Then there are the virtual banks and the virtual ATMs. Through them, bank customers, be they companies or individuals, can access all the information on their deposits (balance, check situation, listing of movements) on the Web and give instructions such as payment orders and giro payments. Here again no new forms of money are involved, since there must be a traditional bank deposit, which remains with a depositary party but which can now be accessed in cyberspace.

Coming now to analyse e-money (or e-cash), we might first ask ourselves: What exactly is electronic money? In reality, in the wholesale segment, it has apparently existed for decades, considering that EFTs permit the electronic transfer of conventional currency. With the movements effected via EFTs, however, what changes is the mode of transfer (much faster) and not the nature of the underlying currency, which is still traditional deposits. To qualify as electronic money, a new medium of payment must meet a few necessary conditions:

- it must be generated and transformed by computers;

- it must be independent of other forms of currency controlled by governments and of bank deposits;
- it must be outside the current monetary aggregates;
- it must not be subject to restriction or regulation by the supervisory authorities of the financial markets;
- it can assume many forms, only a few of which are offered by banks.

E-money does not resemble any of the present monetary aggregates; on the contrary, it is transferred from the stock of traditional money toward accounts denominated in the new form of money. Such e-cash can then be physically stored in a chip mounted on a special card or on the hard·disk of a computer. It can be issued by banks, or by the systems that manage credit cards, as 'smart' cards' or 'electronic purses', both replacements for cash. The issuer could, however, be of non-bank origin and produce cybermoney 'stored' on a computer, from which it could be manipulated and used for online purchases.

Defining exactly what electronic money is can still present a series of difficulties. It may be simpler, therefore, to say what is not e-money, such as all the new modes for transferring the traditional money that we have in a bank account.

Virtual banking services, for example, enable us to transfer our traditional deposits from our homes, just as debit cards cause bank money to be transferred to those who have sold us something. The electronic payment of utility bills is a variant of what we just described, and the same may be said for e-checks, which give us faster access to the deposit of traditional money we have in a bank.

In the case of real electronic money, however, there is a value that is not perceived by the banking system. With smart cards, the 'money' is stored in the memory of the card, called a 'stored value card', used especially for paying small amounts.

In the case of cybermoney, then, the currency could be found in the memory of a computer, after being input there by a party other than a bank. In this way the currency would have no physical manifestation and would only be transferred via computer, as a sort of e-bills for making online purchases.

To obtain security in this type of payment, systems of keys are used: they are assigned univocally to each e-coin and allow it to be used only once without the possibility of counterfeiting.

In both cases the holders of e-money transfer their wealth from one form to another, while the issuers hold the traditional money transferred to them and 'create' electronic money: this money thus presupposes the existence of a liability. If it is a bank that issues an e-cash card, it will have a liability against the customer, which in any case must be separate from traditional deposits. Of course these special accounts may also be subject to central bank regulation, such as an obligation to create a reserve.

If we leave aside the case where a bank is involved in the creation of electronic money and assume that the issuer is a company outside the financial world, such as a software house, the ties with the banking system are tenuous if not nonexistent. The underlying deposit may even be quite small and thus approach a sort of 'free' money. And it may in some cases approach a sort of electronic bartering, which may seem far removed from the current concept of money but is simply a return to a primitive form of money.

In comparing traditional money (cash, for example) and electronic money, we will immediately note that the former is universally accepted (the State imposes this by law), while the latter is not; the former is tangible, while the latter is not. If we compare traditional bank deposits with electronic money, on the other hand, a few of the macro-differences disappear: neither is tangible nor electronically accessible. Deposits, however, are treated as liabilities by banks and are counted as part of the money supply, such that reserve and control obligations (sometimes limits) are imposed on the transformation of maturities by the banks. Electronic money is not part of the money supply, however, and is not counted as deposits in the financial statements of banks (it may be a liability of a non-banking company or an item separate from deposits on the liabilities side of a bank's balance sheet). Its use is not yet regulated in any way by law. Its transformation into loans or investments and the existence of reserves will depend on the reliability of the issuer.

One of the principal differences between bank deposits and the new forms of money is that the former, regardless of their type and geographical location, present common characteristics (such as insurance, for example), while the latter varies significantly from case to case, from one issuer to another (in terms of the various forms of security, the various technological forms and the reputations of the various issuers). In addition, the clearing systems will be as numerous and complex as the number of issuers, thus increasing the level of uncertainty. Without common standards, there will be innumerable types of e-money, and the situation will be more similar to bartering than to the current payments system.

Smart cards, cards that contain a microchip that permits the processing of various types of information usable for individual applications (such as automatic dispensers or road tolls) or multiple applications, have thus far not achieved widespread distribution in the USA, where there are only a few million in circulation, while they assume considerable importance in areas where the access to credit is more difficult, where the inefficiencies of the telecommunications networks make instant authorizations of payment cards difficult, where the currency is unstable or where the government has facilitated their use. Internationally, the number of cards exceeds one billion, and in a few European countries (Germany and Spain, for example), tens of millions have been issued, sometimes linked to a few specific uses, such as the payment of benefits for the social-security system.

Recently, a few of the major players in the payment card field, along with companies in the technology sector, have announced the creation of a common standard that will permit the future development of this new instrument. In any event, some are predicting that its use will be limited to a few specific situations. Smart cards will replace part of the cash payments and will be particularly functional for payments related to travel and entertainment.

Smart cards are direct descendants of credit cards and are often linked to them, often coexisting on the same card.

E-cash cards enable us to transfer currency from a bank deposit directly onto the card (through a special physical ATM or an ATM in cyberspace accessible via the Internet). The currency in this case is not created but is simply transformed by passing from the form of cash or bank deposits into smart card form. Once stored on the card, this new money can be spent (until it is spent, the issuer can freely utilize the transformed amount) or transferred from one card to another (as cash passes from hand to hand), without the need for any bank intervention.

To better understand the differences in operation, we could compare the withdrawal of banknotes from an ATM to the loading of a smart card. In the first case the depositor, leaving the level of his assets unchanged, only sees his credit toward the bank diminish and his cash increase, while the bank experiences a decrease in liabilities (the deposit), assets (cash) and reserves (cash is part of the reserve computation). When the consumer decides to transfer a certain amount from his deposit to an electronic purse, on the other hand, the level of the deposit declines, of course, but the other asset held (e-cash) is increased by the same amount. For the bank, however, the situation is different from cash withdrawal, since it sees a decline in one liability, such as a traditional deposit, but sees an equivalent increase in another liability (the one associated with the e-cash and separate from deposits). It can also utilize the electronic money until it re-enters the banking circuit. The re-entry occurs when a merchant, of whom the issuing bank becomes a debtor from the moment something is purchased, deposits electronic money in the bank, where it once again becomes part of the traditional money supply.

This innovative form thus makes for easy transfer and anonymity that may alarm police forces and anti-laundering authorities (the issuer knows only the amount of electronic money in circulation but not the holders).

Thanks to the chip on the card, we can therefore decide freely how much electronic money to hold, just as we can decide how many banknotes to hold, with the difference that until we spend the e-money, it can be used by the issuer.

In addition to ridding us of cash, smart cards can offer useful extra services, because of the powerful chips used. Among the various functions, it can record our transactions, convert money from one currency to another, compute the value of our investment portfolio and record personal data (all the data recorded could be easily accessed with the use of a computer). Furthermore, they could be used in all types of automatic dispensers and public telephones.

Electronic money could then assume the form of cybermoney, issued by non-banking firms, with a different function from that of smart cards. In essence, a consumer (via the Internet) could transform part of a bank deposit into cybermoney, with the amount being credited by the issuer to the customer's computer. The consumer sees his assets decrease but has a credit towards the issuer, who sees his assets and liabilities increase by the same amount. When the consumer makes an online purchase, the payment occurs immediately and the quantity of cybermoney decreases. The merchant can then decide whether to go to his bank immediately and transform the electronic money into a traditional deposit or use it to make online payments of his own. If more and more merchants decide to circulate this electronic money, circumventing the banks, the banks would see the quantity of traditional money, and thus their activity, decline.

Comparing electronic purses with cybermoney, consumers and merchants might conceivably feel more protected in the first case, since the debt relationship would be created toward the banking system. As we saw earlier, the major telephone and computer companies have not yet become equally reliable in the eyes of customers, but this perception could change with time, and with the offering of guarantees against losses and remunerated accounts. The central banks could also be concerned about the crucial role played by non-financial companies, which could obtain considerable cash to invest with no controls.

In any case, there are grounded fears associated with the spread of cybermoney, and particularly its value between the time it is issued and when it is transformed into traditional money. It could, in effect, be treated 'under par', in case of excessive issues, reducing its effectiveness its value reserve function. And the new currency might not be commonly accepted (due to the reputation of the issuer), the contrary of current legal tender. This would deprive it of two of the three characteristics of a currency.

The future could hold another innovation, which we could describe as free-money. The condition whereby each euro of e-money must be offset by one euro of traditional deposits could be lifted, and the new bankers of cyberspace would be free to decide, as once did the early bankers not controlled by any state authority, the most prudent ratio between traditional money and the free cash (with no law requiring them to hold a predetermined amount of it). The same phenomenon could also occur in a fraudulent manner: virtual bankers could initially ensure the existence of a 100 per cent coverage ratio but then go back on their word, since no laws exist for punishing such actions.

In both cases, issuers of non-banking origin would create the currency and in the better of the two scenarios would hold reserves consisting of bank deposits and not official central bank reserves, as now. In a banking system like that in the USA, this might simply represent the addition of a new level of banks to the three already in existence: already today many small banks ('respondents') hold reserves at larger banks ('city correspondents'), which in turn hold reserves at the central bank. The new non-bank issuers would probably be positioned at the bottom, holding their reserves at first-level banks.

Developments could also be more drastic. A small issuer of cybermoney could decide to hold reserves not with a classic banking institution but with other larger virtual bankers. The reserves would thus be the liability of a non-banking firm and no longer traditional money. The virtual bank could even decide to grant loans by issuing cybermoney to the borrower.

The problem of the reliability of a non-bank issuer of electronic money would become absolutely paramount. While today the liabilities of the central bank, cash and monetary base, are secured by the existence of the government, and bank deposits are secured by the liabilities of the central bank and by the existence of mandatory reserves, in the future scenario described the money system would depend on the judgments formed about a non-banking company.

For some this does not represent a risk, as they feel the market will be able to regulate the money supply better than the central banks (often influenced by political power). The most efficient issuers will survive, and two alternative scenarios could be possible in the near future: either a single type of e-money will prevail at the global level or the system will be fragmented and 'anarchical', like the Internet (with cybermoney used for a sort of electronic bartering, particularly for the transfer of intellectual property).

Per some, the government will be forced to regulate this new situation and, in effect, at level of the European Union there is talk of reserving the issue of e-money to banking institutions, to preserve the integrity of the retail payments system.

Some governments might even decide to issue electronic money directly, particularly if the systems freely created by the market proved a failure. The experiences of countries like Finland and New Zealand have been the first pointing in this direction: the obvious advantages in terms of efficiency and absence of fraud would be mitigated by a few disadvantages, such as the possible limitation of privacy due to the central role played by the government in this field.

This last observation suggests that there are a number of quite different scenarios for the future of electronic money and, as seems logical, the most extreme ones (free cash and e-money managed totally by the government) present threats of various kinds but all serious ones.

One of the practical applications of electronic money that governments might find cost-effective is the management of the food subsidies. The government could furnish the indigents a smart card within a system called EBT (Electronic Benefits Transfer), select a bank (or a financial services company) to manage the system, credit the accounts of the beneficiaries and involve a network of merchants (the type of stores would be selected according to the intended use of the card). Once the system has been created, the beneficiaries could make purchases in the authorized stores (or even withdraw cash from an ATM, if the government wishes to grant this opportunity), in some cases with a few restrictions that could be stored on the card, by the foregoing methods.

In conclusion, the outbreak of the foregoing new technologies in the payments system, and particularly the Internet, poses crucial new challenges to the traditional players, especially to the banks. Until now the revolutions in the form and use of money (such as credit cards) had never challenged the central role of banking institutions in the payments system, while in coming years the entry of new players, coming from successful endeavours in the new technologies and the Internet, could for the first time relegate the established players to a marginal role.

In reality, as in every revolution, the banks will be facing not only risks but major opportunities as well. They may lose enormous market shares, in both the retail and wholesale segments of the payments system, unless they are able to sustain the incessant pace of technological innovation, which in just a few years has altered the structural characteristics of this sector. But they will also be able to exploit their assets of confidential information, and particularly the privileged relationships developed with their customers, whether private individuals or companies, to expand their volume of activity in payment services (the Internet will probably cause commercial volume to mushroom, both business-to-consumer and business-to-business) and to improve their margins (on products like deposits, there may be significant cuts in costs with the transition from traditional branches to the virtual ones).

On-line Trading

On-line trading means the possibility of trading securities, particularly equities, but also bonds and derivatives, through the Internet, i.e. the possibility for retail customers to interact with a trading intermediary (and through him with the market) using only the Internet and thus excluding all the forms requiring further interaction with said intermediary to conclude the execution of the order.

This phenomenon could be viewed as simply an innovation in the process of distributing a product that has always been handled by banks (after the SIM law of 1991) or by the SIMs, such as securities trading. In reality, it can be demonstrated, observing the experience of markets that have already seen online trading develop in recent years, that this is not a simple extension of traditional operating modes but a phenomenon capable of drastically altering the organization of the markets and the activities of existing brokers and investors and cause the birth of a new category of intermediaries.

To appreciate the growth potential of this new type of investment services, we must first determine whether a broad potential user market exists. US experience can be particularly significant from this standpoint: in the United States, in fact, besides a high degree of Internet diffusion among the population, there is a high level of equity investment and a segment of investors that are natural targets: these are the customers of the discount brokers, intermediaries characterized 'by low costs and a modular, efficient level of service'. These investors find it easy and automatic to switch to online trading, since they are particularly active, willing to operate first hand without consulting and attentive in the search for better pricing conditions; regarding commissions, in fact, the Web channel permits enormous cost savings for brokers, who can therefore offer drastically lower commissions, along with an improvement in service, in terms of greater immediacy (great rapidity in placing orders and confirming their execution).

These favourable prospects have in effect been confirmed in reality: it is estimated that there were around 10 million active online accounts in the USA at the end of 1999, with dozens of brokers actively offering online trading, a segment that has come to represent one-third of the retail market. For Forrester, an Internet research and consulting firm, the online accounts in the USA will exceed 20 million by 2003, while in Europe an estimate of JP Morgan Securities talks of over 8 million Web trading accounts by 2002. A further proof is the stock exchange valuations of the principal companies offering online trading, which had grown immeasurably in recent years and are attributed high future profitability levels for this type of intermediaries.

In addition to low costs and rapid execution, there are two more success factors underlying the US experience: technology, which permits both a high level of security (thanks to the use of cryptography) and extremely easy network access (through the use of user-friendly interfaces), and the possibility for intermediaries to differentiate the product, accompanying trading with a vast range of information and analysis (real-time quotations, research on selected industries, information on issuers, etc.). This last aspect lead some to forecast that the process of product differentiation and the transformation of online brokers may spawn new entities known as financial hubs. These intermediaries would specialize in the distribution of low- and medium-value-added financial products: one of the major online trading firms, Charles Schwab, has in effect taken this direction, seeking to furnish ever-better consulting services, greatly expanding its range of products and services and utilizing the multichannel approach, i.e. the possibility for customers to exploit not only the online contact but also the other channels available: telephone, branches and, more recently, television and cellular telephone.

Regarding the categories of securities traded, the vast majority of operations thus far have concerned equities and equity-based derivatives, consistent with the preference of US retail investors, while recently numerous firms have been expressing the intention of shunting a small portion of their bond trading onto the Internet. This trading volume, in fact, amounts in the USA every day to US$350 billion, i.e. eight times the value traded on the two principal stock exchanges. In Italy, on the other hand, in addition to the possibility of bond trading offered by various online brokers, a special circuit had been created on the Internet designed for the retail customers of institutional investors.

In our country this development could encounter difficulties, since the principal intermediaries who might enter this new segment are those already present in the trading sector and possessed of a large customer base, i.e. the current leading banking groups, that would be unlikely to choose to distribute the products of their competitors, since most can offer all the services that could be potentially placed on the Internet. On the other hand, with such an important innovation, that create a technological gap, it is possible that some players outside the sector might find new ways for interacting with customers and divert market share both from intermediaries who continue using traditional trading modes and from those that convert to the new channel too late and too cautiously (in effect, the major banking groups might simply see their customers switch from traditional methods to the new, more economical channel, while the new entrants, with innovative approaches and techniques, could win over vast new segments of customers).

The greatest danger will clearly come from the online brokers already established in other countries. They will find lower entry barriers, since they have already sustained the necessary investments in technology and can wield unique expertise, particularly in the crucial field of marketing. Competition of a much different sort, but just as dangerous, could come from the principal Web portals: since they have hundreds of thousands of habitual users, they would find it simple to add their own vast offering of investment services, in conjunction with the best financial advertizers on their sites. Then there are the telecommunications companies, particularly those that offer Internet access through their own providers: thus far they have chosen to ally themselves with the principal financial operators, that have created virtual banks according to two different approaches, providing just their own services and know-how (but remaining outside those Internet initiatives) or investing directly in the virtual banks (or their parent companies).

We would mention a final category of potential entrants that can boast a highly diversified range of products. A few Italian insurance companies are preparing to enter the Internet, thanks to alliances with online brokers with which they can create portals capable of offering customers a vast range of services, from online trading in Italian and foreign securities to life and casualty policies, along with asset management.

The consequences of this growing activity will not be felt just by the financial intermediaries. For customers, it will not only change their mode of accessing trading services, with the effects seen earlier, but will also probably alter their level of activity and their attitude toward the market, by eliminating the filter between investor and market. Regarding the first aspect, it is estimated that the exodus to online trading, with its low costs and its ease of access, may increase the number of transactions per investor. Regarding the second aspect, Internet traders, feeling more directly involved in their investments, might even decide to participate more in the decisions of the companies on which they have 'wagered', taking part via the Internet in shareholders' meetings or at least assigning their votes to companies that use the Internet to collect proxies.

In Italy, there are already dozens of players capable of offering online trading services, with all the possible options described above (from trading in securities listed in foreign markets to market research, information, real-time quotations, etc.). Even though the phenomenon has only appeared in recent months, the level of activity achieved by the principal players is anything but negligible. Estimates of the entire market, furnished by Prometeia and Intermobliare Securities, speak of commissions equal to ITL 150–200 billion for all of 2000 and more than 500,000 Italian online investors within three years.

The second great impact of the Internet, after the offer of online trading services, is the creation of electronic communication networks (ECNs), trading systems that use the Internet to allow investors – until recently only institutional investors, but now unsophisticated individuals as well – to trade listed securities efficiently and anonymously and at lower costs than those offered by the listing exchange. These advantages derive from the possibility of forwarding orders directly via the Internet to the ECN, eliminating the intermediation of both brokers and traders. Another advantage is the increasingly widespread possibility of operating after hours, i.e. after the market's close.

In the USA, where the phenomenon has already assumed significant proportions, securities can even be traded outside the traditional exchanges, in the over-the-counter markets, through network connections between specialized operators who send their own buy and sell offers (one example is the NASDAQ, the stock exchange that lists most of the technological stocks). In addition, there are the proprietary trading systems (PTSs), operating systems for trading that enable the intermediaries to execute orders automatically. They are used by institutional investors to obtain direct, immediate access to listed securities without the participation of brokers-dealers, intermediaries present on many exchanges, enjoying anonymity and extra-low commissions.

The ECNs have entered this context, have captured significant shares of the trading on the traditional markets (30 per cent on the NASDAQ and 4 per cent on the NY Stock Exchange, according to a few sources) and are about to be officially recognized as exchanges. The success of the ECNs is demonstrated by attracting equity participation from the principal brokerage houses and online brokers and by exporting of this phenomenon outside the USA.

In this way the Internet can become not only a medium for collecting orders, as we saw earlier, but also a trading system in competition with the traditional exchanges. For some, there is an even more extreme scenario: the processes of alliance between the various ECNs, the recognition of the ECNs as markets and the growing number of agreements between stock exchanges could even lead, in the not-too-distant future, to the creation of a single world stock exchange.

For the moment the most advanced initiative for the creation of a global stock exchange for continuous trading in high-tech stocks is the creation of two regional alliances by the NASDAQ, i.e. NASDAQ Japan and NASDAQ Europe. These two exchanges will probably be able to ensure a high degree of liquidity, permitting investors around the globe, institutional or not, to access a single global trading platform, Internet-based, with low transaction costs. In Europe, particularly, the initiative seems destined for probable success, considering that the existing markets for technology stocks have so far been unable to rise above their marginal role and develop adequate levels of liquidity.

Then there is a project to create a European online platform for small investors that would furnish a complete service of trading, settlement, liquidation and custody. These investors could continue to use their own online brokers, but those brokers, in cases of cross-border transactions, could utilize this new platform, with the possibility of cutting costs by as much as half.

Soon all the operators, even in Italy, will have to confront this new reality: the asset managers, who will perhaps find this new trading system cost-effective; the intermediaries that offer online trading services and may find the ECNs a natural evolution of their own online activity; and the Italian Stock Exchange, which will find unexpected competitors seeking to disintermediate it.

In effect, in only a few months' time, the first online brokers have launched or designed organized trading systems outside the organized markets, where by acting as market makers with customers they will make after-hours trading possible. In reality, the possibility of unregulated markets for financial products was already contemplated in the Unified Law on the financial markets, which only requires a minimum level of transparency from promoting intermediaries. But not until today, with the development of trading on the Internet, have large-scale projects in this field had prospects of success.

The effect of this innovation on the supply structure for trading services could be explosive. If for some the birth of online brokers has threatened the very survival of traditional brokers, the possibility of direct contact between investors and market through the ECNs could result in a further degree of disintermediation.

For other observers, however, this concern is unjustified, since there will always be vast market segments, composed of customers in need of consulting and a diaphragm between them and the market. This additional service will always be provided by intermediaries (the traditional brokers can boast a competitive advantage in this field, some say). Banks will therefore be increasingly oriented toward obtaining predominance in information and economic expertise so they can sell effective consulting to customers and thus offset the drop in commissions and loss of the more 'sophisticated' investors. In reality, to this observation one could object that the information 'monopoly' of the full-service brokers has already crumbled. Data on the market and on companies, annual reports and market research are now available to anyone free of charge on the Web. Other increasingly specialized consulting services are sprouting up that can tailor retirement plans to an small investor's needs.

Asset Management

The share of small investors' portfolios allocated to asset management grew considerably during the 1990s, growth that was clearly reflected in a similar increase in the total assets managed by the financial intermediaries present in the asset management field (see Tables 3.6, 3.7, 3.8 and 3.9). Among these asset mangers, bank intermediaries play a significant role. In Italy, in particular, the major banking groups lead the way, well ahead of the insurance groups, while important managers of mutual funds and independent pension funds, on the US model, are basically absent. In addition to their established leadership in the ranks of mutual funds and asset management, banks have recently gained pre-eminence in life insurance, while the prospects for pension funds, an instrument of recent introduction to our country, seem rather more competitive (see Tables 3.6, 3.10, 3.11 and 3.12).

As for all the other sectors of financial intermediation, asset management has begun to exploit the potential of the Internet. This phenomenon, which has been developing for some years in the USA, began to make a serious appearance in Europe and Italy during 1999, and managers have decided to offer a wide range of services via the Internet. They range from the presentation of their own products, with relative costs, to the possibility of subscribing fund shares and managing switches from one type of fund to another, not to mention so-called 'educational' services (see below).

Focusing on Italy, the authority that supervises this sector of financial intermediation was forced to intervene to launch the use of the new channel. CONSOB, in fact, with a recent regulation (7 July 1999) finally authorized mutual funds to operate via the Internet (limited for the time being to redemptions and switching). The Commission then made a pronouncement (3 September 1999) on the subject of remote promotion and placement, specifying the procedure that the savings management companies (SGRs) must follow for the direct placement of mutual fund shares through their Internet sites. In particular, it affirmed that nothing prevents from publishing prospectuses for mutual funds on the website, along with the subscription form, provided that this document can also be acquired by investors in hardcopy form (possibility of printing) and that investors, before accessing the subscription form, have the opportunity to acquire exact information about the risks connected with the investment operation. Likewise, the SGRs must also be able to obtain, by means of an interactive fact-sheet, all the information regarding investors' experience with financial instruments, financial situation, investment objectives and propensity to risk, so that they can determine whether the investment is compatible with the customer's economic-financial profile. In any case, in compliance with the anti-laundering laws, investors must be directly identified by at least one intermediary when they make their first subscription.

The laws to combat the laundering of illegal income thus places a serious limitation on the ease of use of the new channel. In reality, the obvious disadvantages deriving from the mandatory physical contact between intermediary and client can be accommodated in two ways: firstly, investors can send the documentation regarding their first autograph subscription of fund shares to the SGR through the postal service (the law includes post offices, in fact, among the parties authorized to identify investors). Alternatively, customers can ask another intermediary that identified them in the past to certify this fact. Lastly, there is no problem regarding any subscriptions subsequent to the first, and any switching transactions, and confirmation via e-mail is regarded as sufficient, since they are considered parts of a single operation initiated with the first subscription.

In reality, the CONSOB could, in this context, have taken advantage of recent regulations on 'digital signatures', which offers the possibility to electronically sign the trading documents.

The green light of the CONSOB at the end of 1999 found a few managers already prepared to start actual online trading activity in funds (i.e. the possibility to subscribe fund shares via the Internet), while most of the Italian SGRs are well behind on an entire range of services that could potentially be distributed via the Web. On 31 May, according to a report in the newsletter *Internet and Finanza*, our SGRs had not yet made a sufficient effort to develop their presence on the Internet. Only 20 per cent of the Italian management companies already had their own websites (10 cases out of a total of 53); 10 per cent (six cases) were hosted on the sites of parent companies and the remaining 70 per cent were totally absent from the Web. Looking at the United States, on the other hand, the presence of fund management companies on the Web is practically a general phenomenon, and there are also many sites devoted specifically to individual mutual funds.

Regarding the content of the sites, in almost all cases there was a presentation of the company indicating the controlling group. Then they provided information on the products offered by the company; an indication of historical performance (11 cases) was more frequent than an indication on the commissions applied to the funds (eight cases); only three companies had already placed their prospectuses online; only two companies gave information on the mangers. In almost all cases the sites examined provided indications on contacting the company (e-mail, addresses of distributors, etc.).

One of the principal functions of the sites seems to be information: they are primarily a means for delivering information on the management company and on the products readily accessible and comparable. The US authorities (the SEC in particular) have encouraged this use of the Web and have also issued new procedures for absolving disclosure requirements, specially designed to provide online investors with standardized, concise, readily comparable information. For the industry as a whole, the same thing may happen in Italy that happened in the United States in the 1990s: allowing fund management companies to provide online information on their funds will help absorb the enormous growth in the number of customers we are witnessing.

The sites of the Italian management companies are beginning to carry an 'education' section, i.e. a section that we could define as the financial ABCs, where visitors can find basic financial information, financial market research and aids to savings planning. On the sites of US investment companies, the space devoted to education has increased with time and has played an important role in expanding the financial culture of investors and orienting them toward more informed, rational choices. In Italy, this function seems particularly important, given the generally low level of financial knowledge. This knowledge will become increasingly necessary, given the steadily growing percentage of households that own equities, directly or indirectly (through institutional investors), and considering that the future pension schemes of workers will be increasingly dependent on the savings and investment choices of the workers themselves (see the current debate on the role of pension funds). Looking to the future, some feel that asset management services could be partly transformed into 'sales of expertise in asset options'.

In Europe, and particularly in the UK, there a growing number of initiatives by management companies to distribute their funds via the Internet. For the moment, however, the initiatives are limited to the distribution of self-managed funds. The launch of 'supermarkets', based on the US experience, that offer numerous mutual funds of various management companies is blocked, in fact, by the lack of a standardized, centralized system for settling buy and sell orders.

The AUTIF (Association of Unit Trusts and Investment Funds), the British equivalent of Italy's Assogestioni, has been working on such a project since 1998. The project, called EMX (Electronic Messaging Exchange), will offer the British mutual funds sector a common platform for the trading of mutual fund shares. According to the AUTIF, the principal advantages for those offering products to join in the system are a reduction in transaction and banking costs and independence from distributor technology. For distributors, on the other hand, the advantages are the use of a single standard per all trades, the opportunity to offer a uniform service and independence from provider technology.

The birth of the so-called 'supermarkets' could provide a strong boost to the success of the Internet as a channel for mutual fund sales. The activity of these independent distributors is to offer thousands of funds managed by various companies (often 'no load') and placed in direct competition on price (the management commissions) and on performance. In this way investors are offered the possibility to diversify their funds portfolios among a number of management companies (highly specialized in some cases and rather inaccessible otherwise) while centralizing all the administrative operation in a single account. Clearly, because of these characteristics, this type of distributor has found an ideal channel for development in the Internet.

As for the categories of investor that can most easily utilize the 'supermarkets', they include not only the savers capable of navigating through a vast range of products in search of the best conditions (price and/or performance) without the need of consulting. In the USA, in fact, there has been a recent shift in the orientation of small investors toward consulting: the customers of one of the biggest 'supermarkets' are to an increasing extent independent advisors (i.e. consultants) who deal with the numerous final customers requiring a guide to orient their investment decisions.

Another factor that may favour the centrality of the Web as a channel for selling funds is the presence of direct sales. If the management companies are, in fact, directly distributing their products without the help of a distribution network, represented in Italy primarily by bank branches (see Table 3.12), they will find the transition to the new Internet channel even more cost-effective (see below).

One problem pointed out by a few commentators is the risk that the possibility of operating via the Internet, and thus in real time on market trends, may encourage procyclic behaviour on the part of fund subscribers (i.e. subscriptions when the financial markets are rising and redemptions when they decline), with the undesirable effect of amplifying the stock market cycles both up and down. In reality, past experience with subscriber behaviour does not suggest that procyclic behaviour is very likely. On the other hand, any risk of 'panic crises' and widespread exodus from equity investments is not attributable so much to the existence of Internet operations as to the more general fact that a growing share of household financial wealth is invested in equities.

One last consideration concerns the possibility that the increasing online trading of stocks and bonds will promote direct investment by small investors, to the detriment of asset management. In reality, this thesis can only be sustained if we assume that the only motivation behind the institutionalization of savings is the presence of high transaction costs in securities trading, a problem that would be eliminated by trading via the Internet. If investors choose asset management because of the growing complexity of the financial markets and the need for portfolio diversification, however, then the potential conflict between the growth of online trading in securities and mutual funds completely disappears.

As far as Italy is concerned, it has been observed that the start of Internet operations is based on a distribution structure perfectly reflective of that in the USA, characterized by:

- a declining presence of the direct selling channel;
- the absolute prevalence of single-brand networks;
- a lower level of competition among management companies and among distribution networks (the growth of subscriptions has occurred thanks to the transition from administered savings to managed savings, within a given banking group);
- little penetration by foreign players.

The effects of Internet use on such a distribution structure can only be disruptive:

- product comparability and market transparency will increase, with a consequent downward pressure on commissions;
- the Internet will permit the development of multi-brand distribution (the cause-effect relationship in the USA was the opposite);
- there will be a growing presence of foreign players, who will finally be able to hurdle the entry barrier represented by the need for an extensive distribution network;
- the mobility of subscribers from one fund to another will be greatly enhanced, increasing the ratio of the value of redemptions to the value of assets under management.

Clearly these mega-changes could have significant effects on the current ranking of asset management firms, with the possibility of radical changes in the characteristics of the leading players.

Other intermediaries in Italy are involved in asset management of savings and potentially interested in Internet-related developments: besides the SGRs, in fact, there are the SIMs, which with their own networks of financial promoters, represent one of the principal channels for fund sales.

A few of them, in fact, are preparing to enter the Web with mutual funds selling services. For these players the offering of such services may still be problematic, however, since it must be reconciled with their own networks of financial promoters (who today hold a position of leadership in the off-premise marketing of investment services). Some of the intermediaries involved have therefore chosen the multichannel strategy, offering different conditions (in terms of commissions and consulting) for the same products, depending on the channel selected. It will thus be the customers who select the channel best suited to their needs, continuing to work with promoters, for example, if they desire across-the-board assistance. This approach should dispel the threat of 'cannibalization' perceived by the networks, and the presence of new channels could even prove a great opportunity to exploit, as has occurred for the major US online brokers.

They have identified three categories of investor, according to demand for consulting: the first, who wish to choose in total independence, can be offered just the subscription of mutual funds online (or via telephone); the second, who choose for themselves with the aid of a consultant, must be offered online assistance with the advice of brokers; while customers who totally delegate the management of their assets must be offered the possibility to contact an authentic network of financial consultants. By adopting a similar approach, Italian SIMs could concentrate the efforts of their sales networks on higher value added activities, such as consulting to customers and the sale of more sophisticated products.

A final category of intermediaries involved in managed assets, and thus far the only competitors of the banks (or of the companies of banking origin), are insurance companies. A few of them are planning to trade their funds online, while others already distribute insurance products, such as life policies, that have been enormously successful (see above) and now closely resemble those of managed assets.

Lending

The segment of online loans to private individuals, and particularly loans for the purchase of property, has thus far presented the best opportunity for growth, among the various financial services. Three particular factors have favoured the growth of volumes and the central role of this type of loan service within the more general Web activities of banks:

- firstly, the need to seek better conditions (interest rates, in this specific case), to minimize an expense that may constitute a significant item in the family budget, makes it natural to compare the various offerings; operating via the Internet can certainly simplify this form of 'shopping';
- secondly, in some countries where household borrowing is already an established process, loans represent one of the largest classes of financial assets;
- lastly, the strong demand for 'education' associated with lending, caused by the complexity of financial choices implicit in a loan, can be satisfied effectively through the creation of a website where information can be furnished more efficiently, in terms of both quantity and quality.

Certainly these characteristics are not present with the same intensity in every country. The transition to online operation has thus far been more rapid in the USA, where outstanding loans at the end of 1998 amounted to over US$4 trillion, making this the most widespread financial activity, and where the 'financial culture' induces households not merely to accept the services offered by their own banks but to seek better conditions in the market.

While on the one hand this segment offers excellent prospects for growth, on the other banks must not underestimate the risk deriving from the entry of new players of non-financial origin. In fact, the traditional banks that offer loans to private customers on the Web, both under their own names and through specially constituted operating units, have been joined by innovative players such as 'aggregator sites' and 'market places'.

'Internet aggregators' are sites that attract ('aggregate') a large number of consumers, offering them, in the role of brokers, loans originating from traditional banks or from other lenders. Their function, in essence, is to help consumers find the best borrowing conditions and to receive a commission when the transaction has been finalized. These players, at first glance, resemble players highly active, for example, in the US lending market, such as the brokers who now mediate a large share of the loans, earning commissions ranging from 50 to 100 base points and generally offering the products of a restricted number of lenders. In reality, there are many opportunities the new aggregators could exploit to obtain competitive advantages over traditional brokers, and perhaps over banks and traditional lenders as well:

- the breadth of their product range (these sites can easily conclude agreements with all the major lenders and thus offer innumerable combinations of interest rates, repayment terms and duration);
- the particularly low level of their commissions, well below what a traditional broker can offer;
- the possibility of presenting material of an educational and financial advisory nature: potential borrowers can thus use computers to estimate monthly payments or assess refinancing opportunities, can compare the various types of loan and the rates offered by the various lenders, and can then formally apply for a loan by filling in an online application and even finalize the transaction on the website;
- the offer by a few aggregators of loan-related services, such as useful information on the steps to take in the purchase of a home, news on the real estate market, and sometimes agreements with real estate agencies;
- the preference for an anonymous channel, as is certainly manifested by all consumers of the sub-prime category, who are more likely to be rationed using the traditional channels because of their imperfect credit records;
- the possibility of vertical integration, transforming a site that simply directs consumers toward lenders in exchange for a commission into first a Web-based broker and then into a full-fledged lender with its own portfolio.

Let us now examine 'market places'. As their name implies, they perform the function of bringing together the demand for funds by households with the offerings of lenders (or brokers). In some cases, the loan application, along data on the applicant and a credit score, is forwarded by the market place to a restricted number of lenders, selected on the basis of the applicant's preferences. The lenders then make an offer in terms of interest rate, thus proposing different conditions to borrowers based on their different credit scores, which does not usually occur in the private lending market.

To counter the obvious ability of these new players of non-financial origin, and particularly players born and raised on the Web, to contact a vast pool of potential customers and to set up efficient systems for managing and reusing the information gathered, traditional banks certainly must use their capacity to fully exploit their patrimony of confidential information. Particularly in a country like ours, where banks have been the only players in the business of lending to private individuals (see Table 3.4), the ability of banks to evaluate the creditworthiness of potential borrowers cannot be equalled in the short term. Then bank intermediaries, since they have an enormous base of highly faithful customers, to whom they offer a broad range of financial services, can implement strategies of cross-selling, providing a loan service to those who already utilize their payment and investment services, and exploiting the information gained in providing those services to better assess their creditworthiness. Lastly, many consumers, particularly the more 'traditional' one, less familiar with the use of the Web to finalize contracts, will prefer to use sites like the market places or aggregators only to obtain useful information, while they will continue to finalize the transactions with traditional players with well-known names, deemed more trustworthy.

Then there is another competitive advantage for players already operating in the field. New entrants have benefited in the past two years, particularly in the USA, from the high volume of loan origination deriving from the low level of interest rates. But when rates rise, they, like all the others, will suffer a decline in activity. Intermediaries with a large loan portfolio, unlike the new players operating via the Internet, will be able to offset this decline with larger cash flows deriving from variable-rate loans and thus maintain stable profitability.

In reality, the response of banks and other traditional lenders to the new challenges has been weak. In the USA only a small fraction of them offer the possibility of forwarding an application online, and only a very few leading players have adopted a true strategy to use the new channel, integrating it with the other established ones. In our country, then, while many banks are beginning to show their lending conditions on their websites, only a few offer useful information on the process of purchasing property. Very few offer users the possibility of entering their personal data and income and financial situation to obtain a credit score, while the first non-bank players are beginning to develop their own strategies of Web exploitation.

Origination

In investment banking, and especially in the issue of new shares (origination), the key factor has always been played by placement capacity, i.e. ensuring the success of an issue by exploiting contractual power with investors, compared to the other two phases, i.e. the search for companies that constitute a valid source of investment and the structuring of issues. The major Italian banks, in particular, have participated in placement syndicates more for their placement capacity than their ability to find companies in need of restructuring. The advent of the Internet in the issue of equities (called IPOs) and bonds can radically transform the distribution channel and lower its costs, shifting the focus of investment banks to the other two phases of these operations. Italian banks, seeing their only success factor diminish, should thus specialize in search for issuing companies, particularly among those already clients to which they only sell credit products, by exploiting their asset of confidential information.

Starting with equity issues, there are now many intermediaries who have decided to exploit the Internet as a new channel.

In the USA, a new ruling by the Securities and Exchange Commission (the federal regulatory body oversees the financial markets) has simplified the rules that regulate the purchase of IPO share via the Internet. Some of the most interesting new activities are those of the online brokers: three of them have joined forces to offer the placement of new companies on the Stock Exchange. The regulation of these operations is essential to make them transparent and allow small investors to participate in the placement of new companies, which used to be reserved for pension funds and other institutional investors in the USA.

Looking at Europe, we see that the phenomenon has already assumed significant dimensions, particularly in Germany. Of the many online activities there, the most innovative is undoubtedly free online IPOs. The intermediary asks no commission from investors to access this service: they need simply register and receive information about future IPOs via e-mail. In Italy, however, the offering of such services is inhibited by legislative delays, and particularly the lack of regulation regarding electronic signatures, indispensable for finalizing any contract, including the subscription or purchase of equities through public offerings.

As in online trading, the bond sector has lagged somewhat behind equities. Until recently, equity issues over the Internet were not imitated by similar operations for bonds. The beginning of the new millennium has also narrowed this gap, and the new channel will be increasingly used for the primary bond market. Traditionally. Banks participated in placements by collecting orders and so-called 'book-building' through telephone contacts with institutional investors, mutual funds and banks. This will now be replaced with the use of a website. Thanks to the new technologies, it is now possible, in a few seconds, to contact all the institutional investors connected to the banks by means of a special password. The new security issue can also be accompanied by copious documentation including a detailed prospectus, the advice of analysts and charts comparing the yields with those of bonds in circulation.

Bonds issued and placed via the Internet offer other benefits to the issuer and the lead bank beyond mere time considerations: an photograph updated in real time of the inflow of subscription orders, a precise geographical map of the demand distribution and also a picture of the type of yield most attractive to investors. The site can, in fact, allow institutional clients to book the new bond issue directly online for a specific amount and at a desired yield. The issuer also derives advantages, of course. The use of this new technology permits some issuers, who address their offers primarily to institutional investors, to broaden the investor base, in terms of both geography and purchaser category.

Another variant is the possibility of using the Internet to connect not only to institutional investors but also to the online clients of the placement syndicate banks, thus reaching a pool of several million potential purchasers-investors (institutional and private) within a few hours. Obviously, with an issue organized in this way, it would be natural to find online brokers in the placement syndicate. Although these online brokers have no experience in major issues, they can lever on their ability to access millions of potential online subscribers.

The Internet boom would thus seem destined to expand from the equity segment to bonds. This is particularly evident considering the rapidly growing number of issuers desirous of utilizing the new channel, which has already been exploited not only by corporate issuers (both American and European, including Italians) but also by institutions like the BIS and the World Bank (see above) and by sovereign states.

One aspect should be underscored, however: we must consider that fixed-income purchasers are quite different from the less risk-shy investors who have animated online equity trading in recent years. It is the latter who have been involved in online share trading in the last few years. The future of bonds on the Internet is therefore still difficult to project.

Returning to Italy, we stated earlier that the development of a channel like the Internet for the issuing of equities and bonds constitutes a challenge and a present danger for Italian banks, eliminating the only entry barrier to this market represented by placing power. In reality, the challenge may seem even more crucial, if we consider the trend in origination activity. On the equity side, 1999 concluded with record figures from the standpoint of fund raising, through both IPOs and rights issues. The scenarios for coming years are quite similar for a number of reasons: offering of securities range from the still incomplete privatization processes to the current consolidation in several industries (which increasingly results in the spin-off of high-value subsidiaries and the financing of maxi-acquisition on the capital market, the placements of medium-sized companies promoted by the ever more numbers venture capital funds, the numerous IPOs in the high-growth sectors such as technology (particularly the Internet) and telecommunications. On the securities demand side, there is an equivalent change in the portfolio choices of Italian investors, who are increasing the portion assigned to equities to the detriment particularly of public debt issues.

In conclusion, the leadership position of Italian banks (in terms of number of operations led) for the placement of equities in our country, an activity that promises to grow in the immediate future (see above), could be challenged by the advent of a channel that will facilitate the entry of major foreign players, particularly those with strong positions in Europe, which will soon become the single 'domestic' market to follow. Therefore Italian banks, on the one hand, must exploit the new Web-based operating procedures and, on the other, concentrate their efforts on aspects of origination activity they have overlooked until now, such as the search for valid entrepreneurial projects to develop and accompany to the market and expertise in structuring issues.

4   Introducing E-Banking In Italy: A Preliminary Empirical Analysis

After analysing the qualitative macro-phenomena accompanying the introduction of new information technologies in the banking system as a whole, we can ask ourselves a more specific question: how much and how is the introduction of the Internet technologies changing the individual Italian banks?

From this standpoint, for our part, we would like to illustrate a few results of a first systematic analysis of choices by the top 110 Italian banks regarding Internet banking (see Table 3.1). These banks represent the lion's share of the entire Italian financial system and more specifically, for our purposes, hold roughly 90 per cent of the total bank deposits in our country, equal to ITL 2,924,350 billion. On this amount we computed the rate of penetration of online trading, since in the final analysis the assets that can be transacted through this innovative mode correspond to the securities in custody and administration entrusted by customers to the banks and reported in their indirect deposits.

One necessary condition for offering trading services, of course, is the presence of the banking institutes on the Internet. Regarding the major banks we analysed, presence on the Web is now an established fact, with no less

Table 3.1   Top 110 Italian banks

	Bank	Total sssets	Trading online banks			No.	%
1	S.Paolo-Imi	305,336,031					
2	Cariplo	172,570,645					
3	Comit	170,535,238					
4	Banca di Roma	150,055,310	prime	10	banche	7	70.0
5	Bnl	146,821,352	prime	20	banche	13	65.0
6	Montepaschi	119,497,484	prime	30	banche	18	60.0
7	Credito Italiano/						
	UniCredito	116,615,927	prime	40	banche	25	62.5
8	Rolo Banca	67,577,759	prime	50	banche	32	64.0
9	Banco di Napoli	62,350,218	prime	60	banche	36	60.0
10	Ambroveneto	58,062,541	prime	70	banche	39	55.7
11	Banco di Sicilia	55,363,962	prime	80	banche	42	52.5
12	Deutsche Bank	50,452,807	prime	90	banche	47	52.2
13	Pop. Milano	43,454,159	prime	100	banche	52	52.0
14	Banca Crt	41,137,412	prime	109	banche	56	51.4
15	Bna	39,968,292					
16	Pop. Novara	38,177,436					
17	Pop. Bergamo	37,110,357					
18	Cariverona	35,258,121					
19	Crediop	34,490,971					
20	Pop. Verona	30,862,208					
21	Banco di Brescia	29,766,279					
22	Banca Toscana	26,725,948					
23	Carisbo	25,924,332					
24	Banca Antonveneta	25,921,040					
25	CariParma	25,460,208					
26	Pop. Emilia Romagna	22,484,742					
27	Carime	21,196,929					
28	CariPaRo	20,922,559					
29	Banca Intesa	20,058,595					
30	Carige	19,205,475					
31	Carifirenze	18,495,251					
32	Banco di Sardegna	17,807,101					
33	Banca delle Marche	16,682,902					
34	Bipop	16,141,521					
35	Credem	15,544,569					
36	Creberg	14,329,560					
37	Bam	14,127,026					

Table 3.1 cont'd

	Bank	Total sssets
38	Pop. Lodi	12,827,401
39	Bre	12,736,010
40	Pop. C&I	10,872,156
41	Pop. Vicenza	10,350,912
42	Pop. Sondrio	10,207,047
43	CariVenezia	9,374,838
44	Pop. Etruria e Lazio	8,794,926
45	Banca Sella	8,102,128
46	Banca Fideuram	7,822,337
47	CariBolzano	7,117,148
48	Pop. Ancona	7,087,716
49	Biverbanca	7,049,185
50	Creval	6,976,768
51	Cassamarca	6,925,070
52	Banca del Salento	6,690,394
53	Pop. Adriatico	5,932,150
54	CariLucca	5,623,703
55	Carire	5,292,213
56	Pop Friuladria	5,259,877
57	Caritro	5,256,392
58	Credito Artigiano	5,074,189
59	Banca di Legnano	4,827,702
60	CariTrieste	4,781,425
61	Banca dell'Umbria 1462	4,768,839
62	Banca Mediterranea	4,751,994
63	Banco Chiavari	4,250,113
64	BCC Roma	4,235,784
65	Pop. Alto Adige	4,202,674
66	CariUdinePordenone	4,045,643
67	CariAsti	4,040,415
68	Banca Agricola Pop. Ragusa	3,980,197
69	Pop. Puglia e Basilicata	3,911,846
70	Banco di Desio	3,845,045
71	CariPistoiaPescia	3,802,834
72	Tercas	3,733,709
73	CariPisa	3,691,112
74	CariPrato	3,638,058
75	CR S.Miniato	3,633,798

Table 3.1 cont'd

	Bank	Total sssets
76	Banca Trento e Bolzano	3,490,320
77	CariSpezia	3,485,286
78	Pop. Pugliese	3,466,698
79	Pop. Intra	3,450,627
80	Pop. Irpinia	3,428,553
81	CariFerrara	3,337,355
82	Pop. Asolo e Montebellluna	3,335,225
83	Pop. Bari	3,284,301
84	CariRimini	3,274,426
85	Banca di Piacenza	3,214,789
86	Banca Cr. Pop.- T. del Greco	3,074,022
87	CariForlì	3,050,593
88	CariRavenna	2,900,339
89	CariCesena	2,872,457
90	Banca di Sassari	2,841,476
91	Pop. Luino e Varese	2,763,638
92	Pop. Cremona	2,763,251
93	CariAlessandria	2,663,533
94	CariChieti	2,608,737
95	Pop. Abbiategrasso	2,606,219
96	CariRieti	2,343,468
97	Banca Monte Parma	2,312,294
98	Pop. Spoleto	2,302,419
99	CariSavona	2,266,404
100	CariFermo	2,223,032
101	Pop. Udinese	2,213,544
102	CariAscoli	2,210,446
103	CariGorizia	2,162,814
104	Banca Valle Camonica	2,105,887
105	Caripe	2,002,684
106	CariViterbo	1,989,711
107	Carispaq	1,848,170
108	CariTerniNarni	1,490,928
109	CariCivitavecchia	753,790

than 90 per cent of these players (99 out of 110) boasting a website. These sites therefore become an instrument of communication and a medium for conveying services, such as online trading, with the associated information and 'education' services, corporate banking or home banking.

The latter is now furnished by 61 per cent (67) of the major banks, while the former involves 55 per cent (60 banks versus five a year ago). In reality, the penetration of online trading seems much greater if we look at the share of indirect deposits attributable to the banks involved (or rate of penetration of online trading) (Figure 3.1).

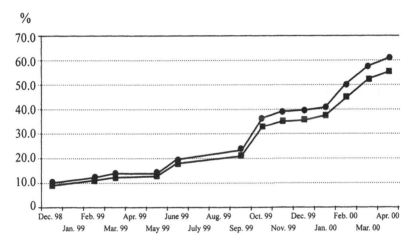

Figure 3.1   Trading online penetration

At the present (last measurement: 3 May 2000) these banks hold 66 per cent of the indirect deposits of the major banks and 60 per cent of those of the entire banking system. This percentage grew sharply over the past year, as it barely approached 10 per cent at the end of the 1998 and 40 per cent at the end of the 1999.

The services offered by the smaller banks are not included in our analysis, but in any case it is unlikely they are able to furnish innovative services and certainly represent a much smaller share both of total assets and indirect deposits of the entire banking system. Also omitted are the players of non-bank origin, certainly present in this field but still few in number and with data difficult to acquire.

If we attempt to interpret what induces banks to offer trading services via the Internet, we discover that the leading determinant is size. Thus far, seven of the top ten banks in total assets have taken this path, and 13 of the top 20 (data from Bankscope, updated to December 1998), while for the entire sample of 110 banks the percentage drops to around 50 per cent.

The importance of the size factor is confirmed by a comparative analysis of a few significant variables, based on financial statements and other sources: total assets are 27 per cent greater, on the average, for the online banks than for the total of the major banks (ITL 28,600 billion versus 22,500 billion) and the number of branches is an average 30 per cent higher (263 versus 202). Another interesting variable to examine is the amount of securities in custody and administration: the 56 online banks safeguard and administer an average of ITL 31,135 billion in securities for their customers, against an average of 25,617 billion for the major banks as a whole.

The 'e-innovative' banks are also more probably listed: 45 per cent are present on the stock exchange versus 32 per cent of major banks as a whole. They are more probably based in northern Italy (Figure 3.2): 60 per cent circa have their head offices in a northern city, a percentage that drops to 50 per cent if we consider the entire sample – the Banca del Salento representing the most famous exception.

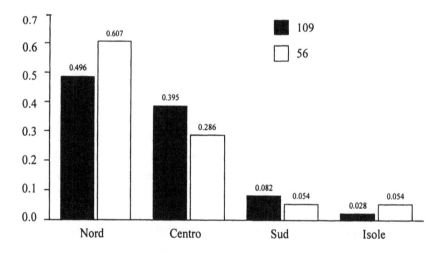

Figure 3.2   Geographic location

They most frequently assume the form of mutual loan banks ('Banche Popolari'): 30 per cent of the online banks have this form, versus 25 per cent of total major banks, while savings banks ('Casse di Risparmio') were less represented among the e-innovative banks (30 per cent versus 38 per cent) (Figure 3.3).

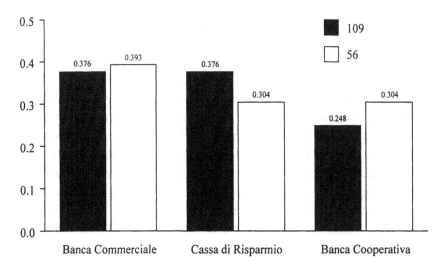

Figure 3.3   Bank governance

Another variable that shows significant values in the two samples is profitability: the return on equity (ROAE) of the online banks is 17 per cent higher (8.2 per cent versus 7 per cent).

Lastly, an econometric analysis was performed on 43 of the 56 banks offering online trading services (more information on the attached regression tables are available on request). In particular, we were seeking to discover what variables determined the speed of entry into this market (the dependent variable is definitely the delay in the offering of these services, measured in months, with respect to the first entrants in February 1997).

This analysis indicated a strong, highly significant inverse correlation between the amount of securities in custody and the delay in market entry. In other words, the larger the customer assets in custody at the banks, the faster the banks decided to offer online service. Looking at the profit variable, both the operating margin and the interest margin and revenues from services seem to have had a positive effect on the speed of entry into online services.

Thus the move to e-banking – at least until now and on the average – seems to have been easier for banks that were already innovative, in terms of ability to create value from indirect deposits, large, private and particular mutual-loan banks and located primarily in the north.

5   Introducing e-banking and Banker Conservatism: Role and Determinants of Managerial Incentives

What are the causes of how and when a traditional bank move into e-banking? The analysis of the facts and data, both macro and micro, contained in the foregoing sections, can only be followed by a few theoretical reflections, which necessarily begins with the 'Internet revolution' that is impacting all the sectors of our banking system, though in different ways and with different timing.

Therefore all the strategies announced in recent months in the Italian financial industry seem to be based on the combination of banking and telecommunications. Not a day goes by that some bank – small, medium-sized or large – does not announce 'something' that concerns the universe of the already legendary 'new economy'.

In general, the challenge of the Internet for banks is linked to two different aspects. In the first place, the Internet can offer important opportunities for bank product distribution. From this standpoint, its development can represent an opportunity to accelerate the rationalization of the distribution network, increasing efficiency in terms of costs. As a new distribution network, the Internet also ensures total market competitiveness, demolishing the residual barriers that are fragmenting international competition in the European banking system.

On the demand side, in fact, it provides customers the possibility to compare different conditions and directly access banking products located even in other countries. From the supply standpoint, it provides the possibility to serve different markets, hurdling even the final non-tariff barriers that continue to isolate some markets.

Secondly, the Internet can be another resource for ensuring a more efficient and effective production of financial services. From the viewpoint, being the first to arrive in the market and anticipating the trends can offer important advantages to first movers, thus providing returns on *expertise* at least in the short term.

Despite its definite potential, the phenomenon of the 'Internetization race' among Italian banks suggests a series of considerations. The most immediate is a reminder that at night all cows are black. In other words, we should be extremely cautious in formulating general opinions, whether positive or negative, when companies like banks, that typically represent the old economy, leap indiscriminately and rapidly into relationships with an industry, in this case typical of the new economy, which is also characterized by significant diversities, current and future, between one company and another in terms of value creation capacity, if applied to the production and distribution of financial products.

The new economy will represent an opportunity for growth and stable development only for those banks with quality management and quality shareholders. In other words, the critical variable of success will not be so much the application of the new technologies of information and communication (ICT) as the ability of each bank to transform them into tangible value creation strategies: an ability, in fact, linked to the quality of the management and the shareholders.

To fully understand the central role of the binomial 'management quality – shareholder quality' some further reflections are necessary.

There is no doubt that finance, by utilizing progress in the production and dissemination of information, is assuming totally new quantitative and qualitative connotations, especially outside Italy, but in our country too.

In a world characterized by imperfect, asymmetrical information, and thus risks, banks have always sought to absolve as best they could their task of conveying the purchasing power of the various economic actors in space and time. The more efficient this vehicle has been, jointly satisfying the risk-return needs of households and companies, the more value has been created.

Today intermediaries have the possibility of performing this function with radically greater potential, in terms of effectiveness and efficiency. But not all will succeed. For the individual banks, the challenge will be met by those companies whose directors and managers possess the professionalism, but especially the cultural sensitivity, to exploit the new opportunities in their own reference markets and therefore respect to their own stakeholders, actual and potential, with shareholders capable of following them but also monitoring them. The importance of the features in the trinomial managerial factor–shareholder factor–stakeholder factor has, in fact, become the pivot around which even the result of the game increasingly revolves.

Our approach adopt the more recent theories on bank behaviour, based on the role of managerial incentives and consequently on the importance of the allocation of control and property rights. The bank is a 'special' firm since most of the capital structure (equity, debt) is external – not owned by management – and their debt is mainly held by small no coordinated operators. The various claims represents the links between the stakeholders' and shareholders' behaviour and the managerial incentives.

Let us assume that a bank manager has a certain sum W available for investing to develop his bank and must choose between traditional channels and e-banking activities.

The traditional channels have lower expected returns, at least in the short term, but at the same time are less volatile that those of e-banking activity. For simplicity's sake, let us call the utility function of the manager U, assuming that if he does not invest in e-banking, the expected utility of the sum is zero, or the extra profits, as it were, whatever their amount:

$$U(W) = 0 \tag{1}$$

But the e-banking investment is risky: if the investment goes well, there will be profits, otherwise losses. The probability of investment failure is equal to p, with 0<p<1, of course.

If the result of the e-banking investment is positive, the sum invested Y will have positive expected profitability, which can be found by imagining that the monetary value B of this benefit is equal to:

$$B = (1 + r)Y = mY \tag{2}$$

where r is the average expected rate of return on the e-banking investment.

But the e-banking investment, like all investments, has an unrecoverable cost: we can assume that this cost C is proportional to the amount of liquidity invested in e-banking, according to a parameter c between 0 and 1:

$$C = cY \tag{3}$$

If the e-banking investment goes badly, there is tangible economic damage (the unrecoverable cost C). There may also be intangible economic damage for management, such as loss of reputation equal to S. What is the monetary value of the damage from intangible loss S? We can assume that, like tangible costs, the intangible costs S are related to the amount of the investment: with the first derivative S' and the second derivative S'' both positive.

And the same possible loss of reputation of the bank manager, associated with the failed investment in e-banking, can be perceived in a more or less direct way depending on the type of institutional context in which the manager works. The relevance of the institutional variable, defined in a uniform way, seeks to gauge the influence of a series of structural factors, such as the governance model:

$$S = sY \tag{4}$$

Having defined the terms of the question, the banker is faced with the problem of deciding if and how much to invest in e-banking. The expected utility E of the banker, expressed earlier in generic terms, can now be better specified as:

$$E = u(1-p)(B-C) + pu(-C-S)$$
$$E = u(1-p)(ay) + pu(-cy-S(y)) = E(y) \quad (5)$$

where a = m – c and where S is a monotone increasing, convex function, with S. The specification of the utility function of the banker is the most general one possible, so as to determine, beyond the propensity to risk, what the other important variables are and what role they play.

The dilemma of choice can be summarized in the following chart:

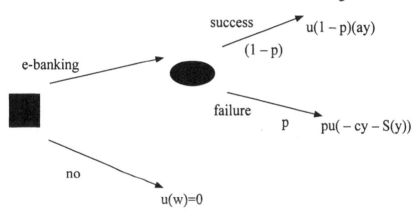

Let us rewrite the utility function as:

$$E = u(ay) + p(u(-cy-S(y)) - u(ay)) \quad (5a)$$

Since – cy – S(y) < ay for y > 0, the expression multiplied by p is negative, so the utility of the banker declines as the probability of failure of the e-banking investment rises. Therefore, whatever the propensity to risk, it is important to understand for each bank what the probabilities of success are when entering activities associated with e-banking. If those probabilities of success vary according to market variables, such as reference type of customers, current and potential, the nature of the products, and the characteristics of the competition, we shall have behavioural differences.

In addition to the probability of success in the areas of e-banking, it is important for the bank manager to perceive the expected losses in case of failure, in terms of reputation. If, for example, for each amount of investment in e-banking we make the expected intangible costs more severe: so that S1 (y) > S(y), the new expected utility will be:

$$E1 = u(ay) + p(u(- cy - S1(y)) - u(ay)) < E \tag{5b}$$

In addition to the intangible expected losses, managers should be sensitive to the net tangible gains, given by the difference between the tangible expected gains and the tangible expected costs. Thus if a = m −c, we must look at the reactivity of the banker's utility as the tangible net gains change, since

$$\frac{dE}{da} = \frac{dE}{dm} \tag{6}$$

$$\frac{dE}{da} = yu'(ay) - pyu'(ay) = yu'(ay)(1-p) < 0$$

The banker's utility increases as the expected net return on the e-banking investment increases.

Now the banker must identify the optimal level Y* of the e-banking investment, bearing in mind the maximum resources at his disposal: the more the e-banking investment is, the less the banker conservatism is. Deriving (5) with respect to that variable subject to the banker's decision – to observe the first necessary and sufficient condition for a maximum – we find that:

$$\frac{dE}{dY} = au'(ay) + p(- cy - S'(y))u'(- cy - S'(y)) - pau'(ay) \tag{7}$$

$$\frac{dE}{dY} = (1 - p)au'(ay) - p(c + S'(y))u'(- cy - S'(y))$$

In (7), the first part is positive, the second negative; this derivative in 0 is valued at:

$$\frac{dE}{dY}(0) = (1 - p)au'(0) - p(c + S'(0)u'(0) \tag{7a}$$

$$\frac{dE}{dY}(0) = u'(0)(a - p(a + c + S'(0))$$

Therefore, for the manager to have an incentive to invest in e-banking (7a) must be positive. This occurs, all other conditions being equal, if a very precise relationship exists between the probability of success of the e-banking investment, the level of intangible expected costs and the level of tangible net expected gains:

$$p < \frac{a}{a + c + S'(0)} \tag{8}$$

We may define (8) as the 'e-banking condition': its likelihood, the banker's propensity to risk being equal, is:

a) directly proportional to the probability of success of the e-banking investment;
b) inversely proportional to the unrecoverable expected costs of the investment;
c) directly proportional to the relative expected profitability;
d) indirectly proportional to the reputation costs for the manager (more precisely, the initial progressiveness of said costs).

It is not important, on the other hand, to compute the second derivative of the utility function with respect to the amount of investment to be chosen, because (5) suggests that the utility function of the banker is a convex linear combination of a concave function (the first addendum) and the superimposition of monotonic and concave functions with a concave known to be concave.

Thus the banker's utility function is concave in y, and therefore if $E'y(0) > 0$ then the optimal level y^* of the e-banking investment exists and is unique. Two cases are possible:

$$\frac{dE}{dY}(W) \geq 0 \rightarrow y^* = W$$

$$\frac{dE}{dY}(W) < 0 \, esiste \rightarrow y^* < W \rightarrow unico$$

In other words, if where the resources available for the investment are maximum, the banker's utility is positive, then those resources will all be invested in e-banking; in the opposite case, only a fraction of them.

In general, we also observe that it is possible to compute the maximum value of the e-banking investment. This critical value Y' indicates the limit beyond which conditions are optimal for the banker to abstain from the investment.

Beyond a certain amount, the economic damage associated with both the tangible and intangible factors, associated with the risk of failure of the e-banking investment, is so high that the expected utility is negative, and it is better to invest in less risky banking activities with a lower expected value.

The critical value Y', which we can define as propensity to e-banking, or space for the investment in e-banking, can be determined as follows: given that u (0) = E(Y') since it is not restrictive to assume u(0) = 0 – with an appropriate choice of origin and unit of measurement, the equation for finding Y' is:

$$(1-p)u(aY') + pu(-cY' - S(Y')) = 0 \tag{9}$$

The critical value Y' or, if we wish, the propensity to invest in e-banking (absolute or, if divided by W, relative), will depend on the structural parameters of the model. In fact:

$$\frac{dY'}{dp} = \frac{-u(aY') + u(-cY' - S'(Y')) - pau'(ay)}{(1-p)au'(aY') - p(c + S'(Y'))u'(cY' - S(Y'))} \tag{10}$$

$$\frac{dY'}{dp} = \frac{u(aY') - u(-cY' - S'(Y'))}{(1-p)au'(aY') - p(c + S'(Y'))u'(cY' - S(Y'))}$$

The numerator is positive, the denominator is the derivative of the banker's utility function compared to Y computed as Y'. Since it is reasonable that Y' > Y*, the denominator is negative, so

$$\frac{dY'}{dp} < 0$$

There is thus an inverse relationship between the propensity to invest in e-banking and the probability of failure in those banking activities.

Lastly, regarding the effect of the expected net probability of those activities:

$$\frac{dY'}{da} = \frac{(1-p)u'(aY')Y'}{(1-p)au'(aY') - p(c + S'(Y'))u'(cY' - S(Y'))} > 0$$

On the contrary, an increase in net expected profitability increases the propensity to invest in e-banking. In conclusion, our model proposed a simple systematic framework to capture together the interaction of the possible key variables in determine the bank behaviour in new information technology investments.

6   Conclusions: From Banks To E-banks in Italy: A New Schumpeterian View?

Drawing conclusions on the topic in question – which is constantly evolving, even day by day – is perhaps a foolhardy undertaking. Nonetheless, we feel prepared to offer a few indications, addressing them ideally to three different audiences: the banks, the monetary and financial authorities and the economic policy makers.

The new information and communications technologies are destined to radically and irreversibly alter the behaviour patterns of households and companies, and thus the mechanisms that lead to choices about purchase and sale, savings and investment, but with timeframes and methods that are difficult to predict in each context.

The Internet, in other words, will represent a structural shock to the behaviour patterns of economic players, with varying intensity and form and difficult to foresee for each environmental, social and institutional context. All other conditions being equal, the 'Internet shock' is augmenting uncertainty, in the double sense of risk and opportunity.

What does this mean for banks? The Internet shock will likely be *structural* – as is obvious – but also *idiosyncratic*. It will be idiosyncratic in nature because today, despite the phenomena of globalization and the standardization of conduct and the harmonization of regulations, each bank still possesses a specific identity of its own, formed by its particular markets, activities and customers. This identity will be impacted, in different ways and time-frames difficult to predict, by the 'Internet shock', which for banks is not just the simple introduction of new instruments of production and distribution but requires a gradual rethinking of the relationships with all their stakeholders, if they wish to continue producing economic value.

If the shock is to be structural and idiosyncratic, the capacity of management to confront events of this scope becomes more a crucial success factor than ever. So in each bank, all other conditions being equal, the *human capital of entrepreneurship* will be decisive: in terms of *propensity to risk*, since, as we stressed, managers will have to confront situations with a higher degree of uncertainty; in terms of *propensity to contamination* between different, heterogeneous approaches and schemes of analysis, since each problem will involve a different mix of economic-financial, legal and technological aspects; in terms of *propensity to flexibility*, since managers will have to interpret highly different and variable scenarios and govern them.

Banks are therefore faced with a situation that, without exaggeration, could be termed epic. We would like to advance a 'new Schumpeterian' thesis which states that Italian banks could become active protagonists in the changes that the way of producing, distributing and purchasing may register, starting from the coming months.

If our banks are able to understand what opportunities are available, in terms of relations with households and companies, they could play a decisive role in the launch of the new economy in Italy. If by 'new economy' we mean the complex of changes caused in production and distribution companies by the increasingly pervasive technologies of information, we can project with reasonable certainty that in the not-too-distant future all consumers and all companies will have to deal with the opportunities and the risks produced in their own areas of interest by the new economy.

For Italian consumers and companies, this may mean having need of parties – the 'navigators' – capable of 'accompanying' users to the network in a professional, reliable way, so as to make their achievement of their various purchasing and selling objectives more efficient.

But who in Italy is still today capable of making simultaneous contact with the greatest number of households and companies? One characteristic of our country is that the banks have traditionally monopolized the management of household savings and the financing of companies.

In other institutional contexts the grid of financial relations, and thus information flows, also passes through the securities markets and other forms of intermediation and service. In Italy the history of fiduciary instruments relates primarily to banking.

Therefore the banking system as a whole (perhaps) and individual banks (definitely) have an extraordinary opportunity to exploit their considerable assets of information and customer loyalty to their advantage and to the benefit of society, bearing in mind, as the point of departure for our reflections, that no one can buy or sell anything without using the payments system.

The implications for the monetary and financial authorities are also significant. Situations of greater uncertainty generate both a *demand for certainty* by the players and a *demand for knowledge* by the authorities. This, in our view, requires a shift toward forms that we might call *concerted regulation*, or self-regulation.

The problem is clear: on the one hand, in a context made dynamic and uncertain by the options and opportunities offered by technology, the players become gradually more sensitive to the certainty of the rules, and to their capacity to ensure the proper, orderly development of the markets. For their part the authorities, in a context of growing complexity and intertwining relations among intermediaries, instruments and markets, which in perspective could throw any system of segmentation or categorization into crisis, feel an increasing need to understand and know what is happening with the least possible delay. Thus new spaces are opening for a vision of good regulation as a market asset, and thus a common objective of the authorities and the players, the healthy, responsible ones, of course, i.e. the majority, if that market exists. Regulation thus becomes less and less an imposition from above and more and more endogenous with regard to the needs of the players, but with the final purpose of satisfying the needs of the users, ensuring ever greater transparency, competition and contendability.

But no industry can be efficient without a suitable institutional framework, made of game rules that respect the needs of an authentic market economy, which first of all means a level playing field for all, combating positions of interest and monopoly wherever they exist. And this is where the responsibilities of policy makers emerge: the more they define laws and regulations to increase competition and contendability in all markets (capital, labour, goods and services), the more the Internet shock will be a growth opportunity for the banking industry and for the economic sector as a whole. The more our banking companies, and thus our users of financial services, households and companies, are hobbled and penalized by labour, tax and governance policies that explicitly restrict the full flexibility of prices and interchange, the dissemination of information and competition, the more difficulties they will encounter with the Internet revolution.

Acknowledgement

The author wishes to thank, without implicating, Simone Puglisi who provided excellent research assistance.

References

Dewatripoint, M. and Tirole, J. (1994), *The Prudential Regulation of Banks*, Boston: MIT Press.

Dorn, J.A. (ed.) (1997), *The Future of Money in the Information Age*, Washington, DC: Cato Institute.

Evans, P. and Wurster, T. (2000), *Blown to Bits*, Cambridge, MA: Harvard Business School.

Freixas, X. and Rochet, J.C. (1997), *Microeconomics of Banking*, Cambridge, MA: MIT Press.

Il Sole 24ore, 1997–2000.

Mcknight, L. and Bailey, J. (1997), *Internet Economics*, Cambridge, MA: MIT Press.

Masciandaro, D. and Riolo, F. (eds) (2000), *Internet Banking. Tecnologia, Economia e Diritto*, Rome: V Rapporto Fondazione Rosselli, Bancaria Editrice.

Schumpeter, J.A. (1939), *Business Cycles. A Theoretical, Historical and Statistical Analysis of the Capitalist Process*, New York.

Solomon, E.H. (1997), *Virtual Money*, New York: Oxford University Press.

Dependent variable: LAG
Method: least squares
Date: 05/04/00 Time: 12:35
Sample: 1 43
Included observations: 43

Variable	Coefficient	Std error	t-statistic	Prob.
C	33.65302	1.471076	22.87647	0.0000
CAP	−4.75E–07	3.57E–07	−1.328432	0.1914
R-squared	0.041266	Mean dependent var		32.53488
Adjusted R-squared	0.017882	SD dependent var.		7.983163
S.E. of regression	7.911463	Akaike info criterion		7.019898
Sum squared resid.	2566.241	Schwarz criterion		7.101814
Log likelihood	−148.9278	F-statistic		1.764733
Durbin-Watson stat.	1.346389	Prob. (F-statistic)		0.191383

Dependent variable: LAG
Method: least squares
Date: 05/04/00 Time: 12:35
Sample: 1 43
Included observations: 43

Variable	Coefficient	Std error	t-statistic	Prob.
C	27.98232	2.916331	9.595043	0.0000
CAP_TOTATT	0.566535	0.331303	1.710018	0.0948
R-squared	0.066573	Mean dependent var.		32.53488
Adjusted R-squared	0.043806	SD dependent var.		7.983163
SE of regression	7.806348	Akaike info criterion		6.993147
Sum squared resid.	2498.502	Schwarz criterion		7.075063
Log likelihood	−148.3527	F-statistic		2.924161
Durbin-Watson stat.	1.404643	Prob. (F-statistic)		0.094821

Dependent variable: LAG
Method: least squares
Date: 05/04/00 Time: 12:36
Sample: 1 43
Included observations: 43

Variable	Coefficient	Std error	t-statistic	Prob.
C	40.45204	4.553916	8.882914	0.0000
COMMATT_RISOP	−28.77543	15.98017	−1.800696	0.0791
R-squared	0.073289	Mean dependent var.		32.53488
Adjusted R-squared	0.050687	SD dependent var.		7.983163
S.E. of regression	7.778212	Akaike info criterion		6.985925

Sum squared resid.	2480.524	Schwarz criterion	7.067842
Log likelihood	−148.1974	F-statistic	3.242507
Durbin-Watson stat.	1.509828	Prob. (F-statistic)	0.079110

Dependent variable: LAG
Method: least squares
Date: 05/04/00 Time: 12:36
Sample: 1 43
Included observations: 43

Variable	Coefficient	Std error	t-statistic	Prob.
C	33.75473	1.386272	24.34928	0.0000
COMMATT	−2.81E–06	1.64E–06	−1.716157	0.0937
R-squared	0.067020	Mean dependent var.		32.53488
Adjusted R-squared	0.044264	SD dependent var.		7.983163
SE of regression	7.804480	Akaike info criterion		6.992668
Sum squared resid.	2497.306	Schwarz criterion		7.074584
Log likelihood	−148.3424	F-statistic		2.945195
Durbin-Watson stat.	1.429594	Prob. (F-statistic)		0.093681

Dependent variable: LAG
Method: least squares
Date: 05/04/00 Time: 12:38
Sample: 1 43
Included observations: 43

Variable	Coefficient	Std error	t-statistic	Prob.
C	31.64688	8.536833	3.707098	0.0006
COS_MARINTERM	0.013981	0.132994	0.105121	0.9168
R-squared	0.000269	Mean dependent var.		32.53488
Adjusted R-squared	−0.024114	SD dependent var.		7.983163
SE of regression	8.078844	Akaike info criterion		7.061770
Sum squared resid.	2675.976	Schwarz criterion		7.143686
Log likelihood	−149.8280	F-statistic		0.011050
Durbin-Watson stat.	1.310450	Prob. (F-statistic)		0.916792

Dependent variable: LAG
Method: least squares
Date: 05/04/00 Time: 12:35
Sample: 1 43
Included observations: 43

Variable	Coefficient	Std error	t-statistic	Prob.
C	34.69247	1.364719	25.42096	0.0000
CUST	–5.46E–05	1.94E–05	–2.810316	0.0076
R-squared	0.161518	Mean dependent var.		32.53488
Adjusted R-squared	0.141067	SD dependent var.		7.983163
SE of regression	7.398687	Akaike info criterion		6.885877
Sum squared resid.	2244.364	Schwarz criterion		6.967794
Log likelihood	–146.0464	F-statistic		7.897874
Durbin-Watson stat.	1.508643	Prob. (F-statistic)		0.007554

Dependent variable: LAG
Method: least squares
Date: 05/04/00 Time: 12:38
Sample: 1 43
Included observations: 43

Variable	Coefficient	Std error	t-statistic	Prob.
C	34.41235	1.386709	24.81584	0.0000
DEPOS	–7.90E–08	3.25E–08	–2.431765	0.0195
R-squared	0.126051	Mean dependent var.		32.53488
Adjusted R-squared	0.104735	SD dependent var.		7.983163
SE of regression	7.553545	Akaike info criterion		6.927306
Sum squared resid.	2339.298	Schwarz criterion		7.009223
Log likelihood	–146.9371	F-statistic		5.913482
Durbin-Watson stat.	1.380012	Prob. (F-statistic)		0.019481

Dependent variable: LAG
Method: least squares
Date: 05/04/00 Time: 12:31
Sample: 1 43
Included observations: 43

Variable	Coefficient	Std error	t-statistic	Prob.
C	34.47934	1.494415	23.07213	0.0000
DIPEN	–0.000452	0.000216	–2.094602	0.0424
R-squared	0.096665	Mean dependent var.		32.53488
Adjusted R-squared	0.074632	SD dependent var.		7.983163
SE of regression	7.679487	Akaike info criterion		6.960378
Sum squared resid.	2417.955	Schwarz criterion		7.042294
Log likelihood	–147.6481	F-statistic		4.387357
Durbin-Watson stat.	1.397071	Prob. (F-statistic)		0.042428

Dependent variable: LAG
Method: least squares
Date: 05/04/00 Time: 12:31
Sample: 1 43
Included observations: 43

Variable	Coefficient	Std error	t-statistic	Prob.
C	34.62267	1.612912	21.46594	0.0000
FILIA	−0.006563	0.003452	−1.900975	0.0644
R-squared	0.081000	Mean dependent var.		32.53488
Adjusted R-squared	0.058585	SD dependent var.		7.983163
SE of regression	7.745786	Akaike info criterion		6.977570
Sum squared resid.	2459.886	Schwarz criterion		7.059487
Log likelihood	−148.0178	F-statistic		3.613704
Durbin-Watson stat.	1.398001	Prob. (F-statistic)		0.064350

Dependent variable: LAG
Method: least squares
Date: 05/04/00 Time: 12:34
Sample: 1 43
Included observations: 43

Variable	Coefficient	Std error	t-statistic	Prob.
C	34.37903	1.461963	23.51566	0.0000
MARINTERE	−2.32E−06	1.10E−06	−2.105422	0.0414
R-squared	0.097568	Mean dependent var.		32.53488
Adjusted R-squared	0.075558	SD dependent var.		7.983163
SE of regression	7.675645	Akaike info criterion		6.959377
Sum squared resid.	2415.537	Schwarz criterion		7.041293
Log likelihood	−147.6266	F-statistic		4.432803
Durbin-Watson stat.	1.398926	Prob. (F-statistic)		0.041424

Dependent variable: LAG
Method: least squares
Date: 05/04/00 Time: 12:40
Sample: 1 43
Included observations: 43

Variable	Coefficient	Std error	t-statistic	Prob.
C	23.48836	4.317815	5.439871	0.0000
MARGINTERE_IMP	2.942293	1.352094	2.176101	0.0354
R-squared	0.103539	Mean dependent var.		32.53488
Adjusted R-squared	0.081674	SD dependent var.		7.983163
SE of regression	7.650210	Akaike info criterion		6.952738
Sum squared resid.	2399.554	Schwarz criterion		7.034655

Log likelihood	−147.4839	F-statistic	4.735415
Durbin-Watson stat.	1.483709	Prob. (F-statistic)	0.035364

Dependent variable: LAG
Method: least squares
Date: 05/04/00 Time: 12:32
Sample: 1 43
Included observations: 43

Variable	Coefficient	Std error	t-statistic	Prob.
C	34.17823	1.446739	23.62433	0.0000
RICSERV	−3.14E–06	1.60E–06	−1.957763	0.0571
R-squared	0.085492	Mean dependent var.		32.53488
Adjusted R-squared	0.063187	SD dependent var.		7.983163
SE of regression	7.726834	Akaike info criterion		6.972671
Sum squared resid.	2447.862	Schwarz criterion		7.054587
Log likelihood	−147.9124	F-statistic		3.832835
Durbin-Watson stat.	1.420549	Prob. (F-statistic)		0.057087

Dependent variable: LAG
Method: least squares
Date: 05/04/00 Time: 12:33
Sample: 1 43
Included observations: 43

Variable	Coefficient	Std error	t-statistic	Prob.
C	32.39489	3.774340	8.582931	0.0000
RICSERV_TOTATT	0.079719	2.031582	0.039240	0.9689
R-squared	0.000038	Mean dependent var.		32.53488
Adjusted R-squared	−0.024352	SD dependent var.		7.983163
SE of regression	8.079781	Akaike info criterion		7.062002
Sum squared resid.	2676.597	Schwarz criterion		7.143918
Log likelihood	−149.8330	F-statistic		0.001540
Durbin-Watson stat.	1.307511	Prob. (F-statistic)		0.968890

Dependent variable: LAG
Method: least squares
Date: 05/04/00 Time: 12:41
Sample: 1 43
Included observations: 43

Variable	Coefficient	Std error	t-statistic	Prob.
C	34.32339	1.456811	23.56063	0.0000
RISOP–1.28E–06	6.20E–07	–2.068608	0.0449	
R-squared	0.094506	Mean dependent var.		32.53488
Adjusted R-squared	0.072421	SD dependent var.		7.983163
SE of regression	7.688659	Akaike info criterion		6.962765
Sum squared resid.	2423.734	Schwarz criterion		7.044681
Log likelihood	–147.6994	F-statistic		4.279139
Durbin-Watson stat.	1.409365	Prob. (F-statistic)		0.044928

Dependent variable: LAG
Method: least squares
Date: 05/04/00 Time: 12:42
Sample: 1 43
Included observations: 43

Variable	Coefficient	Std error	t-statistic	Prob.
C	31.36957	2.545765	12.32226	0.0000
ROAA	1.828770	3.499566	0.522570	0.6041
R-squared	0.006616	Mean dependent var.		32.53488
Adjusted R-squared	–0.017612	SD dependent var.		7.983163
SE of regression	8.053158	Akaike info criterion		7.055401
Sum squared resid.	2658.988	Schwarz criterion		7.137317
Log likelihood	–149.6911	F-statistic		0.273080
Durbin-Watson stat.	1.292634	Prob. (F-statistic)		0.604086

Dependent variable: LAG
Method: least squares
Date: 05/04/00 Time: 12:42
Sample: 1 43
Included observations: 43

Variable	Coefficient	Std error	t-statistic	Prob.
C	33.91489	2.480352	13.67342	0.0000
ROAE	–0.162669	0.254156	–0.640036	0.5257
R-squared	0.009893	Mean dependent var.		32.53488
Adjusted R-squared	–0.014256	SD dependent var.		7.983163
SE of regression	8.039868	Akaike info criterion		7.052097
Sum squared resid.	2650.218	Schwarz criterion		7.134014
Log likelihood	–149.6201	F-statistic		0.409646
Durbin-Watson stat.	1.344905	Prob. (F-statistic)		0.525710

Dependent variable: LAG
Method: least squares
Date: 05/04/00 Time: 12:29
Sample: 1 43
Included observations: 43

Variable	Coefficient	Std error	t-statistic	Prob.
C	34.13444	1.371204	24.89378	0.0000
TOTATT	−4.49E−08	2.03E−08	−2.210516	0.0327
R-squared	0.106489	Mean dependent var.		32.53488
Adjusted R-squared	0.084696	SD dependent var.		7.983163
SE of regression	7.637615	Akaike info criterion		6.949443
Sum squared resid.	2391.660	Schwarz criterion		7.031359
Log likelihood	−147.4130	F-statistic		4.886381
Durbin-Watson stat.	1.386490	Prob. (F-statistic)		0.032707

Dependent variable: LAG
Method: least squares
Date: 05/04/00 Time: 12:42
Sample: 1 43
Included observations: 43

Variable	Coefficient	Std error	t-statistic	Prob.
C	33.16679	1.415503	23.43110	0.0000
UT	−3.06E−06	3.47E−06	−0.881711	0.3831
R-squared	0.018609	Mean dependent var.		32.53488
Adjusted R-squared	−0.005328	SD dependent var.		7.983163
SE of regression	8.004402	Akaike info criterion		7.043255
Sum squared resid.	2626.888	Schwarz criterion		7.125172
Log likelihood	−149.4300	F-statistic		0.777415
Durbin-Watson stat.	1.363767	Prob. (F-statistic)		0.383073

Dependent variable: LAG
Method: least squares
Date: 05/04/00 Time: 12:35
Sample: 1 43
Included observations: 43

Variable	Coefficient	Std error	t-statistic	Prob.
C	33.65302	1.471076	22.87647	0.0000
CAP	−4.75E−07	3.57E−07	−1.328432	0.1914
R-squared	0.041266	Mean dependent var.		32.53488
Adjusted R-squared	0.017882	SD dependent var.		7.983163
SE of regression	7.911463	Akaike info criterion		7.019898

Sum squared resid.	2566.241	Schwarz criterion	7.101814
Log likelihood	−148.9278	F-statistic	1.764733
Durbin-Watson stat.	1.346389	Prob. (F-statistic)	0.191383

Dependent variable: LAG
Method: least squares
Date: 05/04/00 Time: 12:35
Sample: 1 43
Included observations: 43

Variable	Coefficient	Std error	t-statistic	Prob.
C	27.98232	2.916331	9.595043	0.0000
CAP_TOTATT	0.566535	0.331303	1.710018	0.0948
R-squared	0.066573	Mean dependent var.		32.53488
Adjusted R-squared	0.043806	SD dependent var.		7.983163
SE of regression	7.806348	Akaike info criterion		6.993147
Sum squared resid.	2498.502	Schwarz criterion		7.075063
Log likelihood	−148.3527	F-statistic		2.924161
Durbin-Watson stat.	1.404643	Prob. (F-statistic)		0.094821

Dependent variable: LAG
Method: least squares
Date: 05/04/00 Time: 12:36
Sample: 1 43
Included observations: 43

Variable	Coefficient	Std error	t-statistic	Prob.
C	40.45204	4.553916	8.882914	0.0000
COMMATT_RISOP	−28.77543	15.98017	−1.800696	0.0791
R-squared	0.073289	Mean dependent var.		32.53488
Adjusted R-squared	0.050687	SD dependent var.		7.983163
SE of regression	7.778212	Akaike info criterion		6.985925
Sum squared resid.	2480.524	Schwarz criterion		7.067842
Log likelihood	−148.1974	F-statistic		3.242507
Durbin-Watson stat.	1.509828	Prob. (F-statistic)		0.079110

Dependent variable: LAG
Method: least squares
Date: 05/04/00 Time: 12:36
Sample: 1 43
Included observations: 43

Variable	Coefficient	Std error	t-statistic	Prob.
C	33.75473	1.386272	24.34928	0.0000
COMMATT	−2.81E–06	1.64E–06	−1.716157	0.0937
R-squared	0.067020	Mean dependent var.		32.53488
Adjusted R-squared	0.044264	SD dependent var.		7.983163
SE of regression	7.804480	Akaike info criterion		6.992668
Sum squared resid.	2497.306	Schwarz criterion		7.074584
Log likelihood	−148.3424	F-statistic		2.945195
Durbin-Watson stat.	1.429594	Prob. (F-statistic)		0.093681

Dependent variable: LAG
Method: least squares
Date: 05/04/00 Time: 12:38
Sample: 1 43
Included observations: 43

Variable	Coefficient	Std error	t-statistic	Prob.
C	31.64688	8.536833	3.707098	0.0006
COS_MARINTERM	0.013981	0.132994	0.105121	0.9168
R-squared	0.000269	Mean dependent var.		32.53488
Adjusted R-squared	−0.024114	SD dependent var.		7.983163
SE of regression	8.078844	Akaike info criterion		7.061770
Sum squared resid.	2675.976	Schwarz criterion		7.143686
Log likelihood	−149.8280	F-statistic		0.011050
Durbin-Watson stat.	1.310450	Prob. (F-statistic)		0.916792

Dependent variable: LAG
Method: least squares
Date: 05/04/00 Time: 12:35
Sample: 1 43
Included observations: 43

Variable	Coefficient	Std error	t-statistic	Prob.
C	34.69247	1.364719	25.42096	0.0000
CUST	−5.46E–05	1.94E–05	−2.810316	0.0076
R-squared	0.161518	Mean dependent var.		32.53488
Adjusted R-squared	0.141067	SD dependent var.		7.983163
SE of regression	7.398687	Akaike info criterion		6.885877
Sum squared resid.	2244.364	Schwarz criterion		6.967794
Log likelihood	−146.0464	F-statistic		7.897874
Durbin-Watson stat.	1.508643	Prob. (F-statistic)		0.007554

Dependent variable: LAG
Method: least squares
Date: 05/04/00 Time: 12:38
Sample: 1 43
Included observations: 43

Variable	Coefficient	Std error	t-statistic	Prob.
C	34.41235	1.386709	24.81584	0.0000
DEPOS	−7.90E−08	3.25E−08	−2.431765	0.0195
R-squared	0.126051	Mean dependent var.		32.53488
Adjusted R-squared	0.104735	SD dependent var.		7.983163
SE of regression	7.553545	Akaike info criterion		6.927306
Sum squared resid.	2339.298	Schwarz criterion		7.009223
Log likelihood	−146.9371	F-statistic		5.913482
Durbin-Watson stat.	1.380012	Prob. (F-statistic)		0.019481

Dependent variable: LAG
Method: least squares
Date: 05/04/00 Time: 12:31
Sample: 1 43
Included observations: 43

Variable	Coefficient	Std error	t-statistic	Prob.
C	34.47934	1.494415	23.07213	0.0000
DIPEN	−0.000452	0.000216	−2.094602	0.0424
R-squared	0.096665	Mean dependent var.		32.53488
Adjusted R-squared	0.074632	SD dependent var.		7.983163
SE of regression	7.679487	Akaike info criterion		6.960378
Sum squared resid.	2417.955	Schwarz criterion		7.042294
Log likelihood	−147.6481	F-statistic		4.387357
Durbin-Watson stat.	1.397071	Prob. (F-statistic)		0.042428

Dependent variable: LAG
Method: least squares
Date: 05/04/00 Time: 12:31
Sample: 1 43
Included observations: 43

Variable	Coefficient	Std error	t-statistic	Prob.
C	34.62267	1.612912	21.46594	0.0000
FILIA	−0.006563	0.003452	−1.900975	0.0644
R-squared	0.081000	Mean dependent var.		32.53488
Adjusted R-squared	0.058585	SD dependent var.		7.983163
SE of regression	7.745786	Akaike info criterion		6.977570

Sum squared resid.	2459.886	Schwarz criterion		7.059487
Log likelihood	−148.0178	F-statistic		3.613704
Durbin-Watson stat.	1.398001	Prob. (F-statistic)		0.064350

Dependent variable: LAG
Method: least squares
Date: 05/04/00 Time: 12:34
Sample: 1 43
Included observations: 43

Variable	Coefficient	Std error	t-statistic	Prob.
C	34.37903	1.461963	23.51566	0.0000
MARINTERE	−2.32E–06	1.10E–06	−2.105422	0.0414
R-squared	0.097568	Mean dependent var.		32.53488
Adjusted R-squared	0.075558	SD dependent var.		7.983163
SE of regression	7.675645	Akaike info criterion		6.959377
Sum squared resid.	2415.537	Schwarz criterion		7.041293
Log likelihood	−147.6266	F-statistic		4.432803
Durbin-Watson stat.	1.398926	Prob. (F-statistic)		0.041424

Dependent variable: LAG
Method: least squares
Date: 05/04/00 Time: 12:40
Sample: 1 43
Included observations: 43

Variable	Coefficient	Std error	t-statistic	Prob.
C	23.48836	4.317815	5.439871	0.0000
MARGINTERE_IMP	2.942293	1.352094	2.176101	0.0354
R-squared	0.103539	Mean dependent var.		32.53488
Adjusted R-squared	0.081674	SD dependent var.		7.983163
SE of regression	7.650210	Akaike info criterion		6.952738
Sum squared resid.	2399.554	Schwarz criterion		7.034655
Log likelihood	−147.4839	F-statistic		4.735415
Durbin-Watson stat.	1.483709	Prob. (F-statistic)		0.035364

Dependent variable: LAG
Method: least squares
Date: 05/04/00 Time: 12:32
Sample: 1 43
Included observations: 43

Variable	Coefficient	Std error	t-statistic	Prob.
C	34.17823	1.446739	23.62433	0.0000
RICSERV	−3.14E–06	1.60E–06	−1.957763	0.0571
R-squared	0.085492	Mean dependent var.		32.53488
Adjusted R-squared	0.063187	SD dependent var.		7.983163
SE of regression	7.726834	Akaike info criterion		6.972671
Sum squared resid.	2447.862	Schwarz criterion		7.054587
Log likelihood	−147.9124	F-statistic		3.832835
Durbin-Watson stat.	1.420549	Prob. (F-statistic)		0.057087

Dependent variable: LAG
Method: least squares
Date: 05/04/00 Time: 12:33
Sample: 1 43
Included observations: 43

Variable	Coefficient	Std error	t-statistic	Prob.
C	32.39489	3.774340	8.582931	0.0000
RICSERV_TOTATT	0.079719	2.031582	0.039240	0.9689
R-squared	0.000038	Mean dependent var.		32.53488
Adjusted R-squared	−0.024352	SD dependent var.		7.983163
SE of regression	8.079781	Akaike info criterion		7.062002
Sum squared resid.	2676.597	Schwarz criterion		7.143918
Log likelihood	−149.8330	F-statistic		0.001540
Durbin-Watson stat.	1.307511	Prob. (F-statistic)		0.968890

Dependent variable: LAG
Method: least squares
Date: 05/04/00 Time: 12:41
Sample: 1 43
Included observations: 43

Variable	Coefficient	Std error	t-statistic	Prob.
C	34.32339	1.456811	23.56063	0.0000
RISOP	−1.28E–06	6.20E–07	−2.068608	0.0449
R-squared	0.094506	Mean dependent var.		32.53488
Adjusted R-squared	0.072421	SD dependent var.		7.983163
SE of regression	7.688659	Akaike info criterion		6.962765
Sum squared resid.	2423.734	Schwarz criterion		7.044681
Log likelihood	−147.6994	F-statistic		4.279139
Durbin-Watson stat.	1.409365	Prob. (F-statistic)		0.044928

Dependent variable: LAG
Method: least squares
Date: 05/04/00 Time: 12:42
Sample: 1 43
Included observations: 43

Variable	Coefficient	Std error	t-statistic	Prob.
C	31.36957	2.545765	12.32226	0.0000
ROAA	1.828770	3.499566	0.522570	0.6041
R-squared	0.006616	Mean dependent var.		32.53488
Adjusted R-squared	−0.017612	SD dependent var.		7.983163
SE of regression	8.053158	Akaike info criterion		7.055401
Sum squared resid.	2658.988	Schwarz criterion		7.137317
Log likelihood	−149.6911	F-statistic		0.273080
Durbin-Watson stat.	1.292634	Prob. (F-statistic)		0.604086

Dependent variable: LAG
Method: least squares
Date: 05/04/00 Time: 12:42
Sample: 1 43
Included observations: 43

Variable	Coefficient	Std error	t-statistic	Prob.
C	33.91489	2.480352	13.67342	0.0000
ROAE	−0.162669	0.254156	−0.640036	0.5257
R-squared	0.009893	Mean dependent var.		32.53488
Adjusted R-squared	−0.014256	SD dependent var.		7.983163
SE of regression	8.039868	Akaike info criterion		7.052097
Sum squared resid.	2650.218	Schwarz criterion		7.134014
Log likelihood	−149.6201	F-statistic		0.409646
Durbin-Watson stat.	1.344905	Prob. (F-statistic)		0.525710

Dependent variable: LAG
Method: least squares
Date: 05/04/00 Time: 12:29
Sample: 1 43
Included observations: 43

Variable	Coefficient	Std error	t-statistic	Prob.
C	34.13444	1.371204	24.89378	0.0000
TOTATT	−4.49E−08	2.03E−08	−2.210516	0.0327
R-squared	0.106489	Mean dependent var.		32.53488
Adjusted R-squared	0.084696	SD dependent var.		7.983163
SE of regression	7.637615	Akaike info criterion		6.949443

Sum squared resid.	2391.660	Schwarz criterion	7.031359
Log likelihood	−147.4130	F-statistic	4.886381
Durbin-Watson stat.	1.386490	Prob. (F-statistic)	0.032707

Dependent variable: LAG
Method: least squares
Date: 05/04/00 Time: 12:42
Sample: 1 43
Included observations: 43

Variable	Coefficient	Std error	t-statistic	Prob.
C	33.16679	1.415503	23.43110	0.0000
UT	−3.06E−06	3.47E−06	−0.881711	0.3831
R-squared	0.018609	Mean dependent var.		32.53488
Adjusted R-squared	−0.005328	SD dependent var.		7.983163
SE of regression	8.004402	Akaike info criterion		7.043255
Sum squared resid.	2626.888	Schwarz criterion		7.125172
Log likelihood	−149.4300	F-statistic		0.777415
Durbin-Watson stat.	1.363767	Prob. (F-statistic)		0.383073

Chapter 4

Producer Services, Innovation and Outsourcing in the New Economy

Martin Zagler

The aim of this chapter is to explain several distinguished stylized facts of the new economy, the intrinsic inertia of the inflation rate, the low rates of productivity increase, the high rates of economic growth, the cyclical adjustment of growth rates during the emergence of the new economy, the international differences in the development of the new economy, the blurring boundaries of the firm, both in terms of outsourcing on the sales front and in the creation of innovation networks, and the increasing service component of consumer products. This chapter argues that a sound theoretical foundation of the new producer services can explain the above described empirical regularities of the new economy. The characteristic features of producer services are their complementarity to other factors of production, low rates of productivity growth, and a high degree of heterogeneity, which allows rents and fosters entry of innovative market entrants. Both because of heterogeneity and the necessity of joint production with the client, producer services are not storable, which leads to search frictions on the service market, which induces a principal-agent problem that is solved by outsourcing.

1   Introduction

Several distinguished stylized facts form the new economy. The most outstanding empirical regularity associated with the new economy is certainly its low rates of inflation, or the inertia of the inflation rate (Greenspan, 1998). The surprising element is the fact that inflation rates are low despite high aggregate demand and low rates of productivity. Indeed, in a recent article, Gordon (1999) shows that some 99 per cent of the recent productivity gain have been realized in the manufacturing of computers, but not in sectors applying computers, hence in the larger parts of the economy, a phenomenon known as the Solow paradox. In a seminal article, David (1990) gave the first explanation. He suggests that the implementation of information technology, which is a special case of a general purpose technology (Bresnahan and Trajtenberg, 1995), exhibits long lags, that may last decades, before they show up in productivity statistics. The reason is that general purpose technologies render parts of the existing capital, which will continue to remain in the data, obsolete.

What comes even more as a surprise is the fact the American economy has grown at amazing annual 4,8 per cent over the second half of the 1990s, despite low rates of measured total factor productivity growth. Griliches (1994) attributes this to the fact that the driving force behind the growth process are sectors where performance, and therefore productivity, is hard to measure, notably mining, transportation, utilities, construction and most of the services.

When looking in more detail into the growth process of the new economy, we find two further interesting stylized facts. First, we find that economic growth rates seem to decline initially but gain momentum as time evolves, and surpasses the initial rate of economic growth. More precisely, Bassanini, Scarpetta, and Visco (2000) find that this growth cycle is driven by the increase in the share of new technology products in the economy. Second, we observe stark national differences in growth rates in association with the emergence of a new economy. Whereas the new economy, as described by the stylized facts in this introduction, has clearly emerged in the United States, and to some extent in the Netherlands and the United Kingdom, large parts of continental Europe seems to lag behind. Indeed, Euroland is still awaiting the beginning of an economic growth phase at the long end of a business drought.

Another observation in the recent past is the fact that the boundaries of the firm seem to blur. On the one hand, we find that firms pay closer attention as to whether to perform a certain task within or outside the firm, and frequently offer relational contracts which cannot be clearly attributed to either side (Gibbons, 2000). Second, firms have begun to engage in partnerships amongst each other, and form networks which cannot either be attributed to either market relation or hierarchical relation (Powell, 1990).

Last, the new economy comprises new products. These new products are frequently described as weightless goods (Quah, 1997), or products where the manufacturing component is of less and less of importance compared to the service component. In that respect, we do observe a structural shift in the economy from manufacturing goods to service products, as already noted by Clark (1957), Kuznets (1957), and Chenery (1960), and recently confirmed by Echevarria (1997) and Kongsamut, Rebelo and Xie (1997). However, this shift is not so much induced by a shift towards consumption services than by a shift towards producer services, which enter the production process as intermediate products, complementary to other factors of production.

Products of the weightless economy, and in particular their service input factors, are distinct from the conventional manufacturing products of the new economy. This chapter argues that a sound theoretical foundation of the new producer services can explain the above described empirical regularities of the new economy.

Apart from their complementary in production, these new services are very heterogeneous. Whilst manufacturing goods are typically procured by a Fordist production scheme, services are provided individually at the point of sale (Hage, 1998). On the one hand, the service sector exhibits lower rates of productivity gains, in part because permanently novel tasks allow for little learning by doing. On the other hand, the high degree of heterogeneity gives service providers some degree of market power to set prices above marginal costs, and hence to lucrate monopoly rents.

This rents stimulate market entry of new and innovative producer service firms, and it is through this channel, as will be demonstrated below, that the service sector can make up for low productivity growth and still induce high rates of growth. Innovation does not occur in isolation, but requires the formation of an innovation network to gain information. This implies that networks are first and foremost formed for innovative purposes, which is consistent with empirical evidence (Powell, 1990).

Services are much less storable. This is due to the fact that the high degree of heterogeneity would require extremely high storage costs, and hence most services are produced on demand. However, for some services it is even the case that they are produced jointly with the client, which in our case of producer services would be a final product assembly firm. This fact implies that service providers, just like final product assemblers, have to constantly engage in search activities to acquire service factor inputs. Given the large number of available heterogeneous service products, this without doubt leads to a search market friction, as described in some detail in Diamond (1982). These search frictions introduce a principal agent problem. Given that no service innovator can cover the entire market, she will have to hire agents. As there is no possibility to discriminate between unsuccessful searching and shirking agents, she will have to induce effort by delegating all economic incentives to the agent. She will still be able to skim of all the monopoly rents by setting a fixed licensing fee, which corresponds to partnership stakes in American law or consulting firms. Hence, outsourcing and an increasing contractual flexibility of work (Mühlberger, 2000) is an intrinsic feature of the new economy. We shall argue that a correct specification of all of these features of the service economy can account for all the empirical regularities of the new economy.

2   The Model

We shall specify a simple general equilibrium model which takes care in including all the previously mentioned characteristics of producer services, in order to demonstrate that the model can indeed account for the stylized facts of the new economy. This following chapter discusses the supply of final products and the demand for producer service intermediate products. We shall defer the supply of producer services to section 2.1, we discuss the creation of new services in section 2.3, and summarize the equilibrium of the model economy in section 2.4.

Manufacturing

Manufacturers combine labour, capital,[1] and intermediate producer services to assemble final consumer products, according to the following constant returns to scale Cobb-Douglas production function,

$$y_t = (A_t l_t)^\sigma x_t^{1-\sigma}, \tag{1}$$

where y_t is the final product output, A_t is labour augmenting technological progress, potentially accounting for capital inputs, l_t is employment in manufacturing, x_t are producer services entering as an input into the production process, and σ is the output elasticity of labour inputs. It is assumed that labour augmenting technological progress grows continuously by a factor a. We can assure that services and manufacturing labour are indeed complements in production by checking whether an increase in manufacturing labour indeed leads to an increase in the marginal product of services. Making use of manufacturing technology (1), the cross derivative of final product technology equals,

$$\frac{\partial^2 y_t}{\partial x_t \partial e_t} = \sigma(1 - \sigma)\frac{y_t}{x_t l_t} > 0, \tag{2}$$

which proves that the two production factors are complements. Final product suppliers minimize costs, which consist of spending on manufacturing goods and spending on service products,

$$c_t = w_t l_t + q_t x_t,$$ (3)

where w_t is the wage rate, and q_t is the price index for services, to be defined below. Minimising costs subject to technology (1) implies that the relative spending share on the two input factors is equal to $(1 - \sigma)/\sigma$,

$$\frac{q_t x_t}{w_t l_t} = \frac{1 - \sigma}{\sigma}.$$ (4)

Heterogeneity of services is equivalent to stating that two different services are no perfect substitutes. We shall assume that there are n_t differentiated producer services available for manufacturers, a number which may potentially over time. Evidently if producer services gain importance in the production process over time, the reason must lie in there more specific and differentiated availability. Therefore we shall assume that the expenditure share on producer services grows exponentially with the number of differentiated service products,

$$\sigma \equiv \frac{1}{1 + n_t},$$ (5)

an assumption which is consistent with the facts. Heterogeneity of services implies that the elasticity of substitution must lie between unity and infinity, and adopting a constant elasticity specification, the service bundle which enters manufacturing production (1) equals,

$$x_t = [\int_0^{n_t} x_{i,t}^{\frac{\varepsilon-1}{\varepsilon}} di]^{\frac{\varepsilon}{\varepsilon-1}},$$ (6)

where $x_{i,t}$ is a specific service variety. Given homotheticity of technology (1), we can separate the cost minimization problem of manufacturing firms. In addition to minimising total cost of production (3), they will also minimize the cost of their service inputs, defined as

$$q_t x_t = \int_0^{n_t} q_{i,t} x_{i,t} di,$$ (7)

where $q_{i,t}$ is the price of a specific service i. The second stage in the manufacturing problem yields after optimization a demand function for a specific producer service,

$$x_{i,t} = \left(\frac{q_{i,t}}{q_t}\right)^{-\varepsilon} x_t, \tag{8}$$

and we find that ε is the demand elasticity for any particular service. Moreover, we obtain a definition for the price index of services,

$$q_t = [\int_0^{n_t} q_{i,t}^{1-\varepsilon} di]^{\frac{1}{1-\varepsilon}}, \tag{9}$$

Producer Services

The previous chapter has already established the heterogeneous nature of producer services and the complementary character as a production input. We can account for the fact that services experience lower rates of productivity gains by positing that one unit of service work $e_{i,t}$ will produce one unit of service output $x_{i,t}$, implying that service productivity growth equals zero. Then we have argued in the introduction that the heterogeneity of producer services implies that service providers and clients engage in search activities to purchase or sell a particular service. We suppose that a searching service worker will find a client with probability p, whereas a shirking service worker will not find a client for sure. The fact that a service provider cannot observe whether a service worker is unsuccessfully searching or shirking constitutes a principal-agent problem.[2] The principal can solve the principal-agent problem by delegating all economic incentives to the agent,[3] or by outsourcing her sales organization to the agent, for a fixed fee, which corresponds for example to partner stakes common in many producer service firms. An outsourced service worker, or dependent self-employed, will maximize his income relative to the opportunity cost of working in the services, which, ignoring nonpecuniary returns, is equal to the manufacturing wage. Maximising

$$m_t = E_t q_{i,t} x_{i,t} - f_{i,t} - w_t e_{i,t}, \tag{11}$$

where $m_{i,t}$ is relative income, $E_t q_{i,t} x_{i,t}$ is the expected earnings from not shirking if he charges a price $q_{i,t}, f_{i,t}$ is the fee paid to the principal, and $w_t x_{i,t}$

is the opportunity cost. Optimization yields a corner solution with respect to labour supply, and assuming that he can at most supply one unit of labour, we have $e_{i,t} = 1$, as long as

$$pq_{i,t} \geq (f_{i,t} + w_t), \tag{12}$$

that is, as long as expected earnings exceed actual and opportunity costs.

As argued, service are provided in heterogeneous varieties. This implies that the provision of services earns economic rents, as the market setting is monopolistically competitive. Whilst the agent is one of many and operates on a flat demand curve for his particular services variety (12), a provider or principal in the service sector operates along the declining demand function (8) introduced above, and sets the fee charged to the agents in order to maximize profits. However, service suppliers consider their individual influence on aggregate variables, such as the total amount of services x_t and the price index q_t thereof, as negligible. Maximizing the fee $f_{i,t}$ subject to demand (8) and the exit condition for agents in the service sector (12), yields the mark-up of prices over the agents opportunity costs,

$$q_{i,t} = \frac{1}{p} \frac{\varepsilon}{\varepsilon - 1} w_t. \tag{13}$$

Producer service sector firms therefore lucrate rents equal to,

$$f_{i,t} e_{i,t} = \frac{1}{\varepsilon - 1} w_t e_{i,t}. \tag{14}$$

where $e_{i,t}$ now is total outsourced self-employment of a particular service variety i. The mark-up equation (13) is identical to the price setting rule of a monopoly provider of a particular service i who would hire labour at the wage rate w_t, provided that she can ensure without cost that her workers would not shirk. Moreover, the fee which she charges (14) is exactly identical to monopoly profits in the absence of the principal-agent problem, hence she has indeed been able to solve the principal-agent problem, and skim off all economic rents from her agents. This implies that the outsourced self-employed does not participate in sharing the rents. Indeed, there is only one possible price and a corresponding quantity at which he can offer his services without being worse off than in a manufacturing job. Hence, given the fact that the principal implicitly sets prices and quantities through the licensing fee, and therefore takes away from her agents all the economic choices a regular self-employed would have, we may refer to him as dependent self-employed.

Innovation and Entry in the Producer Service Sector

Innovative entrepreneurs should be attracted by the producer service market, given the fact that they can skim off rents from dependent self-employed in this sector. For this purpose, they will engage in costly innovative projects to develop a new producer service. However, innovation does not happen in isolation. Given the fact that much information[4] in this market is private and held by incumbents, innovators have to engage in time-consuming activities to acquire knowledge, by forming internal or external networks. We hence assume that new varieties are created according to,

$$\dot{n}_t = \varphi s_{n,t}^{\beta} \eta_t. \tag{15}$$

Given that it is uncertain whether a single innovation will be successful, φ measures the probability of success in innovation, when the number of attempts to innovate is large, or productivity in innovation. η_t represents the value of the network in the innovation process, $s_{n,t}$ is either the amount of time a particular researcher devotes to the innovation of new products, or the number of scientists engaged in innovative activities, with diminishing marginal product of innovative activities.

There is vast evidence that the size of the network is beneficial for the productivity, and hence the value of the network (e.g. Koput and Powell, 2000). We can in general measure the size of a network in different ways. First, we can measure the nods of a network, or the number of participants. If there are n_t incumbent service firms, the potential number of nods in an innovation network equals n_t. With n_t nods, the number of potential ties within the network would equal $n_t!$, and if we use potential ties as a measure for the size of the network, we would have $\eta_t = \eta(n_t!)$. However, there is a natural frontier to the actual number of network ties in which an innovator can engage, namely when the return in terms of information access of an additional tie just offset the costs in terms of time denoted to networking. There is, however, no natural upper limit to the number of nods in a network, and we shall therefore adopt $\eta_t = \eta(n_t)$, and assume that it is linear in n_t for convenience. Networking capital is therefore acquired according to the following process,

$$\eta_t = \psi n_t s_{\eta,t}^{1-\beta} \tag{16}$$

Productivity in networking is assumed to equal ψ. The time spent in networking activities, $s_{\eta,t} = s_t - s_{n,t}$, exhibits a diminishing marginal product as well. Whilst we may refer to equation (14) as the innovation technology, we may label equation (15) the information technology, as it specifies the process under which innovators acquire information. Note that innovation firms will maximize output by setting $s_{\eta,t} = (1 - \beta)s_t$.

Whilst the positive correlation between the number of innovations and the arrival rate of new innovations is rather arbitrary in conventional growth models (e.g. Romer, 1990), here it represents a true networking externality which is bound to have a positive impact. The growth rate of new innovations in optimum can be derived from the arrival rate of innovations (15) and the information technology (16) to equal,

$$\hat{n}_t = \phi s_t, \tag{17}$$

where $\phi = \varphi\psi\beta^\beta = (1 - \beta)^{1-\beta}$ is a measure of productivity in the innovation sector. Given that it is uncertain whether a single innovation will be successful, ϕ measures the probability of success in innovation, when the number of attempts to innovate is large.

Equilibrium

Innovation requires costs, and in order to simplify matters, we shall assume that firms reinvest all profits into new innovations, whereas consumers do not engage in savings.[5] Then, all fees levied will be redistributed to finance research workers in innovative activities, implying

$$\int_0^{n_t} f_{i,t} e_{i,t} di = w_t s_t. \tag{18}$$

The producer service sector is completely symmetric, which facilitates the description of the equilibrium of the economy. The mark-up equation (13) implies that prices are independent of the specific variety. Quantities are identical due to the demand function (8), which implies that the fee charged in the producer service sector is independent of the specific variety as well. We may therefore set $e_{i,t} = e_t$ for all i without loss of generality, and define total dependent self-employment in the producer service sector by $d_t = n_t e_t$. Then, equation (18) reduces to

$$d_t = (\varepsilon - 1)s_t, \tag{19}$$

implying that research for new services will be proportional to the number of dependent self-employed in incumbent producer service firms. Symmetry also implies that the price index (9) reduces to,

$$q_{i,t} = \frac{1}{p} \frac{\varepsilon}{\varepsilon - 1} n_t^{\frac{1}{1-\varepsilon}}. \tag{20}$$

Ceteris paribus, as the number of varieties increases, the price index declines, implying that even for a given nominal spending share on services (4), they may increase in quantity. Indeed, aggregate producer service supply (6) reduces to,

$$x_t = n_t^{\frac{1}{1-\varepsilon}} d_i, \tag{21}$$

which is increasing for a given number of aggregate sector employment. Substitution of service sector quantities (21) and aggregate service sector prices (20) into the optimality condition (4) yields,

$$d_t = n_t^{\frac{\varepsilon - 1}{\varepsilon}} pn_t l_t, \tag{22}$$

Aggregate service sector employment is proportional to manufacturing employment for a given number of varieties, but increases relatively, as variety increases. The model is closed with a condition for labour market clearing. A fully flexible wage and perfect sectoral mobility ensures that the entire labour force is employed, and we normalize the total labour force to unity for convenience. The labour market clearing condition reads,

$$l_t + d_t + s_t = 1. \tag{23}$$

The labour force is employed either in manufacturing, s_t, dependent self-employed in the producer service sector d_t, or in innovative research activities, s_t. The innovation rate (17), The innovation financing constraint (19), the service to manufacturing employment share (22) and the labour market clearing condition (23) completely summarize the evolution of the economy.

3　The New Economy

This section is devoted at demonstrating that the model economy presented above is indeed capable in explaining the stylized facts of the new economy. The following section presents an easy solution to the productivity puzzle, whereas section 3.2 discusses the reason for the expansion of the producer service sector, the high rates of economic growth, international differences in the emergence of the new economy, and the existence of a growth cycle in association with the evolution of the new economy. The last chapter will discuss the reason for inflation inertia in the new economy.

The Productivity Puzzle

The economy comprises essentially three sectors, and by discussing total factor productivity in each, we may shed some light on this puzzle. First, total factor productivity growth in manufacturing equals output growth per factor inputs,

$$\hat{y}_t - \sigma\hat{l}_t - (1 - \sigma)\hat{x}_t = \sigma\hat{A}_t = \sigma a. \tag{24}$$

Note that manufacturing productivity increases continuously by σa. Given that the share of manufacturing labour in total output, σ, declines continuously as the number of differentiated producer services increases (5), we should observe declining rates of productivity growth in manufacturing as the new economy emerges. Second, productivity both for a particular dependent self-employed in services and even for an entire particular service i equals $x_{i,t}/d_{i,t} = 1$. This is due to our normalization, but accounts for the fact that services are known to have lower rates of productivity growth than other sectors of the economy (Baumol, 1967). Given that service provision may realize some productivity gains, a should be considered as relative productivity changes in manufacturing. However, the service sector as a whole does exhibit productivity gains due to increases in variety. Differentiating equation (21) and rearranging terms, we find that productivity in the producer service sector equals

$$\hat{x}_t - \hat{d}_t = \frac{1}{\varepsilon - 1}\hat{n}_t, \tag{25}$$

which is positive for an increasing number of differentiated producer services. Depending on the parameter values, this may well exceed the rate of manufacturing growth. However, as productivity remains to be measured at the plant level, these sectoral productivity gains will hardly find their way into the total factor productivity statistics, which is an explanation for the productivity puzzle. Finally, note that productivity in the innovation sector, which should cover such narrow sectors as the information technology sector singled out by Gordon (1999), is growing at fast pace. Rearranging innovation technology (31), we find that productivity in this sector equals,

$$\dot{n}_t / s_t = \sigma n_t, \tag{26}$$

which grows at the innovation rate, and hence faster than the aggregate service sector productivity (25), given $\varepsilon > 2$. Hence the fact that productivity rates are declining throughout the economy with the exception of a tiny segment of highly innovative sectors should no longer surprise.

An Expansion of the Service Sector and International Differences in the Emergence of the New Economy

The changing perspective on productivity as discussed in the previous section allows us to endogenously explain the shift in the sectoral composition without relying on non-homothetic preferences or technology (Echevarria, 1997;Kongsamut, Rebelo, and Xie, 1997). First, we have already demonstrated that dependent self-employment in the producer service sector will increase relative to manufacturing labour as the number of producer service varieties increases. Second, profit maximizing final product firms in manufacturing will set wages equal to marginal costs, we can eliminate the wage sum in equation (4) to obtain the nominal service share in total output as increasing function of the diversity in producer services,

$$\frac{q_t x_t}{y_t} = \frac{n_t}{1 + n_t} . \tag{27}$$

Finally, by substituting the price index for producer services, we may even obtain an expression of the real relative share of producer services in total output, which equals,

$$\frac{x_t}{y_t} = A_t^{-\sigma} (\frac{\varepsilon - 1}{\varepsilon} p n_t)^{\sigma} n_t^{\frac{\sigma}{\varepsilon - 1}}, \tag{28}$$

and is increasing in the number of producer service varieties as well, thus completely summarizing the stylized facts on the shift of nominal and real output shares as well as employment shares as described in Echevarria (1997). Whilst an increase in manufacturing productivity unambiguously lowers the ratio of service to manufacturing products, the effect of an increase in service varieties raises the ratio for three reasons. First, there is the direct substitution effect. As manufacturing firms shift their factor demand towards producer services, the share of services in total output evidently increases. This is reflected by the first n_t in expression (28). Second, an increase in varieties reduces the price, enabling a larger quantity of services for a given share of spending, which corresponds to the second n_t in expression (28), Note that the exponent $1/(\varepsilon - 1)$ corresponds exactly to the decline in aggregate service prices due to an increase in producer service varieties (20). Third, as the producer service sector starts to dominate the economy, the share of producer services in aggregate output converges exponentially unity, reflected by the fact that the share of labour in total output, σ, approaches zero as the number of producer services goes to infinity. The ratio of producer services to total output therefore approaches, but never actually reaches, unity. Taking time derivatives, we can identify a development threshold, as we find that the service sector grows relative to manufacturing if and only if

$$a < \frac{\varepsilon}{\varepsilon - 1} \hat{n}_t. \tag{29}$$

The right hand side represents exogenous labour augmenting technical progress in manufacturing, whilst the left hand side of the new economy condition (27) represent productivity in the producer service sector, multiplied with the elasticity of substitution between two differentiated producer services, ε.

The new economy threshold (29) can explain why some economies have not yet been able to develop a new economy, as it implies that not only hard technology, represented by the manufacturing productivity growth rate a and the elasticity of substitution ε, which should both be easily transferable across nations, but as well by the potential of firms to set prices well above marginal costs, as the new economy threshold becomes less binding with the size of the mark-up, $\varepsilon/(\varepsilon - 1)$.

High Rates of Economic Growth and Growth Cycles during the Evolution of the New Economy

The new economy threshold (29) is closely related to the growth rates of a pure manufacturing and a pure service economy. Whilst a pure manufacturing, or old economy, would grow at rate a, a pure service or new economy will grow at the rate $/(\varepsilon - 1)$. With an elasticity of substitution close to unity, the new economy threshold (29) gets identical to a growth accelerating condition, $/(\varepsilon - 1) > a$. The development of a new economy is therefore a precondition for high economic growth. Given that ε is bound to be above unity, we find that the growth condition is more stringent than the new economy threshold, and we have to ask whether the new economy will indeed achieve higher rates of economic growth. We therefore proceed by deriving sectoral and aggregate growth rates of the economy. First, note that diversity of producer services hinges on employment in the innovative activities, s_t, only. We solve for the number of service innovators by substituting the employment sector share (22) and the service innovation employment condition (19) into the labour market clearing condition, to derive an innovation rate equal to,

$$\hat{n}_t = \frac{\phi}{\varepsilon} \frac{n_t}{n_t + p} . \tag{30}$$

The growth rate of innovation converges to ϕ/ε from below as the number of differentiated producer services goes to infinity. Note that the share of innovation workers in total employment converges to the number of innovative service workers relative to employment and self-employment in the services, $s_t/(d_t + s_t) = 1/\varepsilon$, which also determines dependent self-employment relative to innovative service employment, allowing us to solve for producer service sector output via equation (6). Instead, we simply substitute equation (21) into aggregate producer service output (21), to obtain,

$$x_t = \frac{\varepsilon - 1}{\varepsilon} \frac{n_t}{n_t + p} n_t^{\frac{1}{\varepsilon - 1}}. \tag{31}$$

The growth rate of producer services therefore equals,

$$\hat{x}_t = (\frac{1}{\varepsilon - 1} + \frac{p}{n_t + p} = \frac{\phi n_t}{\phi \varepsilon (\varepsilon - 1)(n_t + p)} + \frac{p n_t}{(n_t + p)}, \tag{32}$$

where the parenthesis converges to $1/(\varepsilon - 1)$ as n_t goes to infinity, and hence equals productivity (25) in the limit. Finally, we have to solve for manufacturing employment, which equals

$$l_t = \frac{p}{n_t + p} , \tag{33}$$

which converges to zero as n_t goes to infinity, before solving for the growth rate of aggregate output. Substituting manufacturing employment (32), and producer service intermediate products (31) into manufacturing technology (1) and taking logs and derivatives, we find that the economic growth rate equals,

$$\hat{y}_t = \frac{a}{n_t+1} + \frac{n_t}{n_t+1}\frac{1}{\varepsilon-1}\hat{n}_t + \frac{1}{n_t+1}\frac{p-n_t}{n_t+p}\hat{n}_t \;, \tag{33}$$

where the growth rate of variety is described by equation (30). Manufacturing growth will loose pace as innovation in the service sector draws ever more personnel from manufacturing, which corresponds to the first term in the above expression. The second term then describes the increase of economic growth due to the expansion of the service sector, and it is equal to the service sector share times the aggregate sectoral productivity (25). The third term, then, is due to the fact that the service sector can grow the faster the larger its share in total output, or the more workers it can attract away from manufacturing. As the number of new differentiated producer services increases, both the first and the last term in equation (33) converge to zero, hence economic growth in the new economy will equal $\phi/[\varepsilon(\varepsilon-1)]$.

Whilst the first and second term in the above expression are positive for all possible parameter values, the third term is negative apart from very low levels of diversity, $n_t < p$, but converges to zero as the number of varieties goes to infinity, hence becomes less and less important. Over time, the first and the last term become less and less important, whereas the second term gains weight. We should therefore initially observe declining rates of economic growth as the new economy emerges, but as time evolves and the second term becomes more and more important, economic growth should accelerate and surpass the initial levels of economic growth, which were mainly driven by exogenous labour augmenting technical progress, as indicated for reasonable parameter values in Figure 4.1.

The intuition for the growth cycle described in graph 1 is the following. Initially, a very small producer service sector engages in limited innovative activities, as rents from service provision, and hence investment into new producer services, are low. Therefore, a slow growing service sector draws away employment from a fast growing manufacturing sector, lowering economic growth rates. As the producer service sector gains in size, the funds devoted to innovation increase, fostering the growth in productivity of the aggregate producer service sector. If the growth accelerating holds, $/(\varepsilon-1) > a$, economic growth in the new economy will even surpass economic growth of the old economy after some period of time, and reach a new equilibrium level as time goes to infinity.

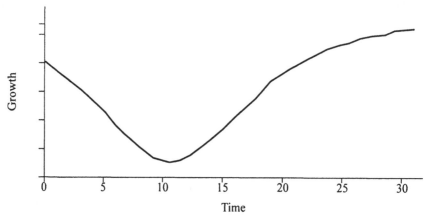

Figure 4.1   A typical growth cycle

Note: Parameter values: relative manufacturing productivity $a = 0.02$, instantaneous probability to find a matching client in producer services $p = 0.1$, elasticity of substitution in producer services $\varepsilon = 5$, relative productivity in innovation $\phi = 1$, n_0 satisfies condition (29).

The driving element of the cyclical behaviour of the growth rate is the number of differentiated service products, n_t. If we interpret the share of producer services relative to manufacturing labour as the share of new technology, the model presented here is consistent with the evidence collected both by David (1990) and Bassanini, Scarpetta, and Visco (2000). The prior has argued that new technologies will not appear in productivity statistics for a long time, and we can attribute the long lag to the transition from an existing widely used technology to a novel technology that requires customary use before developing its productivity potential. The later argue that the introduction of new technologies produces a growth cycle, where output growth declines initially and then surpasses its initial level. Given that the dynamics of the growth cycle described in Figure 4.1 depend crucially on the size of the producer service sector, which corresponds to the new technology, our model can give an endogenous interpretation of this stylized fact.

Inflation Inertia in the New Economy

The most prominent feature of the new economy is certainly the fact prices have not reacted sufficiently to changes in output, or that there is inertia in the inflation rate. The inflation rate of an economy is conventionally measured as the weighted sum of product price changes, which in our case should reflect input price changes of labour in efficiency units and producer service inputs,

$$\pi_t = \sigma(\hat{w}_t - a) + (1 - \sigma)\hat{q}_t. \tag{34}$$

Note that by definition, the inflation rate in the model is zero, hence (34) presents the difference between measured inflation and the fundamental inflation rate, or the bias in the inflation rate. Applying the definition of the price index for producer services (20) and the sector shares (5), we obtain after some rearrangement,

$$\pi_t = \hat{w}_t - \frac{a}{1 + n_t} - \frac{1}{(\varepsilon - 1)(n_t + 1)}\hat{n}_t. \tag{29}$$

The first term on the right hand side is the conventional cost-push element in inflation. If wages rise, inflation will pick up as well. The second part of course corrects for productivity gains. Note however that it depends inversely on the number of varieties in services. If the service sector expands, this element is less and less of importance, which may be the reason why inflation has not increased despite low rates of productivity growth in the recent past. The third term now is the reason for the intrinsic inertia in the new economy. It states that inflationary pressure declines if productivity in the innovative sector increases. Hence productivity gains in small innovative sectors, like the computer service industry, are sufficient to keep inflation low.

4 Conclusions

This chapter has argued that a sound theoretical foundation of the new producer services can explain the empirical regularities of the new economy. In that respect, the fundamental change away from the old economy towards the new economy is the shift away from a simple labour intensive manufacturing economy, where growth is driven by exogenous labour augmenting technical progress, towards an economy where the service component contained in final products gains increasingly in importance. Producer services are different input factors than capital or labour. First, they are distinguished by a high degree of heterogeneity as compared to other factors of production, with a set of consequences. First, as learning by doing is less exploitable, productivity in producer services will lead to low rates of productivity growth, alongside with a general tendency for service products to exhibit low rates of productivity growth (Baumol, 1967).

Secondly, the high degree of heterogeneity gives service providers the potential to set prices and lucrate economic rents. These rents encourage entry of new and innovative producer service providers to the service market. As the service sector as a whole will produce an ever-increasing value added per employee due to the fact that diversity fosters sectoral productivity, service innovators form the essence for the growth of the service sector, and are the key element which fosters the emergence of a new economy. Indeed economic progress is not so much driven by a large service sector, but by a tiny group of highly innovative entrepreneurs, who launch new business concepts in the service sector. It is this group of innovative firms, who operate through the large and growing service sector, which determine the evolution of the economy.

Finally, services heavily alter the production process. Whilst manufacturers could easily disconnect production from purchase, it is in the nature of the service sectors to produce at the point of sale. This of course has strong implications for the stability of the service production function. Efficiency of service provision will depend upon the potential of service providers to transfer the risk of low turnover to the discretion of its employees, which forms the basis for the emergence of dependent self-employment relations in the service sector (Mühlberger, 1999). Whilst service providers can transfer all risk, they can still use their market power to skim of all rents from their workforce, thus making them dependent self-employed. Given the social and institutional consequences of these new forms of work contracts, further inquiries into the causes and nature of dependent self-employment should be the focus of future research.

Whilst the dependent self-employed constitute one important group who blur the boundaries of the firm, the innovative entrepreneurs mentioned above are the other group. Indeed we have shown that innovation cannot occur in isolation, and requires contacts and networks with other firms operating in this market, otherwise innovation would cease and the new economy would never emerge.

Summarizing, we have found that the empirical phenomena associated with the new economy, the structural change, the high rates of economic growth, the low rates of productivity except for a small high technology sector, the low rates of inflation, the stock market boom, and the international differences in the transition to this new economy, the intrinsic inertia of the inflation rate, the low rates of productivity increase, the high rates of economic growth, the cyclical adjustment of growth rates during the emergence of the new economy, the international differences in the development of the new economy, the blurring boundaries of the firm, both in terms of outsourcing on the sales front and in the creation of innovation networks, and the increasing service component of consumer products can be theoretically explained by an endogenous shift from a pure manufacturing economy to an innovative producer service economy, where the shift is endogenously driven by changes in relative prices.

Notes

1   We shall abstract from capital for simplicity. Note however that capital as implicitly included in At. Specifying a general Cobb-Douglas production function, $yt = Btkt\beta$ $lt\gamma$ $xt1 - \beta - \gamma$, and assuming that the capital stock is in optimum, $kt^* = \kappa Btlt$, where κ is the constant capital stock in efficiency units (Solow, 1956), it reduces to $yt = (Atlt)\sigma xt1 - \sigma$, where $At = \kappa\gamma/\sigma Bt(1 + \gamma)/\sigma$, and $\sigma = \beta + \gamma$, as specified in equation (1).
2   We shall assume that the principal is female whereas the agent is male, inverting the empirically more frequent relation, In order to foster our awareness of the problem.
3   We defer the prove that this indeed solves the principal-agent problem below.
4   For instance, which services are demanded and who is demanding these services.
5   This is consistent with a model of capitalists and workers (Kalecki, 1971), and an optimal savings model where some households start out with zero initial wealth (Bertola, 1993). A model where innovators behave optimally by maximizing profits and have full access to capital markets is presented in Zagler (2000b).

References

Bassanini, A., Scarpetta, S. and Visco, I. (2000), 'Knowledge, Technology, and Economic Growth: Recent Evidence from OECD Countries', mimeo, paper presented at the XII Villa Mondragone International Economic Seminar, Paris.

Bertola, G. (1993), 'Factor Shares and Savings in Endogenous Growth', *American Economic Review*, 83(5), pp. 1184–98.

Bresnahan, T. and Trajtenberg, M. (1995), 'General Purpose Technologies: "Engines of Growth"', *Journal of Econometrics*, 65, pp. 83–108.

Baumol, W.J. (1967), *Welfare Economics and the Theory of the State*, London: Bell.

Chenery, H.B. (1960), 'Patterns of Industrial Growth', *American Economic Review*, 50, pp. 624–54.

Clark, C. (1957), *The Conditions of Economic Progress*, London: McGraw-Hill.

David, P.A. (1990), 'The Dynamo and the Computer: An Historical Perspective on the Modern Productivity Paradox', *American Economic Review*, 80 (2), pp. 355–61.

Diamond, P.A. (1982), 'Aggregate Demand Management in Search Equilibrium', *Journal of Political Economy*, 90 (2), pp. 881–94.

Echevarria, C. (1997), 'Changes in Sectoral Composition Associates with Economic Growth', *International Economic Review*, 38 (2), pp. 431–52.

Gibbons, R. (2000), 'Firms (and Other Relationships)', in DiMaggio, P. (ed.), *Firm Futures*, Princeton: Princeton University Press.

Gordon, R.J. (1999), 'Has the "New Economy" Rendered the Productivity Slowdown Obsolete?', mimeo, Northwestern University.

Greenspan, A. (1998), 'Question: Is there a New Economy', http://www.federalreserve.org/boarddocs/speeches/1998/19980904.htm.

Griliches, Z. (1994), 'Productivity, R & D, and the Data Constraint', *American Economic Review*, 84 (1), pp. 1–23.

Hage, J. (1998), 'An Endogenous Theory of Economic Growth from Innovation: Organizational and Institutional Determinants, Feedbacks, and Disequilibria, Presidential Address', Sase 1998, Vienna.

Jorgenson, D.W. and Stiroh, K.J. (2000), 'Raising the Speed Limit: US Economic Growth in the Information Age', mimeo, paper presented at the XII. Villa Mondragone International Economic Seminar, Harvard University and Federal Reserve Bank of New York.

Kaldor, N. (1963), 'Capital Accumulation and Economic Growth', in Lutz, F.A. and Hague, D.C. (eds), *Proceedings of a Conference Held by the International Economics Association*, London: Macmillan.

Kalecki, M. (1971), *Selected Essays on the Dynamics of the Capitalist Economy*, Cambridge: Cambridge University Press.

Kongsamut, P., Rebelo, S. and Xie, D. (1997), 'Beyond Balanced Growth', *NBER Working Paper No. 6159*.

Koput, K.W. and Powell W.W. (2000), 'Science and Strategy: Organizational Evolution in a Knowledge-Intensive Field', mimeo, paper presented at the Organization Science Winter Conference, University of Arizona and Stanford University.

Kuznets, S. (1957), 'Quantitative Aspects of the Economic Growth of Nations: II', *Economic Development and Change*, 4(S), pp. 3–111.

Mühlberger, U. (1999), 'Explaining Atypical Employment', in Kantarelis, D. (ed), *Business and Economics for the 21st Century*, Worcester, pp. 281–92.

Mühlberger, U. (2000), 'Some Empirical Facts of Dependent Self-employment', mimeo, Florence.

Powell, W.W. (1990), 'Neither Market Nor Hierarchy: Network Forms of Organization', *Research in Organitational Behavior*, 12, pp. 295–336.

Quah, D. (1997) 'Increasingly Weightless Economies', *Bank of England Quarterly Bulletin*, 37 (1), pp. 49–56.

Romer, P.M. (1990), 'Endogenous Technological Change', *Journal of Political Economy*, 98(S), pp. 71–102.

Solow, R.M. (1956), 'A Contribution to the Theory of Economic Growth', *Quarterly Journal of Economics*, 71 (1), pp. 65–94.

Unger, B. and Zagler, M. (2000), 'Organizational and Financial Determinants of Innovation', Vienna University of Economics and BA Working Paper, Vienna.

Zagler, M. (1999a), *Endogenous Growth, Market Failures, and Economic Policy*, Basingstoke: Macmillan.

Zagler, M. (1999b), 'Services, Innovation, and the New Economy', mimeo, Firenze.

Zagler, M. (2000a), 'Structural Change, Endogenous Growth, and Search', *European University Institute Working Paper ECO No. 00/14*, Firenze.

Zagler, M. (2000b), 'Sectoral Shifts, Dependent Self-Employment, and the New Economy', mimeo, Firenze.

PART II

Chapter 5

Competition Policy for Network and Internet Markets

Robert D. Willig[1]

The debates that rage around high-technology targets of potential competition policy interventions, like combinations of internet companies and Microsoft's structure and worldwide conduct, cannot avoid the foundational question of whether antitrust should stay away from high-technology markets. This question is inevitably posed by advocates for the commercial freedom of the private targets, and it takes on added significance as it is recurrently raised by neutral observers troubled by the size of the stakes and the depth of the policy challenges that are entailed. There are arguments in favour of the affirmative that deserve to be taken seriously because they are based on intrinsic distinguishing characteristics of high-tech markets.

These same characteristics of high-technology markets lead on deeper consideration to two different conclusions. First, it is vital that competition policy be exercised with vigour and dedication in the context of high-tech. Secondly, it is equally crucial that competition policy be shaped with vigorous dedicated attention to the special characteristics of high-technology markets and to their implications for the structuring of sound antitrust analysis.

Among the themes of this chapter is that the network character of many important high-tech industries, including computer software and the internet, gives rise to competition issues with novel appearances and to types of relevant markets with novel architecture. In my view, many of the apparent difficulties of antitrust analysis of high-tech industries can be much alleviated by means of somewhat novel delineation of what are the relevant markets and novel identifications of what are the key assets that create competitive advantage in them. Once these more novel analytic steps have been taken, the competition analysis that follows can be more conventional and can follow more familiar principles.

In, particular, recent attention to the issues raised in the cases involving Microsoft have led to general suspicion of bundling practices in network and other high-tech settings. This is inappropriate since bundling can bring significant benefits to consumers and to the diversity and dynamism of marketplace offerings, On the other hand, it is true that bundling can be an unfortunately effective vehicle for anti-competitive exclusion. Once the relevant markets have been accurately delineated, a standard test for anti-competitive practices can be gainfully applied to competition policy analyses of bundling and other access issues in network industries.

1   Should Competition Policy be Applied to High-Tech Industries?

The stimulating arguments against the application of competition policy to high-tech industries include the following:

- high-tech markets move too rapidly and unpredictably for government intervention to succeed in achieving its intended goals;
- the critically important performance of high-tech markets is dangerously vulnerable to the delays and uncertainties inevitably introduced by the prospects and realities of government intervention;
- short-run competition is far less important in the setting of high-tech markets than are the special forms of long-run high-tech competition, and these may well be undermined by standard forms of intervention that are aimed at protecting short-term competition;
- high-tech products are especially prone to exhibit extremely crucial economies of scale and scope (due to high R&D investment needs and first-copy costs, learning-by-doing, and network effects arising from the needs for compatibilities and protocols), so interventions based on static views of concentration and competition are apt to be dangerously counterproductive;
- due to the critical roles of entrepreneurship and venture capital, high-tech enterprise is extremely vulnerable to the risks and, dampening of incentives that attend antitrust scrutiny and interventions;
- high-tech markets are too important to the economy to subject to the repression and inevitable mistakes of government intervention.

Each of these arguments has its own stimulating basis in some aspects of the truth. Most striking is the critical importance of technological progress to human welfare and the economies of many nations, throughout the past century even before technology reached the lofty heights we experience today. Despite the challenges of understanding today's information-based version of the industrial revolution while it is in feverish progress, we should all be able to agree that high-tech markets contribute substantially as pivotal forces for continued growth and prosperity – indeed one line of continuing plausible studies (first reported by Amano and Blohm in the *Wall Street Journal*, 17 October 1996) ascribes the entire recent growth of the US economy to the Internet market. And no particular end to this phenomenon is in sight

However, the special importance of high-tech markets does not in itself indicate that competition policy should be kept away – indeed there is an equally compelling implication that, antitrust is all the more vital to our economy when it is employed to protect competition in such critical, sectors. Nevertheless, there are extraordinarily important lessons from the arguments against applying antitrust to high-tech at all that must constrain and shape the way it is to be applied:

- antitrust may be crucial to protect long-run competition over innovation and technological development, and this should be its focus in high-tech markets;
- the pace and unpredictability of change in high-tech markets mean that concentration of contemporaneous market shares and holdings of short-lived assets and elements of competitive advantage should not form the bases of views of monopoly power;
- due to the uncertainties of prediction and the repressing effects of long investigations and the concomitant concerns about interventions, antitrust should be applied only with deep caution and only to the most certain and compelling of threats to competition;
- antitrust analyses of high-tech markets must reflect cognisance of the key economies of scale and scope, in the special network and intergenerational forms that endemically arise, as well as the sunk costs and other consumer and supplier commitments that go along with them;
- the critical importance to the economy of high-tech markets and the innovation competition they are capable of generating means that antitrust should be especially vigilant in protecting against forms of monopolization that become possible in this environment.

Thus, it is absolutely clear that the stakes are extremely high in applying antitrust to technology-driving markets. It is paramount to recognize the great importance to the economy of the competitive performance of high-tech markets, and the vulnerability of that performance to incautious antitrust intervention. It is correspondingly crucial for antitrust to guard high-tech competition appropriately, with respect for the special traits and forms of competition involved. Indeed, some of the special characteristics of high-tech markets make them vulnerable to unconstrained monopolization that would profitably suppress competition and the innovation that would otherwise benefit the economy.

2   Network Industries and their Relevant Markets

Many of the high-technology industries that attract the attention of competition policy have the fundamental properties of network industries. Most succinctly and abstractly, a network industry has the property that its use confers more value on each of its consumers the more users there are. The identification of this characteristic began with telecommunications, where it is relatively clear that the more users there are of a compatible technology, the more people are available for the communications of a given user, and so the greater value there is to any given user. It was less obvious, but is now equally accepted among economists, that products like computer software and playback systems for media have the same network property, inasmuch as the more users there are, the more attention suppliers pay to creating attractive upgrades, additional content, and other complementary products, and so the more value there is to each typical user. In addition, many industries that rely on physical networks, like transport and some financial service providers, also have the economic network property.

Competition policy issues and analyses pertaining to network industries become far clearer and more closely analogous to those arising in more conventional settings when the relevant markets that are appropriate to the network setting are delineated. First, there are the markets for the network services themselves – i.e., the services that cannot effectively be supplied outside the aegis of a network. While different networks can, perhaps, compete with their offerings of their different network services, other supply arrangements without the network characteristics may be unlikely to offer close substitutes, and would thus be unlikely participants in the same relevant market.

The second type of relevant market that aids competition analyses of network industries is delineated in terms of the services of a class of assets, tangible or intangible, that facilitates or that may sometimes be necessary for the effective supply of network services. When such assets are essential for the supply of network services, they can be termed 'bottlenecks', or essential facilities. When they are not essential, such assets may nevertheless underlie elements of competitive advantage, and there may be different such elements that are either complementary or substitutes for one another.

These two generic types of relevant markets in the network setting can provide frameworks for analysing a host of different categories of competition issues. Broadly, there may be horizontal issues in a relevant market for network services arising from a merger or collusion between two suppliers of these services, or from abusive or monopolizing conduct on the part of a dominant supplier of network services. There may be horizontal issues arising from mergers, collusion, or unilateral conduct in a relevant market for the services of assets that provide substitutable elements of competitive advantage in supplying network services, And there may be vertical issues arising from impeded availability or even foreclosed availability to suppliers of network services of these assets that foster effective supply.

Let us now exercise these concepts in the context of several over-simplified examples, at the risk of inaccurate portrayal of the real and more complex cases involved. In the US Visa/MasterCard case, concerns are expressed about competition in the market for 'general purpose card network products and services'. This market definition reflects the view that the value to individual users of Visa and MasterCard is importantly linked to the extent of the network in terms of its commercial and geographic coverage. Consequently, credit arrangements at particular chains of stores or other establishments, or in a particular town, are not participants in this relevant market. As a result of this market delineation, its concentration is far higher than it might otherwise be, and the alleged coordination between Visa and MasterCard becomes a matter of great concern. As a consequence of the network services market definition, competition among the many different issuing banks on the credit interest rates is not evidence of sufficient competition, because possibly significant decisions about product and service design are made at, the overarching network level rather than at the level of the individual bank. When an individual bank is an issuer of a credit card, that relationship fosters the working of that credit card's network, and is an element of competitive advantage for that credit card's network services, Then, competition in the network services market is thought to be suppressed by the alleged agreement between Visa and MasterCard to forbid a bank that issues either of their cards also to be an issuer of any other general-purpose cards.

Competition analysis of airlines issues often rests on the concepts of network services relevant markets and relevant markets for the services of assets that are crucial for the supply of network services. Inasmuch as passengers and corporate customers value more extensive sets of airline operations and frequencies, an airlines network as a whole is important beyond being just a collection of origin-destination markets. Loyalty, frequent-flier, corporate discount, and TACOs programmes all accentuate the relevance of the network markets, and consumers empirically do seem to favour online connection. An airline's hubs provide critical elements of competitive advantage to its network, and the hubs are often the focal points for competitive analysis. In the US combination of Northwest and Continental Airlines, the Department of Justice (DOJ) has complained about seven hub-to-hub routes out of thousands of other overlapping routes. The governmentally proposed competitive mitigations for the American Airlines/British Airlines combination centred on divesting substantial slots at the key hub Heathrow airport, in part on the theory that these assets are essential for other airlines to offer competition on networks that offer services competing with AA's and BA's. Virgin Air has sued BA for monopolizing conduct that levers from BAs holdings of slots at Heathrow.

The joint venture between ATT and BT was analysed in a relevant market of global corporate communications services. To oversimplify, it could be said that this joint venture was allowed to proceed after long analysis for two reasons. First, there was found to be an ample number of equally capable participants in this market for network services. Second, there might have been a serious vertical problem if access to the UK local network had been assessed to be a principal bottleneck to network services that was under the control of the parties. This assessment seems to have come out the other way on the grounds that the joint venture would deal at arms length with BT for local offerings, and that the OFTEL regulator is on the path of opening up UK local access competition.

Several years ago, the US DOJ stopped a proposed merger between Microsoft and Intuit on the grounds that it would diminish competition in the market for personal financial services software. Here, the DOJ viewed this market as having the network property, with the large installed base of Quicken software conferring an important element of competitive advantage on Intuit's ability to sell more into this market. The DOJ perceived Microsoft's dominant position over operating system software as providing it with an important element of competitive advantage in the market for personal financial services software. The DOJ concluded that competition would be diminished if these two important elements of substitutable competitive advantage were merged. It is interesting to note that in some respects the DOJ view in this matter has been borne out, and in others it has been decidedly wrong. Today, as the DOJ would have predicted, the separate Microsoft and Intuit are neck and neck in sales of personal financial services software, and they do seem to compete head-to-head. On the other hand, the sources of competitive advantage that DOJ perceived have turned out to be only two of many, and many types of other enterprises have become successful in offering consumers the same kinds of computerized financial services and information in other ways. Banks, major securities brokers and internet portals have all, moved from their disparate platforms to offer attractive and substitute alternatives to Microsoft's and Intuits personal financial services software.

3   Relevant Markets for Internet 'Sticky Eyeballs' and Reputation

An important set of related considerations arise in competition analyses of internet industry issues. Here, the elements of competitive advantage that are key drivers of success and market participation create repeat and attentive site visits with 'sticky eyeballs' (viewers that remain) by means of reputation for delivering to consumer preferences. While reputation and brand names can always be considered in competition analyses, there are sound reasons for thinking that their analogues in the internet industry are particularly significant, and that as a result a relevant market for competitive advantage over internet audiences can be an insightful tool.

Consider the model of consumer choice over products with different qualities and prices that was originally advanced by Carl Shapiro and by Klein and Leffler. Here, consumers cannot ascertain in advance of the purchase decision what is the quality of the good or service, but the consumer surmises its quality from its price, the identity of the seller, and the seller's reputation. In equilibrium, despite a profusion of sellers, each must charge a mark-up over the marginal cost of supplying the product at the indicated quality. Otherwise, a seller with a reputation for good quality would have an incentive to cut the quality of the good, while leaving the price at the marginal cost of the higher quality good that had been indicated. This would be profitable, even if for only a short while before the consumers notice and stop their patronage, and the alternative to quality cutting is earning zero at a marginal cost price. Thus, any equilibrium where incentives to maintain quality persist must rest on prices above marginal costs, coupled with consumers' rational threats to quit patronage of a supplier who fails to sell the indicated quality. In such an equilibrium, an successfully built reputation for quality is a valuable asset that confers the ability to sell at a persistent mark-up thereafter. Given open entry into the market, these quasi-rents must be counterbalanced by the ex ante costs needed to invest in creating the reputation asset. Thus, the market dynamic has new firms entering, operating in the red while attempting to create a reputation for an attractive high quality product, and then those entrants that are fortunate enough to succeed in this can earn a continuing flow of profits from consumers that trust the firm's reputation for quality and that are not disappointed by their patronage.

This model is an apt description of some forces at work in the internet industry, where consumers cannot ascertain in advance what will be the quality), and appeal of a site visit and its use as a source of entertainment and information, as a portal, or as a vehicle for e-commerce certainly do observe long spells of negative returns, and some firms that emerge with valuable reputational assets that succeed in attracting repeat site visits from attentive consumers with 'sticky eyeballs'. These same forces are surely also in evidence in markets for restaurant meals and magazines, to say nothing of all, branded consumer goods. However, they may be particularly significant in the internet industry, as evidenced by the volatility and variance in equity valuations of internet companies, and by the depth of consumers' ignorance of what they are about to get from a site visit.

From this perspective, combinations of internet firms might insightfully be analysed for impact on competition in terms of the overlap, substitutability and substantiality of their reputational assets in the relevant market for competitive advantage over network services. While there are not very many participants in this market with sufficient share to raise concern, AOL is certainly stands out as a successful holder of this sort of asset, based on its enormous base of paying subscribers, its internal network of 'Instant Messaging', as well as its other attractions and significant reputation. Thus, the proposed deal between Time-Warner and AOL, should be scrutinized from both a horizontal and vertical perspective, with these perspectives in mind.

4   Competition Policy Towards Bottlenecks

The scenario at the centre of many of the expressions of antitrust concerns over high-tech markets focuses on a firm that has control over a 'bottleneck' component of a network system that may include other components that could potentially be more subject to their own competition. The classic antitrust example of such a bottleneck was a unique railroad bridge or railroad terminal controlled by one railroad, but needed for any of the other railroads to be able to haul freight in competition with the bottleneck-holder. Here, the 'network system' included the bottleneck facility together with the potentially competitive line haul services that made up the complementary components of the system. The classic antitrust concern is that the bottleneck-holder would use its control over the 'essential facility' to foreclose rivals from competing for the supply of the complementary services. Today, of course, a leading example of an alleged bottleneck is the operating system software Windows, controlled by the Microsoft Corporation. It is claimed that Windows is a bottleneck component of systems that include applications software such as word processors or Internet browsers, inasmuch as end-users can only be supplied the computing services they demand by employment of applications software in conjunction with use of Windows.

It would not be surprising if Windows were a genuine bottleneck, in view of the economic characteristics of operating systems software (OSS). By its very function, OSS embodies a set of standards or protocols for the ways that the hardware components of a computer work together, the ways that applications software interacts with the computer hardware and with the software functions of the OSS, and the ways that applications software interfaces with the end-user. Such standards and protocols must be reflected in the designs of compatible applications software and computer hardware, as well as in the working habits of end-users. There are substantial to enormous fixed first-copy costs required to write applications software and to design and write OSS, as well as significant fixed costs involved in users' processes of learning and getting acclimated to the computing environment concomitant with an OSS. Consequently, the entire system of OSS, the compatibility features of applications software, the compatibility features of hardware designs, and the compatibility elements of end-users' habits and training might very well constitute a natural monopoly in how deeply they exhibit the economic network property, and in that the excess costs of there being two or more alternative such systems might overwhelm any benefits from diversity. Moreover, the commitments and switching costs of the end-users, hardware manufacturers, and software writers associated with the installed bases of hardware, software, and use patterns may well raise insurmountable barriers to the entry of entrepreneurs seeking to sell alternatives to an established form of OSS.

To assert lack of surprise about operating system software functioning as an economic bottleneck is not to claim the inevitability of such a conclusion, The benefits from a new innovative approach to an OSS might overcome the barriers to entry and the cost disadvantages from breaking into a natural monopoly, and so genuine actual or potential competition might episodically or continuously face the supplier of even a highly popular OSS. Alternatively, the standards and protocols of a highly popular OSS might become freely available to those writing alternatives to the OSS, so that the elements underlying the characteristic natural monopoly and entry barrier traits fall out of the control of the former bottleneck-holder, and competition for the OSS function replaces bottleneck monopoly. Another possibility is that several OSS's coexist, perhaps preponderantly serving different communities of users with different tastes and, needs, but nevertheless each posing an imperialistic threat of extending its empire to the domain largely served by another.

Even if a firm dominates a true bottleneck, it does not necessarily follow that it will employ its control to stifle competition over other system components or to foreclose rivals from participating in the supply of systems to end-users. Instead, the benchmark case is that of the 'perfect squeeze', wherein the bottleneck-holder charges either end-users or suppliers of other component so much for the use of the bottleneck component that the full net value of the system accrues to the bottleneck-holder as profit, and other players are held ('squeezed') to no return in excess of their opportunity costs. In this benchmark scenario, the bottleneck-holder has profit incentives to arrange system participation roles so that systems are configured with optimal efficiency, including the participation of rivals in the supply of system components if they bring lower incremental costs or superior designs. Here, as a matter of economics, there is no problem for antitrust to solve, since market incentives are conducive to efficiency, and only inefficient rivals of the bottleneck-holder are left out of equilibrium market participation. Any apparently high levels of profits that accrue to the bottleneck holder cannot be distinguished from efficient rewards for owning the intellectual property so successfully embodied in the bottleneck.

Outside of the benchmark case of the perfect squeeze, there may well be strong incentives for the bottleneck-holder to employ its control over the bottleneck to disadvantage or disable or foreclose rivals for a variety of different reasons. Rivals who participate in supplying components of the system may become stronger competitors to the bottleneck-holder in other, non-coincident, markets as a result of economies of scale or scope. Then, the bottleneck-holder may profit on net from excluding the rival from efficiently participating in the systems market, because the consequent additional market power in the non-coincident market may generate sufficient additional profits to overcome the losses from tolerating on inefficient configuration of the systems sold to end-users.

Similarly, rivals who participate in the supply of system components may simultaneously provide end-users with an alternative match-up that bypasses the so-called bottleneck, and that accordingly constrains the ability of the dominant firm to earn profits. Then, inefficient foreclosure of the rival may sufficiently weaken its ability to compete together with the bottleneck-bypass against the dominant firm that these gains in market power are worth the losses from the inefficient foreclosure.

In another scenario, the bottleneck-holder is prevented from implementing its profit maximizing (discriminating) pricing strategy as a result of the alternatives offered to end-users by an efficient supplier of other system components. This effect provides yet another motive for the bottleneck-holder to employ its control to disadvantage the rival.

Each of these theories of motives for anticompetitive foreclosure might apply to Microsoft, The Netscape browser might, for example, be viewed as a strong competitor to Microsoft's browser in an incipient non-coincident market for, say, financial services offered over the Internet. Then, even though it might cost MS lost profits from the sale of Windows to exclude the Netscape browser, the strategy might well recoup these losses and more from the resulting additional market power enjoyed in the non-coincident market. The pricing of MS Office suite might assist in effecting profitable price discrimination – charging more to high-willingness-to-pay business end-users than to low-willingness-to-pay household end-users,

Then, MS would have an incentive to foreclose a competing applications suite from the Windows environment, to protect its ability to price discriminate via supra competitive margins on the MS Office suite. Finally, the Netscape browser might be viewed by Microsoft as a precursor to a competitive attack on its OSS monopoly based on network intelligence migrating to the desktop, Then, the non-coincident market is just the market for OSS at a later date, and Microsoft would be motivated to forego maximal profits today by foreclosing Netscape in order to protect future OSS returns against a resurgence of Netscape.

Given the possibility that Microsoft would be motivated to foreclose or competitively weaken a components rival like Netscape or Corel, under any of the theories just described, the next question is how an OSS bottleneck-holder might leverage its control to accomplish the weakening of its intended victim. Perhaps an OSS bottleneck-holder could design the OSS to render the rival applications software ineffective or degraded in its performance or just unattractive in its usage by the end-customer, either absolutely or in comparison to the applications offered by the OSS vendor. This kind of strategy might be implemented under the cover of new positive features of the OSS that were incompatible with rival applications or that rendered the previous functionality of the OSS incompatible with the rival applications. Perhaps the OSS could be sold with an application software module integrated with it, either physically or just commercially, that substituted for the rival's product, thereby undermining the rival's demand. In each of these instances, the diminished demand for and appeal of the rival's product would help raise the bottleneck-holder's profit by diminishing the rival's ability to compete through the effects of lost economies of scale and scope in non-coincident markets, or by diminishing the rival's ability to arbitrage away profitable price discrimination, or by diminishing rival's ability to contribute to bottleneck bypass options.

5   Bundling offers Major Benefits to Consumers

Based (at least implicitly) on theories of this kind, and the press surrounding the Microsoft cases, the public and the competition policy community have lately come to a general suspicion of bundling practices, In an attempt to temper this swing of the pendulum, this section of the chapter will emphasize two key points. First, bundling generally can have powerfully beneficial effects on consumers and on the quality of marketplace offerings. Second, the public policy decision whether to allow bundling should focus on the mark-et power of the enterprise who wishes to engage in such bundling, and on the overall competitive conditions in the relevant markets for the components of the bundle. Bundling decisions by enterprises which face effective competition are unambiguously pro-competitive. There are no plausible competitive harms to offset the significant competitive benefits offered by bundling.

Bundling e-mails selling two or more goods (or services) in a single package. With 'pure' bundling, the seller offers the goods only in a package. With 'mixed' bundling, the seller offers the goods either bundled or unbundled and the price of the bundle is typically set below the sum, of the prices for the unbundled components (Varian, 1989, p. 626). Although 'bundling' and 'one-stop shopping' are sometimes used synonymously, we regard the two practices as distinguishable. In particular, one-stop shopping entails purchasing one's requirements from one seller. Firms may bundle goods for competitive or for anticompetitive reasons. As regulators, courts, antitrust policy-makers, and scholars have recognized, in some market settings, firms with market power over one good can use bundling to extend that market power into markets for other goods. Bundling is also practised in markets that are vigorously and robustly competitive. Manufacturers of radios and CD players bundle them with speakers or headphones. PC manufacturers bundle central processing units with disk drives and operating system software. Cereal and detergent manufacturers offer the same products in varying container sizes; the bundle consists of multiple units of the same commodity. Fast food restaurants offer hamburgers with fries and a drink and a package price that is lower than the sum of individual prices.

Economists have identified a variety of benefits to consumers that can result from allowing suppliers in competitive markets to engage in one-stop shopping generally and bundling specifically. The benefits of these arrangements fall into two general categories: benefits created by reducing transaction costs, for both buyers and sellers, and improved recovery of fixed and sunk costs under competitive conditions.

Bundling, and one-stop shopping, can eliminate or reduce several kinds of transaction costs incurred by customers and suppliers. First, one-stop shopping can greatly reduce purchasers' search costs – the cost of time and effort needed to become informed about the products and services available in the market, to negotiate appropriate purchase terms, and to assemble the desired combination of products (or services). This benefit has particular importance when, as is often true of high-tech network services, the bundled products and services are perceived by consumers to be complex. Second, the ability to bundle gives suppliers incentives to make sure that the complementary goods included in the bundle function properly with each other, and ensures that the vendor will be responsible if they do not function properly. Bundling enables the customer to receive the desired products and services already assembled and working properly, without spending additional time and money assembling, testing and adjusting the components. Moreover, testing systems from the same company are more likely to work better together. In sum, a carrier selling a bundle of network service(s) has the appropriate incentive to ensure that all the components work together well and are fully compatible. On the other hand, a seller who is forced to offer products only à la carte may have lessened incentives to ensure that all complementary components of the package work well together.

Bundling can also reduce the purchasers' transaction costs of verifying that the services and goods actually perform as promised by the seller, and of getting the seller to correct the problem when they do not perform as promised. Plainly, a vendor who values its reputation has an incentive to assume responsibility to the purchaser for the performance of the bundle. Without bundling, the buyer faces a greater risk that individual vendors will try to shun the responsibility when the system needs repair or additional setup work to perform as promised. Indeed, this concern is not merely a reflection of the sellers trying to shirk responsibility, but also of the fact that responsibility is often genuinely difficult to allocate.

Bundling also helps minimize selling and billing costs. Bundling allows the seller to maintain a single inventory entry for the bundle, rather than individual inventory records for each component in the package. Likewise, the seller can submit a single bill for the entire bundle, rather than a separate charge for each component.

Bundling also promotes incentives for sellers to assemble supplies and other complementary goods that work well together. When a durable capital good and other complementary goods are sold separately, purchasers may buy complementary goods of inefficiently low quality, causing the capital good to operate poorly. When the inferior complements make the whole system malfunction, the manufacturer of the core good or service may suffer unwarranted damage to its reputation that may well extend to many potential customers.

This issue is most likely to arise when the technology is complex, and quality differences among competing brands of the complementary goods are hard to detect. First, buyers may simply be poorly informed about the specifications of the complementary goods needed for optimum performance, Moreover, when components are sold on a stand-alone basis, sellers may have inadequate incentives to inform consumers about system requirements. This is a 'free rider' problem: many of the benefits of educating buyers go to sellers of complementary or competing goods, even when these sellers contribute nothing to the cost of the education campaign. Second, because some costs of damage to a manufacturer's reputation are external to any individual buyer, even, educated buyers may buy complements of poorer quality than optimal. Bundling can reduce the informational and other free rider problems. When the same vendor sells the bundle of complementary products – 'the system' – the vendor can set the quality of the complementary goods at the level necessary to make the system work, and can capture (through increased sales or profits) all the benefits of educating purchasers about the requirements for proper system operation.[2]

Likewise, bundling may also facilitate efficient spending on joint marketing and sales complementary components of the bundle. The reason is akin to the 'free rider' problem discussed above: suppliers of complementary or competing products can benefit from one supplier's advertizing without sharing in its cost. Because the supplier that advertizes cannot capture the full benefits of the advertizing, the result is likely to be under-provision of informational advertizing.[3] However, when a vendor sells a package of complementary products in a bundle, it has proper incentives to market and otherwise promote the whole bundle of complements.

The second key benefit that bundling permits is to facilitate efficient recovery of joint and common costs and stimulate usage (sales) of desirable services to a wider range of potential customers. In particular, bundling allows better recovery of the R&D costs of innovative technology, while enabling buyers who are unable or unwilling to pay the stand-alone prices to obtain the new product as part of a bundle (see Levine, 2000).

Expenditures on R&D are an excellent example of a fixed costs: virtually the entire cost must be incurred to produce the first unit of the product while producing the next units requires little or no additional R&D expense. (Software and video recordings exemplify the phenomenon of high fixed costs and very low marginal costs.)

When fixed costs are a significant portion of total costs, marginal cost pricing likely will not recover R&D and other fixed costs. To recover these costs, the innovator must set prices above marginal production cost for at least some customers. Without the opportunity to recover R&D and other fixed costs, suppliers will not invest enough in R&D. Economists have demonstrated that the most efficient way to recover these fixed costs from purchasers in the market, while minimizing the inefficiency that results from pricing above marginal cost, is to charge higher markups to customers with relatively inelastic demand, and lower markups to customers with relatively elastic demand.

For many goods, however, suppliers have no way of determining precisely (if at all) the demand elasticities of potential customers. By offering different bundles, the seller can rely on customer self-selection to facilitate efficient recovery of fixed costs without detailed knowledge of individual consumers' demand elasticities.

Consider, for example, restaurant pricing. Restaurants commonly offer many menu items both individually at separate prices and combined into one or more fixed price meals. MacDonald's and other fast food restaurants offer burgers, fries and shakes both individually and combined as 'value meals'. Even expensive restaurants offer menu items both à la carte and as part of fixed price combinations. The bundled prices are normally below the sum of the corresponding unbundled prices.

The virtue of these arrangements is that they induce diners to sort themselves by the strength of their demands for individual menu items. For example, diners who crave a Big Mac, but are relatively uninterested in fries or a soft drink, can buy the Big Mac alone at a price that makes a higher percentage contribution to MacDonald's common costs than does the pro rata price of a Big Mac in a Value Meal, but at a lower absolute price to the customer. The same holds true for aficionados of fries or soft drinks who buy those items alone. Yet customers who attach a relatively uniform value to each component of a Value Meal can buy it for less than the sum of the à la carte prices of each component.[4] The effect of this mixed bundling strategy is to enable the restaurant to offer customers attractive prices to purchase both complete meals and individually desired items, while earning sufficient contribution to fixed and common costs to support the quality and selection that customers desire.

The same principle applies to the provision of telephone services. By simultaneously offering basic services, enhanced services and CPE alone and in bundled combinations as the marketplace dictates, a nondominant carrier can effect the breadth of sales and financially support the offering of the quality and selection of innovative products and services – including state-of-the-art CPE and enhanced services – that customers demand and that competitive success requires.

A simple example should make this point clear. Consider a competitive interexchange carrier that invents a new messaging service, having substantial R&D and fixed implementation costs. Assume also that the marginal cost of providing the service to an additional customer is low (relative to the fixed costs incurred by the innovator). To recover these fixed costs, the interexchange carrier must charge an average price for the service that greatly exceeds marginal cost. At this price, there is substantial demand from those telecommunications customers who also have high willingness to pay for long-distance services generally. However, long distance customers with low willingness to pay for long-distance service also have a rather low willingness to pay for the innovative new voice messaging service.

The seller faces a marketing dilemma. One strategy could be to charge a very high price to cover costs, At that price, however, many customers would not take the service even though they would be willing to pay a price closer to marginal cost. Another strategy could be to charge a low price, near marginal cost. That strategy would induce (almost) all potential customers to take the service. The problem is that such a strategy would not recover total fixed costs, including the original expenditure on R&D.

Bundling offers a solution to the marketing problem. The carrier offers the messaging service on a stand-alone basis at a price substantially above marginal cost. It also bundles the messaging service with its standard long-distance calling plans. The carrier 'marks-up' those usage plans that appeal to those with a high willingness to pay for interexchange service, and adds the new service to them. The carrier also bundles the messaging service with usage plans that appeal to those with a low willingness to pay for interexchange service, but at a much lower mark-up.[5] Offering both sets of bundles attracts customers from both high-willingness-to-pay and low-willingness-to-pay groups, and thus fosters efficient dissemination of the service. Furthermore, the revenues collected by the interexchange carrier increase, because the revenues secured for the new service from the high willingness-to-pay group are not undermined,[6] while modest additional revenues are secured from the low-willingness-to-pay group.

Competition facing the interexchange carrier further enhances the consumer benefits from this bundling strategy. The competition impels the interexchange carrier to offer the bundle; otherwise the low-willingness-to-pay consumers will be drawn to the competitor who offers his own version of the messaging service bundled with his usage plan for this group. And the competition tends to discipline the prices set for the messaging service both alone and bundled with other interexchange services down toward the necessary economic cost. Here, the added opportunities afforded by bundling do not raise net profit greatly, but they do mean that the interexchange carrier will avail itself of the opportunities and use the added net revenue potential to lower other prices – not because of regulation or altruism, but because of the threat that customers will otherwise divert their business to other interexchange carriers that offer better deals and more attractive bundles of services. Thus, the ability to bundle leads to good outcomes for social welfare and consumers, especially where there is effective competition.

With all these beneficial possibilities to be considered, and with all the ways discussed earlier that bundling and other forms of access impediments can harm competition in network and other high-tech settings, the great challenge for antitrust is to sort out the dangerously anticompetitive conduct. and practices from those that are innocuous or procompetitive, but that cost rivals sufficiently to motivate them to invest in antitrust complaints, lobbying and litigation. It may be entirely efficient for a bottleneck-holder to arrange systems in ways that preclude some or all rivals, and in a perfect squeeze situation, the bottleneck-holder would find it profitable to do so. Yet, the bottleneck-holder might find it profitable to exclude a rival even though the rival were efficient, in order to weaken competition in a market related through a common brand-name or common software platform or user interface. How is antitrust to proceed in this domain to attempt to distinguish the pro- from the anti-competitive?

6   An Economic Test for Anticompetitive Access and Technology Choices

We now delineate a three-prong test that can be used to structure the assessment of the competitive effects of pricing, bundling/packaging, and technological decisions by a bottleneck-holder – i.e., a firm with monopoly power over a 'component' that rivals need in order to offer a viable system.[7] The analysis here of our test builds from stylized facts of the operating system software and browser 'markets', as a example to capture some of the key features of how the test would structure some of the competitive issues that have been brought up by the litigation against Microsoft.

The three-prong test examines whether the actual strategic decisions adopted by a firm make business sense (i.e., are profitable) irrespective of their effect on the economic viability of rivals, or whether these strategic decisions are only profitable because they destroy rivals' ability to compete and, thereby, enable the firm to earn additional monopoly profits in some market. In stylized models, the test has strong economic welfare properties in the sense that pricing, bundling/packaging, and technological decisions that the test does not find to be anticompetitive do improve aggregate economic welfare.

Prong 1: Analysis of the Likelihood and the Sources of Monopoly Profits from Exclusion

The first prong of the test directs the analyst to determine whether the allegedly anticompetitive exclusionary conduct creates a dangerous probability of monopolization of some non-coincident market or markets. In this step, the analysis first focuses on the competitive conditions in the primary market. If the firm engaged in the allegedly exclusionary practice does not have bottleneck market power in the primary market, then any further inquiry is unnecessary and would likely be detrimental to overall economic incentives to compete and innovate. Thus, if there were two or three well-matched vendors of operating system software, licensing practices and software design choices of any one of them would likely not merit antitrust scrutiny. Also at this stage, the analyst must identify rigorously the various non-coincident markets in which the dominant firm can potentially gain market power and earn, monopoly profits from its conduct. The non-coincident market(s) could include the primary market, but at some future date;[8] the same product market but at some other geographic location; or another product market. Finally, the challenged conduct must be shown to be the cause of a dangerous probability of monopolization by virtue of its impact on the ability of rivals to compete. (For example, if the challenged conduct amounts to the placement of a removable browser icon on the OSS opening screen, a nexus between this behaviour and monopolization must be established for an inquiry to proceed.)

Prong 2: Profit Sacrifice

The second prong of the test requires a comparison of the profit flows from the actual challenged conduct *versus* some carefully defined alternative, but less exclusionary course of conduct. The critical step is that the profits from the exclusionary strategy are calculated, on the assumption that the excluded rival remains viable as a competitor. If under the maintained assumption of continued viability of the rival, the exclusionary strategy earns the firm less profit than the alternative, less exclusionary strategy, then the firm is sacrificing profits that it could earn but for the adverse effects of the exclusionary strategy on present and future competition in the relevant markets For example, if consumers value having choices of alternative Internet browsers, then the owner of a bottleneck, such as the operating system software, should possibly welcome the presence of such alternatives in the market because doing so would increase the value of and consumers' willingness to pay for the OSS.

Prong 3: Recoupment of the Foregone Profits

The final step in, the test is the determination of whether the exclusionary strategy is more profitable than the less exclusionary strategy because it has led (or will likely lead) to the already-established diminution of competition in the relevant markets. The rationales for this prong of the test are straightforward.

First, this prong tests the theory of sacrifice that underlay the second prong in the different context where the rival is competitively disabled. The change in the assumed competitive ability of the rival must swing the profit comparison from favouring the less exclusionary to favouring the more exclusionary conduct. This prong also protects the firm from being forced into making strategy choices that accommodate the rival. In particular, a firm should be free to cause rival's exit or foreclose rival from the market, if doing so would be more profitable, whether the rival remains or is excluded, than a more accommodating strategy. For example, if a closed system generates significant efficiencies and consumers do not much value choice, then a closed system may be the right solution, irrespective of its effect on viability of rivals. On the other hand, if a chosen closed system is costly to develop and lessens current demand for the bottleneck, but enables the firm to extract additional profits in the non-coincident market, following the demise of the rival, then this strategic decision is only profitable because the sacrificed profits are more than recouped elsewhere (or at some future time) in the non-coincident market.

7   Applying the Test to Bundling and Network Access

The earlier discussion of the benefits of bundling, together with the structured test above show that bundling itself should not be viewed as a source or cause of competitive concerns. Rather, bundling may be the 'vehicle' for anticompetitive exclusionary conduct – like the refusal of the bottleneck-holder to negotiate a deal at the compensatory price for access to those who would compete in network services. Bundling may merely cover up the fact that the bottleneck-holder's own offering is implicitly priced too low, in order to foreclose competition.

Here, a helpful framework for the needed antitrust analysis is our three-pronged test. The first prong of our suggested test would provide appropriate discipline to the enforcement community to resist the temptation to second guess and intervene in business decisions that are unlikely to render efficient firms competitively disabled. Where serious competitive problems are prevalent, the test would permit consideration of the question of whether the bottleneck-holder had reasonably dealt with rivals' needs for access, in, a fashion permitted to compensate the bottleneck-holder for incremental costs and foregone profits in the primary markets and other markets where the resulting induced monopolization is omitted from the baseline.

This approach does not dwell on the constructs of tying and bundling per se, and avoids the alarmism that increasingly attends bundling characterizations, but rather focuses on the core competitive issue. Adherence to the second and third prongs of the test would provide an appropriate spur for attention to mutually beneficial and serious businesslike negotiations concerning genuine needs for access to bottlenecks and what would constitute genuinely compensatory terms, It has the potential to influence conduct prospectively in the direction of win-win for all parties, outside of denial of the gains from deliberate monopolization – the innovators are protected by the compensatory pricing standard, access to the bottleneck is encouraged in ways that do not undermine the competitive rewards from innovation and entrepreneurial investment, and consumers receive the benefits of incented innovations and a more open set of interfaces available for access to competing network services.

Notes

1   This chapter draws substantially on writings coauthored with Janusz Ordover. Nevertheless, he should not be held responsible for this formulation.
2   The same phenomenon is believed to be responsible for the decline of code-sharing arrangements between major airlines and separately-owned commuter lines. Operating under separate ownership, commuter carriers apparently lacked sufficient incentives to offer high quality service to the passengers interchanged between the commuter lines and the major carriers. The major carriers have moved to replace code sharing equity ownership (100 per cent or partial) of commuter lines (see Levine, 1987). Some observers attribute the growth of equity investments into commuter airlines to the need to capitalize them better and ensure procompetitive benefits of superior service.
3   In some circumstances, joint marketing agreements among all the suppliers can provide an alternative mechanism for internalizing the benefits of advertizing by requiring all of its beneficiaries to share in its costs. Negotiating and administering joint marketing agreements may be infeasible or uneconomic.
4   For a mathematical demonstration of this point, see Adams and Yellen, 1976, or Philips, 1983.
5   Concretely, assume that the high usage plan has a fixed fee of $10 per month and a usage rate of $0.05 per minute and the low usage plan has a usage-only rate of $0.10 per minute, with no monthly fee. Then the carrier may offer the new service to both customer groups by marking up the former plan to $12 in a fixed fee and unlimited voice messaging and the latter plan to $0.105 per minute up to 100 messages per month. Confronted with these options, both groups of customers will stick with their plans *and* receive the new service.
6   As they would, if the vendor tried to attract all customers with low prices.
7   For a prior developments and applications of the test, see Ordover and Willig, 1981, 1983 and 1995.
8   For example, in a standard predatory pricing case, the predator prices aggressively 'now' in order to monopolize the relevant product market at some 'later' time. According to the government, Microsoft's licensing practices would have an adverse effect not only on competition in the browser market but also on future rounds of competition in the OSS market.

References

Adams, W.J. and Yellen, J.L. (1983), 'Commodity Bundling and the Burden of Monopoly', *Quarterly Journal of Economic Research*, 90 (475), August.
Levine, M.E. (1987), 'Airline Competition in Deregulated Markets: Theory, Firm Strategy, and Public Policy', 4 *Yale Journal on Regulation*, 393, pp. 439–40.

Levine, M.E. (2000), 'Trice Discrimination Without Market Power', Harvard Law School Discussion Paper No. 276, February.

Ordover, J.A. (1995), 'Economists' View: The Department of Justice Draft for the Licensing and Acquisition of Intellectual Property', *Antitrust*, 9 (2), Spring, pp. 29–36.

Ordover, J.A. and Willig, R.D. (1981), 'An Economic Definition of Predation: Pricing and Product Innovation', *Yale Law Journal*, 91, November, pp. 8–53.

Ordover, J. and Willig, R.D. (1983), 'The 1982 Department of Justice Merger Guidelines: An Economic Assessment', *California Law Review*, 71, March, pp. 535–74.

Philips, L. (1983), *The Economics of Price Discrimination*, Cambridge, MA: Cambridge University Press. Varian, H.R. (1989), 'Trice Discrimination', in I.R. Schmalensee and R. Willig (eds), *Handbook of Industrial Organization*, North Holland: Amsterdam.

Chapter 6

Mergers between Incumbent Telecom Operators: The Role of Mutual Moderation

Patrick Rey

1   Introduction

This chapter analyses the impact of horizontal mergers between neighbouring incumbent operators. Examples of such mergers can be found on both sides of the Atlantic ocean: they include the wave of mergers between the US incumbent local exchange carriers (the so-called ILECs: SBC-Ameritech, Bell Atlantic-GTE, etc.) as well as the merger projects that have involved the former domestic monopolists in Germany and Italy, and in Sweden and Norway.

Those mergers share common features. In particular, they involve large companies that have (formerly protected) control of local loops in neighbouring territories, but little overlap. For example, SBS and Ameritech have a quasi-monopoly for local calls in their respective territories, and compete with long-distance carriers for intra-LATA communications in their respective territories,[1] but prior to the merger they did not really compete with each other. Similarly, Telia and Telenor have quasi-monopolies for terminating calls in Sweden and Norway, respectively, and have each a dominant position for long-distance and outgoing international calls in their respective countries, but they are not substantially competing with each other in those markets. In that respect, these mergers resemble mergers between 'local monopolies' in distinct territories; such a merger would lead to the creation a single 'local monopoly', in charge of both territories, but in each territory consumers would remain confronted to a monopolistic situation, as before.[2]

The situation involved in those telecom mergers is however slightly different. First, the telecom operators may exchange traffic. For example, Telia relies on Telenor for terminating its Sweden to Norway traffic, and conversely, Telenor relies on Telia for terminating its Norway to Sweden traffic. Furthermore, even if these operators do not compete with each other, they do compete against common rivals. As a result, a merger may allow them to coordinate their strategies against their common rivals, thereby encouraging predatory or foreclosure strategies that prevent the emergence of a level-playing field. This chapter is devoted to a review of these potential anti-competitive effects.[3]

Throughout the chapter, I will consider mergers between local operators that have a legal or de facto monopoly on local telecommunication services, that is, they have (quasi-exclusive) control of the local loops and related infrastructure in their home territories.[4] This assumption fits rather well the situation of the US ILECS and, to a lesser extent, remains a good approximation of the situation of the European former domestic monopolies. Depending on the context, there operators will be exchanging traffic (e.g., cross-border or regional traffic for the European operators) or simply competing with common rivals (e.g., for Intra-LATA traffic in the case of the Baby Bells, and for domestic long-distance and international calls in the case of the European historical operators). The recurring theme of the chapter is that, in each case, the merger significantly increases both the ability and the incentive for the combined entity to distort competition in telecom services (Katz and Salop, 1998).[5]

The basis of the anticompetitive effects described below comes from the merging parties' control of end-user access, access to the local loops and network infrastructure in their home territories. Each party thus has a strong bargaining position, since it can use the access to its own network as a strategic tool to get access to other's network. Therefore, absent the merger, the two operators might constitute an important source of competition for each other, since they would have an incentive to maintain a (mutual) moderation of access prices in their territories. This can be further reinforced by the geographical proximity of their territories, by the importance of the traffic between their territories, by the strength of their existing business relationships, etc. The merger will therefore remove an important source of moderation for access prices in the operators' territories, as well as an important potential or already effective competitor for several telecommunications services.

The chapter is structured as follows. In the next section, I will first consider the competition for cross-border traffic (from one territory to the other) and analyse in detail the role of mutual moderation between the incumbent operators as well as the impact of their merger. Building on this analysis, the last section discusses the impact of the merger on intraterritory telecommunication services.

2   Cross-border Telecommunication Services

I will start with the purest form of mutual moderation, which applies to the competition on calls from one territory to the other.

Cost Internalization of Termination Rates on Cross-territory Calls

To present the argument in its simplest form, consider the following scenario (Figure 6.1): Incumbent 'B' is the sole operator for calls from its territory to the other, while Incumbent 'A' competes with another operator, which will be referred to as the entrant 'E', on calls from its to B's territory.[6] The main working assumption is that the two incumbents have a monopoly on termination in their respective territories.

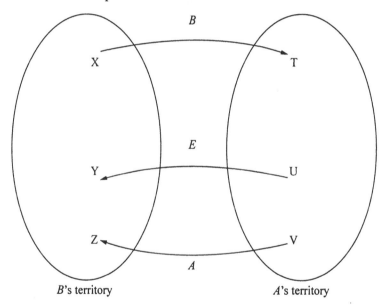

Figure 6.1   An example of cross-border competition between two operators

Each incumbent must choose the level of degradation of call termination. Two cases can be distinguished, according to whether the 'degradation' takes the form of an actual degradation of the quality of termination (for example, a delay in providing circuits, delays in interconnection and all practices which make the entrant a less able competitor) or, alternatively, consists of increasing the termination rates. The difference between the two strategies is that, for a same impact on volume, the latter one generates higher revenues.

Termination fees First, assume that there is no possibility of degrading the quality of termination, and consider the impact of the merger on termination charges. Denote by *a* the termination rate set by *A* and by *b* the rate set by *B*.[7] To simplify, I will also assume that the two incumbents have the same cost of termination, denoted by *c*, that all operators have the same cost of cross-border transport, denoted by *C*, and I will neglect origination costs.[8] These simplifying assumptions are made for expository purposes and do not affect the thrust of the argument. The true cost of carrying a call from one territory to the other is then equal to:

$$C \ (transport) + c \ (termination \ in \ the \ region \ of \ destination) \qquad (1)$$

for all cross-border calls (in both ways).[9]

Before the merger, the total costs of the cross-border calls are (cf. Figure 6.1):

- for *B*: $C + a \ (X \rightarrow T)$ (2)
  (cross-border transport *C* plus *A*'s termination rate, *a*);
- for *A*: $C + b \ (V \rightarrow Z)$;   (3)
- for *E*: $C + b \ (U \rightarrow Y)$.   (3)

A's incentives are to set a high termination charge *b*, but this desire is limited by:

- the loss of revenue generated by the reduction of the volume of calls serviced by both B and E; and
- the possibility of negotiating a reciprocal moderation with B.

Indeed, *B* can equally set a high termination fee. However, the two operators have a mutual interest to reach an agreement over a reciprocal moderation of their termination rates, in order to reduce double marginalization problems on cross-border calls: that is, both incumbents gain from a uniform decrease in the termination rates and thus have an incentive to negotiate a reciprocal reduction of their rates (see remark on double marginalization below). As long as the incumbents are not allowed to price discriminate (i.e., to charge different termination fees to different operators, for the same type of calls), *E* benefits from the reciprocal moderation engaged in by the two operators, even if it is unable to engage in 'competitive' retaliation with *A* or *B*.

Absent any change in regulation, the merger allows the incumbents to:

- *better discriminate*: after the merger, calls from V to Z only cost $C + c$ to A, who no longer pays the termination rate, and similarly for B on calls to A's territory. Since the two firms now constitute a single entity, a payment of a from 'A' to 'B' is merely an internal transfer within this new entity. The resource costs to this new entity are the true costs c even if, formally, A and B keep paying termination rates to each other. Only the entrant effectively pays the termination rate, which is above costs. Hence the entrant is competitively disadvantaged;
- *increase the incentive to raise or not to decrease the termination charge*:
  - the main moderating factor which prevailed before the merger – *t*he two incumbents' incentive to negotiate a mutual reduction of their termination rates – has vanished;
  - the concern about the reduction of the volume of calls from the other of the two merging incumbents has also vanished;
  - for B, the *concern* about the reduction of the volume of calls from the entrant not only has vanished, but it has actually been transformed into a *desire* to reduce the volume of those calls, since this reduces the competitive pressure on A; that is, increasing the rate for call termination in B's territory will now in effect raise the cost of the new entity's only rival (foreclosure).

Therefore, the merger leads to a situation where competition between B and E is distorted, not only because the merger between A and B removes the artificial cost introduced by the termination mark-up (which would in itself tend to lower prices, to the benefit of the customers), but mainly because the new entity will have much higher incentives to raise the termination rates (or resist the pressure for their reduction), thereby imposing a competitive disadvantage on the entrant, reducing the competitive pressure on cross-border calls, and thus eliminating the need for the new entity to pass through its cost reduction to the final users.

Remark on double marginalization In the context just described, where two operators send traffic to each other, it is sometimes argued that removing termination charges has no impact on the operators – particularly if termination rates are symmetric and traffic is balanced, since in that case both operators end up paying nothing. This view, however, presumes that calls will always remain balanced and ignores the fact that the volume of calls *varies* with the final price charged by the operators. Therefore, no operator can guarantee itself that the traffic remains balanced when it adjusts its price: any additional call generated by a price reduction generates an additional cost equal to $C + a$, which thus constitutes the correct *perceived marginal cost*. Therefore, termination charges increase the perceived marginal cost of the calls, which in turn induce the operators to increase the price they charge to their final users: Since each call sent to A costs $C + a$ to B, a price lower than $C + a$ would thus generate a loss on that call. Therefore, B will charge a price above $C + a$, and similarly, A will charge a price above $C + b$; as a result, higher termination rates lead to higher prices.[10] Even if it leads *in fine* to a situation where A sends as much traffic to B as it receives from B and thus pays nothing, because A owes B as much as B owes A, consumer prices will still be driven up by the termination rates.[11]

Access degradation Consider now the alternative case, where the merger does not affect termination rates (because of cost-oriented regulation, say) but the parties can degrade the quality of termination. To fix ideas, I will assume that termination charges are set equal to costs or slightly above them, and I will now denote by a (for A) and b (for B) the 'price equivalent' of the degradation of quality. It can be interpreted as the increase in the cost of the calls that the competitors would have to incur to maintain the quality, or as the users' monetary equivalent of the reduction in quality; that is, the degradation in essence lowers the quality or raises the costs of competitors. A higher level of degradation a or b thus decreases volumes, but does not generate higher revenues.

Before the merger, none of the incumbent operators gains from degrading termination, irrespective of whether regulation is hard or soft, since degrading termination reduces volumes but has no impact on the incumbent operator's margin. As long as termination charges are (even slightly) above cost, degrading termination would thus have a negative impact on the incumbent operator's profit. Therefore, both a and b would be set to zero: neither A or B, behaving individually, would engage in anti-competitive degradation.

However, after the merger, the new entity has an incentive to degrade the termination of calls operated by the entrant because again doing so artificially 'raises the rival's costs'. That is, by reducing the relative quality of the service provided by the entrant, degrading the termination of the entrant's calls distorts competition between the new entity and the entrant on A to B calls. While degradation was competitively self-defeating prior to the merger, after the merger A and B can single out the entrant and not each other for degradation.

The same argument applies as well to competitors servicing international calls from B's region to A's region. And it applies 'twice' to competitors offering international calls both ways. In each case, the merger increases the incumbents' incentives to raise termination rates and degrade termination. This limits the competitive pressures not only because it imposes an artificial competitive disadvantage on the existing competitors, but also because, by imposing such an artificial competitive disadvantage, it reduces the existing competitors' incentives to invest and the incentives for potential additional competitors to effectively enter the market.

A Formal Analysis of the Mutual Moderation Effect

I now develop a formal model to analyse the above issues in more detail. I show that the merger between the two incumbents eliminates the incentive for mutual moderation in termination rates, and introduces an incentive for B to increase its termination rates in order to 'assist' A by reducing competitive pressures for calls from A's to B's region. As a result of this behaviour, the merger places upward pressure on the termination rates between the two territories and eliminates competition on cross-border calls.

a) Framework The basic framework is as described above (see Figure 1). I will furthermore assume that in each country the demand for cross-border calls takes the linear form:

$$D(p) = d - p, \tag{4}$$

where p denotes the retail price and $D(p)$ the volume of calls demanded at that price. The parameter d reflects the size of the demand, and to simplify I will assume that it is the same in both countries.[12] This demand function establishes a standard inverse relationship between price and quantity: that is, the price that will prevail in each country is a decreasing function of the total volume of calls being offered by the operators present in that country. For example, if B offers a volume of calls q_B (where 'q' refers to the 'quantity' being supplied), the price at which it will sell those calls will be given by $d - q_B$. Similarly, if A and the entrant offer a total volume $q_A + q_E$, the price that will prevail in A's territory will be given by $d - q_A - q_E$.

Each operator's profit includes a retail profit, derived from providing international telecommunications services to home country subscribers; this retail profit is of the form:

'volume of (outgoing) calls' times 'retail margin' (5)

where the retail margin is equal to the difference between the price (determined as a function of total supply, see equation (5) above) and the perceived cost of a call (determined from equations (2) through (4) above, as applicable). Therefore, as an example, if A's termination rate is taken as given, the retail profit component for B is:

$$B\text{ 'retail profit'} = q_B(d - q_B - C - a) \qquad (6)$$

In addition, the two incumbent operators obtain a termination profit (derived from providing termination for the operators of the other country). This termination profit takes the form:

'volume of (incoming) calls' times 'termination margin' (7)

where the termination margin is the difference between the termination charge (a for A and b for B) and the actual cost (c) of terminating the call. For example, B would receive ($q_A + q_E$) incoming calls, and therefore its termination profit component is given by:

$$B\text{ 'termination profit'} = (q_A + q_E)(b - c) \qquad (8)$$

B's total profits are therefore given by:

$$B\text{ total profit} = q_B(d - q_B - C - a) + (q_A + q_E)(b - c) \qquad (9)$$

The same analysis determines the other two operators' profit functions, which I summarize below:

- for B: $q_B(d - q_B - C - a) + (q_A + q_E)(b - c)$,   (10)
- for A: $q_A(d - q_A - q_E - C - b) + q_B(a - c)$,   (11)
- for E: $q_E(d - q_A - q_E - C - a)$.   (12)

Finally, I will assume that the two operators in B's region compete à la Cournot (competition in quantities or capacities).[13]

b) Double marginalization in the pre-merger environment I first consider the operators' marketing behaviours, for given termination charges (i.e., for a given set of termination rates). This exercise allows to predict each operator's preferred level of sales as a function of the termination charges set by other operators. Essentially, I compute each operator's 'response' to termination charges set unilaterally by the other operators.

Given A's termination charge a, B will choose a price p_B, or equivalently (given the relationship between price and demand) a volume of traffic q_B that maximize its retail profit as given by equation (7) above (and repeated below):[14]

$$B \text{ 'retail profit'} = q_B(d - q_B - C - a) \tag{6}$$

B's retail profit will be maximized by choosing as a level of output (see Figure 6.2):

$$q_B = (d - C - a)/2 \tag{13}$$

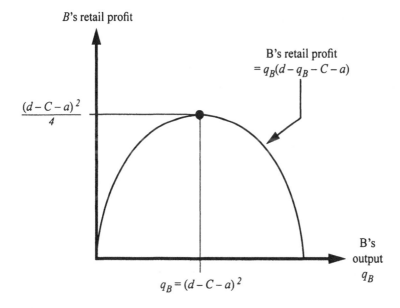

Figure 6.2   Operator B retail profit

By substituting this quantity into the demand function (equation (5) above), we can also write B's profit maximizing decision (taking A's termination rate as given) in terms of the resulting price in B's region:

$$P_B = (d + C + a)/2 \qquad (14)$$

Additionally, by substituting the profit maximizing quantity given by equation (*14*) into the expression for *B*'s retail profit (equation (*7*)), we see that *B*'s maximal retail profit is:

$$(d - C - a)^2/4 \qquad (15)$$

That is, *B*, assumed to enjoy a monopoly position in its territory, acts as a monopolist and chooses monopoly prices and quantities, *but based on a perceived cost (C + a) which is higher than the actual cost of a call (C + c)*. There is thus a double *marginalization problem* (loosely speaking, a form of 'externality,' similar to a sequence of punitive tariffs between sovereign countries).[15] Whenever *A* increases its termination charge *a* over the actual cost of termination *c*, it increases *B*'s *perceived marginal cost*, equal here to $C + a$, and therefore leads *B* to both increase its retail price (above the true monopoly level) and reduce the volume or quantity of its outgoing traffic. As indicated before, this equation measures *B*'s response to the termination rate set unilaterally by *A*. In the particular framework used here, any increase in *A*'s termination charge *a* is half-absorbed by *B* and half-passed through to the final consumers: An increase in *a* of 1€ would translate into an increase of the end user price for cross-border calls to *A*'s territory of 0.50€.[16]

Given *B*'s termination charge *b*, the Cournot equilibrium between *A* and the entrant can be analysed in a similar way to determine both *A*'s and the entrant's responses to the termination rate set unilaterally by *B*. I first characterize each operator's optimal reaction to the volume offered by the other operator. The intersection of the two operators' reaction functions then determines their market behaviour, in response to *B*'s termination charge.

Given the entrant's volume q_E, *A* chooses a price p_A or equivalently, given the relationship between price and demand, a volume of calls q_A so as to maximize its retail profit (given by the first term in equation (12) above):

$$A \text{ 'retail profit'} = q_A(d - q_A - q_E - C - b) \qquad (16)$$

Again, by taking the first derivative of the retail profit with respect to *A*'s output q_A, we find that *A* maximizes its retail profits when:[17]

$$q_A = (d - q_E - C - b)/2 \qquad (17)$$

That is, A acts as a monopolist on its residual demand, given the volume offered by the entrant. Similarly, the entrant chooses a volume of calls maximizing its own retail profit and given (reverting the roles of the two competitors) by:

$$q_E = (d - q_A - C - b)/2 \tag{18}$$

In equilibrium, the two competitors' outgoing traffic volumes are such that neither operator would have an incentive to change its output, taking both the other operator's output and B's termination rate as given. Therefore, the equilibrium in A's region is determined by a pair of quantities (q_A, q_E) that satisfy both conditions as set out in equations (18) and (19) simultaneously, which is:[18]

$$q_A = q_E = (d - C - b)/3 \tag{19}$$

Substituting the values from equation (20) into the demand function in equation (5) determines the retail price for outgoing calls from A's territory:

$$P_A = d - (q_A + q_E) = (d + 2C + 2b)/3 \tag{20}$$

and therefore, by substituting the result from equation (20) into equation (17), A's retail profit, and, by symmetry, the entrant's retail profit are each equal to:

$$(p_A - C - b)q_{operator} = (d - C - b)^2/9. \tag{21}$$

This equilibrium describes the prevailing price and quantities, and demonstrates again a *double marginalization problem*: Any increase in the termination charge b leads both operators in A's region to increase their retail prices – or, equivalently, to reduce their supply – which eventually leads to an equilibrium with higher prices and lower volumes. In particular, two-thirds of any increase in B's termination charge b are passed through to the end users.

Overall, the pre-merger situation is therefore characterized by the existence of double marginalization problems: To maximize its termination profit, each incumbent operator has an incentive to maintain a positive termination margin. This, in turn, leads all operators, which base their retail policies on the perceived cost of calls, to maintain high retail prices: These double marginalization problems lead the monopolist operator to charge a price higher than the true monopoly level in B's region and limit the effectiveness of competition in A's region.

c) *The impact of the double marginalization problem in the pre-merger environment* Having characterized each operator's market response to the termination charges set by the other operators, I now analyse the determination of those termination charges. I first consider a scenario where the two incumbent operators set their termination charges independently from each other, and show that this leads to high termination charges and, therefore, to exacerbated double marginalization problems. I then show that the incumbent operators have an incentive to mutually moderate their termination charges through a symmetrical, reciprocal termination charge (which I refer to as mutual moderation).

Consider first A's choice of termination charge. From the market responses derived above, A knows that an increase in its termination charge will be partly absorbed by B, and partly passed through to consumers. A now has to set its termination charge a to maximize its termination profit, which is given by the second term in equation (12):

$$A \text{ termination profit} = (a - c)q_B \tag{22}$$

Thus, A's termination profit depends on the amount of traffic that B carries its region and hands over to A for termination. However, we have previously determined that B's preferred quantity of cross-border traffic is itself a function of A's termination rate, given by equation (14). Combining equations (23) and (14) we therefore see that:

$$A \text{ termination profit} = (a - c)q_B = (a - c)(d - C - a)/2 \tag{23}$$

This equation takes into account the fact that an increase in the termination charge a generates a reduction in the volume of calls from B. A, who has a monopoly situation for termination in its region, thus faces a standard monopoly trade-off: It has to strike the right balance between increasing its termination margin $a - c$ (by increasing the termination rate a) and maintaining the volume of terminating traffic from B (q_B, which B reduces when facing higher termination charges). A attains this optimal balance (and the revenue profit is therefore maximal) for: [19]

$$a = (d - C + c)/2 \tag{24}$$

Similarly, in this scenario B sets its unilateral termination rate to maximize its termination profit, which we can obtain in terms of its termination charge b by combining its termination profit from equation (11) and the quantity responses by the operators in A's region given by equation (20):

$$(b-c)(q_A + q_E) = 2(b-c)(d-C-b)/3. \tag{25}$$

Again, this equation accounts for the fact that an increase in B's termination charge generates a reduction of the volume of calls serviced by both A and E; this revenue profit is again maximal for:[20]

$$b = (d-C+c)/2 \tag{26}$$

Given these termination charges, we can determine each operator's quantity of traffic by substituting the values given by equations (26) and (27) into equations (14) and (20). Similarly, we can determine each operator's profits by substituting the values from equations (14), (20), (26) and (27) into the profit functions given by equations (11)–(13). The respective traffic quantities q and total profits π for each operator are thus:

- for B: $q_B = (d-C-c)/4$ and $\pi_B = 11(d-C-c)^2/48$;
- for A: $q_A = (d-C-c)/6$ and $\pi_A = 11(d-C-c)^2/72$;
- for E: $q_E = (d-C-c)/6$ and $\pi_E = (d-C-c)^2/36$.

The analysis thus shows that, absent any mutual moderation, in a pre-merger environment both incumbent operators have an incentive to charge rather high termination charges in order to maximize their termination profit. The termination mark-up,

$$a-C = b-c = (d-C-c)/2, \tag{27}$$

is equal to *half* of the maximal surplus generated by a call (this surplus is the difference between the maximal consumer reservation price, equal here to the demand parameter d, and the actual cost of a call, $C+c$). Because double marginalization problems are important in this pre-merger environment, prices are high and volumes of traffic are low. In the absence of mutual moderation and assuming that the parties are setting their respective termination charges independently, B's volume of traffic would be *one fourth* of the competitive level, while the total outgoing traffic from A's region would be equal to one third of the competitive level.[21] In particular, in the pre-merger situation, due to the double marginalization problems, in both directions the *traffic would be lower than in a complete monopoly environment*.[22]

d) Mutual moderation in a pre-merger environment The double marginalization problem identified above, and in particular the fact that it leads to lower volumes of traffic than in a complete integrated monopoly setting, suggests that the incumbent operators have an incentive to mutually moderate their termination charges. This mutual moderation could take the form of reciprocal termination charges negotiated in a bilateral interconnection agreement, or could be achieved as well through tacit cooperation and a mutual understanding of the benefits of a reciprocal reduction of the termination charges. To analyse this issue, I consider below a scenario where A and B negotiate a *reciprocal termination charge t* (that is, $a = b = t$) and study what would be the optimal level of this reciprocal charge for each of the two operators.

Since the termination rates are now symmetrical and reciprocal, the two operators' profits are respectively given by (setting both termination charges to the same value, $a = b = t$, in the previous formulas):

- for B: $q_B(d - q_B - C - t) + (q_A + q_E)(t - c)$ (28)
- for A: $q_A(d - q_A - q_E - C - t) + (q_B)(t - c)$ (29)

For a given level of the reciprocal termination charge, the behaviour of the operators in response to a given termination rate is the same as determined in the previous section. B acts as a monopolist in its region; it therefore offers a quantity of outgoing traffic given by (replacing a with t in equation (14) above) $q_B = (d - C - t)/2$, and thus obtains a retail profit equal to $(d - C - t)^2/4$ (replacing a with t in the equation (16) above). On the other hand, by replacing b with t in equations (20) and (22) above we obtain that A's and E's quantity of outgoing traffic is $q_A = q_E = (d - C - t)/3$, and that their retail profits are each equal $(d - C - t)^2/9$. Therefore, substituting these new quantities in the profit function given by equation (29) above, B's total profit is given by:

$$(d - C - t)^2/4 + 2(t - c)(d - C - t)/3,$$ (30)

where the first term represents B's retail profit and the second term represents its termination profit. The optimal value of the termination charge for B must therefore take into account two aspects:

- as before, from the *termination business standpoint*, the level of the termination charge must strike a balance between increasing the termination margin (which advocates for a high termination charge) and maintaining an adequate flow of incoming traffic (which advocates instead for a low termination charge);
- but there is now another aspect, *retail business standpoint*: Any reduction in t reduces the perceived marginal cost of operating a call to A's region and thus increases B's retail profit.

In the pre-merger situation, this second aspect (the retail business standpoint) clearly ensures that the mutually moderated termination charge that is optimal for B is lower than what B would choose in the absence of mutual moderation (when the two operators were setting their termination charges independently from each other). This is confirmed by the analysis, which shows that, in order to maximize the above profit, B would now ideally choose $t = (d - C + 4c)/5$, that is, a termination margin of:[23]

$$(t - c) = (d - C - c)/5 \tag{31}$$

This margin under mutual moderation is much lower (more than half lower) than the previous equilibrium margin under double marginalization (which was equal to $(d - C - c)/2$), as shown in equation (28) above.

Similarly, A's total profits are given by substituting these new quantities in the profit function given by equation (30) above:

$$(d - C - t)^2/9 + (t - c)(d - C - t)/2, \tag{32}$$

where the first term represents A's retail profit and the second term represents its termination profit.

Again, in this pre-merger situation, in addition to the impact of the termination charge on A's termination profit analysed above, an increase of the reciprocal termination charge has also a negative impact on its retail business; as a consequence, A would now ideally choose $t = (5(d - C) + 9c)/14$, that is, a termination mark-up:[24]

$$(t - c) = 5(d - C - c)/14 \tag{33}$$

This termination mark-up under mutual moderation is also lower than the mark-up that would prevail in the absence of a reciprocal termination charge.

Therefore the two incumbent operators have an incentive to mutually moderate their termination charges: This co-operation or tacit understanding would lead to a reduction in the termination mark-up, from $(d - C - c)/2$ in a double marginalization environment (see equation (28) above) to somewhere between $(d - C - c)/5$ and $5(d - C - c)/14 \approx (d - C - c)/3$ (see equations (32) and (34) above), depending on the two operators' relative bargaining power.[25]

Thus, in the pre-merger environment, mutual moderation reduces double marginalization problems. Mutual moderation is not only good for the incumbent operators (since it benefits them directly), but also for the new entrant (who faces a lower termination charge) and for end users (who benefit from lower retail prices and therefore larger volumes of traffic). For example, if incumbents were to charge a reciprocal termination mark-up smaller than $(d - C - c)/4$, B's volume of traffic would jump to more than $q_B = 3(d - C - c)/8$ (by substituting this mark-up in equation (14) above), which is 150 per cent higher than what would occur in the absence of mutual moderation. Similarly, the total traffic outgoing from A's region would be higher than $q_A + q_E = (d - C - c)/2$ (by substituting this mark-up in equation (20) above), which is not only higher than what would occur in the absence of mutual moderation, but also higher than the level that would occur in the absence of any double marginalization (that is, an integrated single-margin monopoly, as shown below).

e) The impact of the merger The merger allows the incumbents to discriminate against the entrant, as the entrant is the only remaining operator who effectively incurs the termination mark-up. A payment of t from A to B is now an internal transfer within the firm, so that for both A and B the termination costs are the true costs c even if, formally, they keep paying the termination rates. In contrast, the entrant keeps paying the termination charge, which the incumbents have an incentive to maintain way above costs, and is therefore disadvantaged by facing the termination mark-up. In effect, the incumbents have now an additional incentive to maintain a high termination mark-up, as by so doing they raise their rival's cost (and can therefore attempt foreclosure). I show that in this framework the merged companies have an incentive to set the highest termination charge possible, to the point that the entrant is completely foreclosed from operating cross-border calls between the two regions. The intuition is straightforward – any increase in the termination rate leads the entrant to reduce its output, as its margins are squeezed, thereby softening the competitive pressure on A for cross-border traffic. A's business does not suffer as a result of the increased termination rate, as the merger has transformed it into a purely internal transfer rate. Similarly, the profitability of B's traffic into A's region is not affected by increases in the termination rate. Therefore, as all increases in the termination rate increase profits for the merged entity, up to the point that the entrant is driven out of the market.

To show formally that the incumbents indeed set their termination charge sufficiently high to eliminate any competitive pressure from the entrant, I first determine each operator's reaction market response to the termination rate t set by the merged entity. The total profit of the new merged entity is given by:

$$q_B(d - q_B - C - c) + q_A(d - q_A - q_E - C - c) + q_E(t - c) \tag{34}$$

Again, this profit can be interpreted as consisting of B's retail business (the first term, now independent of the termination charge as a result of the merger); A's retail business (the second term, which is not directly affected by the termination charge but indirectly benefits from the reduction in competitive pressures generated by a high termination charge); and B's termination business (now only based upon the entrant's traffic, since A's payment to B is no more than an internal transfer after the merger).

B and A will thus choose quantities of traffic $q_B = (d - C - c)/2$ and $q_A = (d - q_E - C - c)/2$ (obtained by setting $t = c$ in equations (14) and (20) above to reflect the de facto elimination for these two companies of the termination mark-up). The entrant's output decision rule is unchanged (as a function of the termination rate t), and given as before by $q_E = (d - q_A - C - t)/2$. In equilibrium, the volumes of traffic of the two operators active in A's region are therefore given by:[26]

$$q_A = (d - C - c)/3 + (t - c)/3, \tag{35}$$
$$q_E = (d - C - c)/3 - 2(t - c)/3. \tag{36}$$

These two equations represent each operator's market response to a given termination rate set by the merged entity. These equations show that the termination charge (which is only paid by the entrant) introduces an artificial cost disadvantage for the entrant. As a result, for a same level of the termination charge, the entrant's volume of traffic is lower than in the pre-merger situation.

To compute the merged entity's preferred termination charge, I examine its total profits as a function of the termination charge, which are given by (by substituting equations (14), (26) and (27) into equation (20) above):

$$(d - C - c)^2/4 + (d - C + t - 2c)^2/9 + (t - c)(d - C - 2t + c)/3, \qquad (37)$$

where the first term corresponds to the monopoly profits achieved on B's outgoing traffic, while the last two terms correspond to the retail and termination profits realized on B's incoming traffic.[27] The level of the termination charge that maximizes the new entity's profit is thus the one that maximizes the total profit realized on B's incoming traffic, both through retail (for A's traffic) and through termination (for E's traffic). It is straightforward to check that this is achieved for a termination charge equal to:[28]

$$t = (d - C + c)/2 \qquad (38)$$

This termination charge is exactly high enough to completely eliminate the presence of the entrant, as it implies that:

$$q_E = (d - C - c)/3 - 2(t - c)/3 = 0 \qquad (39)$$

In other words, the merged entity has an incentive to raise the termination charge up to the point where entry is no longer viable. In effect, increasing the termination charge 'raises rivals' costs' and thus reduces the competitive pressure from the entrant – and the merged entity has an incentive to increase this termination charge up to the point where those competitive pressures are completely eliminated. Note that this observation is particularly robust: It is independent from any assumption made on the form of the demand, on the common cost structure or on the nature of competition.[29]

The extent to which the new entity can raise its rivals' costs depends on the regulatory environment and on the various possibilities to operate calls from one country to another. For example, in the case of historical operators in neighbouring countries that would set prohibitively high settlement rates for terminating international calls, the entrant could try to build its own cross-border transport capacity and interconnect in the country of destination. However, it would still have to pay an interconnection charge for terminating its calls, and a similar analysis would thus apply. Furthermore, if termination charges were subject to an effective price cap, the incumbents may opt for alternative, non-price degradation strategies, and the thrust of the analysis would again apply, as briefly discussed below.[30]

f) Alternative degradation strategy Consider now the alternative case, where the merger does not affect termination rates (because of cost-oriented regulation, say) but the parties can degrade the quality of termination. To fix ideas, assume that termination charges are set equal to costs or slightly above them. I will now denote by a (for A) and b (for B) the termination cost plus the 'price equivalent' of the degradation of quality. In other words, the increment $(b - c)$ could be interpreted as the additional cost (over and above the termination charge) that the operators terminating their traffic in B's region must incur to maintain the quality of service.[31] A higher level of degradation a or b thus decreases volumes, although it does not generate higher revenues. As termination rates are set at cost, the operators' profits do not include a termination profit, and are therefore given by:

- for B: $q_B(d - q_B - C - a)$,   (40)
- for A: $q_A(d - q_A - q_E - C - b)$,   (41)
- for E: $q_E(d - q_A - q_E - C - b)$.   (42)

Before the merger, no incumbent gains from degrading termination, since doing so reduces volumes but does not generate any revenue. Therefore both a and b would be set to zero: A and B, each behaving individually, would not engage in anti-competitive degradation.

However, after the merger, the new entity has an incentive to degrade the termination of calls operated by the entrant because again doing so artificially 'raises the rival's costs': That is, degrading termination distorts competition between the new entity and the entrant, since it reduces the relative quality of the service provided by the entrant.

g) Summary of results – cross border competition Table 6.1 summarizes the relevant results from the analysis of cross-border competition for each of the cases examined. The merger allows the incumbents to foreclose their markets and eliminate any competitive pressures: By increasing the termination rate, the independent competitor is eliminated, relieving pressure on prices. While the incumbents benefit from the internalization of the termination charges,[32] the entrant is thus clearly hurt, up to the point where he is driven out of the market. Furthermore, provided that mutual moderation was sufficiently effective pre-merger ($t < (d-C + 3c)/4$), consumers in A's region are hurt by the merger, since the difference between the pre-merger termination rate and the lower true cost is fully appropriated by the merged entity, which moreover takes the opportunity of the reduced competitive pressure to raise its price.

Importantly, the model shows that 'efficiency gains' do not form a sufficient defence in this situation. While B and A do lower their costs and increase

Table 6.1   Effect of merger on cross-border services competition

	Pre-merger (Moderation: reciprocal termination rates)	Post-merger
Termination rate	$t - c < (d - C - c)/4$	$t - c = (d - C - c)/2$
Output		
B's region → A's region	$q_B < 3(d - C - c)/8$	$q_B = (d - C - c)/2$
A's region → B's region	$q_A > (d - C - c)/4$	$q_A = (d - C - c)/2$
	$q_E > (d - C - c)/4$	$q_E = 0$
	$q_A + q_E > (d - C - c)/2$	$q_A + q_E = (d - C - c)/2$
Prices		
B's region → A's region	$p_B < (5d + 3C + 3c)/8$	$p_B = (d + C + c)/2$
A's region → B's region	$p_A < (d + C + c)/2$	$p_A = (d + C + c)/2$
Effective competition		
A's region → B's region	Yes	No

their output as a result of the merger, this efficiency gain is appropriated by the producers and not passed on to consumers. The softening of competition in A's region allows instead the merged parties to increase their prices, therefore decreasing consumer welfare. Note that the model predicts a quite substantial increase in interconnection rates: As can be seen fromTable 6.1, the merged entity may have an incentive to increase the interconnection rate to the point that the termination mark-up rate is more than doubled, from $t - c < (d - C - c)/4$ pre-merger to $t - c = (d - C - c)/2$ post-merger.[33]

'Multinational' Customers Residing in both Territories

The merger will also affect competition for 'multinational' customers (MNCs) that are present in both territories.[34] It will both remove an effective potential competitor and also exacerbate the parties' incentive to degrade access, *both on termination and origination,* in order to reduce the competitive pressures from new entrants.

Elimination of most effective competitor A and B are in the best position to enter each other's market for serving the MNCs residing in both countries. Since each of them has control of end user access in its home territory, A needs access to B's facilities and conversely; hence, both parties have an incentive to negotiate a reasonable access to each other's facilities. No other operator is in the same position. Therefore, if one compares the comparative advantage of *A* and *E* in offering services to MNCs located in *A* and *B*'s territories:

- *A* has direct control of end-user access and the local loop infrastructure in its home territory, whereas *E*'s access will have to be negotiated with *A*;
- *B* has an incentive to enter into a reciprocal access agreement with *A* but not to with *E*, so that *A* will have easier access than *E* to end-users and the local loop infrastructure in *B*'s territory.

As a result, *E* is placed at a strategic competitive disadvantage for offering services to the MNCs located in both territories. Similarly, and for exactly the same reasons, *E* is a weaker competitor than *B* for the same services. Therefore, *A* and *B* are the most effective existing or potential competitors for those services, and the merger will eliminate one of these two most effective competitors.

Increased incentives to distort competition for MNCs Beyond the removal of one of the most effective competitors, the merger will give the parties increased incentives to degrade both origination and termination in order to distort the competition for MNCs. To see this, suppose that *E* offers two-way cross-border calls between the two territories, while the two incumbents offer cross-border calls only from their two home countries. MNCs located in both countries can then choose between two formulas: subscribing to *E* (customer located in *Y* and *B*) and subscribing both to *A* and *B* in their respective territories. In this context, the merger affects again the parties' ability and incentives to 'degrade' termination, as explained above, but in addition *it also affects the parties' incentives to 'degrade' origination*.

- *Degradation of termination.* Consider termination first. Before the merger, if *A* increases its termination rate in a non-discriminatory manner for all calls from *B*'s territory, it does not affect the choice offered to MNCs since both *E* and *B* will have to increase their tariffs from *B*'s territory to *A*'s territory. The same argument applies to non-discriminatory increases in *B*'s termination rate for calls from *A*'s territory to *B*'s territory. Therefore, while higher termination charges may lead to lower volumes and higher prices, they do not distort the competition for MNCs between the entrant and the two incumbents. Furthermore, *A* would not have any incentives to degrade the quality of its termination services.

    After the merger, an increase in either termination rate will instead distort competition, since only the entrant will be left facing this charge.

The merged firm does not pay termination rates to itself, while its competitors still pay these rates. As in the previous scenario, the merger both creates the ability to discriminate against competitors and increases the incumbents' incentives to raise or not to lower termination rates and otherwise degrade termination to distort competition for MNCs.

Similarly, the merger will create incentives for the merged entities to degrade the quality of termination for the calls originated by the entrant, using the same incentive mechanism as outlined in the previous section.

- *Degradation of origination.* Consider now the 'degradation' of origination, and suppose first that this 'degradation' consists in adjusting the origination charge that the entrant must pay to A and B. To fix ideas, suppose that all termination charges reflect costs, and denote by a the origination charge set by A and incurred by E for calls originating in A's territory, and by b the origination charge set by B for all calls originating in its own territory.[35] An increase in either incumbent operator's origination charge (or a smaller reduction than what would take place in a competitive situation) distorts competition for MNCs between the incumbents and the entrant: For example, if A increases its origination charge a, E will have to increase its price for all calls from A's territory, which tilts the balance in favour of the '$A + B$' combination. But this distortion of competition benefits B as well as A. That is, there is a spillover benefit to B when A raises origination charges in its home territory. Before the merger, A would not take into account this beneficial impact on B's position, whereas after the merger, it would take into account this impact and would thus have an additional incentive to set a high origination charge. The merger will thus distort competition for MNCs.

3   Intraterritory Competition

The merger will also affect competition in intraterritory services. First, for the same reasons as those developed above for MNCs, the merger eliminates an effective source of competition. Second, the merger increases the parties' incentives to degrade access to their facilities in order to distort competition in their own territories. I will analyse several scenarios, according to the type of competition under consideration; two issues are: (i) whether the entrant is offering intraterritory calls only (i.e., domestic calls in the case of European historical operators, or intra-LATA calls in the case of US ILECs) or both intra- and interterritory calls; and (ii) whether A (or B) is one of the entrants.

Elimination of Effective Actual or Potential Competitor

As already mentioned, *A* and *B* are in a good position to enter each other's market: Since each of them has control of the local loop in its home region, *A* can offer *B* access to its own facilities in exchange to *B*'s facilities and conversely.[36] To be sure, *A* and *B* still have little incentives to mutually create competition in their home markets; that is, even though each party has a strong bargaining position to enter the other's market, both may realize that there is little point for them to mutually compete with the other on both markets: a solution such as 'each one sticks to its own market' may appear more appealing and can be achieved, among other things, by maintaining high access charges for both. Still, several factors may posit those operators as effective sources of competition. First, both parties have even more incentive to foreclose access to other operators, who cannot offer a reciprocal advantage in the access to their own facilities; that, a US ILEC would have more incentive to cooperate with another ILEC than with a long-distance carrier that is not in charge of another local loop; similarly, the former monopolistic operator of one European country will be more open to cooperation with another former monopolist from another country, particularly if there is a large traffic between the two countries, than with an operator that cannot offer access to a local loop of interest. Second, assuming for example that operators offer similarly differentiated services, each incumbent might have an incentive to allow some limited entry (although at a rather high price), since the increase in the variety of services may generate additional business opportunities; however, for the same reason as above, the incentives to allow the entry of the other party (*B* for *A*, and conversely) would then be higher, other things being equal, than the incentives to allow the entry of any other operator. The merger may therefore eliminate an effective source of competition in the two parties' home markets.

Increased Incentives to Degrade Access to the Incumbent's Infrastructure

Beyond the elimination of an effective competitor, the merger increases the parties' incentives to degrade access to their facilities in order to distort competition in domestic telecom services. To see this, I first analyse here several scenarios where each merging party is supposed not to be a competitor in the other's market, and distinguish whether the entrant is offering national calls only or both national and international calls; finally I will discuss the additional motives for anti-competitive behaviour arising from the fact that one of the merging parties is already a competitor in the other's market.

The entrant offers regional calls only This scenario is illustrated in Figure 6.3a: both incumbents offer calls from their home region to both regions, while an 'entrant', different from *A* offers domestic telecom services in *B*'s territory. I will consider here the impact of a uniform increase (again the situation could be reluctance to lower fees) in *B*'s termination charge, which would affect *A* as well as the entrant, which can be interpreted in two ways. First, community-wide regulation may require that termination charges should be the same for all types of calls (e.g., national and international, or intra-Lata and inter-LATA); second, the 'termination charge' may instead refer to the price of leased lines and the interconnection charges that both the entrant and *A* have to lease from *B* in order to operate their calls in *B*'s territory.

Before the merger, a uniform increase in *B*'s termination charge increases *B*'s artificial advantage over the entrant in the competition for intraregion services (calls from *X* to *Y*), but it also harms *A*'s service to *B*'s territory (calls from *V* to *Y*). Such an increase in the termination charge would therefore be limited again (as for cross-border telecom services) by:

• the loss of revenue generated by the reduction of the volume of calls serviced by *A*;
• the possibility of negotiating a reciprocal moderation with *A*, to reduce double marginalization problems on cross-border calls.

The merger allows again the incumbents to:

• discriminate better: after the merger, only the entrant faces the termination charge or the degraded access conditions;
• increase *B*'s incentive to increase (or not reduce) the termination charge, since this in effect raises its domestic rival's cost (foreclosure) and no longer has an adverse effect on *A*'s volume of calls or *A*'s termination charges (that is, there is no scope for the two parties to agree to a mutual reduction in termination charges).

Therefore, the merger leads *B* to further increase its termination charges in order to distort competition in its home market. The same argument applies to each domestic competitor and applies 'twice' to competitors offering domestic telecom services in both regions. That is, if the entrant operates in both markets, the merger will increase each merging party's incentives to degrade access to its infrastructure and, as a result, the entrant will be placed at a competitive disadvantage in each of the two regions.

Similarly, if regulation constrains termination charges to be cost-oriented, then the merger would again exacerbate the incumbents' incentives to degrade the quality of termination. In both cases, the merger reinforces the new entity's incentives to degrade access to the local loop infrastructure in both regions.

The entrant offers both regional and cross-border calls In the previous scenario, the entrant suffers from a competitive disadvantage, since it does not offer cross-border calls. I therefore consider now the case where both the incumbents and the entrant offer calls to the two regions, as shown in Figure 6.3b. Then, even for one-sided entry (in B's region only), the merger affects *both* incumbents' incentives to raise (or not decrease) their termination charges and/or degrade termination.

As developed in the above section, the merger would again exacerbate B's incentive to raise (or not to lower) its termination charge or degrade termination, in order to raise its domestic rival's cost. Furthermore, as shown in the analysis of competition for cross-border calls, the merger would also create a willingness for A to 'raise the rival's costs' and would therefore foster A's incentives to raise (or not to lower) its own termination charge or to degrade termination.

The same argument applies again to each local competitor and applies 'twice' to competitors offering domestic telecom services in both regions (each incumbent would then have two reasons for increasing its termination charge or otherwise degrade termination). In all cases, the merger reinforces the merging parties' incentives to degrade access to their local loops.

A is one of the entrants I now consider the case where both the entrant and A have entered the B's market and offer calls to both regions (Figure 6.3c). In this case, before the merger, A would have an incentive to raise its termination charge (or degrade service to competitors) in its region in order to gain an advantage in the other region. For example, A would benefit when competing for the business of customer X, say, by being able to offer lower prices on calls from X to U). This incentive would be mostly mitigated by B's negotiation power, as B sets the termination charge for A's calls (both the cross-border calls such as those from V to Y and the intraterritory calls such as those from X to Y). The merger, however, removes this mitigation force.

Similarly, before the merger B would have an incentive to raise its termination fee (or degrade service) in its region in order to gain an advantage in the other market (by being able to offer lower prices on calls to its home territory). Again, this incentive would be strongly mitigated by A's negotiation

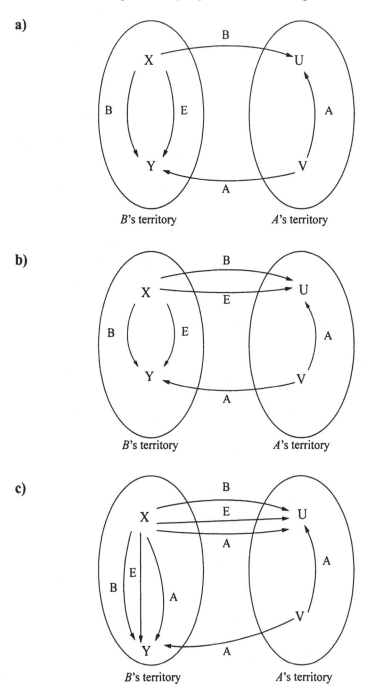

Figure 6.3   Three different hypotheses on cross-competition

power, as *A* sets the termination charge for *B*'s calls to *A*'s territory (for example, calls from *X* to *U*); and the merger would remove this mitigation force too.

Hence, in all instances, the merger exacerbates both incumbents' incentives to 'degrade' termination in their home territories; as a result, competitive pressures from new entrants would be weaker – *a*nd new entrants would have reduced incentives to invest and effectively enter the parties' home markets.

Notes

1   Since the 1984 break-up of ATT, the Baby Bells are restricted to offering local and long-distance communications services *within* their territories, and are prevented from offering long-distance calls outside these territories. Therefore, SBC can offer long-distance services in its territory, but cannot offer communications services within Ameritech's territory, of even from one territory to the other.

2   Another example is provided by mergers between cable TV operators.

3   This is not to say that these mergers cannot have positive efficiency-enhancing aspects as well. For instance, a merger between the local incumbents in two neighbouring countries such as Germany and Italy or Norway and Sweden may allow the new entity to internalize termination charges on cross-border traffic, thereby eliminating the risk of double-marginalization. However, for the sake of the presentation, I will focus here on the anti-competitive effects.

4   While efforts have been made on both sides of the Atlantic Ocean to liberalize the local telephony market, this assumption still constitutes a reasonable first-order approximation.

5   Katz and Salop (1998) offer a first exploration of the impact between ILEC mergers on their incentives to distort competition.

6   For example, the two countries could be Sweden and Norway, and the entrant could refer to operators such as Telenordia, Tele 2 or Tele Danmark, who compete with Telia on communications from Sweden to Norway.

7   I assume here that the termination rates cannot be discriminatory; that is, the termination rate set by A applies to all calls from country *B* to country A, and thus cannot be operator-specific.

8   These costs can be viewed on a per minute basis, although the model does not depend on the units used to measure these costs. It is convenient to analyse costs on a per-minute basis when dealing with circuit switch voice traffic, while other units may be more appropriate when analysing impacts on data traffic.

9   If *C* is interpreted as including origination costs, the true cost of a call would still be *C* (*origination and transport*) + *c* (*termination*). Also, the interpretation of 'transport' and 'termination' depend*s* on whether the operators' interconnection agreement. For example, in the case of international calls the operators can use a settlement regime (in which case 'termination' also covers transportation in the country of destination) or interconnect near the called party (in which case 'transport' covers transportation in the country of destination).

10 See Laffont, Rey and Tirole (1998a and 1998b), Armstrong (1998) and Dessein (1999) for detailed analyses of such two-way interconnection.

11 One way to describe the situation is to distinguish two divisions for each operator, one in charge of the retail business and one in charge of the termination business. Even if termination costs paid by the retail division to the other operator are to some extent compensated by the termination revenues obtained by the other division, the retail division will not charge a price below the perceived marginal cost of its subscribers' calls. Suppose for example that B's retail division adopts a final price p below $C + a$. Then, a small increase in the retail price p:

   • increases the revenue generated by each subscriber's call, which contributes to increase the profits generated by the retail division,

   • probably reduces the number of calls (or their duration), which is also good for retail profits since each call generates less revenue (p) than costs ($C + a$),

   • has no impact on the termination revenue or the profits generated by the termination division.

   Therefore, increasing p necessarily increases the profits of both the retail division and B; and this remains the case as long as the price p remains below the perceived marginal cost $C + a$. In particular, charging a retail price p close to the actual cost of a call, $C + c$, would generate less profits than a price equal to the cost effectively incurred for a call, $p = C + a$: moving B's retail price p from $C + c$ to $C + a$ would not affect the profits generated by B's termination division and would erase the losses generated by B's retail division.

12 The symmetry assumption is also made for exposition purposes and does not affect the thrust of the analysis. Also, note that while potential demand is symmetrical, actual traffic flows are not necessarily symmetric; For example, the model predicts (see below) that, other things being equal, a more competitive environment in one territory would lead to lower prices in that territory and a traffic imbalance from this territory to the other (of course, other factors such as the populations of the two regions, their calling patterns, etc., also affect the traffic balance).

13 The analysis would be similar under Bertrand competition (competition in prices without capacity constraints), but the Cournot assumption seems more realistic as it allows the incumbent operator to maintain some limited margin.

14 Note that B's volume of outgoing traffic, qB, has no impact on B's termination revenue, given by $(q_A + q_E)(a - c)$. Therefore, B's marketing policy is only driven by its retail cost and revenue. (If the price difference between the two regions becomes too large, some subscribers may start asking to be called rather than calling themselves, and some operators may offer 'call-back' services; To keep the analysis simple this is ignored here although it could be incorporated in a more detailed study. It would still be the case, however, that an increase in termination charges would lead the operators to increase retail prices.

15 The term 'double marginalization' refers *here* to the fact that *for each call,* the total margin (difference between the retail price and the actual cost of a call) is given by the sum of B's *retail* margin (difference between the retail price and the cost of a call for B) and A's termination margin (difference between A's termination charge and its termination cost). The addition of those two margins generates higher (and more inefficient) prices.

16 There would not be a double marginalization problem if any increase in A's termination mark-up was fully absorbed by a compression in B's retail margin. Unfortunately, this is highly unlikely: irrespective of the shape of the demand or the cost structure, firms have always an incentive to pass through some of their cost increases as long as the elasticity of their demand is not infinite; Furthermore, even if B was willing to fully absorb *some*

increase in A's termination charge, A would actually have an incentive to increase the termination charge up to a point where B starts passing-through to its customers some of the termination charge increase.

17   This is the same technique employed to determine B's optimal output described in note 16 above, with the only difference being that A's maximal margin is now reduced by the entrant's supply. A's retail profit is still of the form $q(m - q)$, where q represents A's volume, but the maximal margin m is now equal to $d - C - b - q_E$. However, the level of volume that maximizes A's retail profit is still such that $q = m - q = m/2$, with m appropriately redefined.

18   The market outcome is characterized by quantities qA and qE satisfying both $q_A = (d - q_E - C - b)/2$ and $q_E = (d - q_A - C - b)/2$. By symmetry, both volumes are equal and thus satisfy $q_A = q_E = q = (d - q - C - b)/2$ or $2q = d - q - C - b$, the solution to which is $3q = d - C - b$ or $q = (d - C - b)/3$.

19   This uses the technique employed to determine the optimal quantities *described* in note 16 above. To find the top of the bell curve described by the termination profit function, take the derivative of the termination profit with respect to a, which is given by $(d - C + c - 2a)$ *and represents the slope of the termination profit curve, as a function of the termination charge*. The highest point on the termination profit bell curve requires that *its slope to be horizontal and thus* the above derivative be equal to zero, and is therefore given by $a = (d - C + c)/2$.

20   B's termination profit in equation (26) is similar to A's termination profit in equation (24) except that is greater by a factor of 4/3. Therefore, the first derivative will also be identical, except for this scaling factor. As the maximum is achieved by setting the first derivative to zero, the solution for the termination rate that maximizes B's termination profit is symmetrical to that for A. The fact that both incumbent operators have the same optimal value for their respective termination charges is a coincidence due to the linear specification of the final demand. What is robust, however, is that both operators have an incentive to adopt high termination margins (although possibly different ones), thereby exacerbating double marginalization problems.

21   In the absence of fixed costs, the competitive price with free entry would be equal to the constant marginal cost of a call, $C + c$, and would generate a volume of traffic equal to $d - C - c$.

22   If a pure monopolist was servicing cross-border calls in both directions, it would seek to maximize the retail profits, equal in each country to $q(d - q - C - c)$, and would thus choose $q = (d - C - c)/2$, using the same maximization principles *as* set out in note 16 above.

23   Applying the same technique described in note 16, setting to zero the derivative of B's total profit with respect to t, which is $(d - C + 4c - 5t)/6$ and represents the slope of B's profit curve *as a function of t*, yields $t = (d-C + 4c)/5$. Subtracting c from both sides to cast this expression as a margin yields $(t-c) = (d-C-c)/5$.

24   Applying the same technique described in note 16, setting to zero the derivative of A's total profit with respect to t, which is $(5d - 5C + 9c - 14t)/36$ yields $t = (5d - 5C + 9c)/14$. Subtracting c from both sides to cast this expression as a margin yields $(t - c) = 5(d - C - c)/14$.

25   In any event, the difference between the two incumbents' ideal levels is small as compared with the desired reduction from the level that would prevail in the absence of mutual moderation.

26   The traffic quantities for A and the entrant can be rewritten as $2q_A = (d - C - c - q_E)$ and $2q_E = (d - C - t - q_A)$. Subtracting one from the other yields $(q_A - q_E) = t-c$, indicating

that the A will outproduce the entrant by a quantity exactly equal to the termination mark-up, as it exploits the relative advantage provided by the termination mark-up. Therefore, $2q_A = (d-C-c) - (q_A) + (t-c)$, which yields $q_A = (d-C-c)/3 + (t-c)/3$. The entrant's quantity is therefore $q_E = q_A - (t-c) = (d-C-c)/3 - 2(t-c)/3$.

27 This expression assumes that the entrant's traffic quantity is non-negative. Clearly, the lowest traffic quantity that will be provided by the entrant is zero.

28 Applying the same technique described in note 16, setting to zero the derivative of the combined entity's total profit with respect to t, which is $(5d - 5C + 5c - 10t)/9$ (as long as the entrant's traffic *yields* $t = (d - C + c)/2$. Further increases do not increase profits as the effect of driving the entrant out of the market has already been achieved.

29 As long as the entrant offers the same service and faces the same cost as the incumbents (or higher), the new entity's incentive is to completely prevent entry. If the entrant offers a differentiated service or faces a significantly lower cost, the incumbents may choose to let the new operator partially enter, thereby replacing some retail revenue with termination revenue; However, the new entity would still have an incentive to limit the extent of entry and the associated competitive pressures, as compared with the pre-merger situation.

30 Both price and non-price degradation policies constitute foreclosure strategies, where the incumbents raise rivals' costs and, at the same time, enjoy increased supra-competitive rents (these rents may take the form of higher prices, but also of lower quality of service, reduced innovation effort, etc.). Alternatively, the incumbents may adopt predatory strategies, consisting in maintaining low prices for some period, in order to squeeze the entrant (because of the termination charge, which is only paid by the entrant) out of the market, and enjoy afterwards the increased supra-competitive rents.

31 Alternatively, this could be modelled as the reduction in the consumers' willingness to pay, generated by the reduction in the quality of service. The analysis would indeed be the same if the degradation of termination was for example assumed to decrease the demand parameter d rather than to increase the operators' costs.

32 For example, the merger produces a decrease in prices from in B's region since by assumption no competition existed anyway before the merger and the retail prices are now set on the basis of the true cost of termination in A's region instead of the inflated pre-merger interconnection rate.

33 Even if considering the worst scenario for the pre-merger situation, the merging parties would still attempt to increase the termination mark-up from $t - c = 5(d - C - c)/14$ pre-merger to $t - c = (d - C - c)/2$ post-merger, which constitutes a 40 per cent increase.

34 These customers are truly MNCs when the incumbents are two countries' historical operators. In the case of US ILECs, they would include any large customer present in both ILECs' regions.

35 For the sake of presentation, it is assumed here that the entrant's customers pay the entrant, which then pays back the termination charge to the incumbent operator; The same analysis applies when the customer directly pays the origination charge to the incumbent operator and only the price of the long-distance cross-border call to the entrant: In that latter case, the incumbent operator could increase the origination charge and, at the same time, decrease by the same amount its own price for cross-border calls.

36 Various factors can affect the operators' bargaining position and their incentives to cooperate: the regulatory regime in place in each region (an operator benefitting from a laxer supervision will have greater bargaining power), the geographical situation of the two territories and the pattern of the calls between them, the business relationships of the operators – or of their shareholders – in other markets, etc.

References

Armstrong, M. (1998), 'Network Interconnection in Telecommunications', *Economic Journal*, 108, pp. 545–64.

Dessein, W. (1999), 'Network Competition in Nonlinear Pricing', mimeo.

Katz, M.L. and Salop, S.C. (1998), 'Using a Big Footprint to Step on Competition', mimeo, Comments of Sprint, CC Docket No. 98–141.

Laffont, J.J., Rey, P. and Tirole, J. (1998a), 'Network Competition I: Overview and Nondiscriminatory Pricing' *Rand Journal of Economics*, 29 (1), pp. 1–37

Laffont, J.J.,Rey, P. and Tirole, J. (1998), 'Network Competition II: Price Discrimination', *Rand Journal of Economics*, 29 (1), pp. 38–56.

Chapter 7

IPR-based Monopolies and Defensive Leveraging Strategies: Some Reflections on the Essential Facility Doctrine*

Alberto Heimler and Antonio Nicita

In recent years, a growing number of antitrust decisions, in Europe and in the US, has dealt with *ex post* monopolization or abuse of dominant position in industrial sectors characterized by IPR-based monopolies. These examples show that the overlap between antitrust and intellectual property laws is far from being resolved and some boundaries between the different provisions need to be traced. We show that an intellectual property right which generates a 'stable', distinct relevant product market, an IPR-based monopoly, might be classified as an essential facility. The idea that an intellectual property right may be viewed as an essential facility, challenges the optimal 'scope' of legal protection to be granted over an invention. The question addressed here is to what extent increasing the 'scope' of legal protection, by inhibiting third parties access to industrial applications of an IPR technology or input entails a defensive leveraging strategy rather than an efficient device to grant the right incentives to invest. Monopolization of potentially competitive downstream markets must thus be regarded as a way of impeding potential entry in upstream markets. In our concern this is why IPR-based monopolists often refuse to give access to their property rights in order to allow 'newcomers' exploiting rents coming form further industrial applications on the original IPR. Defensive leveraging strategies by the owner of an IPR-based essential facility might thus be the logical explanation for a refusal to deal when the access price is not regulated. By impeding access of a more efficient competitor on a potentially competitive market such a refusal to deal might thus be classified as anti-competitive. This means that downstream markets monopolization by an IPR-based monopolist, and thus the scope of the legal protection over his IPR, should be hindered due to strategic barrier to entry it generates on the upstream markets. However this conclusion puts new puzzles in our framework since it shows 'tragic' trade-off between right *ex ante* incentives to invest and *ex post* competition in the IPR-based market.

1   Introduction

In recent years a growing number of antitrust decisions, in Europe and in the US, has dealt with *ex post* monopolization or abuse of dominant position in industrial sectors characterized by a high degree of technological innovations. The great part of these decisions shares a common feature: dominant firms were charged of having performed exclusionary practices against competitors, by denying access to innovative assets protected by intellectual property rights. Some decisions can be interpreted as implying that those innovative assets are *essential facilities*, and the intellectual property rights over those assets as 'excessive', from an efficiency point of view (see Lipsky and Sidak, 2000; Cotter, 1999). In these cases access to these assets was considered necessary for other firms to compete in downstream (competitive) markets.

Indeed there is an overlap between antitrust and intellectual property laws (see also Pitofsky, 1997 and 2000; Valentine, 1996; De Santi1996). First of all, competition law and intellectual property law share a common objective: increasing social welfare by enhancing the degree of competition through the introduction of appropriate incentives to develop new product and new markets. However, competition law and intellectual property law differ in the instrument chosen to attain that goal: competition law is 'naturally' aimed at delimiting and preventing the exercise of restrictive conduct or abusive market power; intellectual property law is aimed at providing exclusive rights in order to preserve the incentive to create new products (and new markets). As a consequence, inherent in the application of intellectual property law is to protect an inventor from anybody exploiting his invention without his authorization. At the same time, however, intellectual property law meets competition principles, by granting the exclusionary powers only if a patent is filed, which implies widespread information on the characteristics of the new product in order to encourage and enhance competition. Since the market power originating from an IPR finds its origin in the law it would be a deep contrast if the aim of another law would be the elimination of that same market power.

Each time we have an intellectual property product, we face a possible *ex post* monopolistic configuration in the product market, which however, representing a premium for the *ex ante* risk, should be viewed as necessary for inducing R&D investment. At the same time, when the intellectual property has been already developed there is no (short-term) harm in reducing *ex post* profits. Such a puzzle reveals the well known trade-off between the development of *ex post* competition when a dominant firm possesses an essential facility and the protection of property rights in order to induce others to invest in competing facilities.

An essential facility is generally defined as an asset which is necessary in order to enter other competitive (downstream) markets at the minimum efficient scale. An essential facility must satisfy three conditions: i) it has to be essential (not substitutable) for entering competitive downstream markets; ii) it has to be not duplicable (costs subadditivity); iii) it has to be non-rival in consumption.

An intellectual property right which generates a 'stable' distinct relevant product market might be classified an essential facility, since it is: i) not substitutable; ii) not temporarily duplicable (given the legal protection over it); iii) not rival in consumption (the invention could be used by different operators to enter downstream markets).

The notion of essential facility has been used in antitrust practice to impose on the essential facility owner who operates also in complementary competitive markets to grant to competitors access to the essential facility (essential facility doctrine). Thus the essential facility doctrine is not necessarily a tool for eliminating monopoly positions associated with the use of the essential facility, but a way for impeding further monopolization by the essential facility owner of potentially competitive markets. In this sense the regulatory and antitrust conclusions reached with respect to infrastructure based essential facilities can be easily extended to IPR-based ones: access should be granted when the IPR-based facility is essential for entering a complementary market at the minimum efficient scale. As with more traditional essential facilities, also with IPR-based ones the problem is the pricing of access.

The idea that an intellectual property right may be viewed as an essential facility, challenges the optimal 'scope' of legal protection to be granted over an invention. The question addressed here is to what extent increasing the 'scope' of legal protection, by inhibiting third parties access to industrial applications of an IPR technology or input entails a defensive leveraging strategy rather than an efficient device to protect former monopolistic rents. According to this perspective, the refusal to access an essential facility might be viewed not just as a way to keep monopoly profits, or as a way of further monopolizing potentially competitive downstream markets. Rather, it might be regarded as a way of impeding potential entry in markets the development of which might by itself put into question the same monopoly on which the essential facility is based.

Indeed IPR-based monopolists often refuse to give access to their property rights in order to allow 'newcomers' exploiting rents coming from further industrial applications on the original IPR. This apparently irrational behaviour can be explained by defensive leveraging strategies And indeed, by impeding access of a more efficient competitor on a potentially competitive market such a refusal to deal may be anti-competitive. The pricing of access is the critical issue here and the problems are the same if the essential facility is infrastructure or IPR-based and if the essential facility is regulated or not.

In the following sections we briefly summarize the problem of the right incentive to invest in institutional contexts characterized by uncertainty, bounded rationality, asset specificity and contract incompleteness. Next we analyse the economics of essential facility and then turn on the comparison of the *ex ante* legal protection of information goods and the *ex post* efficiency of introducing competition in former monopolized markets, emphasizing the Schumpeterian trade-off between static and dynamic efficiency. We thus examine the rational for imposing obligations to allow access over an essential facility when intellectual property rights are involved and the problem of determining an appropriate price for access.

2   Incentive to Invest, *Ex Post* Competition and the (In)efficiency of Property Rights

As we know since the pioneering works by J.A. Schumpeter the process of innovation is always related to the expected appropriation of (temporary) monopoly rents generated by the adoption of the innovation. The existence of these monopoly rents in a product markets is the main incentive for competitors to enter the market by imitating the dominant firm. Such a process of creative destruction may differ from a market to another, according to level of expected rents, the uncertainty over the return of the investments and the legal protection of intellectual rights.

Legal protection of property rights solves two problems of incentive alignments: the well-known free-rider problem and the hold-up problem. The free rider problem regards the process of investor's rent expropriation by imitators, i.e. by opportunistic agents which replicate the innovative product at zero costs, as *information goods*, once made public, are perfectly known (Arrow, 1962). As a consequence, in the absence of any protection against imitators, no one will be induced to efficiently invest in information goods, and the under-investment choice will characterize a dominant position in the resulting Prisoner dilemma game shown in Figure 7.1. In the absence of legal protection against imitators, the investor will be induced to underinvest since

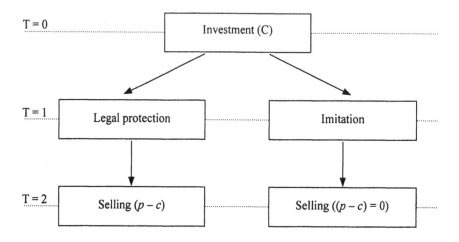

Figure 7.1   Standard free-rider problem

he will gain *ex post* only competitive profits (*P-C = 0*). By contrast, giving the investor a (temporary) property right over its innovation will compensate him for the expenses incurred in R&D and for the risks involved, delaying competition and imitation over time, to the extent it is necessary in order to implement the appropriate *ex ante* incentive to invest. In Figure 7.1 we assume that legal protection is ensured for n periods after the investment is selected, so that imitation can occur only at $t = N$ and competition in the market will be allowed at $t = N + 1$, where firm obtain normal competitive profits ($P - C = 0$). In Figure 7.2 the creation of competitive markets is delayed in order to allow the investor to cover the expenses (C) sustained and receiving the premium for the risk incurred. When legal protection is not attributed to the investor, the main consequence will not be greater competition and lower prices, but the absence of the new product.

Beside the free-rider problem, the *hold-up problem* provides some further rationale for property rights protection in vertically integrated production. The case of hold-up might be particular relevant when strategic complementarities are involved. Suppose that agent *A* has to invest in order to provide a widget (*x*) to agent *B*. Suppose that agent *A* has to make a specific investment, i.e. an investment which, once made, has a value higher than the next best alternative, only if the underlying transaction with agent *B* takes place. Due to contract incompleteness, agent *A* needs to be guaranteed against counterparts' threat of *ex post* renegotiation of contractual terms. In the absence of any contractual safeguards, agent *A* will be induced to underinvest, reducing hence social efficiency. According to Grossmann and Hart (1986) and Hart and Moore

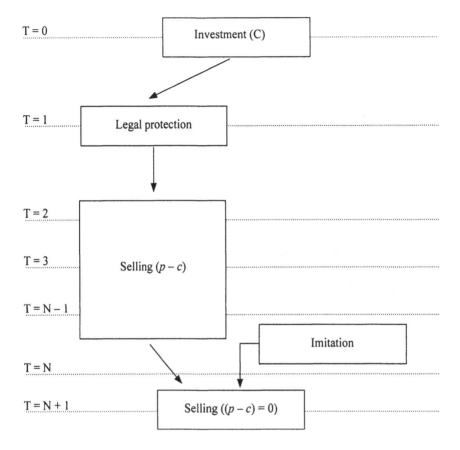

Figure 7.2   Legal protection for N periods against free-riding

(1990), giving the investor property rights over strategic physical assets, will increase the probability of contractual protection, restoring investors' incentives to efficiently invest and thus minimizing the risk of hold-up.

On these lines, Williamson (1985) has emphasized the efficiency role of vertical integration in order to induce specific investment within the firm, when, due to contract incompleteness, the market 'fails' in inducing appropriate investments. Both in the case of free-riding and hold-up the efficiency of property rights implies a reduction of *ex post* competition. However, the static losses associated with the reduction of short-term competition might be outweighed by dynamic efficiency induced by long-term competition.

While property rights are efficient in solving free-riding and hold-up problems, they can also lead to a number of inefficiencies that are mainly addressed by regulators and by antitrust enforcers. Economic regulation impedes (natural) monopolists from gaining monopoly profits, eliminating

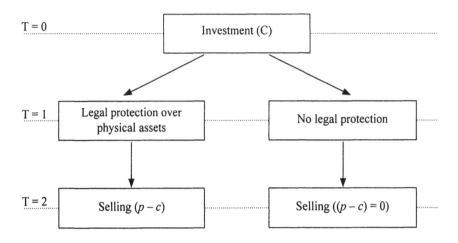

Figure 7.3   Standard hold-up problem

deadweight losses originating from monopoly power. Antitrust laws are also concerned with market power, but these laws do not have the objective of strictly controlling market power by authoritative rules such as, for example, the setting of the 'right' price of different goods and services. Antitrust provisions (with the exception of those about mergers) aim at impeding that companies through restrictive practices or abuse of dominant positions increase artificially their market power.

However, antitrust interventions are particularly difficult for information-based sectors where the owner of a commodity is not always able to exclude others from using it and once a product is on the markets it costs the same irrespective of the number of people that consume it. Both non-excludability and non-rivalry are characteristics of public goods and of market failure.

As for excludability, it does not exist in nature. It is the consequence of our civilization and of law and order. In fact in order to exclude others from exploiting our property not only laws are needed, but also that they are efficiently enforced. What characterizes the information based industry is another peculiarity: The inherent technical difficulty of exclusion which is independent from the existence of any legal protection. For example broadcast television can be consumed by everybody that has a TV set and an antenna. This is why broadcast TV had to find someone else (advertizers) to pay for its services. The development of pay TV was a way to introduce excludability to this market.

Information based products are also generally not rival in consumption in the sense that the product costs the same irrespective of the number of consumers. If the forces of competition would lead prices to fall down to marginal costs, prices would be very close to zero and all producers would get bankrupt, not being able to cover their fixed costs.

Because of non-excludability and non-rivalry information markets are naturally characterized by market failures. However, contrary to what happens with more traditional economies where non-excludability and non-rivalry originates only with public goods and the most natural solution is government supply, information based products continue to be supplied by the market, but ingenuous solutions, like shareware or dual-track products, are found in order to somehow ensure the coverage of costs. However until some form of strong excludability is found the market cannot be stable. And indeed much of technical progress in information technology industries is directed to find ways to guarantee excludability.

Complex governance structures, long-term contracts, IPR and competition laws, emerged in modern capitalistic society in order to deal with the problem of providing optimal *ex ante* incentives alignments so as to increase social welfare. The essential facility doctrine has tried to give a specific answer to the governance of assets which are indispensable for entering downstream markets and are controlled by an integrated monopolistic owner.

3   The Economics of the Essential Facility

The problem of mandatory access to an essential facility falls into the broad area of vertical relations and into the debate about whether antitrust law should intervene in order to guarantee access, which in turn centres around the question of leveraging, that is the possibility that a monopolist 'leverage' its monopoly power in one market in order to extend it into another market. It originally seemed obvious that this was so, a view held in particular by Joe Bain and the Harvard School of the 1950s. Such a common understanding was forcefully put into question by the so-called Chicago Revolution of the 1980s which proved that a firm that has monopoly power at one level can only transmit that same monopoly to another level, but not create more monopoly power than it already has. In this perspective vertical restrictions cannot aim at increasing a 'fixed sum' monopoly profit and therefore, as a matter of logic, should be explained by some other reasoning which it was shown in many cases to be greater efficiency.

Suppose that a private monopolist owns the only possible bridge across a river and that a number of competing railroad companies provide transport services along the bridge. Suppose also that there are no restrictions in the pricing for the use of the bridge (the only restriction is that prices should be linear), nor for transport service charges. In order for the owner of the bridge to gain monopoly profits, he has to charge all railroads a monopoly price to cross. The greater the competition downstream and the lower the profits downstream, the greater the profits the bridge owner would get. Suppose that the bridge owner also owns a railroad company that is providing transport services across the bridge in competition with other railroad companies. His behaviour would not change since all the profits that he could make still depend upon his bridge monopoly: He would continue to charge a monopoly price to everybody. How then would a refusal to grant access be explained? One possibility is that the owner of the bridge might not be able to capture all rents by simple linear pricing, because of double marginalization problems. He might have to use a two part tariff, where the fixed part would be exactly equal to the profit of the downstream firm. Total profits downstream, however, would depend on the structure of the downstream market and be maximized when such a market is a monopoly. As a consequence the bridge monopolist may refuse to deal with competitors in order to remain the only railway company that crosses the bridge and be able to capture all the monopoly profits originating from the bridge. He might reach the same result by auctioning away the right to cross the bridge to the highest bidder. For the consumer it would not matter if the essential facility owner operates downstream or not. In both circumstances he would pay a monopoly price for crossing the bridge.

There has always been a debate on the 'expropriating' role of a mandatory access regime. Indeed, if an essential facility owner is not allowed the possibility of excluding others from exploiting his facility and there are no capacity constraints, all his profits would be reduced to zero: nobody would pay for something everybody has. Indeed with an essential facility, profits arise from the rights to exclusively exploit it. If the facility is made available to everybody its value drops to zero.

As a consequence an IPR owner, who does not face any capacity constraint in granting the use of his IPR, would need always to grant exclusive use of his right if he wants to maximize profits. Following Coase (1972), should the buyer of the services of an upstream monopolist not be assured that the use of his property would not be also given to someone else, he would not be willing to pay for its use a fee equal to the monopoly profits he can gain in the downstream market. In fact, if the possibility of contractual exclusivity is ruled out, the upstream property owner, after having sold the use of his property to one customer in exchange for his monopoly profits, would have the incentive to sell it to others as well, but at prices below the monopoly level. The fear of losses on the part of its first potential customers would make them choose to delay their purchase and such a strategy would impede the upstream monopolist from gaining monopoly profits at all. At the limit, if the services associated to the upstream property could be supplied without any quantitative limit, should it be for example an intellectual property right, the price buyers would be willing to pay (in the absence of exclusivities) would be driven down to zero and all monopoly profits would be dissipated.

If, as in Coase (1972), D in Figure 7. 4 is the demand curve for the use of an essential facility needed in fixed proportions in the production of some other good and q_c is the maximum capacity the property can be put at use, then an upstream monopolist would first sell the profit maximizing quantity q_m at the price p_m. He would then be left with an unused capacity equal to $q_c - q_m$, that he would be willing to sell at any positive price lower than p_m. The first buyer knowing the existence of such an incentive would never accept to purchase q_m at the price p_m in the first place and the equilibrium price for the use of the essential facility would be p_c, where its full capacity is utilized. With the same line of reasoning, if the upstream property is a patent, some other intellectual property right or a franchise the total quantity of which is

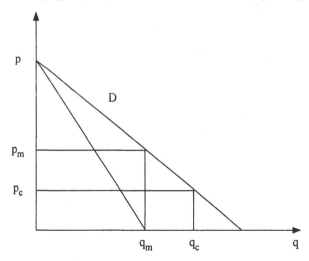

Figure 7.4   Demand curve and marginal revenue for an upstream monopolist

not physically limited, then, without the possibility for the owner of the right to engage in some exclusionary conduct, the equilibrium price would be zero and the total quantity demanded would be q (Figure 7.1).

Certainly the possibility for an upstream monopolist to engage in such an opportunistic strategy is higher the greater the length of the contract. At the limit if the contract is made once and for all (pure durable good), a very strict contractual exclusivity (with high penalties if the upstream monopolist would not comply) will be necessary in order to assure the buyer that the services associated to the upstream property will not be sold to other users at lower prices (see Stokey, 1981 and Butz, 1990). Without such an exclusivity clause the upstream monopolist would never be able to gain his monopoly profits because everyone would refuse to purchase at prices above the competitive level.

On the other hand, should contractual arrangements be valid only for very short periods of time, which is possible when what is sold is a perishable service, pricing would adjust to actual market conditions and this would make it much more difficult for the upstream monopolist to engage in opportunistic practices. He would sell the monopolistic quantity at the monopolistic price and would not sell any additional quantity, because otherwise his reputation as an unfair trader would make it more difficult for him to trade again at profitable (monopolistic) prices in the future. In any case opportunistic practices would not always be to the monopolist advantage in the case of vertical integration, that is if the owner of the facility would himself operate as a monopolist in the downstream market.

The importance of Coase (1972) analysis for the essential facility doctrine is that exclusivities are necessary for the essential facility owner to gain all the profits associated with the use of the essential facility. Coase (1972) also shows that exclusivities are to the advantage of both the buyer of the essential facility services and the supplier. In fact by just eliminating the possibility of contractual exclusivities profits originating from the use of the essential facility may disappear.

4   Essential Facility Doctrine, Mandatory Access and Efficient Pricing

In the United States the main characteristics of antitrust decisions concerning the imposition of a duty to deal with competitors on the part of firms controlling an essential facility have been as follows (see Tye, 1987): a) control of the facility by a monopolist or a group of competitors with monopoly power; b) the inability practically or reasonably for the foreclosed competitor to duplicate the facility or its economic function; c) the denial of use of the facility or the imposition of restrictive terms with the consequence of substantial harm to competition in a relevant market in which the monopolist competes (or would be forced to compete absent the discriminatory practice); d) the absence of a valid business reason. From this definition it is quite clear that a facility is considered 'essential' by US courts only if the services it can provide belong to a relevant market (no duplicability at reasonable costs) controlled by a monopolist. At the same time, the behaviour of the essential facility owner is deemed abusive only insofar as it affects substantially the competitive conditions of the downstream market.

In the European Union the notion of essential facility has been utilized mostly with respect to legal monopolies that tried to extend their dominant position to complementary competitive markets. As a consequence in most of the relevant decisions no explicit reference was given to the possibility (or the cost) of duplication of the facility or to the competitive conditions characterizing the downstream market. Furthermore the reasons considered 'objective' in cases of refusal to access to a legal monopoly have included for the EC only technical feasibility (such as the lack of unused capacity) or compliance with public interest objectives imposed upon the owner of the facility. Only recently the European Court of Justice gave a rigorous interpretation of an essential facility in a case where the owner of the facility was not protected by any special and exclusive right (legal monopoly) (European Court of Justice, 1998; see also Hausman and Sidak, 1999). In that case the court gave a definition of essential facility so rigorous that it would be almost impossible to apply. Indeed the court, denying that Mediaprint, a dominant Austrian newspaper publisher, should give access to its national distribution network (essential facility) to Oscar Bronner, a small newspaper publisher, said that a facility is essential when it is not economically viable to duplicate the facility by an entrant with the same size of the incumbent. The problem with this definition is that there are very few industries where a facility could not be duplicated by a new entrant of the size of the incumbent. Furthermore the new entrant may never reach that scale, while at the minimum efficient scale of operation the duplication of the facility would not be economically viable.

In any case, in the antitrust experience of the US and of the EC, the essential facility doctrine does not introduce a generalized mandatory access regime. The essential facility doctrine introduces a further qualification and that is that access should be granted to competitors wishing to enter complementary markets. This means that profits related to the use of an essential facility are not put into question. The objective of the essential facility doctrine is to grant access to competitors in the complementary market that are more efficient than the incumbent, not necessarily to reduce the profits originating from the use of the essential facility itself.

The essential facility doctrine has not addressed the question of pricing. This is a separate issue which has recently been dealt quite extensively in the literature. According to the efficient component pricing rule (ECPR), proposed by Willig (1979), Baumol and Willig (1995) and Baumol and Sidak (1994), an essential facility owner that operates also in a complementary market would maintain his profits if he would be free to price access in such a way as to charge its competitors the opportunity cost of new entry. If p is the price that the essential facility owner charges for the services sold in the complementary market, it would grant access if the new entrant would be willing to pay a sum equal to $p - c$, where c is the marginal cost saved by the essential facility owner because of entry. The behaviour of the essential facility owner would be profit maximizing. Entry would occur only if the new entrant, being able to produce with lower marginal cost, is more efficient than the incumbent.

ECPR by itself does not eliminate dominant positions originating from the essential facility. This is why in order to be used as an instrument for regulating monopoly power ECPR should be supplemented by some other tool aimed at reducing monopoly profits. Indeed if p, the price that the essential facility owner charges for the services sold in the complementary market is regulated, ECPR, as a rule for identifying access charges, would still apply. If the price in the complementary market is regulated, ECPR, more than a regulatory device is an effective instrument for identifying price abuses, a widely denounced antitrust violation, but a difficult one to prove. Under an antitrust perspective, ECPR is the highest price a monopolist is allowed to charge for granting access. Any price above the ECPR would be 'excessive' and should be considered an abuse. If the new entrant has the same costs as the incumbent any price above the ECPR would be exactly equivalent to a refusal to deal and there would be no entry. On the other hand a competitor more efficient than the incumbent would enter also at access prices above the ECPR. The incumbent could in fact profit from the greater efficiency of a new entrant and, instead of charging an access price equal to $p - c^i$, where c^i is the cost the incumbent avoids because of entry, would charge an access price equal to $p - c^*$, where c^* is the cost of the new entrant and $c^* < c^i$. The incumbent by charging an access price equal to $p - c^*$ would gain from the efficiency of the new entrant and would impede that efficiency gains be transmitted to the consumers. This point leads us to pose the following questions:

a) why an owner of an IPR-based essential facility would refuse to deal with downstream competitors instead of charging a price which would reflect at least ECPR;

b) why and when such a refusal to deal should be judged as anti-competitive.

In the next section we try to give a tentative answer to both questions. What is important here to remind is that ECPR, at least for access to a vertically integrated essential facility, solves the question of identifying the 'right' price, a problem antitrust authorities have been struggling with for many years without actually finding a suitable solution.

In all these cases mandating access is therefore the right solution and the ECPR the maximum price that would keep with the essential facility owner profits originating from the use of it. Indeed when the essential facility is IPR-based the essential facility doctrine, exactly as it is for infrastructure based essential facilities, would imply that access to the essential facility should be granted when it is indispensable for entering into a competitive complementary market.

In such cases the ECPR would not eliminate profits originating from the IPR itself. For example, if a pharmaceutical patent is an essential facility and the owner of the patent also operates as a producers of the drug based on that patent, the essential facility doctrine would imply that any producer of pharmaceuticals should be granted access to the patent. The access price, according to the ECPR, would be $p_j - c_j$, where p_j is the price of the drug and c_j is the cost of production of the drug that the patent owner avoids. A competing producer would enter only if he is more efficient than the incumbent who will in any case continue to earn all the profits associated to the patent.

Of course, if the complementary product is non-rival the avoided cost in the ECPR formula is zero and the new entrant would have to pay the price of the full bundle for the use of the IPR-based essential facility. In theory the major problem with pure non-rival goods is that the marginal cost is zero and there is no way one can be more efficient than that. As a consequence the application of the ECPR to the case of non-rivalry would require a qualitative improvement on the part of the new entrant such that the price of the combined bundle would be greater than p. For rival goods, efficiency requires that entry is accommodated only if the new entrant produces the competitive good at lower costs than the incumbent. For non-rival goods, efficiency requires that the new entrant provides to consumers greater benefits than the incumbent.

5   Optimal Patent Policy, Splintering and Defensive Leveraging

To what extent increasing the 'scope' of legal protection, by inhibiting third parties access to industrial applications of an IPR technology or input, entails a defensive leveraging strategy, aimed at maintaining monopolistic rents in upstream markets, rather than an efficient device to grant the right incentives to invest? Answering this question is very important in order to properly understand the intersection of antitrust and intellectual property.

D'Aveni (1994) and Besanko et al. (1996) show the relationship between time and economic profitability of an innovation. In Figure 7.8a, economic profits rise as the advantage against competing products is developed. Monopoly rents are extracted until an effective substitute comes along and/or expiring date of IPR become closer. One way of impeding erosion of competitive advantage due to imitation and/or expiring date of legal protection over an innovation, is to introduce a new innovation, say *A2* (next generation product or upgrading and updating of existing products), and to start a new development advantage so as to shift customers to a new product protected by IPR legislation, as in Figure 7.8b.

As already mentioned, these monopoly profits can be gained when the downstream market is competitive or, should the downstream market not be competitive, when the monopolist is allowed to use two part prices. However, it is very often the case that IPR-based essential facility owners refuse to deal with competitors in downstream markets. One possible reason for such refusals to deal is that dealing with potential competitors in downstream markets, may allow such competitors, in the medium-long run, to have access to information, knowledge, customers, technology, which in turn may allow them to expand their activity from downstream markets to upstream markets, and thus enabling them to threat upstream monopolistic rents earned by the owner of the essential facility.

In network industries, as in all industries characterized by a relevant degree of vertical integration between upstream and downstream markets, entry generally occurs only in a portion of the network ('splintering'), by licensing or imitating a dominant product or by introducing a generic or lower-end version. As Feldman (1999) has pointed out splintering may harm monopolist's long-term rents: 'entrants in the splintered market are poised to become successful competitors in the broad market'. In this case, entrants in a portion of the market may increase the scope of their economic activity by extending their investment at the upstream level or by promoting forms of backward vertical integration with former competitors of the upstream monopolist.

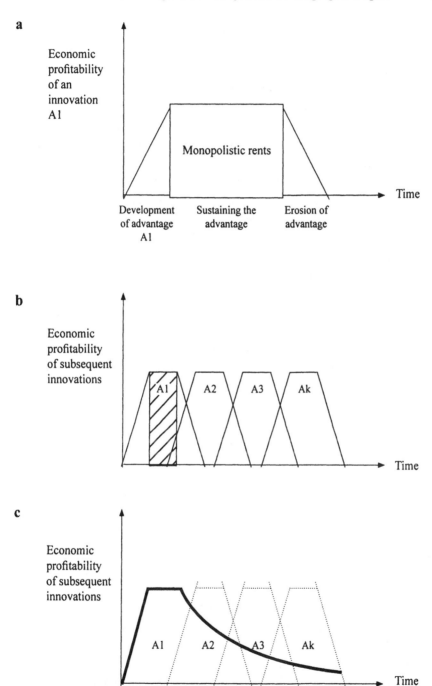

Figure 7.5 **Economic profitability under different hypotheses of innovation**

This means that when giving access to an essential facility the probability that successful splintering occurs may increase and this in turn would threat monopolist market power. In Figure 7.8c we show a possible consequence of 'backward competition' by successful entrants in the splintered market. Suppose, in Figure 7.8b, that after the first innovation, *A1*, is introduced by the owner of an IPR, who does not refuse to deal with downstream competitors, entrants in the downstream market are able to introduce a lower-end version of the input protected by an IPR. This means that a portion of the monopolistic rent earned by the former monopolist is now shared with these newcomers. Suppose that, due to economics of learning, as new innovations are introduced by the former monopolist, imitation by new entrants becomes stronger until monopolistic rents are entirely dissipated. Refusal to deal by the owner of the essential facility might thus be viewed as a rational strategy by the owner of the facility in order to deter potential entry in upstream markets ('defensive leveraging').

In certain circumstances also patent scope and the length of patent protection may help the monopolist in defending his market power. However the enforcement role of patent rights as effective deterrence device against potential competitors in upstream markets, strictly depends on the degree of competition in downstream markets. In order to properly assess this point we need first to briefly analyse the determination of optimal patent scope and length of protection.

Following Gallini (2002), the broader is the scope of the innovation protected by the patent system, the higher is the costs of imitation. Optimal patent scope is thus defined as sufficiently broad to raise the cost of imitation, whereas an optimal patent length is defined as sufficiently short to discourage imitation at that scope.

Consider Figure 9.9. Patent policy F is defined by the pair (T, C), where T is patent life and K is patent breadth measured by imitation costs. For imitation cost, K, $T^K(C)$ is the critical patent life that triggers imitation (derived from the zero-profit entry condition), with $k = 0, 1, 2, ...N$. For $T^* = T^K(C)$ there is no imitation and the return to the innovator increases in patent life.

However, for $T > T^K(C)$, entry keeps the return to the innovator constant at K. The return to innovator is shown for three levels of C, where $C^1 < C^2 < C^*$. If, for example, the innovator faces an investment cost of C^*, optimal patent policy would be a 'scope' implying an imitation cost of C^* and a patent life of $T^{K+2}(C^*)$, as shown in Figure 9.9.

As a consequence, this approach implies that optimal patent scope is set sufficiently broad to raise the cost of imitation (C^*) and patent length is set sufficiently short (T^*) to discourage imitation at that scope.

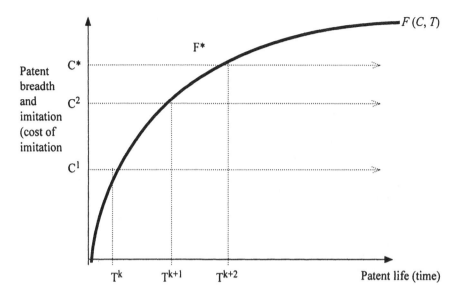

Figure 7.6   Optimal patent policy (breadth and time length)

In Gallini's analysis, the determination of optimal patent policy neglects the externalities originating from downstream markets to the upstream market of the patented innovation. In order to show how the determination of the optimal patent policy depends also on the degree of competition in downstream markets we assume that it is possible to draw alternative patent policies F^1, F^2, F^3, indexed according to an indicator of the degree of competition in downstream market, assuming that H^1, indicates a market with a competition degree higher than H^2.

As we can see from Figure 7.10, introducing the degree of competition in downstream markets may affect, for given imitation costs, the effective life of a patent. We assume that as the degree of competition in downstream markets, increases also the probability of splintering and entry in upstream markets. In Figure 7.10, shifting from F^3 to F^1 decreases the life time associated with the innovation C^1.

The main consequence thus is that the scope of an imitation also produces its effects on downstream markets, i.e. on the market characterized by the industrial applications over the IPR-based essential facility. Entry in these downstream market is not a matter of imitation, rather a matter of developing industrial application in new (potentially) competitive markets.

The analysis above illustrates why the owner of an essential facility might be induced to refusal to deal with downstream competitor, even if the

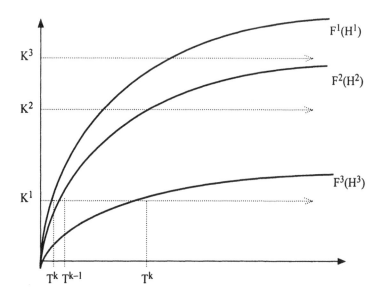

Figure 7.7   Optimal patent policy with 'backward competition'

monopolist could be able to extract all of its monopoly profit by setting a proper selling price. The monopoly holder may fear that competitors entering the complementary market may become stronger competitors also in other contiguous markets because of existing economies of scale and scope, weakening his market position in these markets as well. Also, competitors in the complementary market may develop skills and competence to become effective competitors also in the essential facility market, trying to bypass the original monopoly of the incumbent.

According to this perspective, the essential facility doctrine might be viewed not just as a tool against monopoly positions, or as a way of impeding further monopolization of potentially competitive downstream markets. Rather, it must be regarded as a way of inducing potential entry in upstream markets, from which downstream monopolization is generated. Indeed IPR-based monopolists often refuse to give access to their property rights in order to allow 'newcomers' exploiting rents coming form further industrial applications on the original IPR. Defensive leveraging strategies by the owner of an IPR-based essential facility might thus be the logical explanation for a refusal to deal when the access price is not regulated. By impeding access of a more efficient competitor on a potentially competitive market such a refusal to deal might thus be classified as anti-competitive. This means that downstream markets monopolization by an IPR-based monopolist, and thus the scope of the legal protection over his IPR, should be hindered due to strategic barrier to entry it generates on the upstream markets.

Defensive leveraging represents a further explanation for a refusal to deal by an essential facility owner when the access price is not regulated. Therefore ECPR does not eliminate the 'tension' between antitrust and IPR protection. The purpose of impeding access is not short-term profit maximization that ECPR ensures. Indeed, by impeding access of a more efficient competitor on a potentially competitive market, the essential facility owner impedes competition on the essential facility market itself.

6   Conclusions

Some recent antitrust decisions have dealt with the strategic use by a monopolist of an intellectual property right, defined as an essential facility, in order to deter competitors' entry. Dominant firms, such as Microsoft and Intel, were charged of having performed exclusionary practices against competitors, by denying access to innovative assets protected by intellectual property rights. We have argued in this chapter that the essential facility doctrine is a tool for granting access, not an instrument for eliminating monopoly profits originating from the essential facility. There are other instruments to achieve that. In this perspective it has to be acknowledged that especially for IPR-based essential facilities a complete liberalization' of intellectual property rights will destroy the emergence of new market rather than introducing competition in new markets.

An essential facility is generally defined as an asset which is necessary in order to enter other competitive (downstream) markets at the minimum efficient scale. For this asset being an essential facility is must satisfy three conditions: i) it has to be essential (not substitutable) for entering competitive downstream markets; ii) it has to be not duplicable (costs subadditivity); iii) it has not to be rival in consumption.

An intellectual property right which generates a 'stable' distinct relevant product market might be classified an essential facility, since it is i) not substitutable; ii) not temporarily duplicable (given the legal protection over it); iii) not rival in consumption (the invention could be used by different operators to enter downstream markets).

The idea that an intellectual property right may be viewed as an essential facility, imposing an access obligation on the owners when they operate also in complementary markets, should not lead to the elimination of the market power associated with its exploitation. In order to control for supranormal profits some other instruments (regulatory or antitrust) are needed. The essential facility doctrine is not the tool to be used for eliminating monopoly profits, but a way of impeding further monopolization of potentially competitive markets.

The efficient component pricing rule identifies the proper price for access without considering the problem of eliminating monopoly profits originating from the use of the facility and indeed the method is neutral with respect to the level of profits that the incumbent receives. The ECPR is particularly important when the essential facility is IPR-based and is not price regulated. In fact the utilization of the ECPR would not contradict the objective pursued by the IPR, that is to guarantee *ex post* profits in order to provide the right incentives for *ex ante* R&D investments. The ECPR does not break down when the market for which access is needed is characterized by non-rival products. It is true that avoided costs in the case of non-rival goods are zero, but the ECPR would still be used and a new entrant would pay the full price of the bundle to the incumbent $(p - 0)$. This implies that entry will occur only if the new entrant's bundle is valued by the consumer more than that of the incumbent.

Why, thus, such a rule is not generally followed by owners of IPR? One possible explanation is defensive leveraging, that is the strategy of keeping competitors out downstream in order to protect monopolistic profits upstream.

References

Arrow, K. (1962), 'Economic Welfare and the Allocation of Resources to Invention', in R. Nelson (ed.), *Rate and Direction of Inventive Activity: Economic and Social Factors*, New York: Arno Press.

Baumol, W.J. and Sidak, J.G. (1994), *Toward Competition in Local Telephony*, Cambridge, MA: MIT Press.

Baumol, W.J. and Willig, R. (1995), 'Notes on the Efficient Component Pricing Rule', paper presented at the Montreal Conference on Regulated Industries.

Besanko D., Dranove, D. and Shanley, M. (1996), *The Economics of Strategy*, New York: John Wiley and Sons.

Butz, D.A. (1990), 'Durable-good Monopoly and Best-price Provisions', *American Economic Review*, 80, pp. 1062–76.

Coase, R.H. (1972), 'Durability and Monopoly', *Journal of Law and Economics*, 15, pp. 143–9.

Cotter, R.N. (1999), 'Intellectual Property and the Essential Facility Doctrine', *The Antitrust Bulletin*, Spring, pp. 211–50.

D'Aveni, R. (1994) *Hypercompetition: Managing the Dynamics of Strategic Maneuvering*, New York: Free Press.

DeSanti S. (1996),'The Intersection of Antitrust and Intellectual Property Issues: A Report from the FTC Hearings', paper given at the conference on *Antitrust for High-tech Companies, Business Development Associates*, San Francisco.

Feldman, C.R. (1999) 'Defensive Leveraging in Antitrust', *Georgetown Law Journal*, 87 (6).

European Court of Justice (1998), *Oscar Bronner vs Mediaprint*, case C–7/97, 26 November.

Gallini, N. (2002), 'Intellectual Property Rights: An Efficient Mechanism for Rewarding Innovation', in F. Cafaggi, A. Nicita and U. Pagano (eds), *Legal Orderings and Economic Institutions*, London: Routledge.

Hart, O. and Moore, J. (1990), 'Property Rights and the Nature of the Firm', *Journal of Political Economy*, 98, pp. 1119–58.

Hausman, J.A. and Sidak, G.J. (1999) 'A Consumer-welfare Approach to the Mandatory Unbundling of Telecommunications Networks', *The Yale Law Journal*, 109.

Hirsch, F. (1976), *Social Limits to Growth*, Cambridge, MA: Harvard University Press.

Langlois, R.N. (1999), 'Technological Standards, Innovation, and Essential Facilities: Toward a Schumpeterian Post-Chicago Approach', mimeo.

Lipsky, B. and Sidak, J.G. (2000), 'Essential Facilities', mimeo.

Pitofsky, R. (1997), 'Competition Policy in Communication Industries', Glasser Legal Works seminar on *Competitive Policy in Communication Industries: New Antitrust Aproach*, Washington.

Pitofsky, R. (2000) 'Challenges to the New Economy: Issues at the Intersection of Antitrust and Intellectual Property', paper presented at the American Antitrust Institute, Conference on *Agenda for Antitrust in the 21st Century*, National Press Club, Washington.

Tye, W.B. (1987), 'Competitive Access: A Comparative Industry Approach to the Essential Facility Doctrine', *Energy Law Journal*, 8.

Valentine, D.A. (1996) 'Intellectual Property and Antitrust: Divergent Paths to the Same Goal', *Antitrust 1996*, Washington: Business Development Associates.

Williamson, O. (1985), *The Economic Institutions of Capitalism*, New York: The Free Press.

Willig, R. (1979), 'The Theory of Network Access Pricing', in H.M. Trebing (ed.), *Issues in Public Utility Regulation*, East Lansing, MI: MSU Institute of Public Utilities.

PART III

Chapter 8

The Impact of IT Investment on Productivity and Efficiency

Luigi Paganetto, Leonardo Becchetti and David Andrés Londoño Bedoya

1   Introduction

The relationship between information technology (from now on also IT)[1] and productivity has long been debated over the past three decades (Paganetto and Pietrobelli, 2001). In the 1980s and early 1990s, empirical research generally did not find relevant productivity improvements associated with IT investments. This research showed that there was no statistically significant, or even measurable, association between investments in IT and productivity at any level of analysis chosen. Robert Solow commented this puzzle by saying that 'we find computer everywhere, except in the productivity statistics'. More recently, as new data are made available and new methodologies are applied, empirical investigations have found evidence that IT is associated with improvements in productivity, in intermediate measures and in economic growth. An interpretation consistent with older and more recent results is that micro level data, by allowing the use of more controls, succeed better than aggregate measures in isolating IT effects on productivity from changes in other conditioning variables.

We repropose the two terms of this 'measurement paradox' in this chapter by showing that, simple growth accounting measures do not find a positive and significant effect of IT investment on multifactor productivity. On the contrary, microfounded estimates of efficiency at firm level, which include several quantitative and qualitative controls traditionally used in the literature, reveal a positive and significant impact of IT investment on productive efficiency.[2] We also show that it is possible to understand better the impact of IT investment by decomposing it into software, hardware and telecommunication investment. Software investment has scale effects by increasing labour productivity, the demand for high skilled workers and the overall firm productive efficiency. Telecommunications investment has scope effects by positively affecting the creation of new processes or products, while negatively affecting average labour productivity. The combination of these two effects, increases productive efficiency and utilization capacity.

In the theoretical section of the chapter these results are explained in the framework of the real option theory. We argue that if IT investment reduces lags between knowledge of changing consumer tastes and final production, it generates a flexibility option which, at any instant of time, delays the decision to invest in additional capacity and makes the decision to modify products and processes more likely thereby producing the observed effects on productivity and capacity utilization.

The chapter is divided into seven sections (including introduction and conclusions). The second section presents a review of the literature with a brief illustration of the theoretical predictions and the main empirical findings on the relationship between IT technology and productivity. The third section presents descriptive empirical evidence on the intensity of investment in hardware, software and telecommunications in a representative sample of more than 4,000 Italian firms between 1995 and 1997 showing how IT investment is affected by industry, geographical and qualitative firm characteristics. The fourth section measures the impact of IT investment on multifactor productivity. The fifth section analyses the effects of IT investment on several intermediate variables such as capacity utilization, new product/process introduction and white collars hiring rates at firm level. The sixth section presents several estimates which evaluate the association between IT investment and non-random deviations from the 'efficiency frontier'.

2   The State of Art

Tables 8.1–8.3 present a taxonomy of the empirical studies on IT investment according to industry (manufacturing, services or both) and level of disaggregation (aggregate, industry level or firm level) with a brief comment on their main results. These tables show that the findings of the 1980s and early 1990s mainly evidenced an insignificant, or even negative, relationship between IT and productivity (Strassmann, 1990; Loveman, 1998; Bender, 1986; Franke, 1987; Roach, 1989). These results were puzzling because productivity effects apparently failed to materialize in any sector (neither in services nor in manufacturing), by any measure (a variety of data sets and methods were used), or at any time. Positive effects are reported in the literature, only in case of studies of a single industry or small set of firms.[3]

Various rationales have been suggested to explain this paradox. Firstly, simple bivariate correlations between aggregate productivity and aggregate IT capital stock do not take into account the impact of all controls which also affect aggregate productivity (Lehr and Licthemberg, 1999). Brynjolfsson and Hitt (1995) find in fact that 50 per cent of changes in marginal products are explained by firm level variables. All these variables are neglected in aggregate correlations. Secondly, IT investment has a positive effect on productive variety which in turns negatively affects productivity (Brooke, 1991). Milgrom and Roberts (1988) show for instance that computer aided design (CAD) reduces costs of adjusting products to changing consumer tastes. This shifts productive organization from the Fordist approach to a more flexible network approach which emphasizes economies of scope more than economies of scale. Since variety is more difficult to detect than quantity it is very difficult to find trace of these changes in data. Thirdly, productivity gains from IT investment materialize only after time and depend significantly on network externalities and on changes in the complementary infrastructure (David, 1990). Fourthly, output measurement errors may affect estimates of the impact of IT investment on output as quality improvements in products and in services are not fully reflected in sales. Fifthly, IT accounts for a relatively small share of capital output so that its increase has only small effects on aggregate output.

Only more recently, the implementation of the information available and the disaggregation of IT into different components has led to new empirical findings which show the positive impact of IT on efficiency. Oliner and Sichel (1994) find that, from 1970 to 1992, computer hardware contributed for 0.15 percentage points to the total US output growth rate of 2.8 per cent. When software and computer-related labour are included, this contribution doubles to 0.31 percentage points for the period 1987 to 1993 (or 11 per cent of total growth).[4] Other capital and labour inputs, as well as multifactor productivity gains, account for about 90 per cent of the growth in US output during this period.[5] Lehr and Licthemberg (1999) also find a significant and positive contribution of computers investment to productivity growth on a large sample of US firms between 1977 and 1993. Sichel (1997) argues that computing technologies are part of a 150-year trend toward greater information intensity in the United States, and that we should expect the effects of computers to be modest and part of a historical continuum.

Brynjolfsson and Hitt (1996) analysed the impact of IT on marginal output using a new firm-level database and found large contributions of IT to marginal product for the firms considered in their study. Every additional dollar of computer capital stock was associated with an increase in marginal output of 81 cents, and every additional dollar spent on IT-related labour was associated with an increase in marginal output of $2.62. Their earlier work also demonstrates that firm-level factors account for half of the variability in IT's marginal product contributions (Brynjolfsson and Hitt, 1995).

Several factors may explain the dramatically different findings of Brynjolfsson and Hitt relative to the earlier productivity studies. The more recent time period of their study (1987–91), the use of a larger data set, more detailed firm-level[6] data; and the inclusion of IT-related labour (note that IT capital expenses are typically a small fraction of firm's total IT-related costs) are all reasons why their findings are more positive than those resulting from earlier research. Using similar data and methods, other analysts have also found significant positive rates of return at the firm level (Lichtenberg, 1995).

By commenting their results, Oliner and Sichel (1994), and Bryjolfsson and Hitt (1996) highlight the complexity of research into the effects of IT on productivity. Both sets of findings suggest that IT does have measurable pay-offs for economic productivity, but the orders of magnitude are quite different. Macroeconomic impacts may be quite modest at best (as measured by Oliner and Sichel), whereas firm-level benefits may be more substantial (as measured by Brynjolfsson and Hitt). While they do not indicate that the productivity paradox has been resolved, these findings do suggest that the relationship between IT and productivity may be changing.

A limit of this last vintage of empirical approaches is that they do not disaggregate the impact of IT into the contributions of components with different effects and characteristics (such as software, hardware and telecommunications). In addition, many of them do not microfound their estimates or, when they do it, they generally adopt two-stage estimation procedures (production function and then, separately, an estimation in which the dependent variable is the residual from the first equation) which inconsistently assume the independence of the inefficiency effects in the two estimation stages and are unlikely to be efficient. This chapter will try to amend these shortcomings in the following sections.

3   Descriptive Empirical Findings on IT Investment Intensity in Italy

We evaluate the intensity of IT investment and its impact of various productivity measures using the Mediocredito Survey. The Survey includes a sample of more than 5,000 firms drawn from the whole set of Italian manufacturing firms. The sample is stratified according to industry geographical and dimensional

Table 8.1   Principal empirical studies of IT and productivity

	Cross-sector	Manufacturing	Services
Aggregate level studies	Jonscher (1983) Jonscher (1994)	Morrison and Berndt (1991)	Brand and Duke (1982)
Economy-wide and industry-level	Baily (1986b) Baily and Chakrabarti (1988) Baily and Gordon (1988) Roach (1987) Roach (1988) Roach (1989b) Brooke (1992) Lau and Tokutsu (1992) Oliner and Sichel (1994) Jorgenson and Stiroh (1995)	Berndt, Morrison and Rosenblum (1992) Berndt and Morrison (1995) Siegel and Griliches (1992) Siegel (1994)	Baily (1986a) Roach (1987) Roach (1989a) Roach (1991)
Micro-level studies	Osterman (1986) Dos Santos (1993) Krueger (1993)	Loveman (1994) Weill (1988, 1992) Dudley and Lasserre (1989)	Cron and Sobol (1983) Pulley and Braunstein (1984) Bender (1986) Bresnahan (1986) Franke (1987) Strassmann (1985) Strassmann (1990) Harris and Katz (1987, 1991) Parsons et al. (1990) Diewert and Smith (1994)
Firm and workers	Brynjolfsson and Hitt (1994) Hitt and Brynjolfsson (1994) Lichtenberg (1995) Brynjolfsson and Hitt (1996)	Barua, Kriebel and Mukhopadhyay (1991) Brynjolfsson and Hitt (1993, 1996) Brynjolfsson and Hitt (1995)	

Source: Adapted from Brynjolfsson (1993) and Brynjolfsson and Yang (1996).

Table 8.2   Studies of IT and productivity in manufacturing firms

Study	Data source	Findings
Lefebvre and Lefebvre (1988)	667 manufacturing firms	The impact of IT on employee's productivity was greater for clerical and secretarial personnel, managers, and professionals than for blue-collar workers
Loveman (1988)	PIMS–MPIT	IT investments added nothing to output
Dudley and Lasserre (1989)	US and Canadian aggregate data	IT and communication reduces inventories
Morrison and Berndt (1990)	BEA	IT marginal benefit is 80 cents per dollar invested
Weill (1990)	Interviews and surveys	Contextual variables affected IT performance
Barua, Kriebel and	PIMS–MPIT	IT improved intermediate outputs, if not necessarily final output
Siegel and Griliches (1991)	Multiple government sources	IT-using industries tended to be more productive; government data were unreliable
Weill (1992)	Valve manufacturers	Contextual variables affect IT performance transaction processing IT produce positive results
Brynjolfsson and Hitt (1993)	IDG; Compustat; BEA	The return on IT investment was more than 50% per year in manufacturing firms
Siegel (1994)	Multiple government sources	A multiple-indicators and multiple-causes model captures significant MFP effects of computers
Brynjolfsson and Hitt (1995)	IDG; Compustat: BEA	Firm effects account for half of the productivity benefits of earlier study
Lichtenberg (1995)	IDG; Informationweek (cross-sector)	IT has excess return; IT staff's substitution effect is large

Table 8.2 cont'd

Study	Data source	Findings
Kwon and Stoneman (1995)	UK survey	New technology adoption especially computer use has a positive impacton output and productivity

Notes: BEA, Bureau of Economic Analysis; IDG, International Data Group, Inc.; MPIT, Management Productivity and Information Technology Project; PIMS, Profit Impact of Market Strategy database of the Strategic Planning Institute.

Source: Adapted from Brynjolfsson (1993) and Brynjolfsson and Yang (1996).

Table 8.3   Studies of IT and productivity in services firms

Study	Data source	Findings
Brand (1982)	BLS	Productivity growth of 1.3% per year in banking
Cron and Sobol (1983)	138 medical- supply wholesalers	Bimodal distribution among high IT investors was either very good or very bad
Pulley and Braunstein (1984)	An info-service firm	Significant economies of scope
Clarke (1985)	Case study	Major business process redesign needed to reap benefits in investment firm
Bender (1986)	LOMA insurance data on 132 firms	Weak relationship between IT and various performance ratios
Franke (1987)	Finance industry data stagnant labour productivity	IT was associated with a sharp drop in capital productivity and
Lefebvre and Lefebvre (1988)	996 firms	The impact of IT on employee productivity was greatest for managers in wholesale or retail trade services and for secretarial and clerical personnel in other services firms
Harris and Katz (1989)	LOMA insurance data for 40 companies	Weak positive relationship was shown between IT and various performance ratios
Roach (1989)	Principally BLS, BEA	IT capital per information worker was vastly increased, but measured output decreased
Alpar and Kim (1990)	Federal Reserve data (759 banks)	Performance estimates were sensitive to methodology
Noyelle (1990)	US and French industry	Severe measurement problems occurred in services
Parsons et al. (1990)	Internal operating data from two large banks	IT coefficient in translog production function was small and often negative
Strassmann (1990)	Computerworld survey of 38 companies	No correlation was shown between various IT ratios and performance measures

Table 8.3 cont'd

Study	Data source	Findings
Alpar and Kim (1991)	Large number of banks	IT is cost saving, labour saving, and capital using
Diewert and Smith (1994)	A large Canadian retail firm	Multifactor productivity grows 9.4% per quarter over 6 quarters
Brynjolfsson and Hitt (1995)	IDG; Compustat; BEA	Marginal products of IT do not differ much in services and in the manufacturing; firm effects account for 50% of the marginal product differential

Notes: BEA, Bureau of Economic Analysis; BLS, Bureau of Labor Statistics; IDG, International Data Group, Inc.; LOMA, Life Office Management Association, Inc.

Source: Adapted from Brynjolfsson (1993) and Brynjolfsson and Yang (1996).

distribution of Italian firms for firms from 11 to 500 employees. It is by census for firms with more than 500 employees. For a subsample of 4,404 firms both qualitative and quantitative data (balance sheets for the 1995–97 period) are collected. Qualitative data provide, among other things, information on ownership structure,[7] internationalization, R&D investment, and successful introduction of products and processes.[8]

Descriptive features of this sample illustrate some important characteristics of the Italian IT investment per employee (Tables 8.4a–8.4d) evaluated as the sum of investment in software, hardware and telecommunications in the three considered years. The average IT cumulative investment per employee in the sample is 7 million liras. The following deviations from this value worth noting. Per capita IT investment is on average: i) more than a half lower in firms located in the south; ii) much higher in firms located in the northeast; iii) substantially higher for small firms and (as expected) for firms in the specialized industries according to the Pavitt classification (mechanical equipment and mechanical materials); iv) ownership structure and financial constraints seem to matter as firms with only one controlling shareholder and firms with financial constraints have a relatively lower intensity of IT investment; v) firms participating to credit and export consortia also have relatively lower IT investment per employee.[9]

When we disaggregate IT investment into hardware, software and telecommunications components we find that: i) northeast investment in software and hardware per employee is almost double and south almost half as much as national average; ii) software and hardware investment intensity is also relatively higher in specialized industries and in R&D investing firms. The pattern of telecommunications investment is quite different. Intensity is higher in larger firms and in firms affiliated to groups and its geographical distribution is not so different across macroareas.

4   Evidence of IT effects on productivity from multifactor productivity analyses

As additional descriptive empirical investigation we want to check whether IT investment significantly contributed to multifactor productivity in the Mediocredito Survey. This experiment is only partially comparable with other tests of the impact of IT on TFP as we only dispose of IT investment and not of IT stock.

As it is well known the test is derived from growth accounting at the firm level. If we assume that each firm has a Cobb-Douglas production function, following Stiroh (1998). Multifactor productivity may be estimated as: $\Delta VA = \alpha(\Delta K) + (1 + \alpha)\Delta L + \Delta MFP$ where ΔVA represents the rate of change in value added, α the share of capital in nominal output, ΔK and ΔL respectively the rate of change in the capital stock and in the labour input and ΔMPF the rate of change in multifactor productivity. This equations says that the rate of growth of value added (ΔVA) equals the share-weighted growth in inputs (for example, $\alpha(\Delta K)$ is the rate of growth of stock capital, weighted by the share of stock capital in total output), plus the rate of growth of multifactor productivity.

Descriptive results from the multifactor productivity approach show that IT firms have an average total factor contribution which is superior to that of non-IT firms between 1989 and 1997 but not when we consider the shorter period between 1995 and 1997.

To test whether the relationship between IT investments and multifactor productivity is econometrically robust, the following regression was estimated: $\Delta MFP = \alpha + \beta_1 K_{IT} + \varepsilon$; where ΔMFP represents the average growth rate of multifactor productivity for either 1995–97 or 1989–97, and K_{IT} is the flow of IT investments. A simple dummy which takes value of one for IT investing firms and zero otherwise is considered alternatively to the variable measuring IT intensity. Unlike Stiroh (1998), we estimate multifactor productivity growth rate on the basis of both total output and added value in order to avoid potential errors in measuring output.

The results presented in Tables 8.5 and 8.6 are consistent with findings of Stiroh (1998), Baily and Gordon (1988), and Berndt and Morrison (1995) as the data show the nearly nonexistent relationship between IT investments and multifactor productivity growth.

5 Four Hypotheses on the Impact of IT Investment: Theoretical Rationales and Empirical Tests

Multifactor productivity evidence for our sample does not help to solve the productivity paradox. To find the effects of IT investment we therefore disaggregate it into different components and test their impact on productivity at firm level. The survey of the existing literature and the theoretical analysis which is described in detail in the appendix lead us to formulate five hypotheses which we briefly explain and test in the following sections of the chapter.

Table 8.4a   Descriptive findings on the determinants of IT investment (95–97 IT investments per employees – millions of liras)

Variable	South and isles		Centre		Northwest		Northeast		Italy	
	No. of obs	Mean	No. of obs	Mean	No. of obs	Mean	No. of obs	Mean	No. of obs	Mean
All firms	338	2.87	354	6.05	1386	5.42	802	12.06	2980	7.16
Small size	188	3.00	315	4.65	750	7.23	457	19.57	1710	9.59
Medium size	64	3.04	59	3.21	223	3.36	137	3.19	483	3.25
Large size	86	2.46	80	13.67	413	3.25	208	3.48	787	4.28
Scale sectors	100	2.21	129	6.43	413	10.22	205	4.29	847	7.26
Traditional sectors	163	2.65	223	2.81	483	2.89	302	2.79	1171	2.82
Specialized sectors	37	4.27	80	4.91	424	3.64	264	31.47	805	12.92
High–tech sectors	38	4.19	22	40.81	66	5.28	31	2.33	157	9.41
Industries										
Food, beverages, tobacco	71	3.61	36	2.26	82	3.27	62	2.77	251	3.10
Textile, clothing	33	1.42	87	4.02	198	2.94	48	2.85	366	3.05
Leather, shoes	8	1.01	34	1.37	12	2.95	26	3.00	80	2.10
Wood and wooden furniture	18	1.51	32	1.78	52	2.28	84	2.67	186	2.30
Paper and printing	25	4.15	52	4.50	72	3.80	49	7.90	198	5.04
Chemicals	19	3.38	17	72.48	72	4.52	26	2.88	134	12.66
Rubber and plastics	28	2.38	22	4.85	103	3.24	44	3.53	197	3.36
Glass, ceramics	9	0.87	8	1.70	24	56.75	35	2.26	76	19.25
Construction materials	21	0.53	19	2.57	34	2.75	30	2.38	104	2.16
Metal extraction	10	3.58	13	2.99	73	25.81	16	3.98	112	18.06
Metal products	31	3.11	29	3.15	170	2.77	85	2.63	315	2.80
Mechanical materials	2	1.27	9	3.70	73	4.09	28	2.88	112	3.71
Mechanical equipment	11	3.59	30	4.78	170	3.74	132	59.10	343	25.13

Table 8.4a cont'd

Variable	South and isles		Centre		Northwest		Northeast		Italy	
	No. of obs	Mean	No. of obs	Mean	No. of obs	Mean	No. of obs	Mean	No. of obs	Mean
Industries (cont'd)										
Electronics	11	6.93	16	4.59	37	4.81	19	4.65	83	5.01
Electrical equipment	0	–	4	1.50	16	2.46	13	3.91	33	2.91
Precision instruments and apparel	2	15.70	0	–	12	5.09	19	7.02	33	6.84
Vehicles and vehicle components	14	1.75	9	2.96	56	2.29	21	3.72	100	2.58
Energy	5	1.33	6	1.49	11	3.84	2	2.01	24	2.57
Others manufacturing	5	1.91	6	3.99	4	4.58	2	5.39	17	3.68
Others non-manufacturing	15	3.71	25	5.28	115	3.13	61	3.10	216	3.41
Ownership structure										
Family owned	196	2.40	262	3.77	869	6.70	483	3.77	1810	5.03
Banks among controlling shareholders	8	1.57	12	4.10	63	3.37	33	4.12	116	3.53
Privately owned	193	2.61	265	6.11	813	5.08	496	18.49	1767	8.61
State owned	6	5.90	5	2.70	7	2.73	1	0.39	19	3.60
One controlling shareholder	38	2.00	28	2.33	45	3.06	43	2.17	154	2.42
R&D, external finance, group and consortia affiliation										
R&D investments	88	4.53	178	8.77	607	5.98	333	25.23	1206	11.60
Credit rationed firms	21	2.08	17	2.68	45	3.03	25	2.61	108	2.69
Subsidized firms	241	2.60	210	9.40	609	3.20	350	3.93	1410	4.20
Affiliated to groups	106	3.87	100	12.73	389	3.54	242	4.00	837	4.81
Affiliated to nondiversified group	83	3.12	83	14.90	318	3.65	201	3.99	685	5.05
Affiliated to export consortia	6	3.55	25	2.35	28	2.76	16	4.01	75	2.95
Affiliated to credit consortia	15	2.51	19	4.26	66	2.53	56	3.32	156	3.06

Table 8.4b Descriptive findings on the determinants of telecommunications investment (95–97 IT investments per employees – millions of liras)

Variable IT telecommunication investments/ mean employment 95–97	South and isles		Centre		Northwest		Northeast		Italy	
	No. of obs	Mean	No. of obs	Mean	No. of obs	Mean	No. of obs	Mean	No. of obs	Mean
All firms	333	0.151	443	0.258	1363	0.149	792	0.152	2931	0.167
Small size	186	0.148	304	0.145	737	0.110	449	0.128	1676	0.126
Medium size	63	0.111	59	0.116	222	0.175	136	0.171	480	0.158
Large size	84	0.190	80	0.789	404	0.206	207	0.191	775	0.261
Scale sectors	98	0.140	126	0.081	405	0.151	201	0.210	830	0.153
Traditional sectors	160	0.129	218	0.081	476	0.116	300	0.104	1154	0.108
Specialized sectors	37	0.271	78	0.570	418	0.164	260	0.164	793	0.209
High-tech sectors	38	0.157	21	1.987	64	0.291	31	0.133	154	0.457
Industries										
Food, beverages, tobacco	70	0.177	36	0.131	82	0.112	62	0.128	250	0.137
Textile, clothing	31	0.084	86	0.081	195	0.130	48	0.088	360	0.109
Leather, shoes	8	0.081	32	0.042	12	0.096	26	0.037	78	0.053
Wood and wooden furniture	18	0.087	31	0.059	52	0.095	82	0.104	183	0.092
Paper and printing	24	0.356	51	0.061	70	0.308	49	0.394	194	0.271
Chemicals	19	0.280	17	2.544	72	0.181	26	0.108	134	0.481
Rubber and plastics	27	0.124	21	0.192	99	0.190	43	0.172	190	0.177
Glass, ceramics	9	0.042	7	0.151	24	0.096	35	0.090	75	0.092
Construction materials	21	0.022	19	0.03	34	0.060	30	0.056	104	0.041
Metal extraction	10	0.009	13	0.158	70	0.147	16	0.096	109	0.128
Metal products	31	0.112	28	0.110	166	0.106	84	0.122	309	0.111
Mechanical materials	2	0.473	9	0.046	73	0.190	27	0319	111	0.215

Table 8.4b cont'd

Variable IT telecommunication investments/ mean employment 95–97	South and isles		Centre		Northwest		Northeast		Italy	
	No. of obs	Mean	No. of obs	Mean	No. of obs	Mean	No. of obs	Mean	No. of obs	Mean
Industries (cont'd)										
Mechanical equipment	11	0.145	29	0.430	166	0.171	132	0.175	338	0.194
Electronics	11	0.089	16	0.112	36	0.249	19	0.067	82	0.159
Electrical equipment	0	–	4	0.086	16	0.001	12	0.173	32	0.076
Precision instruments and apparel	2	0.250	0	–	12	0.394	19	0.118	33	0.227
Vehicles and vehicle components	14	0.179	9	0.619	56	0.090	20	0.271	99	0.187
Energy	5	0.028	6	0.016	10	0.150	2	0.439	23	0.114
Others manufacturing	5	0	6	0	4	0.226	2	0	17	0.053
Others non-manufacturing	15	0.327	23	0.956	114	0.112	58	0.152	210	0.236
Ownership structure										
Family owned	193	0.170	257	0.176	857	0.134	474	0.168	1781	0.153
Banks among controlling shareholders	8	0.208	12	0.015	62	0.162	33	0.309	115	0.192
Privately owned	189	0.146	259	0.250	799	0.160	488	0.152	1735	0.170
State owned	6	0.010	5	0.169	7	0.005	1	0	19	0.049
One controlling shareholder	37	0.034	27	0.083	44	0.040	43	0.071	151	0.055
R&D, external finance, group and consortia affiliation										
R&D investment	88	0.145	172	0.550	594	0.191	331	0.185	1185	0.238
Credit rationed firms	20	0.018	16	0.105	43	0.120	20	0.124	104	0.103
Subsidized firms	238	0.174	207	0.470	599	0.136	346	0.182	1390	0.204
Affiliated to groups	104	0.166	100	0.854	383	0.237	241	0.231	828	0.301
Affiliated to nondiversified group	81	0.175	83	1.019	312	0.217	200	0.240	676	0.317
Affiliated to export consortia	6	1.433	25	0.134	28	0.236	16	0.403	75	0.333
Affiliated to credit consortia	15	0.611	19	0.617	66	0.163	56	0.207	156	0.277

Table 8.4c   Descriptive findings on the determinants of hardware investment (95–97 IT investments per employees – millions of liras)

Variable *IT hardware investments/ mean employment 95–97*	South and isles		Centre		Northwest		Northeast		Italy	
	No. of obs	*Mean*	*No. of obs*	*Mean*	*No. of obs*	*Mean*	*No. of obs*	*Mean*	*No. of obs*	*Mean*
All firms	333	1.718	443	3.908	1363	2.811	792	8.207	2931	4.311
Small size	186	1.876	304	2.768	737	3.777	449	13.222	1676	5.914
Medium size	63	1.802	59	1.699	222	1.671	136	1.509	480	1.646
Large size	84	1.304	80	9.867	404	1.675	207	1.728	775	2.494
Scale sectors	98	1.276	126	4.169	405	5.373	201	2.074	830	3.908
Traditional sectors	160	1.614	218	1.443	476	1.461	300	1.399	1154	1.463
Specialized sectors	37	2.507	78	4.735	418	1.858	260	21.642	793	8.437
High-tech sectors	38	2.525	21	33.175	64	2.860	31	1.167	154	6.570
Industries										
Food, beverages, tobacco	70	2.213	36	1.278	82	1.723	62	1.265	250	1.683
Textile, clothing	31	0.716	86	1.999	195	1.408	48	1.542	360	1.507
Leather, shoes	8	0.495	32	0.671	12	1.520	26	1.305	78	0.995
Wood and wooden furniture	18	1.006	31	0.931	52	1.157	82	1.463	183	1.241
Paper and printing	24	2.555	51	2.443	70	1.769	49	3.621	194	2.511
Chemicals	19	1.949	17	56.975	72	2.017	26	1.569	134	8.893
Rubber and plastics	27	1.291	21	2.594	99	1.553	43	1.484	190	1.615
Glass, ceramics	9	0.428	7	1.049	24	34.078	35	1.243	75	11.63
Construction materials	21	0.342	19	1.197	34	1.467	30	1.345	104	1.155
Metal extraction	10	2.170	13	1.580	70	12.479	16	2.111	109	8.711
Metal products	31	1.887	28	1.680	166	1.414	84	1.266	309	1.445
Mechanical materials	2	0.667	9	2.156	73	2.395	27	1.466	111	2.119

Table 8.4c cont'd

Variable IT hardware investments/ mean employment 95–97	South and isles		Centre		Northwest		Northeast		Italy	
	No. of obs	Mean	No. of obs	Mean	No. of obs	Mean	No. of obs	Mean	No. of obs	Mean
Industries (cont'd)										
Mechanical equipment	11	2.540	29	2.529	166	1.880	132	40.703	338	17.119
Electronics	11	4.391	16	2.052	36	2.811	19	3.025	82	2.924
Electrical equipment	–	–	4	0.891	16	1.399	12	2.249	32	1.655
Precision instruments and apparel	2	7.976	–	–	12	3.020	19	3.456	33	3.571
Vehicles and vehicle components	14	0.998	9	1.379	56	1.233	20	1.445	90	1.256
Energy	5	0.752	6	0.838	10	2.271	2	0.439	23	1.408
Others manufacturing	5	0.982	6	1.718	4	2.013	2	0.865	17	1.471
Others non-manufacturing	15	2.149	23	2.638	114	1.683	58	1.607	210	1.800
Ownership structure										
Family owned	193	1.382	257	1.940	857	3.480	474	1.920	1781	2.615
Banks among controlling shareholders	8	0.887	12	1.659	62	1.597	33	2.076	115	1.692
Privately owned	189	1.548	259	4.098	799	2.782	488	12.391	1735	5.547
State owned	6	2.933	5	1.020	7	1.530	1	0.314	19	1.775
One controlling shareholder	37	1.240	27	1.072	44	1.671	43	1.082	151	1.290
R&D, external finance, group and consortia affiliation										
Firm investing in R&D	88	2.569	172	5.823	594	3.275	331	17.057	1185	7.442
Credit rationed firms	20	1.183	16	1.251	43	1.725	25	1.202	104	1.422
Subsidized firms	238	1.475	207	6.502	599	1.688	346	1.939	1390	2.431
Affiliated to groups	104	2.383	100	8.897	383	1.782	241	2.039	828	2.791
Affiliated to nondiversified group	81	1.738	83	10.471	312	1.888	200	2.010	676	2.960
Affiliated to export consortia	6	1.724	25	1.104	28	1.248	16	2.072	75	1.414
Affiliated to credit consortia	15	1.250	19	2.065	66	1.336	56	1.658	156	1.532

Table 8.5d Descriptive findings on the determinants of hardware investment (95–97 IT investments per employees – millions of liras)

Variable IT software investments/ mean employment 95–97	South and isles		Centre		Northwest		Northeast		Italy	
	No. of obs	Mean	No. of obs	Mean	No. of obs	Mean	No. of obs	Mean	No. of obs	Mean
All firms	333	1.022	443	1.982	1363	2.475	792	4.356	2931	2.744
Small size	196	0.997	304	1.824	737	3.361	449	6.513	1676	3.664
Medium size	63	1.179	59	1.397	222	1.516	136	1.514	480	1.457
Large size	84	0.959	80	3.015	404	1.384	207	1.546	775	1.550
Scale sectors	98	0.776	126	2.273	405	4.782	201	1.997	830	3.253
Traditional sectors	160	0.946	218	1.310	476	1.320	300	1.291	1154	1.259
Specialized sectors	37	1.495	78	1.885	418	1.631	260	10.114	793	4.431
High-tech sectors	38	1.514	21	7.572	64	1.976	31	1.031	154	2.435
Industries										
Food, beverages, tobacco	70	1.259	36	0.851	82	1.441	62	1.377	250	1.289
Textile, clothing	31	0.686	86	1.933	195	1.404	48	1.225	360	2.044
Leather, shoes	8	0.435	32	0.731	12	1.340	26	1.663	78	1.105
Wood and wooden furniture	18	0.424	31	0.728	52	1.029	82	1.107	183	0.954
Paper and printing	24	1.325	51	2.051	70	1.537	49	3.887	194	2.240
Chemicals	19	1.159	17	12.963	72	2.324	26	1.211	134	3.293
Rubber and plastics	27	0.882	21	2.280	99	1.387	43	1.879	190	1.525
Glass, ceramics	9	0.405	7	0.686	24	22.579	35	0.935	75	7.774
Construction materials	21	0.168	19	1.375	34	1.225	30	0.982	104	0.969
Metal extraction	10	1.410	13	1.257	70	14.026	16	1.777	109	9.547
Metal products	31	1.115	28	1.440	166	1.268	84	1.277	309	1.270
Mechanical materials	2	0.129	9	1.506	73	1.512	27	1.090	111	1.384

Table 8.5d cont'd

Variable IT software investments/ mean employment 95–97	South and isles		Centre		Northwest		Northeast		Italy	
	No. of obs	Mean	No. of obs	Mean	No. of obs	Mean	No. of obs	Mean	No. of obs	Mean
Industries (cont'd)										
Mechanical equipment	11	0.909	29	1.779	166	1.694	132	18.225	338	8.132
Electronics	11	2.458	16	2.434	36	1.782	19	1.558	82	1.948
Electrical equipment	–	–	4	0.525	16	1.064	12	1.280	32	1.078
Precision instruments and apparel	2	7.476	–	–	12	1.680	19	3.450	33	3.050
Vehicles and vehicle components	14	0.580	9	0.966	56	0.969	20	1.641	99	1.050
Energy	5	0.555	6	0.637	10	1.515	2	1.132	23	1.044
Others manufacturing	5	0.934	6	2.281	4	2.343	2	4.532	17	2.164
Others non-manufacturing	15	1.237	23	1.846	114	1.331	58	1.407	210	1.402
Ownership structure										
Family owned	193	0.850	257	1.699	857	3.104	474	1.689	1781	2.281
Banks among controlling shareholders	8	0.481	12	2.429	62	1.593	33	1.735	115	1.644
Privately owned	189	0.927	259	1.843	799	2.110	488	6.186	1735	3.088
State owned	6	2.959	5	1.517	7	1.196	1	0.078	19	1.778
One controlling shareholder	37	0.784	27	1.248	44	1.395	43	1.020	151	1.112
R&D, external finance, group and consortia affiliation										
R&D investing firms	88	1.819	172	2.587	594	2.537	331	8.126	1185	4.052
Credit rationed firms	20	0.939	16	1.474	43	1.195	25	1.264	104	1.205
Subsidized firms	238	0.953	207	2.540	599	1.365	346	1.831	1390	1.586
Affiliated to groups	104	1.350	100	2.987	383	1.507	241	1.726	828	1.730
Affiliated to nondiversified group	81	1.223	83	3.414	312	1.533	200	1.729	676	1.785
Affiliated to export consortia	6	0.392	25	1.113	28	1.278	16	1.540	75	1.208
Affiliated to credit consortia	15	0.654	19	1.584	66	1.032	56	1.457	156	1.216

Table 8.5   Sources of aggregate growth

	All firms		Non-IT firms		IT firms	
	1995–97	*1989–97*	*1995–97*	*1989–97*	*1995–97*	*1989–97*
No. of obs	2867	806	862	157	2005	649
Output	12.279	7.393	2.478	6.085	16.493	7.710
Contribution of capital	11.591	3.637	3.358	7.151	15.131	2.787
Contribution of labour	1.894	1.588	1.194	1.246	2.196	1.671
Productivity	–1.206	2.167	–2.074	–2.311	–0.833	3.251

	All firms		Non-IT firms		IT firms	
	1995–97	*1989–97*	*1995–97*	*1989–97*	*1995–97*	*1989–97*
No. of obs	2849	802	853	157	1996	645
Value added	4.479	6.770	2.897	5.038	5.155	7.191
Contribution of capital	11.792	3.563	3.411	7.515	15.373	2.689
Contribution of labour	1.652	1.607	1.233	1.246	1.832	1.695
Productivity	–8.965	1.599	–1.748	–3.358	–12.049	2.806

Note: Contribution of an input is the average share – weighted growth rate.

Table 8.6   Multifactor productivity added value

	Added value 1995–97		Real output 1995–97	
	Coefficient	*Coefficient*	*t-ratio*	*t-ratio*
Constant	−0.091	−0.017	−0.153	−1.095
ΔK_{IT}	0.0001	0.0001	1.001	0.896
Constant	−0.017	−0.020	−2.313	−2.171
Dummy IT	−0.103	0.012	0.077	−0.870
Constant	−0.123	−1.029	−0.015	−0.096
ΔK_{IT}	0.0001	0.932	0.0001	1.018

Hypothesis 1: Investment in Software Increases the Demand for Skilled Labour

This hypothesis has been already supported by Roach (1991), Berndt et al. (1992) and Stiroh (1998) which argue that, even though IT may substitute for labour, it also increases white-collar productivity and white-collar hiring rates.

This proposition is the obvious outcome of cost minimization under the assumption that an increase in the stock of IT capital raises more the marginal productivity of skilled vis-à-vis that of unskilled labour (see appendix). In this case, if the market for skilled labour is competitive or if skilled labour wage is not too upward sloping in the number of skilled workers hired, only an increase in the number of skilled workers may restore the equilibrium condition which states that the ratio of wages between two factors must equal the ratio between their marginal productivities. Descriptive evidence does not contradict our hypothesis as software investing firms have an average hiring rate of 0.6 per cent against a 0.3 per cent of the rest of the sample. We test our proposition on a regression model which includes five types of controls (industry, location, identity, ownership, finance, innovation and human and physical capital) and which is described in detail in the Appendix A. The justification for using all these controls is that these five types of variables have been widely demonstrated to affect all relevant firm choices (hiring included).[10] Nonetheless, traditional empirical papers just use the first three types of controls (industry, location and identity) for scarcity of data. The richness of our data set enables us to use all of them reducing the risk that our significant relationships proxy for unobserved variables.

Since the dependent variable is clearly non-normal and left censored we use a Tobit model and evaluate the significance of coefficients with percentile and bias corrected bootstrapping techniques.

By estimating our model we empirically find a positive and significant effect of aggregate IT investment and of software investment on the demand for high skilled workers[11] (telecommunications and hardware seem to have no impact) which supports our theoretical hypothesis (see Table A1.2 in the appendix). This effect is significant net of the relationship that other controls have on the dependent variable (the positive and significant impact of size, export capacity, government subsidies, affiliation to group and rationing and the negative and significant impact of government ownership). Since we are aware that in case of overparametrization the relative significance of individual regressors may be blurred by reduced efficiency and multicollinearity among regressors, we also run a stepwise regression using 95 per cent significance as a threshold to see whether exclusion/inclusion of insignificant controls and eventual correlation among regressors generate a spurious relationship between software investment and the demand for skilled workers. The relationship is confirmed and reinforced under the stepwise procedure (Table A1.3).

Hypothesis 2: Investment in Telecommunications Positively Affects the Introduction of New Products or Processes

Previous papers argue that IT investment has a positive effect on productive variety (Brooke, 1991; Barua, Kriebel and Mukhopadhyay, 1991). We show here that this hypothesis is confirmed but that the increased variety effect must be attributed to telecommunications only and not to software and hardware investment. If telecommunications investment (such as the introduction or implementation of e-commerce and network production) allows the firm to know in real time consumer tastes and to adapt more quickly its productive process to satisfy consumers taste for variety, the introduction of new processes and products should be positively affected by it. Descriptive evidence strongly support this hypothesis as 69 per cent of telecommunication investing firms declare they have introduced new products against 30 per cent of the rest of the sample. Econometric results show that investment in telecommunications for firms participating to groups is positively and significantly related to the decision to introduce new products (Table A1.2). The interesting finding is that the effect is not significant for those firms which invest in telecommunications but are not part of a group. The interpretation is that the scope and flexibility effect of this kind of IT investment can be achieved only in an integrated network productive system which is typical of industrial groups. Logit results also shows that family ownership, participation to traditional sectors and investment in hardware (R&D investment, credit rationing and participation to credit consortia) seem to affect negatively (positively) the dependent variable. The negative impact of hardware may be interpreted by considering that hardware investment is mainly related to an individual and specific production process, entails much more sunk costs and reduces flexibility and opportunities for introducing new processes. Stepwise estimates confirm the effect of all the above mentioned variables while some other controls previously significant in the overall estimate are dropped (Tables A1.1–A1.3). When we consider as a dependent variable the introduction of both products and processes the positive impact of telecommunications investment is confirmed. An interesting result is also the different effect of investment subsidies – negative – and tax allowances – positive – which shows that when government support – as it is in the case of tax allowance – is not related to a specific investment in physical capital (and often to the renovation of the existing capital stock) it increases flexibility and capacity of introducing new products or processes.

Hypothesis 3: The Investment in Information Technology Increases the Value of the Firm by Adding a Flexibility Option whose Effect is that of Increasing Average Capacity Utilization

The hypothesis of a positive relationship between capacity utilization and IT has been formulated by Barua, Kriebel and Mukhopadhyay (1991). We find support for it on our data and provide a theoretical rationale for it by using a simple dynamic programming example (see also Becchetti, Londoño Bedoya and Paganetto, 2003).

Consider the decision to increase productive capacity to satisfy a potential increase in demand under uncertainty as a real option in a simple dynamic approach. If telecommunications investment, reduces lags between knowledge of current customer tastes and final production,[12] it also has the effect of enlarging the time window in which the firm may adapt its capacity to satisfy market demand. Telecommunications investment therefore creates an option for flexibility transforming the investment in the increase of capacity from a 'now or never' investment into a decision which can be postponed. In this framework, for certain values of model parameters, the decision to wait is preferred to the decision to 'invest now' in additional capacity if the firm has previously invested in telecommunications. For the same parameter values the firm would have invested now in additional capacity if the IT investment had not occurred and the opportunity to delay were not available. Given the positive probability *ex post* of the realization of the negative state of nature the non-IT firm will find herself with expected lower additional capacity contrary to the IT firm which can postpone the investment decision after the observation of the stock. In a theoretical appendix we show that this result holds in simple two period examples and in continuous time models (see Appendix B).

Empirical results are consistent with our hypothesis on the effects of telecommunications investment on capacity utilization. The interesting point is that the effect is positive only when firms are part of a group. This may be interpreted by saying that the crucial factor in generating the flexibility option is the network productive organization. In the language of our theoretical model the critical factor is not just the capacity of knowing consumer tastes in real time (B2C effect) but mainly the capacity of a more flexible productive organization (B2C effect) which reduces lags between knowledge of consumers' taste for variety and the final production of a complex diversified range of products which assemble different components.

Hypothesis 4: Investment in Telecommunications Reduces Average Productivity of Labour, While Investment in Software Increases It

Telecommunications investment extends the window in which the decision to increase productive capacity may be taken and gives firms not only the opportunity to expand capacity but also to change products and processes to satisfy consumers taste for variety. If this is true telecommunications investing firms are more likely, at any instant of time, to shift firm activity to new products or processes by paying though, when this decision is taken, the cost of reduced productivity of labour inputs which need to be retrained because of these changes.

On the other hand, the effect of software investment on average labour productivity is the consequence of hypothesis 1 as new workers are hired, the new software technology increases the marginal productivity of each individual worker and average labour productivity is higher.[13] Given the non-normal distribution of the dependent variable (Table A1.1) we evaluate the effect of our set of regressors on two points of the distribution of the dependent variable (conditional mean and conditional median). Empirical results on the determinants of labour productivity seem consistent with our theoretical conclusions. In the estimate with all controls software and telecommunications investments have the expected sign even though the impact of telecommunications is significant only on conditional mean and not on conditional median. These two regressors resist to the stepwise selection and substantially reinforce their significance together with expected controls such as capital stock per employee and multiple borrowing (Table A1.3).

6   IT Investment and Firm Efficiency: A Stochastic Frontier Approach

The empirical approach followed so far has the shortcomings of not being strictly microfounded. The stochastic frontier approach followed in the next section will amend this problem and test whether different types of IT investment significantly affect non-random deviations from the optimal production frontier in our sample. We estimate the impact of IT investment on efficiency at firm level by using a traditional stochastic frontier approach. In this model the inefficiency effects are expressed as an explicit function of a vector of firm-specific variables and a random error.[14]

The first equation is specified as follows:

$$Y/L_{it} = \alpha_0 + \alpha_1 K/L_{it} + \sum_{j+1}^{m-1} \beta_j K/L_{it} * Ind_j + v_{it} - u_{it} \qquad (3).$$

Y/L is the log of real output per worker of the ith firm at time t ($i = 1,...,N$; $t = 1,...,T$); K/L is the log of the capital stock per worker where the capital stock is evaluated at the replacement cost of capital. We rewrite the Cobb-Douglas production function in terms of output per worker and capital per worker in order to remove potential problems of heteroskedasticity, multicollinearity and measurement of output (which should better be physical but is in value in our data) (Hay and Liu, 1997). Since any industrial sector may have in principle a different production function we add to the specification $m-1$ dummies accounting for differences in the output per worker-capital per worker elasticity between the reference sector and all other sectors. We consider 21 sectors aggregated on the basis of the four digit ISTAT-ATECO classification.

The v_{it} are random variables which are assumed to be iid. $N(0,\sigma_V^2)$, and independent of the u_{it} which are non-negative random variables which are assumed to account for technical inefficiency in production and are assumed to be independently distributed as truncations at zero of the $N(m_{it},\sigma_U^2)$ distribution; where: (4) $m_{it} = z_{it}\delta$, where z_{it} is a $p{\times}1$ vector of variables which may influence the efficiency of a firm; and δ is an $1{\times}p$ vector of parameters to be estimated.

We use the parameterization from Battese and Corra (1977), replacing σ_V^2 and σ_U^2 with $\sigma^2 = \sigma_V^2 + \sigma_U^2$ and $\gamma = \sigma_U^2/(\sigma_V^2 + \sigma_U^2)$. The log-likelihood function of this model is described in Battese and Coelli (1993).

The non-zero mean residual of the production function is regressed on a series of factors which are expected to affect efficiency:

$$u_{it} = \alpha_0 + \sum \alpha_i Ind_i + \sum \gamma_k Macroarea_k + \delta_1 Young + \delta_2 Old + \delta_3 Group$$
$$+ \delta_4 Csat + \delta_5 Qtnosep + \delta_6 Family + \delta_7 CSSA + \delta_8 Ration + \delta_9 Rents$$
$$+ \delta_{10} Presfi + \delta_{11} Innovat + \delta_{12} Cap + \delta_{12} Qlowsk + \delta_{13} IT$$

First, we introduce factors traditionally considered in the literature (Hay and Liu, 1997; Nickell, 1996; Nickell, Nicolitsas and Dryden, 1997) such as *CAP* (the degree of capacity utilization), *RENTS* – ((profits before tax + depreciation + interest payments – cost of capital*capital stock)/value added) and *PRESFI* – interest payments/(interest payment + cash flow). *IND, MACROAREA, SIZE, GROUP, QTNOSEP* and *FAMILY* are specified as in Appendix A.

We then add four dummies (*OLD, YOUNG, SMALL* and *BIG*) respectively picking up the older, the younger, the smaller and the larger 20 per cent of sample firms. An additional control (which we expect to be positively related to productive efficiency) is represented by *CSAT* and *CSSA*, two dummies respectively picking up firms monitoring customer satisfaction and firms which created sale structures abroad.[15] *INNOVAT* is a dummy for firms which successfully introduced new products or processes and *QLOWSK* is the share of low skilled on total workers.[16] Finally, *IT* is the dummy for firms investing in IT.

The model is estimated as a cross-section in which all variables are expressed as three year averages. We adopt two different specifications. In the first IT investments are considered jointly, while in the second they are disaggregated into software, hardware and telecommunications.

On the whole the model seems to fit well our data and the presence of technical inefficiencies is supported by the positive and significant gamma coefficient (Table 8.7).

Estimate results show that IT investment has a positive and significant effect on firm efficiency when it is jointly considered and that software (telecommunications) has positive (negative) effect when individually considered. These findings confirm (in direction and significance) results from simple regressions on the determinants of average labour productivity.

Other controls give expected results. Firms located in the south (affiliated to groups) are significantly less (more) efficient than average consistently with previous findings (Becchetti and Santoro, 2000). Firms declaring significant product or process innovation and those with internationalization processes (creation of sales structures abroad) are consistently more efficient than average. Efficiency is also positively related to ownership concentration consistently with the evidence surveyed by Short (1994) on several papers comparing performance of closely held and widely held firms. In small firms it appears obvious that ownership concentration raises controlling shareholders' incentives in managing efficiently their firms.[17] On the other side though, the negative impact of family ownership on efficiency may be explained by the fact that family ties may turn into constraints on the entrepreneurial activity limiting the facto the possibility of choice of the entrepreneur.

The coefficient of the utilization capacity rate is positive as expected since output for a given level of capital inputs is higher the higher the capacity utilization. This variable is useful to correct for inefficiencies determined by demand factors (or by entrepreneurs forecast errors on expected demand).The result on rents is consistent with all the traditional literature on the effects of competition on efficiency. According to it, competition has positive effects on efficiency (Short, 1994; Nickell, 1996; Vickers, 1995): i) by making it easier for owners to compare managerial performance with that of competitors;[18] ii) by increasing the advantage of higher efficiency under the form of cost reductions as the latter are more profitable under competition where demand elasticities are higher; iii) by leading managers to work harder in order to avoid bankruptcy which is more likely to occur in a tight market (Aghion and Howitt, 1996).

The hypothesis that financial pressure increases managerial discipline (Aghion et al. 1995) is not supported by our data. This hypothesis is expected to hold in a corporate governance framework (separation between ownership and control, market for corporate control, significant informational asymmetries between managers and ownership) which is different from that prevailing in our sample firms. We therefore argue that with scarce contendibility and no separation between ownership, control and management, efficiency types are likely to persist over time and high financial pressure may simply signal less efficient types if past negative performance which generated current financial distress is strongly correlated with actual performance.

Table 8.7   IT investment and productive efficiency: a stochastic frontier estimate (1997 cross-section estimate)

	Production function variables					Technical efficiency variables			
	Coef.	t-ratio	Coef.	t-ratio		Coef.	t-ratio	Coef.	t-ratio
Constant	5.340	109.399	5.400	110.620	Constant	0.847	5.707	0.876	5.461
Ln(K/L)	0.227	10.017	0.234	12.266	ind1	-0.708	-5.466	-0.669	-4.801
Ln(K/L)*ind1	0.010	0.369	0.002	0.069	ind2	-0.175	-1.358	-0.207	-1.712
Ln(K/L)*ind2	-0.035	-1.264	-0.046	-1.954	ind3	-0.272	-1.598	-0.297	-1.730
Ln(K/L)*ind3	0.020	0.531	0.009	0.269	ind4	-0.634	-3.263	-0.634	-3.173
Ln(K/L)*ind4	-0.117	-3.666	-0.129	-4.688	ind5	0.026	0.166	0.077	0.542
Ln(K/L)*ind5	0.018	0.582	0.027	1.044	ind6	-0.505	-2.649	-0.439	-2.137
Ln(K/L)*ind6	-0.009	-0.282	-0.010	-0.343	ind7	-0.549	-2.634	-0.482	-2.376
Ln(K/L)*ind7	-0.088	-2.474	-0.087	-3.157	ind8	-0.047	-0.194	0.158	0.754
Ln(K/L)*ind8	-0.070	-1.411	-0.022	-0.518	ind9	-0.408	-2.178	-0.424	-2.183
Ln(K/L)*ind9	-0.098	-2.744	-0.112	-3.505	ind10	0.495	2.262	0.520	2.532
Ln(K/L)*ind10	0.213	4.471	0.216	5.075	ind11	-0.483	-2.739	-0.438	-2.616
Ln(K/L)*ind11	-0.112	-3.638	-0.113	-4.663	ind12	-1.034	-4.291	-1.118	-3.999
Ln(K/L)*ind12	-0.144	-4.491	-0.164	-5.591	ind13	-0.689	-4.553	-0.690	-4.639
Ln(K/L)*ind13	-0.121	-4.655	-0.134	-5.887	ind14	-1.621	-4.047	-1.932	-4.485
Ln(K/L)*ind14	-0.168	-4.969	-0.187	-6.183	ind15	-0.561	-1.143	-1.074	-2.343
Ln(K/L)*ind15	-0.059	-1.365	-0.101	-2.296	Ind16	-0.959	-2.351	-1.175	-2.670
Ln(K/L)*ind16	-0.215	-4.329	-0.241	-5.718	Ind17	-1.358	-4.329	-1.502	-5.902
Ln(K/L)*ind17	-0.160	-5.099	-0.182	-7.015	Ind18	0.124	0.428	0.683	2.147
Ln(K/L)*ind18	-0.001	-0.019	0.134	1.951	Ind19	-1.979	-7.615	-2.414	-9.861
Ln(K/L)*ind19	-0.027	-0.686	-0.050	-1.291	Northwest	0.029	0.656	0.021	0.447
					Northeast	0.077	1.576	0.064	1.172

Table 8.7 con'td

	Production function variables				Technical efficiency variables			
	Coef.	t-ratio	Coef.	t-ratio	Coef.	t-ratio	Coef.	t-ratio
South					0.434	8.125	0.405	7.515
Young					0.058	1.603	0.060	1.577
Old					0.148	4.078	0.099	2.351
Group					-0.060	-1.632	-0.078	-1.938
Csat					-0.032	-0.903	-0.014	-0.361
Qtnosep					-0.001	-1.672	-0.001	-1.316
Family					0.057	1.898	0.070	2.082
CSSA					-0.149	-4.261	-0.118	-3.132
Ration					0.227	3.401	0.218	2.737
Rents					0.005	2.636	0.005	2.392
Presfi					0.004	1.923	0.004	2.057
Innovat					-0.037	-1.196	-0.008	-0.233
Cap					-0.005	-4.931	-0.005	-4.194
Lowsk					0.366	8.494	0.353	8.030
IT investment – aggregate							-0.000	-7.035
IT Hardware investments						0.000	0.598	
IT Software investments						-0.000	-3.432	
IT Telecommunication investments					0.000	2.219		
Sigma-squared					0.312	28.813	0.313	27.267
Gamma					0.164	4.832	0.199	5.393
Log L					2706.97		2714.18	
No. of obs					3392		3392	

Industry legend

ind1: Food, beverages, tobacco
Ind2: Textile, clothing
Ind3: Leather, shoes
Ind4: Wood and wooden furniture
Ind5: Paper and printing
Ind6: Chemicals
Ind7: Rubber and plastics
Ind8: Glass, ceramics
Ind9: Construction materials
Ind10: Metal extraction
ind11: Metal products
ind12: Mechanical materials
ind13: Mechanical equipment
ind14: Electronics
ind15: Electrical equipment
ind16: Precision instruments and apparel
ind17: Vehicles and vehicle components
ind18: Energy
ind19: Other manufacturing

7   Conclusions

Simple intuition from experience in various professional fields (including the academia) suggests that the increase in productivity from an improvement in software technology (more powerful word processing and printing, etc.) is positively related to the skills of the labour inputs. In the same way, an improvement in telecommunications technology (such as the opportunity of Internet or intranet networking, the introduction of e-mail, e-commerce, etc.) increases the inflow of available information thereby generating a flexibility option which will make more expensive and which will delay irreversible decisions such as new investments. This option will generate at the same time the opportunity to differentiate more quickly processes and products in order to satisfy consumers' taste for variety.

We therefore expect that, at any instant of time, a firm investing in telecommunications will delay investment in additional capacity and introduce new products and processes with a higher probability. We also expect this firm to have a higher capacity utilization and a lower average labour productivity if introduction of new products and processes goes together with a learning phase in which productive inputs have to be retrained.

What we should observe therefore is an increase in the demand for skilled workers and in average labour productivity after a software investment and an increase in capacity utilization together with a reduced average labour productivity and an increase introduction of new products and processes after a telecommunications investment.

Empirical results of our investigation support these hypotheses showing: i) the positive impact of software investment on the demand for skilled labour and on average labour productivity; ii) the positive (negative) impact of telecommunications investment on the creation of new products processes (on average labour productivity) and iii) the positive effect of aggregate IT investment on capacity utilization and on average labour productivity.

These results open interesting directions for future research. Which is the combined effect of higher productivity and reduced investment intensity generated by the option to delay on the rate of growth? Is the volume of high-tech investment socially optimal and, if not – considered that increased capacity utilization must be related with a lower rate of growth of the physical capital stock and considered the positive externality of this type of investment on the rest of the economy – which measures can be taken to reduce the incentive of high-tech firms to delay? We think that answers may be found on fiscal and monetary policies and on the governance of financial markets and that the different ability to implement measures in these three directions is significantly affecting the capacity of different countries of translating benefits of the new economy into higher rates of growth.

Notes

1   Information Technology is defined by the US Bureau of Economic Analysis as: 'Office, computing and accounting machinery'. As many researchers do we add to it communication equipment, software and related services.

2   Alpar and Kim (1990) also find, as we do, that key ratios and microfounded econometric approaches give very different results on the same data set.

3   These empirical studies identify another anomaly: industries that are IT intensive are more profitable than others, but, within industries, such intensity is negatively related with profitability (Morrison and Berndt 1990 and Berndt and Morrison 1995).

4   Jorgenson and Stiroh (1995), who also use a growth accounting approach, find an appreciably higher level of contribution by computing hardware to macroeconomic output. These authors estimate that computer hardware contributed 0.38 percentage points to the 2.49 per cent growth rate from 1985 to 1992 – more than double than the 0.15 estimate provided by Oliner and Sichel. These differences are in large part due to the different time periods of the studies and to different assumptions about depreciation rates.

5   Sichel (1997) asserts that there is no additional contribution of IT hidden in the multifactor productivity (MFP) estimate. MFP is a residual element that reflects technical and organizational changes that improve the efficiency of converting inputs into outputs, hence IT could contribute to gains that are captured by MFP. However, given the nature of growth accounting techniques, IT inputs would have to have a 'supernormal' rate of return, and Sichel argues that there is no compelling evidence for such an assumption.

6   Findings are based on a data set of 367 firms generating $1.8 trillion in aggregate sales in 1991.

7   The richness of the data set of Italian firms allows to overcome some traditional problems in the estimates of the impact of ownership and control on firm performance. The first problem is about the proxy adopted to identify ownership-controlled (OC) and manager-controlled (MC) firms which is usually based on percentage ownership criteria (Short, 1994). Cubbin and Leech (1983) and Leech and Leahy (1991) are among the few exceptions to the use of the ownership percentage criteria. They consider complex patterns of shareholdings, kinship networks and interlocking directories. It is well known that, as firms grow in size, control may be exerted with a limited ownership share and that a univocal relationship between the two variables does not exist at low ownership-control shares.

8   The following selection bias of the Mediocredito data set must be taken into account. More than 90 per cent of observed small firms (below 50 employees) are 'società di capitali' (entrepreneurs have limited liability) while this share is much lower and unlimited liability is widespread in the universe of Italian small firms. When interpreting empirical results we must therefore consider that we are analysing the subset of Italian small and medium sized firms with the most 'evolved' form of corporate governance.

9   This last finding could be partially explained by the fact that IT endowment of other participants to consortia and of consortia themselves may partially substitute for their own investment.

10   The reader can check Short (1994) for a detailed survey on the effect of ownership on firm choices (leverage, performance, ecc.); Chirinko (1993) for the impact of the availability of external finance on firm decisions; Gale (1991) and Schwarts and Clements (1999) for the impact of state subsidies on firm performance and Aw and Hwang, (1995), Clerides, Lach and Tybout (1998) and Becchetti and Santoro (2000) for the effect of internationalization on firm efficiency.

11   We use the ratio of high skilled (graduated) workers hired to total firm employees as a dependent variable.

12   As specified in the appendix with more analytical detail we may think of an investment in telecommunications has having a B2C (business to consumer) and a B2B (business to business) effect. The first enable producers to know in real time, through Internet communication, consumer tastes and the demand for differentiated products of the firms. The second allows through Internet and intranet communication the reduction of production lags and informational asymmetries among subcontractors and component producers at different levels of the chain value (i.e. the creation of 'digital auction markets' for specific product chains increase the number of participants, reduce transaction costs and reduce lags between the definition of new product characteristics adapting to changed consumer tastes and its availability to final consumers). In our model this creates for the IT investing firm the possibility to invest and adapt production in the same period in which consumer tastes are known.

13   Only with a wage which is insensitive to the total number of employees the marginal productivity of the last worker hired would be the same as before.

14   This approach has been widely recognized superior to the two-stage estimation which inconsistently assumes the independence of the inefficiency effects in the two estimation stages. The two-stage estimation procedure is unlikely to provide estimates which are as efficient as those that could be obtained using a single-stage estimation procedure.

15   The literature investigating the relationship between efficiency and internationalization usually finds a two-way positive relationship among the two variables (Aw and Hwang, 1995; Clerides, Lach and Tybout, 1998; Becchetti and Santoro, 2000). The variable is therefore an important control to be considered in order to avoid omitted variable biases.

16   This variable is used to evaluate the impact of differences in average human capital on productive efficiency.

17   The idea that ownership concentration has different impact on firm performance according to firm size seems supported by recent empirical evidence. McConnel and Servaes (1990) find a positive relationship on a large sample of listed and unlisted firms, while Leech and Leahy (1991) find a negative relationship on a small sample of large listed firms.

18   The relationship between competition and efficiency becomes unambiguous only when productivity shocks across competitors are more correlated than managerial abilities.

References

Aghion, P. and Howitt, P. (1996), 'Research and Development in the Growth Process', *Journal of Economic Growth*, 1 (1), pp. 49–73.

Ahituv, N. and Giladi, N. (1993), 'Business Success and Information Technology: Are They Really Related', *Proceedings of the 7th Annual Conference of Management IS*, Tel Aviv University.

Allen, T.J. and Scott Morton, M.S. (1994), *Information Technology and the Corporation of the 1990s*, Oxford: Oxford University Press.

Alpar, P. and Kim, M. (1990), 'A Comparison of Approaches to the Measurement of Information Technology Value', *Proceedings of the 22nd Hawaii International Conference on System Science*, Honolulu, HI.

Alpar, P. and Kim, M. (1991), 'A Microeconomic Approach to the Measurement of Information Technology Value', *Journal of Management Information Systems*, Fall, 7 (2), 55–69.

Applegate, L., Cash, J. and Mills, D.Q. (1988), 'Information Technology and Tomorrow's Manager', *Harvard Business Review*, November–December, pp. 128–36.

Attewell, P. and Rule, J. (1984), 'Computing and Organizations: What We Know and What We Don't Know', *Communications of the ACM*, 27 (December), pp. 1184–92.

Aw, B.Y. and Hwang, A. (1995), 'Productivity and Export Marker: A Firm Level Analysis', *Journal of Development Economics*, 47, pp. 209–31.

Ayres, R.U. (1989), 'Information, Computers, CIM and Productivity', Organization for Economic Co-operation and Development paper (June).

Baily, M.N. (1986a), 'Taming the Information Monster', *Bell Atlantic Quarterly*, Summer, pp. 33–8.

Baily, M.N. (1986b), 'What Has Happened to Productivity Growth?' *Science*, 234, pp. 443–51.

Baily, M.N. and Chakrabarti, A. (1988), 'Electronics and White-collar Productivity', in W.C. Brainard, and G.L. Perry (eds), *Innovation and Productivity Crisis*, Washington, DC: Brookings.

Baily, M.N. and Gordon, R.J. (1988), 'The Productivity Slowdown, Measurement Issues and the Explosion of Computer Power', *Brookings Papers in Economic Activity*, 1988(2), pp. 347–31.

Bakos, J.Y. (1987), 'Inter-organizational Information Systems: Strategic Implications for Competition and Cooperation', PhD Dissertation, MIT School of Management.

Bakos, J.Y. and Kemerer, C.F. (1992), 'Recent Application of Economic Theory in Information Technology Research', *Decision Support System*, 8, pp. 365–86.

Banker, R.D. and Kauffman, R.J. (1988), 'Strategic Contributions of Information Technology: An Empirical study of ATM Networks', *Proceedings of the 9th International Conference on Information Systems*, Minneapolis, Minnesota.

Barua, A., Kriebel, C. and Mukhopadhyay, T. (1991), 'Information Technology and Business Value: An Analytic and Empirical Investigation', University of Texas at Austin Working Paper (May).

Baumol, W.J. (1967), 'Macroeconomics of Unbalanced Growth: The Anatomy of Urban Crisis', *American Economic Review*, 57 (3), pp. 415–26.

Baumol, W.J., Blackman, S.A. and Wolff, E.N. (1985), 'Unbalanced Growth Revisited: Asymptotic Stagnancy and New Evidence', *American Economic Review*, 74 (4), pp. 806–17.

Becchetti, L. and Santoro, M. (2000), 'The Determinants of Small-medium Firm Internationalization and its Effects on Productive Efficiency', *Weltwirtschaftliches/Review of World Economics*, 137 (2), pp. 297–319.

Becchetti, L., Londoño Bedoya, D.A. and Paganetto, L. (2003), 'ICT Investment, Productivity and Efficiency: Evidence at Firm Level using a Stochastic Frontier Approach', *Journal of Productivity Analysis*, 20 (2), pp. 143–68.

Bender, D.H. (1986), 'Financial Impact of Information Processing', *Journal of Management Information Systems*, 3 (2), pp. 22–32.

Beniger, J. (1986), *The Control Revolution*, Cambridge, MA: Harvard University Press.

Benjamin, R.I., Rockart, J.F., Scott Morton, M.S. et al. (1984), 'Information Technology: A Strategic Opportunity', *Sloan Management Review*, Spring, pp. 3–10.

Berman, E., Bound, J., and Griliches, Z. (1994), 'Changes in the Demand for Skilled Labour within US Manufacturing: Evidence form the Annual Survey of Manufactures', *Quarterly Journal of Economics*, 109 (2), pp. 367–97.

Berndt, E.R. (1991), *The Practice of Econometrics: Classic and Contemporary*, Reading, MA: Addison-Wesley.

Berndt, E.R. and Malone, T.W. (1995), 'Information Technology and the Productivity Paradox: Getting the Questions Right; Guest Editor's Introduction to Special Issue', *Economics of Innovation and New Technology*, 3, pp. 177–82.

Berndt, E.R. and Morrison, C.J. (1991), 'Computers Aren't Pulling Their Weight', *Computerworld*, December, 9, pp. 23–5.

Berndt, E.R., Morrison, C.J. and Rosenblum, L.S. (1992), 'High-tech Capital Formation and Labour Composition in US Manufacturing Industries: an Exploratory Analysis', National Bureau of Economic Research Working Paper No. 4010 (March).

Berndt, E.R. and Morrison, C.J. (1995), 'High-tech Capital Formation and Economic Performance in US Manufacturing Industries: An Exploratory Analysis', *Journal of Econometrics*, 65, pp. 9–43.

Blinder, A.S. and Maccini, L.J. (1991), 'Taking Stock: A Critical Assessment of Recent Research on Inventories', *Journal of Economic Perspectives*, 5, pp. 73–96.

Brand, H. and Duke, J. (1982), 'Productivity in Commercial Banking: Computers Spur the Advance', *Monthly Labour Review*, 105 (December), pp. 19–27.

Bresnahan, T.F. (1986), 'Measuring Spillovers from Technical Advance: Mainframe Computers in Financial Services', *American Economic Review*, 76 (4) (September).

Bresnahan, T.F. and Trajtenberg, M. (1995), 'General Purpose Technologies and Aggregate Growth', *Journal of Econometrics*, 65, pp. 83–108.

Brooke, G.M. (1992), 'The Economics of Information Technology: Explaining the Productivity Paradox', MIT Sloan School of Management Center for Information Systems Research Working Paper No. 238 (April).

Brynjolfsson, E. (1993), 'The Productivity Paradox of Information Technology: Review and Assessment', *Communications of ACM*, December, 36 (12), pp. 67–77.

Brynjolfsson, E. (1994), 'Technology's True Payoff', *Informationweek*, October. 10, pp. 34–6.

Brynjolfsson, E. (1995), 'Some Estimates of the Contribution of Information Technology to Consumer Welfare', MIT Sloan School of Management Working Paper (August).

Brynjolfsson, E. and Hitt, L. (1993), 'Is Information Systems Spending Productive? New Evidence and New Results', *Proceedings of the 14th International Conference on Information Systems*, Orlando, FL.

Brynjolfsson, E. and Hitt, L. (1994), 'Computers and Economic Growth: Firm-level Evidence', MIT Sloan School of Management Working Paper No. 3714 (August).

Brynjolfsson, E. and Hitt, L. (1995), 'Information Technology as a Factor of Production: the Role of Differences among Firms', *Economics of Innovation and New Technology*, 3, pp. 183–99.

Brynjolfsson. E. and Hitt, L. (1996), 'Paradox Lost? Firm-level Evidence on the Returns to Information Systems Spending', *Management Science* (April).

Brynjolfsson, E., Malone, T. Gurbaxani, V. and Kambil, A. (1991), 'Does Information Technology Lead to Smaller Firms?', *Management Science*, 40 (12) (December), pp. 1628–44.

Champy, J. (1995), *Reengineering Management*, New York: HarperBusiness.

Cecil, J.L. and Hall, E.A. (1988), 'When IT Really Matters to Business Strategy', *McKinsey Quarterly* (Autumn), p. 2.

Chirinko, R.S. (1993), 'Business Fixed Investment Spending', *Journal of Economic Literature*, 31.

Chismar, W.G. and Kriebel, C.H. (1985), 'A Method for Assessing the Economic Impact of Information Systems Technology on Organizations', *Proceedings of the 6th International Conference on Information Systems*, Indianapolis, Indiana.

Clarke, R.F. (1985), 'The Application of Information Technology in an Investment Management Firm', Masters thesis, Massachusetts Institute of Technology, Cambridge, MA.

Clemens, E.K. (1991), 'Evaluation of Strategic Investment in Information Technology', *Communications of the ACM*, 34 (1), pp. 22–36.

Clerides, S.K., Lach, S. and Tybout, J. (1998), 'Is Learning-by-exporting Important? Microdynamic Evidence from Colombia, Mexico and Morocco', *Quarterly Journal of Economics*, CXIII, August, pp. 903–47.

Cooper, R.B. and Mukhopadhyay, T. (1990), 'Research in MIS Effectiveness: A Microeconomic Production View', Carnegie Mellon University Working Paper.

Cron, W.L. and Sobol, M.G. (1983), 'The Relationship Between Computerization and Performance: A Strategy for Maximizing the Economic Benefits of Computerization', *Information and Management*, 6, pp. 171–81.

Crowston, K. and Malone, T.W. (1988), 'Information Technology and Work Organization', in M. Helander (ed.), *Handbook of Human–Computer Interactions*, Amsterdam: Elsevier Science, pp. 1051–70.

Crowston, K. and Treacy, M.E. (1986), 'Assessing the Impact of Information Technology on Enterprise level Performance', MIT Center for Information Systems Research Working Paper, No. 143 (October).

Cubbin, J. and Leech, D. (1983), 'The Effect of Shareholding Dispersion on the Degree of Control in British Companies: Theory and Evidence', *Economic Journal*, 83, pp. 351–68.

Curley, K.F. and Pyburn, P.J. (1982), 'Intellectual Technologies: The Key to Improving White-collar Productivity', *Sloan Management Review*, Fall, pp. 31–9.

Davenport, T.H. (1993), *Process Innovation: Reengineering Work through Information Technology*, Boston, MA: Harvard Business School Press.

Davenport, T.H. and Short, J. (1990), 'The New Industrial Engineering: Information Technology and Business Process Redesign', *Sloan Management Review*, 31(4), pp. 11–27.

David, P.A. (1990), 'The Dynamo and the Computer and Dynamo: A Historical Perspective on the Modern Productivity Paradox', *American Economic Review Papers and Proceedings*, 80 (2) (May), pp. 355–61.

Denison, E.E. (1985), *Trends in American Economic Growth, 1929–1982*, Washington DC: Brookings Institution.

Denison, E.E. (1989), *Estimates of Productivity Change by Industry, an Evaluation and an Alternative*, Washington DC: Brookings Institution.

Diewert, W.E. and Smith, A.M. (1994), 'Productivity Measurement for a Distribution Firm', National Bureau of Economic Research Working Paper No. 4812 (July).

Dos Santos, B.L. Peffers. K.G. and Mauer, D.C. (1993), 'The Impact of Information Technology Investment Announcements on the Market Value of the Firm', *Information Systems Research*, 4 (1), pp. 1–23.

Dos Santos, B.L. Peffers. K.G. and Mauer, D.C. (1991), 'The Value of Investments in Information Technology: An Event Study', Kannert Graduate School of Management, Perdue University.

Dudley, L. and Lasserre, P. (1989), 'Information as a Substitute for Inventories', *European Economic Review*, 31, pp. 1–21.

Dulberger, E.R. (1989), 'The Application of Hedonic Model to a Quality Adjusted Price Index for Computer Processors', in Jorgenson, R. and Landau, D.W. (eds), *Technology and Capital Formation*, Cambridge, MA: MIT Press.

Fisher, F.M. and Griliches, Z. (1995), 'Aggregate Price Indices, New Goods, and Generics', *Quarterly Economics*, CX (1) (February), pp. 229–44.

Franke, R.H. (1987), 'Technological Revolution and Productivity Decline: Computer Introduction in the Financial Industry', *Technological Forecasting and Social Change*, 31, pp. 143–54.

Gale, W.G. (1991), 'Economic Effects of Federal Credit Programs', *American Economic Review*, pp. 133–52.

Gordon, R.J. (1987a), 'Productivity, Wages, and Prices Inside and Outside of Manufacturing in the US, Japan, and Europe', *European Economic Review*, April, 31 (3), pp. 685–739.

Gordon, R.J. (1987b), 'The Postwar Evolution of Computer Prices', National Bureau of Economic Research Working Paper No. 2227, Cambridge, MA.

Gordon, R.J. (1990), *The Measurement of Durable Goods Prices*, Chicago: University of Chicago Press.

Gordon, R.J. and Baily, M N. (1989), 'Measurement Issues and the productivity Slowdown in Five Major Industrial Countries', International Seminar on Science, Technology and Economic Growth, Paris, France.

Gremillion, L.L. and Pyburn, P.J. (1985), 'Justifying Decision Support and Office Automation Systems', *Journal of Management Information Systems*, 2 (1).

Griliches, Z. (1992), 'The Search for R&D Spillovers', *Scandinavian Economics*, 94, Supplement, pp. 29–47.

Griliches, Z. (ed.) (1992) (with the assistance of E.R. Berndt, T.F. Bresnahan and M.E. Manser), 'Output Measurement in the Service Sectors', *NBER Studies in Income and Wealth*, 56, University of Chicago Press.

Griliches, Z. (1994), 'Productivity, R&D, and Data Constraints', *American Economic Review*, 84 (1) (March).

Griliches, Z. (1995), 'Comments on Measurement Issues in Relating IT Expenditures to Productivity Growth', *Economics of Innovation and New Technology*, 3, pp. 317–21.

Griliches, Z. and Cockburn (1994), 'Generics and New Goods in Pharmaceutical Price Indexes', *American Economic Review*, LXXXIV.

Grove, A. S. (1990), 'The Future of the Computer Industry', *California Management Review*, 33 (1), pp. 148–60.

Gurbaxani, V. and Mendelson, H. (1989), 'The Use of Secondary Data in MIS Research', University of California, Irvine (March).

Hammer, M. (1990), 'Reengineering Work: Don't Automate, Obliterate', *Harvard Business Review*, July–August, pp. 104–12.

Hammer, M. and Champy, J. (1993), *Reengineering the Corporation*, New York: HarperBusiness.

Harris, S.E. and Katz, J.L. (1991), 'Organizational Performance and Information Technology Investment Intensity in the Insurance Industry', *Organizational Science*, 2 (3), pp. 263–96.

Hausman, J.A. (1994), 'Valuation of New Goods under Perfect and Imperfect Competition', National Bureau of Economic Research Working Paper No. 4970 (December).

Hay, D. and Lim, G. (1997), 'The Efficiency of Firms: What Difference does Competition Make?', *Economic Journal*, May.

Hitt, L. and Brynjolfsson, E. (1994), 'Three Faces of IT Value: The Theory and Evidence', *Proceedings of the 15th International Conference on Information Systems* (December).

Jonscher, C. (1994), 'An Economic Study of the Information Technology Revolution', in T.J. Allen and M.S. Scott Morton (eds), *Information Technology and the Corporation of the 1990s: Research Studies*, Oxford: Oxford University Press, pp. 5–42.

Jonscher, C. (1983), 'Information Resources and Economic Productivity', *Information Economics and Policy*, 1, pp. 13–35.

Jorgenson, D.W. and Landau, R. (eds) (1989), *Technology and Capital Formation*, Cambridge, MA: MIT Press.

Jorgenson, D.W. and Stiroh, K. (1995), 'Computers and Growth', *Economics of Innovation and New Technology*, 3, pp. 295–316.

Kaplan, R. (1989), 'Management Accounting for Advanced Technological Environments', *Science*, 245 (September), pp. 819–23.

Kaplan, R. and Norton, D.P. (1992), 'The Balanced Scorecard – Measures that Drive Performance', *Harvard Business Review*, January–February, pp. 71–9.

Katz, L.F. and Krueger, A.B. (1994), 'How Computers Have Changed the Workplace, 1984–1993', unpublished paper, Harvard University.

Kemerer, C.F. and Sosa, G.L. (1991), 'Systems Development Risks in Strategic Information Systems', *Information and Software Technology*, 33 (3) (April), pp. 212–23.

Kriebel, C.H. (1989), 'Understanding the Strategic Investment in IT', in K.C. Lauden and J.A. Turner (eds), *Information Technology and Management Strategy*, Englewood Cliffs, NJ: Prentice Hall.

Krueger, A.B. (1993), 'How Computers Have Changed the Wage Structure: Evidence from Micro-data, 1984–1989', *Quarterly Journal of Economics*, 108 (1), pp. 33–60.

Kwon, M.J. and Stoneman, P. (1995), 'The Impact of Technology Adoption on Firm Productivity', *Economics of Innovation and New Technology*, 3, pp. 219–33.

La Porta, R., Lopes de Silanes, F. and Shleifer, A. (1998), 'Corporate Ownership around the World', *Journal of Finance*, 59 (2), pp. 471–517.

Landauer, T.K. (1995), *The Trouble with Computers*, Cambridge, MA: MIT Press.

Lasserre, P. (1988), 'Project on the Impact of Information on Productivity', unpublished paper (September).

Lau, L.J. and Tokutsu, I. (1992), 'The Impact of Computer Technology on the Aggregate Productivity of the United States: An Indirect Approach', unpublished paper, Stanford University (August).

Leech, D. and Leahy, J. (1991), 'Ownership Structure, Control Type Classifications and the Performance of Large British Companies', *Economic Journal*, 101, pp. 1418–37.

Lichtenberg, F.R. (1995), 'The Output Contributions of Computer Equipment and Personal: A Firm-level Analysis', *Economics of Innovation and New Technology*, 3, pp. 201–17.

Loveman, G.W. (1994), 'An Assessment of the Productivity Impact of Information Technologies', in T.J. Allen and M.S. Scott Morton (eds), *Information Technology and the Corporation of the 1990s: Research Studies*, Oxford: Oxford University Press, pp. 84–110.

Malone, T. and Rockart, J. (1991), 'Computers, Networks and the Corporation', *Scientific American*, 265 (3), pp. 128–36.

Mark, J.A. (1982), 'Measuring Productivity in the Service Sector', *Monthly Labour Review* (June).

McKersie, R.B. and Walton, R.E. (1991), 'Organizational Change', in M.S. Scott Morton (ed.), *The Corporation of the 1990s*, Oxford: Oxford University Press, pp. 244–77.

Milgrom, P. and Roberts R. (1988), 'The Economics of Modern Manufacturing: Products, Technology and Organization', Stanford Center for Economic Policy Research Discussion Paper 136.

Morrison, C.J. and Berndt, E.R. (1991), 'Assessing the Productivity of Information Technology Equipment in US Manufacturing Industries', National Bureau of Economic Research Working Paper No. 3582 (January).

Nelson, R.R. (1981), 'Research on Productivity Growth and Productivity Differences: Dead Ends and new Departures', *Journal of Economic Literature*, 29, pp. 1029–64.

Nickell, S.J. (1996), 'Competition and Corporate Performance', *Journal of Political Economcy*, 104, pp. 724–66.

Nickell, S.J., Nicolitses, D. and Dryden, N. (1997), 'What Makes Firms Perform Well 2', *European Economic Review*, 41, pp. 783–96.

Noyelle, T. (1990), *Skills, Wages, and Productivity in the Service Sector*, Boulder, CO: Westview Press.

Oliner, S.D. and Sichel, D.E. (1994), 'Computers and Output Growth Revisited: How Big is the Puzzle?', *Brookings Papers on Economic Activity*, 1994 (2), pp. 273–334.

Osterman, P. (1986), 'The Impact of Computers on the Employment of Clerks and Managers', *Industrial and Labour Relations Review*, 39, pp. 175–86.

Parsons, D.J., Gotlieb, C.C. and Denny, M. (1990), 'Productivity and Computers in Canadian Banking', University of Toronto Department of Economics Working Paper No. 9012 (June).

Porat, M. (1977), *The Information Economy: Definition and Measurement*, Washington, DC: US Government Printing Office.

Porter, M.E. and Miller, V.E. (1985), 'How Information Gives You Competitive Advantage', *Harvard Business Review*, July–August, pp. 149–60.

Pulley, L.B. and Braunstein, Y.M. (1984), 'Scope and Scale Augmenting Technological Change: An Application in the Information Sector', in M. Jussawalla and H. Ebenfield (eds), *Communication and Information Economics: New Perspectives*, Amsterdam: Elsevier.

Roach, S.S. (1989a), 'Pitfalls of the New Assembly Line: Can Service Learn From Manufacturing?', *Morgan Stanley Special Economic Study*, New York (June 22).

Roach, S.S. (1989b), 'America's White-collar Productivity Dilemma', *Manufacturing Engineering*, August , p. 104.

Roach, S.S. (1987), 'America's Technology Dilemma: A Profile of the Information Economy', *Morgan Stanley Special Economic Study* (April).

Roach, S.S. (1991), 'Services under Siege: the Restructuring Imperative', *Harvard Business Review*, 39 (2) (September–October), pp. 82–92.

Romer, P.M. (1986), 'Increasing Returns and Long-Run Growth', *Journal of Political Economy*, 94 (5), pp. 1002–37.

Romer, P.M. (1987), 'Crazy Explanations for the Productivity Slowdown', in S. Fisher (ed.), *NBER Macroeconomics Annual: 1987*, Cambridge, MA: MIT Press.

Scherer, F. (1980), *Industrial Market Structure and Economic Performance*, Chicago, IL: Rand-McNally.

Schneider, K. (1987), 'Services Hurt by Technology: Productivity is Declining', *The New York Times*, 29 June, D1, D6.

Schwarts, G. and Clements, B. (1999), 'Government Subsidies', *Journal of Economic Surveys*, 13 (2), pp. 119–47.

Scott Morton, M.S. (ed.) (1991), *The Corporation of the 1990s: Information Technology and Organizational Transformation*, Oxford: Oxford University Press.

Short, E. (1994), 'Ownership, Control, Financial Structure and the Performance of Firms', *Journal of Economic Surveys*, 8, pp. 203–49.

Siegel, D. (1994), 'The Impact of Computers on Manufacturing Productivity Growth: A Multiple-Indicators, Multiple-Causes Approach', SUNY at Stony Brook Working Paper (May).

Siegel, D. and Griliches, Z. (1992), 'Purchased Services, Outsourcing, Computers, and Productivity in Manufacturing', in Z. Griliches et al. (eds), *Output Measurement in the Service Sectors*, Chicago, IL: University of Chicago Press.

Snow, C.P. (1966), 'Government Science and Public Policy', *Science*, 151, pp. 650–53.

Stabell, C.B. (1982), 'Office Productivity: A Microeconomic Framework for Empirical Research', *Office: Technology and People*, 1, pp. 91–106.

Stiroh, K.J. (1998), 'Computers Productivity and Input Substitution', *Economic Inquiry*, 36 (2), April, pp. 175–91.

Strassmann, P.A. (1985), *Information Payoff: The Transformation of Work in the Electronic Age*, New York: Free Press.

Strassmann, P.A. (1990), *The Business Value of Computers: An Executive's Guide*, New Canaan, CT: Information Economics Press.

Thurow, L. (1987), 'Economic Paradigms and Slow American Productivity Growth', *Eastern Economic Journal*, 13, pp. 333–43.

Trajtenberg, M. (1990), 'Product Innovations, Price Indices and the (Mis)measurement of Economic Performance', National Bureau of Economic Research Working Paper No. 3261 (February).

Vickers, J. (1995), 'Entry and Competition Selection', mimeo.

Watts, L. (1986), 'What Price Automation?', *Northeastern University Alumni Magazine*, pp. 21–24.

Weill, P. (1992), 'The Relationship Between Investment in Information Technology and Firm Performance: A Study of the Valve Manufacturing Sector', *Information Systems Research*, 3 (4), pp. 307–33.

Weitzendorf, T. and Wigand, R. (1991), 'Tasks and Decisions: A Suggested Model to Demonstrate Benefits of Information Technology', Institute for Information Science Working Paper, Graz, Austria.

Wilson, D.D. (1995), 'IT Investment and Its Productivity Effects: An Organizational Sociologist's Perspective on Directions for Future Research', *Economics of Innovation and New Technology*, 3, pp. 235–51.

Zachary, G.P. (1991), 'Computer Data Overload Limits Productivity Gains', *Wall Street Journal*, 11 November, B1.

Appendix A

To consider the impact of IT investment on different dependent variables we formulate a general model with six types of general controls plus specific controls which may be relevant for the selected dependent variable.
The estimated model is:

$$IO = \alpha_0 + \sum_{i-1}^{m-1} \alpha_i Ind_i + \sum_{j-1}^{p-1} \delta_j Pavitt_j + \sum_{k-1}^{n-1} \gamma_k Macroarea_k + \sum_{l-1}^{d-1} \alpha_l Identity_l$$

$$+ \sum_{f-1}^{g-1} \delta_j Ownership_j + \sum_{s-1}^{w-1} \gamma_s Finance_s + \sum_{r-1}^{z-1} \gamma_r IPHC_r + \sum_{q-1}^{y-1} \gamma_q ITV_q + \varepsilon \tag{1}$$

where *IO* is the selected intermediate variable (utilization capacity, hiring rate of skilled workers, introduction of new products or processes, net sales per employee) measured in 1997. Given the distributions of these dependent variables (see Table 8.A1) we adopt a right censored Tobit model for utilization capacity, a left censored Tobit model for the hiring rate of skilled workers, a Logit model for the introduction of new products or processes and least squares for net sales per employee. Since dependent variables are not normally distributed (see Table 8.A1) we estimate confidence intervals for regressors coefficients with bootsrapping techniques (we adopt the percentile method with 1000 replications). In the case of the net sales per employee estimate we check whether the impact of regressors are significant not only on conditional mean but also on conditional median.
Our groups of general controls are:

1 *IND* are $m - 1$ industry dummies based on a three-digit ATECO classification *(m = 1,...,20)*,
2 *PAVITT* are $p - 1$ macrosector dummies *(p = 1,...,4)*,[1]
3 *MACROAREA* are $n - 1$ macroarea dummies *(n = 1,...,4)*,
4 *IDENTITY:* (three variables) *SIZE* are firm's employees in 1995, *BIRTH* is the firm's year of establishment, EXPORT is a dummy for exporting firms.
5 *OWNERSHIP*: (six variables) *GROUP* is a dummy which takes value of one for firms affiliated to groups (subsidiaries or parent companies) and zero otherwise; *FAMILY* is a dummy which takes value of one if the firm is 'family controlled' (all controllers are linked by kinship),[2] *SOCBANK* is a dummy for firms having financial intermediaries among controlling

shareholders.[3] *CONPUB* is a dummy for firms in which the government is a controlling shareholder, *CMS* is a dummy for firms with controlling minority shareholders (the control group owns less than 40 per cent of firm capital), *CNTRNM* is the number of controlling shareholders and is introduced as a proxy for coordination costs.

6 *FINANCE*: (five regressors on the availability and costs of external and internal finance): *SUBSIDY* is a dummy indicating if the firm received soft loans, *AGEVOL* is a dummy for firms which received tax allowances in the 1995–97 period, *RATION* is a dummy indicating type I or type II credit rationing (the firm declares she asked and did not received credit (additional credit) at the prevailing rate in the considered period), *LEV* is the 1995 ratio of debt versus banks to total assets,[4] *CONFIDI* is a dummy for firms affiliated to credit consortia, *PRESFI* measures firm financial pressure and is calculated as interest expenditures /(gross profits + depreciation+ interest expenditures), *NBANC* is a proxy for multiple borrowing and is the number of banks with whom the firm has relationship, *QPBANC* is the share of the first lender on firm debt.

7 *INNOVATION, HUMAN AND PHYSICAL CAPITAL*: (four controls for technological innovation) *INNOVAT* is a dummy taking value of one if the observed firm declares to have successfully innovated their products or processes, *R&DINV* is a dummy for firms with non-zero R&D investment in 1995. *QLWSK* is the 1995 share of low skilled workers on total employees, *CAPAD* is capital intensity or the stock of physical capital per employee.

8 *ITV*: is a vector of information technology variables. *ITXASOF*, *ITXAHAR*, *ITXATEL* and *ITXTELG* are respectively the 1995–97 investment in software, hardware, telecommunications and telecommunication for firms participating to groups only. All these variables are scaled for the total number of firm employees.

We decide to use so many controls in order to reduce the possibility of omitted variable bias. In our case we want to avoid that the significance of IT variables be explained by correlations with omitted regressors and than that the former are in reality significant because they proxy for other hidden variables which are the true determinants of our observed dependent variables. On the other hand, though, we are aware that overparametrization leads to reduced efficiency (too high standard error) and potential multicollinearity among IT regressors. In that case insignificant controls may ultimately reduce the effective impact of the former on the dependent variable. It is well known that a comparison in terms of mean squared errors shows then that it is better to omit the variable if the coefficient of the omitted variable is small and insignificant and if there is small correlation between excluded and included. For this reason after using the overparametrized specification we adopt a stepwise backward approach to reduce the number of regressors. The test for omission of redundant variable is performed at constant number of observations and the order of deletion follows that of the coefficient lowest significance. Results of estimates including all controls are shown in Table 8.A2 while final results from the stepwise backward approach are presented in Table 8.A3.

Table 8.A1 Percentile distribution and normality tests for dependent variables of econometric estimates in Table 8.A2

Percentile	Fatad97	Dhsk	Cap97
10	133.572	0.000	0.70
20	169.263	0.000	0.70
30	200.000	0.000	0.80
40	231.250	0.000	0.80
50	267.653	0.000	0.85
60	309.989	0.000	0.90
70	369.003	0.000	0.90
80	468.196	0.000	0.95
90	637.343	0.011	1.00
100	19417.850	0.654	1.00
Mean	368.634	0.004	0.831
Obs	4445	3317	4309
Normality tests			
Shapiro Wilk Z	19.472	18.109	12.020
P-value (reject the null)	0.9999	0.9999	0.9999
Shapiro Francia Z	4.966	6.565	4.385
P-value(reject the null)	0. 9999	0.9999	0.9999

Notes

1   These are three of the four Pavitt dummies (scale, specialized, high-tech and traditional sectors). We adopt both the Pavitt and the 21-sector extended classification since firms within the same sector often belong to different Pavitt macrosectors. The inspection of the correlation matrix shows that this choice does not create severe multicollinearity problems in the estimate. The correlation matrix is available from the authors upon request.

Table 8.A2 The effect of IT investment on intermediate and productivity variables

	Demand for high skilled workers (l.c. Tobit)		Introduction of new products		Introduction of new products and processes		Capacity utilization (r.c.Tobit)		Net sales per employee (conditional mean)		Net sales per employee (conditional median)	
	Coef.	b.s.e.	Coef.	z	Coef.	Z	Coef.	b.s.e.	Coef.	b.s.e	Coef.	b.s.e.
Ind-01	0.036	0.015**	0.938	1.240	0.664	0.896	-10.410	4.093**	6.002	187.049	209.526	62.461**
Ind-02	0.015	0.011	1.770	2.506	1.101	1.607	-6.505	3.784	-172.770	114.121*	-48.766	43.327
Ind-03	-0.030	0.179	1.010	1.152	0.059	0.062	-1.682	4.659	-58.227	139.481	63.638	72.699
Ind-04	0.024	0.014**	1.998	2.618	1.700	2.274	-8.509	4.327**	-221.035	135.866*	-48.734	47.531
Ind-05	0.005	0.007	0.400	0.766	0.396	0.720	-3.001	3.292	-238.448	178.428	-45.458	39.178
Ind-06	0.006	0.007	0.841	1.748	0.814	1.673	0.005	3.292	-9.306	115.027	97.466	45.626**
Ind-07	-0.003	0.008	0.998	2.305	0.726	1.557	-2.886	2.584	-94.737	99.839	-19.412	28.550
Ind-08	-0.002	0.008	0.417	0.720	0.123	0.200	-2.104	3.055	-197.438	124.696*	-84.863	49.372
Ind-09	0.007	0.022	0.375	0.478	0.584	0.767	-4.762	3.841	-314.336	203.090*	-44.790	54.969
Ind-10	0.008	0.008	0.713	1.379	0.886	1.676	-4.472	3.332	279.151	190.569*	120.110	58.787**
Ind-11	0.017	0.010**	1.660	2.635	1.521	2.503	-6.926	3.262**	-179.947	100.903**	-64.316	34.950
Ind-12	0.004	0.008	1.425	2.792	0.736	1.420	0.610	3.197	-4.201	67.167	40.408	37.749
Ind-13	0.004	0.006	0.755	1.844	0.438	1.004	0.838	2.562	-22.490	52.180	8.283	24.855
Ind-14	0.014	0.010	0.559	0.867	0.211	0.324	2.988	3.926	-1.216	110.228	-2.955	53.772
Ind-15	0.016	0.008**	0.216	0.264	0.009	0.010	-6.115	3.194	-103.205	77.565	-3.145	38.796
Ind-16	n.i.	n.i.	1.167	1.130	1.398	1.336	n.i.	n.i.	-35.736	127.367	-82.528	46.651
Ind-17	0.010	0.007	0.683	1.419	0.461	0.919	-2.416	3.049	-75.139	67.320	-26.499	26.148
Ind-18	n.i.	n.i.	0.575	0.571	0.612	0.630	3.515	5.228	-88.597	136.015	-119.534	106.003
Ind-19	n.i.	n.i.	1.704	1.779	1.729	1.579	n.i.	n.i.	1,644.061	1470.973	346.003	1,919.846
Scala	-0.002	0.007	-0.047	-0.094	-0.129	-0.272	2.619	2.932	34.645	83.799	-39.259	38.930
Special	0.001	0.008	0.024	0.048	-0.081	-0.169	2.296	3.123	-3.492	83.643	-54.724	41.074
Tradiz	-0.002	0.012*	-1.079	-1.462	-0.775	-1.111	5.715	3.658	110.086	112.071	-17.478	46.404
Novest	0.0008	0.004	-0.333	-1.294	-0.421	-1.624	-0.527	1.491	48.773	60.479	4.552	21.785
Nest	0.003	0.005	-0.524	-1.863	-0.751	-2.579	-0.652	1.651	67.393	83.776	8.718	25.804
Sud	-0.009	0.009	-0.311	-0.777	-0.195	-0.502	-2.272	1.998	-80.467	83.497	-3.584	34.163

Table 8.A2 cont'd

	Demand for high skilled workers (l.c. Tobit)		Introduction of new products		Introduction of new products and processes		Capacity utilization (r.c.Tobit)		Net sales per employee (conditional mean)		Net sales per employee (conditional median)	
	Coef.	b.s.e.	Coef.	z	Coef.	Z	Coef.	b.s.e.	Coef.	b.s.e.	Coef.	b.s.e.
Size	0.000001	0.000003**	0.0001	0.574	0.0001	0.722	0.001	0.001	-0.043	0.079	0.010	0.021
Birth	-0.00003	0.00007	0.006	1.214	0.006	1.462	-0.060	0.025**	-1.007	0.804	-0.202	0.328
Export	0.012	0.005**	0.287	1.164	0.144	0.583	-1.091	1.284	-138.596	132.642	20.511	19.517
Gruppo	0.019	0.004**	-0.124	-0.608	0.177	0.925	-0.632	1.057	44.379	34.283	21.470	15.499
Family	-0.004	0.003	-0.373	-1.937	-0.424	-2.134	0.359	1.098	-22.972	66.510	5.984	14.462
Socbank	0.006	0.004*	0.074	0.251	0.169	0.615	-0.380	1.553	210.569	157.923	-9.906	27.136
Contpub	-0.034	0.065**	0.818	1.099	1.133	1.508	-3.510	3.557	-2.242	146.341	-29.447	50.573
Cms	n.i.	n.i.	-1.819	-1.795	-1.386	-1.344	n.i.	n.i.	-145.999	170.874	16.615	85.661
Cntrnm	0.001	0.001	-0.017	-0.160	-0.056	-0.513	0.191	0.568	29.785	27.159	-0.823	7.253
Subsidy	-0.002	0.005	-0.560	-1.354	-0.574	-1.554	1.211	2.383	24.297	57.907	23.045	23.396
Agevol	0.013	0.006**	0.844	2.021	0.926	2.452	-1.928	2.381	-120.599	83.631	-32.625	23.346
Ration	0.014	0.006**	1.611	3.060	1.502	3.198	-3.396	2.912	-179.682	91.874**	-90.852	29.869**
Lev	-0.004	0.008	-0.307	-0.596	-0.150	-0.287	4.856	2.912	426.919	122.973***	182.850	43.559**
Confidi	0.015	0.008**	0.784	2.123	0.704	2.145	-0.640	1.483	-15.364	51.949	-21.284	24.330
Prefi	-0.0001	0.0009	-0.089	-1.451	-0.063	-1.193	0.068	0.418	-0.289	14.116	-0.156	5.645
Nbanc	0.0001	0.0002	0.023	1.338	0.024	1.446	0.049	0.084	12.885	12.125	0.769	1.461
Qpbanc	-0.000001	0.000005	0.002	0.838	0.003	0.980	-0.064	0.017**	1.486	0.977*	0.003	0.252
Innovat	-0.001	0.004					-0.866	1.260	28.496	47.165	25.230	17.414
Rdinv	0.001	0.003	0.569	3.264	0.575	3.207	-1.999	1.014**	30.343	53.129	-21.951	13.633
Qlwsk	0.365	0.267**	0.495	0.132	0.688	0.210	-13.078	27.843	-96.530	1142.75	925.243	921.320
Capad	-0.000001	0.00002	-0.002	-2.078	-0.002	-1.625	0.008	0.010	3.317	1.560**	1.030	0.203**
Amm	0.005	0.010					1.530	4.605				
Itxasof	0.001	0.0008**	-0.006	-0.142	-0.005	-0.108	0.054	0.258	58.973	35.293**	15.442	6.867**
Itxahar	-0.0003	0.0005	-0.076	-2.513	-0.031	-0.946	-0.041	0.197	-2.679	17.210	-2.330	7.010
itxatel	0.002	0.002	0.315	0.881	0.938	2.762	-3.641	1.891	-122.074	81.866**	-6.319	18.215

Table 8.A2 cont'd

	Demand for high skilled workers (l.c. Tobit)		Introduction of new products		Introduction of new products and processes		Capacity utilization (r.c. Tobit)		Net sales per employee (conditional mean)		Net sales per employee (conditional median)	
	Coef.	*b.s.e.*	*Coef.*	*z*	*Coef.*	*Z*	*Coef.*	*b.s.e.*	*Coef.*	*b.s.e*	*Coef.*	*b.s.e*
Itxtelg			1.073	2.105			4.583	2.274**	3.316	1.560**	135.433	60.486**
Cons			−0.823	−1.084	−1.152	−1.505						
F	69.56		Wald		Wald 04.41		Wald 99.75		3.79		2.23	
R sq.	0.18		0.12		0.12		0.09		0.29			
No. of obs	866		761		761		883		905			

** Significant at 95% with two methods to compute confidence intervals: bias-corrected and percentile.
* Significant at 95% with one method to compute confidence intervals: only bias-corrected.
n.i. Not included.

Table 8.A3 The effect of IT investment on intermediate and productivity variables (bootstrap stepwise regression estimates)

Demand for high skilled workers (l.c. Tobit)			Capacity utilization (r.c.Tobit)			Net sales per employee (conditional mean)		
High skill demand	Coef.	b.s.e.	Cap97	Coef.	b.s.e.	Fatad97	Coef.	b.s.e.
Ind-01	0.018	0.009*	Ind-01	-4.086	1.024**	Contban	178.000	129.063
South	-0.014	0.007**	Itxatele	-1.247	1.126	Agevol	-109.660	45.828 **
Ind-03	-0.036	0.144*	Qpbanc	-0.048	0.010**	lev	536.076	94.541**
Agevol	0.010	0.003**	Itxatelg	1.998	1.328*	Itxatel	-98.994	58.788*
Contpub	-0.040	0.078***	Age	-0.025	0.014	stkad95	3.228	1.041**
Export	0.014	0.005**				Itxasof	38.488	21.081**
Itxasoft	0.0007	0.0004***				ind-19	1846.008	1050.796**
Tradiz	-0.011	0.003**				ind-10	272.735	201.016
Size	0.00001	0.000003**				Nbanc	8.467	7.435
Group	0.020	0.003**						
Confidi	0.022	0.007**						
Qlwsk	0.450	0.283**						
LR chi2(12) =	188.30		LR chi2(5) =	42.17				

** Significant at 95% with two methods to compute confidence intervals: bias-corrected and percentile.
* Significant at 95% with one method to compute confidence intervals: only bias-corrected.

2   La Porta et al. (1999) have recently emphasized the importance of family ownership on corporate structure in the world. They find that in 1995, for firms with a market capitalization of at least 500 million dollars, family owned firms represented from 60 to 80 per cent of the sample in Italy, up to 40 per cent in the UK and 20 per cent in the US. Countries like Israel, Honk Kong, Mexico, Argentina and Sweden all had in 1995 a share of family owned firms higher than 50 per cent.

3   When financial intermediaries are also controlling shareholders the traditional divergence of incentives existing between (lenders) financiers and entrepreneurs is eliminated. Therefore it should be easier for firms to finance investment in risky activities.

4   In balance sheet data the following debt items are registered: i) debt versus banks; ii) debt versus partners; iii) debt versus group; iv) debt versus suppliers – customers anticipated payments; v) bonds. Items ii) and iii) should be considered as equity more than debt, because non-individual firms are often participated with a share higher than 50 pre cent. Item iv) is commercial debt more linked to operating expenses than to investment financing. We use total assets and not equity capital as a scale variable because all firms are small and medium sized, not listed in the stock exchange and most of them family owned. As a consequence, equity capital is often a symbolic balance sheet item, extremely volatile and not representative of firm's stock of total assets.

Appendix B

Hypothesis 1: Investment in Software Increases the Demand for Skilled Labour

Consider a cost minimization problem of the type:

min wx
s.t. $f(L_1, L_2, K, K_{it})$

where **x** is the vector of the four inputs which are argument of the profit function (L_1 is skilled labour, L_2 is unskilled labour K is stock of capital, K_{it} is the stock of information technology capital including hardware, software and telecommunications) and **w** is the vector of their prices.

The production possibility set L is the set of all combinations of the input vector **x** producing output y with the usual regularity properties. It is closed, convex, and is bounded from above.

Imagine a technological shift which makes available a new vintage of IT technology under the form of more powerful computer software. IT technology has a stronger complementarity relationhsip with skilled than with non-skilled labour (i.e. more powerful software such as the introduction of an e-mail program in English increases more the productivity of skilled vis-à-vis that of non-skilled workers as the former know English better and have more computing knowledge allowing them to use e-mail more productively).

Since this increases overall productivity the new technology will be adopted and this will correspond to a discrete change in the amount of K_{it}. Which is the effect on the demand of the two labour inputs? By simple inspection of the first order condition from cost minimization we know that:

$$\frac{w_i}{w_j} = \frac{\delta y(.)/\delta x_i}{\delta y(.)/\delta x_j},$$

therefore if $w'_{L1} = 0$ and if $\delta MP_{L1}/\delta K_{it} > \delta MP_{L2}/\delta K_{it}$ then $\delta L*_1/\delta K_{it} > \delta L*_1/\delta K_{it}$.

Hypothesis 3: Investment in Information Technology Increases the Value of the Firm by Adding a Flexibility Option whose Effects is that of Increasing on Average Capacity Utilization

Consider the case of an entrepreneur which must invest in additional capacity and has not invested in IT. The entrepreneur knows that in t_1 there will be a taste shock which will affect the demand of the product generated with additional capacity. The model is in two periods.

Additional capacity will therefore yield to him extra revenues generated by the following process: X in *to* and $X(1 + g)$ in t_1 if the shock increases demand for the product (with prob p) and $X(1 - d)$ if the shock reduces the demand for the product (with prob $1 - p$). The non-IT entrepreneur must decide now because: i) either he has not the technology to know in real time consumer tastes (know in t_1 the realization of the shock in t_1) or; ii) because its productive process cannot be adapted in t_1 (extra additional capacity cannot be added) to produce in t_1. In other terms we postulate that an investment in telecommunications has a B2C (business to consumer) and a B2B (business to business) effect. The first allows through Internet communication to know in real time consumer tastes and the demand for differentiated products of the firms. The second allows through Internet and intranet communication the reduction of production lags and informational asymmetries among subcontractors and component producers at different levels of the chain value (i.e. Internet auctions among subcontractors in 'digital markets' increase the number of participants, reduce transaction costs and reduce lags between the definition of product characteristics and its availability to final consumers). In our model this creates for the IT investing firm the possibility to invest and adapt production in t_1 after knowing consumer tastes in the same period.

The value of its investment in extra capacity will be:

$$\Omega_{NIT} = \max \{V_0 - I, 0\}$$

where $V_0 = X + [X(1 + g)p + X(1 - d)(1 - p)](1/(1 + r))$ or $V_0 = X + [X(1 + p(g + d) - d)](1/(1 + r))$. The entrepreneur which has invested in information technology (and in telecommunications technology) may know in real time consumer tastes on its web site and has eliminated lags between changes in productive capacity and final production. Therefore the value of its investment changes into:

$$\Omega_{NIT} = \max \left\{ V_0 - I, \frac{E_0[F_1]}{1 + r} \right\}$$

where $= p*max[X(1 + g) - I,0] + (1 - p)*max[X(1 - d) - I,0]^1$ is the expected value today of the continuation value. The investment in IT will therefore increase the value of the IT investing firm by the flexibility option which is equal to $\Omega_{IT} - \Omega_{NIT}$. It is obvious then that there will be values of g,d,p such that:

$$0 < V_0 - I < \frac{E_0[F_1]}{1 + r}.$$

If this condition holds the IT entrepreneur will find it optimal to wait in t_0 and the non-IT entrepreneur will find it optimal to invest in additional capacity. As a result, capacity utilization will be higher for the IT entrepreneur in t_1 if the negative shock is realized (with probability $(1 - p)$) as with the negative shock the additional capacity I is too much to produce just $X(1 - d)$. The inequality holds when $V_0 - I > 0$ (NC_1) if

$$X + [X(1 + p(g + d) - d)](1/(1 + r)) - I < [p*max[X(1 + g) - I,0] + (1 - p)*max[X(1 - d) - I,0]] (1/(1 + r))$$

In choosing whether to postpone the investment the IT entrepreneur therefore trades off the advantage from investing soon (the present cash flow from the investment in t_0 (X)) with the advantage from waiting and avoiding to invest under the bad state of nature in t_1 and from reducing the expected cost of the investment. Therefore if $X > Ir/(1 + r)$, it is convenient to wait only if the investment would give nonpositive returns in case the bad state of nature is realized. It is therefore clear that the value of the option to wait is increasing in the discount rate and – if the value of the project is non-positive under the negative shock – in the size of the negative shock and while it is decreasing in the project value.

To check that the same arguments holds in continuous time and with a slightly more complicated stochastic process for returns from the project of investing in additional capacity. Consider the following argument developed by following the standard Dixit-Pindick approach.

Let the return from investing in additional capacity follow the geometric Brownian motion: $dY = \alpha Y dt + \sigma Y dz$ where dz is the increment of a Wiener process so that $E[dz] = 0$ and $Var[dz] = dt$. Remember that Y represents the present value of the investment in additional capacity and therefore the discounted sum of cash flow from the investment at the time the investment itself is taken. Consider the payoff from investing now: $\Omega_{Y_0} = \max\{V_0 - I, 0\}$ and the payoff from holding the option to invest in the future $\Omega_Y = F(Y) \max E\{Y_T - I)e^{-\rho T}\}$ where T is the period in which the firm finally decides to expand its capacity. We are in the continuation region if $\Omega_Y > \Omega_{Y_0}$. In this region the following no arbitrage condition holds: $\rho F(Y)dt = E[dF(Y)]$ where on the left hand side we have the appreciation at the normal market return of a sum corresponding to the value of the option and on the right hand side we have the change in value of the option to wait in the same interval. By applying Ito's lemma, taking expectation and simplifying we get the following second order (homogenous-constant coefficient) differential equation: .

$$F_t + \alpha Y F_y + \frac{1}{2}\sigma^2 Y^2 F_{yy} - \rho F = 0.$$

The differential equation has the usual three boundary conditions:

$$F(0) = 0 \quad (1), \quad F(Y^*) = Y^* - I \quad (2), \quad F'(Y^*) = 1 \quad (3)$$

The first is the obvious consequence of what happens to a geometric Brownian motion when $Y = 0$. The second is the value matching conditions, implying that the gain from investing net of the opportunity cost is equal to the cost of investing. Finally (3) is the smooth pasting conditions requiring that non-only levels but also first derivatives of the holding option and the termination payoff match at the optimum.

The trial solution which satisfies (1) is $F(Y) = AV^{\beta_1}$. By replacing this solution in (2) and (3) we find the usual values for A and Y^* with

$$Y^* = \frac{\beta_1}{\beta_1 - 1} I.$$

To solve the value of β_1 we replace the trial solution in the second order differential equation and simplify to obtain:

$$F_t + \alpha Y F_y + \frac{1}{2}\sigma^2(\beta_1 - 1) + (\rho - \delta) - \rho = 0.$$

This second order equation gives two roots: $\beta_1 > 1$ and $\beta_1 < 0$. Given the range of values that β_1 can take the following inequality may hold: $Y^* < Y < 1$. When Y takes values which respect this inequality the non-IT firm will invest in additional capacity but the IT firm will find it optimal to wait. A subsequent fall of the value of the returns from the project will therefore generate the result of a lower capacity utilization for the IT firm.

$Y^* < Y < I$ may occur even in the case of a deterministic process similar to the previous one except for $\sigma = 0$. In this case in fact it is possible to find the time at which the option to increase productive capacity is exercised. We have in fact $\Omega_Y = \{(Y_e^{-\alpha T} - I)e^{-\rho T}\}$. After rearranging first order condition we get:

$$T^* = \max E\left\{\frac{1}{\alpha}\log\left[\frac{\rho I}{(\rho-\alpha)Y},0\right]\right\}.$$

It is clear than that if Y is not too higher than I it is better to wait for the IT firm while it is impossible to do it for the non-IT firm.

Hypothesis 4: Investment in Telecommunications Reduces Average Productivity of Labour

Consider the same model presented in the previous section with the only difference that now the IT firm not only has the advantage of more productive flexibility, but also that to adapt its product or process to new consumer tastes. For the IT firms now the return from the project assumes the form of $dY^N = \alpha_1 Y^N dt + \sigma Y^N dz$ with Y^N being the return from the new product, $\alpha_1 > \alpha$ and $I_1 > I$. The difference in investment costs is given by the reduction of sales per employee at the moment the new product or process is developed due to training costs of the existing personnel.

Consider the payoff from investing now: $\Omega_{Y_0} = \max\{Y_0 - I, 0$ and the payoff from holding the option to invest in the future $\Omega_Y = F(Y, Y^N) = \max E\{Y^N_T - I_N)e^{-\rho T}\}$. The same analysis of proposition three may be developed with the difference that whenever the IT firm invests it incurs in higher sunk costs than in the previous case as sunk costs include the costs of retraining personnel. Therefore, given that in any instant of time there will be a positive probability that an IT firm invests and incur in labour retraining costs, its average productivity of labour will be lower.

Note

1   Note that, from a mathematical point of view the flexibility option shifts the probability of the realization of the state of nature before the max operator. In other terms, the advantage of postponing the investment decision is that the decision can be taken after the state of nature in t1 has been observed.

Chapter 9

The Economic Impact of the Computer Revolution: A Progress Report

Michael T. Kiley

1 Introduction

The US economy has performed exceptionally well in the 1990s: growth in gross domestic product accelerated sharply in the second half of the decade, the unemployment rate fell to levels not seen in decades, and the level of income inequality between 'skilled' and 'unskilled' workers halted its trend towards greater inequality. Many popular commentaries, and an expanding chorus of economic analysts, point to the expanding influence of the computer revolution as a partial explanation for these and other trends. This chapter summarizes some of this recent research. Computers have lifted the productive capacity of firms, shifted the demand for skills, and reduced the susceptibility of firms to unwanted swings in inventories. The magnitude and timing of these effects is the subject of intense research.

The increased economic importance of computers is readily apparent through a perusal of the US National Income and Product Accounts. In 1999, businesses devoted 20.7 per cent of their expenditures on fixed investment to computers and peripheral equipment and software – five times the share devoted to these assets 30 years earlier. The analysis of this trend increase in the investment share of computers, in conjunction with the cyclical swings in information technology and other forms of investment, is an important first step in understanding the economic impact of the computer revolution. The first section of this chapter presents the data on the increased importance of investment in computers in the US economy, setting up the focus of the remainder of the chapter on the broader economic impact of computers.

One important area examines the link between the cyclical performance of the economy and computers. In recent years, output growth has been very strong while inflation has decelerated (through early 1999). An acceleration in the pace of technological progress in computers and software plays an important role in explaining these events. In addition, a relatively large range of anecdotal literature has linked the rise of information technologies to the trend decline in inventories relative to sales in the US, and consequently to the increased stability of the US business cycle. Economic models and econometric work lags behind these anecdotes. For example, the trend decline in inventories relative to sales since the 1980s lines up well with the timing of the introduction of the personal computer and increased computer networking, but few studies have formally explored the link. Further research on these links is important when considering the increased importance of computers may have for stabilizing the business cycle, as improvements in inventory management are perhaps the most common set of anecdotes suggesting greater stability in the 'new economy'.

A burgeoning literature examines how the combination of rapid improvements in technology and the ever-expanding range of business applications of information technology have boosted the contribution of computer expenditures to 'trend' growth in the economy. The falling price of computer capital has boosted real investment in computers, and the 1990s finally appeared to provide evidence that the computer revolution was providing a substantial boost to labour productivity. The intense pace of recent work in this area – with important contributions from Oliner and Sichel (1994, 2000), Brynjolfsson and Hitt (1995, 1997), Jorgenson and Stiroh (1995, 2000), and Kiley (1999a) – largely agrees on the increased importance of computers in boosting labour productivity through faster capital accumulation. However, researchers disagree on the historical nature of the frictions and dynamics associated with the technological revolution, with some research claiming that computers fall short of 'great invention' status'. Analyses that highlight the frictions in the investment in new technologies that arise from learning problems and business reorganisations emphasize the transition costs of the computer revolution – and hence attempt to explain the evidence that computers may have generated sub-par short-run returns in the early years following their introduction. As the transition to an 'IT-based' economy matures, these transition costs fade and growth picks up (David (1990), Greenwood and Yorukoglu (1997), Kiley (1999a)). An optimistic interpretation of recent experience in the US would attribute some of the recent strength in the economy to the fading of the transition period as businesses finally 'catch on' to the potential of information technology.

Finally, computers and software are often mentioned as a prime example of 'skill-biased technological progress'. The skill bias in technological advances in recent decades is often mentioned as the most important source of widening income inequality in the United States and elsewhere. Recent research has emphasized the potential of technological revolutions to exacerbate wage differentials between skilled and unskilled labour, in the short run, and either widen or leave unchanged wage differentials in the long-run – depending upon the long-run adaptability of technologies to different skill levels. The final section briefly reviews theoretical and empirical work on this subject.

2 Investment in Information Technology

Figure 9.1 presents the ratio of business investment in computers and software to business output in the top panel, and the share of business investment accounted for by computers and software in the bottom panel.[1] It is clear that the importance of these information technologies has increased greatly since the mid-1960s when computers and software first entered widespread use. In part, the trend increase in the importance of information technologies reflects the relative newness of the goods; when a new capital good is introduced, business practices must adjust in order to exploit the potential of the new technology, and this adjustment requires both time and resources.[2] This adjustment process will take centre stage in the discussion of the implications of the computer revolution for productivity and wage inequality below.

Another factor behind the trend increase in the share of investment in computers and software is the sharp decline in the relative price of these goods. Figure 9.2a plots the price of investment in computers and software relative to the price of business output over the period 1966–99; the decline in prices has been phenomenal, averaging 14 per cent per year (measured in terms of the log difference). The decline has been especially rapid for computer prices, which have fallen 22 per cent per year over the same period. The rapid pace of price declines for computers reflects the rapid pace of innovation (and hence productivity growth) in the production of computers and semiconductors.[3]

Figure 9.2b illustrates that the pace of price declines for computers and software has been far from smooth; over the 1966–99 period, the standard deviations of the price declines for computers and software and for computers only were 5.6 per cent and 8.1 per cent per year. This volatility in the pace of technological progress associated with information technologies may have important implications going forward. As computers and software assume a more central role in production processes, the uneven pace of technological progress for these technologies may provide an additional source of business cycle variability in aggregate production. As an example, Figure 9.2 clearly shows that during the period between 1995 and 1998 the pace of price declines

a   Investment in computers and software as a share of business output

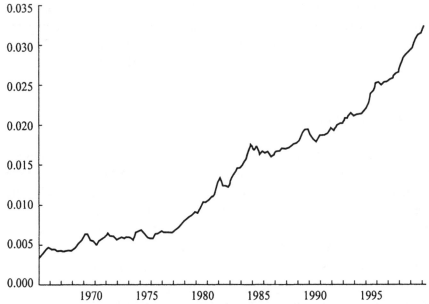

b   Investment in computers and software as a share of business investment

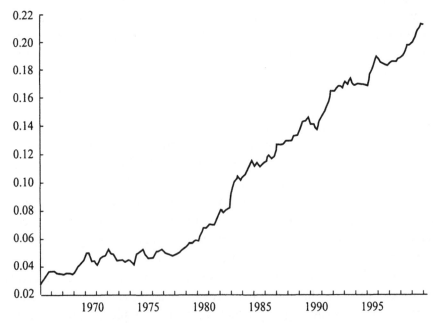

Figure 9.1   Business investment in computers and software

a *Level*

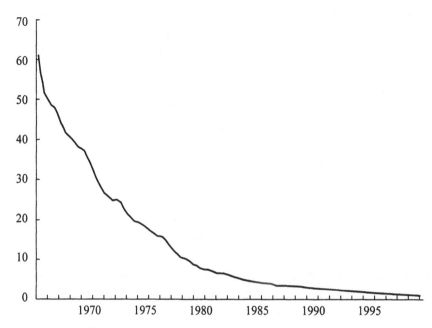

b *Percent change at an annual rate*

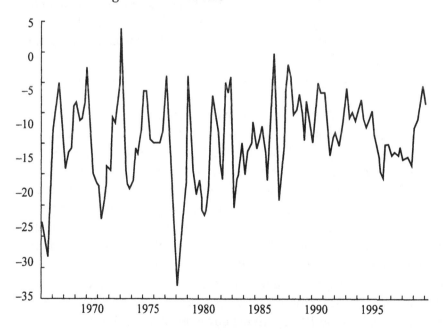

Figure 9.2 Price of investment in computers and software relative to the price of business output

accelerated and was unusually smooth, a combination that provided a steady boost to business investment and production. The acceleration in price declines for computers also helped hold down measures of inflation – one of several favourable supply shocks that partially explain the deceleration in inflation in the US in the late 1990s (Gordon, 1998).

In order to gauge the implications of the increased intensity of information technologies for economic growth and fluctuations, a framework for analysing these trends is required. The appendix provides such a framework, based on the models of Solow (1960) and Greenwood et al. (1997, 2000). The following sections interpret recent data and suggest directions for the future course of the economy in light of the model.

3   The Impact of Computers at the Business Cycle Frequency

Much of the recent enthusiasm about the impact of computers and software on the economy stems from the strong performance of the US economy in the latter half of the 1990s. Table 9.1 presents some statistics on business output growth, the contribution of business fixed investment to output growth, and the contribution of business investment in computers and software to output growth over business cycle periods (as identified by the National Bureau of Economic Research) since 1973.[4] The last period (1991–99) and the subperiods 1991–95 and 1996–99 do not represent complete business cycles, and hence the pace of growth and the contributions in these subperiods are not directly comparable to those of earlier periods.

The pace of growth over the 1990s overall has been slightly better than the average since 1973, but not strongly so. This is consistent with the analysis in Zarnowitz (2000), who shows that the 1990s expansion in the US is not unusually strong relative to the expansion in the 1960s and after 1982. The latter half of the 1990s stand out in one dimension: BFI has accounted for about 30 per cent of GDP growth – a postwar high for a four-year period. Investment in computers and software accounts for half of the contribution of business fixed investment. For the most part, the increased importance of investment in computers and software reflects the trend increase in the share of investment spending devoted to these goods shown in Figure 9.1. In addition, technological progress in computers and software accelerated a bit in the latter half of the 1990s, driving down prices at an above average rate (Figure 9.2b; Table 9.1, line 4). A final factor behind the strength in business investment that is often ignored in discussions of the new economy has been

Table 9.1   Growth in non-farm business output

	1974–79	1980–90	1991–99	1991–95	1996–99
1 Growth in output	3.1	2.9	3.6	2.7	4.8
Contribution of:					
2 BFI	0.7	0.5	1.1	0.7	1.6
3 BFI, computers and software	0.2	0.3	0.6	0.4	0.7
Memo:					
4. Growth in relative price of computers and software	−15.2	−11.7	−11.2	−9.2	−13.7
5 Total government surplus as % of GDP	−1.5	−3.0	−1.9	−3.6	0.3

the improvement in government saving; the total government surplus turned positive in the latter half of the 1990s. While the improvement in government finances in part reflects the strength in the economy – rather than vice versa – the increase in government savings has helped to partially finance the boom in high-tech investment.

The appendix presents a model that illustrates how rapid price declines for computers and software spur investment and provide both a trend or structural boost to output growth, and a cyclical boost to output growth. In the model, the cyclical contribution of computers and software to output growth is the product of the cyclical portion of the decline in the relative price of computers multiplied by the sum of the share of computers and software investment in GDP and the product of capital income share of computers and software and the depreciation rate of computers and software.[5] Over the 1996–99 period, the share of computers and software investment in GDP was 2.8 per cent, while the capital income share of computers and software was around 4.3 per cent and the depreciation rate for computers and software was around 0.35 per cent. Computer and software prices fell 4.5 percentage points faster over the 1996–99 period than over the 1991–95 period. Putting it all together, the *cyclical* acceleration implied by the model is only 0.2 percentage points – close to the increase in the contribution from investment in computers and software, but a far cry from the nearly two percentage point acceleration in the data. Part of the discrepancy probably comes from the simplicity of the model, in which businesses devote a constant share of their revenue to expenditures on computers. In fact, businesses probably accelerate their purchases of computers and software more than proportionately in response to faster-than-average price declines (as in Greenwood et al. (2000)), and this would provide some further boost to output. Even given these qualifications, cyclical factors associated with computers cannot account for all the strength in output growth, and we will return to the acceleration in output growth in the latter half of the 1990s when we discuss trend productivity growth in sections 4 and 5 below.

Computers and software have also contributed to the favourable behaviour of inflation in the US in the late 1990s, both directly and indirectly (Gordon (1998)). The indirect effects are hard to quantify, but work through the acceleration in productivity associated with computers documented below. The direct effects, which come through the increased share of expenditure devoted to computers and their falling prices, are easy to quantify. Figure 9.3 presents the inflation rate derived from the index of prices for business output, including and excluding the effects of prices of investment in computers and software. From the last quarter of 1994 until the last quarter of 1998, inflation in the price of business output decelerated 1.2 percentage points, 0.3 percentage points of which came from the faster pace of declines in computers and software (and the increased share of expenditure devoted to computers and software).

In addition to the direct effects of computers and software on output growth and prices, recent US business cycles also appear to be more stable

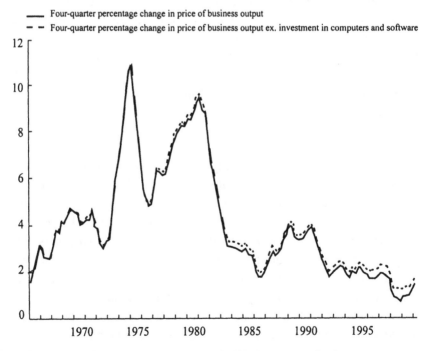

Figure 9.3   Effect of computers and software on inflation

than earlier cycles, and this may reflect the effects of computers on inventory management. Figure 9.4 presents the standard deviation of business output growth over rolling five-year periods. This measure of business cycle volatility has dropped sharply in recent years. In part, this simply reflects the long expansion; for example, volatility was low in the mid-to-late 1960s as well. However, McConnell and Perez-Quiros (forthcoming) present evidence that there has been a significant break in the volatility of the business cycle in the US. They find that the break stems primarily from the decline in the inventory-to-sales ratio (Figure 9.5) and the attendant drop in the importance of inventory swings for output fluctuations. It is tempting to link the decline in the ratio of inventories relative to sales to the rise of computer-based inventory management systems (such as 'just-in-time' inventories), and anecdotal evidence is supportive of a link (Economic Report of the President, 2000, p. 114). Econometric evidence linking the rise of computers and the trend decline in inventories relative to sales is not widespread, although the timing looks about right. The drop off began near the early 1980s, around the same time the personal computer entered business use. Unfortunately, the theoretical link between computer use and inventory-to-sales ratios is not clear. For example, improved information can be used either to lower the

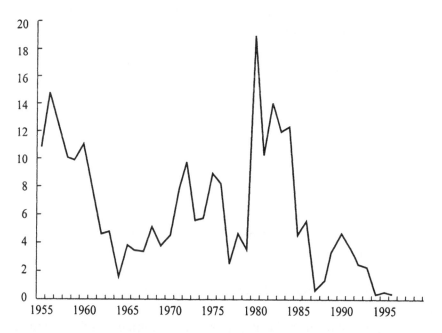

Figure 9.4   **Variance of business output growth: rolling five year intervals**

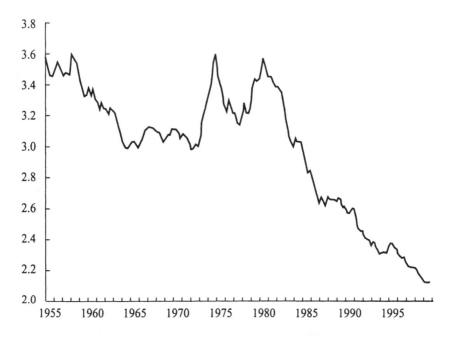

Figure 9.5   Ratio of inventories to final sales (business sector)

inventory on hand to meet a given pace of sales (the 'just-in-time' effect), or to increase the variety of goods kept on inventory, a channel that could raise inventory levels.

One notable recent study is Lehr and Lichtenberg (forthcoming), who find that firms that are more computer-intensive economize a bit on inventories relative to other firms. The small effects found by these authors may reflect the variety channel partially offsetting the 'just-in-time' effect.

4   Productivity Growth and the Computer Revolution

While the overall pace of growth in output and employment in the US during the current expansion has not been remarkable by historical standards, the concentration of output growth in investment, especially in computers and software, has exceeded previous experience. The boom in computers and software has generated speculation that 'trend' growth in labour productivity has accelerated.

A decomposition of productivity growth into contributions from computers and software, other capital, and multifactor productivity growth is possible under a few stringent conditions: competitive output and factor markets, instantaneous adjustment of all factors to frictionless levels, and constant returns to scale.[6] Under these assumptions, the contribution of a capital input to output growth can be measured by the growth of that input multiplied by its income share – because the income share reflects the marginal product of the input at each instant when there are no frictions. Solow (1957) introduced this method of 'growth accounting', and focused primarily on long averages of the resulting decomposition because of the strong assumptions required regarding factor adjustment; the literature on technological revolutions, discussed below, drops the assumption of frictionless factor markets.

A few recent papers proceed under the assumption that factor market frictions are unimportant and focus on the contributions of computers and software to growth in recent years using the Solow approach. Table 9.2 presents averages of labour productivity growth since 1974 and a decomposition of that growth under the Solow approach, taken from Oliner and Sichel (2000).

Table 9.2   Growth in labour productivity in the non-farm business sector

	1974–90	1991–99	1991–95	1996–99
1 Labour productivity	1.4	2.0	1.5	2.6
Contribution of:				
2 Capital per hour	0.8	0.8	0.6	1.1
3 Multifactor productivity	0.6	1.2	0.9	1.5
Memo:				
4 Capital per hour, computers and software	0.3	0.6	0.5	0.9

Note: Multifactor productivity includes labour quality.

Source: Oliner and Sichel, 2000.

Growth in labour productivity clearly accelerated in the latter half of the 1990s, with the acceleration nearly evenly spread across the contributions of capital per hour and multifactor productivity, and a big jump in the contribution of computer and software capital. As always, it is difficult to separate the permanent, or 'trend' component of the fluctuations in labour productivity from the temporary fluctuations. For example, Gordon (forthcoming) suggests that a good portion of the improvement in labour productivity in the latter half of the 1990s reflects cyclical factors (including the unusually rapid pace of price declines for computers in recent years). The Congressional Budget Office (CBO) (2000) takes a more optimistic view, and forecasts that growth in trend labour productivity through 2010 will exceed 2.25 per cent – even stronger than the average for the current expansion.

To interpret reasonable trend values for growth in labour productivity, it is useful to once again return to the model in the appendix. Suppose production takes the Cobb-Douglas form:

$$Y + C^a K^b (ZL)^{1-a-b}$$

where Y is output measured in consumer prices, K is capital input excluding computers and software, C is the stock of computers and software used in production, Z is labour-augmenting technological progress, and L is labour input. It is straightforward to demonstrate (as in Appendix 1) that growth in output per unit of labour input (measured as a log-difference) is given by

$$d(y - l) = \frac{a}{1 - a - b} (dc - dy) + dz$$

where dc – dy equals the excess of growth in computer input over output growth. Along a steady-state growth path, this excess equals the rate of technological progress in computer and software production – which is the negative of the rate of change in the relative price of investment in computers and software (and equals 12.3 per cent over the period 1974–99). In the data, non-farm business output is not measured at consumption prices; instead, output is measured as a chain-weighted aggregate of consumption and investment (and other categories) where each type of expenditure is measured using its own relative price. Equation A9 in the appendix presents the appropriate modifications to the equation for output growth for the Tornqvist approximation to the official measure of output growth.

Under the Solow assumptions (so, for example, learning or adjustment costs associated with computers are unimportant), the parameters a and b can be determined by looking at the income shares of computers and software and other capital. Using data from the Oliner and Sichel (2000), the average capital income shares over 1990–99 imply that b lies between one-quarter and one-third (approximately 0.28) and a equals 0.038. The share of non-farm business output (less housing) devoted to investment in computers and software averaged 2.7 per cent over 1991–99. Growth in labour-augmenting technological progress (dz) averaged 1.2 per cent per year over the period

1974–99; for the more recent 1991–99 period, dz averaged 1.75 per cent per year. [7] Using these parameters and the value of dc reported above yields two possible estimates for trend growth in labour productivity from equation A9:

$$d(y - l) = 1.9 \text{ per cent (using 1974–99 average growth in Z)}$$
$$d(y - l) = 2.4 \text{ per cent (using 1991–99 average growth in Z).}$$

In each of these calculations, computers and software contribute about 1.0 percentage point to trend growth – assuming that price declines for these inputs continue at the same pace as over 1974–99. Note that these figures are below the averages in the late 1990s, although only by a bit in the second case. Some commentators have suggested that nearly all of the late 1990s surge in productivity is a 'trend' increase. This position may be too optimistic, as the pace of declines in the prices of computers and software has been unusually rapid in this period, and the strong performance of the economy probably reflects cyclical factors to at least some extent. Some argue that cyclical factors should be downplayed because the last recession ended at the start of the 1990s; on the other hand, the last recession was relatively mild, and the evidence of 'non-linearities' in business cycles – a necessary condition for treating recessions and expansions as separate processes rather than outcomes of a single cyclical process – is less than overwhelming.

In sum, the conclusion that can be drawn from back-of-the-envelope calculations is that faster growth in labour productivity in the future (relative to averages though 1995) should be expected if the pace of technological progress remains at its average over 1974–99 simply because the composition of capital goods – and consequently investment expenditures – has shifted towards goods with fast rates of technical progress such as computers and software. So long as Moore's law holds up in the near-term, modest optimism regarding productivity growth seems like a good bet.

5 Questions Unanswered by Traditional Approach

The optimistic back-of-the envelope guess for trend growth in labour productivity (between 1.9 and 2.4 per cent per year) might come as quite a surprise to someone who was familiar with research on the topic half a dozen years ago. At that time, optimistic outlooks regarding computers' potential contribution to economic growth were hard to find: computers were everywhere except in the productivity statistics. The economic performance in the US in the 1990s has banished this view, at least for the most part (again, with Gordon (forthcoming) being a sceptic). The most influential work that attempts to explain both the early disappointments and the recent optimism follows the approach discussed in section 3 (such as Oliner and Sichel (1994, 2000) and Jorgenson and Stiroh (1995, 2000). These papers espouse the view that the failure to observe a quantitatively important effect of computers on aggregate productivity growth prior to the 1990s stemmed from the relatively small size of the computer capital stock relative to the stock of other inputs. As computers have become increasingly important as an input, the productivity effect should be bigger, and that is exactly what we see. In other words, we didn't see computers in the productivity statistics earlier because computers were not everywhere.

This view probably captures a significant part of the story. However, this view is inconsistent with a range of empirical evidence that suggests that the learning or adjustment costs associated with adapting to new computer technologies have been substantial and explain an important part of the early disappointments with the computer revolution. Specifically, Oliner and Sichel (1994, 2000) and Jorgenson and Stiroh (1995, 2000) assume that computer investments earn a normal return in every period – i.e., that factor markets are frictionless. Historical analyses of previous 'revolutions' have suggested that such an assumption misses the dynamic adjustment that accompanies new technologies: Initially, new technologies involve large upfront costs as firms reorganize production and train workers to use the new technology, and the returns to these investments arrive after the adjustment period passes. While the adjustment period may not be unduly long for an individual firm, the slow diffusion of new technologies across firms generates a significant delay between introduction of the technology and the aggregate payoff. David (1990) represents an early exposition of this view that compares the computer revolution to electrification.

This view of technological revolutions – that they take time and resources to take effect, and can actually slow economic growth in the decades immediately following their introduction as the economy incurs the resources necessary for the technological transformation – may help to explain the scepticism of some, notably Gordon (forthcoming), about the importance of the computer revolution. Gordon's argument boils down to the view that historically computers have not contributed that much to productivity growth, and the current strong pace of productivity growth in the US reflects a confluence of cyclical factors and some pickup in computers' contribution. The disappointment with the impact of computers to date on aggregate productivity is exactly what the 'revolution' view predicts, because of the delays in the productivity payoff from new technologies.

A Formal Approach to Technological Revolutions

While David (1990) is perhaps the most influential article emphasizing the short-run costs of adopting a new technology and applying this notion to the perception of a small aggregate payoff to computers through the beginning of the 1990s, recent research has presented formal models of the tradeoffs between these short-run costs and the long-run benefits. The discussion below highlights the approaches of both Greenwood and Yorukoglu (1997) and Kiley (1999a); this box will provide a short description of the approach in Kiley (1999a), as that approach can be explained in a more succinct manner.

   Suppose a firm produces output (net of costs of installing capital) according to the production function $Y = G(K,I) = F(K) - C(I,K)$, where G is the net production function, F is the production function gross of installation costs, and C is the installation cost function, which depends on both the investment flow and the stock of capital (and of course, $FK>0$, $CI>0$, and $CK<0$, following a long tradition (e.g., Lucas (1967))). If the price of investment relative to output is given by P, the firm's first order conditions are given by $P + CI = Q$, $FK - CK = (r+d - (dQ/dt)/Q)Q$, where r is the interest rate and d is the depreciation rate. In a steady state, $Q = P$, and the marginal product of capital equals the Jorgensonian user cost. Taking logs of the production function and differentiating with respect to time yields the growth accounting expression (where dx represents the growth rate of x) $dy = (GKK/Y)dk + (GII/Y)di$, which shows that capital contributes positively to growth while investment detracts from growth (because $GI = -CI < 0$). For reasonable degrees of adjustment costs, the negative effect of investment is likely to be small near a steady state (see Kiley (1999a)).

   Suppose the economy is initially in a steady state where $dQ/dt=0$ and marginal adjustment costs are zero. In this situation, the standard Solow growth accounting accurately describes capital's contribution to growth (using the standard user cost formula). Now suppose a 'technological revolution' unexpectedly occurs; FK is fixed in the short run with capital, but investment flows increase, and output growth is depressed by the installation costs. The standard approach followed in Jorgenson and Stiroh (forthcoming) and Oliner and Sichel (2000) ignores this depressing effect, but Kiley (1999a) suggests that this depressing effect may be quite large for computers because firms have been intensively reorganizing work and training employees in new practices. The experimentation with new practices and employee training diverts resources from production and hence involves 'adjustment costs'. See the text for examples.

Of course, the fact that computers have not had a huge impact on productivity in the last 20 years proves neither the revolution view nor Gordon's view that computers do not rank as a 'great invention'. One must look for evidence consistent with the importance of transition costs to provide a guide to the plausibility of the different views. Most evidence relating to the transition issues associated with models of technological revolutions does not deal with computers or software directly. Instead, this research tends to draw analogies with previous innovations or draws on evidence suggesting that equipment generally involves significant transition costs. For example, the literature on learning costs reveals important short-run losses from adopted new equipment. Case studies predominate, with David's (1975) analysis of the slow rise in productivity at a cotton textile mill following the introduction of a new technology, even though there was no new investment in the plant over the period studied, providing a classic example of how the productive impact of new equipment arrives with a lag. More recent case studies are summarized in Argotte and Epple (1990). Bahk and Gort (1993) analyse a large sample of new firms and find that learning at new plants accounts for most of the increase in productivity at those plants.

The emphasis on learning and adjustment costs *for computers and software* has received less attention, but the hypothesis does have testable implications: Firms that invest in a new technology, such as computers, should initially experience *lower* productivity as production processes are shifted and workers adapt to the new equipment. As the adjustment period passes, productivity should advance rapidly. This dynamic process is inconsistent with the growth accounting exercises that assume firms earn normal returns on investment in each period.

Empirical studies that identify learning and adjustment costs associated with computers have not been performed, but a wide range of anecdotal and empirical evidence suggests that such costs are significant. Anecdotally, Sichel (1997) reports that in his focused interviews of seven companies '[t]he one challenge that nearly every company identified and emphasized was that of getting their people up the technology learning curve; that is, the challenge of training employees to use new systems effectively and the challenge of reorganizing work to exploit the new technologies' (p. 108). One telling anecdote on the large costs associated with adjusting to new technologies is the Y2K bug: Firms around the world spent billions of dollars fixing systems at the last minute – even though the problem could be anticipated years or decades in advance – because the disruptions to normal work practices associated with installing a new system were substantial.

Of course, the most widespread 'anecdote' supporting the importance of adjustment costs to computers was the 'productivity paradox' itself, which stemmed from an idea that computers were not delivering much in turns of productivity in their early years. Econometric evidence seems to support the notion that firms face significant costs to adopting new computer systems. For example, Dunne et al. (2000) find that plants that invest in computer technology in the early years of business adoption of computers (early 1970s) had lower labour productivity, but in later years computer intensive establishments had higher then average productivity. Similarly, Yorukoglu (1998) found that firms that had recently adopted computer technologies had lower productivity than firms who had more experience with the technology. Brynjolfsson and Hitt (1997) similarly find that the productive impact of computer investments arrives with a lag. While the results in these papers are difficult to map into particular models of learning or adjustment costs, they all suggest that such costs are important.

The macroeconomic importance of such costs of learning or other adjustments required to effectively utilize computers has been explored in a number of studies recently, most notably Hornstein and Krusell (1996), Greenwood and Yorukoglu (1997), Hornstein (1999), and Kiley (1999a). The first three papers consider the response of the economy to a 'technological revolution', which is defined as a shift in the trend growth rate of technological change embodied in equipment. The widespread business adoption of computers since the 1960s – and the fast pace of technological change in computers and software – makes the computer revolution a good example of such a technological revolution. These authors assume that the learning and diffusion process of new technologies follows patterns observed for other inventions, and consider the macroeconomic effects of revolution. Because learning costs initially lower productivity, and diffusion and learning curves across historical innovations have been slow (Gort and Klepper (1982)), technological revolutions can generate a slowing in aggregate productivity growth in these models.

In fact, Greenwood and Yorukoglu (1997) argued that nearly all of the productivity slowdown that began in the US around 1974 stems from learning costs associated with a technological revolution in equipment (including computers), and predicted an acceleration in productivity growth in the US in coming years (a prediction that looks prescient given the productivity performance since the mid-1990s). One difficulty with these models lies in the choice of parameters governing the costs of adopting technologies – as the learning curve across technologies varies considerably, and the results are sensitive to reasonable changes in the costs of adoption. For example, Figure 9.6 plots the level of output and the growth rate of output following the introduction of a new technology from the model of Hornstein (1999). For these parameter values – which assume a 50 year S-shaped diffusion process and slow learning, the technological revolution leads to sharply lower output growth in the short run, and a long expansion decades later. For other 'reasonable' parameter values governing the learning process, output growth barely slows initially and quickly picks up. Unfortunately, little is known about why new technologies follow the slow diffusion patterns that they do, and the nature of the frictions that generate the slow pace of diffusion is critical in determining the nature of the economy's response to technological revolutions.

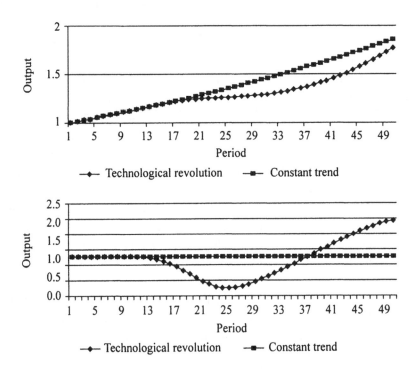

Figure 9.6   The effect of a technological revolution

The approach taken in Kiley (1999a) is similar in emphasizing the short-run costs associated with computer adoption, but models such costs as disruptions to production arising from the investment in new equipment such as computers. Investment adjustment costs have long played a key role in explaining investment behaviour, and this key role is also true in explaining computer investment (Tevlin and Whelan, 2000). Kiley illustrates that such costs are likely to be quite important in explaining the behaviour of productivity if firms must re-arrange production on a massive scale to incorporate an important technology. Using survey data of firms costs of managing information technologies, adoption costs in the US were around 2–3 per cent of non-farm business output in 1997. Costs of this magnitude imply that the reorganisation of production has shaved about .5 of a percentage point off of growth in labour productivity since 1973. The maturation of computer technologies implies that this half point can be expected to reappear in the future.

6 The Computer Revolution and Labour Market Outcomes

The discussion so far has focused primarily on the effects computers and software have had on productivity growth in the 1990s, but another body of research has focused on the transformation computers have wrought on the workplace (McConnell, 1996). Perhaps the most interesting body of work has focused on how the increases in income generated by computers are distributed across workers of different types. It is well-known that income and wage inequality in the United States has expanded rapidly since the mid-1970s, and a large body of research has linked this increase in inequality to skill-biased technological change (e.g., Krugman (1994).

Linking these labour market developments to the computer revolution is difficult. Many authors suggest that 'skill-biased' technological change is a primary culprit. However, most of this research cannot really be linked to any particular technological revolution, as skill-biased technological change essentially is a residual reflecting the unexplained portion of the increase in wage inequality that remains after accounting for shifts in factor supplies and other possible factors, such as greater competition from low-skilled labour through increased exposure to international markets and the decline in union membership. For example, Freeman (1997) attributes a greater portion of the increase in wage inequality in the US to the decline in unionisation and the falling real value of the minimum wage in the US than to technological factors. Nonetheless, skill-biased technological progress remains a primary factor in most economists' assessment.

A few studies have tried to look directly at technology adoption and skill requirements; Bartel and Lichtenberg (1987), Berman et al. (1994), and Autor et al. (1998) find that skilled workers implement more new technologies than unskilled workers. Evidence linking skill-biases to computers is largely anecdotal. For example, the proportion of workers using a computer on the job doubled between 1984 and 1997 (to about 50 per cent (Economic Report of the President, 2000, p. 134) and over 50 per cent of jobs available to workers without a college education required some training in computer skills; these statistics certainly suggest that less-educated workers are seeing shifts in the demand for their labour that are related to computers.

The link between computerisation and shifts in wage inequality is more difficult to pin down. Krueger (1993) finds that workers who use computers earn higher wages than those that do not. However, these results are likely to reflect, at least to some extent, unobserved characteristics of the workers that may have little to do with computers *per se*; for example, DiNardo and Pischke (1997) find that workers who use pencils earn more than other workers. Autor et al. (1998) find that the shift in wage inequality since the mid-1970s is accounted for by skill-upgrading within industries, and that the extent of skill-upgrading is positively correlated with the intensity of computer use in an industry – but again a causal interpretation of these correlations is only one possible reading.

A more direct linkage is presented in Krusell et al. (1997), who present a model with a strong link between movements in overall equipment investment and wage inequality through capital-skill complementarity in the production function. This study does not ascribe much of the growth in wage inequality to computers and software *per se*. Rather, equipment other than computers plays a central role, as Krusell et al. argue that technological progress in equipment outside of computers is substantially understated in the US national accounts (on the basis of Gordon's (1990) findings that quality-adjusted equipment prices fall faster than reported in the national accounts). The fast rate of adoption of new technologies other than computers explains most of Krusell et al.'s finding of increased inequality stemming from capital-skill complementarity.

The difficulty in finding a major role of computers in income inequality is not surprising. The work of Oliner and Sichel (1994, 2000) and Jorgenson and Stiroh (1995, 2000) emphasizes how the historical contribution of computers to productivity growth has been small because computers are a small part of the capital stock. While it is possible to construct a model where an input with a relatively small share of income has large effects on the wages of different skill groups, it is also possible to expect small effects on inequality (a point suggested by Levy (1998)). This uncertainty is even greater when turning to recent years; while the trend towards greater wage inequality in the US halted in the late 1990s (Ilg and Haugen, 2000), it is far too early to suggest that the underlying trend in skill-premia has flattened, especially given the strong cyclical position of the economy in the recent period.

A few theoretical contributions do suggest a linkage between computerisation and wage inequality through the 'technological revolutions' channel. Greenwood and Yorukoglu (1997) present a model in which the introduction of a new technology both disrupts production and hence lowers productivity, and increases the demand for skilled labour at the expense of unskilled labour because skilled labour is required to incorporate new technologies. Interestingly, Greenwood and Yorukoglu's model implies that the demand for skilled labour rises in the medium run because skilled labour adopts new technologies first (following a suggestion in Nelson and Phelps, 1966). Over the long run, skill differentials stop growing, and could even fade – depending on the adaptability of the new technology to different skill levels.

Kiley (1999b) presents a model where a demographic shift towards greater skill-acquisition actually *generates* a technological revolution by spurring the development of skill-intensive sector; the adjustment period is one of stagnation in productivity growth (reflecting the costs of the technological transition) and widening wage inequality.[8] It will be interesting to see how these stories stand the test of empirical scrutiny, and future work will undoubtedly attempt to pin down the links between computerisation and labour market developments more closely.

7   Summary

The experience of the US economy in the late 1990s clearly illustrates the increased economic importance of computers and software. Investment in computers and software has grown rapidly, and this growth has spurred a resurgence in productivity growth in recent years that suggests that computers and software may rank among the major technological developments in terms of economic impact. This view has gained acceptance in recent years, but some observers remain sceptical that computers have or will have such an important effect on the economy (e.g, Gordon (1998)).

In part the scepticism of these commentators reflects the nature of their focus: Computers have not had a major impact on productivity over recent decades. Different researchers attribute the small historical contribution of computers and software to different factors. The view emphasized in the recent work on economic models of technological revolutions is that the response of productivity to the introduction of a new technology is delayed or even negative in the short run as the transition to new modes of production occurs. An optimistic interpretation of recent events in the US is that the delayed response of productivity to computers has finally arrived. However, this interpretation is somewhat speculative, as the analyses of Greenwood and Yorukoglu (1997) or Kiley (1999a) rely on parameters for the nature of the adjustment frictions associated with computers that, while reasonable, are open to question. Hornstein (1999) illustrates this uncertainty well by showing how small changes in parameter values can make the transition issues emphasized in recent papers on technological revolutions not important at all. Future research should place a high priority on trying to assess the quantitative importance of these transition issues.

It is also important to keep in mind that the computer revolution has effects beyond those on productivity. Good examples of these other effects include the lower inflation engendered – both directly and indirectly – by faster technological progress in computers and software in recent years, and the stabilizing effects that computer-based inventory management systems have had on the business cycle through lower inventory levels. The magnitude of these effects is uncertain, and research has only begun to address the importance of these links – although the anecdotal evidence that information technologies are leading to lower and more stable inventory levels seems overwhelming. A similar degree of uncertainty surrounds the effects computers have had on the labour market, although work in this area has proceeded at a fast pace in recent years and the increased importance of computers in influencing the shape of labour demand seems clear from a perusal of the high-tech want ads.

Notes

1   Both ratios are expressed in nominal terms.
2   Tevlin and Whelan (2000) analyse the determinants of business investment in computers. They find a large role for 'adjustment costs' and some evidence that the trend increase in the nominal share of business spending on computers reflects a price elasticity greater than one. However, the point estimate of the price elasticity is statistically indistinguishable from one, so more work is needed to sort out the role of transition effects and price effects.
3   Data on productivity growth in four-digit manufacturing industries can be found at http://www.nber.org/nberprod/ ; computers and peripheral equipment can be found in industries 3571-3579, and semiconductors in industries 3672-3679.
4   The cycle from January 1980 to July 1981 has been combined with the 1980s' expansion.
5   This is the sum of the *impact effects* of the cyclical portion of the decline in computer prices in period t and period t-1 in equation A10 in the appendix (contribution = $[s(IC)+ad(c)L]dq(t)$).
6   Kiley (1999) discusses the importance of the assumption of frictionless factor adjustment and demonstrates that this assumption could be quite misleading during the 'computer revolution'. See the discussion in section 5.

7   Growth in labour augmenting technological progress is multifactor productivity growth divided by the labour income share. Oliner and Sichel report dz* in equation A9.
8   Acemoglu (1998) pursues a similar line of thought.

References

Acemoglu, D. (1998), 'Why Do New Technologies Complement Skills?: Directed Technical Change and Wage Inequality', *Quarterly Journal of Economics*, vol. 113 (November), pp. 1055–89.

Argotte, L. and Epple, D. (1990), 'Learning Curves in Manufacturing', *Science*, 247, pp. 920–24.

Autor, D., Katz, L. and Krueger, A. (1998), 'Computing Inequality: Have Computers Changed the Labor Market?', *Quarterly Journal of Economics*, 113 (November), pp. 1169–213.

Bahk, B.H. and Gort, M. (1993), 'Decomposing Learning-by-Doing in New Plants', *Journal of Political Economy*, 101, pp. 561–83.

Bartel, A. and Lichtenberg, F. (1987), 'The Comparative Advantage of Educated Workers in Implementing New Technologies', *Review of Economics and Statistics*, 69 (February), pp. 1–11.

Berman, E., Bound, J. and Griliches, Z. (1994), 'Changes in the Demand for Skilled Labor Within US Manufacturing Industries: Evidence From the Annual Survey of Manufacturers', *Quarterly Journal of Economics*, 109 (May), pp. 367–98.

Brynjolfsson, E. and L. Hitt (1995), 'Information Technology as a Factor of Production: The Role of Differences Among Firms', *Economics of Innovation and New Technology*, 3 (4), pp. 183–200.

Brynjolfsson, E. and Hitt, L. (1997), 'Computing Productivity: Are Computers Pulling Their Weight?', mimeo.

Congressional Budget Office (2000), *The Budget and Economic Outlook, 2001–2010*, January, US Government Printing Office.

David, P.A. (1975), 'The Horndahl Effect in Lowell, 1834–56: A Short-run Learning Curve for Integrated Cotton Textile Mills', in *Technical Choice, Innovation and Economics Growth: Essays on American and British Economic Experience*, London: Cambridge University Press, pp. 174–91.

David, P.A. (1990), 'The Dynamo and the Computer: An Historical Perspective on the Modern Productivity Paradox', *American Economic Review Papers and Proceedings*, pp. 355–61.

Davis, S.J. (1992), 'Cross-country Patterns of Change in Relative Wages', *NBER Macroeconomics Annual*, pp. 239–300.

Di Nardo, J.E. and Pischke, J.S. (1997), 'The Return to Computer Use Revisited: How Pencils changed the Wage Structure Too', *Quarterly Journal of Economics*, 112, February, pp. 291–304.

Dunne, T., Haltiwanger, J. and Foster, L. (2000), 'Wage and Productivity Dispersion in US Manufacturing: The Role of Computer Investment', NBER Working Paper No. 7465 (January).

Economic Report of the President (2000), Washington, DC: US Government Printing Office.

Federal Reserve Bank of Dallas (1996), *The Economy at Light Speed*.

Freeman, R.B. (1997), 'When Earnings Diverge: Causes, Consequences, and Cures for the New Inequality in the US', National Policy Association Report 284.

Galor, O. and Tsiddon, D. (1997), 'Technological Progress, Mobility, and Economic Growth', *American Economic Review*, 87 (June), pp. 363–82.

Goldin, C. (1996), 'How America Graduated From High School: 1910 to 1960', NBER Working Paper No. 4762 (June).

Goldin, C. and Katz, L. (1998), 'The Origins of Technology-skill Complementarity', *Quarterly Journal of Economics*, 113 (August), pp. 693–732.

Gordon, R.J. (1998), 'Foundations of the Goldilocks Economy: Supply Shocks and the Time-Varying NAIRU', *Brookings Papers on Economic Activity*, 1998(2), pp. 297–333.

Gordon, R.J. (forthcoming), 'Does the New Economy Measure Up to the Great Inventions of the Past?', *Journal of Economic Perspectives*.

Gort, M. and S. Klepper (1982), 'Time Paths in the Diffusion of Product Innovations', *Economic Journal*, 92, pp. 630–53.

Greenwood, J. (1996), 'The Third Industrial Revolution', Rochester Centre for Economic Research Working Paper No. 435.

Greenwood, J., Hercowitz, Z. and Krusell, P. (1997), 'Long-run Implications of Investment-specific Technological Change', *American Economic Review*, 87 (3), pp. 342–62.

Greenwood, J., Hercowitz, Z. and Krusell, P. (2000), 'The Role of Investment-specific Technological Change in the Business Cycle', *European Economic Review*, 44 (1), pp. 91–115.

Greenwood, J. and Yorukoglu, M. (1997), '1974', *Carnegie Rochester Conference Series on Public Policy*, 46 (June), pp. 49–96.

Hercowitz, Z. and Sampson, M. (1991), 'Output Growth, the Real Wage, and Employment Fluctuations', *American Economic Review*, 81 (5), pp. 1215–37.

Hornstein, A. (1999), 'Growth Accounting with Technological Revolutions. Federal Reserve Bank of Richmond', *Economic Quarterly*, 85 (3), pp. 1–22.

Hornstein, A. and Krusell, P. (1996), 'Can Technology Improvements cause Productivity Slowdowns?', *NBER Macroeconomics Annual 1996*, 209–59.

Ilg, R. and Haugen, S. (2000), 'Earnings and Employment Trends in the 1990s', *Monthly Labor Review* (March), pp. 21–33.

Jorgenson, D.W. (1963), 'Capital Theory and Investment Behaviour', *American Economic Review*, 53, pp. 247–59.

Jorgenson, D.W. (1966), 'The Embodiment Hypothesis', *Journal of Political Economy*, 74(1), pp. 1–17.

Jorgenson, D.W. and Stiroh, K.J. (1995), 'Computers and Growth', *Economics of Innovation and New Technology*, 3 (3–4), pp. 295–316.

Jorgenson, D.W. and Stiroh, K.J. (2000), 'Raising the Speed Limit: US Economic Growth in the Information Age', *Brookings Papers on Economic Activity, 2000*.

Katz, L. and Murphy, K. (1992), 'Changes in Relative Wages, 1963–1987: Supply and Demand Factors', *Quarterly Journal of Economics*, 107 (February), pp. 35–78.

Kahn, J. and Lim, J.S. (1998), 'Skilled Labor-augmenting Technical Progress in US Manufacturing', *Quarterly Journal of Economics*, 113 (November), pp. 1281–308.

Kiley, M. (1999a), 'Computers and Growth with Costs of Adjustment: Will the Future Look Like the Past?', Federal Reserve Board FEDS Working Paper 1999–36.

Kiley, M. (1999b), 'The Supply of Skilled Labour and Skill-Biased Technological Progress', *Economic Journal*, 109, pp. 708–24.

Krueger, A.B. (1993), 'How Computers Have Changed the Wage Structure: Evidence from Microdata, 1984–1989', *Quarterly Journal of Economics*, 108(1), pp. 33–60.

Krugman, P. (1994), 'Past and Prospective Causes of High Unemployment', in Federal Reserve Bank of Kansas City, *Reducing Unemployment: Current Issues and Policy Options.*

Krussell, P., Ohanian, L., Rios-Rull, J.V. and Violante, G. (1997), 'Capital Skill Complementarity and Inequality', Federal Reserve Bank of Minneapolis Staff Report 239.

Lehr, B. and Lichtenberg, F. (forthcoming), 'Information Technology and its Impact on Productivity: Firm-level Evidence from Government and Private Data Sources, 1977–1993', *Canadian Journal of Economics.*

Levy, F. (1998), *The New Dollars and Dreams: American Incomes and Economic Change*, New York: Russell Sage Foundation.

Lucas, R.E. (1967), 'Adjustment Costs and the Theory of Supply', *Journal of Political Economy*, 75, pp. 321–34.

McConnell, M.M. and Perez Quiros, G. (forthcoming), 'Output Fluctuations in the United States: What has Changed since the Early 1980s?', *American Economic Review.*

McConnell, S. (1996), 'The Role of Computers in Reshaping the Work Force', *Monthly Labor Review* (August), pp. 3–5.

Nelson, R. and Phelps, E.S. (1966), 'Investment in Humans, Technological Diffusion, and Economic Growth', *American Economic Review*, 56 (February), pp. 69–75.

Oliner, S.D. and Sichel, D.E. (1994), 'Computers and Output Growth Revisited: How Big is the Puzzle?', *Brooking Papers on Economic Activity*, 2, pp. 273–334.

Oliner, S.D. and Sichel, D.E. (2000), 'The Resurgence of Growth in the Late 1990s: Is Information Technology the Story?', Federal Reserve Board FEDS Working Paper 2000–20.

Sichel, D.E. (1997), *The Computer Revolution*, Washington DC: Brookings Institution.

Solow, R. (1957), 'Technical Change and the Aggregate Production Function', *Review of Economics and Statistics*, 39, pp. 312–30.

Solow, R. (1960), 'Investment and Technical Progress', in K. Arrow, S. Karlin and P. Suppes (eds), *Mathematical Methods in the Social Sciences, 1959*, Stanford, CA: Stanford University Press, pp. 89–104.

Tevlin, S. and. Whelan, K (2000), 'Explaining the Investment Boom of the 1990s', Federal Reserve Board FEDS Working Paper 2000–11.

Yorukoglu, M. (1998), 'The Information Technology Productivity Paradox', *Review of Economic Dynamics*, 1, pp. 551–92.

Zarnowitz, V. (2000), 'The Old and the New in US Economic Expansion of the 1990s', NBER Working Paper No. 7721 (May).

Appendix 1

A Simple Model of Computers and Growth

This appendix presents a simple version of a dynamic general equilibrium economy that experiences disembodied productivity shocks and shocks to the productivity of computers (embodied technology shocks). The model is a combination of those presented in Hercowitz and Sampson (1991) and Greenwood et al. (1997, 2000).

Suppose the representative consumer in a closed economy maximizes the following preferences

Equation A1

$$E_t \sum_{j=t}^{\infty} B_{j-t} \log(E(j)),$$

where B is the time discount factor and E(t) is consumption in period t. The consumer accumulates capital assets – denoted computers (C(t)) and other capital (K(t)) according to the accumulation equations

Equation A2

$$C(t+1) = C(t)^{(1-d(c))}(q(t)IC(t))^{d(c)},$$

Equation A3

$$K(t+1) = K(t)^{(1-d(k))}(IK(t))^{d(k)},$$

where d(j) is the depreciation rate of asset j, IC(t) is investment in computer capital, IK(t) is investment in other capital, and q is a factor that adjusts for changes in quality in computer investment (e.g., the rapid rate of technological advance in computers has made a dollar's expenditure on computer power much more productive over time). All quantities are denoted in consumption units.[1] Greenwood et al. show that q equals the inverse of the relative, quality-adjusted price of computer investment under certain conditions in a closely related model. In the calibration exercise in the main body of the chapter, q will be treated as the inverse of the relative price of a unit of computer power.

The consumer's budget constraint is given by:

Equation A4

$$E(t) + IC(t) + IK(t) = W(t)L + rc(t)(IC(t-1) + uc(t)(C(t-1)) + rk(t)(IK(t-1) + uk(t)(K(t-1))$$

where $W(t)$ is the wage rate received for the consumer's inelastically supplied labour input (L), $r.(t)$ is the return in period t to investment in period $t-1$, and $u.(t)$ is the relative price of capital (in terms of investment goods) in period (t).

Production by firms is governed by a Cobb-Douglas production function:

Equation A5

$$Y(t) = C(t)^a K(t)^b (Z(t)L(t))^{(1-a-b)}.2$$

Finally, output is denominated in consumption units and the aggregate resource constraint is given by

Equation A6

$$Y(t) = E(t) + IC(t) + IK(t).$$

Contribution of Computers to Potential Growth

Along a steady-state growth path, the savings rate is constant, and the allocation of the savings pool across investment in computers and other capital implies that investment in each asset is a constant fraction of the savings pool, which in turn implies that other capital input grows at the same rate as output (i.e., balanced growth from equation A3) and computer capital grows at the rate of output growth plus the rate of technological advance in computer power (i.e., balanced nominal growth, where $C(t+1)/q(t)$ grows at the same rate as output from equation A2).[3]

Taking natural logarithms of equation A5, differentiating with respect to time, and inserting the growth implication derived above into the resulting expression yields the following equation for growth in labour productivity:

Equation A7

$$d(y-l) = dz + \frac{a}{1-a-b} \, dz,$$

where dz is the growth rate of labour-augmenting technological progress and dq is the negative of the pace of relative price declines for computers.

Business Cycle Implications

The special form of the capital accumulation equations and consumer preferences guarantees a constant savings rate in each time period, and a constant allocation of this savings pool across investment in computers and investment in other capital. Using this result and manipulating the first-order conditions governing utility maximisation by consumers and cost minimisation by firms yields a convenient stochastic process for output that depends on disembodied technology shocks $(Z(t))$ and embodied technology shocks $(q(t))$. In logs, this process is given by

Equation A8

$$y(t) = \frac{(1 - (1 - d(c)L)(1 - (1 - d(k)L)[(1 - a - b)z(t) + ad(c)Lq(t)]}{(1 - (2 - d(c) - d(k) + ad(c) + bd(k))L + ((1 - d(c)(1 - d(k) + ad(c)(1 - d(k)) + b(d(k)(1 - d(c))L^2)}$$

The short-run impact of computer-specific technological change $(q(t))$ is given by ad(c) – implying that only large shocks have much impact at business cycle frequencies (as a is likely between 0.03 and 0.05 and d(c) lies between 0.3 and 0.5). The business cycle effects of disembodied shocks are more muted in this model than that of Greenwood et al. (2000) because of the special assumption made regarding depreciation (A2 and A3), which generated constant savings rates. In Greenwood et al. (2000), investment responds more than proportionately to disembodied shocks and labour supply is not fixed, and therefore disembodied shocks can generate larger effects at business cycle frequencies than noted here or in the text.

From a Utility-Based Measure of Output to a Production-Based Measure

The discussion above focuses on the trend and cyclical behaviour of a utility-based measure of output – output measured at consumption prices. It is useful to transform this measure to a production based measure, i.e., one in which growth in consumption and investment goods are measured using their good-specific deflators, as this is the convention adopted in the national accounts. Denoting investment measured in investment units as $IC^* = IC/P(IC)$ and $IK^* = IK/P(IK)$, and remembering that $q(IC) = 1/P(IC)$, etc., the Tornqvist approximation to growth in gross domestic product (dy^*) is given by

$$dy^* = dy + s(IK)dq(IK) + s(IC)dq(IC),$$

where $s(X)$ is the nominal share of X in expenditure.

For trend growth calculations, the text uses the decomposition

Equation A9

$$dy^* = dz^* + \frac{a}{1 - a - b} \, dq,$$

$$dz^* = dz + s(IK)dq(IK) + s(IC)dq(IC).$$

Note that it was assumed above that $dq(IK)$ equals zero, which is approximately true in the data. dz^* is referred to as growth in labour-augmenting technological progress or multifactor productivity, although it in fact contains disembodied progress. This is the convention adopted in Oliner and Sichel (1994, 2000) and Jorgenson and Stiroh (1995, 2000) (whereas Greenwood et al. (1997, 2000) adopt the decompositions in A7 and A8).

For the business cycle impact of shocks, the text uses the decomposition

Equation A10

$$dy(t) = \frac{(1 - (1 - d(c)L)(1 - (1 - d(k)L)[(1 - a - b)z(t) + ad(c)Lq(t)]}{(1 - (2 - d(c) - d(k) + ad(c) + bd(k))L + ((1 - d(c)(1 - d(k) + ad(c)(1 - d(k)) + b(d(k)(1 - d(c))L^2)} + s(IC)dq$$

where $dq = dq(IC)$, as $dq(IK)$ is set to zero.

Notes

1   This assumption follows Solow (1960) and Greenwood et al. (1997, 2000). This choice reflects the desire to obtain a measure of output growth that corresponds to the rate of expansion in consumption possibilities – as this is the relevant measure for welfare. The alternative convention, advocated in Jorgenson (1966), focuses on the growth in production possibilities and hence values investment and consumption goods using separate deflators. For the purposes herein, the choice is unimportant, so long as one remembers the convention adopted.

2   Labour input is supplied inelastically at a constant level, normalized to 1.

3   The assumptions made actually imply a constant savings rate in every time period, but this result does not obtain generally (as in Greenwood et al. (1997, 2000), for example). The constant savings rate in steady-state holds under slightly more general conditions than those used herein, implying that the trend growth results herein are more general than the business cycle implications discussed below.

Chapter 10

The 'New Economy' in the OECD

Francesco Daveri

1   Introduction

After two decades of productivity slowdown, the United States is now in the midst of a period of economic rebirth. While a large fraction of this economic miracle is credited to the rapid spreading of information technologies in the economy, a key policy concern everywhere, and notably in Europe, is whether and when the US economic boom will extend abroad, and what role new technologies are about to play.

In this chapter, I collect and supplement the available cross-country evidence on the extent and the contribution to growth of 'new economy' activities in the OECD, and in particular in the EU, in 1991–97. Information technology activities did make a contribution to growth in the EU too, but not equally everywhere. Over the 1990s, the contribution of new technologies to growth was substantial in the UK and the Netherlands – although of a smaller order of magnitude than in the US, Canada Australia – and rapidly increasing over time in Finland, Ireland and Denmark. It was instead less quantitatively relevant in France, Germany, Belgium and Sweden, and outright marginal in Italy and Spain.

How to measure the contribution of information technology to growth has been an issue of public concern in the US for a long time. In his oft-cited 1987 article in the *New York Times Book Review*, Robert Solow concisely summarized the widespread concern that computers had been deeply changing the lives of the Americans without leaving too much of their presence in the official statistics. ('Computers are everywhere, but in the national accounting data'.) Since then, the US Bureau of Economic Analysis (BEA) has undertaken an impressive work of data revision – a concise rendition of which is offered by Moulton (2000). Among other important changes, hedonic (i.e. quality-adjusted) price indexes for computers and semiconductors were constructed. Broadly speaking, this has redistributed the nominal growth of computer-related incomes from prices to quantities.[1]

Overall, the BEA statistical amendments have possibly contributed to the sizable upward revision of the estimated contribution of new technologies to growth shown in recent studies. At first, Oliner and Sichel (1994) and Jorgenson and Stiroh (1995) reported rather low estimates of the contribution of computers to growth – some 0.2 percentage points per year, to be compared with yearly GDP growth rates in the order of 3 percentage points. As more recent evidence became available, these estimates were revised upwards. Oliner and Sichel (2000) provided a comprehensive assessment of the contribution of new technologies to growth. They credited the use of computers, software and communication technologies a hefty yearly contribution of 1.10 percentage points in 1996–99, markedly bigger than 0.57 in 1991–95 and 0.49 in 1974–90 (see Oliner and Sichel, 2000, Table 1).

Their findings did not go unchallenged, however. Jorgenson and Stiroh (2000), while agreeing on the relevance of the contribution of new technologies to today's US economic growth, raised a note of caution about its long-term sustainability, as long as gains in productivity growth do not tangibly materialize outside the high-tech producing sectors. Gordon (1999, 2000) reached a broadly similar conclusion. The growth acceleration in the second part of the 1990s – in Gordon's view – is the combined effect of the BEA revision and of an unusually strong cyclical upswing, originating from, but also largely confined to, the computer-producing sector.

No discussion of this sort and momentum has taken place elsewhere in the world. News and magazines have popularised the view that a large technology gap exists between the US and the rest of the world. A similar view is also held by businessmen and politicians. While episodes and anecdotal evidence on the much advertized 'new economy' abound, little work has been done, though, to reconcile sketchy pieces of evidence from different countries with the impressive amount of work carried out in the US. Stephen Roach and Eric Chaney at Morgan Stanley (Morgan Stanley, 2000) have argued that, while Europe will likely catch up over the next five years in terms of use of new technologies, the ICT production gap is harder to bridge, and is hence bound to persist through 2005, and beyond. In parallel, the Council on Competitiveness, a Washington-based forum of experts, such as Michael Porter and an array of top executives from large US corporations, has recently analysed international patenting, R&D and human capital indicators, reaching the conclusion that Denmark, Finland and Sweden may be the next technological leaders (Porter and Stern, 1999).

My primary undertaking in this chapter is to contribute to lay some numerical basis for this discussion. By taking advantage of data collection at both private (WITSA/IDC) and official (the OECD, the US BEA) sources, I provide a broad picture of the aggregate extent and contribution to economic growth of 'new economy' activities in the EU, and in a sample of OECD countries at large, in the 1990s.

Available evidence indicates that Italy, Spain and, to a lesser extent, France and Germany invest and accumulate fewer resources in new technologies than the US. In 1997, ICT spending and investment in Italy and Spain reached 4.5 and 2.0 per cent of their GDP, which falls short by 3 and 1.5 percentage points of the values recorded for the same items in the US and in other non-European countries. This gap has even widened between 1992 and 1997. But this is not all. Countries in continental Europe also significantly lag behind other countries in the EU (the UK, the Netherlands, Sweden, Finland) and outside the EU (Canada, Australia, New Zealand).

The structure of the chapter is as follows. The size of the new economy in Europe and other OECD countries is measured in terms of ICT spending (section 2) and investment (section 3). In Section 4, nominal data are used to construct real investment series, price deflators, capital stocks and capital income shares. Section 5 concludes.

2   The Depth of the 'New Economy' in the OECD

In 1997 – the latest year for which a full set of comparable data is available – OECD countries as a whole spent about US$1,600 billion in information and communication technologies – a figure higher by one third than in 1992, as a result of yearly growth rates of 6 per cent per year. ICT spending in the US alone amounted to US$640 billion: about one third of the entire world market, 20 per cent higher than the amount spent by the EU15 as a whole, and nearly twice as much as spending in Japan.

These figures concern total spending in new technologies and do not thus provide *per se* an indicator of the depth of 'new economy' activities in each country. That large and rich countries take the lion's share in the world market of ICT goods is hardly surprising: they do the same with world trade at large. However, as made clear below, not all of the large countries have developed equally sizable 'new economy' sectors.

The GDP share of ICT spending is a proxy for the depth of penetration of ICT spending relative to each country's endowment.[2]

Even a cursory look at data availability immediately suggests, however, that the alleged technology gap between the US and the rest of the world manifests itself, first of all, in a data availability gap. In the US, in the last few years, the BEA and the Bureau of Labor Statistics have gradually adjusted their methods of data collection and processing to better incorporate quality improvements. In other countries, instead, most national statistical offices are still taken with surprise as 'new economy' activities show up. This produces a 'data availability gap' between the US and the rest of the world over and above the technological gap.

To gain a sense of the technological revolution occurring around the world, data from private sources must then supplement, or outright substitute for, official ones. The primary data source I am relying on here is WITSA/IDC (1998). In their Report, WITSA[3] and IDC[4] put together ICT spending data for the 50 largest markets in the years between 1992 and 1997 (six years, overall). Aggregate spending data, in current local and dollar values, are obtained by adding up various items, such as information technology hardware, software and related external and internal services, plus telecommunications.

Table 10.1 is a summary of what GDP shares of ICT spending have to tell us about the degree of penetration of new technologies in 18 OECD countries (11 EU countries, the US and a composite 'control' group of countries inclusive of Norway, Switzerland, Canada, Japan, Australia and New Zealand).[5] The GDP shares of ICT spending reported in Table 10.1 are the ratios between nominal spending in local currency from WITSA/IDC, and the nominal GDP in local currency reported in the OECD National Accounts.[6] Morgan Stanley (2000) estimates for 1998 are also reported.

In 1997, ICT spending averaged 6.7 per cent of the GDP of the OECD countries in the sample, up from 6 per cent in 1992. New Zealand, Sweden and Australia showed the highest ratios – all devoting more than 8 per cent of their GDP to new technologies. The United States were actually very close to this group of strong high-tech users, spending 7.7 per cent of their GDP, with Japan ranking slightly lower with its 7.4 per cent.

In the same year, the 11 EU countries in the sample as a whole destined about 6.3 per cent of their GDP to new technologies, hence a smaller fraction than the US and most other Industrial Countries. France, Germany, Belgium and Finland spent in ICT approximately the same as the EU average, with Sweden, the UK, the Netherlands and Denmark clearly above the EU average and Italy and Spain (and Greece and Portugal, not included in this study) lower than the EU average by roughly twp percentage points.

Hence, while the US, Japan and Europe act prominently in the ICT world market, the degree of domestic involvement of the EU, and more markedly of its Southern members, in the 'new economy' is much smaller than that of the US and Japan.

Table 10.1   The use of information and communication technologies in the OECD: nominal ICT spending as a share of GDP (percentage points)

	1992	1997	1998
Germany	5.4	5.7	5.9
France	5.8	6.5	6.7
UK	7.1	7.8	7.6
Italy	3.7	4.4	4.5
Spain	3.9	4.3	4.2
Netherlands	6.6	7.3	7.3
Belgium	5.8	6.2	6.3
Ireland	5.5	5.9	n.a.
Denmark	6.4	6.8	6.8
Sweden	7.6	8.4	8.9
Finland	4.7	6.2	6.2
Norway	5.6	5.8	6.5
Switzerland	7.6	7.9	8.1
Japan	5.7	7.6	NA
Australia	7.2	8.5	n.a.
New Zealand	9.0	8.7	n.a.
Canada	6.8	7.7	n.a.
USA	7.1	7.7	8.1
EU11 (*)	5.7	6.3	n.a.
OECD18 (*)	6.0	6.7	n.a.

Note: (*) = arithmetic averages.

Sources: 1992–97 – WITSA/IDC for ICT spending in local currency; OECD National Accounts for GDP in local currency: 1998 – Morgan Stanley (2000) estimates.

Have these gaps got bigger or smaller over time? In 1992, the US spent in new technologies slightly more than 7 per cent of their GDP – 0.6 percentage points less than in 1997, while the EU11 and Japan destined about 5.7 per cent of their respective GDP. Hence, the EU–US gap has stayed roughly constant since then. Japan, instead, substantially narrowed its distance from the US. Strikingly, the severe economic stagnation experienced by the Japanese economy in the 1990s has not seemingly led to a slowdown in the pace of adoption of new technologies in this country.

Another piece of evidence from Table 10.1 is that, within the EU, countries starting with a low (high) ICT share in 1992 still had a low (high) share in

1997 and 1998. The only notable exception is Finland, a country clearly below the average in 1992 and slightly above the average in 1997, due to an increase in its ICT share of 1.5 points. This outcome was partly driven by the success of Nokia, which now represents the bulk of the capitalization of the Finnish stock market. It also has to do with the unusually rapid diffusion of telecommunications and Internet usage among the Finnish population (as confirmed by the impressive share of population connected to the Internet, and by anecdotal evidence in a recent 'on-line banking' survey in the *Economist* magazine).

To sum up, Europe as a whole indeed lags behind the United States and Japan in the usage of information and communication technologies. Data up to 1998 do not show much evidence of a closing gap between Europe and the US. Moreover, sharp differences exist in the pace of new technology adoption within Europe between the northern front-runners and the southern laggards, with France and Germany in between.

3 Investment and Capital Stocks in 'New Economy' Activities

In the previous section, some evidence on the penetration of information technologies in a sample of OECD countries, and in Europe in particular, was reported. Yet investment, not spending, matters when accounting for the contribution of new technology to growth. It is therefore important to append the description of investment data. As made clear in what follows, the picture on the extent of adoption of information and communication technologies is roughly the same, irrespective of whether we look at spending or investment.

Calculating such investment data implies going through a few steps. First, nominal investment for three categories of ICT capital goods (hardware, software and telecommunication equipment) must be calculated. Then price indices are derived for these same categories, so as to construct series on investment spending in real terms. Finally, capital stocks are computed through the perpetual inventory method, by adding up real investments at various dates in accordance with depreciation and service lives of each capital good.

Nominal Investment

The starting point for computing ICT investment is the WITSA/IDC data on hardware, software and telecommunications spending. WITSA/IDC provides data for hardware, software and telecommunications. Yet none of these items can be included or excluded *as such* in an 'investment spending' item. Each capital good involves separate issues.

Hardware The WITSA/IDC item for 'IT hardware' includes computer system central units, storage devices, printers, bundled operating systems, and data communication equipment bought by corporations, households, schools or government agencies from an external agent or corporation. All of these items would be properly (from a national accounts perspective) assigned to investment, but for household spending. In turn, to calculate investment spending of the business sector, hardware spending by public schools and government agencies should be subtracted out as well. Hence, classifying the WITSA/IDC 'IT hardware' item as investment would introduce an upward bias in the measured value of investment spending. At the same time, though, the WITSA/IDC definition leaves out hardware spending from unincorporated enterprises, which represents a downward bias. Schreyer (2000, p. 9) concludes that 'the two effects roughly cancel out', arguing that 'a comparison for the United States suggests that this approximation is not unreasonable'. I checked this assertion, using the latest available data from the BEA. According to WITSA/IDC, 'IT hardware' amounted to US$138 billion in 1997, while 'computers and other peripherals equipment' added up to some US$88 billion in the BEA national accounts. The same applies to the years back to 1992. Clearly, discrepancies of such magnitudes cannot be easily swept under the rug. Hence, in my calculations, I used BEA data for computers and other peripherals for the US. In the absence of better alternatives, I took the short cut of correcting downwards WITSA/IDC hardware data for the other countries in the sample, picking 0.654 – the 1992–97 average of the ratio between BEA data and WITSA/IDC data for the US – as a correcting factor. Hence, the hardware part of investment spending in this chapter is equal to the original WITSA/IDC datum times 0.654.

Software The treatment of software as a capital good, and not as an intermediate good like in the past, is another result of the major revision of national accounts by the BEA. The WITSA/IDC 'IT software' item includes pre-packaged software as well as software applications, but does not include software spending internal to the firm. The internal fraction of information systems' operating budgets as well as internally customized software expenses are instead lumped together in a residual item, called 'internal services', together with depreciation of physical assets and other expenses that cannot be associated to a vendor. Once again, I double-checked what was available for the US from both WITSA/IDC and BEA sources. WITSA/IDC reports 'IT software' outlays for US$54 billion and 'Internal IT services' outlays for US$98 billion in the US in 1997, while the software item for BEA was US$123 billion. Moreover, the 'Internal services' item stagnated over time, while the narrow software item of WITSA/IDC and the BEA software item kept rising steadily at roughly similar growth rates. In conclusion, as for hardware, I employed BEA data for the US and adjusted data for the other countries in the sample. The adjusted software data for the other countries are generated multiplying the original WITSA/IDC narrow software item – whose trend is similar to the BEA item – by 2.289, the 1992–97 average ratio between the BEA and the WITSA/IDC narrow item for the US.

Telecommunications equipment WITSA/IDC 'telecommunications spending' includes public and private network equipment, which belong to investment spending, and telecommunications services, which do not. Unfortunately, no information is provided in the WITSA/IDC Report as to how to break the total into these two items. I took investment spending for PTOs (Public Telecommunications Operators) reported in the OECD *2000 Telecommunications Database*. These data go back to 1980, something useful for later purposes. In order to come up with a proxy for business sector investment spending, PTO spending was multiplied by 1.786, the 1980–97 average ratio of BEA and OECD data for the US. Thus, as before, I employed BEA data for the US and adjusted data for the other countries in the sample.

ICT investment of the business sector for three categories of ICT capital goods (computers and other peripheral equipment, software and communications equipment) was eventually computed as described above. Table 10.2 presents the GDP shares of business sector investment in information and communication technologies for the 18 OECD countries in the sample in 1992 and 1997 (column [1] and [2]). In the same table, the GDP shares of total (public and private) fixed investment are also shown in column [3] and [4].

Table 10.2 documents the rise of ICT investment over time and its increased importance within total fixed investment in the OECD countries, and in most EU countries in particular.

The United States can be usefully taken as a benchmark. In the US, both the GDP share and the fraction of total ICT outlays devoted to investment went up steadily over time. As a result, in 1997, 3.4 per cent of the US GDP was being invested in information and communication technologies. This figure amounts to 45 per cent of total ICT spending – a very high investment ratio

Table 10.2   Business sector investment in information technology and total investment in the OECD (GDP shares)

	ICT business investment		Total fixed investment	
	[1]	[2]	[3]	[4]
	1992	*1997*	*1992*	*1997*
Germany	2.8 (51.2)	2.5 (44.4)	22.0	21.9
France	1.9 (33.3)	2.3 (35.3)	17.9	20.2˙
UK	2.4 (34.0)	3.9 (49.7)	15.3	14.9
Italy	2.4 (64.7)	1.9 (42.6)	20.9	18.1
Spain	2.2 (56.7)	2.1 (49.6)	20.3	21.4
Netherlands	2.5 (38.3)	3.0 (41.2)	16.9	20.7
Belgium	2.3 (40.3)	2.3 (37.0)	21.3	20.8
Ireland	1.9 (35.3)	2.5 (43.0)	19.9	18.0
Denmark	2.0 (32.2)	2.4 (35.7)	23.0	19.6
Sweden	2.5 (33.5)	2.8 (33.3)	19.9	23.3
Finland	2.2 (46.3)	2.9 (47.3)	24.0	21.4
Norway	2.3 (40.7)	2.6 (44.7)	30.5	28.4
Switzerland	3.1 (41.4)	3.3 (42.1)	16.5	20.2
Japan	2.0 (35.9)	2.7 (35.8)	16.5	16.7
Australia	2.6 (36.4)	3.9 (46.7)	21.5	23.5
New Zealand	3.7 (41.5)	3.4 (39.7)	20.5	18.0
Canada	2.5 (37.4)	3.3 (43.0)	18.5	19.2
USA	2.6 (36.4)	3.4 (44.3)	15.6	17.7
EU11	**2.3** (42.1)	**2.6** (41.6)	**20.1**	**20.0**
OECD 18	**2.5** (40.6)	**2.9** (41.7)	**20.1**	**20.2**

Notes

1   Nominal shares over GDP, current values, percentage points.
2   Second row in column [1] and [2]: share of ICT investment over total ICT spending.

Primary sources: Bureau of Economic Analysis for US data. My calculations from WITSA/
IDC (1998) and OECD (1999) for other OECD countries.

by any standards, and about one-fifth of total investment spending (17.7 per cent of GDP in the same year).

The US data compare with much lower figures for most European countries. In 1997, Italy and Spain invested in information technology around 2 per cent of their GDP – about one-tenth of their total investment. Most other countries in Continental Europe invested less than 2.5 per cent of their GDP, while the Netherlands, Finland and Sweden were close to 3 per cent – a slightly smaller figure than the US. In the UK, ICT investment was close to 4 per cent of GDP – the highest investment share in the sample.

Table 10.2 provides another element to consider. It was emphasized above that the US–EU gap in total ICT spending stayed constant over time. The investment shares gap has instead widened. In 1992, the EU11 invested 2.3 per cent of their GDP, a bare 0.3 points less than the US. By 1997, the difference had nearly tripled, up to 0.8 percentage point of GDP.

It is also worth mentioning, however, that such differences in the amount of ICT investment across countries are not closely associated to remarkable cross-country differences in the propensities to invest in ICT. As shown in the bracketed number in column [1] and [2], the EU11 and the OECD18 (arithmetic) average shares of ICT investment over total ICT spending were rather similar across countries. Most countries, with the exceptions of Denmark, Sweden, France and Japan, devoted 40 to 45 per cent of total ICT spending to investment. Ireland, the UK and the Netherlands markedly increased their propensities to invest over time, from some 35 per cent of total ICT spending in 1992 to 45 per cent, or more, in 1997.

To sum up, Tables 10.1 and 10.2 document existence and persistence of an investment gap in new technologies between the US and other OECD countries (such as New Zealand, Switzerland and Canada) and Europe. This gap is also present within the European Union, too. Wherever this gap shows up, it does not crucially stem from lower propensities to invest, but rather from a smaller amount of resources devoted to information technologies in general.

Prices and Real Investment

Nominal investment flows are routinely converted into real investment flows deflating each nominal series by the appropriate investment price deflator. This is not an easy task to accomplish in a cross-country framework, given that national statistical offices employ different methods to construct such price indexes. The problem here is that the US-BEA employs hedonic price techniques,[7] while most countries in the Industrial world do not.[8]

The hedonic price index for computers in use today in the US is the result of a lengthy process initiated by the BEA in 1985, taking advantage of previous work done at the IBM on mainframe prices in 1969–84. This process has led to improve the methods of accounting for quality changes in output and inputs, as well as to reduce the bias arising from the use of fixed reference points for comparing changes in quantities.

The price index for computers and other peripherals published by the BEA now incorporates all such improvements. Table 10.3 reports the yearly rates of change of such index, of various components of the index (computers and peripherals, software, communications equipment), and of the aggregate equipment and software index for 1988–99. Table 10.3 documents two important facts. First, the price of *all* equipment and software goods declined over the period, more clearly so in 1993–99. Second, while the price of information equipment declined faster than the price of other equipment goods, the difference in the deflation rates between ICT and non-ICT equipment stayed roughly constant, ranging between 3.5 and 4 per cent per year over the period.

Table 10.3   Equipment and software price indices in the US

	Equipment and software : all	Information equipment	Hardware	Software	Communications
1988	1.4	−0.9	−7.4	1.1	1.3
1989	1.5	−1.6	−6.9	−2.4	1.3
1990	1.4	−2.1	−9.7	−1.4	1.2
1991	1.5	−1.6	−10.7	0.6	1.2
1992	−0.7	−4.8	−15.6	−5.9	0.9
1993	−0.5	−3.3	−15.9	0.3	0.4
1994	−0.3	−3.6	−12.6	−2.3	−0.3
1995	−0.8	−4.7	−18.1	0.3	−1.2
1996	−2.1	−7.6	−27.2	−1.9	−0.6
1997	−2.7	−7.3	−25.5	−2.6	−0.4
1998	−3.5	−8.6	−30.1	−2.0	−1.1
1999	−2.6	−6.7	−26.5	0.5	−1.0

Compounded rates of change

1990–93	0.4	−2.9	−12.2	−1.6	0.9
1993–99	−2.0	−6.2	−20.8	−1.3	−0.8
1993–97	−1.5	−5.6	−18.8	−1.6	−0.6
1997–99	−3.0	−7.4	−24.6	−0.7	−1.0

Source: US Bureau of Economic Analysis, www.bea.doc.gov, April 2000.

As mentioned above, no such hedonic price index is available by now in Europe. So here is the problem: sticking to traditional price indices would probably lead to understate the relevance of the 'new economy', but European statistical offices have not produced yet new quality-adjusted price indices.

Schreyer (2000, pp. 10–11) has suggested a way out, which I follow too. The newly constructed US price index and the high tradability of ICT capital goods among countries are exploited to derive a price index for each of the ICT capital goods in all non-US countries. The price index of ICT capital good k in country c can in fact be calculated under the assumption that the rate of change of the price of each ICT good with respect to the other capital goods is the same in each country c as in the US. Hence, knowledge of the hedonic price index for ICT capital good k in the US and of the producer price indices of the other capital goods in the US and in country c suffices to infer the (unobserved) price index of capital good k in country c. This rule amounts to assuming a full pass-through of US ICT price variations into EU or Japanese price variations, once allowance is made for differences in investment good inflation.

Obviously, the real world is possibly far off from the assumptions implied by the pricing rule described above. If perfect substitutability in use, no impediments to foreign trade, uniform domestic regulations, tax regimes and market structures are not observed, the similarity in the price dynamics of information technology capital goods across countries is exaggerated by this procedure, as well as the upward trend in real ICT investment in Europe. This is important to bear in mind when looking at the summary statistics on OECD countries' price trends and real investments reported in Tables 10.4 and 10.5, computed assuming that the mentioned rule holds.

Table 10.4 reports ICT price inflation data and provides a picture of striking similarity in price dynamics across countries. As emphasized above, this is built in the procedure employed to construct the price indices as long as the rates of change of *all* capital goods are roughly similar across countries. If this is the case, price inflation of ICT goods in country c is in practice solely determined by the rate of change in the price of the same good in the US. Hence, unsurprisingly, countries with a consolidated tradition of price stability do not exhibit marked deviations from ICT inflation in the US. Italy, Spain and Ireland, instead, show less pronounced deflation rates for hardware [9] and mildly positive inflation rates for software and communication equipment, whereas the price of both capital goods declined on average by onee or two points per year in the US. In some non-European countries (including the neighbouring Canada), furthermore, the reconstructed deflation rates in hardware prices were

Table 10.4 ICT price inflation in OECD countries

	1990–95			1996–97		
	Communication equipment	Hardware	Software	Communication equipment	Hardware	Software
Germany	0.7	−11.5	−0.3	−2.0	−23.1	−0.9
France	−0.8	−13.0	−1.9	−1.8	−22.9	−0.7
UK	−1.1	−13.4	−02.2	−0.3	−21.4	0.8
Italy	1.9	−10.3	0.9	1.5	−19.6	2.6
Spain	2.2	−10.1	1.1	0.6	−20.5	1.7
Netherlands	−0.5	−12.7	−1.5	−0.9	−21.9	0.3
Belgium	0.2	−12.0	−0.9	−1.1	−22.2	0.0
Ireland	−0.4	−12.6	−1.4	2.0	−19.1	3.1
Denmark	−2.1	−14.4	−3.2	−1.7	−22.7	0.5
Sweden	−0.3	−12.5	−1.4	−1.7	−22.7	−0.5
Finland	0.4	−11.9	−0.7	−1.6	−22.7	−0.5
Norway	0.4	−11.9	−0.7	0.5	−20.5	1.7
Switzerland	−1.8	−14.1	−2.9	−6.2	−27.3	−5.1
Japan	−1.6	−13.8	−2.7	−4.8	−25.9	−3.7
Australia	−1.2	−13.4	−2.3	−3.0	−24.1	−1.9
New Zealand	−0.5	−12.7	−1.5	−5.3	−26.3	−4.1
Canada	−2.8	−15.1	−3.9	−2.1	−23.1	−0.9
USA	−0.7	−12.9	−1.7	−2.5	−23.6	−1.4

Source: BEA for US data, my own calculations for other OECD countries.

actually more pronounced than in the US, as a result of a negative inflation differential with the US producer prices for capital goods.

In Table 10.5, investment price and quantity rates of change in 1992–97 are contrasted. Hardware and software growth rates proved positive in all countries. The same holds for communications equipment, with the exceptions of Germany, Italy, Belgium and New Zealand. The growth rates of hardware investment are the highest, reaching and outweighing a yearly 25 per cent in many cases. Investment spending in software increased a lot too, although at somewhat smaller rates (about less than one half in the US) than hardware. Communication equipment increased more moderately, except for the UK and Ireland, where growth rates of 23.5 and 18.5 were recorded. A somewhat negative relation between prices and quantities can be traced for hardware and software (with some outliers), while no relation at all emerges for communication equipment.[10]

Capital Stocks and Income Shares

In this section, the nominal and real investment series previously derived are employed to obtain nominal and real capital stocks. The perpetual inventory method calculates capital stocks as the cumulated sum of past investment flows, weighted so as to reflect the relative efficiency in production of each vintage of capital.

Capital stocks The availability of quality-adjusted price indices for investment provides a natural weighting scheme.[11] As long as quality improvements are accounted for on the price side, each new vintage of capital is effectively the same as the vintages of the past. Investment flows can then be simply added up to the previous ones, once allowance is made of the loss in productive efficiency of each capital good over time.

The perpetual inventory method also requires assumptions on the service lives of capital goods and their pace of depreciation. The assumptions made on service lives and depreciation determine how far one has to go backwards in time in adding up investment flows to obtain the extent of today's capital stocks. Implicitly, the perpetual inventory method assumes that there is a point in time back in the past when the capital stock was effectively equal to zero. From then onwards, investments cumulate literally from scratch.

Here I have three types of ICT capital goods (communication equipment, hardware and software), plus the aggregate capital stock to be employed in the growth accounting exercise. In line with existing studies on the US,[12]

Table 10.5 ICT investment: prices and quantities in the OECD 1992-97, average rates of change, percentage points

	Communication equipment		Hardware		Software	
	Price	*Quantity*	*Price*	*Quantity*	*Price*	*Quantity*
Germany	-1.7	-4.1	-17.6	25.6	-0.8	11.1
France	-2.2	6.7	-18.0	22.0	-1.3	12.5
UK	-0.4	23.2	-16.6	29.7	0.5	13.9
Italy	1.6	-5.4	-14.9	18.6	2.5	2.9
Spain	1.1	3.2	-15.3	21.6	2.0	1.0
Netherlands	-1.2	1.6	-17.2	26.0	-0.3	13.7
Belgium	-1.1	-2.6	-17.1	24.2	-0.2	4.6
Ireland	1.5	18.5	-15.0	23.5	2.4	11.4
Denmark	-2.4	13.2	-18.2	27.2	-1.5	10.3
Sweden	-1.3	2.7	-17.3	24.7	-0.4	8.4
Finland	-1.0	11.6	-17.1	30.3	-0.1	12.2
Norway	-0.4	9.4	-16.6	27.1	0.5	9.3
Switzerland	-5.3	3.2	-20.7	25.0	-4.4	11.7
Japan	-4.5	14.5	-20.0	23.0	-3.6	12.1
Australia	-2.4	14.8	-18.1	33.8	-1.5	19.0
New Zealand	-3.9	-0.1	-19.5	24.4	-3.0	14.7
Canada	-1.4	6.8	-17.4	27.5	-0.5	16.6
USA	-2.1	10.9	-18.0	31.4	-1.2	13.4

Source: BEA for US data, my own calculations for other OECD countries.

depreciation rates are assumed constant, though different across goods. In particular, software, hardware and communications equipment are assumed to respectively depreciate at yearly rates of 44 per cent, 32 per cent and 15 per cent – much faster than the aggregate capital stock, whose depreciation rate is 7.5 per cent per year.[13] Depreciation rate assumptions are actually immaterial in the stage of calculation of the capital stock, since to evaluate the contribution of capital to the growth rate of *gross* domestic product, I am using the *gross* (productive) capital stock. Depreciation rates are employed, though, when computing the user costs of capital necessary to calculate the value added share of each type of capital good (see below).

Following the same sources as above, service lives for communication equipment, hardware and software are assumed to be equal to eleven, seven and four years, and deterministic retirement at the end of the service life is assumed. No assumption is employed for the aggregate capital stock, instead, for I am using capital stocks of the business sector computed by the OECD (for their *Economic Outlook*), and BEA data for the US. In the absence of better alternatives, US depreciation and scrapping rates are assumed to equally apply to all other countries in the sample.

Finally, productive stocks obtain by appending an age-related rule for the loss of efficiency of each capital good. Here I simply assume that the loss of productive efficiency is zero in the early years of life of an ICT capital good – respectively, three, four and five years for software, hardware, and communication equipment – and then it starts gaining momentum at an increasing rate as the capital good 'ages'. The rule chosen for each capital good is consistent, however, with the assumed rule for depreciation. The efficiency loss rate in the final period of use of the capital good is such that, at the time of scrapping, the fraction of the capital good still not depreciated equals the fraction of the initial efficiency left after the age-related loss has occurred.

Now, suppose that investment at time *t* enters the capital stock immediately at the end of time *t*.[14] Then, investment flows must go back to 1980 for telecommunications investment, to 1984 for hardware and to 1987 for software, to enable one to compute capital stocks from 1990 onwards. Accordingly, the series of hardware and software investment had to be projected backwards for a few years. In doing so, I took what happened in the US as an educated guess for the other countries. Hence, I computed the compounded growth rate of the nominal GDP share of software in the US in 1987–91 (+7.5 per cent per year) and took that as the growth rate of the investment spending shares in software in the other countries in the sample. I did the same for hardware, with one notable difference. While the software growth rate was relatively constant in 1987–91, the same does not apply to the growth rate of the hardware share. Hence I computed two different average growth rates for the US: +7.2 per cent in 1990–92 and –4.5 per cent in 1984–89. These growth rates were then used to backward project existing hardware series for the other countries in the sample.

This may look rough. However, the marked decline in ICT prices and the steady rise in nominal spending experienced throughout 1992-97 tend to reduce the importance of investment flows before 1992 in the determination of the total capital stocks. This is particularly true for hardware.

The growth rates of real capital stocks in the three ICT goods in the 1990s are reported in Table 10.6, together with the growth rates of the aggregate capital stocks in the business sector taken from the OECD. The growth rates of hardware and software outweighed by far the growth rates of communications equipment and aggregate capital stocks everywhere. This is well known from the US-based literature. The growth rates of software capital in Canada, the UK and the Netherlands were markedly bigger than in the US (12.6 per cent per year). Instead, hardware capital grew in the US faster (25.7 per cent per year) than in any other country, but Australia. The data for the US in Table 10.6 are consistent with the summary statistics on growth rates of the various capital goods reported in Oliner and Sichel (2000, Table 10.1, which refers to 1991–95 though).

ICT value added shares Finally, the capital share of capital good k in value added is equal to:

$$(r + \ \delta_k - \dot{p}_k)\frac{P_k K}{PY} \tag{1}$$

i.e. the product of the gross rate of return on capital (the term in parentheses) and the capital-output ratio in nominal terms. In turn, r is the nominal market rate of return on investment,[15] δ_k is the depreciation rate of good k, dotted p_k is the capital gain or loss on the possess of capital good k, and P_k equals the purchasing price of a new capital good (and p_k being its log). Overall, the expression in parentheses times P_k is the user cost of capital, i.e. the rental price charged if capital good k were to be rented for one period. This rental price (and the implied gross rate of return) is supposed to be high enough to compensate an asset holder for the opportunity cost of not investing elsewhere, plus the loss due to depreciation less asset price inflation.

Can the value added shares of capital be computed from the pieces of information put together so far? Yes, following the method used by Oliner

Table 10.6 ICT and aggregate capital stocks in OECD countries 1991–97, average rates of change, percentage points

	Communication equipment	Hardware	Software	All capital goods (business sector)
Germany	4.0	24.8	12.8	2.5
France	1.6	20.2	12.6	2.2
UK	5.7	25.7	14.0	2.5
Italy	3.0	18.7	7.5	2.6
Spain	5.4	20.7	6.2	3.9
Netherlands	6.7	22.5	13.8	2.2
Belgium	2.6	21.2	7.7	2.8
Ireland	3.0	22.4	12.9	2.6
Denmark	2.5	24.1	11.6	2.7
Sweden	3.6	22.0	10.4	2.1
Finland	3.4	22.6	10.8	0.3
Norway	2.3	19.6	9.8	1.6
Switzerland	4.1	22.7	12.6	2.9
Japan	8.7	21.9	12.3	4.3
Australia	6.9	28.2	9.1	3.4
New Zealand	5.0	24.4	12.5	1.3
Canada	5.5	25.0	15.9	3.3
USA	4.6	25.7	12.6	2.2

and Sichel (1994, 2000) and first suggested by Hall and Jorgenson (1967). Expression (1) requires imputation of depreciation rates, rates of inflation/deflation and nominal capital-output ratios for each of the capital good. Depreciation rates are known from above. The rates of change of P_k can be approximated by three-year moving averages of the growth rates of each investment deflator. Both P_k and, as shown below, r are specified in nominal terms. Capital-output ratios obtain from the perpetual inventory method, once nominal rather than real investment is used. Wherever needed, the 'other capital' item is computed residually. Capital stocks data for hardware – evaluated, following Schreyer (1998),[16] at quality-unadjusted prices – and communications equipment are thus subtracted out of aggregate capital stocks, and the 'other capital' item obtains.[17]

Having done so, the net rate on return on investment r remains to be calculated to be able to compute capital income shares. One possibility is to plug a market rate of return, such as the yearly growth rate of the share prices in the stock market, into (1). Here, instead, I follow Oliner and Sichel once again.

The net rate of return obtains, under the restriction that the same rate of return r be earned on all types of capital onto the identity: $s_K = s_{COM} + s_{HW} + s_{OTK}$.[18] Once the aggregate share s_K is computed from aggregate data, each of the three shares depends on one unknown only. Then the net rate of return r can be computed right away.

In turn, once the net rate of return is calculated, the gross rate of return on each capital good and its income share can be derived as well. Table 10.7 presents summary evidence on OECD capital output ratios and income shares in information and communication technologies in 1997. The ICT capital-output ratio in the US was 0.135 and the income share of information technology capital in the economy was 0.053, about one-sixth of the economy-wide income share of all capital. The implied net rate of return was about 5.7 percentage points in nominal terms (see the last column in Table 10.7) and 4.1 in real terms, quite close to the value of 4.4 computed by Oliner and Sichel. The overall gross rates of return tend instead to take on large values, the more so the higher the depreciation rate of the capital good and the capital loss anticipated by capital owners. Hence, as a result of a depreciation rate of 44 per cent, the gross (nominal) rate of return on software was 51.1 per cent, while the gross return on hardware reached 61.3 per cent, since a depreciation rate of 32 per cent cumulated to an expected capital loss of 23.6 per cent.

Within the EU, the UK and the Netherlands exhibit very similar figures to those obtained for the US. The rest of the countries in the EU show lower capital-output ratios and income shares. All such ratios and shares steadily increased over time in the 1990s. Switzerland and New Zealand, in particular, even exhibit higher capital-output ratios than the US in 1997 (0.17 against 0.14).

In any case, in spite of rapidly increasing real investment flows and capital stocks, ICT capital still remains a rather modest fraction of overall capital stocks in the OECD. The rapid pace of ICT capital accumulation has instead made ICT capital shares over value added less negligible over time. In 1997, they range between one sixth and one seventh of the value added share of total capital.

4   Conclusions

In this chapter the existing evidence on the extent of adoption and capital accumulation in information and communication technologies in OECD countries was put together and surveyed.

Table 10.7 ICT capital-output ratios, capital income shares and net rates of returns

1997	Capital-output ratios				Income shares				Net rates of return
	TLC	Hardware	Software	ICT	TLC	Hardware	Software	ICT	r
Germany	0.085	0.023	0.026	0.134	0.019	0.011	0.013	0.043	0.051
France	0.059	0.022	0.027	0.108	0.014	0.011	0.014	0.039	0.067
UK	0.058	0.035	0.042	0.135	0.012	0.017	0.021	0.050	0.061
Italy	0.072	0.015	0.019	0.106	0.016	0.007	0.010	0.033	0.088
Spain	0.094	0.016	0.013	0.123	0.023	0.008	0.007	0.038	0.105
Netherlands	0.055	0.030	0.041	0.127	0.014	0.015	0.022	0.051	0.042
Belgium	0.044	0.024	0.037	0.104	0.009	0.011	0.018	0.038	0.047
Ireland	0.062	0.021	0.016	0.099	0.015	0.010	0.008	0.033	0.112
Denmark	0.042	0.031	0.026	0.100	0.008	0.014	0.012	0.034	0.015
Sweden	0.066	0.041	0.028	0.134	0.013	0.014	0.013	0.041	0.033
Finland	0.069	0.030	0.024	0.123	0.017	0.015	0.012	0.044	0.074
Norway	0.052	0.028	0.025	0.105	0.010	0.013	0.012	0.035	0.054
Switzerland	0.095	0.034	0.040	0.168	0.019	0.019	0.019	0.057	0.012
Japan	0.086	0.029	0.015	0.130	0.018	0.014	0.008	0.040	0.010
Australia	0.101	0.037	0.031	0.169	0.024	0.018	0.016	0.058	0.052
New Zealand	0.089	0.037	0.042	0.168	0.019	0.018	0.021	0.058	0.015
Canada	0.072	0.032	0.034	0.139	0.018	0.016	0.018	0.052	0.079
USA	0.055	0.039	0.041	0.135	0.013	0.019	0.021	0.053	0.057

Note: all variables are in *nominal* terms.

Among the 18 OECD countries in the sample, most countries in Continental Europe appear to be at a significant disadvantage in ICT adoption compared not just to the US, but also to countries in Northern Europe and Switzerland, as well as other non-European countries, such as Australia and New Zealand. The available evidence shows that Italy and Spain in particular, but also France and Germany, significantly lag behind in terms of spending and investment rates. This gap has even been widening over time.

This represents a worrisome feature, especially in consideration of the slow rates of change experienced by spending and investment ratios in the past. Differences, when technology adoption is involved, tend to persist for quite a long time.

Notes

1   Now the quality-adjusted price index for IT hardware exhibits a marked reduction over time, at yearly rates of 20 per cent or so in the last twenty years. The price index of semiconductors – a key input in computer production – was adjusted for quality as well, which helped achieve a sensible balance between cost and revenue effects of quality improvements over time. Finally, the traditional fixed-weight indexes were supplemented, and soon replaced, by chained price indexes. Indeed, chained data provide better measures of economic growth when innovation makes the shares of activities subject to the fastest pace of technical progress rapidly diminishing over time.

2   At the same time, the amount of spending is *not* a measure of the technological capability of a particular country in producing new technologies. ICT production is much more geographically concentrated than ICT spending. Yet the extraordinary economic performance of technology-importing countries, such as Italy and Japan in the post-World War II, also suggests that perhaps a handful of technological leaders may suffice for a technological revolution to get started. Here I stick to usage data as measures of diffusion and omit analysing ICT production data. OECD (1999) provides a broad and documented survey of high-tech production and trade.

3   WITSA stands for World Information Technology and Services Alliance – a consortium of 32 information technology industries associations around the world.

4   IDC is for International Data Corporation – a research and consulting company on hi-tech industries.

5   The 11 EU countries included are: Germany, France, the UK, Italy, Spain, the Netherlands, Belgium, Ireland, Denmark, Sweden, Finland. Sample size is dictated by unavailability of the values for the aggregate capital stocks necessary to carry out the growth accounting exercise in the sections to follow. No large ICT market within the Industrialized world is left out, though.

6   As long as one is not interested in world market shares, sticking to *local currency* flows, as opposed to flows denominated in current dollars, is preferable. WITSA/IDC (1998, p. 35, Figure 18) shows that the occasionally wild year-to-year fluctuations of nominal exchange rates have sometimes dominated the fluctuations of dollar-denominated flows.

In particular, given the depreciation of EU currencies vs the dollar, converting ICT flows into dollars in 1992–97 implies a reduction of the growth rate of ICT spending in EU countries with respect to the US.

7   The hedonic function relates changes in the price of a product to product characteristics, unlike the traditional matched-model technique, which computes price changes by comparing identical products over time. For computers, this amounts to considering its speed, memory and disk capacity, and processor speed as determinants of the computer price.

8   Scarpetta, Bassanini, Pilat and Schreyer (2000, p. 92) report, however, that progress is being made in a variety of countries in Europe and outside Europe in this area.

9   As shown in Table 10.4, the reduction of hardware prices in Italy, Spain and Ireland was in the order of an yearly 10 per cent in 1990–95, and 20 per cent in 1996–97, whereas hardware prices fell by 13 per cent and 23.6 per cent, respectively, in the US.

10 This is not particularly striking if one considers that the use of hedonic pricing by the BEA to deflate software and communications spending is so far limited. Jorgenson and Stiroh (2000) evaluate that only about one third of software spending (prepackaged software only) and few items within communications equipment are deflated using constant-quality techniques. This may lead to severe underestimates of both software and communications equipment quantities in the figures reported by the BEA.

11 See Appendix B in Jorgenson and Stiroh (2000) for a rigorous discussion of the issues on the measurement of capital services within the perpetual inventory method.

12 Here I mostly refer to the work by Fraumeni (1997), where a detailed table of service lives based on used-asset data is provided. Estimates for software depreciation and service lives are in Seskin (1999, pp. 37–9).

13 The 7.5 per cent depreciation rate is the weighted average of the depreciation rates of 25 equipment goods and 18 structures listed in Fraumeni (1997). Residential buildings are left out.

14 This is not the usual practice in national accounting, where a gestation lag of one year is customarily assumed. I simply found this practice meaningless when dealing with such capital goods as software and computers, and thus I decided to omit the gestation lag. Jorgenson and Stiroh (2000) did the same.

15 Note that r is non-indexed, which implies the existence of well functioning capital markets.

16 Schreyer (1998l, p. 10, Box) surveys the studies aimed at quantifying the difference between quality-adjusted and unadjusted price indices for computers in the US, concluding that 10 percentage points is a plausible lower bound for such difference. I concur with his conclusion and accordingly compute a new real investment series for hardware, to be used to obtain the 'other capital' residual item.

17 Software is not subtracted out, for it was not included in the OECD measure of aggregate capital stock either.

18 I.e., that the aggregate share of capital equals the sum of the two ICT capital shares (with software left out) plus the share of all other capital goods.

References

Bassanini, A., Scarpetta, S. and Visco, I. (2000), 'Knowledge, Technology and Economic Growth: Recent Evidence from OECD Countries', mimeo, May, OECD: Paris.

Blanchard, O.J. (1997), 'The Medium Run', *Brookings Papers on Economic Activity*, 2, pp. 89–158.

Fraumeni, B. (1997), 'The Measurement of Depreciation in the US National Income and Production Accounts', *Survey of Current Business*, July, pp. 7–17.

Gordon, R.J. (1999), 'Has the "New Economy" Rendered the Productivity Slowdown Obsolete?', mimeo, June, Northwestern University.

Gordon, R.J. (forthcoming), 'Does the "New Economy" Measure up to the Great Inventions of the Past?', *Journal of Economic Perspectives*.

Hall, R.E. and Jorgenson, D.W. (1967), 'Tax Policy and Investment Behavior', *American Economic Review*, 57, pp. 391–414.

Jorgenson, D.W., and Stiroh, K.J. (1995), 'Computers and Growth', *Economics of innovation and new technologies*, 3, pp. 295–316.

Jorgenson, D.W., and Stiroh, K.J. (2000), 'Raising the Speed Limit: US Economic Growth in the Information Age', *Brookings Papers on Economic Activity*, pp. 125–235.

Morgan Stanley Dean Witter (2000), 'The Globalization of the Information Age', *Special Economic Study*, 17 February.

Moulton, B. (2000), 'Improved Estimates of the National Income and Product Accounts for 1929–99: Results of the Comprehensive Revision', *Survey of Current Business*, 11–16 April.

Oliner, S. and Sichel, D. (1994), 'Computers and Output Growth Revisited: How Big is the Puzzle?', *Brookings Papers on Economic Activity*, 2, pp. 273–317.

Oliner, S. and Sichel, D. (forthcoming), 'The Resurgence of growth in the Late 1990s: Is Information Technology the Story?', *Journal of Economic Perspectives*.

Porter, M.E. and Stern, S. (1999), *The New Challenge to America's Prosperity: Findings from the Innovation Index*, Washington DC; Council on Competitiveness.

Scarpetta S., Bassanini, A., Pilat, D. and Schreyer, P. (2000), 'Economic Growth in the OECD Area: Recent Trends at the Aggregate and Sectoral Level', Economics Department Working Papers No. 248, 26 June.

Schreyer, P. (1998), 'Information and Communication Technology and the Measurement of Real Output, Final Demand and Productivity', OECD, Directorate for Science, Technology and Industry, STI Working Paper 1998/2, 15 July.

Schreyer, P. (2000), 'The Contribution of Information and Communication Technology to Output Growth: A Study of the G7 Countries', OECD, Directorate for Science, Technology and Industry, DSTI/DOC(2000)2, 23 March.

Stern, S., Porter, M.E. and Furman, J.L. (2000), 'The Determinants of National Innovative Capacity', NBER Working Paper No. 7876, September.

WITSA/IDC (1998), *Digital Planet. The global Information Economy*, Volume 1, October.

Chapter 11

Reorienting Training Policies to Meet the Challenges of Information and Communication Technologies

Lisa M. Lynch

Over the past 20 years, workers with the right training and educational foundation have discovered that new information and communication technologies, ICTs, have helped them leverage their ability to create economic value. At the same time, firms have found that by investing in both information capital and human capital they experience higher productivity. This paper will briefly summarize current evidence on the economic returns to productivity and wages associated with ICTs with a special focus on micro-level studies of enterprises and establishments. I will review some of the descriptive evidence on the preparedness of workers to utilize ICTs in the workplace and discuss how effective are our current training and education institutions are in generating the skills necessary to work with new ICTs. I also examine how new innovations in ICTs may also influence the way in which workers acquire skills. Finally, I present alternative strategies policy makers may wish to consider as they reform educational and training institutions to meet the challenges associated with ICTs.

1   The Impact of ICTs on Workers and Firms: A Brief Summary

While the impact of computers on aggregate productivity growth continues to be a hotly debated topic (see Gordon, 1999; Jorgenson and Stiroh, 2000; Oliner and Sichel, 1994, 2000) researchers using micro enterprise or plant level continue to find a positive relationship between computers and plant level productivity. Examples of such studies include Brynjolfsson and Hitt (1993) and Bresnahan, Brynjolfsson and Hitt (1999), Greenan and Mairesse (1996), Doms et al. (1997), Dunne et al. (2000) and Black and Lynch (1996, 1997, 2000).

More specifically, using data from a US nationally representative sample of manufacturing and non-manufacturing establishments in the US in 1993, Black and Lynch (1996) find that computer skills development has a significant impact on productivity in non-manufacturing productivity, even after controlling for wide range of workplace practices and worker characteristics. Within manufacturing, Black and Lynch (1997) find that increasing the proportion of non-managers using computers has a significant and positive effect on productivity. More recently, using longitudinal data on US manufacturing plants to control for time invariant unobserved heterogeneity (over the period 1993–96), Black and Lynch (2000) find that changes in the proportion of non-managers using computers is positively associated with changes in productivity.

But ICTs may have more than just a direct effect on productivity of firms. As discussed in Bresnahan, Brynjolfsson, and Hitt (1999), ICTs can also have an important effect on the ability of firms to implement organizational changes such as reorganizing production and giving workers more power in decision making. Figure 11.1 presents some descriptive evidence from Black and Lynch (2000) indicating just how extensive ICTs, organizational change and skills needs are in US establishments. As shown in this figure, by 1996 41 per cent of US employers reported that 75 per cent or more of their workers used computers on the job. Twenty-six per cent of establishments had undergone major re-engineering efforts over the period 1993–96 and almost half reported that a majority of their workers were meeting on a regular basis to discuss workplace issues.

In one of the few empirical studies of investments in information technologies and organizational change, Bresnahan, Brynjolfsson, and Hitt (1999) find evidence for complementarities between technology, organizational changes and skills. Unfortunately their work uses just cross sectional micro data. However, using longitudinal data on manufacturing establishments, Black and Lynch (2000) find that those establishments that increased the proportion of workers involved in decision making or who re-engineered their production processes also have higher productivity.

There is a large literature that has provided empirical evidence on skilled biased technological change with specific reference to the impact of computers on the demand for labour by skill type. Studies using US data such as Berman, Bound and Griliches (1994) and Autor, along with Machin and Van Reenen (1998) using data from seven OECD countries, find evidence of skill-biased technological change at the industry level. In other words, investments in computers are found to have a positive and significant effect on the growth in the wage bill share of non-production workers.

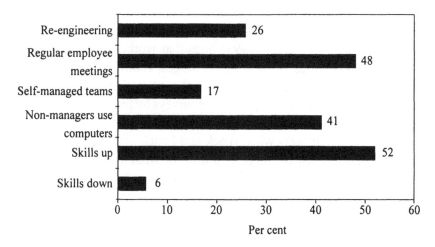

Figure 11.1   Incidence of workplace practices

Notes

1   Re-engineering – any re-engineering efforts between 1993–96.
2   Regular employee meetings – per cent of businesses reporting 75 per cent or more of employees meet regularly to discuss workplace issues.
3   Self-managed teams – per cent of employers reporting 25 per cent or more of their employees are in self-managed teams.
4   Non-managers use computers – per cent of employers reporting that 75 per cent or more of their employees use computers.
5   Text of the survey and a public use file are available on the internet at www.irhe.upenn.edu/ ~shapiro.

Source: EQW 2nd Round Survey. Weighted data on US Establishment practices in 1996.

But as discussed in Chennells and Van Reenen (1999), aggregation may be a problem industry based studies, so increasingly researchers have examined whether technological change is biased in favour of non-production workers using micro level enterprise or establishment data. This allows for more proxies for technical change including various dimensions of ICTs. Many studies using micro level plant level data have found evidence of skilled-biased technological change in favour of non-production or more highly skilled workers. Some of these studies include Bresnahan, Brynjolfsson, and Hitt (1999), Lynch and Krivelyova (2000), Caroli and Van Reenen (1999), Doms et al. (1997), Greenan and Mairesse (1996) and Dunne et al. (2000). But while these findings remain even after controlling for unobserved time invariant heterogeneity, there is a potential problem with the endogeneity of technology that has not been addressed in most of these studies.

Finally, information and communication technologies have also been associated with higher wages. Using individual data obtained from household surveys Krueger (1993) finds that workers who use computers have approximately 20 per cent higher wages, controlling for a wide range of personal, geographic, and occupational characteristics. Black and Lynch (2000), using wage data from plant level surveys by five occupational classes, find that as computer usage increases within a business, wages also increase. But this effect disappears when Black and Lynch control for time invariant unobserved fixed effects. This is similar to what was found in Doms et al. (1997). As Chennells and Van Reenen (1999) discuss, the fact that the computer-wage effect is not robust to attempts to control for endogeneity and fixed effects suggests that ICTs may be more likely used by the most able workers who were already earning higher wages.

In sum, using data from recent micro level surveys of enterprises/establishments we see that the introduction of new technologies, especially ICTs, appears to have raised the productivity of businesses, reduced the demand for unskilled labour, and raised the payoff to advanced skills. However, much more work will need to be done to address more satisfactorily problems of the endogeneity of the technology choice, the presence of unobserved heterogeneity, and measurement error before the true impact of ICTs on these outcomes can be fully assessed.

2   Worker Preparedness and ICTs

In this section I briefly summarize some of the descriptive evidence on the preparedness of workers to utilize ICTs in the workplace and discuss how effective are our current training and education institutions are in generating the skills necessary to work with new ICTs. I also examine how new innovations in ICTs may also influence the way in which workers acquire skills.

New Entrants and Initial Human Capital

As shown in Table 11.1, there is significant variation across countries in terms of the basic preparation of youths as they enter the labour force. For example, in Sweden only 3 per cent of youth age 16–25 years of age have low literacy skills while in the US almost one in four youths in this age range suffer from low literacy skills. Since we know that workers in the US with less education are also less likely to obtain skills training from their employer (see Lynch 1992 and Lynch 1994), this creates a vicious circle for youth who enter the labour market poorly prepared to work with most technologies, let alone ICTs.

Table 11.1   Percentage of 16–25 year olds with low literacy skills

Sweden	3.1
Germany	5.2
Belgium	5.8
Netherlands	6.1
Switzerland (German speaking)	7.1
Switzerland (French speaking)	8.7
Australia	9.7
Canada	10.4
Ireland	17.0
United Kingdom	17.8
New Zealand	18.3
United States	24.7

Source: OECD (1997), *Literacy Skills for the Knowledge Society.*

There have been several different strategies followed by countries to equip young workers with the skills they need to face the changing labour market. As discussed in a recent OECD paper (1999), those countries that have historically relied on vocational education to prepare youth for work have tried to find ways to continuously update the content of education (in part to reflect innovations in ICTs) so that youth are receiving relevant vocational education. In those countries with less emphasis on vocational education, there have been attempts to keep at risk youth in school longer. Part of this dropout prevention effort has included bringing work-based learning within schools to help motivate the learning process of at risk youths. Unfortunately when one examines the evaluation of programmes targeted at unemployed and disadvantage youths the results are mixed. In the US, with the important exceptions of residential youth programmes such as Job Corps or CET in San Jose (see US Deparment of Labor, 1995), the impact of programmes for youth funded by the Job Training Partnership Act have had little impact on their subsequent employment or earnings. In the Nordic countries however there has been more success. The Nordic training programmes have provided a multitude of services to disadvantaged youths tailored to their specific needs but including remedial education and training, work experience (in part obtained through wage subsidies to employers who hired these youth), job-search assistance, and support for returning to formal education.

New information and communication technologies (the Internet in particular) may be an important new tool to meet the skill deficiencies of disadvantaged youth. However, computers are not equally available, as advantaged families are much more likely to have computers at home than disadvantaged families. As a result, children from advantaged households become more proficient with the technology earlier than those from disadvantaged households. The same inequality can occur in public access to computers. Schools and libraries in affluent communities (or countries) are much more likely to have computers than schools and libraries in less affluent areas.

No matter what countries do, it is clear that the transition of a young worker from formal education into the workplace will more complicated than in the past. It is also clear that learning will not stop the moment a student exits from the classroom. So perhaps one of the most important aspects of initial education is to ensure that it provides a solid basis on which workers can build as they acquire new skills in the workplace.

Incumbent Workers and Life-long Learning

What innovations in ICTs have highlighted is the necessity of acquiring new skills after workers have completed their formal education. One of the most common places workers acquire training after school is at the workplace. This is especially true for training associated with ICTs since some of the technology may be proprietary or so new that there are not sufficient trainers outside the firm to train workers. Workplace training differs from other forms of human capital investment such as education and governmental training programmes, since there are at least two parties in the training decision – the worker (who may or may not be represented by a union) and the firm. Firms who are concerned with the skills upgrading of their workforce are constantly facing two possible strategies – 'make' the skills in-house or 'buy' the skills from outside. If employee turnover is high firms may be reluctant to train workers in-house. If new skills such as skills associated with ICTs are valuable to other employers, firms run the risk of having a newly trained worker hired away by another employer and may be less likely to provide these skills. As a result, investments in non-portable firm-specific training are typically more attractive investments to firms than more general training. In addition, smaller firms often face higher training costs per employee because they can not spread the training costs across a wider group of employees. As a result, employers may end up investing in a suboptimal level of training.

Since the training investment for incumbent workers is two-sided, even if a worker wants and needs training, this is still no guarantee that they will actually be able to obtain it. As human capital theory argues, employees who have already shown an aptitude to learn new skills by having completed more years of schooling are more likely to receive additional human capital investments provided by an employer. Research has shown that firm provided training is much more likely to be obtained by more educated employees (see for example Lynch, 1992). This results in the creation of both a 'virtuous' circle and a 'vicious' circle of human capital accumulation. Individuals who acquire more schooling are also more likely to receive post-school employer provided training, while those with minimal education find it extremely difficult to make up this deficiency in human capital once they enter the labour market.

None of these issues would necessarily result in under investment in training as long as capital markets were perfect so that workers could borrow to finance more general training, if the government subsidized general training, or workers accepted lower wages during training spells. However, capital markets are far from perfect, and workers differ from employers in their attitudes towards risk and time horizons. As a result, there may be a market failure in the provision of general training and the proportion of workers trained in more general skills.

Recent work by Stevens (1994) and Acemoglu and Pischke (1998, 1999) re-examines this issue of market failure in the context of imperfection competition. In particular, these papers try to develop the theoretical basis for understanding investments in general training by relaxing the assumption that the labour market is characterized by perfect competition. More specifically, Acemoglu and Pischke show how a firm can exhibit *ex post* monopsony power and as a result workers decide not to invest in general training because they realize that part of the return will be appropriated by the firm. So workers could end up not investing in general training even if they were not credit constrained. Acemoglu and Pischke (1998) argue that there may be multiple training equilibriums – low training and high quit rates or low quit rates and high training with the US representing a high quit rate and low training equilibrium and Germany and Japan representing a low quit rate and high training equilibrium. Booth and Chatterji (1998) argue that unions in this context of firm ex-post monopsonistic power can increase social welfare by counterbalancing the firm's *ex post* monopsonistic power in wage determination. As a result, local union-firm wage bargaining ensures that the post-training wage is set sufficiently high to deter at least some quits so that the number of workers that the firm trains is nearer the social optimum.

Given this discussion, what do we actually observe in terms of the amount of training incumbent workers are receiving? As shown in Figure 11.2 there are large variation across countries in the probability that a worker will actually receive training. For example, Swedish employees are approximately seven times as likely as French employees to have participated in job training annually. This is in spite of the fact that initial skills of Swedish workers, as measured by the International Adult Literacy Survey, are considerably higher than in many other European countries.

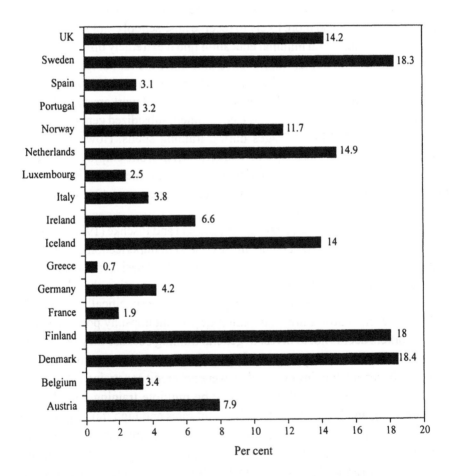

Figure 11.2   Participation rate (%) in job training in Europe

Source: EUROSTAT as reported in OECD *Employment Outlook 1999.*

A recent study by Leuven and Oosterbeek (1999) on the demand and supply of training in Canada, the Netherlands, Switzerland and the US found that one in five workers in the Netherlands reported that they were not receiving the training they needed, one in four in the US reported they were under trained, almost 30 per cent of workers reported insufficient training in Switzerland, and one-third of Canadian workers responded that they were not obtaining sufficient workforce development training. In addition, as summarized in Lynch (1994) and the ILO's *World Employment Report, 1998–99*, workers typically less likely to receive employer sponsored training include women, minorities, and those employed in the informal sector.

Not surprisingly, one reason cited for the increased demand for learning by workers is the rapid rate of technological change including ICTs. One group particularly vulnerable to change associated with ICTs is older workers. If ICTs increase the depreciation rate of both physical and human capital due to obsolescence, and the payoff period to investments in human capital is shortened, older workers may become more marginalized in the workforce. This is particularly of concern in advanced industrialized economies that are facing rapidly aging workforces over the next ten years. In an increasingly skills-driven economy a key issue is the extent to which the growing number of mid and late-career workers are able to refresh, expand and redeploy their job skills.

Human capital theory does not provide an unambiguous prediction of the effect of technological change on the optimal level of on-the-job training. As discussed by Bartel and Sicherman (1993), technological change may be positively or negatively correlated with training. The eventual sign will be determined by the degree of complementarity or substitutability between schooling and training and the impact of technological change on the marginal returns to training. In addition, new technologies themselves may lower the cost of providing training to workers. With marginal costs of training potentially being as low as zero, smaller firms may be able to overcome one of the obstacles they face in investing in their employees.

Innovation in information and communication technologies could in principal be a powerful tool in helping workers acquire the skills to keep up with changes in technology. For small firms the development of distance learning may go some way to lowering the marginal costs of training workers much lower. Computer based learning can also potentially address a second deficit that many unskilled workers face – the time deficit. In the face of falling hourly wages many unskilled workers have taken on second jobs or increased their hours of work to try to maintain standards of living. What this means though is that they have little time outside of work to engage in new learning activities. For women, this can be especially difficult has many finish the paid work day and return home to start the 'second shift'. But a pressing policy issue seems to be how to get unskilled workers who are not computer literate sufficiently 'skilled' so that they can take advantage of additional training through the Internet. At the moment information technology is more likely to play a role in skill development along the skill ladder rather than basic skill development which will still remain more person-to-person intensive.

3   Policy Tools to Stimulate Investment in Training.

Since economic theory suggests that there can be a market failure in the provision of more general training, we may be especially worried about the capacity of the marketplace to generate sufficient skills training in the area of ICTs given that these skills are likely to be portable across employers. Additionally, empirical evidence across countries suggests that there are many workers who would like and/or need more training who are not currently receiving it. Consequently, many countries have tried different strategies to stimulate additional investment in skills training. One method that has been used in countries such as France, Korea, Australia, Quebec, and Hungary to stimulate and finance additional training is a training levy. Training levies are potentially useful in that they can set a level playing field across employers in terms of the investment that they make in their employees. This would overcome concerns about poaching of trained workers and it theory raise the overall level of training. However, if the rate is set 'too high' employers may protest calling it an unfunded mandate and a burden especially on smaller employers who are struggling to establish their businesses. If the rate is set too low then it will do little to affect the overall level of workforce development investments. In practice the tax can be manipulated and quickly revert to an exercise in creative accounting or in the case of France, employer provided training is still more likely to be acquired by skilled workers in large firms (see Lynch, 1994).

Another strategy that some unions have pursued at the national level in Europe (for example Denmark and the Netherlands) and at the sectoral level in the US (in telecommunications and automotive) is to establish training funds through the collective bargaining process. This has had a positive impact on the training of workers, especially those covered by collective bargaining agreements. But in those countries with a substantial informal sector or low union coverage this strategy will have a limited impact.

In the US much of the federal training policy has devolved to the state and local level. During this current economic expansion states have increased their spending on workforce development dramatically. In particular, ten states have now established training funds that are financed by a training tax associated with employers' unemployment insurance tax payments. Employers and other appropriate groups can then apply to these funds for training targeted at employed but 'at risk' workers. Many states have also tried to encourage greater collaboration between employers and community colleges to develop training modules (especially in the area of ICTs) for workers and employers.

Most industrialized economies allow for immediate and full tax deductibility of training expenses incurred by firms. But firms' financial statements provide little or no indication of the value of these knowledge investments for the bottom line of the company (see O'Connor, 1998). Many countries have also tried using targeted tax incentives directed at smaller firms or specific categories of workers. Depending on the way in which the tax incentive is structured firms may or may not take advantage of it. Many small firms face constant cash flow problems. Receiving a tax rebate 12 months after incurring an expensive may be too little, too late. Finally, some European countries have legislation that provides workers the right to paid training leave. The advantage of this approach is that workers can choose to take the leave and select the course they feel would be most relevant for their skill development. However, if a firm needs to raise skills for a group of workers (e.g. introduce a new technology, or improve team skills and problem solving) this training leave policy may not be the most appropriate mechanism for ensuring that this training happens.

4   Concluding Remarks

As a result of the perceived positive impact of ICTs on productivity and wages, more governments have been formulating policies to increase investments in worker training. The hope is that with increased training more workers will be better equipped to meet the challenges associated with ICTs and share in the gains associated with these technologies. However, there is considerable debate on just how to accomplish this. In particular, there is little consensus on how to share training policy responsibility across levels of government, and the roles of training providers, employers, and workers themselves in decision-making about job training.

One of the biggest issues is where policy-making authority and financial responsibility for worker training should be concentrated – the national, regional, sectoral or local level. In theory, there are arguments for, and against, almost any imaginable degree of centralization in who pays and who decides. For example, in the United States during the 1950s and 1960s, federal manpower programmes proliferated to produce a confusing array of training efforts run by different agencies, for different clienteles, with different permutations of federal, state, and local funding and authority. The norm, however, was substantial federal funding but state or local implementation.

Whether national, regional, sectoral or local interests take the lead on the public sector side, workforce investment involves at least four other players: Training providers, employers, organized labour, and individuals themselves. Defining their respective roles and responsibilities is a perennial issue in training policy. How are decision-making authority, control over resources, and the right to specify goals and define success allocated among these players? A workforce development system that ignores any one of these players would rapidly and dramatically fail. In practice, debates on the focus and structure of training programmes always turn on questions of balance – how much, and how, to incorporate the interests of and the information commanded by each party.

But to better understand these practical debates, consider for a moment the impractical extremes as described in Donahue, Lynch and Whitehead (1999). Imagine first a simple-minded training system that relied only on the judgment and motives of individual trainees, with no role for employers or training providers, by providing vouchers or tax incentives for training but nothing further. An advantage of this model is that the trainee may be strongly motivated to choose the training that's right for her. She would presumably avoid training in obsolete skills, or training providers that are ineffective or (unless her voucher is unlimited) wasteful. But an individual trainee might not know what skills are in demand, or she may have too little information to distinguish between effective and ineffective providers. So to the extent workforce policy puts individuals in control, government's job is to define eligibility, police the definition of 'training', and ensure access to reliable information about the market for skills and the performance of training providers to help individuals make well-informed choices.

Next, imagine that public training policy is limited to providing grants or tax incentives to subsidize workforce investments chosen exclusively by the private sector. The great advantage here is that employers tend to have privileged information about the demand for skills. They may also be able to provide training more efficiently by integrating it with their other operations, or procure training cheaply though hard bargaining with providers, in ways that individuals cannot. In addition some skills such as the ability to function as part of a workplace team may be hard to deliver outside the workplace. But the primary downside of employer-centred training policy is that any rational employer may be tempted to use public resources to train the same way as she would have in any event in firm-specific skills, instead of training different people, or training them more extensively in more broadly marketable skills. So to the extent employers are in control, government's job is to try to ensure that public resources supplement, rather than substitute for, private resources.

Finally, imagine that the government promotes workforce investments by sending resources to schools, community-based organizations, and other sources of training (excluding employers) and counts on them to do useful things with the money. This could be a simple and direct way to get training done, but it also has some fairly fundamental defects. For example, providers may do a poor job at developing appropriate skills, especially if they are not familiar with rapid innovations such as we have seen in information and communication technology. They may make decisions about which trainees to accept, which skills to concentrate on, and how long training should last based on their own convenience rather than the needs of employers or the interests of workers. So to the extent providers are at the centre of workforce policy, government needs to have the data and the analytic capacity to distinguish between efficient and inefficient providers and some way to ensure that training content is appropriate for current market needs.

The design of an effective training and education policy to meet the skill needs associated with ICTs will vary considerably across countries. But while the goals of publicly funded and privately funded training programmes are not always the same, there are some common features in the best practice of the delivery of training across the public and private sectors. First there should be a detailed 'needs' analysis completed before any training intervention occurs. In the public sector this needs analysis would examine (at the local, regional or national level) the specific labour markets needs/gaps to ensure that training is targeted at those jobs with the greatest potential to expand but provide career advancement. One of the better ways to ensure this is the establishment of partnerships between local employers, community based organizations, and training and education providers so that the training programmes are responsive to the increasing rate of change in technology and demand. For the private sector this needs analysis would identify what are the skills currently lacking in the firm and the best way to meet those needs – hire new skilled workers or retrain current employees in specific areas of deficiency.

The second step in the successful delivery of training is the design of the training programme. The public sector needs to decide how much of the design it should do itself versus allowing more competition among public and private vendors to design the programme. One risk with only relying on the private sector to design training programmes is that the programmes will be designed to meet areas of expertise of the private vendor rather than the specific needs of the targeted training group.

The next step is implementation of the training programme. The public sector needs to decide to what degree it will rely on the private sector to bid on training programmes that the government sector may have designed. In the private sector, employers need to decide to what degree they will conduct training in-house, on-the-job, off-the-job, with outside vendors, and how to time the training to minimize disruption to production.

Finally, the establishment of a set of performance measures is critical for the success of any training system. Without better measurement of the amount and quality of training being provided in an economy it is difficult to evaluate the effectiveness of training. With poor data, public policy can end up being driven by what is easy to measure rather than what is needed to be measured. It also makes it much more difficult to create a training system that is sufficiently flexible to adapt to changes in the workplace so that it continues to meet the needs of workers and employers.

From a public policy perspective it is important to realize that there are numerous barriers to reform of training and education institutions to ensure that they are able to meet the new demands of new information and communication technologies. For example, it is important to recognize that not all education and training institutions may be willing to surrender their control or influence in a country's training strategy. It is also important to ensure that the government is not funding what the private sector would have done anyway. At the same time, as more countries develop partnerships between the government and the private sector to improve skills development, it is important to find ways to reach out to those groups of workers that have been historically underserved.

References

Acemoglu, D. and Pischke, J.-S. (1999), 'Beyond Becker: Training in Imperfect Labor Markets', *Economic Journal*, 109.

Autor, D., Katz, L.F. and Krueger, A.B. (1998), 'Computing Inequality: Have Computers Changed the Labor Market?', *Quarterly Journal of Economics*, 113 (4), pp. 1169–213.

Bartel, A. and Sicherman, N. (1993), 'Technological Change and Retirement Decisions of Older Workers', *Journal of Labor Economics*, 11 (1), Part 1, January, pp. 162–83.

Berman, E., Bound, J. and Griliches, Z. (1994), 'Changes in the Demand for Skilled Labor Within US Manufacturing: Evidence from the Annual Survey of Manufactures', *Quarterly Journal of Economics*, May, pp. 367–97.

Black, S.E. and Lynch, L.M. (1996), 'Human-Capital Investments and Productivity', *American Economic Review*, May, pp. 263–7.

Black, S.E. and Lynch, L.M. (1997. 'How to Compete: The Impact of Workplace Practices and Information Technology on Productivity', NBER Working Paper No. 6120, August.

Black, S.E. and Lynch, L.M. (2000. 'What's Driving the New Economy: The Benefits of Workplace Innovation', NBER Working Paper, No. 7479, January.

Booth, A. and Chatterji, M. (1998), 'Unions and Efficient Training', *Economic Journal*, 108 (447), pp. 328–43.

Bresnahan, T., Brynjolfsson, E. and Hitt, L. (1999), 'Information Technology, Workplace Organization, and the Demand for Skilled Labor: Firm-Level Evidence', NBER Working Paper 7136, May.

Caroli, E. and van Rennen, J. (1999), 'Organization, Skills and Technology: Evidence from a Panel of British and French Establishments', Institute for Fiscal Studies Working Paper Number W99/23, London.

Chennells, L. and van Rennen, J. (1999), 'Has Technology Hurt Less Skilled Workers?: An Econometric Survey of the Effects of Technical Changes on the Structure of Pay and Jobs', Institute of Fiscal Studies Working Paper W99/27, London.

Doms, M., Dunne, T. and Troske, K. (1997), 'Workers, Wages and Technology', *Quarterly Journal of Economics*, 112, February, pp. 235–90.

Donahue, J., Lynch, L.M. and Whitehead, R. (2000), *Opportunity Knocks: Training the Commonwealth's Workers for the New Economy*, Boston, MA: MASSINC.

Dunne, T., Foster, L., Haltiwanger, J. and Troske, K. (2000), 'Wage and Productivity Dispersion in US Manufacturing: The Role of Computer Investment', NBER Working Paper No. 7465, January.

Gordon, R.J. (1999), 'Has the "New Economy" Rendered the Productivity Slowdown Obsolete?', mimeo, Northwestern University, 12 June.

Greenan, N. and Mairesse, J. (1996), 'Computers and Productivity in France: Some Evidence', NBER Working Paper No. 5836, November.

Jorgenson, D. and Stiroh, K. (forthcoming), 'Raising the Speed Limit: US Economic Growth in the Information Age', *Brookings Papers on Economic Activity*, 2.

Krueger, A. (1993), 'How Computers Have Changed the Wage Structure: Evidence from Micro Data, 1984–1989'. *Quarterly Journal of Economics*, February, pp. 33–60.

Leuven, E. and Oosterbeek, H. (1999), 'Demand and Supply of Work-related Training: Evidence from Four Countries', *Research in Labor Economics*.

Lynch, L.M. (1992), 'Private Sector Training and the Earnings of Young Workers', *American Economic Review*, March, pp. 299–312.

Lynch, L.M. (ed.) (1994), *Training and the Private Sector: International Comparisons*, Chicago: University of Chicago Press.

Lynch, L.M. and Krivelyova, A. (2000), 'How Workers Fare When Employers Innovate', mimeo, Tufts University, June.

Machin, S. and van Reenen, J. (1998). 'Technology and Changes in Skill Structure: Evidence from Seven OECD Countries', Berkeley Center for Labor Economics Working Paper No. 3.

Mincer, J. and Higuchi, Y. (1988), 'Wage Structure and Labor Turnover in the United States and Japan', *Journal of the Japanese and International Economics*, 2 pp. 97–133.

O'Connor, M.A. (1998), 'Rethinking Corporate Financial Disclosure of Human Resource Values for the Knowledge-based Economy', *Journal of Labor and Employment Law*, Fall, pp. 527–44.

OECD (1999), 'Preparing Youth for the 21st Century: The Policy Lessons from the Past Two Decades', background paper for the conference with the same title, February.

Oliner, S. and Sichel, D. (1994), 'Computers and Output Growth Revisited: How Big is the Puzzle?', *Brookings Papers on Economic Activity*, 2, pp. 273–334.

Oliner, S. and Sichel, D. (forthcoming), 'The Resurgance of Growth in the Late 1990s: Is Information Technology the Story?', *Journal of Economic Perspectives*.

Stevens, M. (1994), 'A Theoretical Model of On-the-Job Training with Imperfect Competition', *Oxford Economic Papers*, 46, pp. 537–62.

US Department of Labor (1995), 'What's Working (and What's Not)', monograph, Office of the Chief Economist.

Chapter 12

Raising the Speed Limit: US Economic Growth in the Information Age

Dale W. Jorgenson and Kevin J. Stiroh

1   Introduction

The continued strength and vitality of the US economy continues to astonish economic forecasters.[1] A consensus is now emerging that something fundamental has changed with 'new economy' proponents pointing to information technology as the causal factor behind the strong performance of the US economy. In this view, technology is profoundly altering the nature of business, leading to permanently higher productivity growth throughout the economy. Sceptics argue that the recent success reflects a series of favourable, but temporary, shocks. This argument is buttressed by the view that the US economy behaves rather differently than envisioned by new economy advocates.[2]

While productivity growth, capital accumulation, and the impact of technology were once reserved for academic debates, the recent success of the US economy has moved these topics into popular discussion. The purpose of this chapter is to employ well-tested and familiar methods to analyse important new information made available by the recent benchmark revision of the US National Income and Product Accounts (NIPA). We document the case for raising the speed limit – for upward revision of intermediate-term projections of future growth to reflect the latest data and trends.

The late 1990s have been exceptional in comparison with the growth experience of the US economy over the past quarter century. While growth rates in the 1990s have not yet returned to those of the golden age of the US economy in the 1960s, the data nonetheless clearly reveal a remarkable transformation of economic activity. Rapid declines in the prices of computers and semiconductors are well known and carefully documented, and evidence is accumulating that similar declines are taking place in the prices of software and communications equipment. Unfortunately, the empirical record is seriously incomplete, so much remains to be done before definitive quantitative assessments can be made about the complete role of these high-tech assets.

Despite the limitations of the available data, the mechanisms underlying the structural transformation of the US economy are readily apparent. As an illustration, consider the increasing role that computer hardware plays as a source of economic growth.[3] For the period 1959 to 1973, computer inputs contributed less than one-tenth of one percent to US economic growth. Since 1973, however, the price of computers has fallen at historically unprecedented rates and firms and households have followed a basic principle of economics – they have substituted towards relatively cheaper inputs. Since 1995 the price decline for computers has accelerated, reaching nearly 28 per cent per year from 1995 to 1998. In response, investment in computers has exploded and the growth contribution of computers increased more than fivefold to 0.46 percentage points per year in the late 1990s.[4] Software and communications equipment, two other information technology assets, contributed an additional 0.29 percentage points per year for 1995–98. Preliminary estimates through 1999 reveal further increases in these contributions for all three high-tech assets.

Next, consider the acceleration of average labour productivity (ALP) growth in the 1990s. After a 20-year slowdown dating from the early 1970s, ALP grew 2.4 per cent per year for 1995–98, more than a percentage point faster than during 1990–95.[5] A detailed decomposition shows that capital deepening, the direct consequence of price-induced substitution and rapid investment, added 0.49 percentage points to ALP growth. Faster total factor productivity (TFP) growth contributed an additional 0.63 percentage points, largely reflecting technical change in the production of computers and the resulting acceleration in the price decline of computers. Slowing labour quality growth retarded ALP growth by 0.12 percentage points, relative to the early 1990s, a result of exhaustion of the pool of available workers.

Focusing more specifically on TFP growth, this was an anaemic 0.34 per cent per year for 1973–95, but accelerated to 0.99 per cent for 1995–98. After more than 20 years of sluggish TFP growth, four of the last five years have seen growth rates near 1 per cent. It could be argued this represents a new paradigm. According to this view, the diffusion of information technology improves business practices, generates spillovers, and raises productivity throughout the economy. If this trend is sustainable, it could revive the optimistic expectations of the 1960s and overcome the pessimism of *The Age of Diminished Expectations*, the title of Krugman's (1990) influential book.

A closer look at the data, however, shows that gains in TFP growth can be traced in substantial part to information technology industries, which produce computers, semiconductors, and other high-tech gear. The evidence is equally clear that computer-using industries like finance, insurance, and real estate (FIRE) and services have continued to lag in productivity growth. Reconciliation of massive high-tech investment and relatively slow productivity growth in service industries remains an important task for proponents of the new economy position.[6]

What does this imply for the future? The sustainability of growth in labour productivity is the key issue for future growth projections. For some purposes, the distinctions among capital accumulation and growth in labour quality and TFP may not matter, so long as ALP growth can be expected to continue. It is sustainable labour productivity gains, after all, that ultimately drive long-run growth and raise living standards.

In this respect, the recent experience provides grounds for caution, since much depends on productivity gains in high-tech industries. Ongoing technological gains in these industries have been a direct source of improvement in TFP growth, as well as an indirect source of more rapid capital deepening. Sustainability of growth, therefore, hinges critically on the pace of technological progress in these industries. As measured by relative price changes, progress has accelerated recently, as computer prices fell 28 per cent per year for 1995–98 compared to 15 per cent in 1990–95. There is no guarantee, of course, of continued productivity gains and price declines of this magnitude. Nonetheless, as long as high-tech industries maintain the ability to innovate and improve their productivity at rates comparable to their long-term averages, relative prices will fall and the virtuous circle of an investment-led expansion will continue.[7]

Finally, we argue that rewards from new technology accrue to the direct participants; first, to the innovating industries producing high-tech assets and, second, to the industries that restructure to implement the latest information technology. There is no evidence of spillovers from production of information technology to the industries that use this technology. Indeed, many of the industries that use information technology most intensively, like FIRE and services, show high rates of substitution of information technology for other inputs and relatively low rates of productivity growth. In part, this may reflect problems in measuring the output from these industries, but the empirical record provides little support for the 'new economy' picture of spillovers cascading from information technology producers onto users of this technology.[8]

The chapter is organized as follows. Section 2 describes our methodology for quantifying the sources of US economic growth. We present results for the period 1959–98, and focus on the 'new economy' era of the late 1990s. Section 3 explores the implications of the recent experience for future growth, comparing our results to recent estimates produced by the Congressional Budget Office, the Council of Economic Advisors, and the Office of Management and Budget. Section 4 moves beyond the aggregate data and quantifies the productivity growth at the industry level. Using methodology introduced by Domar (1961), we consider the impact of information technology on aggregate productivity. Section 5 concludes.

2   The Recent US Growth Experience

The US economy has undergone a remarkable transformation in recent years with growth in output, labour productivity, and total factor productivity all accelerating since the mid-1990s. This growth resurgence has led to a widening debate about sources of economic growth and changes in the structure of the economy. 'New economy' proponents trace the changes to developments in information technology, especially the rapid commercialization of the Internet, that are fundamentally changing economic activity. 'Old economy' advocates focus on lacklustre performance during the first half of the 1990s, the increase in labour force participation and rapid decline in unemployment since 1993, and the recent investment boom.

Our objective is to quantify the sources of the recent surge in US economic growth, using new information made available by the benchmark revision of the US National Income and Product Accounts (NIPA) released in October 1999, BEA (1999). We then consider the implications of our results for intermediate-term projections of US economic growth. We give special attention to the rapid escalation in growth rates in the official projections, such as those by the Congressional Budget Office (CBO) and the Council of Economic Advisers (CEA). The CBO projections are particularly suitable for our purposes, since they are widely disseminated, well documented, and represent 'best practice'. We do not focus on the issue of inflation and do not comment on potential implications for monetary policy.

Sources of Economic Growth

Our methodology is based on the production possibility frontier introduced by Jorgenson (1966) and employed by Jorgenson and Griliches (1967). This captures substitutions among outputs of investment and consumption goods, as well inputs of capital and labour. We identify *information technology* (IT) with investments in computers, software, and communications equipment, as well as consumption of computer and software as outputs. The service flows from these assets are also inputs. The aggregate production function employed by Solow (1957, 1960) and, more recently by Greenwood, Hercowitz, and Krusell (1997), is an alternative to our model. In this approach a single output is expressed as a function of capital and labour inputs. This implicitly assumes, however, that investments in information technology are perfect substitutes for other outputs, so that relative prices do not change.

Our methodology is essential in order to capture two important facts about which there is general agreement. The first is that prices of computers have declined drastically relative to the prices of other investment goods. The second is that this rate of decline has recently accelerated. In addition, estimates of investment in software, now available in the NIPA, are comparable to investment in hardware. The new data show that the price of software has fallen relative to the prices of other investment goods, but more slowly than price of hardware. We examine the estimates of software investment in some detail in order to assess the role of software in recent economic growth. Finally, we consider investment in communications equipment, which shares many of the technological features of computer hardware.

i) Production possibility frontier Aggregate output Y_t consists of investment goods I_t and consumption goods C_t. These outputs are produced from aggregate input X_t, consisting of capital services K_t and labour services L_t. We represent productivity as a 'Hicks-neutral' augmentation A_t of aggregate input:[9]

$$Y(I_t, C_t) = A_t \cdot X(K_t, L_t) \tag{1}$$

The outputs of investment and consumption goods and the inputs of capital and labour services are themselves aggregates, each with many subcomponents.

Under the assumptions of competitive product and factor markets, and constant returns to scale, growth accounting gives the share-weighted growth of outputs as the sum of the share-weighted growth of inputs and growth in *total factor productivity* (TFP):

$$\bar{w}_{I,t}\,\Delta\ln I_t + \bar{w}_{C,t}\,\Delta\ln C_t = \bar{v}_{K,t}\,\Delta\ln K_t + \bar{v}_{L,t}\,\Delta\ln L_t + \Delta\ln A_t, \tag{2}$$

where $\bar{w}_{I,t}$ is investment's average share of nominal output, $\bar{w}_{C,t}$ is consumption's average share of nominal output, $\bar{v}_{K,t}$ is capital's average share of nominal income, $\bar{v}_{L,t}$ is labour's average share of nominal income, $\bar{w}_{I,t} + \bar{w}_{C,t} = \bar{v}_{K,t} + v_{L,t} = 1$, and Δ refers to a first difference. Note that we reserve the term *total factor productivity* for the augmentation factor in Equation (1).

Equation (2) enables us to identify the contributions of outputs as well as inputs to economic growth. For example, we can quantify the contributions of different investments, such as computers, software, and communications equipment, to the growth of output by decomposing the growth of investment among its sub-components. Similarly, we can quantify the contributions of different types of consumption, such as services from computers and software, by decomposing the growth of consumption. As shown in Jorgenson and Stiroh (1999), both computer investment and consumption of IT have made important contributions to US economic growth in the 1990s. We also consider the output contributions of software and communications equipment as distinct high-tech assets. Similarly, we decompose the contribution of capital input to isolate the impact of computers, software, and communications equipment on input growth.

Rearranging Equation (2) enables us to present our results in terms of growth in *average labour productivity* (ALP), defined as $y_t = Y_t / H_t$, where Y_t is output, defined as an aggregate of consumption and investment goods, and $k_t = K_t / H_t$ is the ratio of capital services to hours worked H_t:

$$\Delta \ln y_t = \bar{v}_{K,t} \, \Delta \ln K_t + \bar{v}_{L,t}(\Delta \ln L_t - \Delta \ln H_t) + \Delta \ln A_t \qquad (3).$$

This gives the familiar allocation of ALP growth among three factors. The first is *capital deepening*, the growth in capital services per hour. Capital deepening makes workers more productive by providing more capital for each hour of work and raises the growth of ALP in proportion to the share of capital. The second term is the improvement in *labour quality*, defined as the difference between growth rates of labour input and hours worked. Reflecting the rising proportion of hours supplied by workers with higher marginal products, labour quality improvement raises ALP growth in proportion to labour's share. The third factor is TFP growth, which increases ALP growth on a point-for-point basis.

i) Computers, software, and communications equipment We now consider the impact of investment in computers, software, and communications equipment on economic growth. For this purpose we must carefully distinguish the *use* of information technology and the *production* of information technology.[10] For example, computers themselves are an output from one industry (the computer-producing industry, commercial and industrial machinery), and computing services are inputs into other industries (computer-using industries like trade, fire, and services).

Massive increases in computing power, like those experienced by the US economy, therefore reflect two effects on growth. First, as the production of computers improves and becomes more efficient, more computing power is being produced from the same inputs. This raises overall productivity in the computer-producing industry and contributes to TFP growth for the economy as a whole. Labour productivity also grows at both the industry and aggregate levels.[11]

Second, the rapid accumulation of computers leads to input growth of computing power in computer-using industries. Since labour is working with more and better computer equipment, this investment increases labour productivity. If the contributions to output are captured by the effect of capital deepening, aggregate TFP growth is unaffected. As Baily and Gordon (1988, p. 378) remark, 'there is no shift in the user firm's production function', and thus no gain in TFP. Increasing deployment of computers increases TFP only if there are spillovers from the production of computers to production in the computer-using industries, or if there are measurement problems associated with the new inputs.

We conclude that rapid growth in computing power affects aggregate output through both TFP growth and capital deepening. Progress in the technology of computer production contributes to growth in TFP and ALP at the aggregate level. The accumulation of computing power in computer-using industries reflects the substitution of computers for other inputs and leads to growth in ALP. In the absence of spillovers this growth does not contribute to growth in TFP.

The remainder of this section provides empirical estimates of the variables in Equations (1) through (3). We then employ Equations (2) and (3) to quantify the sources of growth of output and ALP for 1959–98 and various sub-periods.

Output

Our output data are based on the most recent benchmark revision of NIPA.[12] Real output Y_t is measured in chained 1996 dollars, and $P_{Y,t}$ is the corresponding implicit deflator. Our output concept is similar, but not identical, to one used in the Bureau of Labor Statistics (BLS) productivity programme. Like BLS, we exclude the government sector, but unlike BLS we include imputations for the service flow from consumers' durables and owner-occupied housing.

These imputations are necessary to preserve comparability between durables and housing and also enable us to capture the important impact of information technology on households.

Our estimate of current dollar, private output in 1998 is $8,013B, including imputations of $740B that primarily reflect services of consumers' durables.[13] Real output growth was 3.63 per cent for the full period, compared to 3.36 per cent for the official GDP series. This difference reflects both our imputations and our exclusion of the government sectors in the NIPA data. Appendix Table 12.A1 presents the current dollar value and corresponding price index of total output and the IT assets – investment in computers I_c, investment in software I_s, investment in communications equipment I_m, consumption of computers and software C_c, and the imputed service flow from consumers' computers and software, D_c.

The most striking feature of these data is the enormous price decline for computer investment, 18 per cent per year from 1960 to 1995 (Figure 12.1). Since 1995 this decline has accelerated to 27.6 per cent per year. By contrast the relative price of software has been flat for much of the period and only began to fall in the late 1980s. The price of communications equipment behaves similarly to the software price, while consumption of computers and software shows declines similar to computer investment. The top panel of Table 12.1 summarizes the growth rates of prices and quantities for major output categories for 1990–95 and for 1995–98.

In terms of current dollar output, investment in software is the largest IT asset, followed by investment in computers and communications equipment (Figure 12.2). While business investments in computers, software, and communications equipment are by far the largest categories, households have spent more than $20B per year on computers and software since 1995, generating a service flow of comparable magnitude.

Capital Stock and Capital Services

This section describes our capital estimates for the US economy from 1959 to 1998.[14] We begin with investment data from the Bureau of Economic Analysis, estimate capital stocks using the perpetual inventory method, and aggregate capital stocks using rental prices as weights. This approach, originated by Jorgenson and Griliches (1967), is based on the identification of rental prices with marginal products of different types of capital. Our estimates of these prices incorporate differences in asset prices, service lives and depreciation rates, and the tax treatment of capital incomes.[15]

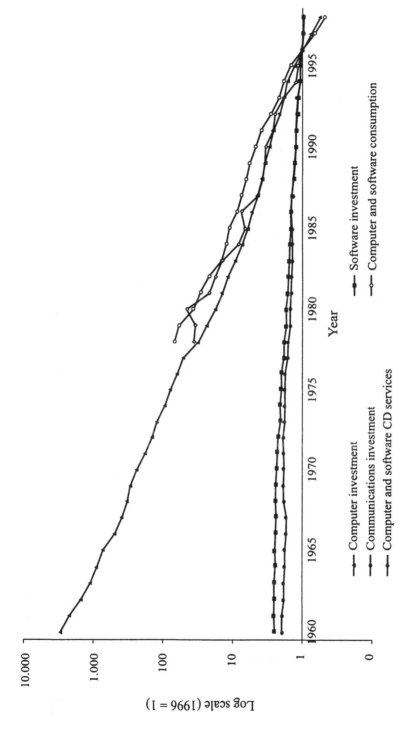

Figure 12.1   Relative prices of information technology outputs, 1960–98

Note: All price indexes are relative to the output price index.

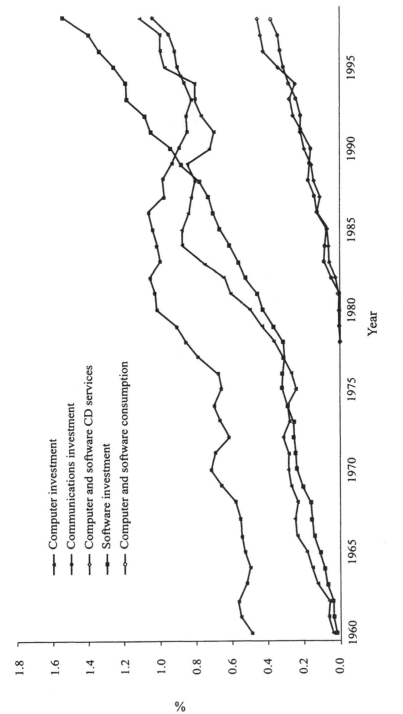

Figure 12.2   Output shares of information technology, 1960–98

Note: Share of current dollar output.

Table 12.1 Average growth rates of selected outputs and inputs

	1990–95		1995–98	
	Prices	Quantities	Prices	Quantities
Outputs				
Private domestic output (Y)	1.70	2.74	1.37	4.73
Other (Y_n)	2.01	2.25	2.02	3.82
Computer and software consumption (C_c)	−21.50	38.67	−36.93	49.26
Computer investment (I_c)	−14.59	24.89	−27.58	38.08
Software investment (I_s)	−1.41	11.59	−2.16	15.18
Communications investment (I_m)	−1.50	6.17	−1.73	12.79
Computer and software CD services (D_c)	−19.34	34.79	−28.62	44.57
Inputs				
Total capital services (K)	0.60	2.83	2.54	4.80
Other (K_n)	1.00	1.78	4.20	2.91
Computer capital (K_c)	−10.59	18.16	−20.09	34.10
Software capital (K_s)	−2.07	13.22	−0.87	13.00
Communications capital (K_m)	3.10	4.31	−7.09	7.80
Total consumption services (D)	1.98	2.91	−0.67	5.39
Non–computer and software (D_n)	2.55	2.07	0.54	3.73
Computer and software CD services (D_c)	−19.34	34.79	−28.62	44.57
Labour (L)	2.92	2.01	2.80	2.81

Notes

2 CD refers to consumers' durable assets.
1 All values are percentages.

We refer to the difference between growth in capital services and capital stock as the growth in *capital quality* $q_{K,t}$; this represents substitution towards assets with higher marginal products.[16] For example, the shift toward IT increases the quality of capital, since computers, software, and communications equipment have relatively high marginal products. Capital stock estimates, like those originally employed by Solow (1957), fail to account for this increase in quality.

We employ a broad definition of capital, including tangible assets such as equipment and structures, as well as consumers' durables, land, and inventories. We estimate a service flow from the installed stock of consumers' durables, which enters our measures of both output and input. It is essential to include this service flow, since a steadily rising proportion is associated with investments in IT by the household sector. In order to capture the impact of information technology on US economic growth, investments by business and household sectors as well as the services of the resulting capital stocks must be included.

Our estimate of capital stock is $26T in 1997, substantially larger than the $17.3T in fixed private capital estimated by BEA (1998b). This difference reflects our inclusion of consumer's durables, inventories, and land. Our estimates of capital stock for comparable categories of assets are quite similar to those of BEA. Our estimate of fixed private capital in 1997, for example, is $16.8T, almost the same as that of BEA. Similarly, our estimate of the stock of consumers' durables is $2.9T, while BEA's estimate is $2.5T. The remaining discrepancies reflect our inclusion of land and inventories. Appendix Table 12.B1 list the component assets and 1998 investment and stock values; Table 12.B2 presents the value of capital stock from 1959 to 1998, as well as price indices for total capital and IT assets.

The stocks of IT business assets (computers, software, and communications investment equipment), as well as consumers' purchases of computers and software, have grown dramatically in recent years, but remain relatively small. In 1998, combined IT assets accounted for only 3.4 per cent of tangible capital, and 4.6 per cent of reproducible, private assets.

We now move to estimates of capital services flows, where capital stocks of individual assets are aggregated using rental prices as weights. Appendix Table 12.B3 presents the current dollar service flows and corresponding price indexes for 1959–98, and the second panel of Table 12.1 summarizes the growth rates for prices and quantities of inputs for 1990–95 and 1995–98.

There is a clear acceleration of growth of aggregate capital services from 2.8 per cent per year for 1990–98 to 4.8 per cent for 1995–98. This is largely due to rapid growth in services from IT equipment and software, and reverses the trend toward slower capital growth through 1995. While information technology assets are only 11.2 per cent of the total, the service shares of these assets are much greater than the corresponding asset shares. In 1998 capital services are only 12.4 per cent of capital stocks for tangible assets as a whole, but services are 40.0 per cent of stocks for information technology. This reflects the rapid price declines and high depreciation rates that enter into the rental prices for information technology.

Figure 12.3 highlights the rapid increase in the importance of IT assets, reflecting the accelerating pace of relative price declines. In the 1990s, the service price for computer hardware fell 14.2 per cent per year, compared to an increase of 2.2 per cent for non-information technology capital. As a direct consequence of this relative price change, computer services grew 24.1 per cent, compared to only 3.6 per cent for the services of non-IT capital in the 1990s. The current dollar share of services from computer hardware reached nearly 3.5 per cent of all capital services in 1998.[17]

The rapid accumulation of software, however, appears to have different origins. The price of software investment has declined much more slowly, –1.7 per cent per year for software versus –19.5 per cent for computer hardware for 1990 to 1998. These differences in investment prices lead to a much slower decline in service prices for software and computers, –1.6 per cent versus –14.2 per cent. Nonetheless, firms have been accumulating software quite rapidly, with real capital services growing 13.3 per cent per year in the 1990s. While lower than the 24.1 per cent growth in computers, software growth is much more rapid than growth in other forms of tangible capital. Complementarity between software and computers is one possible explanation. Firms respond to the decline in relative computer prices by accumulating computers and investing in complementary inputs like software to put the computers into operation.[18]

A competing explanation is that the official price indexes used to deflate software investment omit a large part of true quality improvements. This would lead to a substantial overstatement of price inflation and a corresponding understatement of real investment, capital services, and economic growth. According to Moulton, Parker, and Seskin (1999) and Parker and Grimm (2000), only prices for prepackaged software are calculated from constant-quality price deflators based on hedonic methods. Prices for business own-account software are based on input-cost indexes, which implicitly assume no change in the productivity of computer programmers. Custom software prices are a weighted average of prepackaged software and own-account software,

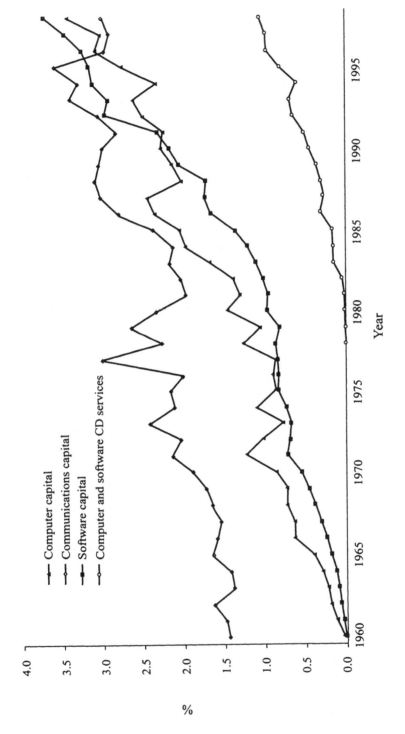

Figure 12.3   Input shares of information technology, 1960–98

Note: Share of current dollar capital and consumers' durable services.

with an arbitrary 75 per cent weight for business own-account software prices. Thus, the price deflators for nearly two-thirds of software investment are estimated under the maintained assumption of no gain in productivity.[19] If the quality of own-account and custom software is improving at a pace even remotely close to packaged software, this implies a large understatement in investment in software.

Although the price decline for communications equipment during the 1990s is comparable to that of software, as officially measured in the NIPA, investment has grown at a rate that is more in line with prices. However, there are also possible measurement biases in the pricing of communications equipment. The technology of switching equipment, for example, is similar to that of computers; investment in this category is deflated by a constant-quality price index developed by BEA. Conventional price deflators are employed for transmission gear, such as fibre-optic cables, which also appear to be declining rapidly in price. This could lead to an underestimate of the rate of growth in communications equipment investment, capital stock, and capital services, as well as an overestimate of the rate of inflation.[20] We return to this issue at the end of section 2.

Measuring Labour Services

This section describes our estimates of labour input for the US economy from 1959 to 1998. We begin with individual data from the Census of Population for 1970, 1980, and 1990, as well as the annual Current Population Surveys. We estimate constant quality indexes for labour input and its price to account for heterogeneity of the workforce across sex, employment class, age, and education levels. This follows the approach of Jorgenson, Gollop and Fraumeni (1987), whose estimates have been revised and updated by Ho and Jorgenson (1999).[21]

The distinction between labour input and labour hours is analogous to the distinction between capital services and capital stock. Growth in labour input reflects the increase in labour hours, as well as changes in the composition of hours worked as firms substitute among heterogeneous types of labour. We define the growth in labour quality as the difference between the growth in labour input and hours worked. Labour quality reflects the substitution of workers with high marginal products for those with low marginal products, while the growth in hours employed by Solow (1957) and others does not capture this substitution. Appendix Table 12.C1 presents our estimates of labour input, hours worked, and labour quality.

Our estimates show the value of labour expenditures to be \$4,546B in 1998, roughly 57 per cent of the value of output. This value share accurately reflects the NIPA measure of output and our imputations for capital services. If we exclude these imputations, labour's share rises to 62 per cent, in line with conventional estimates. As shown in Table 12.1, the growth of the index of labour input L_t appropriate for our model of production in Equation (1) accelerated to 2.8 per cent for 1995–98, from 2.0 per cent for 1990–98. This is primarily due to the growth of hours worked, which rose from 1.4 per cent for 1990–98 to 2.4 per cent for 1995–98, as labour force participation increased and unemployment rates plummeted.[22]

The growth of labour quality decelerated in the late 1990s, from 0.65 per cent for 1990–98 to 0.43 per cent for 1995–98. This slowdown captures well-known underlying demographic trends in the composition of the work force, as well as exhaustion of the pool of available workers as unemployment rates have steadily declined. Projections of future economic growth that omit labour quality, like those of CBO, implicitly incorporate changes in labour quality into measured TFP growth. This reduces the reliability of projections of future economic growth. Fortunately, this is easily remedied by extrapolating demographic changes in the work force in order to reflect foreseeable changes in composition by characteristics of workers such as age, sex, and educational attainment.

Quantifying the Sources of Growth

Table 12.2 presents results of our growth accounting decomposition based on Equation (2) for the period 1959 to 1998 and various subperiods, as well as preliminary estimates through 1999. As in Jorgenson and Stiroh (1999), we decompose economic growth by both output and input categories in order to quantify the contribution of information technology (IT) to investment and consumption outputs, as well as capital and consumers' durable inputs. We extend our previous treatment of the outputs and inputs of computers by identifying software and communications equipment as distinct IT assets.

To quantify the sources of IT-related growth more explicitly, we employ the extended production possibility frontier:

$$Y(Y_{it}, C_c, I_c, I_s, I_m, D_c) = A \cdot X(K_{it}, K_c, K_s, K_m, D_{it}, D_c, L) \qquad (4)$$

where outputs include computer and software consumption C_c, computer investment I_c, software investment I_s, telecommunications investment I_m, the services of consumers' computers and software D_c, and other outputs Y_n, Inputs include the capital services of computers K_c, software K_s, telecommunications equipment K_m, and other capital assets K_n, services of consumers' computers and software D_c and other durables D_n, and labour input L.[23] As in Equation (1), total factor productivity is denoted by A and represents the ability to produce more output from the same inputs. Time subscripts have been dropped for convenience.

The corresponding extended growth accounting equation is:

$$\bar{w}_{Yn}\Delta \ln Y_n + \bar{w}_{Cc}\Delta \ln C_c + \bar{w}_{Ic}\Delta \ln I_c + \bar{w}_{Is}\Delta \ln I_s + \bar{w}_{Im}\Delta \ln I_m \bar{w}_{Dc}\Delta \ln D_c =$$
$$\bar{v}_{Kn}\Delta \ln K_n + \bar{v}_{Kc}\Delta \ln K_c + \bar{v}_{Ks}\Delta \ln K_s + \bar{v}_{Km}\Delta \ln K_m + \bar{v}_{Dn}\Delta \ln D_n \qquad (5)$$
$$+ \bar{v}_{Dc}\Delta \ln D_c + \bar{v}_L\Delta \ln L + \Delta \ln A$$

where $\bar{w}$ and $\bar{v}$ denote average shares in nominal income for the subscribed variable $\bar{w}_{Yn} + \bar{w}_{Cc} + \bar{w}_{Ic} + \bar{w}_{Is} + \bar{w}_{Im} + \bar{w}_{Dc} = \bar{v}_{Kn} + \bar{v}_{Kc} + \bar{v}_{Ks} + \bar{v}_{Km} + \bar{v}_{Dn} + \bar{v}_{Dc} + \bar{v}_L = 1$, and we refer to a share-weighted growth rate as the *contribution* of an input or output.

Output Growth We first consider the sources of output growth for the entire period 1959 to 1998. Capital services make the largest growth contribution of 1.8 percentage point (1.3 percentage points from business capital and 0.5 from consumers' durable assets), labour services contribute 1.2 percentage points, and TFP growth is responsible for only 0.6 percentage points. Input growth is the source of nearly 80 per cent of US growth over the past 40 years, while TFP has accounted for approximately one-fifth. Figure 12.4 highlights this result by showing the relatively small growth contribution of the TFP residual in each sub-period.

More than three-quarters of the contribution of broadly defined capital reflects the accumulation of capital stock, while increased labour hours account for slightly less than three-quarters of labour's contribution. The quality of both capital and labour have made important contributions, 0.45 percentage points and 0.32 percentage points per year, respectively. Accounting for substitution among heterogeneous capital and labour inputs is therefore an important part of quantifying the sources of economic growth.

A look at the US economy before and after 1973 reveals some familiar features of the historical record. After strong output and TFP growth in the 1960s and early 1970s, the US economy slowed markedly through 1990, with output growth falling from 4.3 per cent to 3.1 per cent and TFP growth falling almost two-thirds of a percentage point from 1.0 per cent to 0.3 per cent.

Table 12.2 Growth in US private domestic output and the sources of growth, 1959–99

	1959–98	1959–73	1973–90	1990–95	1995–98	Preliminary* 1995–99
Growth in private domestic output growth (Y)	3.630	4.325	3.126	2.740	4.729	4.763
Contribution of selected output components						
Other (Yn)	3.275	4.184	2.782	2.178	3.659	3.657
Computer and software consumption (Cc)	0.035		0.000	0.023	0.092	0.167
Computer investment (Ic)	0.150	0.067	0.162	0.200	0.385	0.388
Software investment (Is)	0.074	0.025	0.075	0.128	0.208	0.212
Communications investment (Im)	0.060	0.048	0.061	0.053	0.122	0.1288
Computer and software CD services (Dc)	0.036	0.000	0.023	0.089	0.187	0.204
Contribution of capital services (K)	1.260	1.436	1.157	0.908	1.611	0.923
Other (Kn)	0.936	1.261	0.807	0.509	0.857	0.490
Computers (Kc)	0.177	0.086	0.199	0.187	0.458	0.2054
Software (Ks)	0.075	0.026	0.071	0.154	0.193	0.109
Communications (Km)	0.073	0.062	0.080	0.058	0.104	0.608
Contribution of CD services (D)	0.510	0.632	0.465	0.292	0.558	0.403
Other (Dn)	0.474	0.632	0.442	0.202	0.370	0.204
Computers and software (Dc)	0.036	0.000	0.023	0.089	0.187	1.438
Contribution of labour (L)	1.233	1.249	1.174	1.182	1.572	0.991
Aggregate total factor productivity (TFP)	0.628	1.009	0.330	0.358	0.987	
Growth of capital and CD services	4.212	4.985	3.847	2.851	4.935	2.575
Growth of labour input	2.130	2.141	2.035	2.014	2.810	

Table 12.2 cont'd

	1959–98	1959–73	1973–90	1990–95	1995–98	Preliminary* 1995–99
Contribution of capital and CD quality	0.449	0.402	0.405	0.434	0.945	1.225
Contribution of capital and CD stock	1.320		1.664	1.217	0.765	0.248
Contribution of labour quality	0.315	0.447	0.200	0.370	0.253	1.190
Contribution of labour hours	0.918	0.802	0.974	0.812	1.319	
Average labour productivity (*ALP*)	2.042	2.948	1.437	1.366	2.371	2.580

Notes

1 A contribution of an output and an input is defined as the share-weighted, real growth rate.
2 CD refers to consumers' durable assets.
3 All values are percentages.
4 1995–99 results include preliminary estimates for 1999; see the Appendix for details on estimation and data sources.

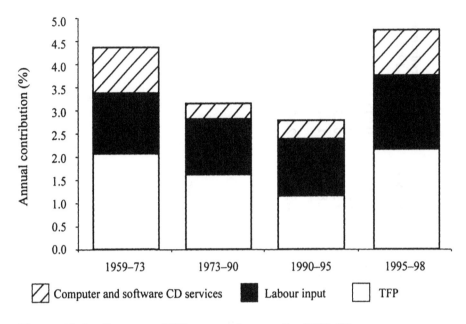

Figure 12.4   Sources of US economic growth, 1959–98

Notes

1   An input's contribution is the average share-weighted, annual growth rate.
2   TFP defined in Equation (2) in text.

Growth in capital inputs also slowed, falling from 5.0 per cent for 1959-73 to 3.8 per cent for 1973–90, which contributed to sluggish ALP growth, 2.9 per cent for 1959–73 to 1.4 per cent for 1973–90.

We now focus on the period 1995–98 and highlight recent changes.[24] Relative to the early 1990s, output growth has increased by nearly two percentage points. The contribution of capital jumped by 1.0 percentage point, the contribution of labour rose by 0.4 percentage points, and TFP growth accelerated by 0.6 percentage point. ALP growth rose 1.0 percentage point. The rising contributions of capital and labour encompass several well-known trends in the late 1990s. Growth in hours worked accelerated as labour markets tightened, unemployment fell to a 30-year low, and labour force participation rates increased.[25] The contribution of capital reflects the investment boom of the late 1990s as businesses poured resources into plant and equipment, especially computers, software, and communications equipment.

The acceleration in TFP growth is perhaps the most remarkable feature of the data. After averaging only 0.34 per cent per year from 1973 to 1995, the acceleration of TFP to 0.99 per cent suggests massive improvements in technology and increases in the efficiency of production. While the resurgence in TFP growth in the 1990s has yet to surpass periods of the 1960s and early 1970s, more rapid TFP growth is critical for sustained growth at higher rates.

Figures 12.5 and 12.6 highlight the rising contributions of information technology (IT) outputs to US economic growth. Figure 12.5 shows the breakdown between IT and non-IT outputs for various sub-periods from 1959 to 1998, while Figure 12.6 decomposes the contribution of IT outputs into its components. Although the role of IT has steadily increased, Figure 12.5 shows that the recent investment and consumption surge nearly doubled the output contribution of IT for 1995–98 relative to 1990–98. Figure 12.6 shows that computer investment is the largest single IT contributor in the late 1990s, and that consumption of computers and software is becoming increasingly important as a source of output growth.

Figures 12.7 and 12.8 present a similar decomposition of the role of IT as an input into production, where the contribution is rising even more dramatically. Figure 12.7 shows that the capital and consumers' durable contribution from

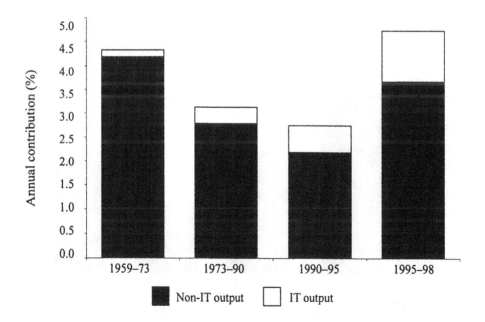

Figure 12.5   Output contribution of information technology, 1959–98

Note: An output's contribution is the average share-weighted, annual growth rate.

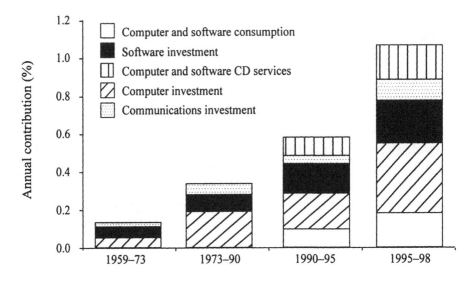

Figure 12.6   Output contribution of information technology assets, 1959–98

Note: An output's contribution is the average share-weighted, annual growth rate.

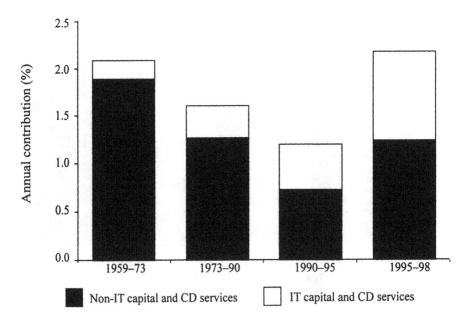

Figure 12.7   Input contribution of information technology, 1959–98

Note: An output's contribution is the average share-weighted, annual growth rate.

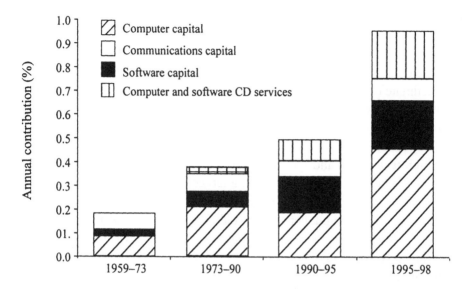

Figure 12.8 Input contribution of information technology assets, 1959–98

Note: An output's contribution is the average share-weighted, annual growth rate.

IT increased rapidly in the late 1990s, and now accounts for more two-fifths of the total growth contribution from broadly defined capital. Figure 12.8 shows that computer hardware is also the single largest IT contributor on the input side, which reflects the growing share and rapid growth rates of the late 1990s.

The contribution of computers, software, and communications equipment presents a different picture from Jorgenson and Stiroh (1999) for both data and methodological reasons. First, the BEA benchmark revision has classified software as an investment good. While software is growing more slowly than computers, the substantial nominal share of software services has raised the contribution of information technology. Second, we have added communications equipment, also a slower growing component of capital services, with similar effects. Third, we now incorporate asset-specific revaluation terms in all rental price estimates. Since the acquisition prices of computers are steadily falling, asset-specific revaluation terms have raised the estimated service price and increased the share of computer services. Finally, we have modified our timing convention and now assume that capital services from individual assets are proportional to the average of the current and lagged stock. For assets with relatively short service lives like IT, this is a more reasonable assumption than in our earlier work, which assumed that it took a full year for new investment to become productive.[26]

This large increase in the growth contribution of computers and software is consistent with recent estimates by Oliner and Sichel (2000), although their estimate of contribution is somewhat larger. They report that computer hardware and software contributed 0.93 percentage points to growth for 1996–99, while communications contributed another 0.15. The discrepancy primarily reflects our broader output concept, which lowers the input share of these high-tech assets, and also minor differences in tax parameters and stock estimates. Whelan (1999) also reports a larger growth contribution of 0.82 percentage points from computer hardware for 1996–98. The discrepancy also reflects our broader output concept. In addition, Whelan (1999) introduces a new methodology to account for retirement and support costs that generates a considerably larger capital stock and raises the input share and the growth contribution from computer capital.

Despite differences in methodology and data sources among studies, a consensus is building that computers are having a substantial impact on economic growth.[27] What is driving the increase in the contributions of computers, software, and communications equipment? As we argued in Jorgenson and Stiroh (1999), price changes lead to substitution toward capital services with lower relative prices. Firms and consumers are responding to relative price changes.

Table 12.1 shows the acquisition price of computer investment fell nearly 28 per cent per year, the price of software fell 2.2 per cent, and the price of communications equipment fell 1.7 per cent during the period 1995–98, while other output prices rose 2.0 per cent. In response to these price changes, firms accumulated computers, software, and communications equipment more rapidly than other forms of capital. Investment other than information technology actually declined as a proportion of private domestic product. The story of household substitution toward computers and software is similar. These substitutions suggest that gains of the computer revolution accrue to firms and households that are adept at restructuring activities to respond to these relative price changes.

Average labour productivity growth   To provide a different perspective on the sources of economic growth we can focus on ALP growth. By simple arithmetic, output growth equals the sum of hours growth and growth in labour productivity.[28] Table 12.3 shows the output breakdown between growth in hours and ALP for the same periods as in Table 12.2. For the period 1959–98,

ALP growth was the predominant determinant of output growth, increasing just over 2 per cent per year for 1959–98, while hours increased about 1.6 per cent per year. We then examine the changing importance of the factors determining ALP growth. As shown in Equation (3), ALP growth depends on a capital deepening effect, a labour quality effect, and a TFP effect.

Table 12.3 The sources of ALP growth, 1959–98

Variable	1959–98	1959–73	1973–90	1990–95	1995–98
Growth of private domestic output (*Y*)	3.630	4.325	3.126	2.740	4.729
Growth in hours (*H*)	1.588	1.377	1.689	1.374	2.358
Growth in ALP (*Y/H*)	2.042	2.948	1.437	1.366	2.371
ALP contribution of capital deepening	1.100	1.492	0.908	0.637	1.131
ALP contribution of labour quality	0.315	0.447	0.200	0.370	0.253
ALP contribution of TFP	0.628	1.009	0.330	0.358	0.987

Notes

1   ALP Contributions are defined in Equation (3).
2   All values are percentages.

Figure 12.9 shows the importance of each factor, revealing the well-known productivity slowdown of the 1970s and 1980s, and highlighting the acceleration of labour productivity growth in the late 1990s. The slowdown through 1990 reflects less capital deepening, declining labour quality growth, and decelerating growth in TFP. The growth of ALP slipped further during the early 1990s with the serious slump in capital deepening only partly offset by a revival in the growth of labour quality and an up-tick in TFP growth. Slow growth in hours combined with slow ALP growth during 1990–98 to produce a further slide in the growth of output. This stands out from previous cyclical recoveries during the postwar period, when output growth accelerated during the recovery, powered by more rapid hours and ALP growth.

For the most recent period of 1995–98, strong output growth reflects growth in labour hours and ALP almost equally. Comparing 1990–98 to 1995–98, output growth accelerated by nearly 2 percentage points due to a 1

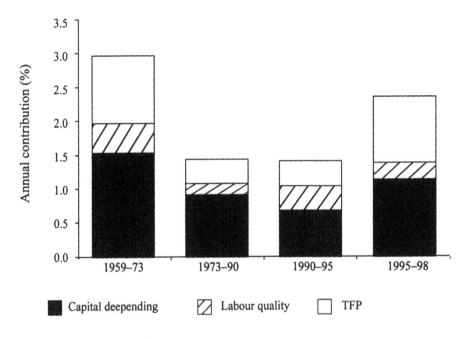

Figure 12.9   Sources of US labour productivity growth, 1959–98

Note: Annual contributions are defined in Equation (3) in text.

percentage point increase in hours worked, and a 1 percentage point increase in ALP growth.[29] Figure 12.9 shows the acceleration in ALP growth is due to capital deepening from the investment boom, as well as faster TFP growth. Capital deepening contributed 0.49 percentage points to the acceleration in ALP growth, while acceleration in TFP growth added 0.63 percentage points. Growth in labour quality slowed somewhat as growth in hours accelerated. This reflects the falling unemployment rate and tightening of labour markets as more workers with relatively low marginal products were drawn into the workforce. Oliner and Sichel (2000) also show a decline in the growth contribution of labour quality in the late 1990s, from 0.44 for 1991–98 to 0.31 for 1996–99.

Our decomposition also throws some light on the hypothesis advanced by Gordon (1999b), who argues the vast majority of recent ALP gains are due to the production of IT, particularly computers, rather than the use of IT. As we have already pointed out, more efficient IT-production generates aggregate TFP growth as more computing power is produced from the same inputs, while IT-use affects ALP growth via capital deepening. In recent years, acceleration of TFP growth is a slightly more important factor in the acceleration of ALP growth than capital deepening. Efficiency gains in computer production are important part of aggregate TFP growth, as Gordon's results on ALP suggest. We return to this issue in section 3.

iii) Total factor productivity growth Finally, we consider the remarkable performance of US TFP growth in recent years. After maintaining an average rate of 0.33 per cent for the period 1973–90, TFP growth rose to 0.36 per cent for 1990–95 and then vaulted to 0.99 per cent per year for 1995–98. This jump is a major source of growth in output and ALP for the US economy (Charts 4 and 9). While TFP growth for the 1990s has yet to attain the peaks of some periods in the golden age of the 1960s and early 1970s, the recent acceleration suggests that the US economy may be recuperating form the anaemic productivity growth of the past two decades. Of course, caution is warranted until more historical experience is available.

As early as Domar (1961), economists have utilized a multi-industry model of the economy to trace aggregate productivity growth to its sources at the level of individual industries. Jorgenson, Gollop, and Fraumeni (1987) and Jorgenson (1990) have employed this model to identify the industry-level sources of growth. More recently, Gullickson and Harper (1999) and Jorgenson and Stiroh (2000) have used the model for similar purposes. We postpone more detailed consideration of the sources of TFP growth until we have examined the implications of the recent growth resurgence for intermediate-term projections.

Alternative Growth Accounting Estimates

Tables 12.1–12.3 and Figures 12.1–12.9 report our primary results using the official data published in the NIPA. As we have already noted, however, there is reason to believe that the rates of inflation in official price indices for certain high-tech assets, notably software and telecommunications equipment, may be overstated. Moulton, Parker, and Seskin (1999) and Parker and Grimm (2000), for example, report that only the pre-packaged portion of software investment is deflated with a constant-quality deflator. Own-account software is deflated with an input cost index and custom software is deflated with a weighted average of the prepackaged and own-account deflator. Similarly, BEA reports that in the communications equipment category, only telephone switching equipment is deflated with a constant-quality, hedonic deflator.

This subsection incorporates alternative price series for software and communications equipment and examines the impact on the estimates of

US economic growth and its sources. Table 12.4 presents growth accounting results under three different scenarios. The Base Case repeats the estimates from Table 12.2, which are based on official NIPA price data. Two additional cases, moderate price decline and rapid price decline, incorporate price series for software and communications equipment that show faster price declines and correspondingly more rapid real investment growth.[30]

The moderate price decline case assumes that prepackaged software prices are appropriate for all types of private software investment, including custom and business own-account software. Since the index for prepackaged software is based on explicit quality adjustments, it falls much faster than the prices of custom and own-account software, −10.1 per cent vs. 0.4 per cent and 4.1 per cent respectively, for the full period 1959–98 according to Parker and Grimm (2000). For communications equipment, the data are more limited and we assume prices fell 10.7 per cent per year throughout the entire period. This estimate is the average annual 'smoothed' decline for digital switching equipment for 1985–96 reported by Grimm (1997). While this series may not be appropriate for all types of communications equipment, it exploits the best available information.

The rapid price decline case assumes that software prices fell 16 per cent per year for 1959–98, the rate of quality-adjusted price decline reported by Brynjolfsson and Kemerer (1996) for microcomputer spreadsheets for 1987–92. This is a slightly faster decline than the −15 per cent for 1986–91 estimated by Gandal (1994), and considerably faster than the 3 per cent annual decline for word processors, spreadsheets, and databases for 1987–93 reported by Oliner and Sichel (1994). For communications equipment, we used estimates from the most recent period from Grimm (1997), who reports a decline of 17.9 per cent per year for 1992–96.

While this exercise necessarily involves some arbitrary choices, the estimates incorporate the limited data now available and provide a valuable perspective on the crucial importance of accounting for quality change in the prices of investment goods. Comparisons among the three cases are useful in suggesting the range of uncertainty currently confronting analysts of US economic growth.

Before discussing the empirical results, it is worthwhile to emphasize that more rapid price decline for information technology has two direct effects on the sources of growth, and one indirect effect. The alternative investment deflators raise real output growth by reallocating nominal growth away from prices and towards quantities. This also increases the growth rate of capital stock, since there are larger investment quantities in each year. More rapid price declines also give greater weight to capital services from information technology.

The counter-balancing effects of increased output and increased input growth lead to an indirect effect on measured TFP growth. Depending on the relative shares of high-tech assets in investment and capital services, the TFP residual will increase if the output effect dominates or decrease if the effect on capital services dominates.[31] Following Solow (1957, 1960), Greenwood, Hercowitz, and Krusell (1997) omit the output effect and attribute the input effect to 'investment-specific' (embodied) technical change. This must be carefully distinguished from the effects of industry-level productivity growth on TFP growth, discussed in section 4.

Table 12.4 reports growth accounting results from these three scenarios – base case, moderate price decline, and rapid price decline. The results are not surprising – the more rapid the price decline for software and communications, the faster the rate of growth of output and capital services. Relative to the base case, output growth increases by 0.16 percentage points per year for 1995–98 in the moderate price decline case and by 0.34 percentage points in the rapid price decline case. Capital input growth shows slightly larger increases across the three cases. Clearly, constant-quality price indexes for information technology are essential for further progress in understanding the growth impact of high-tech investment.

The acceleration in output and input growth reflects the increased contributions from IT, as well as the effect on the TFP residual. In particular, the output contribution from software for 1995–98 increases from 0.21 percentage points in the base case to 0.29 percentage points under moderate price decline to 0.40 percentage points with rapid price decline. Similarly, the capital services contribution for software increase from 0.19 to 0.29 to 0.45 percentage points. The contribution of communications equipment shows similar changes. Residual TFP growth falls slightly during the 1990s, as the input effect outweighs the output effect, due to the large capital services shares of IT.

This exercise illustrates the sensitivity of the sources of growth to alternative price indexes for information technology. We do not propose to argue the two alternative cases are more nearly correct than the base case with the official prices from NIPA. Given the paucity of quality-adjusted price data on high-tech equipment, we simply do not know. Rather, we have tried to highlight the importance of correctly measuring prices and quantities to understand the dynamic forces driving US economic growth. As high-tech assets continue to proliferate through the economy and other investment goods become increasingly dependent on electronic components, these measurement issues

Table 12.4 Impact of alternative deflation of software and communications equipment on the sources of US economic growth, 1959–98

	Base case				Moderate price decline				Rapid price decline			
	1959–73	1973–90	1990–95	1995–98	1959–73	1973–90	1990–95	1995–98	1959–73	1973–90	1990–95	1995–98
Growth in private domestic output growth (Y)	4.33	3.13	2.74	4.73	4.35	3.30	2.90	4.89	4.36	3.38	3.03	5.07
Contribution of selected output components												
Other (Y_n)	4.18	2.78	2.18	3.66	4.12	2.76	2.17	3.66	4.08	2.75	2.16	3.66
Computer and software consumption (C_c)	0.00	0.02	0.09	0.17	0.00	0.02	0.09	0.17	0.00	0.02	0.09	0.17
Computer investment (I_c)	0.07	0.16	0.20	0.39	0.07	0.16	0.20	0.39	0.07	0.16	0.20	0.39
Software investment (I_s)	0.03	0.08	0.13	0.21	0.04	0.14	0.22	0.29	0.05	0.17	0.29	0.40
Communications investment (I_m)	0.05	0.06	0.05	0.12	0.12	0.19	0.13	0.21	0.16	0.25	0.19	0.27
Computer and software CD services (D_c)	0.00	0.02	0.09	0.19	0.00	0.02	0.09	0.19	0.00	0.02	0.09	0.19
Contribution of capital services (K)	1.44	1.16	0.91	1.61	1.54	1.39	1.15	1.83	1.61	1.51	1.32	2.09
Other (Kn)	1.26	0.81	0.51	0.86	1.25	0.80	0.51	0.86	1.25	0.79	0.51	0.85
Computers (Kc)	0.09	0.20	0.19	0.46	0.09	0.20	0.19	0.46	0.09	0.20	0.19	0.46
Software (Ks)	0.03	0.07	0.15	0.19	0.05	0.15	0.28	0.29	0.06	0.18	0.36	0.45
Communications (Km)	0.06	0.08	0.06	0.10	0.16	0.25	0.18	0.23	0.22	0.34	0.27	0.33
Contribution of CD services (D)	0.63	0.47	0.29	0.56	0.63	0.46	0.29	0.56	0.63	0.46	0.29	0.56
Non-computers and software (Dn)	0.63	0.44	0.20	0.37	0.63	0.44	0.20	0.37	0.63	0.44	0.20	0.37
Computers and software (Dc)	0.00	0.02	0.09	0.19	0.00	0.02	0.09	0.19	0.00	0.02	0.09	0.19
Contribution of Labour (L)	1.25	1.17	1.18	1.57	1.25	1.17	1.18	1.57	1.25	1.18	1.18	1.57
Aggregate total factor productivity (TFP)	1.01	0.33	0.36	0.99	0.94	0.27	0.27	0.93	0.88	0.22	0.23	0.85
Growth of capital and CD services	4.99	3.85	2.85	4.94	5.24	4.40	3.43	5.44	5.41	4.70	3.84	6.02
Growth of labour input	2.14	2.04	2.01	2.81	2.14	2.04	2.01	2.81	2.14	2.04	2.01	2.81

Table 12.4 cont'd

	Base case				Moderate price decline				Rapid price decline			
	1959–73	1973–90	1990–95	1995–98	1959–73	1973–90	1990–95	1995–98	1959–73	1973–90	1990–95	1995–98
Contribution of capital and CD quality	0.40	0.41	0.43	0.95	0.48	0.59	0.63	1.11	0.54	0.70	0.78	1.34
Contribution of capital and CD stock	1.66	1.22	0.77	1.23	1.68	1.26	0.82	1.28	1.69	1.27	0.84	1.31
Contribution of labour quality	0.45	0.20	0.37	0.25	0.45	0.20	0.37	0.25	0.45	0.20	0.37	0.25
Contribution of labour hours	0.80	0.97	0.81	1.32	0.80	0.97	0.81	1.32	0.80	0.98	0.81	1.32
Average labour productivity (ALP)	2.95	1.44	1.37	2.37	2.98	1.61	1.52	2.53	2.99	1.69	1.65	2.72

Notes

1 base case uses official NIPA price data.
2 Moderate price decline uses pre-packaged software deflator for all software and annual price changes of –10.7 per cent for communications equipment.
3 Rapid price decline uses annual price changes of –16 per cent for software and –17.9 per cent for communications equipment.
4 See text for details and sources.
5 A contribution is defined as the share-weighted, real growth rate.
6 CD refers to consumers' durable assets.
7 All values are percentages.

will become increasingly important. While the task that lies ahead of us will be onerous, the creation of quality-adjusted price indexes for all high-tech assets deserves top priority.

Decomposition of TFP estimates

We next consider the role of high-tech industries as a source of continued TFP growth. As discussed above, increased output of high-tech investment goods has made important contributions to aggregate growth.[32] CEA (2000) allocates annual TFP growth of 0.39 percentage points to the computer production, while Oliner and Sichel (2000) allocate 0.47 percentage points to the production of computers and computer-related semiconductor production for the period 1995–99.

We employ a methodology based on the price 'dual' approach to measurement of productivity at the industry level. Anticipating our complete industry analysis (section 4, below), it is worthwhile to spell out the decomposition of TFP growth by industry. Using the Domar approach to aggregation, industry-level productivity growth is weighted by the ratio of the gross output of each industry to aggregate value-added to estimate the industry contribution to aggregate TFP growth. In the dual approach, the rate of productivity growth is measured as the decline in the price of output, plus a weighted average of the growth rates of input prices.

In the case of computer production, this expression is dominated by two terms; namely, the price of computers and the price of semiconductors, a primary intermediate inputs into the computer-producing industry. If semiconductor industry output is used only to produce computers, then its contribution to computer industry productivity growth, weighted by computer industry output, precisely cancels its independent contribution to aggregate TFP growth.[33] This independent contribution from the semiconductor industry, based on the complete Domar weighting scheme, is the value of semiconductor output divided by aggregate value added, multiplied by the rate of price decline in semiconductors.

We report details of our TFP decomposition for 1990–95 and 1995–98 in Table 12.5 and summarize the IT vs non-IT comparison in Figure 12.10. In our Base Case, using official NIPA data, we estimate the production of information technology accounts for 0.44 percentage points for 1995–98, compared to 0.25 percentage points for 1990–95. This reflects the accelerating relative price changes prices due to radical shortening of the product cycle for semiconductors.[34]

Table 12.5 Information technology decomposition of TFP growth for alternative deflation cases, 1990–98

	Base case		Moderate price decline		Rapid price decline	
	1990–95	1995–98	1990–95	1995–98	1990–95	1995–98
Aggregate TFP growth	0.36	0.99	0.27	0.93	0.23	0.85
			TFP contribution			
Information technology	0.25	0.44	0.46	0.64	0.64	0.87
Computers	0.16	0.32	0.16	0.32	0.16	0.32
Software	0.05	0.08	0.17	0.18	0.28	0.34
Communications	0.04	0.04	0.13	0.13	0.21	0.20
Non-information technology	0.11	0.55	-0.19	0.29	-0.41	-0.01
			Relative price change			
Computers	-16.6	-29.6	-16.6	-29.6	-16.6	-29.6
Software	-3.4	-4.2	-11.3	-9.7	-18.0	-18.0
Communications	-3.5	-3.8	-12.7	-12.7	-19.9	-19.9
			Average nominal share			
Computers	0.96	1.09	0.96	1.09	0.96	1.09
Software	1.54	1.88	1.54	1.88	1.54	1.88
Communications	1.05	1.02	1.05	1.02	1.05	1.02

Notes

1 Base case uses official NIPA price data.
2 Moderate price decline uses pre-packaged software deflator for all software and –10.7 per cent for communications equipment.
3 Rapid price decline uses –16 per cent for software and –17.9 per cent for communications equipment.
4 See text for details and sources.
5 A TFP contribution is defined as the share-weighted, growth rate of relative prices.

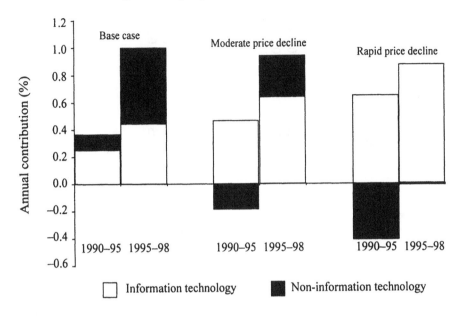

Figure 12.10 TFP decomposition for alternative deflation cases

Note: Annual contribution of information technology is the share-weighted decline in relative prices.

As we have already suggested, the estimates of price declines for high-tech investments in our base case calculations may be conservative; in fact, these estimates may be *very* conservative. Consider the moderate price decline case, which reflects only part of the data we would require for constant-quality estimates of the information technology price declines. This boosts the contribution of information technology to TFP growth to 0.64 percentage points, an increase of 0.20 percentage points for 1995–98. Proceeding to what may appear to be the outer limit of plausibility, but still consistent with the available evidence, we can consider the case of rapid price decline. The contribution of information technology to TFP growth is now a robust 0.86 percentage points, accounting for all of TFP growth for 1995–98.

3   Setting the Speed Limit

We next consider the sustainability of recent US growth trends over longer time horizons. Rapid output growth is highly desirable, of course, but cannot continue indefinitely if fuelled by a falling unemployment rate and higher labour force participation. Output growth driven by continuing TFP improvements, on the other hand, is more likely to persist. The sustainability of growth has clear implications for government policies. Since economic growth affects tax revenues, potential government expenditures, and the long-term viability of programs like Social Security and Medicare, it is closely studied by government agencies. This section examines the impact of the recent success of the US economy on official growth forecasts.

A Brief Review of Forecast Methodologies

The importance of economic growth for the US government is evident in the considerable effort expended on projecting future growth. No fewer than five government agencies – the Congressional Budget Office (CBO), the Social Security Administration (SSA), the Office of Management and Budget (OMB), the Council of Economic Advisors (CEA), and the General Accounting Office (GAO) – report estimates of future growth for internal use or public discussion. This section briefly discusses the methodologies used by these agencies.[35]

All five agencies employ models that rest securely on neoclassical foundations. While the details and assumptions vary, all employ an aggregate production model similar to Equation (1), either explicitly or implicitly. In addition, they all incorporate demographic projections from the SSA as the basic building block for labour supply estimates. CBO (1995, 1997, 1999a, 1999b, 2000) and GAO (1995, 1996) employ an aggregate production function and describe the role of labour growth, capital accumulation, and technical progress explicitly. SSA (1992, 1996), OMB (1997, 2000), and CEA (2000) on the other hand, employ a simplified relationship where output growth equals the sum of growth in hours worked and labour productivity. Projections over longer time horizons are driven by aggregate supply with relatively little attention to business cycle fluctuations and aggregate demand effects.

Given the common framework and source data, it is not surprising that the projections are quite similar. Reporting on estimates released in 1997, Stiroh (1998b) finds that SSA and GAO projections of per capita GDP in 2025 were virtually identical, while CBO was about 9 per cent higher due to economic feedback effects from the improving government budget situation. More recently, CBO (2000) projects real GDP growth of 2.8 per cent and OMB (2000) projects 2.7 per cent for 1999–2010, while CEA (2000) reports 2.8 per cent for 1999–2007. Although the timing is slightly different – CBO projects faster growth than OMB earlier in the period and CEA reports projections only through 2007– the estimates are virtually identical. All three projections identify the recent investment boom as a contributor to rising labour productivity and capital deepening as a source of continuing economic growth. We now consider the CBO projections in greater detail.

CBO's Growth Projections

Of the five government agencies CBO utilizes a sophisticated and detailed long-run growth model of the US economy.[36] The core of this model is a two-factor production function for the non-farm business sector with CBO projections based on labour force growth, national savings and investment, and exogenous TFP growth. Production function parameters are calibrated to historical data, using a Cobb-Douglas model:

$$Y = A \cdot H^{0.7} \cdot K^{0.3} \tag{6}$$

where Y is potential output, H is potential hours worked, K is capital input, and A is potential total factor productivity.[37]

CBO projects hours worked on the basis of demographic trends with separate estimates for different age and sex classifications. These estimates incorporate SSA estimates of population growth, as well as internal CBO projections of labour force participation and hours worked for the different categories. However, CBO does use this demographic detail to identify changes in labour quality. Capital input is measured as the service flow from four types of capital stocks – producers' durable equipment excluding computers, computers, nonresidential structures, and inventories. Stocks are estimated by the perpetual inventory method and weighted by rental prices, thereby incorporating some changes in capital quality. TFP growth is projected on the basis of recent historical trends, with labour quality growth implicitly included in CBO's estimate of TFP growth.

Turning to the most recent CBO projections, reported in CBO (2000), we focus on the non-farm business sector, which drives the GDP projections and is based on the most detailed growth model. Table 12.6 summarizes CBO's growth rate estimates for the 1980s and 1990s, and projections for 1999–2010. We also present estimates from BLS (2000) and our results.[38]

CBO projects potential GDP growth of 3.1 per cent for 1999–2010, up slightly from 3.0 per cent in the 1980s and 2.9 per cent in the 1990s. CBO expects actual GDP growth to be somewhat slower at 2.8 per cent, as the economy moves to a sustainable, long-run growth rate. Acceleration in potential GDP growth reflects faster capital accumulation and TFP growth,

Table 12.6 Growth rates of output, inputs, and total factor productivity: comparison of BLS, CBO, and Jorgenson-Stiroh

	BLS Non-farm business		CBO Overall economy		CBO Non-farm business			Jorgenson-Stiroh	
	1990–99	1980–90	1990–99	1999–2010	1980–90	1990–99	1999–2010	1980–90	1990–98
Real output	3.74	3.0	2.9	3.1	3.2	3.4	3.5	3.48	3.55
Labour input								2.14	2.34
Hours worked	1.68	1.6	1.2	1.1	1.6	1.5	1.2	1.81	1.76
Labour quality								0.33	0.58
Capital Input					3.6	3.6	4.4	3.68	3.63
TFP – not adjusted for labour quality					0.9	1.2	1.4	0.91	0.97
TFP – adjusted for labour quality								0.73	0.63
ALP	2.06	1.4	1.7	1.9	1.5	1.9	2.3	1.67	1.79

Note: CBO estimates refer to 'potential' series that are adjusted for business cycle effects. Growth rates do not exactly match Table 12.5 since discrete growth rate are used here for consistency with CBO's methodology. Hours worked for CBO Overall Economy refers to potential labour force.

partly offset by slower growth in hours worked. Projected GDP growth is 0.4 per cent higher than earlier estimates (CBO (1999b)) due to an upward revision in capital growth (0.1 per cent), slightly more rapid growth in hours (0.1 per cent), and faster TFP growth, reflecting the benchmark revisions of NIPA and other technical changes (0.2 per cent).[39]

CBO's estimates for the non-farm business sector show strong potential output growth of 3.5 per cent for 1999–2010. While projected output growth is in line with experience of the 1990s and somewhat faster than the 1980s, there are significant differences in the underlying sources. Most important, CBO projects an increasing role for capital accumulation and TFP growth over the next decade, while hours growth slows. This implies that future output growth is driven by ALP growth, rather than growth in hours worked.

CBO projects potential non-farm business ALP growth for 1999–2010 to rise to 2.3 per cent, powered by capital deepening (3.2 per cent) and TFP growth (1.4 per cent). This represents a marked jump in ALP growth, relative to 1.5 per cent in the 1980s and 1.9 per cent in the 1990s. In considering whether the recent acceleration in ALP growth represents a trend break, CBO 'gives considerable weight to the possibility that the experience of the past few years represents such a break (CBO, 2000, p. 43)'. This assumption appears plausible given recent events, and low unemployment and high labour force participation make growth in hours worked a less likely source of future growth. Falling investment prices for information technology make capital deepening economically attractive, while the recent acceleration in TFP growth gives further grounds for optimistic projections.

As the investment boom continues and firms substitute toward more information technology in production, CBO has steadily revised its projected growth rates of capital upward. It is worthwhile noting just how much the role of capital accumulation has grown in successive CBO projections, rising from a projected growth rate of 3.6 per cent in January 1999 (CBO (1999a)) to 4.1 per cent in July 1999 (CBO (1999b)) to 4.4 per cent in January 2000 (CBO (2000)). This reflects the inclusion of relatively fast-growing software investment in the benchmark revision of NIPA, but also extrapolates recent investment patterns.

Similarly, CBO has raised its projected rate of TFP growth in successive estimates – from 1.0 per cent in January 1999 to 1.1 per cent in July 1999 to 1.4 per cent in January 2000.[40] These upward revisions reflect methodological changes in how CBO accounts for the rapid price declines in investment, particularly computers, which added 0.2 per cent. In addition, CBO adjustments for the benchmark revision of NIPA contributed another 0.1 per cent.

Table 12.6 also reports our own estimates of growth for roughly comparable periods. While the time periods are not precisely identical, our results are similar to CBO's. We estimate slightly faster growth during the 1980s, due to rapidly growing CD services, but slightly lower rates of capital accumulation due to our broader measure of capital. Our growth of hours worked is higher, since we omit the cyclical adjustments made by CBO to develop their potential series.[41] Finally, our TFP growth rates are considerably lower, due to our labour quality adjustments and inclusion of consumers' durables. If we were to drop the labour quality adjustment, our estimate would rise to 1.0 per cent per year from 1990 to 1998, compared to 1.2 per cent for CBO for 1990–99. The remaining difference reflects the fact that we do not include the rapid TFP growth of 1999, but do include the services of consumers' durables, which involve no growth in TFP.

Evaluating CBO's Projections

Evaluating CBO's growth projections requires an assessment of their estimates of the growth of capital, labour, and TFP. It is important to emphasize that this is not intended as a criticism of CBO, but rather a description of 'best practice' in the difficult area of growth projections. We also point out comparisons between our estimates and CBO's estimates are not exact due to our broader output concept and our focus on actual series, as opposed the potential series that are the focus of CBO.

We begin with CBO's projections of potential labour input. These data, based on the hours worked from BLS and SSA demographic projections, show a decline in hours growth from 1.5 per cent in the 1990s to 1.2 per cent for the period 1999–2010. This slowdown reflects familiar demographic changes associated with the aging of the US population. However, CBO does not explicitly estimate labour quality, so that labour composition changes are included in CBO's estimates of TFP growth and essentially held constant.

We estimate growth in labour quality of 0.57 per cent per year for 1990–98, while our projections based on demographic trends yield a growth rate of only 0.32 per cent for the 1998–2010 period. Assuming CBO's labour share of 0.70, this implies that a decline in the growth contribution from labour quality of about 0.18 percentage points per year over CBO's projection horizon. Since this labour quality effect is implicitly incorporated into CBO's TFP estimates, we conclude their TFP projections are overstated by this 0.18 percentage points decline in the labour quality contribution.

TFP growth is perhaps the most problematical issue in long-term projections. Based on the recent experience of the US economy, it appears reasonable to expect strong future productivity performance. As discussed above and shown in Table 12.2, TFP growth has increased markedly during the period 1995–98. However, extrapolation of this experience runs the risk of assuming that a temporary productivity spurt is a permanent change in trend.

Second, the recent acceleration of TFP growth is due in considerable part to the surge in productivity growth in industries producing IT. This makes the economy particularly vulnerable to slowing productivity growth in these industries. Computer prices have declined at extraordinary rates in recent years and it is far from obvious that this can continue. However, acceleration in the rate of decline reflects the change in the product cycle for semiconductors, which has shifted from three years to two and may be permanent.

We conclude that CBO's projection of TFP growth is optimistic in assuming a continuation of recent productivity trends. However, we reduce this projection by only 0.18 percent per year to reflect the decline in labour quality growth, resulting in projected TFP growth of 1.22 per cent per year. To obtain a projection of labour input growth we add labour quality growth of 0.32 per cent per year to CBO's projection of growth in hours of 1.2 per cent per year. Multiplying labour input growth of 1.52 per cent per year by the CBO labour share of 0.7, we obtain a contribution of labour input of 1.06 per cent.

CBO's projected annual growth of capital input of 4.4 per cent is higher than in any other decade, and 0.8 per cent higher than in the 1990s. This projection extrapolates recent increases in the relative importance of computers, software, and communications equipment. Continuing rapid capital accumulation is also predicated on the persistence of high rates of decline in asset prices, resulting from rapid productivity growth in the IT producing sectors. Any attenuation in this rate of decline would produce a double whammy – less TFP growth and reduced capital deepening.

Relative to historical trends, CBO's capital input growth projection of 4.4 per cent seems out of line with the projected growth of potential output of 3.5 per cent. During the 1980s capital growth exceeded output growth by 0.4 per cent, according to their estimates, or 0.1 per cent by our estimates. In the 1990s capital growth exceeded output growth by only 0.2 per cent, again according to their estimates, and 0.1 per cent by our estimates. This difference jumps to 0.9 per cent for the period of CBO's projections, 1999–2010.

Revising the growth of capital input downward to reflect the difference between the growth of output and the growth of capital input during the period

1995–98 of 0.2 per cent would reduce the CBO's projected output growth to 3.34 per cent per year. This is the sum of the projected growth of TFP of 1.22 per cent per year, the contribution of labour input of 1.06 per cent per year, and the contribution of capital input of 1.06 per cent per year. This is a very modest reduction in output growth from CBO's projection of 3.5 per cent per year and can be attributed to the omission of a projected decline in labour quality growth.

We conclude that CBO's projections are consistent with the evidence they present, as well as our own analysis of recent trends. We must emphasize, however, that any slowdown in technical progress in information technology could have a major impact on potential growth. Working through both output and input channels, the US economy has become highly dependent on information technology as the driving force in continued growth. Should productivity growth in these industries falter, the projections we have reviewed could be overly optimistic.

4　Industry Productivity

We have explored the sources of US economic growth at the aggregate level and demonstrated that accelerated TFP growth is an important contributor to the recent growth resurgence. Aggregate TFP gains – the ability to produce more output from the same inputs – reflects the evolution of the production structure at the plant or firm level in response to technological changes, managerial choices, and economic shocks. These firm- and industry-level changes then cumulate to determine aggregate TFP growth. We now turn our attention to industry data to trace aggregate TFP growth to its sources in the productivity growth of individual industries, as well as reallocations of output and inputs among industries.

Our approach utilizes the framework of Jorgenson, Gollop, and Fraumeni (1987) for quantifying the sources of economic growth for US industries. The industry definitions and data sources have been brought up-to-date. The methodology of Jorgenson, Gollop, and Fraumeni for aggregating over industries is based on Domar's (1961) approach to aggregation. Jorgenson and Stiroh (2000) have presented summary data from our work; other recent studies of industry-level productivity growth include BLS (1999), Corrado and Slifman (1999), and Gullickson and Harper (1999). The remainder of this section summarizes our methodology and discusses the results.

Methodology

As with the aggregate production model discussed in section 2, we begin with an industry-level production model for each industry. A crucial distinction, however, is that industry output Q_i is measured using a 'gross output' concept, which includes output sold to final demand as well as output sold to other industries as intermediate goods. Similarly, inputs include all production inputs, including capital services K_i and labour services L_i, as well as intermediate inputs, energy E_i and materials M_i, purchased from other industries.[42] Our model is based on the industry production function:

$$Q_i = A_i \cdot X_i(K_i, L_i, E_i, M_i) \tag{7}$$

where time subscripts have been suppressed for clarity.

We can derive a growth accounting equation similar to Equation (2) for each industry to measure the sources of economic growth for individual industries. The key difference is the use of gross output and an explicit accounting of the growth contribution of intermediate inputs purchased from other industries. This yields:

$$\Delta \ln Q_i = \bar{w}_{Ki} \Delta \ln K_i + \bar{w}_{Li} \Delta \ln L_i + \bar{w}_{Ei} \Delta \ln E_i + \bar{w}_{Mi} \Delta \ln M_i + \Delta \ln A_i \tag{8}$$

where $\bar{w}_i$ is the average share of the subscripted input in the ith industry and the assumptions of constant returns to scale and competitive markets imply $\bar{w}_{Ki} + \bar{w}_{Li} + \bar{w}_{Ei} + \bar{w}_{Mi} = 1$.

The augmentation factor $\Delta \ln A_i$ represents the growth in output not explained by input growth and is conceptually analogous to the TFP concept used above in the aggregate accounts. It represents efficiency gains, technological progress, scale economies, and measurement errors that allow more measured gross output to be produced from the same set of measured inputs. We refer to this term as *industry productivity* or simply *productivity* to distinguish it from TFP, which is estimated from a value-added concept of output.[43]

Domar (1961) first developed an internally consistent methodology that linked industry-level productivity growth in Equation (8) with aggregate TFP growth in Equation (2). He showed that aggregate TFP growth can be expressed as a weighted average of industry productivity growth:

$$\Delta \ln A = \sum_{i=1}^{37} \bar{w}_i \cdot \Delta \ln A_i, \quad \bar{w}_i = \frac{1}{2} \left(\frac{P_{i,t} \cdot Q_{i,t}}{P_{Y,t} \cdot Y_t} + \frac{P_{i,t-1} \cdot Q_{i,t-1}}{P_{Y,t-1} \cdot Y_{t-1}} \right) \tag{9}$$

where $\bar{w}_i$ is the 'Domar weight', $P_i \times Q_i$ is current dollar gross output in sector i, and $P_Y \times Y$ is current dollar aggregate value-added. This simplified version of the aggregation formula given by Jorgenson, Gollop, and Fraumeni (1987), excludes re-allocations of value added, capital input, and labour input by sector. Jorgenson and Stiroh (2000) show that these terms are negligible for the period 1958–96, which is consistent with the results of Jorgenson, Gollop, and Fraumeni (1987) and Jorgenson (1990) for periods of similar duration.

Domar weights have the notable feature that they do not sum to unity. This reflects the different output concepts used at the aggregate and industry levels in Equations (1) and (7), respectively. At the aggregate level, only primary inputs are included, while both primary and intermediate inputs are included in the industry production functions. For the typical industry, gross output considerably exceeds value added, so the sum of gross output across industries exceeds the sum of value added. This weighting methodology implies that economy-wide TFP growth can grow faster than productivity in any industry, since productivity gains are magnified as they work their way through the production process.[44]

In addition to providing an internally consistent aggregation framework, industry-level gross output allows an explicit role for intermediate goods as a source of industry growth. For example, Triplett (1996) shows that a substantial portion of the price declines in computer output can be traced to steep price declines in semiconductors, the major intermediate input in the computer-producing industry. Price declines in semiconductors reflect technological progress – Moore's law in action. This should be measured as productivity growth in the industry that produces semiconductors. By correctly accounting for the quantity and quality of intermediate inputs, the gross output concept allows aggregate TFP gains to be correctly allocated among industries.

Data Sources

Our primary data include a set of interindustry transactions accounts developed by the Employment Projections office at the BLS. These data cover a relatively short time period from 1977 to 1995. We linked the BLS estimates to industry-level estimates back to 1958, described by Stiroh (1998a), and extrapolated to 1996 using current BLS and BEA industry data.[45] This generated a time series for 1958 to 1996 for 37 industries, at roughly the two-digit standard industrial classification (SIC) level, including private households and general government.[46] Table 12.7 lists the 37 industries, the relative size in terms of 1996 value-added and gross output, and the underlying SIC codes for each industry.

Table 12.7   1996 value-added and gross output by industry

Industry	SIC codes	Value-added	Gross output
Agriculture	01–02, 07–09	133.3	292.2
Metal mining	10	8.8	10.7
Coal mining	11–12	14.7	21.1
Petroleum and gas	13	57.4	83.3
Nonmetallic mining	14	10.5	17.0
Construction	15–17	336.0	685.5
Food products	20	147.2	447.6
Tobacco products	21	26.7	32.7
Textile mill products	22	19.9	58.9
Apparel and textiles	23	40.7	98.5
Lumber and wood	24	34.2	106.7
Furniture and fixtures	25	23.4	54.5
Paper products	26	68.3	161.0
Printing and publishing	27	113.5	195.6
Chemical products	28	184.0	371.2
Petroleum refining	29	44.7	184.3
Rubber and plastic	30	64.1	148.9
Leather products	31	3.4	8.1
Stone, clay, and glass	32	40.4	79.1
Primary metals	33	57.6	182.1
Fabricated metals	34	98.4	208.8
Industrial machinery and equipment	35	177.8	370.5
Electronic and electric equipment	36	161.9	320.4
Motor vehicles	371	84.9	341.6
Other transportation equipment	372–379	68.0	143.8
Instruments	38	81.3	150.0
Miscellaneous manufacturing	39	24.8	49.3
Transport and warehouse	40–47	258.6	487.7
Communications	48	189.7	315.
Gas utilities	492, %493, 496	32.9	57.9
Trade	50–59	1,201.2	1,606.4
Fire	60–67	857.8	1,405.1
Services	70–87, 494–495	1,551.9	2,542.8
Goverment enterprises		95.2	220.2
Private households	88	1,248.4	1,248.4
General government		1,028.1	1,028.1

Note: All values are in current dollars. Value-added refers to payments to capital and labour;
      Gross output includes payments for intermediate inputs.

Before proceeding to the empirical results, we should point out two limitations of this industry-level analysis. Due to the long lag in obtaining detailed inter-industry transactions, investment, and output data by industry, our industry data are not consistent with the BEA benchmark revision of NIPA published in December 1999; they correspond to the NIPA produced by BEA in November 1997. As a consequence, they are not directly comparable to the aggregate data described in Tables 12.1–12,6. Since the impact of the benchmark revision was to raise output and aggregate TFP growth, it is not surprising that the industry data show slower output and productivity growth. Second, our estimates of rental prices for all assets in this industry analysis are based on the industry-wide asset revaluation terms, as in Stiroh (1998a). They are not directly comparable to the aggregate data on capital input, where asset-specific revaluation terms are included in the rental price estimates. The use of industry-wide revaluation terms tends to reduce the growth in capital services since assets with falling relative prices, such as computers, have large service prices and rapid accumulation rates.

Empirical Results

i) Sources of industry growth Table 12.8 reports estimates of the components of Equation (8) for the period 1958–96. For each industry, we show the growth in output, the contribution of each input (defined as the nominal share-weighted growth rate of the input), and productivity growth. We also report average labour productivity (ALP) growth, defined as real gross output per hour worked, and the Domar weights calculated from Equation (9). We focus the discussion of our results on industry productivity and ALP growth.

Industry productivity growth was the highest in two high-tech industries, industrial machinery and equipment, and electronic and electric equipment, at 1.5 per cent and 2.0 per cent per year, respectively. Industrial Machinery includes the production of computer equipment (SIC #357) and Electronic Equipment includes the production of semiconductors (SIC #3674) and communications equipment (SIC #366). The enormous technological progress in the production of these high-tech capital goods has generated falling prices and productivity growth, and fuelled the substitution towards information technology.

An important feature of these data is that we can isolate productivity growth for industries that produce intermediate goods, for example, electronic and electric equipment.[47] Consider the contrast between computer production and semiconductor production. Computers are part of final demand, sold as

Table 12.8   Sources of US economic growth by industry, 1958–96

Industry	Output growth	Contributions of inputs				Productivity growth	ALP growth	Domar weight
		Capital	Labour	Energy	Materials			
Agriculture	1.70	0.19	-0.13	-0.04	0.51	1.17	3.21	0.062
Metal mining	0.78	0.73	-0.07	-0.07	-0.26	0.44	0.99	0.003
Coal mining	2.35	0.82	-0.01	0.06	0.63	0.84	2.32	0.005
Petroleum and gas	0.43	0.61	-0.01	0.06	0.20	-0.44	0.88	0.022
Nonmetallic mining	1.62	0.59	0.18	0.06	0.34	0.46	1.52	0.003
Construction	1.43	0.07	0.87	0.02	0.91	-0.44	-0.38	0.113
Food products	2.20	0.21	0.18	0.00	1.27	0.54	1.59	0.076
Tobacco products	0.43	0.59	0.05	0.00	-0.01	-0.20	0.88	0.004
Textile mill products	2.23	0.12	0.02	0.01	0.86	1.23	2.54	0.013
Apparel and textiles	2.03	0.24	0.17	0.00	0.82	0.80	2.01	0.022
Lumber and wood	2.24	0.21	0.33	0.02	1.70	-0.02	1.55	0.015
Furniture and fixtures	2.91	0.31	0.58	0.02	1.44	0.56	1.78	0.007
Paper products	2.89	0.50	0.40	0.05	1.51	0.42	1.96	0.022
Printing and publishing	2.51	0.55	1.20	0.02	1.19	-0.44	0.14	0.024
Chemical products	3.47	0.74	0.47	0.09	1.58	0.58	2.02	0.048
Petroleum refining	2.21	0.44	0.24	0.49	0.71	0.33	0.80	0.033
Rubber and plastic	5.17	0.47	1.16	0.08	2.43	1.04	1.94	0.016
Leather products	-2.06	-0.11	-1.13	-0.02	-1.08	0.28	2.08	0.004
Stone, clay, and glass	1.86	0.26	0.37	0.00	0.82	0.41	1.30	0.014
Primary metals	1.14	0.13	0.05	-0.03	0.77	0.22	1.51	0.040
Fabricated metals	2.28	0.26	0.28	0.00	1.09	0.65	1.88	0.035
Industrial machinery and equipment	4.79	0.52	0.75	0.02	2.04	1.46	3.15	0.048
Electronic and electric equipment	5.46	0.76	0.65	0.03	2.04	1.98	4.08	0.036

Table 12.8 cont'd

Industry	Output growth	Contributions of inputs				Productivity growth	ALP growth	Domar weight
		Capital	Labour	Energy	Materials			
Motor vehicles	3.61	0.28	0.29	0.02	2.78	0.24	2.28	0.043
Other transportation equipment	1.31	0.23	0.37	0.00	0.52	0.18	1.00	0.027
Instruments	5.23	0.65	1.44	0.03	1.99	1.12	2.57	0.017
Miscellaneous manufacturing	2.53	0.34	0.41	0.00	0.95	0.82	2.08	0.008
Transport and warehouse	3.25	0.20	0.72	0.12	1.34	0.86	1.74	0.061
Communications	5.00	1.62	0.53	0.02	1.95	0.88	3.93	0.033
Electric utilities	3.22	1.01	0.20	0.67	0.83	0.52	2.52	0.026
Gas utilities	0.56	0.66	-0.04	0.14	0.05	-0.24	0.94	0.016
Trade	3.66	0.62	0.83	0.04	1.19	0.98	2.49	0.195
Fire	3.42	1.14	0.94	-0.00	1.52	-0.18	0.66	0.131
Services	4.34	0.84	1.70	0.07	1.92	-0.19	0.92	0.208
Government enterprises	2.86	1.24	1.08	0.23	0.83	-0.52	0.49	0.022
Private households	3.50	3.55	-0.06	0.00	0.00	0.00	5.98	0.137
General government	1.35	0.60	0.75	0.00	0.00	-0.00	0.46	0.131

Notes

1　Output growth is the average annual growth in real gross output.
2　Contributions of inputs are defined as the average, share-weighted growth of the input.
3　Productivity growth is defined in Equation (8).
4　ALP growth is the growth in average labour productivity.
5　Domar weight is the average ratio of industry gross output to aggregate value added as defined in Equation (9).
6　All numbers except Domar weights are percentages.

consumption and investment goods, and can be identified in the aggregate data, as we did in Table 12.2. Semiconductors, on the other hand, do not appear at the aggregate level, since they are sold almost entirely as an input to computers, telecommunications equipment, and an increasingly broad range of other products such as machine tools, automobiles, and virtually all recent vintages of appliances. Nonetheless, improved semiconductor production is an important source of aggregate TFP growth since it is ultimately responsible for the lower prices and improved quality of goods like computers produced for final demand.

The enormous price declines in computer equipment and the prominent role of investment in computers in the GDP accounts have led Gordon (1999b), Whelan (1999), and others to emphasize technological progress in the production of computers. Triplett (1996), however, quantifies the role of semiconductors as an intermediate input and estimates that falling semiconductor prices may account for virtually all of the relative price declines in computer equipment. He concludes, 'productivity in the computer industry palls beside the enormous increases in productivity in the semiconductor industry' (Triplett, 1996, p. 137).[48]

The decline in prices of semiconductors is reflected in the prices of intermediate input into the computer industry, effectively moving productivity away from computers and toward semiconductor production. Building on this observation, Oliner and Sichel (2000) present a model that includes three sectors – semiconductor production, computer production, and other goods – and shows that semiconductors productivity is substantially more important than computer productivity. Our complete industry framework with Domar aggregation over all industries captures the contributions of productivity growth from all industries.

The impact of intermediate inputs can be seen in Table 12.8 in the large contribution of material inputs in the industrial machinery industry. Since a substantial portion of these inputs consists of semiconductors purchased from the electronic equipment industry, productivity gains that lower the price of semiconductors increase the flow of intermediate inputs into the industrial machinery industry. By correctly accounting for these inputs, industry productivity growth in the industrial machinery industry falls, and we can rightly allocate technological progress to the electronic equipment industry, which produces semiconductors. while this type of industry reallocation does not affect aggregate productivity growth, it is important to identify the sources of productivity growth and allocate this among industries in order to assess the sustainability of the recent acceleration.

The two high-tech industries also show high rates of average labour productivity (ALP) growth of 3.1 per cent and 4.1 per cent per year. This reflects an underlying relationship similar to Equation (3) for the aggregate data, where industry ALP growth reflects industry productivity growth, labour quality growth, and increases in input intensity, including increases in capital as well as intermediate inputs per hour worked. As implied by Table 12.8, these industries showed rapid accumulation of capital and intermediate inputs, which raised ALP growth above productivity growth. It is also worthwhile to note that communications, another high-tech industry, shows ALP growth much faster than industry productivity growth due to the rapid accumulation of inputs, notably intermediate materials. These results highlight the crucial importance of accounting for all inputs when examining the sources of industry growth.

Productivity growth in information technology provides a final perspective on the conclusions of Greenwood, Hercowitz, and Krusell (1997) and Hercowitz (1998). They argue that some 60 per cent of postwar US growth can be attributed to investment-specific (embodied) productivity growth, which they distinguish from input accumulation and (disembodied) productivity growth. As evidence, they note the relative price of equipment in the US has fallen 3 per cent per year, which they interpret as evidence of technical change that affect capital goods, but not consumption goods. Our decomposition, however, reveals that declines in the prices of investment goods are the consequence of improvements in industry (disembodied) productivity. Domar aggregation shows how these improvements contribute directly to aggregate TFP growth. There is no separate role for investment-specific technical change.

Other industries that show relatively strong productivity growth include agriculture, textile mill products, rubber and plastic, instruments, trade. All of these industries experienced productivity growth in the 1.0 per cent per year range, and ALP growth in the 2–3 per cent range. Industries with the slowest productivity growth include petroleum and gas, construction, printing and publishing, and government enterprises, all of which showed a declines in productivity of nearly 0.5 per cent per year.

It is worth emphasizing that nine industries showed negative productivity growth for the entire period, a counter-intuitive result, if we were to interpret productivity growth solely as technological progress. It is difficult to envision technology steadily worsening for a period of nearly 40 years as implied by these estimates. The perplexing phenomenon of negative technical progress was a primary motivation for the work of Corrado and Slifman (1999) and Gullickson and Harper (1999), who suggest persistent measurement problems as a plausible explanation. Corrado and Slifman (1999) conclude, 'a more likely statistical explanation for the implausible productivity, profitability, and price trends ... is that they reflect problems in measuring prices' (p. 331). If prices are systematically overstated because quality change is not accurately measured, then output and productivity are correspondingly understated. We do not pursue this idea here, but simply point out that measurement problems are considered a reasonable explanation by some statistical agencies.[49]

An alternative interpretation for negative productivity growth is the possibility of declines in efficiency that have no association with technology. These might include lower quality of management and worsening of industrial organization through the growth of barriers to entry. This appears to be plausible explanation, given the widespread occurrence of negative productivity growth for extended periods of time. Until more careful research linking firm- and plant-level productivity to industry productivity estimates has been done, it would be premature to leap to the conclusion that estimates of economic performance should be adjusted so as to eliminate negative productivity growth rates, wherever they occur.

Low productivity growth rates are surprising in light of the fact that many of the affected industries are heavy investors in information technology. Stiroh (1998a), for example, reports nearly 80 per cent of computer investment in the early 1990s was in three service-related industries, Trade, FIRE, and Services. Triplett (1999) reports a high concentration in service industries using the BEA's capital use survey. The apparent combination of slow productivity growth and heavy computer-use remains an important obstacle for new economy proponents who argue that the use of information technology is fundamentally changing business practices and raising productivity throughout the US economy.

ii) Comparison to other results Before proceeding to the Domar aggregation results, it is useful to compare these results to three other recent studies – BLS (1999), Corrado and Slifman (1999) and Gullickson and Harper (1999). BLS (1999) reports industry productivity growth ('industry multifactor productivity' in their terminology) for 19 manufacturing industry for 1949–96. Corrado and Slifman (1999) report estimates of ALP growth for selected one- and two-digit SIC industries for the period 1977–97. Gullickson and Harper (1999) report industry productivity growth for certain one and two-digit SIC industries based on two output series for the period 1947–92. Similar to BLS (1999), Gullickson and Harper use a 'sectoral output' concept estimated by the Employment Projections staff at BLS and also, for 1977–92, use BEA's gross output series, 'adjusted for consistency'.[50] Note that none of these studies reflect the BEA benchmark revision of NIPA.

Time period, industry classification, and methodological differences make a definitive reconciliation to our results impossible. For example, BLS (1999) reports detailed manufacturing industries; Corrado and Slifman (1999) use a value-added concept, BEA's 'gross product originating', for output; Gullickson and Harper (1999) use the same data sources as we do, but make different adjustments for consistency and do not account for labour quality growth. Nonetheless, it is useful to compare broad trends over similar time periods to assess the robustness of our findings.

We first consider the ALP estimates from Corrado and Slifman (1999). We can compare similar time periods, but there are relatively few overlapping industries since our industry breakdown focuses on manufacturing industries, while they provide details primarily for service industries. For comparable industries, however, the results are quite similar. For seven industries with comparable definitions, five show differences in ALP growth of less than 0.25 per cent when we compare our estimates for 1977–96 to Corrado and Slifman's estimates for 1977–97 (Corrado and Slifman, 1999, Table 2).[51] Our ALP growth rates for communication and trade are below theirs by 1.3 per cent and 0.4 per cent, respectively, for these periods.

Our productivity estimates for 1977–92 for the majority of industries are similar to those of Gullickson and Harper (1999). The range of discrepancies is somewhat greater due to the difficulty of linking the various data sets needed to estimate intermediate inputs and industry productivity growth. For 7 of the 11 comparable industries productivity differences are below 0.5 per cent, while we found larger discrepancies for metal mining, coal mining, petroleum and gas, and services.[52] Similar differences can also be seen in Gullickson and Harper's comparison of productivity growth estimated from the BLS and BEA gross output series, where they find differences of 0.5 percentage points or more in 17 out of 40 industries and aggregates. Methodological differences, such as the inclusion of labour quality growth in our estimates of labour input growth, contribute to this divergence, as do different methods for linking data sets.

Neither Corrado and Slifman (1999) nor Gullickson and Harper (1999) break out ALP growth or industry productivity growth for detailed manufacturing industries. To gauge these results, we have compared our manufacturing results to the manufacturing industry estimates in BLS (1999). For the 18 industries that are comparable, ten showed productivity differences of less than 0.25 per cent for 1979–96; two showed differences between 0.25 per cent and 0.5 per cent; and the remaining six industries, textile mills, lumber and wood, petroleum refining, leather, stone, clay and glass, and instruments, showed differences greater than 0.5.[53]

iii) Domar aggregation We now turn to the aggregation of industry productivity growth described by Equation (9). This is not directly comparable to our estimates of aggregate productivity, due to different vintages of data and a broader definition of output. Nonetheless, it is useful to quantify an industry's contribution to aggregate TFP growth and to trace aggregate productivity growth back to its sources at the level of the individual industry. These results update the earlier estimates of Jorgenson, Gollop, and Fraumeni (1987). Gordon (1999b) presents a similar decomposition for ALP growth, although he focuses exclusively on the contribution from computer production.

We present our estimates of each industry's contribution to aggregate TFP growth for the period 1958–96 in Figure 12.11. This follows Equation (9) by weighting industry productivity growth by the 'Domar weight', defined as industry gross output divided by aggregate value-added. Summing across industries gives an estimate of aggregate TFP growth of 0.48 for 1958–96. This is lower than the number implied by Table 12.2 for two reasons. First, the data are prior to the BEA benchmark revision, which raised output and TFP growth. Second, these estimates include a broader output concept that includes government enterprises, which we estimate has negative industry productivity growth, and the general government, which has zero productivity growth by definition. The estimate is consistent, however, with the estimates in Ho, Jorgenson, and Stiroh (1999) and Jorgenson and Stiroh (1999), which are based on the same vintage of data.

The most striking feature of Figure 12.11 is the wide range of industry contributions. Trade, industrial machinery, and electronic equipment make the largest contribution, although for different reasons. Trade has solid, but not exceptionally strong productivity growth of almost 1 per cent per year, but makes the largest contribution due to its large relative size; Trade receives a Domar weight of nearly 0.20. Industrial machinery and electronic equipment, on the other hand, make important contributions due to their rapid productivity growth, 1.5 per cent and 2.0 per cent, respectively, in spite of their relative small sizes with Domar weights of 0.05 and 0.04, respectively. An industry's contribution to aggregate productivity growth depends on both productivity performance and relative size.

Figure 12.11 also highlights the impact of the nine industries that experienced negative productivity growth over this period. Again, both performance and relative size matter. Services makes a negative contribution of 0.07 due to its large weight and productivity growth of –0.19 per cent. Construction, on the other hand, shows even slower industry productivity growth, –0.44 per cent per year, but makes a smaller negative contribution,

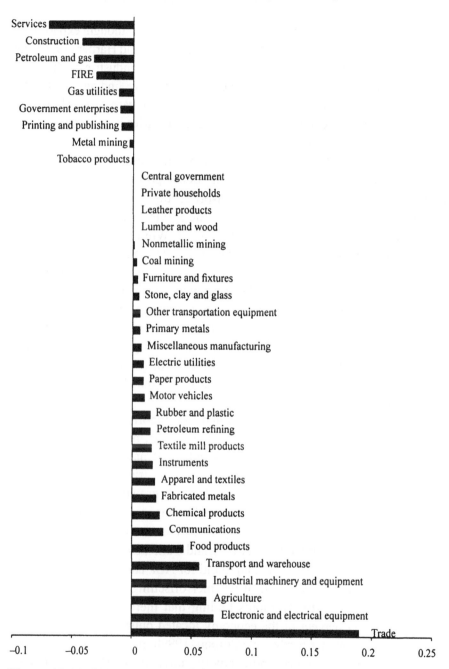

Figure 12.11 Industry contributions to aggregate total factor productivity growth, 1958–96

Note: Each industry's contribution is calculated as the product of industry productivity growth and the industry Domar weight, averaged for 1958–96.

since it is so much smaller than services. We can also do a 'thought experiment' similar to Corrado and Slifman (1999) and Gullickson and Harper (1999) and imagine that productivity growth is zero in these nine industries rather than negative. By zeroing out the negative contributions, we find aggregate TFP growth would have been 0.22 per cent higher, an increase of nearly half.[54] Clearly, negative productivity growth in these industries is an important part of the aggregate productivity story.

Finally, these data enable us to provide some new perspective on an argument made by Gordon (1999b), who decomposes trend-adjusted ALP growth into a portion due to computer-production and a residual portion for the rest of the economy.[55] He finds the former accounts for virtually all of the productivity acceleration since 1997. While we cannot comment directly on his empirical estimates since our industry data end in 1996 and we examine TFP growth rather than ALP growth, we can point to an important qualification to his argument. The US economy is made up of industries with both positive and negative productivity growth rates, so that comparing one industry to the aggregate of all others necessarily involves aggregation over off-setting productivity trends. The fact that this aggregate does not show net productivity growth does not entail the absence of gains in productivity in any of the component industries, since these gains could be offset by declines in other industries.

Consider our results for 1958–96 and the importance of the negative contributions. The five industries with the largest, positive contributions – trade, electronic equipment, agriculture, industrial machinery, and transport – cumulatively account for the sum across all industries, about 0.5 per cent per year. Nonetheless, we find sizable productivity growth in some remaining industries that are offset by negative contributions in others. This logic and the prevalence of negative productivity growth rates at the industry level, in BLS (1999), Corrado and Slifman (1999), and Gullickson and Harper (1999), suggest that a similar argument could hold for ALP and for the most recent period. This raises the question of whether offsetting productivity growth rates are responsible for Gordon's finding that there is '*no* productivity growth in the 99 percent of the economy located outside the sector which manufactures computer hardware' (Gordon, 1999b, p, 1, italics in original). Assessing the breadth of recent productivity gains and identifying the sources in productivity growth at the industry level remains an important question for future research.

5   Conclusions

The performance of the US economy in the late 1990s has been nothing short of phenomenal. After a quarter century of economic malaise, accelerating total factor productivity growth and capital deepening have led to a remarkable growth resurgence. The pessimism of the famous Solow (1987) paradox, that we see computers everywhere but in the productivity statistics, has given way to optimism of the information age. The productivity statistics, beginning in 1995, have begun to reveal a clearly discernible impact of information technology. Both labour productivity and TFP growth have jumped to rates not seen for such an extended period of time since the 1960s. While a substantial portion of these gains can be attributed to computers, there is growing evidence of similar contributions from software and communications equipment – each equal in importance to computers.

The forces shaping the information economy originate in the rapid progress of semiconductor technology – Moore's Law at work. These gains are driving down relative prices of computers, software, and communications equipment and inducing massive investments in these assets by firms and households. Technological progress and the induced capital deepening are the primary factors behind accelerating output growth in recent years. The sustainability of recent growth trends therefore hinges to a great degree on prospects for continuing progress, especially in the production of semiconductors. While this seems plausible and perhaps even likely, the contribution of high-tech assets to the growth resurgence remains subject to considerable uncertainty, owing to incomplete information on price trends for these assets.

The strong performance of the US economy has not gone unnoticed. Forecasters have had to raise their projected growth rates and raise them again. The moderate speed limits set by Blinder (1997) and Krugman (1997), reflecting the best evidence available only a few years ago, have given way to the optimism of the ordinarily conservative community of official forecasters. Our review of the evidence now available suggests that the official forecasters are relying very heavily on a continuation of the acceleration in US economic growth since 1995.

What are the risks to the optimistic view of future US economic growth in the information age? Upward revision of growth projections seems a reasonable response as evidence accumulates of a possible break in trend productivity growth. Nonetheless, caution is warranted until productivity patterns have been observed for a longer time period. Should the pace of technological progress in high-tech industries diminish, economic growth would be hit with a double whammy – slower total factor productivity growth in important industries that produce high-tech equipment and slower capital accumulation in other sectors that invest in and use the high-tech equipment. Both factors have made important contribution to the recent success of the US economy, so that any slowdown would retard future growth potential.

At the same time we must emphasize that the uncertainty surrounding intermediate term projections has become much greater as a consequence of widening gaps in our knowledge, rather than changes in the volatility of economic activity. The excellent research that underlies estimates of prices and quantities of computer investment in NIPA has provided much needed illumination of the impact of information technology. But this is only part of the contribution of information technology to economic growth and may not be the largest part. As the role of technology continues to increase, ignorance of the most basic empirical facts about the information economy will plague researchers as well as forecasters. The uncertainties about past and future economic growth will not be resolved quickly. This is, of course, a guarantee that the lively economic debate now unfolding will continue for the foreseeable future.

The first priority for empirical research must be constant-quality price indexes for a wider variety of high-tech assets. These assets are becoming increasingly important in the US economy, but only a small portion have constant-quality price deflators that translate the improved production characteristics into accurate measures of investment and output. This echoes the earlier findings of Gordon (1990), who reported that official price measures substantially overstate price changes for capital goods. In fact, Gordon identified computers and communications equipment as two assets with the largest overstatements, together with aircraft, which we have not included.[56] Much remains to be done to complete Gordon's program of implementing constant-quality price deflators for all components of investment in NIPA.

The second priority for research is to decompose the sources of economic growth to the industry level. Fortunately, the required methodology required is well established and increasingly familiar. Domar aggregation over industries underlies back-of-the-envelope calculations of the contribution of information technology to economic growth in section 3, as well as the more careful and comprehensive view of the contributions of industry-level productivity that we have presented in section 4. This view will require considerable refinement to discriminate among alternative perspectives on the rapidly unfolding information economy. However, the evidence already available is informative on the most important issue. This is the 'new economy' view that the impact of information technology is like phlogiston, an invisible substance that spills over into every kind of economic activity and reveals its presence by increases in industry-level productivity growth across the US economy. This view is simply inconsistent with the empirical evidence.

Our results suggest that while technology is clearly the driving force in the growth resurgence, familiar economic principles can be applied. Productivity growth in the production of information technology is responsible for a sizable part of the recent spurt in TFP growth and can be identified with price declines in high-tech assets and semiconductors. This has induced an eruption of investment in these assets that is responsible for capital deepening in the industries that use information technology. Information technology provides a dramatic illustration of economic incentives at work! However, there is no corresponding eruption of industry-level productivity growth in these sectors that would herald the arrival of phlogiston-like spillovers from production in the information technology sectors.

Many of the goods and services produced using high-tech capital may not be adequately measured, as suggested in the already classic paper of Griliches (1994). This may help to explain the surprisingly low productivity growth in many of the high-tech intensive, service industries. If the official data are understating both real investment in high-tech assets and the real consumption of commodities produced from these assets, the underestimation of US economic performance may be far more serious than we have suggested. Only as the statistical agencies continue their slow progress towards improved data and implementation of state-of-the-art methodology will this murky picture become more transparent.

Notes

*   We are indebted to Mun S. Ho for his comments and assistance with the industry and labour data. We are also grateful to Bob Arnold of CBO for helpful comments and discussions of the CBO's results and methods and Bruce Grimm and Dave Wasshausen of BEA for details on the BEA investment data and prices. Our thanks are due to Erwin Diewert, Robert Gordon, Steve Oliner, Dan Sichel, as well as seminar participants at the Brookings Panel on Economic Activity, the Federal Reserve Bank of New York, and the Federal Reserve Board for helpful comments and advice. Dave Fiore provided excellent research assistance. The views expressed in this chapter are those of the authors only and do not necessarily reflect the views of the Federal Reserve Bank of New York or the Federal Reserve System.

1   Labour productivity growth for the business sector averaged 2.7 per cent for 1995–99, the four fastest annual growth rates in the 1990s, except for a temporary jump of 4.3 per cent in 1992 as the economy exited recession (BLS, 2000).

2   Stiroh (1999) critiques alternative new economy views, Triplett (1999) examines data issues in the new economy debate, and Gordon (1999b) provides an often-cited rebuttal of the new economy thesis.

3   Our work on computers builds on the groundbreaking research of Oliner and Sichel (1994, 2000) and Sichel (1997, 1999), and our own earlier results, reported in Jorgenson and Stiroh (1995, 1999, 2000) and Stiroh (1998a). Other valuable work on computers includes Haimowitz (1998), Kiley (1999), and Whelan (1999). Gordon (1999a) provides valuable historical perspective on the sources of US economic growth and Brynjolfsson and Yang (1996) review the micro evidence on computers and productivity.

4   See Baily and Gordon (1988), Stiroh (1998a), Jorgenson and Stiroh (1999) and Department of Commerce (1999) for earlier discussions of relative price changes and input substitution in the high-tech areas.

5   BLS (2000) estimates for the business sector show a similar increase from 1.6 per cent for 1990–95 to 2.6 per cent for 1995–98. See CEA (2000, p. 35) for a comparison of productivity growth at various points in the economic expansions of the 1960s, 1980s, and 1990s.

6   See Gullickson and Harper (1999), Jorgenson and Stiroh (2000), and section 4, below, for industry-level analysis.

7   There is no consensus, however, that technical progress in computer and semiconductor production is slowing. According to Fisher (2000), chip processing speed continues to increase rapidly. Moreover, the product cycle is accelerating as new processors are brought to market more quickly.

8   See Dean (1999) and Gullickson and Harper (1999) for the BLS perspective on measurement error; Triplett and Bosworth (2000) provide an overview of measuring output in the service industries.

9   It would be a straightforward change to make technology labour-augmenting or 'Harrod-neutral', so that the production possibility frontier could be written: $Y(I, C) = X(K, AL)$. Also, there is no need to assume that inputs and outputs are separable, but this simplifies our notation.

10 Baily and Gordon (1988), Griliches (1992), Stiroh (1998a), Jorgenson and Stiroh (1999), Whelan (1999), and Oliner and Sichel (2000) discuss the impact of investment in computers from these two perspectives.

11 Triplett (1996) points out that much of decline of computer prices reflects falling semiconductor prices. If all inputs are correctly measured for quality change, therefore, much of the TFP gains in computer production are rightly pushed back to TFP gains in semiconductor production since semiconductors are a major intermediate input in the production of computers. See Flamm (1993) for early estimates on semiconductor prices. We address this further in section 4.

12 See Appendix A for details on our source data and methodology for output estimates.

13 Current dollar NIPA GDP in 1998 was $8,759.9B. Our estimate of $8,013B differs due to total imputations ($740B), exclusion of general government and government enterprise sectors ($972B and $128B, respectively), and exclusion of certain retail taxes ($376B).

14 See Appendix B for details on theory, source data, and methodology for capital estimates.

15 Jorgenson (1996) provides a recent discussion of our model of capital as a factor of production. BLS (1983) describes the version of this model employed in the official productivity statistics. Hulten (2000) provides a review of the specific features of this methodology for measuring capital input and the link to economic theory.

16   More precisely, growth in capital quality is defined as the difference between the growth in capital services and the growth in the average of the current and lagged stock. Appendix B provides details. We use a geometric depreciation rate for all reproducible assets, so that our estimates are not identical to the wealth estimates published by BEA (1998b).

17   Tevlin and Whelan (1999) provide empirical support for this explanation, reporting that computer investment is particularly sensitive to the cost of capital, so that the rapid drop in service prices can be expected to lead to large investment response.

18   An econometric model of the responsiveness of different types of capital services to own- and cross-price effects could be used to test for complementarity, but this is beyond the scope of the chapter.

19   According to Parker and Grimm (2000), total software investment of $123.4B includes $35.7B in prepackaged software, $42.3B in custom software, and $45.4B in own-account software in 1998. Applying the weighting conventions employed by BEA, this implies $46.3B = $35.7B + 0.25*$42.3B, or 38 per cent of the total software investment, is deflated with explicit quality adjustments.

20   Grimm (1997) presents hedonic estimates for digital telephone switches and reports average price declines of more than 10 per cent per year from 1985 to 1996.

21   Appendix C provides details on the source data and methodology.

22   By comparison, BLS (2000) reports growth in business hours of 1.2 per cent for 1990–95 and 2.3 per cent for 1995–98. The slight discrepancies reflect our methods for estimating hours worked by the self-employed, as well as minor differences in the scope of our output measure.

23   Note we have broken broadly defined capital into tangible capital services, K, and consumers' durable services, D.

24   Table 12.2 also presents preliminary results for the more recent period 1995–99, where the 1999 numbers are based on the estimation procedure described in Appendix E, rather than the detailed model described above. The results for 1995–98 and 1995–99 are quite similar; we focus our discussion on the period 1995–98.

25   See Katz and Krueger (1999) for explanations for the strong performance of the US labour market, including demographic shifts toward a more mature labour force, a rise in the prison age population, improved efficiency in labour markets, and the 'weak backbone hypothesis' of worker restraint.

26   We are indebted to Dan Sichel for very helpful discussions of this timing convention.

27   Oliner and Sichel (2000) provide a detailed comparison of the results across several studies of computers and economic growth.

28   See Krugman (1997) and Blinder (1997) for a discussion of the usefulness of this relationship.

29   BLS (2000) shows similar trends for the business sector with hours growth increasing from 1.2 per cent for 1990–95 to 2.3 per cent for 1995–98, while ALP increased from 1.58 per cent to 2.63 per cent.

30   The notion that official price deflators for investment goods omit substantial quality improvements is hardly novel. The magisterial work of Gordon (1990) successfully quantified the overstatements of rates of inflation for the prices of a wide array of investment goods, covering all producers' durable equipment in the NIPA.

31   This point was originally made by Jorgenson (1966); Hulten (2000) provides a recent review.

32   CEA (2000), Gordon (1999a), Jorgenson and Stiroh (1999), Oliner and Sichel (2000), Stiroh (1998), and Whelan (1999) have provided estimates.

33 This calculation shows that the simplified model of Oliner and Sichel (2000) is a special case of the complete Domar weighting scheme used in section IV.

34 elative price changes in the Base Case are taken from the investment prices in Table 12.5. Output shares are estimated based on final demand sales available from the BEA website for computers and from Parker and Grimm (2000) for software. Investment in communications equipment is from the NIPA, and we estimate other final demand components for communications equipment using ratios relative to final demand for computers. This is an approximation necessitated by the lack of complete data of sales to final demand by detailed commodity.

35 Stiroh (1998b) provides details and references to supporting documents.

36 The five sectors – non-farm business, farm, government, residential housing, and households and non-profit institutions – follow the breakdown in Table 1.7 of the NIPA.

37 See CBO (1995, 1997) for details on the underlying model and the adjustments for business cycle effects that lead to the potential series.

38 Note the growth rates in Table 12.5 do not exactly match Table 12.2 due to differences in calculating growth rates. All growth rates in Table 12.5 follow CBO's convention of calculating discrete growth rates as $g = [(X_t / X_0)^{1/t} - 1] * 100$, while growth rates in Table 12.2 are calculated as $g = [\ln(X_t / X_0)/t] * 100$.

39 See CBO (2000, pp. 25 and 43) for details.

40 Earlier upward revisions to TFP growth primarily reflect 'technical adjustment ... for methodological changes to various price indexes' and 'increased TFP projections' (CBO, 1999b, p. 3).

41 See CBO (1995) for details on the methodology for cyclical adjustments to derive the 'potential' series.

42 This is analogous to the sectoral output concept used by BLS. See Gullickson and Harper (1999), particularly pp. 49–53 for a review of the concepts and terminology used by the BLS.

43 BLS refers to this concept as *multi-factor productivity* (MFP).

44 Jorgenson, Gollop, and Fraumeni (1987), particularly Chapter 2, provide details and earlier references; Gullickson and Harper (1999, p. 50) discuss how aggregate productivity can exceed industry productivity in the Domar weighting scheme.

45 We are grateful to Mun Ho for his extensive contributions to the construction of the industry data.

46 Appendix D provides details on the component data sources and linking procedures.

47 Our industry classification is too broad to isolate the role of semiconductors.

48 This conclusion rests critically on the input share of semiconductors in the computer industry. Triplett reports Census data estimates of this share at 15 per cent for 1978–94, but states industry sources estimate this share to be closer to 45 per cent. This has an important impact on his results. At one end of the spectrum, if no account is made for semiconductor price declines, the relative productivity in computer equipment increases 9.1 per cent for 1978–94. Assuming a 15 per cent share for semiconductors causes this to fall to 9 per cent; assuming a 45 per cent share causes a fall to 1 per cent.

49 Dean (1999) summarizes the BLS view on this issue. McGuckin and Stiroh (2000) attempt to quantify the magnitude of the potential mismeasurement effects.

50 See Gullickson and Harper (1999), particularly pp. 55–6, for details.

51 These five industries are Agriculture, Construction, Transportation, FIRE and Services. Note that our estimates for 1977–96 are not given in Table 12.10.

52 These seven other industries that are comparable are agriculture, nonmetallic mining, construction, transportation, communications, trade, and FIRE.

53 The ten industries with small differences are food products, apparel, furniture and fixtures, paper products, printing and publishing, chemical products, primary metals, industrial and commercial machinery, electronic and electric machinery, and miscellaneous manufacturing. The two industries with slightly larger differences are rubber and plastic, and fabricated metals.

54 This aggregate impact is smaller than that estimated by Gullickson and Harper (1999), partly because our shares differ due to the inclusion of a household and government industry. Also, as pointed out by Gullickson and Harper, a complete re-estimation would account for the change in intermediate inputs implied by the productivity adjustments.

55 Oliner and Sichel (2000) argue that Gordon's conclusion is weakened by the new NIPA data released in the benchmark revision, which allow a larger role for ALP growth outside of computer production.

56 Gordon (1990), Table 12.3, p. 539.

References

Baily, M.N. and Gordon, R.J. (1988), 'The Productivity Slowdown, Measurement Issues, and the Explosion of Computer Power', *Brookings Papers on Economic Activity*, 2, pp. 347–420.

Blinder, A.S. (1997), 'The Speed Limit: Fact and Fancy in the Growth Debate', *The American Prospect*, No. 34, September–October, pp. 57–62.

Brynjolfsson, E. and Kemerer, C.F. (1996), 'Network Externalities in Microcomputer Software: An Econometric Analysis of the Spreadsheet Market', *Management Science*, Vol. 42, No. 12, December, pp. 1627–47.

Brynjolfsson, E. and Yang, S. (1996), 'Information Technology and Productivity: A Review of the Literature', *Advances in Computers*, 43, February, pp. 179–214.

Bureau of Economic Analysis (1998a), *Fixed Reproducible Tangible Wealth of the United States, 1925–96*, NCN–0136, May.

Bureau of Economic Analysis (1998b), 'Fixed Reproducible Tangible Wealth in the United States: Revised Estimates for 1995–97 and Summary Estimates for 1925–97', *Survey of Current Business*, 36–45, September.

Bureau of Economic Analysis (1998c), 'Investment Estimates of Fixed Reproducible Tangible Wealth, 1925–1997.

Bureau of Economic Analysis (1999), 'National Accounts Data – Data from the Latest GDP Release', http://www.bea.doc.gov/bea/dn/niptbl-d.htm.

Bureau of Labor Statistics (1983), *Trends in Multifactor Productivity, 1948–1981*, Washington DC: US Government Printing Office.

Bureau of Labor Statistics (1997), *BLS Handbook of Methods*, Washington DC: US Government Printing Office.

Bureau of Labor Statistics (1999), 'Multifactor Productivity Trends', USDL 99–36, 11 February.

Bureau of Labor Statistics (2000), 'Productivity and Costs: Preliminary Fourth Quarter and Annual Averages, 1999', USDL 00–37, 8 February.

Christensen, L.R. and Jorgenson, D.W. (1973) 'Measuring Economic Performance in the Private Sector', in M. Moss (ed.), *The Measurement of Economic and Social Performance*, New York: Columbia University Press, pp. 233–8.

Congressional Budget Office (1995), 'CBO's Method for Estimating Potential Output', *CBO Memorandum*, October.

Congressional Budget Office (1997), 'An Economic Model for Long-run Budget Simulations, *CBO Memorandum*.

Congressional Budget Office (1999a), *The Economic and Budget Outlook: Fiscal Years 2000–2009*, January, Washington DC: Government Printing Office.

Congressional Budget Office (1999b), 'The Economic and Budget Outlook: An Update', *CBO Papers*, July.

Congressional Budget Office (2000), *The Budget and Economic Outlook: Fiscal Years 2001–2010*, January, Washington DC: US Government Printing Office.

Corrado, C. and Slifman, L. (1999), 'Decomposition of Productivity and Unit Costs', *American Economic Review, Papers and Proceedings*, Vol. 89, No. 2, May, pp. 328–32.

Council of Economic Advisors (2000), *The Annual Report of the Council of Economic Advisors*, Washington, DC: US Government Printing Office.

Dean, E.R. (1999), 'The Accuracy of the BLS Productivity Measures', *Monthly Labor Review*, February, pp. 24–34.

Denison, E.F. (1962), *Sources of Economic Growth in the US and the Alternatives before Us*, New York: Committee for Economic Development.

Department of Commerce (1999), *The Emerging Digital Economy II*, June.

Diewert, E. (1980), 'Aggregation Problems in the Measurement of Capital', in D. Usher (ed.), *The Measurement of Capital*, Chicago, IL: University of Chicago Press.

Domar, E. (1961), 'On the Measurement of Technological Change'. *Economic Journal*, Vol. 71, No. 284, December, pp. 709–29.

Federal Reserve Board (1995), 'Balance Sheets for the US Economy', Release C.9, June.

Federal Reserve Board (1997), 'Flow of Funds Accounts of the United States', Release Z.1.

Fisher, F.M. (1992), *Aggregation – Aggregate Production Functions and Related Topics*, Cambridge, MA: The MIT Press.

Fisher, L.M. (2000), 'New Era Approaches: Gigabyte Chips'. *New York Times*, 7 February, C8.

Flamm, K. (1993), 'Measurement of DRAM Prices: Technology and Market Structure', in M.F. Foss, M.E. Manser and A.H. Young (eds), *Price Measurements and their Uses*, Chicago, IL: University of Chicago Press.

Fraumeni, B. (1997), 'The Measurement of Depreciation in the US National Income and Product Accounts', *Survey of Current Business*, July, pp. 7–23.

Gandal, N. (1994), 'Hedonic Price Indexes for Spreadsheets and an Empirical Test for Network Externalities', *RAND Journal of Economics*, Vol. 25, No. 1, Spring, pp. 160–70.

General Accounting Office (1995), 'The Deficit and the Economy: An Update of Long-term Simulations', GAO/AIMD/OCE–95–119.

General Accounting Office (1996), 'Deficit Reduction and the Long Term', GAO/T–AIMD–96–66.

Gordon, R.J. (1990), *The Measurement of Durable Goods Prices*, Chicago, IL: University of Chicago Press.

Gordon, R.J. (1999a), 'US Economic Growth Since 1870: What We Know and Still Need to Know', *American Economic Review, Papers and Proceedings*, Vol. 89, No. 2, May, pp. 123–8.

Gordon, R.J. (1999b), 'Has the "New Economy" Rendered the Productivity Slowdown Obsolete?', manuscript, Northwestern University, 12 June.

Greenwood, J., Hercowitz, Z. and Krusell, P. (1997), 'Long-run Implications of Investment Specific Technological Change', *American Economic Review*, Vol. 87, No. 3, pp. 342–63.

Griliches, Z. (1992), 'The Search for R&D Spillovers', *Scandinavian Journal of Economics*, Vol. 94, pp. 29–47.

Griliches, Z. (1994), 'Productivity, RD, and the Data Constraint', *American Economic Review*, Vol. 84, No. 1, March, pp. 1–23.

Grimm, B.T. (1997), 'Quality Adjusted Price Indexes for Digital Telephone Switches', Bureau of Economic Analysis, unpublished memo.

Gullickson, W. and Harper, M.J. (1999), 'Possible Measurement Bias in Aggregate Productivity Growth', *Monthly Labor Review*, February, pp. 47–67.

Haimowitz, J.H. (1998), 'Has the Surge in Computer Spending Fundamentally Changed the Economy?', *Economic Review*, Federal Reserve Bank of Kansas City, Second Quarter, pp. 27–42.

Hercowitz, Z. (1998), 'The "Embodiment" Controversy: A Review Essay', *Journal of Monetary Economics*, 41, pp. 217–24.

Ho, M.S. and Jorgenson, D.W. (1999), 'The Quality of the US Workforce, 1948–95', Harvard University, manuscript.

Ho, M.S., Jorgenson, D.W. and Stiroh, K.J. (1999), 'US High-tech Investment and the Pervasive Slowdown in the Growth of Capital Services', mimeo, Harvard University.

Hulten, C.R. (2000), 'Total Factor Productivity: A Short Biography', NBER Working Paper 7471, January.

Jorgenson, D.W. (1966), 'The Embodiment Hypothesis', *Journal of Political Economy*, Vol. 74, No. 1, pp. 1–17.

Jorgenson, D.W. (1990), 'Productivity and Economic Growth', in E. Berndt and J. Triplett (eds), *Fifty Years of Economic Measurement*, Chicago, IL: University of Chicago Press.

Jorgenson, D.W. (1996), 'Empirical Studies of Depreciation' *Economic Inquiry*, Vol. 34, No. 1, January, pp. 24–42.

Jorgenson, D.W. (1999), 'Information Technology and Growth', *American Economic Review, Papers and Proceedings*, Vol. 89, No. 2, May, pp. 109–15.

Jorgenson, D.W. (2000), 'US Economic Growth at the Industry Level', *American Economic Review, Papers and Proceedings*, May, forthcoming.

Jorgenson, D.W., Gollop, F. and Fraumeni, B. (1987), *Productivity and US Economic Growth* Cambridge, MA: Harvard University Press.

Jorgenson, D.W. and Griliches, Z. (1967), 'The Explanation of Productivity Change', *Review of Economic Studies*, Vol. 34, No. 3, July, pp. 249–83.

Jorgenson, D.W. and Stiroh, K.J. (1995), 'Computers and Growth', *Economics of Innovation and New Technology*, Vol. 3, No. 3–4, pp. 295–316.

Jorgenson, D.W. and Yun, K.Y. (1991), *Tax Reform and the Cost of Capital*, Oxford: Oxford University Press.

Katz, A.J. and Herman, S.W. (1997), 'Improved Estimates of Fixed Reproducible Tangible Wealth, 1925–95, *Survey of Current Business*, May, pp. 69–92.

Katz, L.F. and Krueger, A.B. (1999), 'The High-pressure US Labor Market of the 1990s', *Brookings Papers on Economic Activity*, 1, pp. 1–87.

Kiley, M.T. (1999), 'Computers and Growth with Costs of Adjustment: Will the Future Look Like the Past'. mimeo. Federal Reserve Board, July.

Krugman, P. (1990), *The Age of Diminished Expectations: US Economic Policy in the 1990s*, Cambridge, MA: MIT Press.

Krugman, P. (1997), 'How Fast Can the US Economy Grow?', *Harvard Business Review*, July–August, Vol. 75, No. 4, pp. 123–9.

Lum, S.K.S. and Yuskavage, R.E. (1997), 'Gross Product by Industry, 1947–96', *Survey of Current Business*, November, pp. 20–34.

McGuckin, R.H. and Stiroh, K.J. (forthcoming), 'Do Computers Make Output Harder to Measure?', *Journal of Technology Transfer*.

Moulton, B.R., Parker, R.P. and Seskin, E.P. (1999), 'A Preview of the 1999 Comprehensive Revision of the National Income and Product Accounts, Definitional and Classification Changes', *Survey of Current Business*, August, pp. 7–19.

Office of Management and Budget (1997), *Analytical Perspectives, Budget of the United States Government, Fiscal Year 1998*, Washington DC: US Government Printing Office.

Office of Management and Budget (2000), *Analytical Perspectives, Budget of the United States, Fiscal Year 2001*, Washington DC: US Government Printing Office.

Oliner, S.D. (1993), 'Constant-quality Price Change, Depreciation, and the Retirement of Mainframe Computers', in M.F. Foss, M.E. Manser, and A.H. Young (eds), *Price Measurement and Their Uses*, Chicago, IL: University of Chicago Press, pp. 19–61.

Oliner, S.D. (1994), 'Measuring Stocks of Computer Peripheral Equipment: Theory and Application', Board of Governors of the Federal Reserve System, May.

Oliner, S.D. and Sichel, D.E. (1994), 'Computers and Output Growth Revisited: How Big Is the Puzzle?', *Brookings Papers on Economic Activity 2*, pp. 273–334.

Oliner, S.D. and Sichel, D.E. (2000), 'The Resurgence of Growth in the Late 1990s: Is Information Technology the Story?', mimeo, Federal Reserve Board, February.

Parker, R. and Grimm, B. (2000), 'Software Prices and Real Output: Recent Developments at the Bureau of Economic Analysis', paper presented at the NBER Program on Technological Change and Productivity Measurement, 17 March.

Sichel, D.E. (1997), *The Computer Revolution: An Economic Perspective*, Washington, DC: The Brookings Institution.

Sichel, D.E. (1999), 'Computers and Aggregate Economic Growth', *Business Economics*, Vol. XXXIV, No. 2, April, pp. 18–24.

Social Security Administration (1992), 'Economic Projections for OASDI Cost and Income Estimates: 1992', Actuarial Study No. 108, SSA Pub. No. 11–11551, December.

Social Security Administration (1996), *1996 Annual Report of the Board of Trustees of the Federal Old-Age and Survivors Insurance and Disability Trust Funds*, Washington, DC: US Government Printing Office.

Solow, R.M. (1957), 'Technical Change and the Aggregate Production Function', *Review of Economics and Statistics*, Vol. 39, No. 2, August, pp. 312–20.

Solow, R.M. (1960), 'Investment and Technical Progress', in K.J. Arrow, S. Karlin and P. Suppes (eds), *Mathematical Methods in the Social Sciences, 1959*, Stanford, CA: Stanford University Press.

Solow, R.M. (1987), 'We'd Better Watch Out', *New York Times Book Review*, 12 July.

Stiroh, K.J. (1998a), 'Computers, Productivity, and Input Substitution', *Economic Inquiry*, Vol. XXXVI, No. 2, April, pp. 175–91.

Stiroh, K.J. (1998b), 'Long-run Growth Projections and the Aggregate Production Function: A Survey of Models Used by the US Government', *Contemporary Economic Policy*, Vol. XVI, October, pp. 467–79.

Stiroh, K.J. (1999), 'Is There a New Economy?', *Challenge*, July–August, pp. 82–101.

Tevlin, S. and Whelan, K. (1999), 'Explaining the Equipment Investment Boom of the 1990s', mimeo, Division of Research and Statistics, Federal Reserve Board, 29 December.

Triplett, J.E. (1986), 'The Economic Interpretation of Hedonic Methods', *Survey of Current Business*, 66, January, pp. 36–40.

Triplett, J.E. (1989), 'Price and Technological Change in a Capital Good: A Survey of Research on Computers', in D.W. Jorgenson and R. Landau (eds), *Technology and Capital Formation*, Cambridge, MA: The MIT Press.

Triplett, J.E. (1996), 'High-tech Industry Productivity and Hedonic Price Indices', *OECD Proceedings: Industry Productivity, International Comparison and Measurement Issues*, pp. 119–42.

Triplett, J.E. (1999), 'Economic Statistics, the New Economy, and the Productivity Slowdown', *Business Economics*, Vol. XXXIV, No. 2, April, pp. 13–17.

Triplett, J. and Bosworth, B. (2000), 'Productivity in the Service Sector', mimeo, The Brookings Institutions, 5 January.

Whelan, K. (1999), 'Computers, Obsolescence, and Productivity', mimeo, Division of Research and Statistics, Federal Reserve Board, 29 December.

Appendix A

Estimating Output

We begin with the National Income and Product Accounts (NIPA) as our primary source data. These data correspond to the most recent benchmark revision published by the Bureau of Economic Analysis (BEA) on 29 October 1999. These data provide measures of investment and consumption, in both current and chained 1996 dollars. The framework developed by Christensen and Jorgenson (1973), however, calls for a somewhat broader treatment of output than in the national accounts. Most important, consumers' durable goods are treated symmetrically with investment goods, since both are long-lived assets that are accumulated and provide a flow of services over their lifetimes. We use a rental price to impute a flow of consumers' durables services included in both consumption output and capital input. We also employ a rental price to make relatively small imputations for the service flows from owner-occupied housing and institutional equipment.

Table 12.A1 presents the time series of total output in current dollars and the corresponding price index from 1959–98. The table also includes the current dollar value and price index for information technology output components – computer investment, software investment, communications investments, computer and software consumption, and the imputed service flow of computer and software consumer durables – as described in Equation (4) in the text.

Table 12.A1 Private domestic output and high-tech assets

Year	Private domestic output		Computer investment		Software investment		Communications investment		Computer and software		Computer and software consumption services	
	Value	Price	Value	Price	Value	Price	Value	Price	Value	Price	Value	Price
1959	484.1	0.25	0.00	0.00	0.00	0.00	1.80	0.47	0.00	0.00	0.00	0.00
1960	472.8	0.24	0.20	697.30	0.10	0.61	2.30	0.47	0.00	0.00	0.00	0.00
1961	490.1	0.24	0.30	522.97	0.20	0.62	2.70	0.47	0.00	0.00	0.00	0.00
1962	527.1	0.25	0.30	369.16	0.20	0.63	3.00	0.46	0.00	0.00	0.00	0.00
1963	562.1	0.25	0.70	276.29	0.40	0.63	2.90	0.46	0.00	0.00	0.00	0.00
1964	606.4	0.26	0.90	229.60	0.50	0.64	3.00	0.47	0.00	0.00	0.00	0.00
1965	664.2	0.26	1.20	188.74	0.70	0.65	3.50	0.47	0.00	0.00	0.00	0.00
1966	728.9	0.27	1.70	132.70	1.00	0.66	4.00	0.47	0.00	0.00	0.00	0.00
1967	763.1	0.28	1.90	107.71	1.20	0.67	4.20	0.49	0.00	0.00	0.00	0.00
1968	811.0	0.28	1.90	92.00	1.30	0.68	4.70	0.51	0.00	0.00	0.00	0.00
1969	877.7	0.29	2.40	83.26	1.80	0.70	5.80	0.54	0.00	0.00	0.00	0.00
1970	937.9	0.31	2.70	74.81	2.30	0.73	6.70	0.57	0.00	0.00	0.00	0.00
1971	991.5	0.32	2.80	56.98	2.40	0.73	6.80	0.60	0.00	0.00	0.00	0.00
1972	1,102.9	0.33	3.50	45.93	2.80	0.73	6.80	0.62	0.00	0.00	0.00	0.00
1973	1,255.0	0.36	3.50	43.53	3.20	0.75	8.40	0.64	0.00	0.00	0.00	0.00
1974	1,345.9	0.38	3.90	35.55	3.90	0.80	9.40	0.69	0.00	0.00	0.00	0.00
1975	1,472.7	0.42	3.60	32.89	4.80	0.85	9.70	0.76	0.00	0.00	0.00	0.00
1976	1,643.0	0.44	4.40	27.47	5.20	0.87	11.10	0.80	0.00	0.00	0.00	0.00
1977	1,828.1	0.47	5.70	23.90	5.50	0.89	14.40	0.78	0.00	0.00	0.00	0.00
1978	2,080.4	0.50	7.60	16.17	6.60	0.90	17.70	0.81	0.10	33.68	0.02	17.84
1979	2,377.8	0.56	10.20	13.40	8.70	0.95	21.40	0.83	0.10	32.81	0.07	19.01

Table 12.A1 cont'd

Year	Private domestic output		Computer investment		Software investment		Communications investment		Computer and software		Computer and software consumption services	
	Value	Price	Value	Price	Value	Price	Value	Price	Value	Price	Value	Price
1980	2,525.9	0.59	12.50	10.46	10.70	1.01	25.70	0.88	0.20	22.11	0.20	25.93
1981	2,825.6	0.65	17.10	9.19	12.90	1.07	29.00	0.96	0.40	18.79	0.25	13.90
1982	2,953.5	0.69	18.90	8.22	15.40	1.12	31.10	1.01	1.40	15.12	0.74	11.96
1983	3,207.7	0.72	23.90	6.86	18.00	1.13	31.90	1.03	2.90	10.71	2.07	10.39
1984	3,610.3	0.75	31.60	5.55	22.10	1.14	36.60	1.07	3.00	9.41	2.37	6.07
1985	3,844.1	0.76	33.70	4.72	25.60	1.13	39.90	1.09	2.90	8.68	2.70	4.93
1986	3,967.4	0.76	33.40	4.06	27.80	1.12	42.10	1.10	5.20	6.54	4.84	5.61
1987	4,310.8	0.79	35.80	3.46	31.40	1.12	42.10	1.10	6.20	5.91	4.91	3.54
1988	4,766.1	0.84	38.00	3.21	36.70	1.14	46.70	1.10	8.20	5.41	6.65	3.24
1989	5,070.5	0.86	43.10	3.00	44.40	1.11	46.90	1.10	8.30	5.02	7.89	2.85
1990	5,346.8	0.89	38.60	2.72	50.20	1.09	47.50	1.11	8.90	4.22	10.46	2.97
1991	5,427.2	0.91	37.70	2.45	56.60	1.10	45.70	1.11	11.90	3.53	11.66	2.44
1992	5,672.4	0.92	43.60	2.09	60.80	1.04	47.80	1.10	12.10	2.68	14.96	2.25
1993	5,901.8	0.93	47.20	1.78	69.40	1.04	48.20	1.09	14.50	2.07	16.26	1.71
1994	6,374.4	0.96	51.30	1.57	75.50	1.02	54.70	1.07	18.00	1.81	16.14	1.17
1995	6,674.4	0.97	64.60	1.31	83.50	1.02	60.00	1.03	21.00	1.44	22.64	1.13
1996	7,161.2	1.00	70.90	1.00	95.10	1.00	65.60	1.00	23.60	1.00	30.19	1.00
1997	7,701.8	1.02	76.70	0.78	106.60	0.97	73.00	0.99	26.20	0.69	33.68	0.71
1998	8,013.3	1.01	88.51	0.57	123.41	0.96	83.60	0.97	30.40	0.48	36.53	0.48

Notes   1   Values are in billions of current dollars.   2   All price indexes are normalized to 1.0 in 1996.

Appendix B

Estimating Capital Services

i) Capital Services Methodology

We begin with some notation for measures of investment, capital stock, and capital services, for both individual assets and aggregates. For individual assets:

$I_{i,t}$ = quantity of investment in asset i at time t
$P_{i,,t}$ = price of investment in asset i at time t
δ_i = geometric depreciation rate for asset i
$S_{i,t}$ = quantity of capital stock of asset i at time t
$P_{i,t}$ = price of capital stock of asset i at time t
$K_{i,t}$ = quantity of capital services from asset i at time t
$c_{i,t}$ = price of capital services from asset i at time t

where the i subscript refers to different types of tangible assets – equipment and structures, as well as consumers' durable assets, inventories, and land, all for time period t.

For economy-wide aggregates:

I_t = quantity index of aggregate investment at time t
$P_{I,t}$ = price index of aggregate investment at time t
S_t = quantity index of aggregate capital stock at time t
$P_{S,t}$ = price index of aggregate capital stock at time t
K_t = quantity index of aggregate capital services at time t
c_t = price of capital services at time t
$q_{K,t}$ = quality index of aggregate capital services at time t

Our starting point is investment in individual assets we assume that the price index for each asset measures investment goods in identically productive 'efficiency units' over time. For example, the constant-quality price deflators in the NIPA measure the large increase in computing power as a decline in price of computers.[1] Thus, a faster computer is represented by more $I_{i,t}$ in a given period and a larger accumulation of $S_{i,t}$, as measured by the perpetual inventory equation:

$$S_{i,t} = S_{i,t-1}(1 - \delta_i) + I_{i,t} = \sum_{\tau=0}^{\infty}(1 - \delta_i)^{\tau} I_{i,t-\tau} \tag{B1}$$

where capital is assumed to depreciate geometrically at the rate δ_i.

Equation (B1) has the familiar interpretation that the capital stock is the weighted sum of past investments, where weights are derived from the relative efficiency profile of capital of different ages. Moreover, since $S_{i,t}$ is measured in base-year efficiency units, the appropriate price for valuing the capital stock is simply the investment price deflator, $P_{i,t}$. Furthermore, $S_{i,t}$ represents the installed stock of capital, but we are interested in $K_{i,t}$, the flow of capital services from that stock over a given period. This distinction is not critical at the level of individual assets, but becomes important when we aggregate heterogeneous assets. For individual assets, we assume the flow of capital services is proportional to the average of the stock available at the end of the current and prior periods:

$$K_{i,t} = q_i \frac{(S_{i,t} + S_{i,t-1})}{2} \tag{B2}$$

where q_i denotes this constant of proportionality, set equal to unity. Note that this differs from our earlier work, e.g., Jorgenson (1990), Jorgenson and Stiroh (1999) and Ho, Jorgenson, and Stiroh (1999), where capital service flows were assumed proportional to the lagged stock for individual assets.

Our approach assumes any improvement in input characteristics, such as a faster processor in a computer, is incorporated into investment $I_{i,t}$ via deflation of the nominal investment series. That is, investment deflators transform recent vintages of assets into an equivalent number of efficiency units of earlier vintages. This is consistent with the perfect substitutability assumption across vintages and our use of the perpetual inventory method, where vintages differ in productive characteristics due to the age-related depreciation term.

We estimate a price of capital services that corresponds to the quantity flow of capital services via a rental price formula. In equilibrium, an investor is indifferent between two alternatives: earning a nominal rate of return, i_t, on a different investment or buying a unit of capital, collecting a rental fee, and then selling the depreciated asset in the next period. The equilibrium condition, therefore, is:

$$(1 + i_t)P_{i,t-1} = c_{i,t} + (1 - \delta_i)P_{i,t} \tag{B3}$$

and rearranging yields a variation of the familiar cost of capital equation:

$$c_{i,t} = (i_t - \pi_{i,t})P_{i,t-1} + \delta_i P_{i,t-1} \tag{B4}$$

where the asset-specific capital gains term is $\pi_{i,t} = (P_{i,t} - P_{i,t-1})/P_{i,t-1}$.

This formulation of the cost of capital effectively includes asset-specific revaluation terms. If an investor expects capital gains on his investment, he will be willing to accept a lower service price. Conversely, investors require high service prices for assets like computers with large capital losses. Empirically, asset-specific revaluation terms can be problematic due to wide fluctuations in prices from period to period that can result in negative rental prices. However, asset-specific revaluation terms are becoming increasingly important as prices continue to decline for high-tech assets. Jorgenson and Stiroh (1999), for example, incorporated economy-wide asset revaluation terms for all assets and estimated a relatively modest growth contribution from computers.

As discussed by Jorgenson and Yun (1991), tax considerations also play an important role in rental prices. Following Jorgenson and Yun, we account for investment tax credits, capital consumption allowances, the statutory tax rate, property taxes, debt/equity financing, and personal taxes, by estimating an asset-specific, after-tax real rate of return, $r_{i,t}$, that enters the cost of capital formula:

$$c_{i,t} = \frac{1 - ITC_{i,t} - \tau_t Z_{i,t}}{1 - \tau_t}\left[r_{i,t}P_{i,t-1} + \delta_i P_{i,t}\right] + \tau_p P_{i,t-1} \tag{B5}$$

where $ITC_{i,t}$ is the investment tax credit, τ_t is the statutory tax rate, $Z_{i,t}$ is the capital consumption allowance, τ_p is a property tax rate, all for asset i at time t, and $r_{i,t}$ is calculated as:

$$r_{i,t} = \beta[(1 - \tau_t)i_t - \pi_{i,t}] + (1 - \beta)\left[\frac{\rho_t - \pi_{i,t}(1 - t_g^q)}{(1 - t_g^e)a + (1 - t_g^q)(1 - a)}\right] \tag{B-6}$$

where β is the debt/capital ratio, i_t is the interest cost of debt, ρ_t is the rate of return to equity, a is the dividend pay out ratio, and t_g^q and t_q^e are the tax rates on capital gains and dividends, respectively. $\pi_{i,t}$ is the inflation rate for asset i, which allows $r_{i,t}$ to vary across assets.[2]

Equations (B1) through (B6) describe the estimation of the price and quantity of capital services for individual assets: $P_{i,t}$ and $I_{i,t}$ for investment; $P_{i,t}$ and $S_{i,t}$ for capital stock; and $c_{i,t}$ and $K_{i,t}$ for capital services. For an aggregate production function analysis, we require an aggregate measure of capital services, $K_t = f(K_{1,t}, K_{2,t}...K_{n,t})$ where n includes all types of reproducible fixed assets, consumers' durable assets, inventories, and land.

We employ quantity indexes of to generate aggregate capital services, capital stock, and investment series.[3]

The growth rate of aggregate capital services is defined as a share-weighted average of the growth rate of the components:

$$\Delta \ln K_t = \sum_i \bar{v}_{i,t} \Delta \ln K_{i,t} \tag{B7}$$

where weights are value shares of capital income:

$$\bar{v}_{i,t} = \frac{1}{2} \left(\frac{c_{i,t} K_{i,t}}{\sum_i c_{i,t} K_{i,t}} + \frac{c_{i,t-1} K_{i,t-1}}{\sum_i c_{i,t-1} K_{i,t-1}} \right) \tag{B8}$$

and the price index of aggregate capital services is defined as:

$$c_t = \frac{\sum_i c_{i,t} K_{i,t}}{K_t} \tag{B9}$$

Similarly, the quantity index of capital stock is given by:

$$\Delta \ln S_t = \sum_i \bar{w}_{i,t} \Delta \ln S_{i,t} \tag{B10}$$

where the weights are now value shares of the aggregate capital stock:

$$\bar{w}_{i,t} = \frac{1}{2} \left(\frac{P_{i,t} S_{i,t}}{\sum_i P_{i,t} S_{i,t}} + \frac{P_{i,t-1} S_{i,t-1}}{\sum_i P_{i,t-1} S_{i,t-1}} \right) \tag{B11}$$

and the price index for the aggregate capital stock index is:

$$P_{S,t} = \frac{\sum_i P_{i,t} S_{i,t}}{S_i} \tag{B12}$$

Finally, the aggregate quantity index of investment is given by:

$$\Delta \ln I_t = \sum_i \bar{u}_{i,t} \Delta \ln I_{i,t} \tag{B13}$$

where the weights are now value shares of aggregate investment:

$$\bar{u}_{i,t} = \frac{1}{2} \left(\frac{P_{i,t} I_{i,t}}{\sum_i P_{i,t} I_{i,t}} + \frac{P_{i,t-1} I_{i,t-1}}{\sum_i P_{i,t-1} I_{i,t-1}} \right) \tag{B14}$$

and the price index for the aggregate investment index is:

$$P_{I,t} = \frac{\sum_i P_{i,t} I_{i,t}}{I_i} \qquad \text{(B15)}$$

The most important point from this derivation is the difference between the growth rate of aggregate capital services, Equation (B7), and the growth rate of capital stock, Equation (B10); this reflects two factors. First, the weights are different. The index of aggregate capital services uses rental prices as weights, while the index of aggregate capital stock uses investment prices. Assets with rapidly falling asset prices will have relatively large rental prices. Second, as can be seen from Equation (B2), capital services are proportional to a two-period average stock, so the timing of capital services growth and capital stock growth differ for individual assets. In steady-state with a fixed capital to output ratio, this distinction is not significant, but if asset accumulation is either accelerating or decelerating, this timing matters.

A second point to emphasize is that we can define an 'aggregate index of capital quality', $q_{K,t}$, analogously to Equation (B2). We define the aggregate index of capital quality as $q_{K,t} = K_t / ((S_t + S_{t-1}) / 2)$, and it follows that the growth of capital quality is defined as:

$$\Delta \ln q_{K,t} = \Delta \ln K_t - \Delta \ln\left(\frac{(S_t + S_{t-1})}{2}\right) = \sum_i (\bar{v}_{i,t} - \bar{w}_{i,t}) \Delta \ln\left(\frac{(S_{t,i} + S_{t-1,i})}{2}\right) \qquad \text{(B16)}$$

Equation (B16) defines growth in capital quality as the difference between the growth in capital services and the growth in average capital stock. This difference reflects substitution towards assets with relatively high rental price weights and high marginal products. For example, the rental price for computers is declining rapidly as prices fall, which induces substitution towards computers and rapid capital accumulation. However, the large depreciation rate and large negative revaluation term imply that computers have a high marginal product, so their rental price weight greatly exceeds their asset price weight. Substitution towards assets with higher marginal products is captured by our index of capital quality.

Investment and Capital Data

Our primary data source for estimating aggregating the flow of capital services is the 'Investment Estimates of Fixed Reproducible Tangible Wealth, 1925–

1997' (BEA, 1998b, 1998c). These data contain historical cost investment and chain-type quantity indices for 47 types of non-residential assets, five types of residential assets, and 13 different types of consumers' durable assets from 1925 to 1997. Table 12.B1 shows our reclassification of the BEA data into 52 non-residential assets, five residential assets, and 13 consumers' durable assets.[4]

Table 12.B2 presents the value and price index of the broadly defined capital stock, as well as individual information technology assets. Table 12.B3 presents similar data, but for capital service flows rather than capital stocks.[5] The price of capital stocks for individual assets in Table 12.B2 is the same as the investment price in Table 12.A1, but the prices differ for aggregates due to differences between weights based on investment flows and those based on asset stocks. The price index for investment grows more slowly than the price index for assets, since short-lived assets with substantial relative price declines are a greater proportion of investment.

An important caveat about the underlying the investment data is that it runs only through 1997 and is not consistent with the BEA benchmark revision in October 1999. We have made several adjustments to reflect the BEA revision, make the data consistent with our earlier work, and extend the investment series to 1998. First, we have replaced the vh series on 'computers and peripherals equipment' and replaced it with the NIPA investment series for 'computers and peripherals equipment', in both current and chained 1996 dollars. These series were identical in the early years and differed by about 5 per cent in current dollars in 1997. Similarly, we used the new NIPA series for investment in 'software', 'communications equipment', and for personal consumption of 'computers, peripherals, and software' in both current and chained 1996 dollars. These NIPA series enable us to maintain a complete and consistent time series that incorporates the latest benchmark revisions and the expanded output concept that includes software.

Second, we have combined investment in residential equipment with 'other equipment', a form of non-residential equipment. This does not change the investment or capital stock totals, but reallocates some investment and capital from the residential to the non-residential category.

Third, we control the total value of investment in major categories – structures, equipment and software, residential structures, and total consumers' durables – to correspond with NIPA aggregates. This adjustment maintains a consistent accounting for investment and purchases of consumers' durables as inputs and outputs. Computer investment, software investment, communications investment, and consumption of computers, peripherals, and software series not adjusted.

Table 12.B1 Investment and capital stock by asset type and class

Asset	Geometric depreciation rate	1998 Investment	1998 Capital stock
Total capital	*n.a.*	*27,954.7*	
Fixed reproducible assets	*n.a.*	*4,161.7*	*20,804.2*
Equipment and software	*829.1*	*4,082.0*	
Household furniture	0.1375	2.3	13.1
Other furniture	0.1179	37.6	224.4
Other fabricated metal products	0.0917	15.9	134.5
Steam engines	0.0516	2.7	60.1
Internal combustion engines	0.2063	1.6	6.9
Farm tractors	0.1452	10.8	60.7
Construction tractors	0.1633	2.9	15.3
Agricultural machinery, except tractors	0.1179	13.1	89.2
Construction machinery, except tractors	0.1550	20.6	99.5
Mining and oilfield machinery	0.1500	2.4	15.6
Metalworking machinery	0.1225	37.1	228.6
Special industry machinery, n.e.c.	0.1031	38.6	288.7
General industrial, including materials handling, equipment	0.1072	34.5	247.5
Computers and peripheral equipment	0.3150	88.5	164.9
Service industry machinery	0.1650	17.9	92.0
Communication equipment	0.1100	83.6	440.5
Electrical transmission, distribution and industrial apparatus	0.0500	26.7	313.0
Household appliances	0.1650	1.5	6.9
Other electrical equipment, n.e.c.	0.1834	15.2	64.5
Trucks, buses, and truck trailers	0.1917	104.5	367.0
Autos	0.2719	19.4	70.2
Aircraft	0.0825	23.0	174.5
Ships and boats	0.0611	3.0	48.4
Railroad equipment	0.0589	5.3	69.1
Instruments (scientific and engineering)	0.1350	30.9	172.6
Photocopy and related equipment	0.1800	22.6	103.0
Other non-residential equipment	0.1473	35.4	184.3
Other office equipment	0.3119	8.4	24.536
Software	0.3150	123.4	302.4

Table 12.B1 cont'd

Asset	Geometric depreciation rate	1998 Investment	Capital stock
Non-residential structures		*2,271.3*	*5,430.6*
Industrial buildings	0.0314	36.4	766.6
Mobile structures (offices)	0.0556	0.9	9.82
Office buildings	0.0247	44.3	829.8
Commercial warehouses	0.0222	0.0	0.0
Other commercial buildings, n.e.c.	0.0262	55.7	955.8
Religious buildings	0.0188	6.6	155.3
Educational buildings	0.0188	11.0	157.4
Hospital and institutional buildings	0.0188	17.76	355.12
Hotels and motels	0.0281	17.08	210.57
Amusement and recreational buildings	0.0300	9.14	103.55
Other non-farm buildings, n.e.c.	0.0249	2.07	67.68
Railroad structures	0.0166	5.78	210.36
Telecommunications	0.0237	13.19	282.09
Electric light and power (structures)	0.0211	12.12	490.04
Gas (structures)	0.0237	4.96	170.98
Local transit buildings	0.0237	0.00	0.00
Petroleum pipelines	0.0237	1.11	39.20
Farm-related buildings and structures	0.0239	4.59	202.73
Petroleum and n.a.tural gas	0.0751	22.12	276.99
Other mining exploration	0.0450	2.03	38.96
Other non-farm structures	0.0450	6.39	107.70
Railroad track replacement	0.0275	0.00	0.00
Nuclear fuel rods	0.0225	0.00	0.00
Residential structures		*363.18*	*8,309.62*
1–4-unit homes	0.0114	240.27	5,628.27
5-or-more-unit homes	0.0140	21.11	871.81
Mobile homes	0.0455	14.64	147.17
Improvements	0.0255	86.29	1,634.15
Other residential	0.0227	0.87	28.23
Consumer durables		*698.20*	*2,981.97*
Autos	0.2550	166.75	616.53
Trucks	0.2316	92.53	327.85
Other (RVs)	0.2316	18.63	64.98
Furniture	0.1179	56.02	372.26

Table 12.B1 cont'd

Asset	Geometric depreciation rate	1998	
		Investment	Capital stock
Consumer durables cont'd			
Kitchen appliances	0.1500	29.83	161.75
China, glassware	0.1650	29.65	141.44
Other durables	0.1650	64.03	309.67
Computers and software	0.3150	30.40	52.30
Video, audio	0.1833	75.15	289.22
Jewellery	0.1500	44.58	228.38
Ophthalmic	0.2750	16.53	53.44
Books and maps	0.1650	25.34	132.51
Wheel goods	0.1650	48.76	231.66
Land	*0.0000*		*5,824.18*
Inventories	*0.0000*		*1,326.31*

Notes

1 Values of investment and capital stock is in millions of current dollars.
2 Equipment and software and other non-residential equipment includes NIPA residential equipment.

Sources: BEA (1998a, 1999b, 1999c) and author calculations.

Table 12.B2 Total capital stock and high-tech assets

Year	Total stock of capital and CD assets		Computer capital stock		Software capital stock		Communications capital stock		Computer and software CD stock	
	Value	Price	Value	Price	Value	Price	Value	Price	Value	Price
1959	1,300.3	0.17	0.00	0.00	0.00	0.00	9.97	0.47	0.00	0.00
1960	1,391.0	0.18	0.20	697.30	0.10	0.61	11.11	0.47	0.00	0.00
1961	1,478.5	0.18	0.40	522.97	0.27	0.62	12.53	0.47	0.00	0.00
1962	1,583.6	0.19	0.50	369.16	0.39	0.63	14.06	0.46	0.00	0.00
1963	1,667.7	0.19	0.95	276.29	0.67	0.63	15.50	0.46	0.00	0.00
1964	1,736.0	0.19	1.44	229.60	0.97	0.64	16.99	0.47	0.00	0.00
1965	1,848.3	0.19	2.01	188.74	1.37	0.65	18.56	0.47	0.00	0.00
1966	2,007.7	0.20	2.67	132.70	1.95	0.66	20.69	0.47	0.00	0.00
1967	2,150.6	0.21	3.38	107.71	2.55	0.67	23.21	0.49	0.00	0.00
1968	2,394.9	0.22	3.88	92.00	3.09	0.68	26.38	0.51	0.00	0.00
1969	2,670.4	0.24	4.81	83.26	3.98	0.70	30.57	0.54	0.00	0.00
1970	2,874.8	0.24	5.66	74.81	5.12	0.73	35.16	0.57	0.00	0.00
1971	3,127.9	0.26	5.75	56.98	5.91	0.73	39.66	0.60	0.00	0.00
1972	3,543.0	0.28	6.68	45.93	6.86	0.73	43.77	0.62	0.00	0.00
1973	4,005.0	0.30	7.83	43.53	8.04	0.75	48.30	0.64	0.00	0.00
1974	4,250.3	0.31	8.28	35.55	9.77	0.80	55.98	0.69	0.00	0.00
1975	4,915.0	0.35	8.85	32.89	11.89	0.85	64.49	0.76	0.00	0.00
1976	5,404.1	0.37	9.46	27.47	13.52	0.87	71.56	0.80	0.00	0.00
1977	6,151.9	0.41	11.34	23.90	15.01	0.89	76.27	0.78	0.00	0.00
1978	7,097.4	0.45	12.86	16.17	17.00	0.90	88.54	0.81	0.10	33.68
1979	8,258.3	0.50	17.50	13.40	21.01	0.95	101.62	0.83	0.17	32.81
1980	9,407.4	0.56	21.85	10.46	25.93	1.01	122.33	0.88	0.28	22.11
1981	10,771.2	0.62	30.26	9.19	31.72	1.07	146.61	0.96	0.56	18.79

Table 12.B2 cont'd

Year	Total stock of capital and CD assets		Computer capital stock		Software capital stock		Communications capital stock		Computer and software CD stock	
	Value	*Price*	*Value*	*Price*	*Value*	*Price*	*Value*	*Price*	*Value*	*Price*
1982	11,538.6	0.66	37.45	8.22	38.14	1.12	168.74	1.01	1.71	15.12
1983	12,033.2	0.67	45.29	6.86	44.40	1.13	185.59	1.03	3.73	10.71
1984	13,247.3	0.71	56.70	5.55	52.68	1.14	207.81	1.07	5.25	9.41
1985	14,837.5	0.77	66.72	4.72	61.66	1.13	228.43	1.09	6.21	8.68
1986	15,985.5	0.81	72.77	4.06	69.38	1.12	246.93	1.10	8.41	6.54
1987	17,137.5	0.85	78.26	3.46	79.17	1.12	262.59	1.10	11.40	5.91
1988	18,632.2	0.90	87.79	3.21	91.54	1.14	280.64	1.10	15.35	5.41
1989	20,223.2	0.96	99.26	3.00	105.64	1.11	297.05	1.10	18.06	5.02
1990	20,734.0	0.96	100.29	2.72	121.57	1.09	311.95	1.11	19.30	4.22
1991	21,085.3	0.97	99.42	2.45	140.37	1.10	324.37	1.11	22.97	3.53
1992	21,296.9	0.96	101.84	2.09	151.41	1.04	334.48	1.10	24.05	2.68
1993	21,631.7	0.96	106.68	1.78	173.39	1.04	342.48	1.09	27.20	2.07
1994	22,050.0	0.96	115.74	1.57	191.63	1.02	353.46	1.07	34.28	1.81
1995	23,346.7	0.99	130.78	1.31	215.13	1.02	362.23	1.03	39.71	1.44
1996	24,300.2	1.00	139.13	1.00	239.73	1.00	380.00	1.00	42.49	1.00
1997	26,070.4	1.04	150.57	0.78	266.63	0.97	407.58	0.99	46.20	0.69
1998	27,954.7	1.08	164.87	0.57	302.41	0.96	440.52	0.97	52.30	0.48

Notes

1 Values are in billions of current dollars.
2 Total capital stock includes reproducible assets, consumers' durable assets (CD), land, and inventories.
3 All price indexes are normalized to 1.0 in 1996.

Table 12.B3 Total capital services and high-tech assets

Year	Total service flow from capital and CD assets		Computer capital service flow		Software capital service flow		Communications capital service flow		Computer and software CD service flow	
	Value	Price	Value	Price	Value	Price	Value	Price	Value	Price
1959	214.7	0.32	0.00	0.00	0.00	0.00	2.55	0.50	0.00	0.00
1960	183.7	0.26	0.05	407.59	0.02	0.64	2.65	0.47	0.00	0.00
1961	192.3	0.26	0.25	602.38	0.08	0.61	2.85	0.45	0.00	0.00
1962	211.9	0.28	0.41	480.68	0.15	0.65	3.44	0.48	0.00	0.00
1963	241.7	0.30	0.56	291.73	0.22	0.60	3.32	0.42	0.00	0.00
1964	260.2	0.31	0.77	196.86	0.34	0.59	3.68	0.42	0.00	0.00
1965	289.2	0.32	1.15	169.47	0.52	0.64	4.73	0.50	0.00	0.00
1966	315.4	0.33	1.99	161.83	0.74	0.65	5.00	0.48	0.00	0.00
1967	333.8	0.33	2.13	103.65	1.03	0.68	5.14	0.45	0.00	0.00
1968	330.2	0.31	2.40	81.43	1.29	0.69	5.43	0.44	0.00	0.00
1969	349.2	0.31	2.54	63.64	1.57	0.69	6.02	0.44	0.00	0.00
1970	382.5	0.33	3.27	61.40	2.09	0.74	7.23	0.48	0.00	0.00
1971	391.4	0.32	4.83	68.40	2.83	0.83	8.34	0.51	0.00	0.00
1972	439.6	0.35	4.44	45.09	3.01	0.77	8.86	0.51	0.00	0.00
1973	517.9	0.38	4.02	30.87	3.47	0.77	12.48	0.68	0.00	0.00
1974	546.6	0.38	6.04	36.38	3.99	0.78	11.48	0.58	0.00	0.00
1975	619.2	0.42	5.36	26.49	5.17	0.88	13.41	0.64	0.00	0.00
1976	678.1	0.44	6.01	24.25	5.60	0.84	13.61	0.62	0.00	0.00
1977	742.8	0.47	6.35	19.16	6.26	0.86	22.37	0.94	0.00	0.00
1978	847.5	0.51	10.71	20.84	7.31	0.91	19.02	0.72	0.02	17.84
1979	999.1	0.57	10.45	12.30	8.19	0.89	26.30	0.89	0.07	19.01
1980	1,026.9	0.56	15.03	10.96	9.99	0.93	23.94	0.72	0.20	25.93

Table 12.B3 cont'd

Year	Total service flow from capital and CD assets		Computer capital service flow		Software capital service flow		Communications capital service flow		Computer and software CD service flow	
	Value	*Price*	*Value*	*Price*	*Value*	*Price*	*Value*	*Price*	*Value*	*Price*
1981	1,221.4	0.66	15.92	7.33	11.76	0.94	23.89	0.64	0.25	13.90
1982	1,251.7	0.65	17.29	5.47	12.54	0.87	25.32	0.62	0.74	11.96
1983	1,359.1	0.71	22.77	5.06	15.11	0.92	29.54	0.67	2.07	10.39
1984	1,570.1	0.79	30.79	4.54	19.02	0.99	33.20	0.70	2.37	6.07
1985	1,660.5	0.79	33.72	3.43	22.41	0.99	39.30	0.77	2.70	4.93
1986	1,559.9	0.71	36.44	2.82	25.88	0.99	43.39	0.79	4.84	5.61
1987	1,846.6	0.80	45.07	2.76	31.84	1.07	55.49	0.94	4.91	3.54
1988	2,185.3	0.89	43.85	2.18	37.72	1.11	67.22	1.07	6.65	3.24
1989	2,243.0	0.89	47.89	1.97	45.96	1.16	67.90	1.02	7.89	2.85
1990	2,345.0	0.90	53.28	1.89	51.07	1.10	69.86	1.00	10.46	2.97
1991	2,345.8	0.88	52.65	1.69	54.07	1.01	66.05	0.91	11.66	2.44
1992	2,335.4	0.86	57.69	1.60	69.11	1.12	70.72	0.94	14.96	2.25
1993	2,377.4	0.85	62.00	1.42	69.32	0.98	80.23	1.02	16.26	1.71
1994	2,719.6	0.94	63.16	1.17	84.14	1.05	89.16	1.09	16.14	1.17
1995	2,833.4	0.94	77.77	1.11	89.18	0.99	101.18	1.17	22.64	1.13
1996	3,144.4	1.00	96.36	1.00	101.46	1.00	92.91	1.00	30.19	1.00
1997	3,466.3	1.05	103.95	0.77	119.80	1.04	100.13	1.00	33.68	0.71
1998	3,464.8	0.99	118.42	0.61	128.32	0.97	103.35	0.94	36.53	0.48

Notes

1 Values are in billions of current dollars.
2 Service prices are normalized to 1.0 in 1996.
3 Total service flows include reproducible assets, consumers' durable assets (CD), land, and inventories.
4 All price indexes are normalized to 1.0 in 1996.

Fourth, we extended the investment series through 1998 based on NIPA estimates. For example, the 1998 growth rate for other fabricated metal products, steam engines, internal combustion engines, metalworking machinery, special industry machinery, general industrial equipment, and electrical transmission and distribution equipment were taken from the 'other' equipment category in NIPA. The growth rate of each type of consumers' durables was taken directly from NIPA.

These procedures generated a complete time series of investment in 57 private assets (29 types of equipment and software, 23 types of non-residential structures, and five types of residential structures) and consumption of 13 consumers' durable assets in both current dollars and chained-1996 dollars from 1925 to 1998. For each asset, we created a real investment series by linking the historical cost investment and the quantity index in the base-year 1996. Capital stocks were then estimated using the perpetual inventory method in Equation (B1) and a geometric depreciation rate, based on Fraumeni (1997) and reported in Table 12.B1.

Important exceptions are the depreciation rates for computers, software, and autos. BEA (1998a) reports that computer depreciation is based on the work of Oliner (1993, 1994), is non-geometric, and varies over time. We estimated a best-geometric approximation to the latest depreciation profile for different types of computer assets and used an average geometric depreciation rate of 0.315, which we used for computer investment, software investment, and consumption of computers, peripherals, and software. Similarly, we estimated a best geometric approximation to the depreciation profile for autos of 0.272.

We also assembled data on investment and land to complete our capital estimates. The inventory data come primarily from NIPA in the form of farm and non-farm inventories. Inventories are assumed to have a depreciation rate of zero and do not face an investment tax credit or capital consumption allowance, so the rental price formula is a simplified version of Equation (B5).

Data on land are somewhat more problematic. Through 1995, the Federal Reserve Board published detailed data on land values and quantities in its 'Balance Sheets for the US Economy' study (Federal Reserve Board, 1995, 1997), but the underlying data became unreliable and are no longer published. We use the limited land data available in the 'Flow of Funds Accounts of the United States' and historical data described in Jorgenson (1990) to estimate a price and a quantity of private land. As a practical matter, this quantity series varies very little, so its major impact is to slow the growth of capital by assigning a positive weight to the zero growth rate of land. Like inventories, depreciation, the investment tax credit, and capital consumption allowances for land are zero.

A final methodological detail involves negative service prices that sometimes result from the use of asset-specific revaluation terms. As can be seen from the simplified cost of capital formula in Equation (B-5), an estimated service price can be negative if asset inflation is high relative to the interest and depreciation rates. Economically, this is possible, implying capital gains were higher than expected. Negative service prices make aggregation difficult so we made adjustments for several assets. In a small number of cases for reproducible assets and inventories, primarily structures in the 1970s, we used smoothed inflation for surrounding years rather than the current inflation in the cost of capital calculation. For land, which showed large capital gains throughout and has no depreciation, we used the economy-wide rate of asset inflation for all years.

Notes

1   See BLS (1997), particularly Chapter 14, for details on the quality adjustments incorporated into the producer prices indexes that are used as the primary deflators for the capital stock study. Cole et al. (1986) and Triplett (1986, 1989) provide details on the estimation of hedonic regressions for computers.
2   A complication, of course, is that ρt is endogenous. We assume the after-tax rate of return to all assets is the same and estimate ρt as the return that exhausts the payment of capital across all assets in the corporate sector. In addition, tax considerations vary across ownership classes, e.g., corporate, non-corporate, and household. We account for these differences in our empirical work, but do not go into details here. See Jorgenson and Yun (1991, Chapter 2).
3   See Diewert (1980) and Fisher (1992) for details.
4   Katz and Herman (1997) and Fraumeni (1997) provide details on the BEA methodology and underlying data sources.
5   Note that these price indices have been normalized to equal 1.0 in 1996, so they do not correspond to the components of the capital service formula in Equation (B5).

Appendix C

Estimating Labour Input

i)   Labour Input Methodology

We again begin with some notation for measures of hours worked, labour inputs, and labour quality for worker categories:

$H_{j,t}$ = quantity of hours worked by worker category j at time t
$w_{j,t}$ = price of an hour worked by worker category j at time t
$L_{j,t}$ = quantity of labour services from worker category j at time t

and for economy-wide aggregates:

H_t = quantity of aggregate hours worked at time t
W_t = average wage of hours worked at time t
L_t = quantity index of labour input at time t
$P_{L,t}$ = price index of labour input at time t
$q_{L,t}$ = quality index of labour input at time t

In general, the methodology for estimating labour input parallels capital services, but the lack of an investment-type variable makes the labour input somewhat more straightforward. For each individual category of workers, we begin by assuming the flow of labour service is proportional to hours worked:

$$L_{j,t} = q_{L,j} H_{j,t} \tag{C1}$$

where $q_{L,j}$ is the constant of proportionality for worker category j, set equal to unity.

The growth rate of aggregate labour input is defined as the share-weighted aggregate of the components as:

$$\Delta \ln L_t = \sum_j \bar{v}_{j,t} \Delta \ln L_{j,t} \tag{C2}$$

where weights are value shares of labour income:

$$\bar{v}_{j,t} = \frac{1}{2} \left(\frac{w_{j,t}L_{j,t}}{\sum_i w_{j,t}L_{j,t}} + \frac{w_{j,t-1}L_{j,t-1}}{\sum_i w_{j,t-1}L_{j,t-1}} \right) \tag{C3}$$

and the price of aggregate labour input is defined as:

$$P_{L,t} = \frac{\sum_j w_{j,t}L_{j,t}}{L_t} \tag{C4}$$

We define the 'aggregate index of labour quality', $q_{L,t}$, $q_{L,t} = L_t/H_t$, where H_t is the unweighted sum of labour hours:

$$H_t = \sum_j H_{j,t} \tag{C5}$$

The growth in labour quality is then defined as:

$$\Delta \ln q_{j,t} = \sum_j \bar{v}_{j,t} \Delta \ln H_{j,t} - \Delta \ln H_t \tag{C6}$$

Equation (C6) defines growth in labour quality as the difference between weighted and unweighted growth in labour hours. As with capital, this reflects substitutions among heterogeneous types of labour with different characteristics and different marginal products. As described by Ho and Jorgenson (1999), one can further decompose labour quality into components associated with different characteristics of labour, such as age, sex, and education.

i)   Labour Data

Our primary data sources are individual observations from the decennial Censuses of Population for 1970, 1980, and 1990, the NIPA, and the annual Current Population Survey (CPS). The NIPA provide totals for hours worked and the Census and CPS allows us to estimate labour quality growth. Details on the construction of the labour data are in Ho and Jorgenson (1999). Table C1 reports the primary labour used in this study, including the price, quantity, value, and quality of labour input, as well as employment, weekly hours, hourly compensation, and hours worked.

Briefly, the Censuses of Population provide detailed data on employment, hours, and labour compensation across demographic groups in census years. The CPS data are used to interpolate similar data for intervening years and the NIPA data provide control totals. The demographic groups include 168 different types of workers, cross-classified by sex (male, female), class (employee, self-employed or unpaid), age (16–17, 18–24, 25–34, 45–54, 55–64, 65+), and education (0–8 years grade school, 1-3 years high school, 4 years high school, 1–3 years college, 4 years college, 5+ years college).[1] Adjustments to the data include allocations of multiple job-holders, an estimation procedure to recover 'top-coded' income data, and bridging to maintain consistent definitions of demographic groups over time.

These detailed data cover 1959 to 1995 and are taken from Ho and Jorgenson (1999). This allows us to estimate the quality of labour input for the private business sector, general government, and government enterprises, where only the private business sector index is used in the aggregate growth accounting results. For the years 1996–98, we estimate labour quality growth by holding relative wages across labour types constant, and incorporating demographic projections for the labour force. Hours worked by employees are taken from the latest data in the NIPA; hours worked by the self-employed are estimated by Ho and Jorgenson (1999).

Table 12.C1 Labour

Year	Price	Labour input Quantity	Value	Quality	Employ-ment	Weekly hours	Hourly compensation	Hours worked
1959	0.15	1,866.7	269.8	0.82	58,209	38.0	2.3	115,167
1960	0.15	1,877.5	289.1	0.82	58,853	37.7	2.5	115,403
1961	0.16	1,882.0	297.7	0.83	58,551	37.4	2.6	113,996
1962	0.16	1,970.7	315.3	0.86	59,681	37.5	2.7	116,348
1963	0.16	2,000.2	320.4	0.86	60,166	37.5	2.7	117,413
1964	0.17	2,051.4	346.2	0.87	61,307	37.4	2.9	119,111
1965	0.18	2,134.8	375.1	0.88	63,124	37.4	3.0	122,794
1966	0.19	2,226.9	413.7	0.89	65,480	37.1	3.3	126,465
1967	0.19	2,261.8	429.3	0.90	66,476	36.8	3.4	127,021
1968	0.21	2,318.8	480.8	0.91	68,063	36.5	3.7	129,194
1969	0.22	2,385.1	528.6	0.91	70,076	36.4	4.0	132,553
1970	0.24	2,326.6	555.6	0.90	69,799	35.8	4.3	130,021
1971	0.26	2,318.3	600.2	0.90	69,671	35.8	4.6	129,574
1972	0.28	2,395.5	662.9	0.91	71,802	35.8	5.0	133,554
1973	0.29	2,519.1	736.4	0.91	75,255	35.7	5.3	139,655
1974	0.32	2,522.2	798.8	0.91	76,474	35.0	5.7	139,345
1975	0.35	2,441.8	852.9	0.92	74,575	34.6	6.3	134,324

Table 12.C1 cont'd

Year	Price	Labour input Quantity	Value	Quality	Employ-ment	Weekly hours	Hourly compen-sation	Hours worked
1976	0.38	2,525.6	964.2	0.92	76,925	34.6	7.0	138,488
1977	0.41	2,627.2	1,084.9	0.92	80,033	34.6	7.5	143,918
1978	0.44	2,783.7	1,232.4	0.93	84,439	34.5	8.1	151,359
1979	0.48	2,899.6	1,377.7	0.93	87,561	34.5	8.8	157,077
1980	0.52	2,880.8	1,498.2	0.94	87,788	34.1	9.6	155,500
1981	0.55	2,913.8	1,603.9	0.94	88,902	33.9	10.2	156,558
1982	0.60	2,853.3	1,701.6	0.94	87,600	33.6	11.1	153,163
1983	0.64	2,904.9	1,849.0	0.94	88,638	33.9	11.9	156,049
1984	0.66	3,095.5	2,040.2	0.95	93,176	34.0	12.4	164,870
1985	0.69	3,174.6	2,183.5	0.95	95,410	33.9	13.0	168,175
1986	0.75	3,192.8	2,407.1	0.95	97,001	33.5	14.2	169,246
1987	0.74	3,317.1	2,464.0	0.96	99,924	33.7	14.1	174,894
1988	0.76	3,417.2	2,579.5	0.96	103,021	33.6	14.3	179,891
1989	0.80	3,524.2	2,827.0	0.96	105,471	33.7	15.3	184,974
1990	0.84	3,560.3	3,001.9	0.97	106,562	33.6	16.1	186,106
1991	0.88	3,500.3	3,081.4	0.97	105,278	33.2	16.9	181,951
1992	0.94	3,553.4	3,337.0	0.98	105,399	33.2	18.3	182,200
1993	0.95	3,697.5	3,524.4	0.99	107,917	33.5	18.8	187,898
1994	0.96	3,806.4	3,654.6	0.99	110,888	33.6	18.9	193,891
1995	0.98	3,937.5	3,841.2	1.00	113,707	33.7	19.3	199,341
1996	1.00	4,016.8	4,016.8	1.00	116,083	33.6	19.8	202,655
1997	1.02	4,167.6	4,235.7	1.01	119,127	33.8	20.3	209,108
1998	1.06	4,283.8	4,545.7	1.01	121,934	33.7	21.3	213,951

Notes

1 Quantity of labour input is measured in billions of 1996 dollars; value of labour input is measured in billions of current dollars.
2 Employment is thousands of workers, hourly compensation is in dollars, and hours worked is in millions.
3 Price of labour input and index of labour quality are normalized to 1.0 in 1996.

Note

1 There is also an industry dimension, which we do not exploit in this aggregate framework, but is used in the industry productivity analysis discussed below.

Appendix D

Estimating industry-level productivity

Our primary data are annual time series of interindustry transactions in current and constant prices, including final demands by commodity, investment and labour inputs by industry, and output by industry. The first building block is a set of interindustry transactions produced by the Employment Projections Office at the Bureau of Labour Statistics (BLS). These data report intermediate inputs and total value-added (the sum of capital and labour inputs and taxes) for 185 industries from 1977 to 1995. A major advantage of this BLS inter-industry data is that they provide the necessary interpolations between benchmark years.

We aggregate the data from the 'Make' and 'Use' tables to generate inter-industry transactions for 35 private business industries at approximately the two-digit Standard Industrial Classification (SIC) level. These tables enable us to generate growth rates of industry outputs, growth rates of intermediate inputs, and shares of intermediate inputs as needed in Equation (29). They also provide control totals for value-added in each industry, the sum of the values of capital and labour services and taxes.

Estimation of capital services and labour input follows the procedures described above for each industry. We collected information from three sources to estimate prices and quantities of capital and labour inputs by industry. An industry-level breakdown of the value of capital and labour input is available in the 'gross product originating' series described in Lum and Yuskavage (1997) of the BEA. Investments by asset classes and industries are from the BEA Tangible Wealth Survey (BEA (1998a), described by Katz and Herman (1997)). Labour data across industries are from the decennial Census of Population and the annual Current Population Survey. We use employ the prices and quantities of labour services for each industry constructed by Ho and Jorgenson (1999).

We also generate capital and labour services for a private household sector and the government sector.[1] For private households, the value of labour services equals labour income in BLS's private household industry, while capital income reflects the imputed flow of capital services from residential housing, consumers' durables, and household land as described above. For government, labour income equals labour compensation of general government employees and capital income is an estimate flow of capital services from government capital.[2] Note government enterprises are treated as a private business industry and are separate from the general government.

Notes

1 The private household and government sectors include only capital and labour as inputs. Output in these sectors is defined via a Tornqvist index of capital and labour inputs, so productivity growth is zero by definition.

2 BEA includes a similar imputation for the flow of government capital services in the national accounts, but our methodology includes a return to capital, as well as depreciation as estimated by BEA.

Appendix E

Extrapolation for 1999

Table 12.2 presents primary growth accounting results through 1998 and preliminary estimates for 1999. The data through 1998 are based on the detailed methodology described in Appendices A–D; the 1999 data are extrapolated based on currently available data and recent trends.

Our approach for extrapolating growth accounting results through 1999 was to estimate 1999 shares and growth rates for major categories like labour, capital, and information technology components, as well as the growth in output. The 1999 labour share was estimated from 1995–98 data, hours growth are from BLS (2000), and labour quality growth came from the projections described above. The 1999 growth rates of information technology outputs were taken from the NIPA, and shares were estimated from 1995–98 data. The 1999 growth rates of information technology inputs were estimated from recent investment data and the perpetual inventory method, and shares were estimated from 1995–98 data. The 1999 growth of other capital were estimates from NIPA investment data for broad categories like equipment and software, non-residential structures, residential structures, as well as consumers' durable purchases; the income share was calculated from the estimated labour share. Output growth was estimated from growth in BLS business output and BEA GDP, with adjustment made for different output concepts. Finally, TFP growth for 1999 was estimated as the difference in the estimated output growth and share-weighted input growth.

PART IV

Chapter 13

The Location of Industry in a Knowledge-driven European Economy

Adriaan Dierx and Fabienne Ilzkovitz

1   Introduction

European industry is facing significant changes in its business environment. New technologies and globalization have modified the conditions of competition and accelerated the diffusion of knowledge, leading to new production patterns and wider consumer choices. These changes have been accompanied by the European integration process which has seen the abolition of trade barriers, the creation of a single market and now of the world's second largest single currency area in terms of economic size after the United States. The future enlargement of the EU to the Central and Eastern European countries should also significantly affect the business conditions in Europe.

Closer European integration has had an important impact on the location of economic activities within the EU. Industries have been given the opportunity to exploit differences in comparative advantages, creating the potential of an increased specialization of countries and regions. There are gains to be expected from these developments as international competition and specialization associated with economies of scale increase productive efficiency. However, there are also adjustment costs and risks associated with such developments. Economic integration and the resulting fall in trade costs tend to raise the attractiveness of central areas relative to peripheral ones and may thus result in an increased concentration of industries in central locations. In other words, the gains of increased integration may be unevenly distributed. Also, the increasingly specialized countries or regions may become more vulnerable to the effects of shocks affecting particular industries.

The rising importance of electronic commerce may have some of the same effects as the European integration process. In particular, the electronic delivery of knowledge-based products is becoming more and more common. Digital information products can be transferred instantly and with minimal costs across national borders, leaving producers a wider choice to locate their production facilities. On the other hand, the production of such digital information products often requires intensive interaction between those involved, giving rise to economies of scale and a clustering of economic activities in attractive locations. However, as final delivery costs are no longer important, such locations are no longer necessarily at centres of final demand and other location factors may become more important. It is the investigation of these other location factors that is one of the aims of this chapter.

The chapter also analyses the changes in industrial location that have occurred in Europe in recent decades and aims to develop an understanding of the underlying forces that influence these changes. Section 2 presents the theoretical framework for investigating the effects of European integration and e-commerce on the location of industry. Section 3 looks at the issue of location from an economic policy perspective. Section 4 presents empirical evidence on recent trends in industrial specialization and geographic concentration in Europe. It highlights some of the major industry and country characteristics driving the location patterns across the EU. A comparison with the US serves to place the changing location patterns in the EU in the right context. The final section discusses policy implications and presents the conclusions that may be drawn from the analysis.

2   Theoretical Framework

This section presents a short survey of the theoretical literature, which can be used to better understand the effects of European integration and e-commerce on specialization and concentration. Specialization is defined as the extent to which a given country or region limits its activities to a small number of industries. The production structure of a country or region is highly specialized if a small number of industries account for a large share of its production or value added. The Nordic countries, for example, are highly specialized in the production of timber, pulp and paper. Geographic concentration is defined as the extent to which EU activity in a given industry is concentrated in a few member states. For example, 70 per cent of European value added in motor vehicles is concentrated in Germany, France and the United Kingdom.

Three strands in economic theory have a bearing on how specialization and concentration may develop with the increasing market integration associated with the Single Market Programme, Economic and Monetary Union, EU enlargement and e-commerce: traditional trade theory, new trade theory and economic geography. Using these theories as a base, the following questions will be considered:

* will integration increase the specialization of countries;
* will this specialization take place between different industries or within industries (inter versus intra-industry specialization);
* will integration increase the concentration of activities in large core markets (core-periphery model) or will other areas be favoured?

Traditional Trade Theory and Interindustry Specialization

Traditional trade theory explains trade specialization patterns by concentrating on the characteristics of each country, which in turn give rise to relative cost differences, called 'comparative advantages'. Ricardian models focus on international differences in the productivity of labour as a source of cost differences while Heckscher-Ohlin model stresses endowment differences or the relative abundance of factors of production. In the two-factor economy of the H-O world, countries will tend to specialize in the export of goods using intensively factors with which they are abundantly endowed.

In more recent models (see Wolfmayr-Schnitzer (1999) for a detailed survey of the literature), technological differences are added as a determinant for industrial specialization. More advanced countries have a special ability to develop new products that they will export to less developed countries. Therefore, the pattern of trade is determined by a continuing process of innovation and technology transfer from the more developed to the less developed countries. In these models, the ability to produce new products is also a source of comparative advantage for more advanced countries.

The traditional trade theory literature can thus explain how countries at different stages of development engage in trade that is characterized by an exchange of goods from different industries (interindustry trade). Taking differences in endowments and in technology across member states as given, traditional trade theory suggests that intensified integration will tend to increase interindustry specialization: with the reduction in trade barriers, industries are better able to exploit differences in countries' comparative advantages. Countries with highly skilled labour and a good infrastructure will tend to specialize in capital intensive, skill intensive and research intensive industries while countries with abundant and cheap labour will tend to specialize in labour-intensive industries. This specialization of countries in different industries should also result in a greater concentration of economic activities across countries. Labour-intensive industries, for example, should be mainly located in countries relatively abundant in cheap labour.

On the other hand, as integration deepens, labour mobility and technological transfers may rise and lead to some convergence of endowments, resulting in a decline in interindustry specialization. In the presence of both forces – lower trade costs and converging endowments – the outcome in terms of the degree of interindustry specialization is indeterminate.

New Trade Theory and Intra-industry Specialization

Comparative advantage is insufficient as the only explanation of specialization as the bulk of trade takes place among industrialized countries despite the fact that these countries share similar factor endowments and technologies. Most trade occurring between these countries is an exchange of differentiated products that fall into the same product category (intra-industry trade). Empirical evidence of this nature led to the development of the new trade theory, which takes into account economies of scale and product differentiation to explain simultaneous imports and exports of similar products between countries.

A first group of new trade theory models assumes that a firm's costs decrease with the size of the local industry but maintains the assumption of perfect competition and constant internal costs. Economies of scale external to the firm form the basis for a regional concentration of industries.

A second group of models is based on internal economies of scale and monopolistic competition. Consumers derive utility from product variety and each variety is produced with increasing returns to scale. In these models, trade becomes a way of extending the market and allowing the exploitation of economies of scale and intra-industry trade is the natural outcome, independent from international differences in technologies and factor endowments.

Finally, a third group of models shifts the interest to the input side. Inputs are produced with economies of scale, and a larger variety of components yield economies of specialization. Trade provides each country with access to the components produced elsewhere, giving rise to 'international economies of scale', leading to intra-industry trade for inputs.

An another important distinction in the various models explaining intra-industry trade is that between horizontal and vertical product differentiation[1]. Intra-industry trade may also involve an exchange of vertically differentiated products, with the rich or capital abundant countries producing goods of higher quality. Income and endowment differences can thus form the basis for vertical intra-industry trade, which is an exchange of different varieties that are of different qualities.

The effects of market integration on trade and specialization are therefore complex. In the traditional analysis of international trade, market integration should lead to a greater specialization of countries and regions according to their respective comparative advantages, leading to an increase in interindustry trade and a greater concentration of economic activities. Interindustry trade brings efficiency gains, with each country or region specializing in those sectors where it is relatively efficient, whilst consumers gain lower prices as a consequence. But this implies a deeper specialization between the less developed and the more advanced regions, each experiencing a contraction of some of its sectors and an expansion of others. For example, high-tech and capital-intensive industries should expand in the more developed regions and labour-intensive industries in the less developed regions. There are important adjustment costs and redistributive implications associated with this evolution.

However, if we take into account imperfect competition, economies of scale and product differentiation, market integration could also lead to intra-industry trade. This last effect is likely to predominate in the European Union, as the factor endowments of the different member states (but not necessarily of the different regions) are converging (WIFO, 1999). This also implies that the industrial structures of these countries are likely to become more similar and that the concentration of specific industries in particular countries may weaken. Intra-industry trade benefits consumers by raising the variety of products on the market. Adjustment takes place amongst firms within industries and thus adjustments costs are lower. However, if intra-industry trade consists of an exchange of vertically differentiated products with the more developed member states specializing in higher quality products, the redistributive effects may nevertheless be significant.

New Economic Geography and Concentration

Traditionally, economic geography models have focused on the forces of agglomeration and dispersion which influence the concentration of economic activities. The interplay between the existence of economies of scale and a reduction of transport costs associated with market integration leads to the prediction that industries with increasing returns should limit the number of their production sites.

Economic geography shows that locations with optimal market access (defined by size, income level, and centrality) may profit first and stronger from integration, as industries with important scale economies have a clear interest to locate near these markets (the 'market access' effect). As large and central markets tend to pay higher wages in order to attract and retain labour, purchasing power is relatively high, causing a positive demand effect and leading to a further concentration of activity in the core. Furthermore, areas that produce a larger variety of related products tend to benefit more from knowledge spillovers and from forward and backward linkages[2] (the 'agglomeration' effect). By contrast, the periphery tends to become more specialized in low wage industries and in industries with constant returns.

Krugman (1991 and 1993), for example, argued that closer European integration could result in a greater specialization and concentration of activities. National obstacles to trade and high transport costs had limited specialization in Europe in the past. However, with the Single Market Programme reducing these barriers and EMU making prices more transparent, the incentive to reap scale economies and agglomeration benefits would rise and production could thus become more concentrated in the regions closest to the largest markets.

However, the arrival of electronic commerce transport cost are becoming insignificant, at least for electronically delivered products. As a result, the importance of the 'market access' effect is greatly diminished in this segment of the market. New economic geography models show that there is a u-shaped relationship between the level of transport costs and the degree of geographical concentration: very low and very high transport costs favour dispersion, but intermediate levels a concentration of economic activity. When transport costs are initially very high and then reduced, production will move to the larger markets because of economies of scale and this will lead to an increased concentration of activities. But, as the concentration of industry increases in the core, this will give rise to an increase in the price of immobile factors[3] or to congestion costs. A further reduction in trade costs and a decline in the relative prices of immobile factors in the periphery therefore may allow a re-dispersion of economic activities over space.

This does not imply that industries producing digital information products will become fully dispersed. Knowledge spillovers between firms are especially important in high-tech industries, as are forward and backward linkages with enterprises engaged in related activities. The agglomeration effects will continue be important even if outputs and inputs are transferred electronically. The concentration of economic activity in one location will continue to create a favourable environment that supports further concentration and the spatial concentration of economic activity will continue to be a self-reinforcing process. However, this process need no longer occur in an area close to the main centres of consumer demand. Production clusters may equally well develop in more peripheral areas if other location factors, such as the quality of the labour force or the research infrastructure, are favourable.

3 Why is the Location Issue Relevant from an Economic Policy Perspective?

From an economic policy perspective, there are three major reasons why it is important to monitor the changes in specialization and concentration in Europe. They are briefly explained hereafter.

Competitiveness

A first reason why it is necessary to monitor the specialization and concentration movements in Europe is to see whether the structural changes needed for catching up to the US are taking place. In this respect, Figure 13.1 shows that Europe is still lagging behind the US, in terms of standards of living, productivity and employment while European price levels remain well above those in the US.

The ability to exploit the existing comparative strengths of the member states and to take advantage of new opportunities is a key determinant of the competitiveness of Europe's manufacturing industry. In a world where new technologies are changing production patterns and consumer demand, enterprises need to adjust continuously. The Single Market, by deepening integration and reinforcing the degree of competition in the EU, has contributed to a better operation of product and capital markets and has encouraged European companies to reorganize their production processes and to re-deploy their activities on the whole European market. The introduction of the euro and the increased importance of electronic commerce will likely reinforce some of the benefits associated with the Single Market Programme by making prices and costs more transparent and by facilitating cross-border transactions (see Ilzkovitz and Dierx (1999)).

In this period of deeper European integration, it is crucial to monitor the speed and direction of changes in specialization and concentration of economic activities within the Single Market. On the one hand, to see whether European companies exploit the opportunities created and adapt to the new

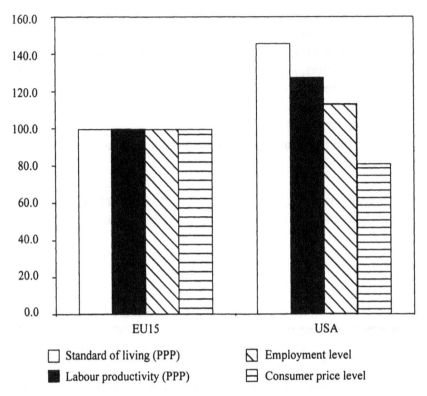

Figure 13.1   A comparison of the EU and US economic performance in 1996

Source: Commission Services.

economic conditions because these are the driving forces of Europe's increased competitiveness. In this respect, the European Commission (1999b) shows that those member states exhibiting the most dynamic industrial structures over the last ten years have tended to enjoy faster growth. On the other hand, to be able to detect whether the risks associated with such a process of specialization and concentration do materialize. These risks are described below.

Risk of asymmetric shocks in EMU

In a monetary union, an increase in interindustry specialization may create a particular problem, which is exacerbated by the loss of the exchange rate as an instrument for adjustment to economic disturbances: an over-specialization of individual countries or regions in narrow product groups might render them more vulnerable to sector-specific shocks.

The vulnerability of EMU to this type of asymmetric shock depends on the impact of EMU on specialization. The literature holds two opposing views on this issue (see Buti and Sapir, 1998). The first, associated with Krugman, claims that European integration is likely to increase regional specialization in Europe, implying greater vulnerability to sector-specific shocks. The second view, based on empirical findings (European Commission, 1996 and 1997) showing that European integration tends to promote intra-industry trade and income convergence, argues that EMU is likely to reduce national specialization and thereby, lower the vulnerability of member states to asymmetric shocks. It is difficult to settle this question as empirical results depend critically on the level of aggregation of the data considered. We will nevertheless attempt to touch on this issue in Section 4.

Risk of Polarization and Regional Imbalances

The economic geography theory shows that, when trade costs fall, location decisions of firms are driven more and more by motives related to the external environment and economies of scale. Factors such as the availability of good transportation and communication infrastructure, the presence of a highly skilled and specialized labour force and the proximity of customers and suppliers influence the location decisions of firms. Agglomeration economies arising with the clustering of firms, workers and consumers in certain locations are an explanation for geographical concentration of economic activities.

From a regional policy point of view, the danger lies in the fact that these agglomeration forces may strengthen the imbalances between richer and poorer regions. Knowledge-based industries are most likely to develop in economically advanced areas where the demand for their innovative products emerged. Once the industry has reached a certain size, there is often little reason to move elsewhere. Other areas might be locked into mature, declining industries or low quality products. History plays a key role in all of this, as cumulative and circular causation will maintain and magnify specialization patterns, once they have been established. Even though such patterns are driven by economic motives and may enhance productivity and competitiveness at the European level, it may endanger the real convergence process, which would not be politically and socially sustainable in the long run. It is therefore important to understand whether such a process is currently going on and if this is the case, in which industries.

4   Recent Empirical Evidence

The theoretical approaches presented in Section 2 do not permit one to draw clear-cut conclusions on the effects of EU market integration on the specialization and concentration of economic activities. The predictions from theory suggest that specialization and concentration may go either way, especially in the longer run. From an economic policy perspective it is nevertheless important to develop a better understanding of ongoing changes in the location of economic activity within the EU. As argued in Section 3, one needs to know what changes have occurred in the past and what future developments will be like.

This section describes recent developments in the industrial specialization of the EU member states and the country concentration of the various industries. This description is based on results from two recent studies (see Box 13.1) carried out for the Commission by WIFO (1999) and the CEPR (Midelfart-Knarvik et al., 2000). Other relevant empirical literature is considered as well. The description will be followed by a comparison of the degree of industrial specialization and spatial concentration in the EU with that in the USA. The part concludes with an analysis of the main determinants of location of economic activity within the EU.

Industrial Specialization of EU Member States

Both the value-added data used by WIFO and the production data used by the CEPR show an increase in country specialization from the early 1980s onwards. Such increase might have been expected in light of the Single Market Programme and other measures taken towards EU market integration. The more integrated markets are, the more likely countries are to specialize. It is therefore not so surprising that specialization is increasing but rather that the rate of change is so modest (see Table 13.1).[4] However, WIFO makes the observation that the speed of change has accelerated, being faster through the nineties than it was at the end of the 1980s.

The CEPR study, going back further in time, makes the reminder that in the 1970s the industrial structures of the European economies were still converging, implying that from a long-run perspective there has been a definite change in trend, which has been particularly striking for the countries that have recently entered into the European Union (see Figure 13.2). While the degree of industrial specialization in the original six has risen gradually, change was rather more abrupt for the Austria, Finland and Sweden and to a lesser degree

Box 1: Data issues

A first look at the empirical literature on industrial location shows that the analysis is very much data-driven. The measures that immediately come to mind when trying to determine a country's industrial specialization or the distribution over space of an industry are value added or production. WIFO has chosen to work with value-added data for 22 manufacturing sectors and 95 manufacturing industries. At this level of disaggregation, annual data were available for the period 1988-1998 only, which is a relatively short period when looking at changes in location patterns. This is the reason why the CEPR choose to work with production data. Their database ran from 1970 to 1997, but covered 36 manufacturing industries only. The problem is that these relatively aggregate data are often insufficiently detailed, especially when investigating intra-industry specialization. The alternative is to look at trade data, which are capable of providing a high level of detail. Both WIFO and the CEPR have taken this route, but with certain qualms as to whether trade patterns are a true reflection of location patterns.

All of the above refers to the manufacturing sectors for which data are relatively abundant. This is not the case for the services sectors, which are continuously rising in economic importance. The CEPR has chosen to use employment data to carry out an initial but still inconclusive investigation of the location of services activities, while WIFO has decided to leave the services sectors aside for the moment.

There are numerous indicators of specialization and concentration. The annex to this chapter presents an overview of the indicators used by WIFO: concentration ratios (CR3, CR5 and CR10), the Herfindahl index, the standard deviation of the shares, the specialization rate, the dissimilarity index (used by Krugman in his 1991 book), and the Gini coefficient. The CEPR study focuses on the last two indicators.

Table 13.1   Evolution of the production and trade specialization of the EU member states (1970–97)

Krugman specialization index	1970/73	1980/83	1988/91	1994/97
Production	0.43	0.40	0.44	0.47
Exports	0.67	0.62	0.63	0.63

Source: Midelfart-Knarvik et al. (1999).

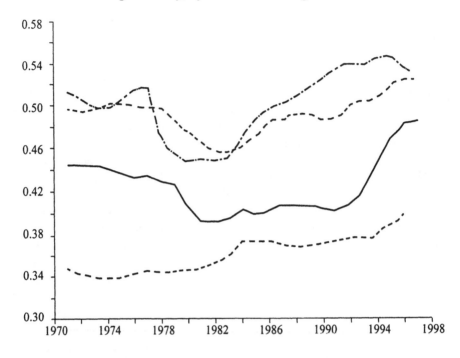

Figure 13.2   Production specialization of EU entrants: Krugman[7] specialization index (two-year moving average, unweighted)

Source: Midelfart-Knarvik et al. (1999).

for Greece, Spain and Portugal. The effects of EU enlargement on industrial specialization appear to be stronger than the effects of market integration (including the Single Market Programme) amongst existing member states. Nevertheless, the steady rise in industrial specialization amongst the six original member states seems to suggest that markets are becoming more integrated.

There are significant other differences between countries. Small countries like Ireland, Greece, Finland and Denmark tend to be more specialized than larger countries such as France, Italy and the UK (see Figure 13.3). A priori, one would expect the more sizeable changes over time to occur in these smaller countries as well. An analysis of the data presented by the CEPR confirms this expectation. In Ireland and Finland, for example, the composition of industry has changed in favour of high technology and increasing returns to scale industries. The labour skills intensity of Irish industry has also risen dramatically. These examples also illustrate the potential for the development

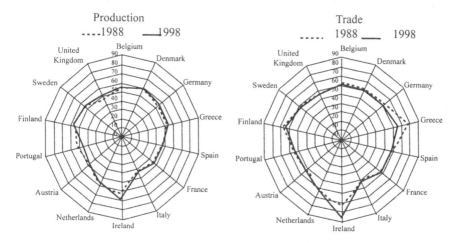

Figure 13.3 Changes in production and trade specialization (1988-98)

Source: WIFO (1999).

of high-tech industries some of the more peripheral regions of the European Union. France, the UK and Germany, which are more centrally located and have large home markets, remain specialized in high technology and high returns to scale industries. Their degree of specialization, however, has been declining slightly. In spite of these changes, the usual division between the North and Central Europe, on the one hand, and the South, on the other, remains valid with the Northern countries more specialized in increasing returns, high-tech and high-skilled labour industries. Amongst the southern countries, Greece and Portugal are the least specialized in these industries. However, in these two countries, the capital-labour ratios in industry have been rising relative to the other EU member states, albeit from moderate levels.

The data reported on export specialization are not always consistent with those on the specialization of production and value added (see Table 13.1). Even though specialization has been increasing consistently since the early 1980s for production, it has remained relatively stable for exports.

The CEPR report suggests that the rapid growth of intra-industry trade has tended to make the still aggregate trade vectors more similar between countries. A number of empirical studies confirm that the share of intra-industry trade in total EU trade has indeed been rising (see Table 13.2 and Commission, 1997, 1999a). This explanation is consistent with the argument that, due to deeper integration and the catching-up process, there is a convergence of factor

Table 13.2   Evolution of intra-industry trade inside the EU (1970–97)

Grubel-Loyd index[1]	1970	1980	1987	1995	1997
Belgium-Luxembourg	0.69	0.76	0.77	0.77	0.81
Denmark	0.41	0.52	0.57	0.65	0.67
Germany	0.73	0.78	0.76	0.80	0.80
Greece	0.22	0.24	0.31	0.27	0.27
Spain	0.35	0.57	0.64	0.72	0.72
France	0.76	0.83	0.83	0.86	0.87
Ireland	0.36	0.61	0.62	0.53	0.53
Italy	0.63	0.55	0.57	0.61	0.60
Netherlands	0.67	0.73	0.76	0.61	0.61
Austria	n.a.	Na	n.a	0.71	0.75
Portugal	0.23	0.32	0.37	0.52	0.55
Finland	n.a	n.a	n.a	0.51	0.50
Sweden	n.a	n.a	n.a	0.69	0.70
UK	0.74	0.81	0.77	0.80	0.80

Note

1   The closer the indicator is to one, the more a member state's trade with its EU partners is intra-industry in nature, and so the more comparable are their industrial structures.

Source: Eurostat and Commission services.

Table 13.3   Convergence of factor endowments between EU member states

Share of the top three member states	1980	1995	Change
R&D capital stock[1]	80.1%	75.9%	–4.2%
Physical capital stock[2]	62.4%	61.5%	–0.9%
Active population[3]	54.4%	56.5%	2.1%

Notes

1   Out of DK, D, E, F, I, Irl, NL, Fin, S and the UK.
2   Out of B, DK, D, EL, E, F, I, NL, A, P, Fin, S and the UK.
3   Out of B, DK, D, EL, E, F, I, Irl, NL, A, P, Fin, S and the UK.

Source: WIFO (1999).

endowments and technology between European countries (see Table 13.3), making intra-industry specialization more likely.

However, the CEPII-report (Commission, 1997) also shows that a rising majority of intra-industry trade involves the exchange of vertically differentiated products. This implies that countries may not be specialized in specific industries but rather in quality ranges within the same industry. The Northern member states are more specialized in the medium and high-quality products while the Southern member states (Greece, Italy, Portugal and Spain) in the low-quality range. However, even in these countries, the share of high-quality products in intra-EU trade has increased over the recent period.

Spatial Concentration of EU Industries

At the aggregate level the degree of spatial concentration of manufacturing industry in the EU has declined (see Table 13.4). Value added, production and trade data all support the message that manufacturing activity has become slightly more dispersed between the EU member states. At first sight this may seem inconsistent with the observed increase in product specialization of these same member states. The most simple explanation for this combination of developments is the fact that the smaller member states have tended to grow faster than the larger ones. Assuming no change in product specialization, more rapid growth for the smaller producers automatically implies a decline in spatial concentration.

Table 13.4   Evolution of the concentration of EU manufacturing production (1970–97)

	1970/73	1982/85	1988/91	1994/97
EU share (D+F+UK)	63.2	59.6	58.7	59.0
Gini coefficient	0.58	0.55	0.56	0.55

Source: Midelfart-Knarvik et al. (1999).

At the level in individual industries, more significant changes in the degree of concentration can be observed. During the 1990s, concentration levels have declined in a majority of industries (see Figure 13.4).

The highly concentrated industries tend to be high- to medium-tech industries with high increasing returns that are both skill and capital intensive.

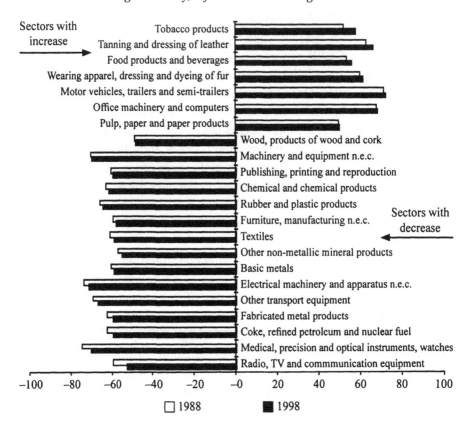

Figure 13.4   Geographic concentration of production (1988–98): share of the largest three producers

Source: WIFO (1999).

Amongst these industries the sharpest declines in concentration have occurred for medical and precision instruments; and radio, television and communication equipment. In these generally rapid-growth industries, the periphery, including in particular Ireland and Finland, has made inroads at the expense of Germany, France and the UK. For motor vehicles, on the other hand, the already high level of concentration has risen further, as Germany has reinforced its position at the expense of both France and the UK.

By contrast, low-tech and labour-intensive industries tend to be more dispersed. However, geographic concentration in such industries as food, beverages and tobacco; and textiles and clothing has increased over the course of the last decade. In textiles and clothing, for example, France, Germany and the UK experienced a decline in market share, while the already important share of the Southern European countries rose further. Dispersion in advertising-intensive industries such as non-metallic minerals; metal products; and printing and publishing, on the other hand, has remained at relatively high levels.

The discussion above has focused on the concentration of industry in the larger EU member states. Nothing is really said about the geographical location of industry, and whether the main locations of an industries are close together or far apart. The only way to resolve such questions is to introduce the concept of geographical distance into the debate. A preliminary analysis by the CEPR at the country level[5] shows a substantial increase in geographical dispersion of manufacturing in the 1970s and early 1980s, which slowed down in the mid 1980s before reversing in the 1990s.

A Comparison with the US

The United States has been an integrated economy much longer than the European Union. Assuming that market integration initially leads to increased specialization and concentration, a first hypothesis can be derived. The current level of regional specialization and industrial concentration in the US should be well above specialization and concentration levels within the EU. Second, assuming that the US and the EU are subject to similar forces of globalization and technological change having an effect on industrial location, recent development in the US may be used as a benchmark to assess the trends observed within the EU.

Due to their different sizes and geographical features a comparison of the levels of specialization and concentration between the EU and the US is difficult. Nevertheless, the data presented in the CEPR report seem to confirm that the US manufacturing industry as a whole is more specialized and more spatially concentrated than EU industry (see Table 13.5). However, important differences between individual manufacturing sectors can be observed. While the motor vehicle sector is relatively more dispersed in the EU, the electronic equipment sector with its important clusters on both sides of the US continent shows appears to be relatively more concentrated in the EU core.

Looking at development over time, two studies by Kim (1995, 1997) on the US economy correspond to some, but not all of the observations made above on the EU economy. He finds for instance that in services, regional specialization has been consistently low. As a result of the increased economic weight of the services sector, regional specialization at the most aggregate level has declined. For manufacturing, an initial phase of greater regional

Table 13.5   Specialization and concentration of manufacturing in the EU[1] and the US (1970–97)

Gini coefficient	1970/73	1980/83	1988/91	1994/97
– of specialization				
EU (production)	0.25	0.23	0.25	0.26
US (employment)	0.45	0.41	0.39	0.37
– of concentration				
EU (production)	0.59	0.57	0.58	0.57
US (employment)	0.68	0.65	0.64	0.62

Note

1   Due to the fact that the EU sectors are aggregated up to the 21 US sectors before the Gini coefficients are calculated, the EU figures reported in Table 13.5 are different from those reported in Table 13.4.

Source: Midelfart-Knarvik et al. (1999).

specialization was observed, followed by phase of dispersion of economic activity during the second half of the century. The CEPR study confirms that this process of US spatial dispersion is continuing.

In Europe, the forces of market integration appear to have had only limited effects thus far. Krugman's argument that these forces may result in a greater industrial specialization of the member states seems to have some, although weak support. No greater concentration of economic activity has been observed, however, which may be attributed in part to the convergence of the factor endowments of the member states associated with the integration process as well as changes in the relative importance of the various determinants of location.

Changing Determinants of Location in the EU

The previous sections gave a plain description of the observed changes over time in location patterns. Changes in location patterns may occur because factor and other endowments of regions or countries change over time, making some locations more attractive and others less attractive. Alternatively, the relative importance of the different locational endowments may change over time.

The more traditional studies (e.g., Ernst & Young, 1998) give an assessment of the relative importance of a wide variety of factors taking into consideration by companies when making a location decision. Such factors may include labour market characteristics including in particular the skills and educational qualifications of the local labour force; infrastructure (transport, telecommunications, energy) and environmental considerations; as well as financial aspects (cost of capital, taxation and financial incentives). These factors vary in importance depending on the sector, project type and country of origin. The different factor endowments of alternative locations, regions or countries may then serve to explain the industrial location patterns observed. Most of these studies are carried out at one point in time and give a snapshot of the relative attractiveness of different locations.

The CEPR study (see Box 2), however, follows the changing interactions between factor endowments and economic geography determinants over time. It shows that a high proportion of the cross-country variation in industrial structure between EU member states can be explained by the interaction between country and industry characteristics. The location of R&D intensive industries, for example, has become increasingly responsive to countries' endowments of researchers. In light of the significantly different R&D skills endowments of the different EU member states, one would expect this development to lead to an increased concentration of R&D intensive industries in a limited number of countries. However, as the WIFO study points out, factor endowments between European countries are converging and less research intensive countries such as Italy and Spain are catching up through the improvement of the research skills of their populations. This trend of converging factor endowments counteracts the rise in country specialization that would result from the increased responsiveness of industry to differences in such endowments.

A similar story would apply to industries that require an abundant supply of skilled labour. The educational level of the population is a highly significant determinant of location and even increasing in importance over time. As educational skills are converging between member states, this does not necessarily imply a rise in concentration levels.

A couple of other results from the CEPR study deserve mentioning:

- backward linkages between industrial sectors are becoming increasingly important determinants of location. Industries which sell a high share of output to industry are, other things being equal, increasingly likely to locate in countries where this industry is located. Auto parts suppliers, for example, will more and more locate close to motor vehicle assembly plants;

Box 2: The model proposed by the CEPR study

Location decisions are driven by interactions between country and industry characteristics. The model used in the CEPR study considers four country characteristics (market potential, agricultural production as a percentage of GDP, secondary and higher education as a percentage of the population and researchers and scientists as a percentage of the labour force) and six industry characteristics (sales to industry as a percentage of output, intermediate goods as a percentage of total costs, economies of scale, agricultural inputs as a percentage of total costs, non-manual workers relative to manual workers, and the R&D share in value added) and analyses six interactions.

There are three interactions between the country abundance in a given factor (agricultural products, skilled labour and R&D) and the intensity of the use of that factor in each industry. For example, one can expect that high-tech industries may tend to concentrate in countries with a high share of researchers and scientists in their labour force. There are three other interactions between market potential, on the one hand, and the importance of economies of scale, forward and backward linkages in each industry, on the other hand. Here it is assumed that central locations will tend to attract industries with high economies of scale and industries with strong forward and backward linkages because the latter will want to be near their suppliers and industrial customers.

A model combining these country and industry characteristics is estimated by OLS covering 14 countries and 32 manufacturing industries for the years 1970, 1980, 1985, 1990 and 1997. The specification chosen is such that the sensitivity of a given industry to a particular factor endowment is a function of the intensity with which the industry uses the factor in question (see Midelfart-Knarvik et al. (1999) for the precise specification of the model). This estimation makes it possible to describe the changing interaction between country and industry characteristics as determinants of industry location. For example, it points to the increasing importance of the supply of researchers in determining the location of high-tech industries.

- forward linkages are becoming increasingly important as well. Industries that are heavily dependent on intermediate goods are locating in central regions with good access to intermediate supplies;
- economies of scale, on the other hand, have been steadily declining in importance as a location factor in the European Union, whereas earlier studies (Brülhart and Torstensson, 1996) still had stressed the importance of this factor.

5 Policy Implications and Conclusions

Current economic analysis does not make it possible to draw unambiguous conclusions about the impact of European integration and the rising importance of electronic commerce on the location of economic activities and about the future direction of changes in specialization and concentration of European industries. First, the theoretical models show that with increased market integration, specialization and concentration may go either way, especially in the longer run. But more importantly, data currently available are not sufficiently up-to-date and disaggregated to give a clear picture of the changes under way. Ideally, data would be both sectorally and regionally disaggregated, because on the one hand, specialization processes sometimes develop at the level of firms or at the level of products rather than at that of industries and one needs very sectorally disaggregated data to capture these developments. On the other hand, it would be necessary to combine sectoral and regional data to better monitor the changes in the distribution over space of industries as there may be changes in specialization and concentration within countries. But again, data unavailability, and in particular the lack of sectoral disaggregation of regional data, prevents such analysis. With these caveats in mind we would like to put forward some conclusions and policy implications from the recent empirical work presented in this chapter.

A first conclusion is that the changes in the specialization and concentration of European industries observed over the recent period are modest and are likely to remain so. There is some evidence of marginally increasing specialization in production since the early 1980s. The Northern countries have become more specialized in increasing returns, high-tech and high-skill industries, with Ireland and Finland having recorded the most important gains. By contrast, trade specialization is slightly less now than it was in the early 1980s, but it has remained relatively stable since the end of the 1980s.

The diverging trend in production and trade specialization might be explained by an increase in intra-industry trade, rendering trade vectors more similar. This explanation is consistent with the observation that, due to deeper integration and the catching-up process, there is some convergence of factor endowments and technology between European countries, making intra-industry specialization more likely. This increase in intra-industry trade is confirmed by several studies.

A second result to be highlighted is that the largest part of intra-industry trade as well as the largest increase has occurred for the exchange of vertically differentiated products. This implies that countries may not be specialized in specific industries but rather in quality ranges within the same industry. The northern member states are more specialized in the medium and high-quality products and the southern member states (Greece, Italy, Portugal and Spain) in the low-quality range. However, even in these countries, the share of high-quality products in intra-EU trade has increased over the recent period.

Third, the available evidence does not support the view that the market integration has led to increased concentration. At the aggregate level, the degree of geographical concentration of manufacturing industries has declined. However, this aggregate picture masks diverging evolutions in the concentration of individual industries.

Geographically concentrated industries are mostly high increasing returns, high and medium-tech, capital intensive and skill intensive industries. Two evolutions are worthwhile to highlight. First, some high-tech and rapid growth industries, such as communication equipment, have become more dispersed and the periphery has made some inroads in these industries. By contrast, some low-tech and labour-intensive industries, such as textiles and wearing apparel, which were more dispersed, have become increasingly concentrated and have reinforced their position in the Southern member states. These evolutions show that there are movements working in opposite directions. However, there are no clear signs of a strengthening of the core at the expense of the periphery.

Companies consider a wide variety of factors when making a location decision and in this respect, country characteristics interact with industry characteristics. Country characteristics include factor endowments (capital and labour intensity but also R&D potential and skill-intensity of labour), size and centrality of markets, infrastructure in transport and telecommunications and business environment (financial and fiscal incentives, state aids). Industry characteristics include factor intensities, economies of scale, the importance of forward and backward linkages, etc. For example, high-tech and high-skill intensive industries tend to locate in countries with a highly educated population with a large proportion of researchers, even if such countries are located in Europe's periphery.

This leads up to our fourth main conclusion: high-tech and high-growth industries are becoming more sensitive to the countries' endowments in research and education. Central locations are increasingly attracting industries higher up in the value added chain (i.e., which are highly dependent on conventionally transported intermediate inputs) while market potential is becoming more and more important for industries with strong backward linkages. By contrast, market potential is becoming less important for industries with high economies of scale. Policy measures, including offers of financial support, do not seem to be a determining element in the location decision of companies.

Coming back to the economic policy issues, it appears that the specialization pattern emerging in Europe should not result in a greater sensitivity of countries to asymmetric shocks. The increase in production specialization is very modest and the trade specialization is more intra-industry in nature. Similarly, there is no very pronounced risk of a strengthening of imbalances between the core and the periphery, though there are forces working in opposite directions. On the one hand, the periphery remains specialized in low-quality products and has increased its position in labour intensive industries. On the other hand, the periphery is becoming increasingly attractive to selected high-tech and high-growth industries because of a relative improvement in its factor endowments. Both movements are related as it appears that endowments such as research and education play a greater role in attracting high-tech and high-skill intensive industries. This implies that investment in education and training and support for basic research are policy measures which should continue to be promoted.

Finally, the slowness of the structural adjustments observed over the last decade is a cause for concern. There is a continuing gap in terms of productivity and growth between the EU and the US. Unless the ability of Europe's manufacturing industry to exploit the existing comparative strengths of the member states and to adapt to new opportunities improves, this gap will not be closed. The US manufacturing industry as a whole is more specialized and more spatially concentrated than the EU industry. This seems to indicate that, despite the success of the Single Market Programme, a number of barriers continue to fragment the European markets and reduce their efficiency. However, with the arrival of the euro and additional economic reforms, the prospects for an improvement in EU market functioning are good.

Notes

1   Horizontal differentiation refers to different varieties of a product that are of similar quality while vertical differentiation refers to different varieties that are of different qualities.
2   Forward linkages refer to the dependence on intermediate products from other producers. Backward linkages refer to the importance of output sold to other producers, as opposed to final consumers.
3   The critical assumption for the u-shaped relationship between transport costs and the geographic concentration of industry is that relative factor costs diverge. Anything that impedes the emergence of such differences (for example, internationally mobile labour and capital) will reinforce the centripetal tendencies (see WIFO, 1999).

4   WIFO defines the speed of change as the sum of the absolute changes in sector shares.
5   This type of analysis is more appropriately done at the regional level.

References

Brülhart, M. and Torstensson, J. (1996), 'Regional Integration, Scale Economies and Industry Location in the European Union', CEPR Discussion Paper No. 1435.

Buti, M. and Sapir, A. (1998), *Economic Policy in EMU*, Oxford: Clarendon Press.

Commissariat Général du Plan (1999), 'Marché unique, monnaie unique : quel scénario pour une nouvelle géographie économique de l'Europe?', Rapport du groupe 'Géographie Economique', April.

Ernst & Young (1998), 'Choosing your European Business Location: A Comparative Assessment of Key Strategic Factors', Research Report, The Economist Intelligence Unit.

European Commission (1996), 'Economic Evaluation of the Internal Market', *European Economy*, No. 4.

European Commission (1997), 'Trade Patterns inside the Single Market', *The Single Market Review*, Rapport CEPII.

European Commission (1999a), 'Economic Reform: Report on the Functioning of Community Product and Capital Markets'.

European Commission (1999b), 'The Competitiveness of European Industry. 1999 Report', Working Document of the Services of the European Commission.

Ilzkovitz, F. and Dierx, A. (1999), 'Du marché unique à la monnaie unique. L'impact sectoriel de l'euro', *Economie Internationale*, 4th quarter.

Kim, S. (1995), 'Expansion of Markets and the Geographic Distribution of Economic Activities: The Trends in US Regional Manufacturing Structure, 1860–1987', *Quarterly Journal of Economics*, Vol. 70, pp. 881–908.

Kim, S. (1997), 'Economic Integration and Convergence: US Regions, 1840–1987', NBER Working Paper No. 6335.

Krugman, P. (1991), *Geography and Trade*, Cambridge, MA: MIT Press.

Krugman, P. (1993), 'Lessons from Massachusetts for EMU', in F. Torres and F. Giavazzi (eds), *Adjustment and Growth in the European Monetary Union*, Cambridge, MA: Cambridge University Press.

Midelfart-Knarvik, K.H., Overman, H.G., Redding, S. and Venables, A.J. (2000), 'The Location of European Industry', Economic Papers No. 142, Economic and Financial Affairs Directorate General of the European Commission, April.

OECD (1999), 'EMU. Facts, Challenges and Policies', OECD Publications.

WIFO (1999), 'Specialisation and (Geographic) Concentration of European Manufacturing', Working Paper No. 1, Enterprise Directorate General of the European Commission.

Wolfmayr-Schnitzer, Y. (1999), 'Globalisation, Integration, and Specialisation of Countries: A Survey of the Literature', WIFO Working Paper No. 12.

Appendix

Indicators of Specialization and Concentration: An Overview[1]

Concentration Ratios (CR3, CR5 or CR10)

This indicator calculates the share of the largest n units in the total and is called CRn, e.g. CR3, if we are talking about the share of the largest three industries. It is easy to calculate and easy to interpret. Its disadvantages are that it makes use only of the information provided by the largest units, that the relative size of each unit within the group of large units is not accounted for, and that there is no good guide as to how large n should be.

Herfindahl Index

This measure is popular in industrial economics and in competition policy. It sums up the squared share of each sector or industry in total manufacturing. Though the measure formally makes use of all information, its value is heavily influenced by the largest (market, export, country) shares.

Standard Deviation of the Shares

This indicator takes into account all available information, highly weighting positive and negative outliers. It is regularly used in specialization studies, but less often in industrial organization.

Specialization Rates (SR)

This indicator uses all available information and gives a rather large weight to small industries and countries. For country specialization, it is the sum of the country's shares in each industry relative to each industry's share of total manufacturing; for geographic concentration of an industry, it is the sum of the industry's share in each country relative to that country's share in total manufacturing. Since these ratios are not symmetric (being between 1 and infinity for positive specialization and between zero and one for negative specialization, e.g.), they are commonly transformed into an SRA index defined as follows: $SRA = (SR - 1)/(SR + 1)$. This transformation is especially useful in econometric work. Its standard deviation is known as sd-SRA.

Dissimilarity Index

This is the sum of the absolute differences between the shares in a country and the norm. All available information is used. Since absolute differences are added together, problems do not arise from relations and the weight assigned to small industries is correctly sized. Krugman (1991) used this index in his analysis of specialization.

Gini Coefficient

This indicator sums up differences in the specialization rates by accumulating the (differences in the) shares of a country and the shares of the norm (EU), after ranking the industries according to their specialization ratios. It is a summary measure using all information, and weighting it. Its advantages and disadvantages are discussed in the literature on income distribution (Lorenz curves). A specific Gini coefficient can correspond to different distributions, and it is difficult to interpret the absolute value derived.

Note

1   Source: WIFO (1999).

Chapter 14

Regional Specialization, Local Externalities and Clustering in Information Technology Industries

Gilles Le Blanc

1   Introduction

Although the theory behind it still remains incomplete and unsatisfactory, the prevalence of geographical specialization is for sure one of the most spectacular stylized facts of the real-world economy. In the US, everyone would for example immediately associate the car industry with Detroit, movies production with Hollywood, aircraft manufacturing with Seattle, defence and microelectronics with California and so on. At the country level, specific policies labelled as regional development, structural cohesion or country planning are precisely set up to address the economic and social consequences of such specialization: disparities between regions, between metropolitan and rural areas, and even sometimes inside cities. In academic research, there has been in the last few years a spectacular renewal of interest in the economic theory of local specialization and growth. A new literature developed on this classic but somehow neglected topic, with many innovative contributions, such as the emergence of a 'new economic geography' (Fujita, Venables and Krugman, 1999), the breaking down of the dynamic components of agglomeration externalities (Dumais, Ellison and Glaeser, 1997; Henderson, 1999) or the revival of the industrial district's idea in an information economy (Porter, 1998).

The amazing growth of the information technology (IT) industries making the digital economy[1] offers in this context an exciting 'natural experiment' and an appealing opportunity for revisiting alternative theories of industrial location, regional specialization and local clustering. First of all, what we call IT-related industries such as telecommunications, software, or internet services, could be strictly considered as disrespectful of geography in the traditional sense. However, various case studies and regional data on employment in the US show that these industries exhibit a high level of geographical concentration. Interestingly enough, we also have empirical evidence of the emergence of brand new IT industrial clusters (e.g. in Virginia, Colorado, Delaware), amid the traditional high-tech states specialized in software, electronics or biotechnology (California, Massachusetts). Even in a world where transportation and communications costs keeps on decreasing, location still matters. But how can one then account for regional specialization in the digital economy? And, to which extent do the alternative theories of agglomeration externalities apply to the IT sectors?

Very little has been said so far about the specific geographical patterns of the digital economy. In fact, because of the lack of consistent and relevant statistics, research efforts logically first concentrated on the overall evaluation of the economic and financial weight of Internet-related activities (e.g. in 1999, the US Department of Commerce report 'Emerging Digital Economy II' or the CREC study on the 'Internet Economy Indicators' at the University of Texas). These macroeconomic overviews measure classic aggregate variables (production, added value, investment, employment, growth) in the IT sectors but without any geographical distribution. Besides, the latest comprehensive statistical survey on the US economy (*Economic Census*) available until the end of 1999 was dating from 1992, i.e. several years before the diffusion of the World Wide Web as the universal navigation tool on Internet for millions of users and the fast growth of electronic commerce. This meant that data on a crucial segment of the digital economy (Internet service providers, portals, electronic financial, security or certification services, etc.) is missing. The regional implications of the structural change driven by the digital economy have therefore not been systematically investigated (the issue is mentioned in a very indirect way – focusing on negative disparities rather than positive features – in the various appraisal of the 'digital divide' in the US).

Existing information is limited to qualitative ranking of the US states according to different variables supposed to capture the main patterns of the new economy (Atkinson and Court, 1999), or sector data on jobs, turnover, exports gathered at the state level by professional bodies such as the American Electronics Association (1999 *Cyberstates 3.0*). One should also mention the great number of management studies devoted to the new firms of the digital economy that underline the very close link between the company and its city of origin: Amazon in Seattle, Dell in Austin, AOL in Virginia near Washington. Despite their informative interest, these stories only focus on one or two exemplary companies and tell us very little on the local industrial structure, the former and existing specialization, inter-firms links. Moreover, it would be quite risky to derive any generalization from some isolated special cases. By examining the state specialization in IT industries, this chapter aims at filling the gap between fragmented company cases and aggregate macro evaluations.

In spring 1999, an extensive fieldwork survey in Denver (Colorado) on the telecommunications industry first suggested that the forces pushing for agglomeration not only arise from increasing returns (such as in the Marshallian tradition extended by Arrow and Romer) but also from the local complementarity between different IT industries. It actually emerged that what we initially considered as a telecom cluster is in fact not restricted to one sector or industry, but rather includes several IT industries (telephony, cable, software, Internet services, data processing). This suggests a specific class of agglomeration externalities, which do not operate within an industry but between different industries, and are usually known as Jacobs diversity externalities (from Jacobs' 1969 pioneering work on the determinants of cities growth). In a similar way, the Denver case appears quite different from the traditional models of industrial districts, where the competitive advantage come from labour market proximity and flexibility (the textile Italian cities) or top University and research environment (the Silicon Valley). From these empirical observations, we derived the 'convergence' hypothesis, which states that the new linkages between telecoms, computer and media industries support new agglomeration externalities, and correspondingly new industrial clustering and regional specialization. This chapter builds on this initial intuition and uses recent data from the 1997 Economic Census to test it in the US case.

The first motivation of this research is to get a better understanding of regional patterns of the digital economy and to contribute that way, with a new applied case, to the current economic debate on the source and scope of agglomeration externalities. Our second motivation comes from a larger research prospect dealing with competition and market structure in the digital economy. It actually turns out that the main engine driving the growth of Internet and electronic commerce is the transformation of a mono-product (telephony) network into multiple interconnected networks, upon which many goods and services of different nature – data, voice, music, video – are transmitted. However, the radical economic consequences of such situation are yet to be systematically explored. This is where comes the widely found idea of convergence, supposed to capture the entire story. Of course, the technological side of the process is extensively studied and supports quite convincingly the concept of convergence: demonstrating how voice telephony might be transmitted over the Internet, Internet on cable networks, or high speed services such as video on an ordinary residential copper line. But a proper economic content of this convergence is clearly lacking. It is nevertheless regularly put forward to explain and justify the on-going wage of mergers in IT industries these last few years (in particular the recent merger between AOL and Time Warner presented as the paradigmatic convergence case). In the present lack of rigorous and homogeneous data at the industry or firm level, we find it necessary to make a detour at the regional level (state in the US case), to rigorously determine the existence and magnitude of the convergence between different IT industries. Once significant evidence have been assembled, it could then motivate and justify future research on the IO foundations of this convergence process and how it translates at the market and industry level. Hence the two questions discussed in this chapter are the following:

- what are the effects of convergence between these industries on local growth and specialization? Does it correspond to the emergence of new industrial clusters? Which theoretical models help explaining the econometric results?
- What is the relative weight of the different agglomeration externalities in 'digital clusters': localization, urbanization, scale and scope economies, input sharing, technological spillovers?

Section 2 presents the different theories of agglomeration externalities and regional specialization, emphasizing their differences according to the source, the scope and the conditions strengthening local effects. Section 3 describes the data, our definition of IT industries and the geographical specialization variables used. Section 4 presents the overall 1997 picture of regional IT specialization in the US. Section 5 tests the convergence externalities with alternative specialization and urbanization theories in fostering employment growth across state-IT industry between 1992 and 1997. Section 6 presents conclusions and possible research extensions.

2   Theories of Regional Specialization and Agglomeration Externalities

While the whole literature on agglomeration externalities stems from the shared need to explain the emergence and persistence of economic geographical concentration, it in fact encompasses quite different approaches and concerns. To simplify, one may distinguish three main strands:

- geographical economy;
- urban growth and specialization;
- industrial clusters.

The first one deals with the economics of industrial location, the resulting regional differences in growth, productivity or employment across the country. Without directly addressing the question of why concentration occurs, it focuses on the reasons why it should persist, self-reinforce and increase, generating huge national discrepancies on observable parameters such as jobs growth, productivity or investment (Krugman, 1991a; Rauch, 1993; Ciccone and Hall, 1996; Ellison and Glaeser, 1999; Fujita and Krugman, 1999). The second strand focuses on the city as the unit for analysis and tries to assess the emergence, the specialization and the growth patterns of cities (Jacobs, 1969; Henderson, 1988, 1999; Glaeser et al., 1992; Holmes, 1999). The final one directly consider what are referred as industrial clusters or districts to explore the determinants of their success, and the reasons that lead firms to co-locate in a specific area (Porter, 1990, 1998; Saxenian, 1994; Roelandt and Hertog, 1998; Baptista and Swann, 1999).

These disparate approaches explain the somehow confusing diversity and heterogeneity of the vast literature on regional specialization and agglomeration externalities. As a matter of fact, depending on the case, these externalities will refer to a firm, an industry, the industrial district, the city, the metro area, the whole state, etc. Some papers might strictly consider the scale economies at the level of the individual firms, whereas some others discuss the overall benefits of local concentration and the corresponding competitive advantage for the cluster or the industrial district as a whole. Finally, many papers mix up in a puzzling way the investigation of externalities' nature and how they work, with the study of the factors reinforcing their magnitude. For these reasons, any reference to the literature of industrial clustering and economy geography should be cautiously used. To avoid any confusion, we first list the different types of externalities examined by the literature, before summing up the unresolved debate on which attributes of the local environment generate and increase externalities.

The easiest way to sort out the different agglomeration externalities is to take up Marshall's (1920) classic view on geographic concentration. Marshall argues that a firm receives three kinds of benefits by locating near other firms in the same industry: information spillovers amongst producers, more efficient labour markets, and savings in transport costs of suppliers' parts and distribution to retailers. Let us then consider three categories of agglomeration externalities: those directly impacting firms' productive efficiency, those related with the labour force, and finally the knowledge spillovers.

The first group includes local scale externalities mentioned by Marshall as a direct effect of industry concentration: the proximity of suppliers and customers or, in the modern vocabulary of development theory, the forward and backward linkages (Bartelsman et al., 1994). In its very basic formulation, this is the argument of natural resource advantage (whose decisive role in oil, coal or steel industries' location during the last century is well documented in Bairoch, 1988; Chandler, 1978). In a broader perspective, transport costs induce firms to locate close to their input suppliers as well as their customers to reduce their shipment and distribution costs. This intense activity of local markets eventually gives rise to another external effect. A high local demand actually allows a greater number of intermediate inputs producers to break-even. And an increased variety of intermediate goods will in turn make the production of final goods more efficient (Krugman, 1991; Ciccone and Hall, 1996). In addition to that, the scale of existing local production of differentiated goods also increases enabling new scale economies through a second-margin effect (Holmes, 1999).

If we now turn to the labour market side, we find several converging external effects. The main one stressed by Marshall – labour market pooling – is that a large local base in a specific industry protects workers from business uncertainty and potential demand-shocks. The idea is that firm demand may wildly and suddenly vary, while industry demand commonly remains roughly stable. Local industry concentration gives workers many other opportunities in case of layoff, without having to move away, nor losing their specific skills. They know that, if they loose their jobs, they should find easily new opportunities from nearby firms, in their very specific skills and qualifications, and without having to relocating. On the other hand, companies benefit from a large market of skilled and experienced employees and can therefore reduce their search and recruitment costs. Local industry success finally plays a major role in attracting and retaining trained and motivated young people (this point is of decisive importance in industries that face national and worldwide skilled labour shortages such most of the IT sectors).

The third group of externalities builds on the idea that geographical proximity facilitates and intensifies transmission of information (often called Marshall-Arrow-Romer externalities after the successive contributions from Marshall, 1920; Arrow, 1962; Romer, 1986). These knowledge spillovers are particularly important in the technological field and may take many forms. Spying, imitation, business interactions, inter-firm circulation of skilled employees, informal exchanges, all this promotes the quick dissemination of innovation or ideas from one firm to the others, without monetary transactions (Saxenian, 1994).

For metering reasons, this last effect is however very difficult to assess empirically. However, several estimations suggest their importance. Ellison and Gleaser (1999) have for instance imagined an indirect method for evaluating them. They put together a set of variables, supposed to capture all sorts of natural advantages in industrial location (state structural characteristics, basic inputs costs, labour inputs, transportation costs, etc.) and found that only 20 per cent of geographical concentration can be attributed to these variables. They argue that the remaining 80 per cent must be explained by knowledge spillovers.

All these kinds of agglomeration externalities differ in what they consider the source of externalities and which factors fosters their effects. One of the main divisions running through the literature opposes the localization to the urbanization theories, depending on whether externalities work within or between industries. In the first case, agglomeration externalities operate within an industry and are best stimulated by local own industry specialization (Henderson, 1988). On the opposite, the urbanization theory argues such specialization hurts and that the local external economies of scale are mostly achieved outside the home-industry through cross-fertilization (Jacobs, 1969). It then claims industry growth will first depend on the overall economic activity in the area, whose measure could be its absolute size, its density or the degree of industrial diversity). The form of externalities at work underlies opposite growth predictions. If localization externalities prevail in an industry, firms are likely to cluster in a few cities or regions, where the high geographical specialization will foster their growth. But in a context of urbanization economies, industries should need a diversified industrial environment to grow faster.

This distinction provides us with a nice model for testing the convergence in IT industries. This hypothesis actually assumes that local externalities first derive from the proximity of several IT industries, which looks like a specific case of Jacobs diversity externalities. We will then study how the local IT industrial diversity explains the growth of a particular industry, in comparison with other explanatory variables such as this specific industry specialization or the cumulative local weight of IT-related activities.

The extension of the notion of geographical concentration beyond a single industry follows two different but complementary ways. The first one, which will prove quite relevant and useful for our topic, argues that an industrial cluster and its boundaries are defined in the first place by competition (Porter, 1990, 1998). Since there is no standard economic definition of a cluster, the identification and the lay out of a regional cluster is often a controversial and disputed issue. Rather than following a technological description, the successive transactions along the chain value or statistical classification, Porter draws the boundaries by searching the linkages across industries and institutions that are most important to competition. Hence he proposes an original definition of a clusters as 'critical masses in one place of unusual competitive success in one field'. Porter still retains the idea of local specialization 'in a particular field' as the foundation of a local cluster and the source of positive dynamic externalities. He however does not restrict it to a single industry and enlarge the scope to include vertically or horizontally related industries, supporting services and specialized infrastructure, all closely interconnected with the initial one through competition. Local scale effects and locational decisions are thus not restricted to the input cost dimension alone but take into account innovation, total systems costs, and the overall productivity gains achieved in being part of a cluster. Even in labour-intensive industries, Porter then argues that the vibrancy and the dynamism of the cluster could easily overturn a relative factor cost disadvantage.

The second approach emphasizes the role of technological change in leading firms to cluster together. Building on the evolutionary economics perspective, it uses at the regional level the concept of national system of innovation (Freeman, 1982; Lundvall, 1992) to suggest another widening of the cluster's scope. The cluster of manufacturers, services providers, and their suppliers encompass users (who are a major source of product or process innovation through so-called learning-by-using process) and many local institution (government, regional and city administration, universities, research centres, professional and trade bodies). Applying at the local level the same systemic approach of the innovation process developed by evolutionary economics, this view focuses on relationships between different agents, and knowledge interactions (Roeland and Hertog, 1998). Geographic concentration clearly favours innovation (technological but also organisational or commercial) through information exchanges or knowledge spillovers between close firms. By locating close to one another, businesses are able to acquire information, communicate and share inputs and benefit from a 'collective' advantage that could not otherwise be achieved alone, while keeping their flexibility and autonomy. Note that in this context, the definition of the cluster is no more industry-based but rather on the strong inter-relationships among firms. The cluster agglomeration's coherence now stems from common goals, a shared vision of local development, and trust sustained by repeated formal and informal cooperation between firms (Saxenian, 1994; Rosenfeld, 1997).

The competition and innovation mechanisms described in the two above literatures put strong objections to the popular view that geography no longer matters for business in the digital economy (Negroponte, 1995). In fact, since market globalization and the ease of transportation and communications allow firms to move their operations virtually anywhere, they now get free from the former natural or inputs constraints and can choose the best place for maximising clustering effects. Two questions then come up: first, is there evidence of regional concentration and clustering in IT industries; second, since, as we have seen, there are a wide range of local externalities, which theory best contribute to the understanding of observed clustering dynamics? The following table summarizes the different theories of agglomeration, and underlines in each case the key variable to consider to test their existence and magnitude in a particular geographical area.

To test the relative importance of each type of agglomeration externalities in the IT industries, we will use geographical data from the US Census Bureau on industry employment across the 51 states. However, in implementing this study, a key issue concerns how to define the IT industries and to appropriately measure regional concentration. The next section deals with these problems.

3   The Data Set

Definition of IT Industries

The choice of the set of industries making the IT sector upon which to base our study is not an easy task: governmental, professional and academic bodies use their own definition (SIC and NAICS statistical system, OECD, Department of Commerce, American Electronics Association, WTO, etc.). The most common method (DoC, 1999) consists in an extensive view bringing together three categories labelled as hardware, software and services, communications (equipment and services):

> IT industries produce, process or transmit information goods and services as either intermediate demand (inputs to production to other industries) or as final products to consumption, investment, government purchases, or exports. Other industries were considered to be IT industries since they provide the

Table 14.1 Theories of agglomeration externalities

References	Cluster approach	Externalities and cluster dynamics	Key variable
Marshall, 1890; Arrow, 1962; Romer, 1986; Henderson, 1986	Industry concentration in a geographical area	Saving on transport costs, labour market pooling, information spillovers within industry	Local industry specialization
Porter, 1990, 1998	Vertical (buyer/supplier) and horizontal (shared resources, technology or market) links	Ibid. + competition	Industry specialization + competition
Jacobs 1969; Glaeser et al. 1992	Interindustry links in a geo area (city)	Knowledge transmission between sectors	Industry variety
Krugman, 1991; Ciccone, Hall, 1996; Holmes, 1999	Spatial concentration and regional productivity differences	Local demand, variety of differentiated products	Scale of local economic activities
Saxenian, 1994; Rosenfeld, 1997	Active channels supporting commercial and information flows	Cooperation, social interaction (trust, shared vision)	Interfirms linkages

necessary infrastructure (communications) or the Internet to operate (DoC, 1999, Appendices, pp. A1–18).

The *Internet Economy Indicators* of the University of Texas (1999) similarly follow a chain value-oriented classification, with three levels: infrastructure, application and intermediary and Internet commerce. A common feature of these classifications is that they include computer and electronic spare components production (such as semiconductors, electronic tubes or printed circuit boards which of course have many different uses outside the IT activities). However, as goods such as computers and hardware electronics are increasingly used in almost every industry or service sector of the economy, it is more and more difficult and debatable to draw accurate boundaries of these sectors. Moreover, the traditional distinction between infrastructure and applications is getting less and less valid in IT industries (for example, does an Internet service provider (ISP) belong to the first or the latter category?). We have therefore chosen not to include hardware manufacturing in our definition and to strictly focus on activities producing final and self-sufficient services to business or individual customers. So, we do not consider computer manufacturing, but we include the numerous services related to the design, installation, maintenance, upgrading and repair of computer systems and networks.

Once the scope of IT activities selected, a second problem lies in the identification of the appropriate statistics to measure them. This task is complicated by the change in US statistical system implemented in 1998. The Standard Industrial Classification (SIC) system has been used to classify employment sectors by the type of activity in which they are engaged throughout the late 1900s. It is based on a four-digit industry coding system and groups industries by sectors such as wholesale trade, services, and manufacturing. Today, new driving industries like biotechnology, software, environmental technology, and communications do not fit into the classic SIC definitions of manufacturing or service sectors. Industries broadly labelled 'biotech' or 'online services' straddle sector definitions, refusing to fall neatly into the categories outlined by the SIC system. The US have launched in 1998 a new industry classification system called NAICS in order to better take into account the growing importance of the IT sectors. This in-depth revision of the economy statistical description aims at capturing new businesses, fast developing high-tech sectors and detailing the various activities confused in indiscriminate and obsolete industries groupings. Therefore the boundaries of the former sectors and industries were redefined; the former SIC four and five-digit classification reshuffled; new numeric codes introduced with detailed codes of maximum six digits. A new Information sector has been defined, bringing together 34 industries that produce, process and distribute information. This major statistical change translates the growing weight of these activities in the US economy. An interesting feature of the NAICS system is that hardware and software industries, which used to be traditionally mixed up within aggregated data, now belong to separate industry classifications. This fits nicely with our definition and our wish to take away hardware manufacturing from our calculations. We eventually distinguish six different IT industries: cable, telecommunications, online services, software, data processing and computer systems design. Table 14.2 presents them, their statistical code and the corresponding scope of activities.

Note the first five industries all belong to the new introduced Information Sector (51), while the sixth one is classified in professional, scientific, and technical services. This subgroup of the vast Services sector brings together activities where human capital is the major input (hence a disparate list mixing lawyer, architecture, design, marketing, consulting, advertising, etc.).

Construction of the Data Set

Our data set is constructed from the Geographical Industry Series of 1997 Economic Census, displaying data at the state level for up to the six-digit industries. It contains information on employment, number of establishments, payroll in 1992 and 1997 for the six IT industries in 51 states. State-industry wages are obtained by dividing annual payroll by the number of paid employees. Data on total state employment come from the US Bureau of Labor Statistics (seasonally adjusted non-farm payroll in March of the selected year). When for confidentiality reasons, employment information is not disclosed, we use the midpoint of the range provided by the Census report. The scale used in employment statistics is rather detailed: 0–19, 20–49, 50–99, 100–249, 250–499, 500–999, 1,000–2,499, 2,500–4,999, 5,000–9,999, etc. When employment in the state-industry is reported to be e, meaning the true number is between 250 and 499, we used 375. The estimation uncertainty so remains limited, except when employment exceeds 5,000.

IT Specialization Measures

Our measure of local specialization in a specific industry is classically the fraction of that industry's employment in the state, relative to its national share

Table 14.2 Description of the IT industries

Industry	NAICS classification	Activities
Telecommunications	5133 Telecommunications	Firms engaged in operating, maintaining or providing access to facilities for the transmission of voice, data, text, video: wired local and long-distance carriers, wireless carriers, telecom resellers, satellite operators.
Cable	5132 Cable networks and programme distribution	Programming material production and broadcast through cable-systems or direct-to-home satellite systems. It comprises the distribution firms that market these programmes to consumers.
Online services	514191 Online information services (subsector of 5141 information services)	Providers of information services (except news) such as Internet Service Providers, online (search routines, browsers, electronic mail) or telephone-based (toll call) information services.
Software	5112 Software publishers	Computer software design, development, publishing and distribution. Includes support operations such as documentation design, installation assistance or support to customers.
Data processing	5142 Data process. services	Electronic data processing services (processing and preparation of reports from customers data bases, automated entry data services, etc.).
Computer services	5415 Computer systems design and related services	Customized software development (e.g. CAD). Design of computer systems integrating hardware, software and communication technologies. On-site management of clients' computer systems and data processing facilities. Disaster recovery services.

of US employment. State s specialization in industry i is then

$$\sigma_{is} = \frac{e_{is}/e_s}{E_i/E},$$

where e_{is} is industry i employment in state s, e_s the employment in state s, E_i the national employment in industry i, and E the US total employment. This ratio measures how specialized is a state in a particular industry relative to what it would be if the employment in this industry was randomly scattered across the country.

We then introduce three variables to capture the state specialization in IT industries.

First, the *state IT mean specialization*, i.e. the average regional specialization in the six selected industries. In state s,

$$MS_s = \frac{1}{6}\sum_i \sigma_{is}.$$

Second, the *IT convergence factor* measuring how close and homogeneous are the six IT industry specializations in that state. Base on an inverse standard deviation form,

$$CF_s = 1/\sqrt{\frac{1}{6}\sum_i \sigma_{is} - MS_s}.$$

And third, the *state adjusted iT specialization* is the IT mean specialization weighted by the convergence factor $AS_s = MS_s \cdot C_s$.

4   IT Regional Specialization in the US: The 1997 Picture

Before discussing state specialization results, it is useful to start with a simple description of the data. Table 14.3 presents for each IT industry the total employment, the state employment mean and standard deviation, the largest state employer and its share of national industry employment (primacy), the share of the five and ten largest state employers, the Herfindhal index (sum over the 51 states of the squared state's share of industry employment), and finally, the Ellison-Glaeser index (an adjusted version of the previous parameter obtained by summing the squared deviations of state employment share in the industry from its share of national total employment). To compare the economic size of these industries, we also report 1997 revenue.

Table 14.3 1997 data by IT industry

1997 data	Cable	Telecoms	Online services	Software	Data processing	Computer systems
Total US employment	174,580	1,012,220	50,280	266,380	263,600	764,660
State employment mean	3,423	19,847	986	5,223	5,169	14,993
Standard deviation	4,057	24,149	1,842	11,560	6,249	20,283
Highest level	20,243 (CA)	116,253 (CA)	9,822 (CA)	77,277 (CA)	27,088 (TX)	101,494 (CA)
Average primacy	0.12	0.11	0.2	0.29	0.1	0.13
5 first states	38%	40%	56%	55%	40%	41%
10 first states	57%	59%	73%	70%	58%	64%
Herfindhal index	0.047	0.048	0.087	0.113	0.048	0.055
Concentration index	0.0036	0.0036	0.029	0.045	0.0077	0.0089
Revenue (billion $)	45.4	260.5	8	61.7	30.8	109

The sum of employment in the six industries amounts to 2,.5 millions, which is comparable to DoC (1999) estimations of 2.6 millions, and slightly lower than the 1.5 millions of the CREC, Univ. of Texas study, which only consider Internet activities. The panel shows that the IT industries, despite huge differences in revenue and total employment, exhibit a common high geographical concentration. In each case, 50 per cent of industry employment in obtained in less than 12 states. The following Lorenz curve, drawing the cumulative geographical concentration for three industries (online services, cable and computer systems design) clearly illustrates this point. The slope for telecoms is very much the same as for cable, while software reproduces the online services' curve, as data processing with computer systems design.

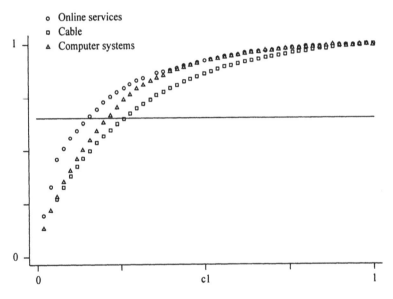

Figure 14.1   1997 geographical cumulative concentration in IT industries

Table 14.3 also gives three widely expected results. First, two key industries – telecoms and computer systems – concentrate 70 per cent of total IT employment. Second, California appears five times out of six as the largest state employer in the industry, amounting to between 10 and 30 per cent of industry national employment. Finally, the most recent and fast-growing industries – Internet online services and software – exhibit a higher level of geographical concentration, than the four other industries, whose concentration measures are roughly similar.

Table 14.4 IT state specialization in 1997

State	IT mean specialization	Convergence factor	Cable specialization	Telecoms specialization	Online services specialization	Software specialization	Data processing specialization	Computer systems specialization
Virginia	2.11	0.64	0.97	1.34	5.10	0.99	1.00	3.27
Massachusetts	1.99	0.89	1.18	1.03	2.14	4.38	1.54	1.68
Colorado	1.90	2.62	1.19	2.01	2.21	1.39	1.34	2.22
Delaware	1.88	0.45	6.72	1.10	0.38	0.41	2.04	0.67
California	1.45	1.53	1.09	1.08	1.83	2.72	0.73	1.24
Nebraska	1.44	0.54	0.92	0.88	0.33	0.30	5.53	0.66
Maryland	1.39	1.80	1.20	1.13	1.08	0.92	1.44	2.59
New Jersey	1.35	1.57	1.17	2.26	0.60	1.01	0.89	2.18
Connecticut	1.29	1.95	2.04	1.04	0.83	0.91	1.98	0.93
New York	1.23	2.36	1.48	1.16	1.93	0.64	1.32	0.83
Georgia	1.21	2.50	1.81	1.56	0.60	0.91	1.15	1.21
Utah	1.12	1.99	0.50	0.89	0.83	2.10	1.29	1.09
Washington	1.10	1.93	0.77	1.10	1.57	1.93	0.37	0.85
North Dakota	1.05	1.38	0.65	0.58	0.47	1.43	2.52	0.67
District of Columbia	1.03	2.95	1.23	1.11	1.45	0.35	0.95	1.08
Texas	1.00	3.84	0.86	1.20	0.68	0.86	1.47	0.94

Let us now present specialization results by state in the US in 1997. Table 14.4 lists the 16 states where the IT mean specialization is greater than one. It shows that a high average specialization can be achieved, either with a very strong (greater than four or five) specialization in one or two industries such as in Virginia (with online services) or in Nebraska (with data processing), either with an homogeneous high specialization in the six industries such as in Colorado, Texas and New York. The third column shows that, whereas the measure of average specialization only varies from 1 to 2.1, the convergence factor is much more contrasted ranging from 0.45 to 3.84 (an 8:5 ratio). The interest of this parameter comes exactly from the fact that it captures the differences above underlined and tells us where the average specialization result comes from. Virginia and Nebraska have precisely amongst the lower convergence factors (respectively 0.64 and 0.54), while Texas which only just passes the required level of one for mean IT specialization, has an almost equal specialization in the six selected industries obtains a record 3.8 convergence measure.

However, these figures only inform us about the intensity of IT activities in the different states. To get the right economic picture, one must take into account their absolute size and regional magnitude. We therefore include in the next table the total number of IT jobs in the state and the corresponding percentage of total regional employment. Note our measure of employment is the total civilian labour force, which not limited to industry employment but also includes government jobs. This is why the results are notably smaller than similar evaluations by the AEA (1999) or Atkinson, Court (1999). In this table, we eliminated three formerly selected states: Delaware for data uncertainties (four out of the six 1997 industry employment are actually estimated figures), North Dakota and the District of Columbia, because the total IT jobs is lower than 10 000 (which gives little significance to later growth and specialization calculations). To support the discussion, we also indicate the adjusted specialization (i.e. mean specialization weighted by the convergence factor), the state IT overall specialization (i.e. the measure of specialization obtained when adding up the six IT industries employment figures instead of taking the mean of the six specialization levels), and finally the employment growth in the six IT industries between 1992 and 1997, both in absolute value and in percentage.

The panel emphasizes the impressive performance of Colorado over the period. It also points out the interest of the specific IT specialization index defined in Section 3, instead of specialization ratio or labour intensity for a single aggregated IT sector. Clearly our procedure of using the mean specialization

Table 14.5 Description of IT industries size and growth in the most specialized states

State	IT mean specialization	IT adjusted specialization	IT jobs	% of local employment	IT state specialization	1992–97 job creation (1,000s)	1992–97 job growth (%)
Virginia	2.11	1.35	127.0	4.0	1.90	35.9	39
Massachusetts	1.99	1.77	107.0	3.5	1.67	36.6	52
Colorado	1.90	4.96	79.5	4.1	1.96	37.4	89
California	1.45	2.21	345.8	2.7	1.28	94.2	37
Nebraska	1.44	0.78	21.7	2.6	1.23	4.9	29
Maryland	1.39	2.50	74.3	3.3	1.59	15.6	27
New Jersey	1.35	2.12	142.7	3.9	1.86	2.80	24
Connecticut	1.29	2.51	38.5	2.4	1.16	9.1	31
New York	1.23	2.90	176.9	2.2	1.06	45.8	35
Georgia	1.21	3.02	99.9	2.8	1.34	26.8	37
Utah	1.12	2.22	22.3	2.3	1.09	6.1	38
Washington	1.10	2.12	52.8	2.1	1.02	16.9	47
Texas	1.00	3.84	190.7	2.2	1.08	56.1	42

of the six IT industries rather than their overall weight, introduces a strong voluntary bias, since it gives after all equal importance to each IT industry despite huge differences in employment levels. This is however the best way to take seriously the convergence assumption, and to argue that, whatever strong specialization might be achieved in one industry, the decisive factor in fostering IT employment growth is the local and significant presence of all six of them. The convergence factor and the adjusted IT specialization afterwards attempt to give quantitative measures. The figures in Table 14.5 provides in this context evidence in favour of this theory (consider for example Texas, California, and the differences between California and Colorado). This however merely suggests the existence of the convergence mechanism, which we should now spot and evaluate in a comprehensive and rigorous manner. This is the objective of the following section.

Before that, we conclude with a brief comment on two reports supporting the previous results. First, the need to take into account the convergence factor to get the right picture of a state IT specialization, is confirmed by data collected, on a quite different methodology, by the American Electronics Association (1999) on state jobs creation between 1990 and 1997. The results are summarized in Table 14.6. Though AEA counts so-called high-tech jobs, the method allows useful comparison with our calculations. Actually, for measurement problems, AEA adopted a fairly conservative and restricted definition of high-tech industries, excluding biotechnology, engineering services, research and testing activities. This eventually leads us to three main categories: electronic and computer production, communication services, software and computer services. The two latter roughly corresponds to our definition of IT industries.

This table shows again the dynamism of states such as Texas, Georgia, who display just average level of state or mean IT specialization, but take profit of an homogeneous and balanced specialization in all IT key industries, as illustrated by their high convergence factor. But since the basis for jobs calculation is not identical, we cannot push further ahead the comparison with our results.

Atkinson and Court (1999) survey of the *State New Economy Index* also brings an interesting complementary perspective. They actually build up a ranking of the US states according to their average performance in a set of 17 indicators, aimed at capturing the main features of the 'New Economy'. Colorado ranks again at the third place, behind Massachusetts and California. This podium underlines how, contrary to the first two states where the high-tech specialization now dates back to several decades, the specialization of Colorado

Table 14.6 AEA estimation of state high-tech employment evolution 1990–97

State	Job creation	Job growth (%)	1998 total jobs	% of local employment	1998 exports (billion $)	1990–98 exports growth (%)
Texas	101,700	37	375,933	5.4	41	173
California	66,100	9	784,151	6.9	64	113
Georgia	46,400	54	132,524	4.4	4	135
Colorado	40,000	44	131,854	8.0	4	100
Washington	35,900	59	97,025	4.7	3,3	135
Virginia	33,000	27	154,712	6.0	4	90
Illinois	25,800	14	207,201	4.2	16	92
Massachusetts	–16,600	–7	205,091	7.7	11,5	40
New York	–30,200	–9	320,410	4.9	15	38
Maryland	–	–	97,484	5.4	1,8	64

in the digital economy is the outcome of a new powerful local growth. The detailed results, in particular the criteria where Colorado ranks first or second, is very informative. The unexpected first rank in labour education is obviously an indirect result of the local IT cluster success. Rather than the product of an effective superiority of regional college and universities, this stems from the continuous attraction and growth of IT companies in the area, whose highly skilled and educated workers now become residents. Other variables in which Colorado ranks within the first four states underline the strength of the local growth: start-up versus bankruptcies rate, cumulated value of IPOs, percentage of high-tech employment, capital-risk investment.

5   Dynamics of IT Specialization between 1992 and 1997

To evaluate the role of agglomeration externalities in IT industries' growth, we now consider one IT industry in a state and look at the growth rate of these regional industries as a function of the different agglomeration externalities discussed in section 2: localization, urbanization, convergence.

1992 Data Set

To do that, we first need to collect older data on IT industry state employment, to measure their recent growth. To get comparable data, we must not go too much further into the past, and decided to use 1992 Census results. However, because of the change in the classification system in 1998, this is not a straightforward task. We actually first have to map the IT industries defined in the new NAICS system with the former SIC classification, as explained in Table 14.7.

In this mapping, we ignore, with the NAICS 5142/SIC 7374 equivalence, two partial SIC categories usually fitting within NAICS 5142 scope: 7379 and 7389. We include the first one in totality in 5415, since it covers three main activities related with computer services: computer consultants, disk conversion, other computer related services. The second one is a disparate set of business services (audio taping, mapmaking, fashion design, translation services, etc.). Among them, only one falls within IT field: microfilm services, but we can ignore it because it is a very small industry. When switching NAICS 5112 software publishers, with SIC 7372 prepackaged software, we include software reproducing (classified somewhere else in NAICS as 334611). But this remains a reasonable approximation since it does not represent many jobs.

Table 14.7 1997 NAICS and 1992 SIC data compatibility by IT industry

NAICS code	Business description	SIC code	Business description
5132	Cable networks and programme distribution	4841	Cable and other pay television services
5133	Telecommunications	481	Telephone
		482	Telegraph communications
		489	Communications services
514191	Online services	7375	Information retrieval services
5112	Software publishers	7372	Prepackaged software
5142	Data processing services	7374	Computer processing and data preparation and processing services
		7	
5415	Computer systems design and related services	371	Computer programming services
		7373	Computer integrated systems design
		7379	Computer related services

Preliminary Facts

We begin with a quick review of the most striking evolutions at the regional and industry level. Table 14.8 first presents the change observed in the size and intensity of state IT activities.

Table 14.8   Means and standard deviations of IT industries variables in 1992 and 1997*

Variable	Mean	Standard deviation
1997 state IT jobs (000s)	49.64	63.45
1997 state IT jobs (% total employment.)	1.79	0.86
1997 state IT specialization	0.86	0.41
1997 IT industries mean specialization	0.87	0.44
1997 convergence factor	3.23	1.89
1997 state IT adjusted specialization	2.38	1.32
1992 state IT jobs (000s)	36.54	46.36
1992 state IT jobs (% total employment)	1.48	0.64
1992 state IT specialization	0.86	0.37
1992 IT industries mean specialization	0.82	0. 40
1992 convergence factor	2.92	1.17
1992 state IT adjusted specialization	2.10	0.96

*   For 50 states: Wyoming was not considered because the local total number of IT jobs is under 1200, i.e. three times smaller than the next state when ranked according to IT jobs.

This table shows an interesting empirical finding, confirming the convergence hypothesis and the design of the following econometric regression. On average, IT industries experienced an impressive growth over the period: State jobs increase by 36 per cent. Meanwhile, standard index such as state overall IT specialization merely changes. But, if we consider the state IT mean specialization, we notice that, while the variable's mean remains fairly the same between 1992 and 1997, the standard deviation increases by 10 per cent. The trend is more marked when we take into account the convergence factor: mean and standard deviation of the state adjusted specialization variable respectively grows by 13 and 37 per cent. The growing heterogeneity and variance in IT industries average specialization at the state level is illustrated by the following figures.

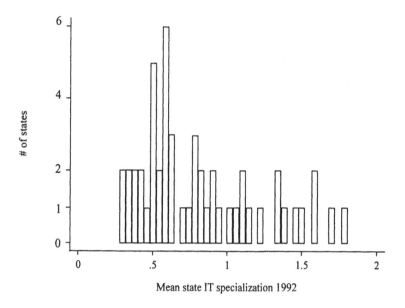

Figure 14.2   1992 IT mean specialization in the US

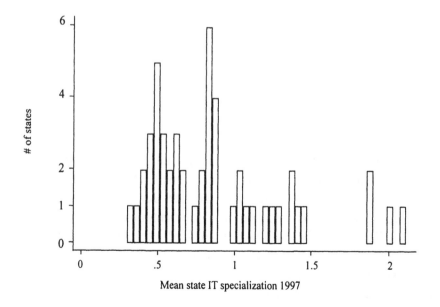

Figure 14.3   1997 IT mean specialization in the US

Figure 14.4 pictures at the same time the evolution of IT state mean specialization and IT local employment growth (given by the disk's size) between 1992 and 1997. It generally illustrates the correlation between both variables, but to get an accurate picture, we have to break down the state data and directly consider state-industry employment's evolution.

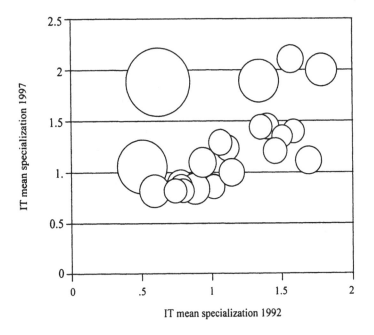

Figure 14.4   Growth and IT specialization 1992–97

Table 14.9 shows how this massive growth of the IT industries drives considerable change in the geographical distribution of employment. Overall jobs creation in the industry actually hides considerable transfers between states, as the jobs destruction and 'churn' indicate. Besides, the relative value of the mean and standard deviation in IT state employment points out the enormous dispersion of growth records. A third interesting feature is that, though between 62 and 82 per cent of employment change is carried out in only ten states, California is no more the permanent leader in jobs' creation either in percentage or, more surprisingly, in absolute term.

Table 14.9 1992–97 growth patterns by IT industry

1992–97 growth	Cable	Telecoms	Online services	Software	Data processing	Computer systems
Employment change	45,327	69,122	18,385	135,353	33,882	366,509
Growth	35.1%	7.3%	57.8%	103.3%	14.8%	92.1%
Job creation	46,357	94,390	24,701	137,249	52,837	367,103
Job destruction	1,030	25,268	–6,316	–1,896	–18,955	–594
(NB states)	(7)	(19)	(10)	(3)	(14)	(1)
Job 'churn'*	2%	27%	26%	1%	36%	0%
State change mean	1,216	3,764	1,272	6,132	2,455	9,427
Standard deviation	6,338	10,205	2,825	19,560	5,258	51,371
Largest job creation	4,627 (GA)	18,786 (TX)	6,081 (VA)	40,748 (CA)	10,477 (NY)	47,598 (CA)
Share of 5 and 10 first states in employment change	41%/65%	50%/71%	66%/82%	57%/74%	52%/68%	39%/62%
First state growths (with job creation greater than 2,000, 1,000 for online services	Colorado 260%	Utah 60%	Virginia 880%	New Hampshire 240%	New York 84%	Arkansas 484%
services	Georgia 99%	Colorado 52%	Colorado 372%	Pennsylvania 195%	Nebraska 78%	Kentucky 232%
	Illinois 56%	Arizona 34%	Washington 359%	Arizona 194%	Connecticut 71%	Georgia 140%

Growth Model

Based on Glaeser et al. (1992), we present a growth model's specification where the growth rate of the firm's technological ability has both national and local components, the latter depending on three agglomeration externalities: localization, urbanization (here considered measured by the size of local population, as a proxy for economic overall activity) and convergence (homogeneous local specialization in the six selected IT industries).

We consider a firm in industry i and the state s. Its production function has the form $A_t f(l_t)$, where A_t represents the level of technology and l_t labour input at time t. For each firm, technology, prices and wages w_t are given.

$Max\{A_t f(l_t) - wl_t\}$ leads to (labour input set to equate marginal productivity to the wage).

Assume now A_t that has both notional and local components: $A_t = A_{national,t} \cdot A_{local,t}$ and set $f(l) = l^{1-\lambda}$ with $0 < \lambda < 1$.

The growth rate of industry employment in that state will then be:

$$\lambda Log\left(\frac{l_{t+1}}{l_t}\right) = Log\left(\frac{A_{t+1}}{A_t}\right) - Log\left(\frac{w_{t+1}}{w_t}\right)$$

Finally, we assume that local technology grows at a rate depending on the three different externalities in the industry and the geographical area:

$$Log\left(\frac{A_{local,t+1}}{A_{local,t}}\right) = S(localization,\ urbanization,\ convergence,\ intialconditions) + \varepsilon_{t+1}$$

The growth model is then defined in equation (1) as:

$$\lambda Log\left(\frac{l_{t+1}}{l_t}\right) = Log\left(\frac{A_{national,t+1}}{A_{national,t}}\right) - Log\left(\frac{w_{t+1}}{w_t}\right) \qquad (1)$$

Econometric Results

We examine employment changes at the state-IT industry level between 1992 and 1997 using the regression specified in equation (1). The measure of localization is given by the industry specialization in the state, σ_{is} defined in section 3. To address the urbanization theory in its simplest form, we use the total employment in the state as a measure of local economic activity. Finally, we test two different measures of the convergence process: the state IT mean and adjusted specialization. Table 14.10 describes the variables. The dependent variable is (log of) the ratio of employment in that industry and the state between 1992 and 1997. The mean of this variable is 0.41 (this corresponds to an 8.5 per cent annual growth). The standard deviation of 0.47 again indicates the great dispersion of growth performance.

Table 14.10 Variables means and standard deviations

Variable	Mean	Standard deviation
Log(1997 employment/1992 employment) in state and IT industry	0.411	0.467
Log(1997 US employment/1992 US employment) in the IT industry	0.383	0.264
1992 wages in the state and in the IT industry (in thousands of dollar per quarter)	8.648	2.339
1992 state-industry specialization	0.877	0.701
1992 State average specialization in the six IT industries	0.889	0.440
1992 state IT adjusted specialization	2.302	1.043
1992 state total employment(in millions)	2.351	2.322

Table 14.11 presents our results of the regression of employment growth across state-IT industry, with 225 observations. Given definition problems, and the fact that in 1992 this activity merely existed, we actually did not consider the online services data. In addition to that, we also eliminated 25 other observations, corresponding to situations where one of the data either in 1992 or 1997 was estimated, or where the total number of jobs did not exceed 500 and would lead to unrealistic growth figures. Therefore, we only kept exact employment figures. We include as control in the regression the 1992 log of wage in the state-IT industry (to control the potential move of firms or workers to low wages states). According to equation (1), we also include national employment variations in the IT industry. This factor aims at correcting for changes in national industry demand, to only consider city-industry changes.

As in Glaeser et al. (1992), we find that initial wages are uncorrelated with employment growth, while the coefficient on national industry employment

Table 14.11 State-IT industry growth between 1992 and 1997

Dependent variable	Log(1997 employment/1992 employment) in the state and the IT industry				
	(1)	(2)	(3)	(4)	(5)
Constant	0.044	0.07	0.1	0.02	−0.06
	(0.19)	(0.19)	(0.19)	(0.19)	(0.19)
Log(1997 national employment/ 1992 national employment) in the industry	1.12	1.10	1.15	1.15	1.09
	(0.1)	(0.1)	(0.1)	(0.1)	(0.1)
State-industry wage in 1992	−0.02	0.006	−0.08	−0.09	−0.007
	(0.1)	(0.1)	(0.1)	(0.1)	(0.1)
State employment in 1992	−0.04	–	–	–	−0.05
	(0.02)				(0.03)
State-industry specialization in 1992	–	−0.1	–	–	−0.09
		(0.03)			(0.03)
Mean state IT specialization in 1992	–	::	0.06	–	–
			(0.06)		
IT convergence index in 1992	–	–	–	0.06	0.08
				(0.02)	(0.02)
Adjusted R^2	0.397	0.413	0.393	0.410	0.438

Note: standard error in parentheses.

change is above one in the five models. The table shows that the effects of agglomeration externalities we investigate are second-order magnitude behind national industry evolution.

The overall results on externalities support the convergence hypothesis, and object to localization and urbanization theories' predictions. Column 1 shows that the undifferentiated weight of economic activity, here measured by total state employment, hurts growth in the city-industry, but the effect is not statistically significant. The following column gives opposite results to the localization theory's prediction. The coefficient on the local specialization variable is actually negative and significant, though quantitatively small. If we raise the measure of state-industry specialization by one standard deviation, the cumulative growth of employment over the five years slows by 7 per cent total, which is about one-seventh of a standard deviation.

On the contrary, the results of column 3 and 4 are consistent with the convergence hypothesis. We put aside the IT state mean specialization variable, which effect is not statistically significant, to focus on the adjusted IT specialization. Equation (4) shows that industries in states where the 'convergence' of the six IT industries is more intense grow faster. The final column uses the three measures of externalities at the same time. The previous findings are confirmed, with similar signs and coefficient for the three explanatory variables. Local specialization and overall state size continue to exert a negative impact on growth of city-industry employment. On the contrary, local convergence between IT industries has a positive and significant influence. An increase of one and a half standard deviation in the adjusted IT specialization (1,56), as in Texas, actually raises growth of employment in the city-industry by 13 per cent over the period (30 per cent of a standard deviation).

6   Conclusions

We have shown in this chapter that IT industry employment growth in a state is fostered by the co-location of close IT industries, whereas local specialization hurts. The interpretation proposed of this evidence is that the deregulation of the telecoms sector combined with the pace of innovations in IT support a process of convergence between formerly distinct industries such as telecoms, cable, software, internet services, data processing and computer design. Jacobs' diversity externalities – labelled as 'convergence externalities' in this specific context – appears to be the most consistent with the evidence.

This convergence mechanism also helps explaining the present geographical specialization patterns of the IT sector across the US. In particular, it accounts for the emergence of new clusters (in Colorado or Texas), amid the long-lasting well-documented clusters in Santa Clara, California (Silicon Valley) and the area around Boston-Cambridge Route 128 (Arthur, 1990; Saxenian, 1994).

This study could be extended in three ways. First of all, the econometric analysis of US data can be improved by adding complementary variables and using a smaller geographical unit. In this chapter, the regional unit for analysis is actually the state. However, it is clear, as the Denver case illustrates, that a cluster is usually much smaller than a state. Since Glaeser et al. (1992) have shown that the magnitude of external effects increases as the geographical unit becomes smaller, we should expect better econometric results by using data at the MSA (Metropolitan Area) level. The US Census Bureau has however not yet released these 1997 data. It would also be interesting to use other variables than employment to evaluate the local benefits generated by agglomeration externalities and measure industry growth: labour or total factor productivity, per capita income. A second avenue for research consists in applying the same method to European countries to discuss the policy implications of the digital economy's fast growth on regional development and cohesion. Finally, the third direction consists in exploring and modelling the IO-foundations of the 'convergence process' at the industry and firm levels. A possible solution to tackle this issue could be to examine equilibrium configurations models where the independence assumption between submarkets is relaxed and the bundling of technology different and hardly substitutable products allowed (Sutton, 1998).

Note

1   We adopt on purpose in this chapter the digital term instead of the common internet, it or new economy names to underline that the numerization of information to process, transmit and store it is actually the main engine driving the structural changes transforming our economy (see Bomsel and Le Blanc, 2000).

References

American Electronics Association (1999), *Cyberstates 3.0: A State-by-state Overview of the High-technology Industry*, Washington: AEA.

Aoki, M. (forthcoming), 'Information and Governance in the Silicon Valley Model', in *Toward a Comparative Institutional Analysis*, Stanford University Press.

Arrow, K. (1962), 'The EcoNo.mic Implications of Learning by Doing', *Review of EcoNo.mic Studies*, No. 29, pp. 155–93.

Arthur, B. (1990), 'Silicon Valley Locational Clusters: Do Increasing Returns Imply MoNo.poly?', *Mathematical Social Sciences*, No. 19, pp. 235–51.

Atkinson, R. and Court, R. (1998), *The New EcoNo.my Index: Understanding America's EcoNo.mic Transformation*, No.vember, Washington: Progressive Policy Institute.

Atkinson, R. and Court, R. (1999), *The State New EcoNo.my Index, Benchmarking EcoNo.mic Transformation in the States*, July, Washington: Progressive Policy Institute.

Bairoch, P. (1988), *Cities and EcoNo.mic Development*, Chicago: Chicago University Press.

Baptista, R. and Swann, G. (1999), 'A Comparison of Clustering Dynamics in the US and UK Computer Industries', *Journal of Evolutionary EcoNo.mics*, Vol. 9, No. 3, pp. 373–99.

Bartelsman, E., Caballero, R. and Lyons R. (1994), 'Customer- and Supplier-Driven Externalities', *American EcoNo.mic Review*, Vol. 84, No. 4, pp. 1075–84.

Barua, A., Pinnell, J., Shutter, J. and Whinston, A. (1999), 'Measuring the Internet Economy: an Exploratory Study', Center for Research in Electronic Commerce, University of Texas at Austin (quarterly results of The Internet Economy Indicators at http://www.internetin dicators.com/).

Black, D. and Henderson, V. (1999), 'A Theory of Urban Growth', *Journal of Political Economy*, Vol. 107, No. 2, pp. 252–84.

Black, D. and Henderson, V. (1999), 'Spatial Evolution of Population and Industry in the United States', *American Economic Review*, AEA Papers and Proceedings, pp. 321–27.

Bomsel, O. and Le Blanc, G. (2000), 'Qu'est ce que l'économie numérique?', *La Recherche*, No. 328, pp. 82–7.

Castells, M. (1989), *The Informational City: Information Technology, Economic Restructuring, and the Urban-Regional Process*, Cambridge: Basil Blackwell.

Chandler, A. (1978), *The visible hand*, Cambridge : Harvard University Press.

Ciccone, A. and Hall, R.E. (1996), 'Productivity and the Density of Economic Activity', *American Economic Review*, Vol. 86, No. 1, pp. 54–70.

Dumais, G., Ellison G. and Glaeser, E. (1997), 'Geographic Concentration as a Dynamic Process', NBER Working Paper 6270.

Ellison, G. and Glaeser, E. (1999), 'The Geographic Concentration of Industry: Does Natural Advantage Explain Agglomeration?', *American Economic Review*, AEA Papers and Proceedings, pp. 311–16.

Freeman, C. (1982), *The Economics of Industrial Innovation*, 2nd edn, London: Frances Pinter.

Fujita, M., Krugman, P. and Venables, A. (1999), *The Spatial Economy, Cities Regions, and International Trade*, Cambridge, MA: MIT Press.

Glaeser, E., Kallak, H., Scheinkman, J. and Shleifer, A. (1992), 'Growth in Cities', *Journal of Political Economy*, Vol. 100, No. 6, pp. 1126–52.

Harrison, B., Kelley, M.R. and Gant, J. (1996), 'Specialization Versus Diversity in Local Economies: The Implications for Innovative Private Sector Behavior', *Cityscape: A Journal of Policy Development and Research*, Vol. 2, No. 2, pp. 61–93.

Henderson, V. (1983), 'Industrial Bases and City Sizes', *American Economic Review*, Vol. 73, No. 2, pp. 164–8.

Henderson, V. (1988), *Urban Development, Theory, Fact and Illusion*, Oxford: Oxford University Press.

Henderson, V. (1999), 'Marshall's Scale Economies', NBER Working Paper 7358.

Holmes, T. (1999), 'Scale of Local Production and City Sizes', *American Economic Review*, AEA Papers and Proceedings, pp. 317–20.

Jacobs, J. (1969), *The Economy of Cities*, New York: Vintage.

Krugman, P. (1991a), 'Increasing Returns and Economic Geography', *Journal of Political Economy*, Vol. 99, No. 3, pp. 483–99.

Krugman, P. (1991b), 'History Versus Expectations', *Quarterly Journal of Economics*, pp. 651–67.

Lundvall, B. (1992), *National Systems of Innovation*, London: Pinter Publishers.

Mansell, R. and Wehn, U. (eds) (1998), *Knowledge Societies: Information Technology for Sustainable Development*, New York: United Nations, Oxford University Press.

Markusen, A., Hall, P. and Glasmeier, A. (1986), *High-tech America: The What, Where and Why of the Sunrise Industries*, Boston: Allen and Unwin.

Marshall, A. [1920] (1949), *Principles of Economics*, 8th edn, London: Macmillan.

Moomaw, R. (1998), 'Agglomeration Economies: Are They Exaggerated by Industrial Aggregation?', *Regional Science and Urban Economics*, No. 28, pp. 199–211.

Morgan Stanley Dean Witter (1999), *The Internet Data Services Report*, August.

Morrison, P.C. and Siegel D. (1999), 'Scale Economies and Industry Agglomeration Externalities: A Dynamic Cost Function Approach', *American Economic Review*, Vol. 89, No. 1, pp. 272–90.

Negroponte, N. (1995), *Being Digital*, New York: Vintage Books.

Newman, N. (1998), 'Net Loss: Government, Technology and the Political Economy of Community in the Age of the Internet', PhD dissertation, University of California, Berkeley.

Persson, F., Rosengren, J. and Wilshire, M. (1999), 'The Soft Side of telecoms', *McKinsey Quarterly*, No. 4, pp. 134–43.

Porter, M. (1990), *The Competitive Advantage of Nations*, New-York: Free Press.

Porter, M. (1998), *On Competition*, Boston: Harvard Business School Press.

Rauch, J. (1993), 'Does History Matter Only When it Matters Little? The Case of City-industry Location', *Quarterly Journal of Economics*, pp. 843–67.

Reich, R. (1991), *The Work of Nations: Preparing Ourselves for 21st Century Capitalism*, New York: Alfred Knopf.

Ricci, L. (1999), 'Economic Geography and Comparative Advantage: Agglomeration Versus Specialization', *European Economic Review*, No. 43, pp. 357–77.

Rivera-Batiz, F. and Rivera Batiz, L. (1998), 'Agglomeration Externalities, Geography, and the Labor Market: Theory and Evidence', mimeo.

Roelandt, T. and den Hertog, P. (1998), 'Cluster Analysis and Cluster-based Policy Making', *OECD NIS Focus Groups Summary Reports*, pp. 20–31.

Romer, P. (1986), 'Increasing Returns and Long-run Growth', *Journal of Political Economy*, Vol. 94, No. 5, pp. 1002–37.

Rosenfeld, S. (1997), 'Bringing Business Clusters into the Mainstream of Economic Development', *European Planning Studies*, Vol. 5, No. 1, pp. 3–23.

Saxenian, A. (1994), *Regional Advantage:Culture and Competition in Silicon Valley and Route 128*, Cambridge: Harvard University Press.

Sutton, J. (1998), *Technology and Market Structure*, Cambridge: MIT Press.

US Department of Commerce (1998), *The Emerging Digital Economy*, Washington, April.

US Department of Commerce (1999), *The Emerging Digital Economy II*, Washington, May.

Chapter 15

Direct Communication, Networking and Location of Innovative Activities

Andreas Kopp

1   Introduction

This chapter starts out from the observation that research firms or individual researchers seek locations close to each other because proximity facilitates the exchange of technical information. The chapter is motivated by the fact that the observations of cooperation among researchers (e.g. von Hippel, 1987; Schrader, 1991) and the fact that this cooperation seems to require geographical proximity (Saxenian, 1994) are in stark contrast to economic theory.[1]

The questions concerned are not only reflected in contradictions between empirical and theoretical research but also in puzzles raised by popular public debates: On the one hand innovative activities are perceived as being localized, leading to demands for government actions to 'create Silicon Valleys', to the strong believe that research of private companies and public institutions depends on 'networking' between individual producers. On the other hand there is the public presumption that geographic distance loses economic importance due to the progress in information and telecommunication technologies. Against this backdrop two major economic questions arise:

- first, why should agents who dispose of proprietary knowledge of economic value reveal such knowledge to competitors? Why should researchers believe than informally traded information is reliable? The theoretical model on innovation races (Loury, 1979; Lee and Wilde, 1980; Reinganum, 1989) predict, in complete contrast to the above mentioned empirical studies that researchers will not cooperate, neither by sharing information. The general non-cooperative behaviour is seen as the reason for an inefficient R&D sector at large, calling for corrective government action (cf. Mortensen, 1982; Stewart, 1983);
- a second major question is, why, given that researchers cooperate in research activities, they benefit from locating close to each other. In view of

the dramatic increase of technical communication possibilities, it appears to be striking that communication is facilitated to a significant degree by geographical proximity. Why has the decrease of communication costs not led to a dissolution of geographic clusters of innovative activities? The assertion that to convey technical information requires face-to-face communication (von Hippel, 1988; Schrader, 1991; Audretsch, 1998; Feldman and Audretsch, 1999) entails the question why this sort of information cannot be transferred via e-mail, facsimile or phone.

The consequences of the localized exchange of information have been investigated at different levels of aggregation: at the industry level as Marshallian localization effects (Arrow, 1962), at the urban interindustry level as urbanization effects (Jacobs, 1984), in non-price interaction models of agglomeration (Papageorgiu and Thisse, 1985; Fujita and Ogawa, 1982a; Imai, 1982b) and in relation to national endogenous growth (Lucas, 1988, 1993; Dudley, 1999).

In the second subsection we present traditional arguments on competition in innovative activities. Researchers compete for the value of an innovation that is completely protected against imitation and duplication. As the research process is stochastic all researchers could gain from coordination of strategies but are unable to ex ante commit to cooperation. In the third subsection we first review the evidence of the behaviour of researchers: Contradicting the predictions of the models on innovation races researchers do share proprietary know-how which is relevant for the ongoing research process, even without having explicit contracts and without any accounting of the mutual support. We then formulate a hypothesis as to why the cooperation of researchers requires face to face communication, which is facilitated by geographical proximity, and develop our argument on how networking between researchers to communicate past experiences in bilateral information trades leads to a 'community enforcement' of cooperative behaviour in a matching market for know-how. A general cooperation of researchers results if a system of overlapping networks is exogenously given. Localization arises if the bilateral network links are the more costly the larger the geographic distance between any two potential network members. These costs of maintaining network links induce networks to locate at single points in geographic space. Depending on whether relocation costs of firms are distance dependent, one or several centres of specific research activities may form.

2   Competition and Cooperation of Innovative Activities

The environment that is considered here is one in which a particular invention is sought simultaneously by identical researchers or research firms. We consider the benchmark case where an invention is completely protected. The winner of the innovation race is completely protected against imitation or duplication of the research results. Entry to the innovation process is associated with fixed costs. To avoid that competition in innovative activities boils down to a sort of an auction we assume that the research process is stochastic: Research results arrive according to a stochastic process whose speed is controlled by variable research expenditures. This implies that the instantaneous probability of making an invention at any point in time is a positive function of own research expenditures and a negative function of the aggregate research expenditures of the competitors, the rival hazard rate. The invention has a fixed monetary value which is equal to the discounted worth of the profit stream generated by the its use over time.

- As the intermediate results obtained in the research process is proprietary knowledge, and this strengthens the competitive position of the competitive position of the individual firm, firms behave strictly in a non-cooperative way. Each firm determines the current research expenditures as a best response function to the rival hazard rate. Excluding characteristics of the stochastic process which make it unprofitable to do research altogether, the symmetric industry equilibrium has the following characteristics:
- Research expenditures are an increasing function of the number of firms or researchers pursuing the same research objective. An increase of the number of firms is associated with an earlier invention date on average as there are more firms and each firms invests at a higher rate.
- The value of taking part in the innovation race is a decreasing function of the number of firms. With free entry expected profits in equilibrium are equal to zero.
- Even with a fixed number of firms each firm invests at a higher rate than jointly optimal. Free entry results in too many firms, each having too high a level of research expenditures compared to the cooperative solution.

Mortensen (1982) and Stewart (1983) have discussed the normative question whether a mechanism could be implemented to correct for the externalities associated with the innovation race. A social optimum would be reached if the winning firm receives the value of the invention less a compensation paid to each losing firm, the compensation being equivalent to the foregone value of continuing the research process. Such an institution would induce non-cooperative firms to select the socially optimal level of research expenditures.

Two major problems prevent that such a mechanism could indeed be implemented. First, a regulating agency or a cooperative agreement to work would require that the research expenditures of the individual researchers or firms must be public information. There is no obvious solution to the moral hazard problem of revealing these information. Second even if the information problems were negligible there is the additional problem of preventing further entry: The compensation of losers of the innovation race by the winners increases the expected profits of the representative firm. The increase of the expected profits would induce entry by other firms and upset the optimal solution the mechanism aimed at.

These policy problems depend on the supposition that the firms will have an incentive to cooperate as long as the individual research processes are not perfectly correlated but that they are unable to commit to any cooperative behaviour. As the review in the next subsection will show, empirical investigations of researchers with similar research interests report a behaviour that must appear striking in the light of the models of innovation races. The empirical studies show that the researchers do cooperate during the research process and share information which is of economic value with respect to achieving the desired research results. This sharing of information works much the same way as the compensation of losers by winners of the innovation race: It reduces the individual incentives to invest in the research process as they can draw upon resources of the competitors.

3   The Informal Trade of Technical Know-how

Before we explain why researchers do cooperate in their professional activities, we report the results of empirical investigations on the trade of proprietary information whose use is non-rival. This empirical literature suggests that the cooperation is based on the informal sharing of information during the research process in networks of research departments of firms (von Hippel, 1987, 1988; Schrader, 1991; Allen 1983a; Allen, Hyman and Pinckney, 1983). As von Hippel (1987, p. 292) notes:

> A firm's staff of engineers is responsible for obtaining or developing the know-how its firm needs. When required know-how is not available in-house, an

engineer typically cannot find what he needs in publications either. Much is very specialized and not published anywhere. He must either develop it himself or learn what he needs to know by talking to other specialists. Since in-house development can be time-consuming and expensive, there can be a high incentive to seek the needed information from professional colleagues. And often, logically enough, engineers in firms which make similar products or use similar processes are the people most likely to have that needed information. But are such colleagues willing to reveal their proprietary know-how to employees of rival firms? Interestingly, it appears that the answer is quite uniformly 'yes' in at least one industry, and quite probably in many.

He reports in his study of US steel minimill firms that there was no explicit accounting of favours given and received but that the obligation to return a favour seemed to be strongly felt by the recipient. The supply of information is restricted to the network, according to the findings of von Hippel, in contrast to the interpretation of historical evidence by Robert Allen (1983, p. 2) that all competitors were given free access to proprietary know-how.

In trying to explain the cooperation in R&D it was however only shown that there is a prisoners' dilemma situation with potential gains from cooperation when the competitive advantage of obtaining information and withholding the own know-how is small relative to the payoff using the non-cooperative strategy (von Hippel, 1987, pp. 297–300). It does not explain why the informal trade of know-how occurs. In fact, to withhold information is a dominant strategy independent of the value of the competitive advantage obtained by receiving information from a competitor and keeping the own knowledge secret. In our attempt to explain the informal exchange of proprietary technical knowledge we draw on the literature which gives reason to the cooperative behaviour of sellers who have private information on the product quality and nevertheless refrain from providing low quality. 'Community enforcement' provides a mechanism that induces sellers to behave cooperatively even when they meet particular buyers only infrequently and have a short-term incentive to cheat (Klein and Leffler, 1981; Okuno-Fujiwara and Postlewaite, 1995; Kandori, 1992; Milgrom et al., 1990).

We consider a finite population of researchers who compete with each other in the sense that they have identical research interests. In consecutive periods pairs of these researchers are randomly matched to bilaterally exchange technical information which is of interest for the common research objectives. The quality of the information is not recognized immediately but becomes evident in the course of the ongoing research activities. Both have a short term incentive to cheat: To withhold useful information while the opponent reports truthfully leads to an increase of the individual's instantaneous probability of making the desired research progress and avoids an enhancement of the imitation possibilities of the competitors in case they loose the innovation race:

Table 15.1   Gains from the informal trade of know-how

		Player i Disclose	Player i Withhold
	Disclose	1,1	-k,(1+g)
Player j			
	Withhold	(1+g),-k	0,0

If both players refuse to communicate there is no change compared to the situation of the non-cooperative behaviour which is central to the models of the innovation race. The change of the value of continuing the innovation race for one more period with mutual disclosure of information is set equal to one. (1+g) is the value of continuing one more round receiving information, g being positive, but without revealing the own know-how and k the absolute loss resulting from revealing information while being cheated by the opponent. To receive information while refusing to offer a return increases the player's instantaneous probability of winning the innovation race and avoids increasing the re-engineering and imitation possibilities of the competitors in case of being the winner. A researcher who reports truthfully and is cheated weakens his position even relative to not communicating at all, as the share of the capital value of the innovation is reduced when that researcher wins the innovation race. Consequently, the strategy pair {withhold, withhold} is the only Nash equilibrium of the one-shot trade game. Without any further information, both parties would try to win the innovation race in isolation.

However, the opponents are able to detect useless or misleading information with the continuation of the research process. Due to this fact, private reputations evolve. If we confine our attention to bilateral cooperation among researchers, cooperative behaviour could only result from infinite repetitions of the interactions. For our concerns another class of models is of much greater importance, namely the class of models where players are unable to recognize their opponents in a large but finite population setting. In these models sequential equilibria have been shown to exist on the basis of contagious strategies: All players who have been disappointed once stop cooperating with any of the potential opponents, understanding that the whole society is in a process of switching to non-cooperative behaviour. In the sequential equilibrium the players stick to the cooperative strategy to avoid the general switch to the socially negative behaviour (Kandori 1992 and Ellison 1994). Community enforcement due to contagious strategies has the problematic consequence that cooperation is unstable in the sense that a single defection would render cooperation impossible for all other agents.

To avoid this instability we employ the concept of Ahn and Suominen (1996),[2] that information on the reputation of fellow researchers is disseminated in face-to-face communication among subsets of the researchers. That is, networks are defined here as subsets of the set of all relevant agents which serve as a platform of communicating not technical information but the experience of individual researchers with respect to the conduct of fellow researchers in previous trading rounds.

Each round of trading technical information is then associated with preplay communication on the reputation of the fellow researchers. The expected overall payoffs of the agents are then the discounted sums of payoffs from the repetition of the trade game.

Networks with Exogenous Connections and Community Enforcement

Contacts to other researchers or firms arrive according to a Poisson process with an arrival rate such that there is exactly one encounter per round.

Each firm is a member of an exogenously given network with a fixed number of members. In this subsection we assume that all After each round of matching each player recognizes the identity of his own trading partner. As set out before if an exchange of information materializes, the quality of the information provided is not publicly observable but is discovered by the receiving party during the subsequent research process before the next matching.

After the occurrence of the next matching and before the informal trading of know-how takes place each player sends a signal to the members of his network on his past experience with their current trading partners. Thus each player receives one or more messages on the reputation of his current partner if the latter is not unknown to all members of the network. All players keep records of the experience and the signals received of all past trading rounds.

The researchers then play the above bilateral game on giving information concerning the ongoing research project.

The equilibrium concept we apply is the sequential equilibrium. The sequential equilibrium requires that after any history a player's equilibrium strategy maximizes the expected payoff, taken as given the expected strategies of the other players, the expectations being based on the actions of and the signals received on the other players in all previous rounds. The expectations have to be consistent with the equilibrium strategy profile. One admissible strategy profile is the refusal to provide know-how after any history. In what follows we disregard this possibility and focus on identifying a sequential equilibrium which supports a stable system of informal trades of technical know-how.

The analysis concentrates on a particular strategy profile which is called 'unforgiving'. This is justified by its tractability and by the fact that it provides a benchmark of maximum punishment without leading to immediate contagion of non-cooperation like in the above-mentioned models of community enforcement. That is, the players do exchange information relevant to the research process if they have never experienced or heard of bad behaviour of the matching partner. That is, information about an agent's bad behaviour spreads through personal experience and pre-trade communication of the members of a networks. The effectiveness of this spread depends on the size of the networks relative to the set of all researchers.

The unforgiving behaviour reduces to the following strategy profile in each round of bilateral encounters:

- communicate honestly in the first round;
- in consecutive rounds give a good signal to a network member who is matched with a trading partner who has cooperated in the past. Give a bad signal to a network member who is matched with a trading partner that has cheated in the past or on whom you have received a bad signal;
- do not cooperate with partners with whom you have a bad experience or on whom you received a bad signal in the past, cooperate otherwise.

In each round of the matching process two incentive compatibility constraints must be met:

1. each agent must find it optimal to cooperate when everyone else cooperates;
2. each agent must find it optimal to play non-cooperatively, after having obtained a bad reputation.

In this subsection we assume that we have a system of exogenous overlapping networks of equal size, i.e. some members of each network belong to more than one network. This implies that information on the individual researchers conduct in bilateral trade meetings can spread to all other members of the overall research community.

The individual decisions whether to cooperate or not now results from the fact whether the incentive compatibility constraints are met: First, the researchers will act according to the first incentive compatibility constraint if the total discounted sum of payoffs of behaving cooperatively in an infinite horizon innovation race is higher than cheating in all bilateral meetings while all other fellow researchers behave cooperatively. Second the researchers will act cooperatively, if the discounted payoff of starting with non-cooperative behaviour and switching to cooperative behaviour at a later period is lower than continuing to cheat once a researcher has obtained a bad reputation with some of the fellow researchers.

Checking for the conditions of the first incentive compatibility constraint to be met and taking the payoff values of Table 15.1 we see that, with all potential partners of trading research information behaving cooperatively the period payoff of behaving cooperatively is equal to one. The total discounted sum of payoffs is therefore a decreasing function of the discount factor only. Playing non-cooperatively, the individual researcher is able to cheat if he or she is matched with a researcher who has never been a trading partner before and who belongs to a network with no other member who knows his type. Acting non-cooperatively in all rounds of the overall play, the probability of realizing the surplus g over the payoff of playing cooperatively depends on the size of the networks relative to the total population of researchers and the number of periods in which he or she has taken part in the innovation race. The smaller the size of the networks, given the number of all researchers, the lower is the probability of being matched with a partner in a network where the non-cooperative behaviour is known. The longer the innovation race lasts the greater is the number of networks where the past cheating is known. That is, the total payoff of cheating with all other players acting cooperatively is a decreasing function of the network size and an increasing function of the discount factor. Taken together these derived conditions form a lower bound of the surplus of cheating g in Table 15.1 as a function of the network size relative to the total population of researchers and the discount rate.

The conditions under which the second incentive compatibility constraint holds follow from the calculations of individual researchers of whether it makes sense to postpone cooperative behaviour to later periods. By the principle of dynamic programming it suffices to check that a one-time switch to cooperative behaviour is profitable after any history of having obtained a bad status. Comparing the discounted sum of payoffs of cooperating after k periods of cheating with the discounted sum of payoffs if the researcher continues to cheat leads to a lower bound for g, the surplus of non-cooperation over cooperation in the period game, as a function of the discount rate and the size of the network relative to the total population of researchers. The largest value for the lower bound gives the minimum size the network must have for the second incentive compatibility constraint to be met.

The individual researchers cannot gain by giving wrong signals in the communication game preceding the sharing of research information if the conditions for cooperative behaviour hold.

Networks with Endogenous Connections

In the previous subsection we spanned the parameter space which ensures the existence of a cooperative sequential equilibrium overcoming the prisoners' dilemma associated with information sharing in the research process in as set out in Table 15.1. In this subsection we extend the discussion by taking account of the fact that networks are not exogenously given, that the maintenance of network connections requires resources and that therefore the decision on the network sizes has an economic dimension. As has been set out in the introduction we follow the hypothesis that the communication on the reputation of the potential partners in the information trades requires confidential and personal contacts. We therefore assume that the costs of maintaining bilateral network links depend on geographical distances between the locations of any two network members. The costs of such contacts decrease with the geographical proximity of the researchers. That is, each firm will order potential network members according to the distances between locations. As a consequence the costs of networking are the lower the higher the density of researchers in the neighbourhood of an individual firm.

Whether firms will want to bear the costs of maintaining network relations at all depends on the total size of the population of researchers as this determines the potential gains to be had from cooperation. Given the values of the surplus of cheating in the period game g and the discount rate we can identify the conditions under which networking will emerge at all. This size is small for moderate values of g and in the relevant range of possible discount factors.

As the model is symmetric all network links will be reciprocal: If a firm i maintains a network link to another firm j, firm j will also bear the costs of having a link to firm i. Unless all of the potential network members are located in a single geographical point the costs of being a member of a network is a progressively increasing function of the number of network members due to the increasing distances between their locations. On the other hand, the larger the network the higher the costs of outsiders of cheating a member of the respective network. From this follows that firms will choose a minimal network size that is large enough to protect its members from being cheated by members of other networks.

Relocation of firms with negligible relocation costs If we allow for firms being able to relocate we are able to study the localization of innovative activities as a function of the costs of relocating. If no relocation costs existed or if relocation costs are negligible, the dependence of the costs of networking on the geographical distances between network members entails a relocation of all firms to the geographical point with the highest initial density of researchers. Such a unique centre of activities with a particular research objective results if the total number of researchers is larger than the minimum number required for a networking incentive to exist and the following simple relation between the surplus of cheating in the period game and the discount factor holds:

$$g < \frac{\delta}{1 - \delta},$$

with δ denoting the discount factor.

With no relocation costs, a complete localization of the research activities and the consequent zero networking costs there will be only one network comprising the total population of researchers. The pre-play communication on the reputation of the partners to trade information with and the informal trade of technical or organizational knowledge may therefore be very hard to distinguish empirically.

With free entry the number of researchers will increase up to a point where expected profits are zero. That is, the cooperation between firms or researchers reduces excessive expenditures in research activities but does not resolve the problem of excessive entry.

Relocation of firms with distance-dependent relocation costs With distance dependent relocation costs a multiplicity of centres of identical or similar research interests may emerge: If there is an unequal geographical distribution of researchers in the initial situation firms will choose those locations they can move to without the costs of relocation being higher than the overall benefit of cooperating with other researchers. As a consequence a system of disjoint networks will emerge depending on the initial geographical densities of researchers. The fact that these networks are disjoint implies that the incentive compatibility constraints for the cooperative behaviour between researchers are violated. In other words, we observe centres of localized research activities where all local researchers communicate on the reputation of the local research population and cooperation among these researchers if the conditions for a community enforcement of cooperation hold at the local level. There will be no informal trades of research information across different geographical research centres. As the networks are disjoint, there is no spread of information on the past conduct of researchers in the trading activities beyond the boundaries of individual networks. If there are no spatial frictions on the output market for innovations such research centres must be of equal size.

4   Conclusions

We have studied the clustering of researchers or research firms in geographical space to facilitate the beneficial sharing of information in the course of the research process. The inability to commit to the truthful revelation of proprietary know-how is overcome by local networking of researchers. The networks serve to communicate on the reputation of potential partners of cooperation. We identify the conditions under which such a networking leads to a general cooperation among researchers. If the costs of maintaining network links depend on the distances between the locations of any two researchers the localization of specialized technical knowledge results. Depending on whether relocation costs are distance dependent one or more centres of technical know how will form.

Against the backdrop of the analysis of this chapter the possibilities of economic policy to newly create research centres appear to be limited. If non-cooperation among researchers is due to fact that conditions for the community enforcement of cooperation do not hold, subsidies will have no effect on the cooperation of researchers as government agencies will be unable to control effective trade of information relevant for achieving research objectives. If the government policies are associated with the postulate to relocate into a geographical research centre, subsidies will have an effect only if they are higher than the relocation costs, albeit without having necessarily an effect on the decisions to cooperate in research activities.

Notes

1   A competing hypothesis of the localization of technologies is based on labour market pooling arguments (David and Rosenbloom, 1990; Antonelli, 1995). In this literature there is, however, no explanation of why R&D staff should be particularly immobile.
2   On its empirical importance cf. Bröcker (1995).

References

Ahn, I. and Suominen, M. (1996), 'Word-of-mouth Communication and Community Enforcement', CARESS Working paper 96-02. Department of Economics, University of Pennsylvania, Philadelphia.

Allen, R.C. (1983), 'Collective Invention', *Journal of Economic Behavior and Organization*, 4, pp. 1–26.

Allen, T.J., Hyman, D.B. and Pinckney, D.L. (1983), 'Transferring Technology to the Small Manufacturing Firm: A Study of Technology Transfer in Three Countries', *Research Policy* 12, pp. 199–211.

Antonelli, C. (1995), *The Economics of Localised Technological Change and Industrial Dynamics. Economics of Science, Technology and Innovation*, Vol. 3, Dordrecht: Kluwer.

Arrow, K.J. (1962), 'The Economic Implications of Learning by Doing', *Review of Economic Studies*, 29, pp. 155–73.

Audretsch, D.B. (1998), 'Agglomeration and the Location of Innovative Activity', *Oxford Policy Review*, 14, pp. 18–29.

Bröcker, J. (1995), 'Korreferat zum Referat Dietmar Harhoff', in B. Gahlen, H. Hesse and H.-J. Ramser (eds), *Standort und Region. Neue Ansätze zur Regionalökonomik*, Tübingen.

David, P. and Rosenbloom, J.I. (1990), 'Marshallian Factor Market Externalities and the Dynamics of Industrial Location', *Journal of Urban Economics*, 28, pp. 340–70.

Dudley, L. (1999), 'Communications and Economic Growth', *European Economic Review*, 43, pp. 595–619.

Ellison, G. (1994), 'Cooperation in the Prisoners' Dilemma with Anonymous Random Matching', *Review of Economic Studies*, 61, pp. 567–88.

Feldman, M.P. and Audretsch, D.B. (1999), 'Innovation in Cities: Science-based Diversity, Specialization and Localized Competition', *European Economic Review*, 43, pp. 409–29.

Fujita, M. and Ogawa, H. (1982), 'Multiple Equilibria and Structural Transition of Non-monocentric Urban Configurations', *Regional Science and Urban Economics*, 12, pp. 160–96.

Imai, H. (1982), 'CBD Hypothesis and Economies of Agglomeration', *Journal of Economic Theory*, 28, pp. 275–99.

Jacobs, J. (1984), *Cities and the Wealth of Nations. Principles of Economic Life*, New York: Random House.

Kandori, M. (1992), 'Social Norms and Community Enforcement', *Review of Economic Studies*, 59, pp. 63–80.

Klein, B. and Leffler, K. (1981), 'The Role of Market Forces assuring Contractual Performance', *Journal of Political Economy*, 89, pp. 615–41.

Lee, T. and Wilde, L. (1980), 'Market Structure and Innovation: A Reformulation', *Quarterly Journal of Economics*, 94, pp. 429–36.

Loury, G.C. (1979), 'Market Structure and Innovation', *Quarterly Journal of Economics*, 93, pp. 395–410.

Lucas, R.E. (1993), 'Making a Miracle', *Econometrica*, 61, pp. 251–72.

Lucas, R.E. (1988), 'On the Mechanics of Economic Development', *Journal of Monetary Economics*, 22, pp. 3–22.

Milgrom, P., North, D. and Weingast, B. (1990), 'The Role of Institutions in the Revival of Trade: The Law Merchant, Private Judges, and the Champagne Fairs', *Economics and Politics*, 2, pp. 1–23.

Mortensen, D.T. (1982), 'Property Rights and Efficiency in Mating, Racing and Related Games', *American Economic Review*, 72, pp. 968–79.

Okuno-Fujiwara, M. and Postlewaite, A. (1995), 'Social Norms and Random Matching Games', *Games and Economic Behaviour*, 9, pp. 79–109.

Papageorgiu, Y.Y. and Thisse, J.F. (1985), 'Agglomeration as Spatial Interdependence between Firms and Households', *Journal of Economic Theory*, 37, pp. 19–31.

Reinganum, J. (1989), 'The Timing of Innovation: Research, Development and Diffusion', in R. Schmalensee (ed.), *Handbook of Industrial Organization*, Vol. I, Amsterdam: Elsevier.

Saxenian, A. (1994), *Regional Advantage: Culture and Competition in Silicon Valley and Route 128*, Cambridge, MA: Harvard University Press.

Schrader, S. (1991), 'Informal Technology Transfer between Firms: Cooperation through Information Trading', *Research Policy*, 20, pp. 153–70.

Stewart, M.B. (1983), 'Noncooperative Oligopoly and Preemptive Innovation without Winner-take-all', *Quarterly Journal of Economics*, 98, pp. 681–94.

von Hippel, E. (1987), 'Cooperation between Rivals: Informal Know-how Trading', *Research Policy*, 16, pp. 291–302.

von Hippel, E. (1988), *The Sources of Innovation*, New York: Oxford University Press.

Chapter 16

Post-Fordism, New Economy and the Case of the Italian 'Mezzogiorno'

Luigi Paganetto and Pasquale L. Scandizzo

1 South Italy and the New Industrial Structure

South Italy has participated to the post-Fordist revolution in an important way, both because the breakdown of the vertical structure of the traditional firm has been intense, and because its less developed areas have been more strongly object of the lower part, so to say, of the so called delocalization processes. It is thus appropriate to ask whether and in what measure the South may profit of the second phase of post-Fordism, that is, of what is more commonly called the 'new economy'.

The phenomenon of light industrialization, which has interested large areas of the southern part of our country, has already indicated some important tendencies) the spontaneous diffusion of clusters of small manufacturing firms, in large part constituted by subcontractors, localized in areas often far away from the cities or even the metropolitan areas; (b) the disappearance or the vertical decomposition of medium and medium-large firms, which had been the protagonists of the industrialization attempts of the years 1960s and 1970s; (c) a new push towards the foreign markets, with a rate of increase of exports as percentage of GNP systematically larger in the South than in the North in the past 10 years; (d) the growth of a 'grey' sector, combining tax evasion and precarious employment with a certain amount of positive entrepreneurial tension and with a robust orientation toward the export markets.

This process of light industrial development, which presents both a positive and a negative side, has not avoided a substantial stagnation of the economy of the South. This region, in the period 1992–98, has displayed an average GNP growth of about 0.4 per cent against 1.4 per cent of the central and northern regions. This meagre growth performance, moreover, has been associated with an average rate of decrease of gross fixed investment of 3.7 per cent per year against an increase of 0.5 per cent per year in the Centre-North for the same period. The gap between the 'two Italies' has in fact worsened, as shown by a comparison of per capita incomes. In 1991 p.c. income in the South was almost 59 per cent of the Centre-North (17 million liras instead of 30), but in 1998 this figure was only 55 per cent (23 million liras rather than 41 million).

Against these discomforting data, some recent information suggests that hope may not be completely lost. A 1999 study of the computer market, for example, concluded that the apparent disinvestment realized in the South may have been caused by a resource movement from traditional hardware to the more modern combination of hardware and software, characteristic of the new technologies. The study demonstrated that the computer market in the Centre-South of Italy represents an extremely interesting share of the national market. According to the study, significant sales are already realized both in the visible market, where transactions in the Centre-South are 40 per cent of the national total, and in expenditure, which is more than 42 per cent of the national total. The study also shows how the market in the South is more dynamic than in the North. This is due mainly to a greater share of computer hardware optionals (in particular CD readers) and to a much broader base of small and new business initiatives, rather than households, as in the Northern part of the country. Another study, performed by the national union of chambers of commerce (Unioncamere) revealed that the firms producing computer hardware have grown in 1999 of 18.5 per cent in the South, and only 6.4 per cent for the whole country, while software companies have grown 6.2 per cent for South Italy and only 3.6 per cent for the entire country. This trend has been confirmed by the data for the first semester of 2000, and is not limited to small firms: to illustrate, think of names like Tiscali, with 800 workers in Cagliari, Finmatica in Salerno, Alcatel, Sema, Gec Marconi in Naples, ST Microelectronics, Olin e Nokia in Catania. For the *call centres*, in particular, Tim, Omnitel, Wind and Blu have all allocated their main plants and directional centres in the South.

But let's see, more in particular, why the perspectives of the 'new economy' might constitute a real opening with respect to blind alley where the post-Fordist revolution appears to have pushed the Mezzogiorno.

The 'new economy' is characterized by three main elements: (i) the use, at the same time intensive and diffused, of the modern information and telecommunication technologies (the so called ICTs); (ii) the prevalence of the network structure inside and outside the firm; (iii) the absolute importance of knowledge and information in determining competitive advantage. For many aspects, we may interpret the vertiginous changes of industrial organization, by hypothesizing that we face a second post-Fordist revolution (PF). This hypothesis is justified by the fact that the so called 'internet revolution' (IR) displays, within a broadly different context, numerous elements of similarity with the processes of deverticalizing and reorganizing the firm that have characterized the 1980s and the 1990s.

The point of departure, in IR as in PF, is given by the exhaustion of some important scale economies. In the PF case, these were mainly directed to the fact that the assembly line could be substituted by more flexible production tools, capable of insuring a larger and more pervasive automation, greater modularity and, as a consequence, an ever increasing recourse to outsourcing.In the IR case, the disappearing scale economies are linked to transaction costs. These costs become so low on the electronic network, that one might possibly state that they threaten the very existence of the firm (at least as a nexus of standardized contracts in the Coasian tradition). Entry barriers shrink, since they depended on the fact that the firm was forced to put together, to start its business, a critical mass of resources, precisely to exploit the scale economies generated by its functioning as a broker of contracts on various markets.

The loss of the traditional scale economies, in IR as in PF, appears to translate itself into a push towards a reduction of the size of the firm and the increase of outsourcing. Here, however, some important differences emerge. In PF, the reduction of firm size was aimed at transforming the old firm into a network, with the so called 'core business' at its centre and, around it, a series of more or less captive subcontractors. The PF organizational model is similar to a small solar system, dominated of what is left of the traditional firm (transformed into a centre irradiating strategic knowledge), with many planets and satellites. These are situated at various distances from the centre, according to their strategic importance, the degree of captivity and other characteristics. The PF mode of production has thus been associated with *delocalizing* and *decentralizing* phenomena, since the traditional firm, in addition to perceiving the end of scale economies, is stimulated by the possibility of exploiting the economies of scope through outsourcing, and, by using a plurality of subcontractors, of optimizing a sort of extended location, given the space structure of prices, wages and transportation costs.

On the whole, the post-Fordist revolution, even though it has signed a fundamental step forward in the conquest of new spaces to increase the productivity of the firm, at the same time has been an organizational revolution based an exploiting inequality across labourers and geographical areas. It has primarily concerned the firms that were already operating, and, by differentiating the workers by the degree of strategic knowledge, has created new classes of *insiders* and *outsiders*. It has also stratified the firm over space, creating new classes of areas less developed, depressed and trapped within low level equilibria (many 'local Koreas'). It has been limited, in its capacity to deverticalize the firm, by the persistence of scale economies in the distribution, publicity, marketing and finance. Finally, it has created company networks, but has not affected the traditional structure of the market, except in a minor form: almost always the subcontractors remain 'captive' of one or more mother companies, and outsourcing networks mostly remain both vertically and horizontally small.

In South Italy, in particular, PF has given some impulse to a new process of 'light' industrialization. It has mostly done so, however, by dissolving the traditional firms, too large and inefficient, and exploiting characteristics such as low salaries, fiscal evasion, the availability of low cost skills in the areas of craftsmen and non specialized intellectual labour. The construction of penetrating networks for outsourcing, which has concerned many areas of the South, has been associated with a new development of the 'underground economy' in all its different shades (from the grey to the black) and with a sort of 'unholy' pact among the firms of the Northern part of the country. These firms remained in the formal economy, prosperous and law abiding in the control of the 'superior' phases of the production cycle. At the same time, they were amenable to delocalize in the South the 'lower end' production phases, without being too fussy on the ways that the subcontractors used to reconcile the quality of the products requested with the prices paid.

The activity of enterprise creation, furthermore, even though notable in size and dynamics, showed two main negative characters. First, the competitive advantage of the new firms often depended on their capacity to evade taxes and elude labour legislation to survive. Second, both from the point of view of marketing and credit, the firms created were completely dependent on the mother companies, with very limited perspectives of growing out of such dependence. This process and these characteristics, incidentally, are common to many less developed areas (for example, in the Mediterranean region, Tunisia and Morocco), but are emblematic in the Mezzogiorno, that constitutes a sort of *enclave* within an industrial economy such as the European Union.

In partial contrast with these characteristics, the IR appears to have found an angle of success based on additional economies with much greater potential and, what is more important, with end results much more virtuous on the industrial structure of the less developed areas. In the first instance, in fact, the reduction of firm size, which is linked , but not totally identified with deverticalization, in the case of IR is based on the disappearance of barriers to entry. The network is in fact available to all, practically at zero cost. Furthermore, it is increasingly easier to find financing for the new firms and the present euphoria renders this financing even more attractive. The development of e-commerce and of its interbusiness components (the so called b2b) will make possible a network of subcontractors to outsource any business. This implies that the degree of captivity of the small subcontractors will diminish drastically. But also the scale economies linked to marketing and the related entry barriers appear destined to dissolve. The possibility thus transpires of a global network constituted of small firms, with very low entry costs and highly competitive with one another on both products and processes: something very similar to the paradigm of perfect competition dear to the heart of the neoclassical economists.

The characteristics of the network are, in effects, the most interesting elements of this new revolution. As we have already mentioned, the IR network is different from the PF network mainly because, instead of being a network embedding a plurality of independent networks, it tends to integrate even the smallest unit as a full member of the total network. The emerging structure thus tends to be a network whose constituent parts are individual subjects, and where everybody tend to develop connections and is potentially connected with everybody else. The scale economies (the so called 'network' economies) of such a network are thus the largest possible ones: they are of the same type of the other single largest individual network that we have experienced, that is, the telecommunication network. Not surprisingly, telecommunications are the basis of Internet, which is, however, a much more complex and dynamic graph, where knots and links display an intensity of proliferation an intrinsic stability, greatly transcending the pattern of fixed or mobile telephone connections.

The PF revolution has been, for many aspects, a computer revolution: numerical control machines, automation and development of programming and control have all conspired to give the computer a crucial role in re-organizing the firm. The computer technology has led the process of deverticalizing the Fordist company, by forming a network of firms integrated by a virtual texture of computerized programs and controls. In this phase, the role of Internet has been, everything considered, marginal, while intranets and the other tools of enterprise integration have proliferated. It is not thus surprising that this phase of industrial transformation has also been characterized by an expansion of computing capacity, the personal computer has taken off, becoming ever more powerful, lighter and inexpensive.

In an economy characterized by a global network, however, the computing power of the individual units is less important, because it is the network itself that presents the greater potential to contain and elaborate information. Communication capacity becomes thus critical. A reasonable prediction, even though not agreed on by everybody, is thus that IR, in spite of having based its take off on the development of 'computing power' and of personal computers, will be itself the main cause of obsolescence of the present combination of computing power and communication capacity. Computers will become increasingly 'stupid', even though smaller and lighter, and will instead develop capacity for speedy interaction, which they lack now. The network, in turn, will grow like an enormous super-computer capable of utilizing the power of the million (billion?) machines permanently connected. Together with the development of new 'speed' telecommunication methods, based on a plethora of new technologies that are just entering now the scene, Internet could evolve, and this is the right word, because of the unpredictable and mutation-like character of these developments, into the ultimate communication technology. Something that, like language, connects all men, instantly, but is infinitely less constrained than language by linguistic and geographical barriers. The battle for the new standard, the so called 'wide band', has to be understood in this perspective: a telematic network of permanent connection, like the electrical network, where, however, marginal connection and communication costs are truly zero.

2   The New Model of Division of Labour

The reasoning above may be extended to the network of economic relations over space. At present, these are mostly based on localized availability of economic and financial resources, as well as on the commercial and monetary flows that are derived from it. In this context, it is not surprising that the model of international trade that the economists still use is based on the idea that trade derives from comparative advantage, which in turn is determined by the different resource endowment of each country. But in an economy organized around a network of very small units, which tend to the limit of the individual or the single enterprises, commercial and financial flows do not depend any longer from the differential endowment of fixed resources over wide geographical areas, with high rates of internal cohesion. They tend instead to be determined by the possession of specialized knowledge, and by the capacity to take from the network everything is necessary to complement this fundamental resource.

Because of its reliance on outsourcing, establishing the PF paradigm, in fact, has already entailed a change of the pattern of trade, which has increasingly exploited comparative advantage in exchanging intermediates, rather than final products. The modified pattern of international specialization from products to processes, however, is likely to be only the first step of more far-reaching changes, based on the global and integrating nature of the IR pattern of resource use. In order to glimpse into some of the possible modifications of the economic activity and exchange, we must firstly reflect on the fact that, due to the increasingly intangible nature of the key factors and products of the new economy, the very concept of property is rapidly changing. The concept of endowment, which is commonplace in traditional economic theory, is based on the idea that property is the right to exclude someone else from resource use and, as a consequence, trade is a form to exchange the products of differential property rights. Trade may be seen as a partial remedy to the inequality of the distribution of resources, which are exchanged, in a way that may be beneficial to all parties, through the fruits of specialized production. The products are thus proxies of resource endowments and the ensuing specialization that they induce among trading partners.

But assume now that the advantage of relatively immobile resources may be overturned by knowledge and talent, i.e. resources that can be accessed without holding property rights of the traditional, excluding form. If the new concept of property is the right not be excluded, rather than the right to exclude others, and if it applies in the first place to intangibles, the way comparative advantage and trade work and link to one another could be completely changed. In the usual model of trade, in fact, countries are heterogeneous from the point of view of the endowment of domestic resources. Each country is thus characterized by one or more scarce resource, basically untradable, and comparative advantage exists if these resources are more (comparatively) productive, in terms of value added at international prices, in producing a particular good than other (comparable) goods. If a country can produce only two goods, for example, it necessarily holds a comparative advantage in one of them and a comparative disadvantage in the other one, and, for this reason any country that can produce at least two goods will hold a comparative advantage in one of them.

If the only limiting resource is knowledge, however, countries are no more heterogeneous in resource endowment, except in the limiting sense that one may have a higher concentration of locally based knowledge than others. Even though knowledge is local in the sense that it is incorporated into people and institutions, its intangible nature makes it also rather mobile, and relatively easy to share with partners and allies regardless of time and space constraints. The model of division of labour in the knowledge based society has thus very broad micro-foundations. Rather than a pattern of specialization of countries, it tends to generate specialized clusters of regions, not necessarily contiguous, characterized by a common pool of knowledge-based resources. In this sense, what appears to be a revival of locality turns out to be a powerful step towards a global economy, where the importance of the local subjects is magnified by the possibility of immediate connection on a world scale with other local subjects.

An alternative hypothesis, consistent with the concept of knowledge-base, but more intimately linked to the theories of endogenous growth, is that ideas, rather than knowledge, are the engine of development and the real key to the new comparative advantage. If ideas are not a function of pre-existing knowledge, but are relatively autonomous in their genesis and possibilities of application, the division of labour in the international arena may not be justified any longer by comparative advantage, since there is no systematic relation between countries and the production of ideas. A higher rate of production of ideas will imply, however, that, at times certain countries may capture a higher amount of trade in the more innovative sectors. This apparent specialization will be swept away by the process of diffusion of technologies, so that the diffusion of the old ideas and the emergence of the new ones will continuously reshuffle production across countries.

The above process is reminiscent of Schumpeter's depiction of the innovation process, with two major differences: first, the Schumpeterian sequence of creative destruction concerned the entrepreneurs rather than the countries, because the barrier of localized resource endowment still acted as the main determinant of the international division of labour. Once knowledge and ideas are the resources of overriding importance, however, their international, instant mobility ensures makes traditional comparisons of localized opportunity costs (the basis of comparative advantage) obsolete. Goods may continue to move in apparent response to fixed resource endowment, but the movement that counts will concern the perfectly mobile, disembodied factors of information, technology and science. Furthermore, in an economy organized around a network of very small units, that tend to the limit of the individual or the single enterprise, the trade and financial flows do not depend any longer on the differential endowment of fixed resources of rather large and internally integrated geographical regions. In addition to the possession of specialized knowledge, they may depend critically on the capacity to draw from the net everything is necessary to complement this fundamental resource.

In this economy, the traditional disadvantage of South Italy should gradually be attenuated for two main reasons: on one hand, Southern companies should not be forced to procure their critical inputs from an underdeveloped area, lacking infrastructures and institutions. The weight of the new, pervasive super-infrastructure, constituted by the envelope of the new generation Inter and Intranets, should in fact progressively reduce the weight of the comparative disadvantage in the supply of local public goods, in the relationship with the institutions and in the generalized lack of social capital. On the other hand, the fact that competition will be increasingly based on the capacity to acquire and coordinate information and knowledge will increase the incentives to engage in activities such as research and innovation. These are today confined in an uneasy low level equilibrium by the lack of interest of the private and the benign neglect of the public sector. They will become, instead, the new frontier on which the local communities will play their capacity to attract and construct human capital and thus to develop and prosper.

3   A Model of Participation to the New Economy

The Participation Value

We consider the case of an economy that may choose to allocate its resources to two alternative uses. On one hand, it may produce 'traditional' goods through industries whose performance is predictable in terms of expected cash flows. On the other hand, it may allocate resources to a set of high risk, innovative industries (the 'new economy'), whose performance is largely unpredictable and whose value depends on the outcome of a large number of independent stochastic variables. Entering the 'new economy', however, will entail up-front costs for three reasons: first, it will cause total production in the traditional sector to fall; second, it will require information costs in the form of money and time loss; third, it may cause a loss of resources in the 'weeding process' of competition and selection of the new firms.

We assume that participation costs can be expressed as a commitment of non-recoverable resources and that the economy decides the regime that it will follow on the basis of a discounted cash flow (DCF) analysis (possibly adjusted for risk aversion) over an infinite time horizon. We model resource allocation in the new economy as a search process, whereby the agents sample business opportunities from an underlying random distribution. Corporate income in the new economy is thus assumed to change according to two principles: (i) a continuous increase in mean income, due to the growth of existing firms, and the increase in the ability of the agent to find better opportunities, because of increased experience both on the search and on the business side; and (ii) a parallel increase in the variance of mean income, as participation to the new industries increases and firms confront a higher degree of product differentiation.. The 'new economy' is thus assumed to yield a net cash flow y evolving according to a stochastic process of the geometric, Brownian motion variety:

$$dy = aydt + \sigma dz \qquad (1)$$

where α and σ^2 are respectively the drift and variance parameters and dz is a normally distributed random variable such that $Edz = 0$ and $Edz^2 = dt$.

The value of the option $F(y)$ to participate to allocate a unit of capital (or other resources) to the new industries can be determined using dynamic programming. Bellman equation, in fact, prescribes:

$$rF(y) = EdF(y) \qquad (2)$$

where r is an appropriate rate of discount reflecting the opportunity cost of the resource concerned..

Equation (2) states that, in order to maximize the present value of the option, the representative firm is to equate, in continuing time (that is, at the margin between holding and exercising the option), the value that it would obtain by exercising the option, to the expected present value of the future capital gains obtained by holding the option.

Solving equation (1) as an ordinary differential equation, after applying Ito's lemma, yields:

$$F(y) = A_1 y^{\beta_1} + A_2 y^{\beta_2} \qquad (3)$$

where A_1 and A_2 are constants determined by boundary conditions and β_1 and β_2 are, respectively, the positive and the negative root of the characteristic equation:

$$r - \beta a - \frac{\beta}{2}(\beta - 1)\sigma^2 = 0 \qquad (4)$$

The value of the option to participate in the new economy (NE) should increase with any increase in the cash flow generated by the new industries. But the second term on the right hand side of (3) goes to infinity as y declines without limits. Thus, if we assume that the representative firm is endowed with one unit of capital and that it can decide to put a share equal to 1 – p of this unit in NE, and that, once a firm has switched to the mixed regime (with a given rate of participation) it will not return to full participation in the traditional economy (TE), the constant A_2 can be set to zero.

To determine the value of A_1 in principle there are several possibilities. They all depend, however, on the alternative sources of income open to the firm. Sometimes these are represented by other options, but for the time being we assume that they are characterized by a flow of income created by the combination of the income w from participating to TE at the rate p and the income from NE at the rate $1 - p$. Our key assumption is that increased NE participation has the effect of increasing productivity in TE activities This may occur for various reasons: because the new activities provide services and technology to the old, because TE industries are less crowded and workers may become more competent and specialized, because the culture of enterprise creation grows more rapidly in the NE industries, but then spills over the TE sector. Defining total income as

$$U = p(\frac{w}{\rho} + A_1^* y^{\beta_1}) + (1 - p)(\frac{y}{\delta} + B_1 y^{\beta_1} - C),$$

with

$$w' = \frac{\delta w}{\delta p} = -\frac{\delta w}{\delta(1-p)} < 0,$$

maximizing behaviour requires:

$$\frac{w}{\rho} - p\frac{|w'|}{\rho} + A_1^* y^{\beta_1} = \frac{y}{\delta} + B_1 y^{\beta_1} - C \tag{5}$$

that is, the proportion between the two sectors should be such that marginal net incomes should be equalized.

$$\beta_1 A_1 y^{\beta_1 - 1} = (\frac{1-p}{\delta}) \; ; A_1 = A_1^* - B_1 \tag{6}$$

Note that we have divided the option value in (5) in two parts: the first one on the left hand side denotes the option to wait, while the second one, on the right hand side, denotes the option that is acquired by participating to NE activities, thereby assuming a position for a higher degree of participation in the future.

Equations (5) and (6) are called, respectively, the value-matching and the smooth-pasting conditions. They both require that the 'activity mix' between TE and NE be decided on the basis of comparing the expected cash flows with the option value of the new industries. This implies that NE participation not only entitles to a share $1 - p$ of its expected income, but also to hold the option to acquire a greater share in the future. The value y_e of y at which the above equations are satisfied represent the threshold of entrance into NE type activities.

Solving equations (5) and (6) for y_e and A_1, we obtain:

$$\frac{y_e}{\delta} \geq (\frac{\beta_1}{\beta_1 - 1}) [\frac{w}{\rho} - \frac{|w'|}{\rho} p + C] \tag{7}$$

$$A_1 = \frac{y_e^{-(\beta_2+1)}}{\delta\beta_1} \tag{8}$$

Expression (7) indicates the intuitive fact that , for any participation rate p, the switching from the traditional economy to a mixed regime will occur at a higher level of income, the higher the cash flow expected from the new activities and the lower the costs of switching.

On the other hand, for any given y, the equilibrium rate of participation can be obtained by solving the disequation in (7) for $1 - p$:

$$1 - p_e \leq 1 - \frac{\frac{w}{\rho} - (\frac{\beta_1 - 1}{\beta_1} \frac{y}{\delta} - C)}{\frac{|w'|}{\rho}} = 1 + [(\frac{\beta_1 - 1}{\beta_1}) \frac{y}{|w'|} \frac{\rho}{\delta} \frac{C}{|w'|} \frac{w}{|w'|}] \tag{9}$$

Given that the condition for an internal solution is met

$$(p \leq 1 \Rightarrow \frac{\beta_1}{\beta_1 - 1} \frac{y}{\delta} - C + \frac{|w'|}{\rho} \geq \frac{w}{\rho},$$

expression (9) states that for any given y, equilibrium and diversification (i.e. indifference between TE and NE and a positive level for both activities) will require that the firms allocate capital between the NE and the TE as a function of the difference between NE income adjusted for risk, entry costs and TE income adjusted for the marginal increase due to higher NE participation.

Differentiating $1 - p_e$ with respect to y and C, we find $\delta(1 - p_e) / \delta y \geq 0$, $\delta(1 - p) / \delta\sigma \leq 0$, and $\delta(1 - p_e) / \delta V \leq 0$. Thus, NE participation will be higher, the higher the ratio between NE and TE expected income, but the lower, ceteris paribus, is NE volatility . A decrease in the NE cash flows should thus decrease equilibrium NE participation unless it is associated with a decrease in volatility or entry costs. Similarly, we should find that firms with lower expected TE incomes would be associated with higher NE participation rates unless their entry costs are higher than those with higher TE incomes. On the other hand, an increase in the incomes associated with NE activities will be generally met by an increase in participation of higher income firms and we should also find that a successful performance of NE firms will induce better TE performers to increase their NE participation rate. Recalling that NE expected income increases at rate a, we further find:

$$d(1 - p_e) = \frac{\beta_1}{\beta_1 - 1} \frac{\rho}{\delta} \left(\frac{a}{2} + \frac{w''}{|w'|} \right) y \qquad (9 \text{ bis})$$

Expression (9 bis) may be interpreted as a prediction of a continuous rise of the NE sector under the joint impulse of both the trend in its own productivity and the positive effect on the productivity of the other sector. If $w'' \leq 0$, however, this second effect would be negative and a stationary state would be reached at the point where $|w''| = a|w'/2|$.

An Alternative Model of Dual Option Value

An alternative assumption of the choice open to the firms is that it is possible to switch back and forth from the TE to the NE activities. The participation rate is thus determined endogenously by the number of switches and by the time spent in each form of resource allocation. In this case there are two value matching conditions:

$$\frac{w}{\rho} - C + A_1 y_e^{\beta_1} = y + A_2 y_e^{-\beta_2} \qquad (10)$$

$$\frac{w}{\rho} + A_1 y_u^{\beta_1} = \frac{y}{\delta} + A_2 y_u^{-\beta_2} - E \qquad (11)$$

where y_e and y_u denote, respectively, the entry and the exit threshold value of income into the NE industries and C and E are the corresponding TE and NE exit costs.

Expressions (10) and (11), and the related smooth pasting conditions form a highly non-linear system that cannot be solved explicitly (Dixit and Pindyck, 1994, p. 218). If the two threshold values are not far apart, however, we can approximate the solution by expressing the option value gained by entry (i.e. the exponential term on the RHS of (10)) as a function of the exit value y_u and the option value gained by exit (the exponential term on the left hand side of (11) as a function of the entry value. Using a Taylor expansion we can write:

$$y_i^\beta = y_j^\beta \left[1 + (y_i - y_j) + 0.5(y_i - y_j)^2 + \ldots\ldots + \frac{1}{n!}(y_i - y_j)^n\right] \tag{12}$$

where i,j = e,u and $\beta = \beta_1$ for i = e, j = u and β_2 for i = u, j = e. For n is arbitrarily large and y_e sufficiently close to y_u, we can write: $y_i = y_j + dy$, take the expected value of the RHS of (12) and use Ito's lemma to obtain:

$$y_i^\beta = y_j^\beta \left[1 + (\beta_1 a + 0.5\sigma^2\beta_1(\beta_1 - 1))dt\right] \tag{13}$$

But the term in square parenthesis is equal, by virtue of (4), to $1 + rdt$. Thus, for $r < 1$, we can neglect the term in *dt* and write:

$$\frac{w}{\rho} + A_1 y_e^{\beta_1} = \frac{y_e}{\delta} + A_2 y_u^{-\beta_2} - C \tag{14}$$

$$\frac{w}{\rho} + A_1 y_u^{\beta_1} - E = \frac{y_u}{\delta} + A_2 y_u^{-\beta_2} \tag{15}$$

The presence of the exit term on the RHS of (14) can be interpreted as a form of rational expectation by the firm that enters the NE on the value that will determine the switching back to the TE activities. Similarly, the presence of the entry term on the LHS of (15) is the rational expectation of the value that will determine the return to the NE activities.

The smooth pasting conditions corresponding to (14) and (15) are:

$$A_2 y_u^{-\beta_2} = \frac{y_u}{\delta\beta_2} \tag{16}$$

$$A_1 y_e^{-\beta_2} = \frac{y_e}{\delta\beta_1} \tag{17}$$

Solving the system of equations (14)–(16), we find:

$$\frac{y_e}{\delta} = \frac{\beta_1[\beta_2\frac{w}{\rho} + E + (\beta_2 + 1)C]}{\beta_1 - \beta_2 - 1} \tag{17}$$

$$\frac{y_u}{\delta} = \frac{\beta_1[\beta_2\frac{w}{\rho} + (1 + \beta_2)C + E]}{\beta_1 - \beta_2 - 1} \tag{18}$$

Expression (17) confirms the earlier result (expression (7)), whereby, as intuition suggests, the entry level of income in the NE will be higher, the higher the income expected from the new activities, the higher, *ceteris paribus*, the costs of switching back to TE in the future, and the *higher* the NE entry costs. Expression (18), on the other hand, states that the TE earning prospects that will convince the firms to exit the new sectors will have to be higher, the higher the NE earnings, the higher the costs of entering the TE activities and the *higher* the costs of re-entering NE in the future.

Equations (17) and (18) suggest that higher NE expected earnings will tend to select higher performers for two concurring reasons: on one hand, increasing the NE net incomes will induce a higher proportion of higher income firms to leave the TE industries for the NE industries. On the other hand, higher NE incomes will also make fewer higher income firms leave the NE in response to expected income increase from the traditional industries. Because higher expected incomes can be used to offset entry and exit costs, furthermore, the new economy will also tend to select a higher proportion of higher performers, becausethey can afford to switch back and forth more easily (beingable to pay the related costs) than marginal firms.

In order to see more clearly what the results obtained imply for program participation, assume that at the beginning of the planning period all firms make their decision by comparing the realized value of y (i.e. the earnings promised by NE for their performance group) with the entry value y_e. For the same performance group, we will thus have an NE participation rate equal to 1 if current NE income is above the critical value and zero otherwise. For any given performance group, the number of switches to and from NE should be a function of the entry and exit critical levels of stochastic income. More specifically, denoting with e_t and u_t the number of switches respectively into and out the NE at the time t for a firm respectively in the NE and in the TE sector at the same time, we can write: $e_t = e_{t-1} + \lambda(1 - G_t(y_e))$ and $u_t = u_{t-1} + \gamma G_t(y_u)$, where $G_t(y)$ is the distribution function of earnings at time t and λ and γ are two scaling constants. By assumption, this distribution is log-normal with mean equal to $y_0 e^{at}$ and variance equal to $y_0^2 e^{2at}(e^{\sigma^2 t} - 1)$ so that, over an extended period of time, we should observe that $prob(\log y_t \leq (a \pm h\sigma^2)t = \emptyset(h)$, where $h = h(y_i)$, $i = e,u$. By integrating the two difference equations corresponding to e_t and u_t, for $t = T$, where T denotes the numbers of units of time considered, we obtain:

$$e_T = \lambda \sum_{i=0}^{T} (1 - G_{T-1}(y_e)) \tag{19}$$

$$u_T = \gamma \sum_{i=0}^{T} G_{T-1}(y_u) \tag{19}$$

Equations (19) and (20) can be tested against the empirical data by nesting them in a regression model of the type:

$$e_{Tj} = \lambda \sum_{i=0}^{T} (1 - G_{T-1j}(y_{ej})) + b \sum_{j} X_{Tj} + v_{Tj} \tag{21}$$

where j denotes the j-th firm, X_{Tj} a vector of shifters and v_{Tj} a well-behaved random disturbance.

4   A Quantitative Analysis

In order to test some of the hypotheses presented in this paper, we use a model developed by Feder (1983) and, more recently, by Scandizzo (1999). Assume that the economy can be divided in two sectors: a traditional sector (TE) and a 'new economy' sector (NE) both characterized by neoclassical production functions:

$$T = F(K^T, L^T, Y)$$
$$Y = G(K^y, L^y,) \tag{22}$$

where T and Y indicate respectively the TE and the NE sector, K and L stand for capital and labour, Y enters the TE function as a positive externality (thereby enhancing productivity of both factors, and $F(.)$ and $G(.)$ are such that:

$$\frac{G_K}{F_K} = \frac{G_L}{F_L} = 1 + \delta \tag{23}$$

where $G_j, F_j; K,L$ denote marginal productivities. Expression (23) hypothesizes that factors in the NE sector are more productive than in the TE sector. This may be the consequence of a more competitive environment, as well as of the fact that the NE sector is just starting its growth and is not hampered by external diseconomies as much as the TE sector is. The positive externality effect on TE, on the other hand , has already been discussed before: it may depend on the gradual extension of the new technology to traditional activities as well as to the efficiency of NE in acting as input supplier for TE.

Defining GNP as $Q = T + Y$ and assuming for simplicity a Cobb-Douglas form for the two production functions (i.e. at least local stability of factor elasticities), we find:

$$g = ag_k + \lambda n + (\frac{\delta}{1 + \delta} \frac{Y}{Q} + \theta)g_y \qquad (24)$$

where are a, λ, θ the factor elasticities of the TE function w.r.t. capital, labour and NE activities, g is the growth rate of GNP, g_k the growth rate of capital, n and g_y, respectively the growth rate of labour (in its various forms of human capital) and of NE activities.

Table 16.1 Regression analysis. Dependent variable: average growth rate of p.c. GNP (1987–99)

Variables (logarithms)	Economic variables		Infrastructure		Human and social capital		'New economy'	
	Coef.	t	Coef.	t	Coef.	t	Coef.	t
Constant								
p.c. GNP 1987	−0.20	−0.31	−0.038	−0.063	−0.17	−0.30	−2.42	−2.19
R&D companies/pop. 1999	42.79	2.28	49.30	2.72	41.72	2.70	51.14	3.02
Exports +imports 97/pop. 97	0.17	2.42	0.16	2.28				
Kms of railway/pop. 97			1.76	1.82			1.68	1.73
University graduates/pop. 97					2.46	2.94		
Unemployment rate/pop. 97					0.30	2.8		
Banking outlets/pop. 97					−0.02	−2.29	36.88	2.37
Technological exports 97/pop. 97							0.77	1.46
R²	0.37		0.49		0.64		0.58	

References

Dixit, A.K. and Pindyck, R.S. (1994), *Investment under Uncertainty*, Princeton: Princeton University Press, pp. 1–19.

Feder, G. (1983), 'On Exports and Economic Growth', *Journal of Development Economics*, 12 (1–2), pp. 59–73.

Levine, R. and Renelt, D. (1992), 'A Sensitivity Analysis of Cross-country Growth Regressions', *American Economic Review*, 82 (4), pp. 942–63.

Mankew, N.G., Romer, D. and Weil, D.N. (1992), 'A Contribution to the Empirics of Economic Growth', *Quartely Journal of Economics*, 107(2), pp. 407–37.

Scandizzo, P.L. (1998), *Growth Trade and Agriculture an Investigative Survey*, FAO, Economic an Social Development Paper, 143, Rome.

Scandizzo, P.L. (1999), 'Ownership, Appropriation and Risk', in McCarthy, N., Swallow, B., Kirk, M. and Hazell, P. (eds), *Property Rights, Risk, and Livestock Development in Africa*, Washington DC: IFPRI, pp. 211–39.

Scandizzo, P.L. (2000), *Le Banche Locali. Progettazione, strategie e tecniche di analisi*, Milan: Giuffrè.

Index

For Product Safety Concerns and Information please contact our EU
representative GPSR@taylorandfrancis.com Taylor & Francis Verlag GmbH,
Kaufingerstraße 24, 80331 München, Germany

Printed and bound by CPI Group (UK) Ltd, Croydon, CR0 4YY
01/05/2025
01858348-0003